DATE DUE

HISTORICAL DICTIONARIES OF ANCIENT CIVILIZATIONS AND HISTORICAL ERAS
Series editor: Jon Woronoff

1. *Ancient Egypt*, Morris L. Bierbrier, 1999. *Out of print. See No. 22.*
2. *Ancient Mesoamerica*, Joel W. Palka, 2000.
3. *Pre-Colonial Africa*, Robert O. Collins, 2001.
4. *Byzantium*, John H. Rosser, 2001.
5. *Medieval Russia*, Lawrence N. Langer, 2001.
6. *Napoleonic Era*, George F. Nafziger, 2001.
7. *Ottoman Empire*, Selcuk Aksin Somel, 2003.
8. *Mongol World Empire*, Paul D. Buell, 2003.
9. *Mesopotamia*, Gwendolyn Leick, 2003.
10. *Ancient and Medieval Nubia*, Richard A. Lobban Jr., 2003.
11. *The Vikings*, Katherine Holman, 2003.
12. *The Renaissance*, Charles G. Nauert, 2004.
13. *Ancient Israel*, Niels Peter Lemche, 2004.
14. *The Hittites*, Charles Burney, 2004.
15. *Early North America*, Cameron B. Wesson, 2005.
16. *The Enlightenment*, by Harvey Chisick, 2005.
17. *Cultural Revolution*, by Guo Jian, Yongyi Song, and Yuan Zhou, 2006.
18. *Ancient Southeast Asia*, by John N. Miksic, 2007.
19. *Medieval China*, by Victor Cunrui Xiong, 2008.
20. *Medieval India*, by Iqtidar Alam Khan, 2008.
21. *Ancient South America*, by Martin Giesso, 2008.
22. *Egypt*, 2nd ed., Morris L. Bierbrier, 2008.
23. *India*, by Kumkum Roy, 2009.

Historical Dictionary of Ancient India

Kumkum Roy

Historical Dictionaries of Ancient Civilizations and Historical Eras, No. 23

The Scarecrow Press, Inc.
Lanham, Maryland • Toronto • Plymouth, UK
2009

SCARECROW PRESS, INC.

Published in the United States of America
by Scarecrow Press, Inc.
A wholly owned subsidiary of
The Rowman & Littlefield Publishing Group, Inc.
4501 Forbes Boulevard, Suite 200, Lanham, Maryland 20706
www.scarecrowpress.com

Estover Road
Plymouth PL6 7PY
United Kingdom

British Library Cataloguing in Publication Information Available

Library of Congress Cataloging-in-Publication Data

Roy, Kumkum.
Historical dictionary of ancient India / Kumkum Roy.
p. cm. — (Historical dictionaries of ancient civilizations and historical eras; no. 23)
Includes bibliographical references.
ISBN-13: 978-0-8108-5366-9 (cloth : alk. paper)
ISBN-10: 0-8108-5366-3 (cloth : alk. paper)
ISBN-13: 978-0-8108-6279-1 (ebook)
ISBN-10: 0-8108-6279-4 (ebook)
1. India—History—To 324 B.C.—Dictionaries. 2. India—History—324 B.C.–1000 A.D.—Dictionaries. I. Title. DS451.R66 2009
934.003—dc22 2008031648

∞™ The paper used in this publication meets the minimum requirements of American National Standard for Information Sciences—Permanence of Paper for Printed Library Materials, ANSI/NISO Z39.48-1992. Manufactured in the United States of America.

For Romila

Contents

Editor's Foreword

The older events are and the less we know about them, the harder it is to understand and interpret them—the temptation being to imagine or invent what happened. This is a problem for all historians, particularly when events play into the national pride and sentiments of outsiders and insiders alike, as can be seen in the case of ancient India. So rather than guess at what might have been, this *Historical Dictionary of Ancient India* adheres to the facts we do know and limits interpretation to what can be legitimately extrapolated.

From the Paleolithic age until roughly the year 1000 was an extremely important period of time for a vast region. It was a time of extraordinary happenings, including the emergence of the Harappan civilization and later the rise of the Maurya and Gupta Empires, sometimes under the rule of exceptional leaders such as Asoka, and more broadly the formation of major religions, among them Buddhism and what has been called Hinduism, all this accompanied by memorable cultural achievements such as the composition of the Vedas and Purāṇas.

The introduction provides the basic context and raises important questions. The chronology traces major periods and events, showing how they fit together and contribute to India's development. The dictionary, with its hundreds of entries, describes the most salient events; outstanding rulers and others, including religious and cultural figures; memorable writings; and crucial aspects of the politics, economics, and culture of the time. It describes not only kingship and warfare but also the lives of ordinary people and the role of women. And considerable attention is devoted to the archaeological sites that have given us as much information as we currently have. Finally, the bibliography provides resources for further reading.

This volume was compiled by Kumkum Roy, who has studied and taught ancient Indian history for nearly three decades, earning her doctorate at the Centre for Historical Studies of Jawaharlal Nehru

University. Since then she has taught at two eminent institutions, first the University of Delhi and then her alma mater, the Centre for Historical Studies. During this time, she has written extensively, including numerous research papers, articles, and the book *The Emergence of Monarchy in North India*, while also editing the anthology *Women in Early Indian Societies*. Her knowledge of the period is thus substantial and the way she imparts it is impressive, providing the essential information while warning against facile interpretations.

Jon Woronoff
Series Editor

Acknowledgments

When I accepted this project several years ago I did not quite realize what I had let myself in for. The work proved to be far more challenging than I had anticipated. By definition, a dictionary is authoritative. Yet, it sometimes seemed virtually impossible to make authoritative statements with the foresight that many of these would be overturned in the light of new evidence or with the development of fresh frames of reference. Also, there were times when it was frustrating to grapple with the problem of being precise and prosaic about situations and processes that were fluid. Besides, there was the constant dilemma of handling the dynamism and dialogue, often polemical, which has animated historical discourse on early India. Nevertheless, I have enjoyed the challenge and would like to thank those who provided me with the opportunity to work my way around and through these issues: Narayani Gupta, Surjit Mansingh, and the general editor of the series, Jon Woronoff. The last-named has been both patient and persistent: besides, his incisive comments and suggestions have helped me improve substantially on earlier drafts.

Part of the work on the dictionary, including a trip to Pune to consult material in the libraries of the Deccan College and the University of Poona, was made possible through financial assistance from the Department of Special Assistance Programme, Centre for Historical Studies, Jawaharlal Nehru University. I would like to thank the coordinator of the program, Prof. Dilbagh Singh, for his support. I am also grateful to Prof. K. Paddayya, director of the Deccan College Post-Graduate and Research Institute, the staff of the college library for the access to their facilities during my stay in Pune, and also Dr. S. Gaekwad and the members of the Department of History, University of Poona, for their kind hospitality.

Friends and colleagues have contributed to the making of the dictionary in a variety of ways. Vijaya Ramaswamy shared the tribulations and triumphs of her own project with warmth and enthusiasm, while Kunal and Shubhra Chakrabarti offered support and encouragement. Bharati Jagannathan and Naina Dayal read through sections of the text and offered painstakingly detailed suggestions. Samira Verma helped me in technical matters with patience and care. My grateful thanks to them, as also to Mr. K. Varghese, who prepared the maps, and Dr. Vandana Sinha, director of archives at the American Institute of Indian Studies, Gurgaon, India, who provided the photos used in the book.

Others who endured the ups and downs of the long-drawn project, generally cheerfully but with occasional exasperation, include my family: my parents and Sumanto, Asha, Shimul, and Shubinoy. Work on the dictionary would not have been possible without their unqualified affection and the support of Lokkhon dada, Sontosh, Rina, and Manoj. I would also like to thank my aunt, Mira Guha, for presenting me with one of the earliest historical dictionaries published in India, authored by Sachidananda Bhattacharya. Finally, I would like to thank my teachers—those who encouraged and often compelled me to express myself precisely and concisely. It was often painful to have excess verbiage—which seemed beautiful if not relevant—ruthlessly excised; however, those lessons acquired fresh meaning as I tried to compress pages of information and analysis into paragraphs. Therefore, this work, with all its shortcomings, is dedicated to Romila Thapar, a teacher and friend I have known and learned from for 30 years.

Reader's Note

There are some general points that the reader may find worth bearing in mind.

Diacritics

These have been used in the text in order to facilitate pronunciation. A guide to approximate phonetic equivalents in English is as follows:

Vowels

Ā/ā is a long sound, as in *bath*.
Ī/ī is a long sound, as in *steep*.
ū is a long sound as in *stoop*.

Consonants

C/c is pronounced as ch as in *chocolate*.
Ch/ch is a harder sound, with no phonetic equivalence in English.
L̲/l̲ is somewhat like l, but a slightly harder sound.
ṅ is generally combined with k, kh, g, or gh, as in *bank* or *bang*.
ṇ is a nasal/palatal sound, somewhat like *run*.
Ś/ś is a sibilant, as in *sharp*.
Ṣ/ṣ is also a sibilant, pronounced as a palatal sound, again close to that in *sharp*.
Ṭ/ṭ is a palatal sound, as in *tea*.
Ṭh/ṭh is a harder sound, with no phonetic equivalence in English.

Dates

Those indicated are often approximate (c.). In the case of archaeological sites, finds are occasionally dated using radiocarbon techniques (r.).

More frequently, however, dating is on the basis of the stratigraphy of finds, established internally within each site as well as externally, through comparison with other more or less similar sites. Uncertain dates have been indicated with a question mark (?). Dates for texts are also subject to considerable speculation and debate.

General

Italics have been used for words in languages other than English as also for the names of books.

Bold type has been used to indicate terms for which entries are available in the dictionary. Where other entries provide additional information, these are listed at the end of the entry.

Spellings can vary depending on the language from which the words are transliterated. For instance, the River Ganges is known as the Ganga in most Indian languages. In the case of place names, present-day spellings have been adopted in most instances.

The name of the Mauryan emperor Asoka (Prakrit) is spelled as Aśoka in Sanskrit. These variations can be problematic in a dictionary. In some instances, variants are noted through cross-references. In other instances, as in the case of Asoka, we have adopted the spelling most commonly used in ancient sources, in this case his own inscriptions and early Buddhist texts. Diacritics have not been used for the names of languages.

Words with more than one meaning have been numbered. The word *brāhmaṇa*, for instance, can refer to the category of priests as well as to a certain class of priestly literature. The term *brahmanical*, which is also highlighted, includes both categories. However, *brahmanical* literature or tradition was not confined to the category of texts that are designated as *brāhmaṇas*.

Visuals

Two maps—one with the present-day political boundaries and another showing the subcontinent during the time of the Mauryan Empire—are included. The latter also shows the major rivers. The photos pertain primarily to ancient Indian architecture and sculpture.

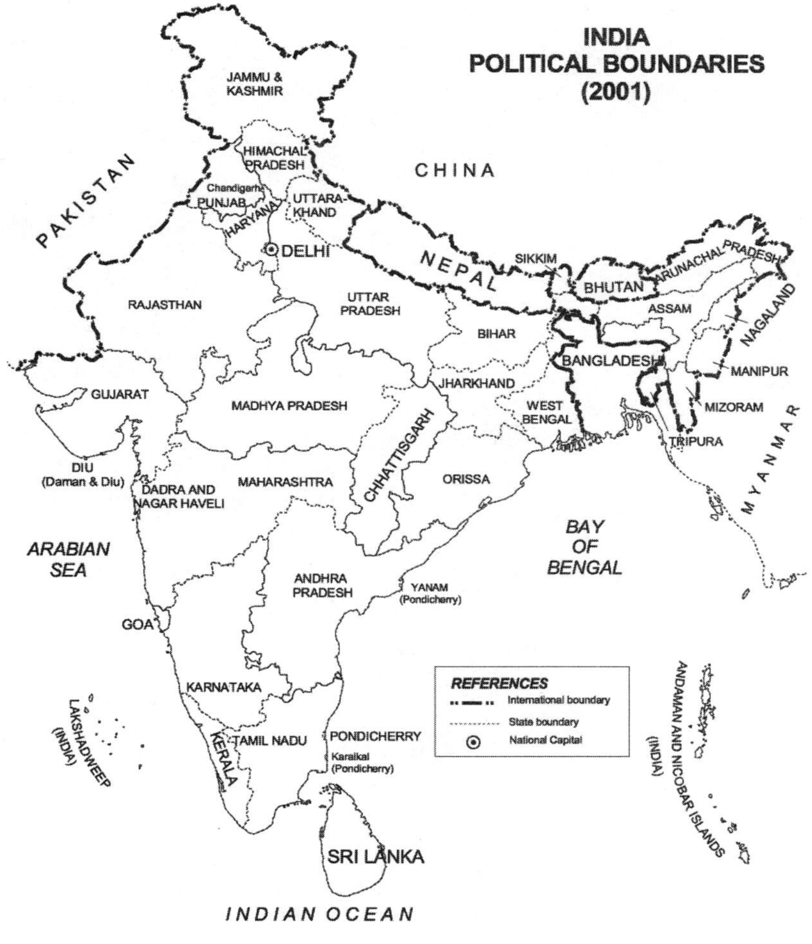

INDIA
POLITICAL BOUNDARIES
(2001)
JAMMU & KASHMIR
HIMACHAL PRADESH
PAKISTAN
CHINA
Chandigarh
PUNJAB
HARYANA
UTTARA-KHAND
DELHI
NEPAL
SIKKIM
BHUTAN
ARUNACHAL PRADESH
RAJASTHAN
UTTAR PRADESH
ASSAM
NAGALAND
BIHAR
BANGLADESH
MANIPUR
GUJARAT
MADHYA PRADESH
JHARKHAND
WEST BENGAL
MIZORAM
CHHATTISGARH
TRIPURA
MYANMAR
DIU (Daman & Diu)
DADRA AND NAGAR HAVELI
MAHARASHTRA
ORISSA
ARABIAN SEA
BAY OF BENGAL
ANDHRA PRADESH
YANAM (Pondicherry)
GOA
REFERENCES
International boundary
State boundary
National Capital
KARNATAKA
LAKSHADWEEP (INDIA)
KERALA
TAMIL NADU
PONDICHERRY
Karaikal (Pondicherry)
ANDAMAN AND NICOBAR ISLANDS (INDIA)
SRI LANKA
INDIAN OCEAN

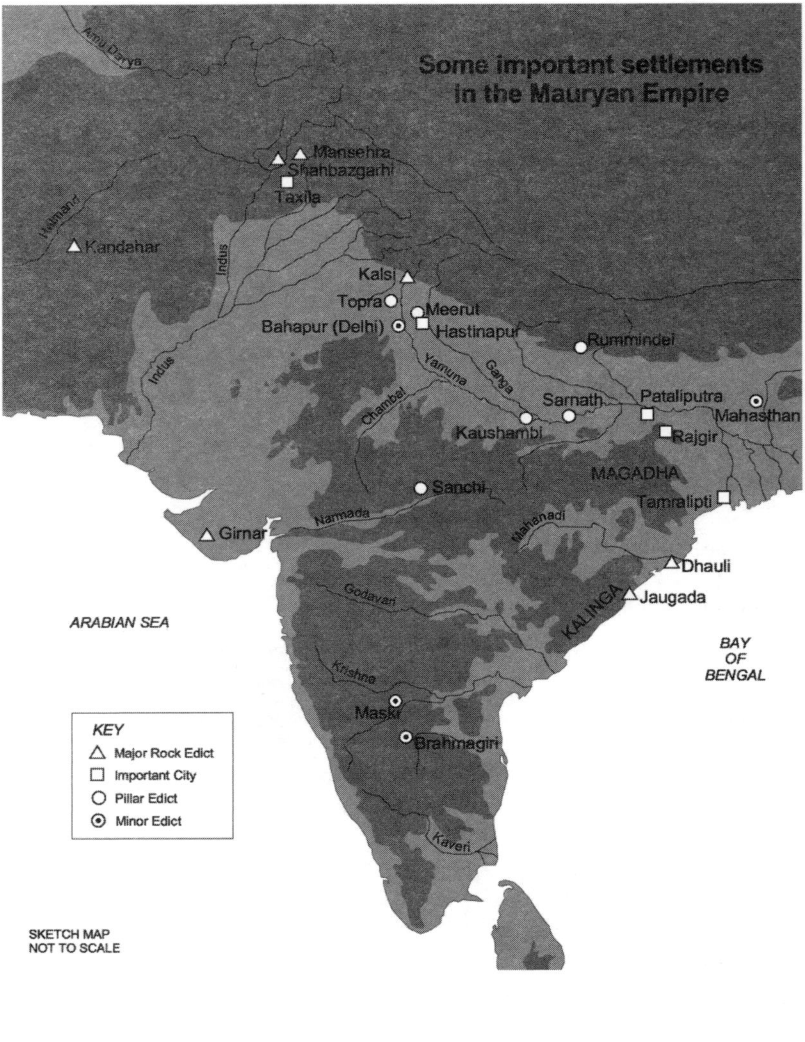
Some important settlements in the Mauryan Empire
Amu Darya
Mansehra
Shahbazgarhi
Taxila
Helmand
Kandahar
Indus
Kalsi
Topra
Meerut
Bahapur (Delhi)
Hastinapur
Rummindei
Yamuna
Ganga
Chambal
Sarnath
Pataliputra
Mahasthan
Kaushambi
Rajgir
MAGADHA
Sanchi
Tamralipti
Narmada
Mahanadi
Girnar
Dhauli
Godavari
KALINGA
Jaugada
ARABIAN SEA
BAY OF BENGAL
Krishna
Maski
Brahmagiri
Kaveri
KEY
Major Rock Edict
Important City
Pillar Edict
Minor Edict
SKETCH MAP
NOT TO SCALE

Chronology

Note: Several historical phases have overlapped and coexisted in different parts of the subcontinent. Uncertain or disputed dates are indicated with a question mark. Certain processes, such as socioeconomic changes or cultural developments, are far more difficult to date than political events.

1.9 million years ago Evidence of Paleolithic tools from Riwat, Pakistan.

500,000–50,000 Before Present (BP) Lower Paleolithic cultures in several parts of the subcontinent. Tools found from Paleolithic sites include hand axes, cleavers, and choppers.

350,000 BP Lower Paleolithic in Hunsgi, Karnataka.

170,000–39,000 BP Middle Paleolithic cultures.

25,000–18,000 BP Upper Paleolithic cultures.

10,000–3000/2000 BP Mesolithic cultures, evidence of open-air settlements as well as habitations in caves and rock shelters, paintings at sites such as Bhimbetka, and burials.

8000 BCE onward Neolithic settlement in Mehrgarh in Baluchistan, Pakistan, evidence of agriculture, domestic architecture, and crafts, including pottery.

7000 BCE? Neolithic settlements in the Belan valley, Uttar Pradesh.

c. 6000 BCE Mesolithic settlement at Adamgarh, Madhya Pradesh, with evidence of microliths, paintings, and domesticated and wild animals.

c. 5000 BCE onward Mesolithic settlement at Bagor, Rajasthan, with evidence of contact with contemporary Chalcolithic settlements as well as with the Harappan civilization.

c. 4000 BCE Mesolithic settlement at Damdama, Uttar Pradesh.

Late fourth–early third millennium BCE Pre-/early Harappan cultures such as the Amri-Nal, Kot Diji, and Sothi–Siswal in Sind, Baluchistan, and the Ghaggar–Hakra valley with evidence of subsistence based on agriculture and pastoralism, distinctive pottery, mud-brick architecture, craft production, and traces of fortifications.

c. 2700–1800 BCE Mature Harappan civilization with evidence of cities and settlements along the Indus and its tributaries. Indications of complex economic networks and town planning, with evidence of a distinctive urban architecture. Extensive use of copper–bronze technology, wide range of crafts, as well as long-distance exchange. Representational art, as evident from seals and sculpture, was highly developed. There is evidence of the use of writing on seals. Contemporary Neolithic settlements include that at Burzahom, Kashmir.

c. 2300–2000 BCE Chalcolithic settlement at Kayatha, Madhya Pradesh.

c. 2300–1800 BCE Neolithic settlements in south India, including ash mounds; Chalcolithic settlements in Navdatoli, Madhya Pradesh, and Ahar, Rajasthan.

c. Second millennium BCE onward Evidence of the use of black and red ware.

c. 2000 BCE Neolithic settlement at Chirand, Bihar.

c. 1800–1000 BCE Evidence of post-Harappan cultures as well as Neolithic–Chalcolithic cultures in several parts of the subcontinent. These include the Cemetery H and Jhukar cultures in the Punjab and Sind, Lustrous Red Ware sites in Gujarat, Ochre-Coloured Pottery sites, sites with copper hoards and Narhan culture sites as well as sites with an overlap between the late Harappan and Painted Grey Ware cultures in north India, and cultures such as the Malwa and Jorwe in the Deccan. Composition and compilation of early Vedic literature, pertaining to Vedic religion, focused on the sacrificial cult in the northwest of the subcontinent, containing descriptions of a predominantly pastoral society, led by chiefs and priests.

c. 1600–500 BCE Gandhara Grave Culture in the northwest of the subcontinent, with possible links with Iran and Central Asia.

c. 14th century BCE Inscription at Bogazkoy, Turkey, mentions Vedic deities.

c. First millennium BCE onward Evidence of megalithic burials from several parts of the Deccan and peninsular India, with typical grave goods including a wide range of iron equipment, and Black and Red Ware. Evidence for the use of black slipped ware in north India. Growing textual references to social stratification, including the *varṇa-jāti* order, and to the practice of untouchability in Brahmanical and other textual traditions.

c. 1000–600 BCE Growing evidence of the manufacture of iron tools and weapons in several parts of the subcontinent. Other distinctive cultural markers include finds of Painted Grey Ware in settlements in the Ganga–Yamuna doab and the mid–Ganga valley. Some of the earliest references to chiefdoms and kingdoms in north India, including those of the Kurus and Pañcālas in the Ganga–Yamuna doab. Rituals to legitimize kingship, such as the *rājasūya* and *aśvamedha*, prescribed in later Vedic texts such as the *Brāhmaṇas*. Other texts composed during this period related to the Vedic tradition include the *Nighaṇṭu*, *Nirukta*, and the earliest Śrautasūtras.

c. Sixth–fifth centuries BCE Increasing evidence of the manufacture and use of iron equipment for agriculture, craft production, and warfare. The first coins in the subcontinent (punch-marked and cast copper coins), indicating the growing importance of commercial exchanges. Evidence of Northern Black Polished Ware at several sites in the subcontinent, with a major concentration in the Ganga valley. (Finds of Northern Black Polished Ware dwindle by the beginning of the first millennium CE.) Beginning of urban settlements in north India, with features such as ring wells and fortification. Emergence of *mahājanapadas* or states in several parts of north and central India. Lists of these states were compiled in Buddhist and Jaina texts. Many of these were monarchies, but some were republics or oligarchies. Some of the latter survived until the mid–first millennium CE. Some of these had standing armies and developed a rudimentary bureaucracy. Bimbisāra and Ajātaśatru, rulers of the *mahājanapada* of Magadha (part of present-day Bihar) adopt policies aimed at ensuring its supremacy. Social categories such as the *gṛhapati*, or head of the peasant household, become important. Earliest references to guilds of merchants and craftsmen. Composition of some of the earliest Upaniṣads expounding philosophical ideas that became extremely influential subsequently, including those of *advaita* or monotheism and *karma*, suggesting that present action could determine future states of existence. A wide range of philosophical ideas gain currency. These include those of the Ājīvikas, Jainism, and Buddhism as well as schools that advocated fatalism and materialism. Composition of the *Aṣṭādhyāyī*, a work on Sanskrit grammar, by Pāniṇi.

c. Sixth–fourth centuries BCE Achaemenid control over the northwest part of the subcontinent.

Composition of the Gṛhyasūtras and Dharmasūtras, Brahmanical texts laying down norms for domestic rituals, including rites of passage, and for the fourfold *varṇa* order. Development of the notion of *daṇḍa*, or the administration of justice as a royal function.

c. Fifth century BCE onward Evidence of urbanism in the Deccan and in peninsular India. By c. second century BCE, there is evidence for the construction of *stūpas* at several sites, as also indications of manufacture of beads and of long-distance exchange with Rome.

c. Fourth century BCE onward Compilation of the early Buddhist texts, development of the Sāṃkhya school of philosophy. Development of the notion of the *cakravartin* or universal ruler.

326 BCE Invasion of the northwest part of the subcontinent by Alexander of Macedon. His conquests extend up to the river Beas. Although he retreated after this conquest, Greek influence in the northwest was in evidence for several centuries.

c. 321–298 BCE Reign of Candragupta Maurya, the founder of the Mauryan Empire.

c. Fourth–third centuries BCE Initial composition of the *Arthaśāstra*, a text laying down norms of statecraft. Megasthenes, the Greek ambassador sent to the Mauryan court by Seleucus Nicator, writes an account describing what he saw.

c. Third century BCE onward The emergence of the chiefdoms and kingdoms of the Co!as, Ceras, and Pāṇḍyas in south India. Initial compilation of the *Ācārāṅga Sūtra*, a Jaina canonical text. Beginning of the compilation of *Sangam* literature in Tamil.

c. 300–272 BCE Reign of Bindusāra, the second Mauryan ruler.

c. 273–232 BCE Reign of Asoka, the Mauryan ruler, renowned for renouncing war and advocating *dhamma*, propagated through some of the earliest known inscriptions in Brāhmī and Kharoṣṭhī from the subcontinent, also associated with some of the earliest and finest examples of stone sculpture and the construction of the earliest surviving *stūpas* and rock-cut caves. According to Buddhist tradition, the third Buddhist Council was held during his reign.

c. Third–second centuries BCE Bactrian Greek rulers in Afghanistan.

c. Second century BCE onward Growth of Bhakti, or devotionalism, within several religious traditions. Earliest examples of Tamil Brāhmī inscriptions. Rock-cut caves constructed at sites along the Western Ghats to serve as shrines and monasteries for Buddhist monks.

c. 185/181 BCE Puṣyamitra Śuṅga overthrows the last Mauryan ruler of north India and establishes the Śuṅga dynasty.

c. Second century BCE–second century CE Composition of the *Manusmṛti*, the best-known Dharmaśāstra, and the *Mimāṃsā sūtra*, a text on the sacrificial ritual.

c. Second century BCE Indo-Greek rulers including Menander establish control over the northwest. Sātavāhanas gain ascendancy in the Deccan. Khāravela rules over parts of Orissa.

Construction and embellishment of the *stūpa* at Bharhut with some of the earliest surviving examples of narrative sculpture. Emergence of the Digambara and Śvetāmbara sects within Jainism.

c. First century BCE onward Establishment of Śaka rule in the northwestern parts of the subcontinent, extending up to Gujarat, parts of central India, and Maharashtra. Construction of rock-cut caves in the Western Ghats. Emergence of the Gandhara School of Art in the northwestern part of the subcontinent, showing Hellenistic influence, and producing some of the earliest anthropomorphic representations of the Buddha.

c. First century BCE The Kuṣāṇas, a Central Asian people, establish control over the northwestern part of the subcontinent. Compilation of the *Dhammapada*, a major Buddhist text.

c. First century CE onward Emergence of Vaiṣṇavism and Śaivism as major theistic traditions. Emergence of Mahāyāna Buddhism. Growing visibility of goddess cults. Tradition of erecting hero stones in south India. Evidence of land grants to religious institutions.

c. First century CE Composition of a major medical treatise, the *Caraka Saṃhitā*. Composition of the *Periplus of the Erythraean Sea*, containing a detailed account of ports along the coasts of the subcontinent.

c. First–second centuries CE Reign of Gautamīputra Sātakarṇi, one of the best-known Sātavāhana rulers. Reign of the Kuṣāṇa king Kaniṣka. Bhāsa, a playwright, composes several plays in Sanskrit. Composition of the *Buddhacarita* by Aśvaghoṣa.

c. Second century CE Reign of Rudradāman, a Śaka ruler, in western India. The Digambara Jaina teacher Kundakunda composes several texts in Prakrit.

c. Second–fourth centuries CE Ikṣvākus establish control over Andhra Pradesh. Composition of the *Silappadikāram*, a Tamil epic. Composition of the *Kāmasūtra*, a Sanskrit text on erotics.

c. Third century CE Composition of the *Sāmkhyakārikā*, a philosophical text.

319–320 CE Beginning of the Gupta era, dating from the reign of Candragupta I.

c. Fourth century CE onward Western Gangas emerge as a major ruling lineage in Karnataka. Compilation of the Purāṇas, encyclopedic texts containing myths, legends, and prescriptions about modes of worship of deities such as Viṣṇu, Śiva, and the goddess.

c. Fourth–fifth centuries CE Gupta rulers in north India, including Samudragupta, Candragupta II, Kumāragupta, and Skandagupta. Kālidāsa, arguably the best-known Sanskrit poet, possibly the poet of the Gupta ruler Candragupta II. Composition of the *Amarakośa*, a dictionary in Sanskrit. Beginning of the composition of the *āgamas*, a category of literature delineating the modes of worship of a wide variety of deities.

The Sanskrit epics, the *Mahābhārata* and the *Rāmāyaṇa*, attain their present form. Compilation of the *Pañcatantra*, a collection of fables that attained widespread popularity. Construction of brick and stone temples at sites such as Bhitargaon. Chinese Buddhist pilgrim Fa Xian visits the subcontinent.

c. Fourth–sixth centuries CE The Kadambas become dominant in Karnataka. Construction and painting of the Buddhist caves at Ajanta under the patronage of the Vākāṭakas. Paintings in the caves at Bagh. Composition and compilation of the *Devīmāhātmya*, one of the most important texts associated with the cult of the goddess.

c. Fifth century CE onward Growing importance of land grants to Brahmanical religious institutions, generally documented in copper plate inscriptions. Badami emerges as an important political and cultural center in Karnataka. Temples for the worship of Brahmanical deities constructed in several parts of the subcontinent.

c. Fifth century CE Hūṇas arrive in northwestern India. Council of Valabhi in Gujarat, in which Jaina texts were finally compiled and codified. Composition of the *Nāṭyaśāstra*, a Sanskrit text codifying the performative arts, attributed to Bharata. Bhartṛhari, linguist, philosopher, and poet, composes several works. Noted mathematician Āryabhaṭa propounds theories about the revolution of the earth. *Jātakas*, birth stories of the Buddha, including folk tales, composed in Pali, receive their final form. Composition of the *Tolkāppiyam*, on Tamil grammar.

c. Sixth century onward Establishment of Gurjara Pratihāra power in north India. The Kalacuris gain control over parts of western and central India. Kanauj, a city in Uttar Pradesh, emerges as a major political and cultural center. Prakrit commentaries on Jaina canonical works written.

c. Sixth–eighth centuries CE Rule of the Cālukyas of Badami, Karnataka; rule of the Maitrakas in Gujarat. The Pallavas of Kanchipuram gain control over the Tamil region.

c. Sixth century CE Nalanda, a Buddhist monastery in Bihar, emerges as a major educational center. Sanskrit author Bhāravi composes the *Kirātārjunīya*. Cāttanār composes the *Maṇimekalai*, a Tamil epic. Composition of the *Tirukkuraḷ*, an anthology of didactic verses, in Tamil. Astronomer Varāhamihira composes major text. Cosmas Indikopleustes, a Greek merchant, writes an account of maritime trade routes linking the subcontinent with other areas.

Beginning of construction of temples at Aihole, in Karnataka, under the patronage of the Cālukyas.

c. Sixth–seventh centuries CE Reign of the Pallava ruler Mahendravarman I.

c. Seventh century CE onward Rāṣṭrakūṭas emerge as a major power in the Deccan.

Construction of rock-cut temples and monasteries at Ellora, Maharashtra, under the patronage of the Rāṣṭrakūṭas.

c. Seventh century CE Reign of the Cālukya ruler Pulakeśin II in the western Deccan; Harṣavardhana rules over parts of north India; Bhāskaravarman rules over eastern India.

Bāṇabhaṭṭa, the court poet of Harṣavardhana, composes the biography of his patron. Sanskrit author Dandin composes several works, including the *Daśakumāracarita*. Chinese Buddhist pilgrims Xuan Zang and I Ching visit India. Growth of devotional traditions associated with the Āḻvārs in the Tamil region.

c. Seventh–eighth centuries CE Noted Sanskrit playwright Bhavabhūti composes plays under the patronage of Yaśovarman, the ruler of Kanauj. Rule of Dharmapāla, one of the major Pāla rulers. Construction of the Shore Temple at Mahabalipuram. Śaṅkarācārya, the most noted exponent of monistic philosophy or *advaita*, propounds his ideas.

712 CE Arab conquest of Sind.

c. Eighth century CE Establishment of Rāṣṭrakūṭa power in Karnataka and of the Eastern Gangas in Orissa. Reign of Lalitāditya Muktāpīḍa in Kashmir. Haribhadra Sūrī, a Jaina author, composes several works in Sanskrit and Prakrit. Buddhist and Brahmanical shrines built at Paharpur, Bangladesh.

c. Ninth century CE The Pallavas superseded by the Coḻas as the dominant power in the Tamil region. Amoghavarṣa, one of the most powerful rulers of the Rāṣṭrakūṭas, rules over the western Deccan from Mānyakheṭa. Avantivarman rules over Kashmir. Mihira Bhoja, the Pratihāra ruler, among the most powerful rulers of north India. The Pālas dominate eastern India. Ānandavardhana composes a work on poetics (Sanskrit) in Kashmir. Kampan composes a version of the *Rāmāyaṇa* in Tamil. Śaiva poet Māṇikkavācakar composes devotional songs in Tamil. Vaiṣṇava poet Nammāḻvār composes devotional songs in Tamil. Earliest surviving works in Apabhraṃśa. Establishment of a Buddhist monastery at Vikramaśilā by the Pāla ruler Dharmapāla.

c. 9th–10th centuries CE Mahendrapāla, one of the most powerful Pratihāra rulers, exercises control over north India. Mahipāla, a ruler of the Pāla dynasty, exercises control over eastern India. Arab historian Al Masudi leaves an account of his travels in the subcontinent.

10th–11th centuries CE Reign of Diddā, one of the few women to exercise power independently, in Kashmir. Abhinavagupta, author of works on aesthetics in Sanskrit literature, in Kashmir.

12th century CE Kalhana composes the *Rājataraṅginī*, a history of Kashmir.

1784 Founding of the Asiatic Society.

1813 Thomas Young classifies certain languages as Indo-European.

1837 Decipherment of Asokan inscriptions by James Prinsep.

1849–1875 Friedrich Max Muller edits and publishes the *Ṛgveda*.

1856 Robert Caldwell identifies languages spoken in south India as belonging to the Dravidian family.

1863–1884 Survey of prehistoric sites in the subcontinent by Robert Bruce Foote.

1871 Establishment of the Archaeological Survey of India.

1875 Establishment of the Indian Museum, Calcutta.

1881 Pali Text Society founded in London.

1883 Establishment of the Department of Epigraphy, Government of India.

1930–1962 P. V. Kane publishes the *History of the Dharmaśāstras*.

Introduction

Historical explorations of the ancient past of the subcontinent are relatively recent. In fact, the earliest systematic studies on the subject were closely linked with the establishment of the Asiatic Society in Calcutta in 1784, when the British East India Company was firmly entrenched in Bengal. History, almost inevitably, was implicated within a colonial discourse whose shifting contours shaped the ways in which the discipline developed. Before turning to the specificities of the relationship between the colonial context and the development of the discipline, as well as its aftermath, let us turn to the three grids on which the present enterprise rests.

DEFINING "INDIA"

The Indian subcontinent has frontiers that are deceptively well defined. To the north are the Himalayas, one of the longest chains of mountains in the world, stretching across in a magnificent arc, including some of the highest peaks, and separating the subcontinent from China/Tibet. To the west, south, and east are the Arabian Sea, the Indian Ocean, and the Bay of Bengal, respectively. However, each of these frontiers has always been permeable—and contacts with lands beyond have been virtually continuous throughout history. In other words, the mountains and seas have never functioned as watertight boundaries: For millennia, influences from beyond the subcontinent have shaped developments within, just as people, ideas, and goods from the subcontinent reached distant lands.

The Himalayas have shaped human existence on the subcontinent in at least two other ways. Virtually all the major rivers that drain the northern plains originate from the snow-fed heights of the mountains and are consequently perennial, and, for large stretches of their course, navigable. These include the tributaries of the Indus (the Indus itself rises from the Tibetan plateau, as does the Brahmaputra) and the northern tributaries of the Ganga. As important, the Himalayas trap the moisture-bearing monsoon winds, leading to reasonably heavy rainfall, which decreases from the east to the west. This, in its turn, is a critical determinant for agriculture. Winter rainfall is relatively low and occurs in the northwest and in the southeast.

South of the Himalayas is a vast expanse of alluvial plains, drained by the Indus, flowing in a roughly southwesterly direction to the Arabian Sea, and the Ganga or Ganges, which flows southeastward into the Bay of Bengal. Each of these rivers is joined by a number of tributaries. The fertility of the land as well as facilities of communication has led to extremely dense concentrations of population in the river valleys. Some of the earliest cities and states in the subcontinent developed in this zone.

Given the nature of the land, most rivers have changed their course several times through history. While some of these changes have been gradual and barely perceptible, the others have been more drastic. Floods, especially in the low-lying deltaic areas, have also shaped human history. The plains become more arid toward the west, and give way to the Thar Desert, which stretches from Rajasthan to the adjacent regions of Pakistan. The desert is relatively sparsely populated, but routes of communication have been developed and used for millennia.

The Vindhyas, a mountain range running through the subcontinent in an east–west direction, roughly along the line of the Tropic of Cancer, are generally used to demarcate the northern plains from the Deccan plateau. The plateau itself is shaped like a rough triangle, with two chains of mountains, the Western Ghats and the Eastern Ghats, converging in the Nilgiris, literally the Blue Mountains, near the southern tip of the subcontinent. The Western Ghats are far steeper than the Eastern Ghats. Consequently, the drainage of the plateau is generally from west to east. The two exceptions are the rivers Narmada and the Tapti, which drain into the Arabian Sea. Some of the earliest traces of human settlement in the subcontinent have been found along the Narmada valley.

All the other major rivers, such as the Mahanadi, Godavari, Krishna, and Kaveri, drain into the Bay of Bengal, and as the gradient is relatively gentle, most of these rivers have extensive deltaic zones, which are generally areas of intensive agriculture. These have also been the nuclei of regional kingdoms, such as those of the Coḻas centered on the Kaveri.

The Deccan plateau and the adjoining coasts also constitute what is known as peninsular India. The Eastern Ghats offer few barriers to communication. The Western Ghats are broken by passes at a number of points, and both archaeological and inscriptional evidence testify to the antiquity of human settlements around such nodes of communication. Although there are few natural harbors along the extensive coastline, maritime routes, both coastal and with regions such as West Asia, Southeast Asia, and even China, were evidently used since the early historic period (mid–first millennium BCE), if not earlier.

It is also worth keeping in mind the vastness of the subcontinent. The area enclosed within the present-day frontiers of India is about 4.4 million square kilometers, while the distance from north to south, as also east to west from one end to another, is about 3,200 kilometers. Today, there are several independent nation-states within the subcontinent, including India, Pakistan, Bangladesh, Nepal, and Bhutan, with Sri Lanka as a neighbor with long and enduring historical links.

As may be expected, regional diversities have been a characteristic of the history of the subcontinent. In fact, it is likely that these differences were sharper in the past, when modes of communication were far slower than at present. As such, any statements about historical trends need to be made and evaluated with extreme caution. While there has been a tendency to generalize on the basis of developments in the Ganga valley, which has often been regarded as the core or heartland of the subcontinent, recent scholarship has been more critical about this assumption. Increasingly, it is evident that trajectories of historical development in the northeast, or in south India, to cite just two instances, were different, and cannot be measured by the yardsticks of the Ganga valley. While some of these autonomous developments have received the attention of scholars, others await systematic investigation.

At the same time, there is evidence of contact and communication among these regions, whose frontiers were often fluid. Thus, an understanding of early India involves, among other things, an examination of intra- and interregional relationships and an exploration of the ways in which these shaped historical processes.

Terms used to designate large geographical entities already occur in Sanskrit and Prakrit texts and inscriptions. These include *āryāvarta*, *madhaydeśa/majjhimadesa*, Jambudvīpa, Bhāratavarṣa. Of these, the last two occasionally (but not invariably) approximated to the subcontinent as we understand it today. Terms that provide the ancestry of the name "India" were derived from the river Indus and were used by peoples such as the Persians, Greeks, and Arabs who came into contact with the subcontinent through the northwest. What is evident is that the definitions of each of these terms varied according to context. It is these amorphous elements that constitute the spatial framework for the present exercise.

PIECING TOGETHER THE PAST

Our understanding of early Indian history has changed substantially over the past two centuries. This has been the result of two distinct but interrelated processes: one, the incremental growth of the sources available for investigating the past; and second, changes in the questions posed of the data and shifts in the foci of historical investigation. Let us begin by examining the kinds of sources available.

The earliest phases of the history of the subcontinent, designated as the Paleolithic, Mesolithic, and Neolithic, have been reconstructed entirely from archaeological evidence, available from several regions. As the nomenclature indicates, characteristic artifacts consist of stone tools. The Paleolithic repertoire, for instance, includes hand axes, cleavers, choppers, and scrapers; the characteristic tools of the Mesolithic consist of microliths; and the Neolithic is associated with ground or polished stone equipment, including axes, mortars, and pestles. While initially tools were classified according to typologies that focused on their formal elements such as shape, texture, size, and so on, more recent studies have focused on functional analyses, which have enriched our understanding of how these tools may have been made and used.

While tools constitute the most prolific and durable equipment associated with these historical phases, other traces of material culture have also been subjected to detailed analyses. These include traces of habitations, including evidence for the use of natural caves and rock shelters. Evidence of domestic architecture, such as remains of huts, is available from some Mesolithic and several Neolithic sites. Attempts have also been made to study subsistence strategies on the basis of plant and animal remains as well as by examining the locations of settlements and contextualizing these in terms of possible paleoenvironments. Besides, there are indications of other crafts such as pottery, the making of terracotta sculpture, and paintings on the walls of rock shelters. The latter as well as the evidence of burials have been used to reconstruct cultural practices and religious beliefs.

Although specialists find the evidence of such archaeological cultures fascinating, interested lay readers usually identify the Harappan civilization (c. 2700–1800 BCE) as one of the most dramatic examples of the achievements of archaeological investigation. In fact, the discovery of the earliest evidence of urbanism in the subcontinent, more or less contemporaneous with cities in Mesopotamia and Egypt, sparked considerable excitement in the 1920s and subsequently. Investigations over decades have uncovered the extent of the civilization as well as its unique characteristics, including town planning, standardized craft production, and the development of a system of writing that is as yet undeciphered.

The late/post-Harappan phase is not as well understood. While urban life disintegrated, populations that survived evidently persisted and continued to use some of the earlier subsistence strategies. However, to suggest that this meant a continuation of the Harappan way of life seems unwarranted at present. Besides, in comparison to the enthusiasm evoked by the discoveries of the Harappan civilization, subsequent phases have been relatively less intensively excavated. While some Neolithic–Chalcolithic cultures in the Deccan, south India, Uttar Pradesh, and Rajasthan (c. second millennium CE) have been carefully explored, others remain relatively unknown. To some extent, this has fueled speculation about the end of the Harappan civilization.

Archaeological evidence for subsequent periods (c. first millennium BCE onward) includes that of megalithic burials from central and south India, with distinctive grave goods, including iron equipment and Black and Red Ware. The elaborate sepulchral structures bear testimony to the ability of leaders or chiefs to mobilize labor, and the recurrent use of some of these sites indicates an attempt to perpetuate collective memory. These structures thus offer a tantalizing glimpse of a set of complex social and political relations.

To the north, during the same period, two archaeological cultures have been considered as significant. These are the Painted Grey Ware sites, clustered around the Ganga–Yamuna doab, but extending both westward and eastward, and the somewhat later Northern Black Polished Ware sites, most prolific around the mid–Ganga valley, but with a subcontinent-wide distribution. The former sites generally appear to be rural settlements, whereas the latter include some of the earliest evidence of towns outside the geographical horizons of the Harappan civilization. Many of these cities were fortified and contained terracotta ring wells that were probably used for sewage or garbage disposal. Other distinctive artifacts include punch-marked and cast copper coins, among the earliest in the subcontinent.

While some of these sites have been systematically excavated, many more are known from small vertical trenches and surface explorations. Typical finds include evidence for the use of iron weapons and tools; signs of local smelting; traces of craft production, especially the manufacture and use of beads of semiprecious stone; and finds of terracotta artifacts. These allow a glimpse into the material culture of urban centers, which are often somewhat stereotypically described in contemporary texts.

Archaeologists have found evidence of religious architecture from several sites in the subcontinent from the end of the first millennium BCE onward, and for the entire period of the first millennium CE and beyond. These include some of the earliest Buddhist *stūpas*, rock-cut cave monasteries, shrines, and temples. It is likely that many of these architectural forms evolved from wooden prototypes that have not survived. What is also increasingly evident is that there were distinct regional styles that emerged in different parts of the subcontinent.

From the second millennium BCE, we also have evidence of textual traditions. It is likely that the *Ṛgveda*, a text containing prayers and chants invoking deities such as Agni, the fire-god, Indra, a warrior god, and Soma, a plant used to prepare a special drink, was composed in Vedic Sanskrit and compiled in the northwest, the region drained by the Indus and its tributaries, during this period. Subsequently, in the first half of the first millennium BCE, an enormous corpus of later Vedic texts, exegeses on an increasingly complex ritual tradition, were composed and compiled by various schools of priests. While localizing these texts has been a matter of scholarly debate, their focus on the Ganga–Yamuna doab is indisputable.

As may be expected, there have been attempts to correlate archaeological and textual evidence. Some of these, suggesting parallels between the

Ṛgveda and the Harappan civilization, have been rather far-fetched. Most such attempts have been hampered by the fact that the material does not lend itself to easy comparison: The preoccupations of ritual specialists are not easy to translate into the traces of pots, pans, tools, and plant and animal remains that archaeologists find. What is also apparent is that the elements of material culture represented in the text, such as the horse-drawn chariot and a predominance of pastoralism, have little in common with the complex urban milieu of the Harappan civilization.

From the mid– and late–first millennium BCE onward, a variety of texts is available in languages such as Pali, Prakrit, and Tamil. Some of these were composed, compiled, and preserved within specific religious traditions: Early Buddhist texts, for instance, were preserved in Pali, while Jaina works were recorded in Prakrit. Early Tamil literature, as compiled in the Sangam/Caṅkam anthologies, on the other hand, represented the vibrant world of a heroic society. This period also witnessed the proliferation of Sanskrit texts: Several of these were *śāstras*, texts that purported to lay down the norms or rules governing various aspects of life or even disciplines such as grammar; others were literary compositions, including plays.

By the mid–first millennium CE, the two major Sanskrit epics, the *Mahābhārata* and the *Rāmāyaṇa*, received their final form, as did the Purāṇas. Written in relatively simple Sanskrit verse, these texts, of which the first and the last were explicitly encyclopedic in nature, recorded genealogies of ruling lineages as well as norms of social behavior, besides containing narratives about heroes who were occasionally deified, and gods and goddesses. The Purāṇas included cosmogonic narratives as well.

Almost simultaneously, an elaborate commentarial tradition developed: These included commentaries on several *śāstras*. This period also witnessed the growth of courtly literature in Sanskrit, including the plays of Kālidāsa, often regarded as the epitome of Sanskrit literature, as well as eulogistic biographies of rulers. Somewhat later, some of the earliest devotional poems in praise of deities such as Viṣṇu and Śiva were composed in Tamil.

As is probably evident, virtually none of these texts were explicitly historical chronicles. In fact, the only work resembling a chronicle that has survived, the *Rājataraṅgiṇī*, an account of the history of Kashmir written by Kalhaṇa, was a work of the 12th century. Interestingly,

Kalhaṇa described himself as a *kavi* or poet rather than as a historian.

While the absence of obvious historical works has often been visualized as a problem, historians have to grapple with other issues as well. With rare exceptions, the dates of texts and authors are generally unknown. In most cases, these can be established only within approximate limits—in some instances, as for example in the case of the Sanskrit epics, it is evident that the texts evolved over a period of nearly a thousand years. Using texts to reconstruct historical processes, then, becomes a task fraught with obvious pitfalls.

As significant, the perspectives of the authors and intended readers of these texts shaped what was documented and how. More often than not, these works represent historical processes from the point of view of elite, literate groups, which constituted a minority within the complex social universe of the subcontinent. Using these texts to recover other points of views remains a challenge.

Apart from texts produced in the subcontinent, historians have frequently drawn on the accounts left by men who visited India. These include those who accompanied Alexander of Macedon, Megasthenes (the Greek ambassador to the Mauryan court), Chinese Buddhist pilgrims, and Arab travelers. Most of these accounts have the advantage of being securely dated, and can and have been fruitfully contextualized and analyzed to yield historical insights.

Other sources such as inscriptions, and to a lesser extent coins, have yielded vast quantities of data that have been tapped by epigraphists, numismatists, and historians. The earliest major corpus of inscriptions that has been deciphered is that of the Mauryan emperor Asoka (c. third century CE). These edicts were found in several parts of the subcontinent. Subsequently, inscriptions, often composed as panegyrics, celebrated the achievements of rulers. While not literally true, they provide an understanding of notions of kingship.

Besides, votive inscriptions, found in thousands from several sites, recorded gifts made by men and women to religious institutions. By the mid–first millennium CE, these often took the form of records of land grants inscribed on copper plates. These have been used to recover political, social, economic, and cultural histories.

The earliest coins issued in the subcontinent, in silver and copper (mid–first millennium BCE), were uninscribed, but were marked with symbols that probably represented ruling lineages and/or dominant urban groups, including merchants. By the end of the first millennium BCE, the subcontinent emerged as a major node along the Silk Route. Indo-Greek and later Kuṣāṇa coinage in gold (often following Roman standards) testifies to the importance of these exchanges, as do finds of hoards of Roman coins in south India.

Apart from attesting to economic transactions, coins have been studied for the representations of rulers and deities, as well as for their inscriptions. These have proved invaluable in the case of the Indo-Greek rulers, as well as for communities such as the Yaudheyas in the northwest.

As is evident, the sources used for reconstructing the history of ancient India are diverse. Using them effectively demands a wide range of expertise and collaboration among specialists in different disciplines and having a familiarity with a variety of languages. While the field has advanced enormously, there still remain areas of uncertainty and ignorance.

THE LIMITS OF CHRONOLOGY

The earliest traces of Paleolithic settlements in the subcontinent date back to nearly 2 million years before present (BP). That provides a convenient though almost inconceivably remote starting point for the Dictionary. However, defining a terminal point is far more arbitrary.

It has been fairly conventional to classify early Indian history into three phases—prehistory, encompassing the Paleolithic, Mesolithic, and Neolithic phases; protohistory, including the Harappan civilization, contemporary and later Neolithic–Chalcolithic cultures, and the Vedic tradition; and history, beginning from the mid–first millennium BCE. This classification was based on the assumption that the first two phases could be understood primarily if not only on the basis of archaeological evidence, whereas the last phase could be reconstructed on the basis of textual sources. This divide has been called into question in recent decades, as it is evident that archaeological data remain important for the so-called historical phase. What is more, the divide between literate and non- or preliterate societies or social strata was by no means watertight. Clearly, the use of writing is not particularly effective as a chronological marker.

Some of the earliest modern historical accounts of ancient India dealt primarily with dynastic history, focusing on ruling lineages that established what were regarded as empires. From this perspective, two or three terminal points were identified with a fair degree of clarity and consistency. One was around the sixth century CE, associated with the breakdown of the Gupta state in north India; the second in the seventh century, with the death of Harṣavardhana, one of the last rulers to control several parts of north India; and a third, in the 12th century, with the establishment of the Delhi sultanate.

In recent decades, all three terminal points have been called into question. The first two have been dismissed as being Ganga valley centric—it is evident that even while certain state structures collapsed in this area, political developments in other parts of the subcontinent were different. In the Deccan and further south, for instance, new polities emerged initially under the Pallavas and Cālukyas and subsequently under the Rāṣṭrakūṭas and Coḻas. Historians have also become increasingly skeptical about the notion that the establishment of the Delhi sultanate, with Muslim rulers, marked a sharp historical break. In fact, several elements of continuity have been traced between this political formation and its predecessors.

At a more fundamental level, the significance assigned to these dates has been reassessed. Scholars have pointed out that the first two dates were chosen because they marked the breakdown of centralized polities. They suggest that this tends to valorize centralization as a political strategy, ignoring the histories of relatively decentralized polities that may have been less visible and spectacular but often proved more enduring than the so-called empires.

Alternative criteria for assigning dates have also been suggested. Some of these are based on identifying crucial technological changes and/or economic developments. Thus, the earliest phases, where the archaeological evidence consists of stone tools, have been designated as Paleolithic, Mesolithic, and Neolithic. Subsequently, the Harappan evidence is often regarded as exemplifying a Bronze Age civilization in the subcontinent.

Within this framework, the evidence for the use of iron, which is far more easily available than copper and lends itself to the making of more durable tools and weapons, acquires a certain centrality. In this context, the impact of iron technology on warfare has been discussed occasionally. More frequently, however, it is the use of the iron plowshare and the iron axe that have been taken as markers of the expansion of agriculture. The former, it is often argued, was indispensable for tapping the fertility of heavy alluvial soils, while the latter has been considered equally crucial as a tool for clearing dense tropical forests. This in turn has been regarded as providing the basis for the development of more complex economic, social, and political institutions. From this perspective, the first millennium BCE is often designated as a formative period in the history of the subcontinent.

The technological determinism implicit, and occasionally explicit, in this formulation has often been called into question. Increasingly, it is evident that the use of iron did not automatically or inevitably transform social and economic relations. In fact, it is obvious that the impact of this and other technological innovations varied according to socioeconomic, political, and cultural contexts. Also, the chronology of the use of iron within the subcontinent shows regional variations. So there are problems in using these dates to project a neat, linear historical trajectory.

Do economic developments in themselves provide us with a more stable chronology? Attempts have been made to both identify significant economic activities and trace changes in these. One criterion that is frequently adopted is the spread of plow agriculture. This is very often taken to be symbolic of intensive, settled agriculture and consequently as marking a transformation in relations of production. While this seems plausible and logical, there is now a realization that the impact of plow agriculture could have varied from region to region, given the enormous environmental diversity within the subcontinent.

Attempts have also been made to use the growth and decline of long-distance exchange, correlated with the presence and absence of coinage and the prosperity or otherwise of urban centers, as a yardstick for measuring historical change. From this perspective, the period between c. second century BCE and second century CE is often regarded as marking the apex of these developments, with the preceding phase as one of gradual but sustained growth and the subsequent phase as typified by a decline that was only sporadically and partially reversed over several centuries. As in other instances, this framework captures certain important economic trends but fails to take into account the myriad economic processes that circumvented these developments in regions such as Rajasthan, Bengal, and Karnataka, which have been studied systematically, and possibly in other areas as well.

If "hard" evidence such as lists of dynasties and technological criteria has its limitations as a chronological marker, the situation becomes even more complicated if we focus on religious, cultural, or linguistic developments. For instance, it is tempting to think of religious history in terms of the growth and elaboration of Vedic religion, followed by a reaction evident in Buddhism, Jainism, and a host of other philosophical traditions, in turn succeeded by the growth of theism within several religious traditions. While this outline is by no means inaccurate, it conceals the complex interaction among traditions that were often not as sharply differentiated as we tend to imagine. Such interactions ranged from outright hostility and conflict, on the one hand, to a wide spectrum of dialogic processes, which often produced assimilations where the "original" was virtually impossible to identify.

It is perhaps evident by now that virtually all the chronological markers that we may choose have their shortcomings. None is universally applicable for the entire subcontinent. Thus, any terminal point can be dismissed as arbitrary. The year 1000 CE that we have chosen is one such marker. Obviously, the millennium of the Common/Christian Era was not a significant date in early Indian history. The only political events that were more or less coeval were the raids of Sultan Mahmud of Ghazni, the significance of which has been debated. In the present work, as for instance in entries on the history of the Co̲las, we have in fact overshot this chronological marker, including later developments as well. Once we acknowledge that these dates are not sacrosanct, we can work toward a more nuanced understanding of the complex past of the subcontinent. This may be somewhat untidy, but will hopefully be fruitful in conveying a sense of the multiple and by no means uniform strands that went into the making of the history of ancient India. While we have chosen the year 1000 CE as an approximate marker, the interested reader who wishes to follow developments in the subsequent period can consult *A Historical Dictionary of Medieval India* by Iqtidar Alam Khan (Scarecrow Press, Lanham, Maryland, 2008).

HOW CONSEQUENTIAL WERE KINGS?

Dynastic history occupied a place of honor among the themes in early Indian history that received attention in the late 18th century, 19th century, and the first half of the 20th century. Names of rulers were retrieved from texts such as the Purāṇas, which contained genealogies of several ruling lineages as well as from inscriptions that also often included genealogies. Besides, names of kings who issued coins were carefully collated and listed.

Many of these early attempts at reconstructing political history were characterized by a preoccupation with "fitting" in names that were discovered within existing or established genealogies. This was painstaking scholarship, marked by efforts to match names that sounded similar, work out relative chronologies, and establish possible sequences of succession, with an attention to minute details often absent from present-day scholarship on the theme.

At the same time, there were certain preconceptions that framed these enterprises. For instance, succession was assumed to be patrilineal—any other mode(s) that surfaced in the sources was generally ignored or at best grudgingly acknowledged. This attempt to tidy up masses of often intractable data thus often led to a tendency to gloss over anything that did not conform to what was valorized as normative.

The other overarching concern, something we have noted earlier, was with empires. This is not surprising, given that the earliest studies of the ancient past were located within the colonial context, with India as a part of the British Empire. Interestingly, the intellectual enterprise of uncovering imperial precedents was something that attracted the attention of both imperial as well as nationalist scholars. The former focused on early empires such as those of the Mauryas (c. fourth–second centuries BCE) and the Guptas (c. fourth–sixth centuries CE) as possible points of comparison with the British Empire in India, uncovering structures of administration as well as military and judicial institutions, focusing also on imperial ideologies and the personalities of individual rulers. Nationalist scholars also covered the same terrain but from a slightly different perspective, reinterpreting the evidence to argue that India had respectably old imperial traditions of its own, and that the present state of dependence was only a passing phase: New heroes, suitably inspired by accounts of their illustrious predecessors from the past, were expected to reverse the fortunes of the country that were at a temporary low.

Yet, to dismiss all these historical studies as merely instrumental in strengthening colonial or nationalist ideologies would be simplistic. In fact, the excitement and challenge of these intellectual endeavors often went beyond their stated objectives. This created the space for investigating and attempting to understand rulers such as the Mauryan emperor Asoka—a successful conqueror who subsequently gave up war. Not surprisingly, several historians wrote biographies of the ruler. Some of these were almost hagiographical; others attempted to locate him within the contemporary context, defined in terms of extra-subcontinental networks as well as the complex sociocultural and economic context within the subcontinent. And yet others blamed him squarely for what was regarded as a misplaced policy of pacifism. This in turn was regarded as encouraging what were defined as "foreign invasions"—the incursions of groups such as the Indo-Greeks, Śakas, and Kuṣāṇas into the northwest (c. second century BCE onward).

While several nationalist historians mined the evidence in search of heroic figures, others tried to trace the roots of democratic institutions and processes in the past. This led to collating information about assemblies, mentioned in texts such as the *Ṛgveda* (c. second millennium BCE) and inscriptions, and examining the ways in which these functioned. Also significant were studies of *gaṇas* or *saṃghas*, often considered synonymous with republics, described in texts from the mid–first millennium BCE onward. By the 20th century, archaeological evidence indicated that some of these polities issued coins in their own name. It was also evident that they continued to flourish in some parts of the subcontinent until the mid–first millennium CE. More detailed studies led to the recognition that many of these polities were in fact oligarchies rather than true democracies: Nevertheless, evidence for nonmonarchical forms of government was often used to argue that India was fit for parliamentary democracy in the 20th century.

Other political processes that have attracted attention include the emergence of regional political formations. The earliest tangible evidence for these is provided in the lists of *mahājanapadas* (literally great *janapadas*, areas where people settled down), available from the mid–first millennium BCE. In the case of the *mahājanapada* of Magadha (part of present-day Bihar), we can trace its development from a state to the nucleus of an empire within the course of a couple of centuries.

In other instances, it is increasingly evident that political structures centered on regions were often far more stable than those that attempted to encompass the entire subcontinent. In fact ruling lineages sometimes had relatively short-term histories of spectacular rises and declines that were often described with poetic flourish in inscriptions that contain panegyrics. At the same time, the more or less autonomous region often continued to flourish in spite of these apparently dramatic changes. Regions such as the northwest of the subcontinent, with its links with Central Asia and Iran, the western areas, the Deccan, the Tamil lands, and the eastern parts of the subcontinent all bear testimony to these long-term trends. As noted earlier, the complex process whereby regional identities were consolidated can be traced back to the first millennium CE, if not earlier, in several cases.

Regional historiographies, often representative of what have been defined as subnationalisms, sometimes replicate the preoccupations of earlier nationalist historians. So it is not unusual to find the Sātavāhanas (c. second century BCE–second century CE) being projected in the heroic mode in histories of Maharashtra and Andhra Pradesh. Other ruling lineages often similarly claimed by historians working within sub nationalist frameworks include the Cālukyas (c. sixth–eighth centuries) and the Rāṣṭrakūṭas (c. 8th–10th centuries CE) in Karnataka and the Co̲las (c. 9th–13th centuries CE) in Tamil Nadu.

At another level, the very relevance of studying political history through the framework of narratives of the rise and fall of dynasties has been called into question. Earlier writing often classified virtually everything, from scripts to pots, in terms of dynastic labels. So it was not unusual to find references to Mauryan Brāhmī, Śunga sculpture, or Śaka–Kuṣāṇa pottery. Increasingly, however, scholars have realized that such classifications emanate from a framework that assumes that dynastic changes influence a whole range of economic, technological, social, and cultural developments, an assumption that is at best simplistic and at worst misleading. Scholars now face the challenge of evolving more complex frameworks that can create space for an understanding of the past that is at once more holistic and pluralistic.

TRACKING RELIGIOUS TRADITIONS

If kings attracted the attention of early Western scholars, so did what was often perceived as the bewildering plethora of religious beliefs and practices in the subcontinent. Here again, we can trace a range of perspectives. On the one hand were scholars who looked to the East as a source of spiritual enlightenment and guidance for what was regarded as the eternal quest of the human soul. On the other hand were those with an evangelizing mission, who felt that an acquaintance with indigenous traditions would help them to further their objectives of converting the heathen. What is interesting is that although their perspectives were divergent, both tended to focus on elements that they found most exotic if not bizarre—the former in order to evoke awe and the latter to provoke horror.

In the early 19th century, the focus was initially on what was defined as Hinduism. This was reconstructed on the basis of practices that were observed, as well as on studies of texts such as the Vedas, including the Upaniṣads and the Purāṇas. Visual sources such as temple architecture and sculpture were also explored. While visual sources seemed apparently accessible, western scholars gained access to texts through a complex process of mediation and frequently depended on *brāhmaṇa* pundits. The history of this interaction, located in a context where the informant was both crucial and subordinate, is in itself a fascinating one. There were several problems: the obvious one of rendering the language, especially that of sacred and ritual texts, accessible as well as the more complicated ones of understanding and evaluating the significance of the texts and of locating them within historical contexts.

The responses of nationalist scholars to these endeavors were varied. Some accepted the framework advocated by Western scholars, suggesting that monotheistic or monistic ideas marked the apex of human philosophical insight, and sifted through texts to argue that instances of such "lofty" ideals could be recovered from some if not all texts that were classified as Hindu. Others adopted a more defensive strategy, providing elaborate justifications for precepts and practices that seemed the furthest removed from Anglican Christianity. Inevitably, polemics and scholarship jostled with each other in a situation where religious traditions, especially those that seemed older than and distinct from Christianity, posed a challenge to the beliefs and practices of the ruling elite.

It was also evident that the diversity of textual traditions was matched if not exceeded by countless variations observed in contemporary ritual praxis. Attempts to document and explain these ran into all the pitfalls of the ethnographic enterprise but were, nonetheless, pursued zealously. In some instances, practices that seemed strange were taken as "proof" of the inferiority of the "degenerate" East. In other cases, Western scholars succumbed to the fascination of the esoteric.

Some of these complications are evident in the discussion on the chronologies of textual traditions. The Purāṇas purported to provide an account that began from remote antiquity but were composed in accessible Sanskrit. The Vedas, on the other hand, were written in archaic Sanskrit. The process of dating the texts was hampered by an initial reluctance to move beyond the framework of Biblical chronology. However, when that was overthrown by 19th-century geological discoveries and Darwinian evolutionism, indigenous claims were considered with less skepticism. Comparative philology, the evidence of the *Avesta*, and inscriptions found from present-day Turkey were used to date the Vedas, with the *Ṛgveda*, the earliest text, being placed in the second millennium BCE.

However, fixing the dates of individual texts or of genres was only part of the problem. What needed to be taken into consideration was that religious traditions coexisted and interacted with one another for several centuries. Thus, while it was possible to suggest that Vedic religion was superseded by Purāṇic traditions, this was qualified by the realization that most subsequent traditions, no matter how disparate and different they appeared, continued to appeal to the Vedas as the authority from which they derived legitimation.

To add to the complexity, it was soon evident that Hinduism, no matter how loosely defined, was not the sole religion for which ancient texts were available. Other traditions, such as Buddhism and Jainism, were "discovered" in the course of the 19th century. The former, in particular, received considerable scholarly attention, as it was evident that it was virtually a world religion, having spread through vast tracts of Central, East, and Southeast Asia, among people who differed widely in terms of language and culture.

For several decades, scholars interpreted the rise of these traditions as a reaction to Vedic religion, with its emphasis on sacrifices. They were also regarded as marking a growing concern with the individual, in turn related to the complexities of urban life and the emergence of stratified societies in the Ganga valley. However, as noted earlier, the relations between religious traditions was often more complicated than this formulation suggests.

Some of these complications are evident in the institutionalization of theistic beliefs and practices, including devotionalism, within each of the major traditions, as well as the incorporation of Tantric ideas within

Hinduism and Buddhism. The latter development was one indication of an enormous substratum of popular cults and practices. These included worship of sacred trees and stones, designating certain spaces as sacred, a wide range of fertility cults, and cults centered on a variety of spirits and demigods. Each of the dominant religious traditions had to engage with these practices, accommodating, transforming, and assimilating them through a virtually unending dialogue. While many of these traditions were initially dismissed as "low" by historians, they have attracted considerable attention in recent decades.

EXPRESSIONS OF CULTURAL PRACTICE: LANGUAGE, PAINTING, SCULPTURE, AND ARCHITECTURE

The discussions on religious traditions were inextricably interwoven with certain other issues: those of language and what may be broadly classified as artistic expression. Textual explorations of religious traditions led to an awareness of the variety of languages that were in use in early India: Vedic Sanskrit, classical Sanskrit, Pali, Prakrit, and Tamil. Almost simultaneously, scholars became aware of other, more or less secular, compositions in these languages. These included literary works such as plays, epics, poems, and prose compositions, as well as treatises on a variety of subjects ranging from grammar, to astronomy, mathematics, medicine, and philosophy. Grappling with these textual traditions was and remains a major plank of the scholarly enterprise, at once challenging and rewarding.

Early attempts to reconstruct histories of languages and literary genres were inevitably shaped by the concern with and implications of identifying the Indo-Aryan and Indo-European families of languages. Indigenous Sanskritic scholarly tradition claimed that all the languages used in the subcontinent were derived from Sanskrit: This claim was soon contested as there was a growing awareness of the Dravidian, Austro-Asiatic, and Tibeto-Burman languages in use in different parts of the subcontinent.

At another level, Western scholars initially tended to evaluate subcontinental literary productions using yardsticks derived from Western traditions. This occasionally led to dismissive statements about works that were thought to be too ornate, abstruse, or even simply boring.

Nationalist scholars often responded to these critiques by sifting through texts to produce excerpts that appeared to conform to Western aesthetic norms. In addition, they attempted to foreground the elaborate discussions on aesthetics within Sanskrit, for instance, to argue for alternative criteria for evaluation. This latter endeavor has proved extremely fruitful.

Similar trends can be discerned in attempts to make sense of visual material. Paintings have been recovered from several cave and rock-shelter sites in the subcontinent. These range from those produced in the context of Mesolithic hunting–gathering societies to the more elaborate works under royal patronage at sites such as Ajanta (mid–first millennium CE). Once again, scholars have shifted from measuring these against the yardsticks of European art to a more contextualized understanding of their meanings, exploring the extent to which these were shaped by patrons, spectators, and the artists themselves.

Analyses of stone (and metal) sculpture have also proceeded along identical lines. Initially several Western scholars were horrified to find representations of deities with multiple arms and heads, which were often dismissed as grotesque. It was only with the understanding of the complex and sophisticated iconographical principles at work that such representations were better appreciated.

At another level, the ubiquitous terracotta figurines, initially dismissed as relatively "low" artistic works, are now receiving considerable attention. It is evident that they were used for a variety of purposes—some may have been toys, others venerated as objects of worship or auspicious symbols, and yet others were probably meant for relatively secular displays. They remain as reminders of the multiplicity of artistic traditions that flourished in the subcontinent, as also of the more ephemeral visual displays mentioned in texts that have left no traces in the archaeological record.

In architecture too, earlier comparisons with Persian or Hellenistic styles (almost invariably to the detriment of what was found in the subcontinent) have made way for contextual evaluations of surviving structures—ranging from *stūpas* and temples, to rock-cut caves, monasteries, and fortification walls, as also of traces of domestic architecture that are at least occasionally visible in the archaeological record. The meanings of architectural symbols have been opened up for exploration. There is also a deeper appreciation of the expertise involved in such constructions.

FOREGROUNDING THE ECONOMY: NEW CRITERIA FOR HISTORICAL INVESTIGATION

By the early 20th century, a new focus on the economy was apparent in historical investigations. These studies gained in momentum around the mid–20th century, and the theme continued to attract scholarly attention for several decades. While some of these studies were located within an explicit or implicit Marxist framework, others were inspired by nationalist ideals and suggested that the subcontinent had been the site of spectacular advances in craft production, including metal and especially iron working, trade, seafaring, and of course, agriculture. Vast quantities of data were collated from texts, inscriptions, coins, and archaeological reports to substantiate these claims.

Marxist historiography on the subject was particularly stimulating. Briefly, it involved a rejection of Karl Marx's own understanding of the subcontinent as a changeless, stagnant society and an attempt to understand early historical processes in terms of the categories and stages Marx deployed in his analysis of European history—primitive communism and the slave mode of production and feudalism.

It soon became evident that although there was evidence of economic change within the subcontinent, it did not conform to the stages delineated for European history, which were, in any case, being subjected to revisions within Marxist historiography. For instance, while slavery as an institution could be documented fairly easily, it was clear that slaves had never constituted the dominant labor force in the crucial sectors of the economy in the subcontinent. It is in this context that categories such as "Indian Feudalism" were evolved to take into account what were seen as variations on the European model.

Indian feudalism was visualized primarily on the basis of the evidence from inscriptions that documented land grants, which became particularly prolific in certain areas. These were construed as leading to the emergence of self-sufficient village communities, under the dominance of *brāhmaṇas* who were the major beneficiaries of these grants. Other elements that were highlighted included political decentralization, the decline of long-distance exchange, the paucity of coins, and the decline of urban centers. Occasionally, this was regarded as a phase of cultural decadence as well.

It was in this context that the categories of early historic and early medieval came into use. The first was used to designate the period from the mid–first millennium BCE to the early centuries CE (with considerable variations regarding the terminal point). This was characterized by the intensification of agriculture in areas such as the Ganga valley, typified by the use of the iron-tipped plowshare and transplantation of paddy, accompanied by growing differentiation within rural society, including the emergence of a category of landless laborers. Other developments that were considered critical included the emergence of urban centers, characterized by markets, craft production, and the presence of an urban elite, consisting of rich merchants, bankers, rulers, and courtesans. In terms of political structures, the early historic phase was associated with the emergence of early states.

By the early medieval period, it was argued, the dominant social category was that of landed intermediaries, who offered military support and (in the case of *brāhmaṇa* intermediaries, usually the recipients of land grants), legitimacy to rulers in return for recognition of their economic and political status. Political relations were fluid, with intermediaries asserting control whenever the overlords appeared to be weak.

More recently, there have been attempts to redefine the early medieval as a period when dominant clans consolidated control over specific localities and regions. The proliferation of regional states, it is suggested, far from marking a collapse of central authority, represented an intensification of political processes in new areas. This was accompanied by socioeconomic transformations that are often categorized as peasantization, drawing attention to the incorporation of agricultural populations within state structures and to differentiation within rural society. Another feature that is often highlighted is the integration of local and regional cults within major religious traditions. This was also the period when regional linguistic and cultural identities gradually crystallized.

Both these formulations have been refined, qualified, and questioned over the past few years. What is evident is that they have drawn attention to a whole range of issues—the importance or otherwise of technology; the significance if any of irrigation; the socioeconomic position of producers, whether of crafts or agricultural produce; and the ways in which resources were defined, mobilized, distributed, and controlled. Strategies for regulating access to resources such as land, labor, and technologies have also been opened up for investigation. In other words, the focus on the economy has generated some of the most fruitful and interesting debates about early Indian history.

SOCIAL HISTORY: BEYOND THE "RIGID" CASTE SYSTEM

If one were to identify one of the most resilient stereotypes about early India, it would probably be the perceived continuity of the caste system from remote antiquity to the present. There have been suggestions that caste, often regarded as synonymous with *varṇa* or the fourfold division of society into priests, warriors, independent producers and traders, and servile groups, existed in the Harappan civilization. However, while Harappan society was certainly differentiated, it is not possible to determine whether status was assigned on the basis of birth, one of the hallmarks of caste society.

The first textual reference to the fourfold order occurs in a late section of the *Ṛgveda.* Subsequently, later Vedic literature indicates that establishing and maintaining social differences was a major preoccupation of the priesthood. Occasionally, both early and later Vedic texts envisaged a twofold social order, consisting of two opposed groups, the *Ārya* and the *Dāsa*. While the texts suggested that the opposition rested on different cultural, social, and linguistic practices, early 19th-century scholarship often interpreted these differences in racial terms. This has had a long and bitter legacy, both within the subcontinent and outside. Even today, claims to the heritage of the *Āryas* and the *Dāsas* are often made by groups aspiring to or contesting social identities.

The history of contestation is, however, not new. As early as the mid–first millennium BCE, Buddhist and Jaina traditions insisted that the category of *khattiya/kṣatriya*, the warriors, was superior to the priesthood, and suggested that social identities based on birth were irrelevant for those who renounced the world.

The same period witnessed the development of a major textual tradition, that of the Dharmasūtras and Dharmaśāstras, marking an attempt by *brāhmaṇas* to codify social practice. These texts in general and the *Manusmṛti* in particular, along with the commentaries on them, were used by the colonial authorities to determine Hindu law in the late 18th and 19th centuries. They thus acquired an authority that their authors had claimed much earlier, but perhaps with less success.

Toward the end of the first millennium BCE and through the first millennium CE, inscriptional evidence indicates that men and women often used other modes of identifying themselves. Some of these were derived from their occupations, others from place names, yet others from kinship affiliations. As these inscriptions were analyzed, it became evident that the *varṇa* system was by no means the sole or even the most important mode of defining social identities.

At the same time, it became apparent that the normative *varṇa* order influenced social relations. Historians have tried to capture this process by using categories such as brahmanization and ksatriyization to demonstrate how those who aspired to upward social mobility adopted and adapted practices associated with the two top-ranking *varṇas*.

Studies have also revealed that the adoption of the *varṇa*-based social order varied substantially from one region to the next—in some areas, a virtually twofold division between *brāhmaṇas* and the rest seems to have operated. Besides, there were several areas, such as the northeastern parts of the subcontinent and parts of central India, where societies that had virtually no resemblance to the *varṇa* order survived for centuries.

Equally important, social histories are now attempting to focus on hitherto-marginalized groups. These include people living in the forests, those engaged in hunting, gathering, and in shifting cultivation. Their visibility within early Indian textual traditions was characterized by considerable ambivalence.

Textual traditions often represented the forest as a retreat from the pressures of worldly existence and, in some instances, as an idyllic, almost utopian world. These romanticized descriptions of the forest often had very little to say about real hunters. On a less exalted plane, texts such as the *Arthaśāstra*, which dealt with questions of statecraft, depicted the forest as an area from which resources such as timber, elephants, medicinal plants, honey, and other produce could be appropriated.

Attitudes toward hunting were also fraught with tension. On the one hand, the ability to hunt was considered as a symbol of virility: The king as hunter is a recurrent image in textual traditions as well as in visual representations. On the other hand, actual hunters were almost invariably assigned a low status in Sanskrit textual traditions. At the same time, there are occasional indications that forest peoples were included in state militias. Reading these texts against the grain to recover histories of forest peoples (among others) is attracting academic attention.

Other marginalized groups that are receiving attention include those designated as untouchable in Brahmanical and other texts. The experience of such groups has been retrieved and analyzed, with special attention being paid to indications of resistance and/or upward mobility within the social order. Such instances were generally viewed with disfavor by Brahmanical authors; nonetheless, their existence points to fissures in the normative social order.

Histories of gender relations, too, have received renewed attention. These have moved away from the earlier preoccupation of nationalist historians, who sought to claim that women in early India were better off than their counterparts in the Western world. There is now far more attention to differences among women, as also between women and men, to regional variations, and to issues ranging from participation in productive and reproductive processes, socialization into gender roles, sexuality, kinship structures, and access to and spaces within religious traditions, to name a few.

It is evident, then, that studies of early Indian history are being enriched and reshaped in several ways. The dynamism of the discipline, developing in several directions, would indicate that our understanding of the past will be transformed in the future.

THE DICTIONARY

– A –

ABASTANOI. Greek name for people living in the northwest of the subcontinent, on the **Chenab**, mentioned in accounts (c. fourth century BCE) of the campaigns of **Alexander (of Macedon)**, identical with the **Sanskrit** Ambasṭḥa, mentioned in the ***Aitareya Brāhmaṇa*** and the ***Mahābhārata***, and the **Pali** Ambaṭṭha. They may have been a martial **tribe** who, with the breakdown of the tribal social structure, took to other occupations, functioning as priests, farmers, and physicians. According to Greek accounts, their **army** consisted of 60,000 infantry, 6,000 cavalry, and 500 chariots.

ABHIDHAMMA PIṬAKA. The third and latest of the **Pali** canonical texts recognized in the early **Buddhist Theravāda** tradition. Its compilation is dated to the third **Buddhist Council**, held during the reign of the **Mauryan** emperor **Asoka**, that is, c. third century BCE. The text focuses on **philosophy** and psychology and lays down methods for training the mind. *See also* LITERATURE.

ABHIJÑĀNA ŚĀKUNTALAM. Perhaps the best-known play in **Sanskrit**, written by **Kālidāsa**, c. fourth–fifth centuries CE. This was among the earliest works to be translated into a number of European languages. The play draws on an old legend of love, separation, and the ultimate union of Duśyanta, recognized as an important ancestor of the protagonists of the ***Mahābhārata***, and Śakuntalā, the daughter of a heavenly nymph and foster child of a sage. Kālidāsa reworked the story into a courtly romance, marked by an extremely skillful use of similes and metaphors, often regarded as one of the distinctive features of classical Sanskrit **literature**.

ABHINAVAGUPTA. Sanskrit scholar who lived in Kashmir (10th–11th centuries CE) and contributed to the development of aesthetics. His works include the *Locana*, a commentary on **Ānandavardhana**'s ***Dhvanyāloka***, and the *Abhinavabhārati*, a commentary on the ***Nāṭyaśāstra***, attributed to **Bharata (2)**. He also composed several treatises on Kashmiri **Śaivism**. His works, marked by an ornate style, influenced subsequent generations of scholars. *See also* LITERATURE.

ABHĪRA. Name of a **tribe** first mentioned in the ***Mahābhāṣya*** of **Patañjali** (c. second century BCE). Initially associated with the lower **Indus** valley and western Rajasthan, its leaders served as generals under the **Śakas**, with some chiefs taking on the title of ***mahākṣatrapa***. After the decline of the **Sātavāhanas**, they extended control over north Maharashtra by the mid–third century CE. The Abhīras are listed among those who rendered homage to **Samudragupta**.

ABHISĀRA. Name of a people and, by extension, the land inhabited by them, identified with the hills between the **Jhelum** and the **Chenab**, corresponding with parts of present-day Kashmir. The Abhisāras and their ruler, **Abhisares** or Abisares, are mentioned in Greek accounts (c. fourth century BCE) of the invasion of **Alexander (of Macedon)**.

ABHISARES. Chief of the **Abhisāras**, also known as Abisares, who offered resistance to **Alexander (of Macedon)** (c. 326 BCE).

***ABHIṢEKA*. Sanskrit** term meaning "sprinkling (or anointing) with water or other substances," the central element of rituals for the proclamation of royal power. The earliest references to the *abhiṣeka* were in **later Vedic** texts (c. 10th–6th centuries BCE).

ABISARES. *See* ABHISARES.

***ĀCĀRANGA SŪTRA*.** *See ĀYĀRA.*

ACHAEMENID. Iranian dynasty that established a vast empire in western Asia. Achaemenid contact with and control over the northwestern part of the subcontinent is attested to by the **inscriptions** of rulers such as **Darius I** and contemporary and later Greek works, including that of **Herodotus**. **Cyrus**, the founder of the Achaemenid Empire (c. sixth century BCE) may have advanced up to the Kabul valley. Darius I extended control over **Gandhara** as well as "India," probably the lands along the **Indus** valley. Troops were recruited from both provinces during **Xerxes**'s campaign against the Greeks. Achaemenid presence in the region continued until the invasion of **Alexander (of Macedon)** (c. 326 BCE). The Achaemenids drew both military support as well as other resources, including gold, from these provinces or *satrapies*. ***Satraps*** or provincial governors combined civil and military functions. Contact with the Achaemenids led to the use of **Aramaic** and the development of the **Kharoṣṭhī script**. More generally, the imperial model provided by the Achaemenids may have influenced the **Mauryas**. This is suggested by certain parallels in **architecture**, in the decorative motifs used on pillars, and in the terminology used in **Asokan inscriptions**.

ACYUTA. King, probably of **Ahichchhatra**, c. fourth century CE, mentioned as being defeated and deposed by the **Gupta** ruler **Samudragupta** in the **Allahabad Pillar Inscription**. **Copper coins** bearing the word *acyu* are attributed to him.

ADAM. Archaeological site in Maharashtra, with evidence of five major occupational phases. Finds from Period I (c. third–second millennium BCE) included microliths and remains of circular huts. Period II (c. last quarter of the second millennium BCE) provided evidence of **pottery**, including **black slipped ware** and **black and red ware**, and microliths and bone artifacts. Other finds included **copper** rings, crucibles, and evidence of post holes. Period III (c. 1000–500 BCE) yielded **iron** artifacts such as points, arrowheads, chisels, knives, plowshares, rods, and nails in addition to the earlier equipment, beads of semiprecious stone, and black and red ware. Traces of a rampart have also been assigned to this phase. Period IV, assigned to pre-**Mauryan** and Mauryan levels (c. 500–150 BCE), yielded iron and bone **tools**, stone artifacts with a typical Mauryan polish, **terracotta** figurines, and beads of semiprecious stone. Other finds included **Northern Black Polished Ware** and ring wells. Period V was associated with local lineages such as the Bhadras, Mitras, Mahārathis, and **Sātavāhanas**. Finds included iron equipment such as plowshares, chisels, knives, and arrowheads. Other artifacts included a sealing bearing the legend *asaka* ***janapada***, silver **punch-marked coins**, lead coins of the Sātavāhanas, terracotta figurines, ivory artifacts, several hundred beads of glass, which may have been locally manufactured, and beads of ivory, bone, copper, and semiprecious stone. Also found were remains of burnt-brick structures, ring wells, and hearths. Other structural remains included a ***stūpa***. There was also evidence of **burials**.

ADAMGARH. Archaeological (natural rock shelter) site near the **Narmada** valley, Madhya Pradesh. There is evidence for occupation during the **Mesolithic** phase (c. 6000–5000 BCE). The site has yielded several thousand microliths made of chert, chalcedony, jasper, and agate. There is evidence for domesticated animals, including cattle, sheep, goat, pig, and dog, as well as wild animals, such as deer, hare, and porcupine. The walls of the rock shelter contain **paintings**, including representations of hunting scenes.

ADHYAKṢA*. Sanskrit** term used in texts such as the ***Arthaśāstra (c. fourth century BCE onward) to designate officials in charge of a variety of departments, including those responsible for regulating **agriculture**, **craft** production, and **trade**, mobilizing resources from **forests** and mines, and administering settlements. Some historians suggest that the *adhyakṣa* was identical with the ***agronomoi*** mentioned in **Megasthenes**'s account of **Mauryan** administration.

ADICHANNALLUR. Megalithic site in Tamil Nadu, with evidence of several urn **burials** (c. first millennium BCE). Grave goods include **iron** artifacts such as knives, swords, and spearheads and **Black and Red Ware**. Also found were red ware and black ware, **copper** ornaments such as bangles and rings, and beads made of **terracotta** and semiprecious stones. Traces of grain, especially rice, were recovered. Remains of a settlement have also been excavated. This included traces of a rampart and kilns for the manufacture of **pottery**. Some potsherds contain graffiti, possibly in **Tamil Brāhmī**.

ADITI. Early **Vedic** (c. 1800–1000 BCE) **goddess**, recognized as the mother of the principal male deities, known as the Ādityas. Goddesses were relatively insignificant in the Vedic pantheon, and the worship of Aditi faded out by the mid–first millennium BCE. *See also* RELIGION.

ĀDITYA. One of the first major rulers (r.c. 871–907 CE) of the **Coḻa** dynasty, known from his **inscriptions**. He extended the kingdom at the expense of the **Pallavas** and the **Pāṇḍyas**. He is associated with the construction of some early **Śaiva temples** on the banks of the **Kaveri**.

ADURRU. Archaeological site in Andhra Pradesh, find spot of a ***stūpa*** built on a spoke-wheeled plan. Other structures include remains of a **Buddhist monastery** and shrine, all of which were probably built between the second and third centuries CE.

ADVAITA. Monistic **philosophical** system, whose origins can be traced from the early **Upaniṣads**, c. sixth century BCE. The best-known advocate of this school of thought was **Śaṅkarācārya**.

AGALASSOI. Tribe mentioned in Greek accounts (c. fourth century BCE) of the invasion of **Alexander (of Macedon)**, as living in the northwest of the subcontinent, with an **army** consisting of 40,000 infantry and 3,000 cavalry.

ĀGAMA. **Sanskrit** term, meaning "coming" or "approaching," used to designate a variety of texts dealing with rituals and associated with **Purāṇic** (c. fourth century CE onward) or **Tantric** (c. sixth century CE onward) deities such as **Viṣṇu**, **Śiva**, or the **goddess**. The texts emphasize devotional modes of worship, including worship in **temples**, and pilgrimages. Several subdivisions are recognized within each stream of āgamic literature. *See also* PĀÑCARĀTRA; RELIGION.

AGASTYA. Sage mentioned in the **Sanskrit epics** and the **Purāṇas**, regarded as responsible for the introduction of Sanskritic and **Brahmanical** traditions south of the **Vindhyas**. While the historicity of these narratives has not been established, Agastya is recognized as symbolic of the process of the Brahmanization of the southern part of the subcontinent.

AGATHOKLES. Bactrian Greek ruler, c. second century BCE, who issued **coins** bearing legends in the **Brāhmī script**.

AGESILAOS. Greek **architect** (c. first–second century CE) associated with the **Kuṣāṇa** ruler **Kaniṣka**, who is attributed with the construction of a number of ***stūpas*** in the northwest of the subcontinent.

AGIABIR. Archaeological site in Uttar Pradesh with evidence of five major occupational phases. Period I (c. 1300–900 BCE) had parallels with the **Narhan** culture and yielded **black and red ware**. Period II (c. 900–600 BCE) provided evidence of the use of **iron**. Period III (c. 600–200 BCE) yielded **Northern Black Polished Ware** and evidence of a bead-making workshop that may have dated to the preceding phase. Finds from Period IV (c. 200 BCE–300 CE) include burnt-brick houses, ring wells, **copper coins**, and **terracotta** figurines. Period V (300–700 CE) was defined as **Gupta**/post-Gupta.

AGNI. Fire, among the principal deities of the **Vedic** pantheon (c. second millennium BCE), identified with the **sacrificial** fire and regarded as mediating between gods and men. *See also* HINDUISM; RELIGION.

AGNIMITRA. Son of **Puṣyamitra Śuṅga**, the founder of the **Śuṅga** dynasty, second century BCE. Agnimitra ruled over **Vidisha** on behalf of his father and succeeded to the throne on Puṣyamitra's death. He is represented as a romantic hero in **Kālidāsa**'s play, *Mālavikāgnimitram*. Agnimitra may have issued **copper coins** bearing his name.

***AGRAHĀRA*. Sanskrit** term used especially c. mid–first millennium CE onward to designate a category of **land grants** made to ***brāhmaṇas* (1)** or Brahmanical institutions, usually by members of the ruling elite. Generally these grants were in perpetuity, and donees were given the right to organize production and collect **revenue** and other resources from the land.

AGRICULTURE. The beginnings of agriculture in the subcontinent may be traced to the **Neolithic** phase. The earliest evidence comes from **Mehrgarh** (c. 8000 BCE onward) in the northwest and, somewhat later, from sites in the Deccan, Central India, Kashmir, and the northeast. Evidence of agriculture includes finds of charred grain, traces of other parts of domesticated plants, stone **tools** such as hoes and grinding stones, and storage facilities. These are often found in **archaeological** sites belonging to later historical phases as well, including **Harappan** and **early historic** sites. The latter (as also **megalithic** sites) have yielded evidence of **iron** tools. A wide variety of crops are in evidence, including wheat, barley, rice, millets, pulses, gram, peas, oilseeds, especially mustard and sesame, sugarcane, and cotton. Sites that have yielded evidence of domesticated plants include **Adichannallur**, **Ahar**, **Atranjikhera**, **Babarkot**, **Bahal**, **Balathal**, **Balu**, **Banawali**, **Bhagimohari**, **Burzahom**, **Chirand**, **Chopani Mando**, **Daimabad**, **Golbai Sasan**, **Gufkral**, **Hallur**, **Hastinapura**, **Hulas**, **Hulas Khera**, **Imlidih Khurd**, **Inamgaon**, **Kaothe**, **Koldihwa**, **Kunal**, **Lal Qila**, **Mahagara**, **Maheshwar**, **Manamunda**, **Manjhi**, **Maski**, **Nagiari**, **Narhan**, **Navdatoli**, **Noh**, **Pandu Rajar Dhibi**, **Rehman Dheri**, **Rojdi**, **Sanghol**, **Songaon**, **Sonpur**, **Taradih**, **Tuljapur Garhi**, **Valmiyo Timbo**, and **Wina**.

From the early historic period onward, texts and **inscriptions** in **Pali**, **Prakrit**, **Tamil**, and **Sanskrit** provide occasional descriptions of agricultural practices and rural society. It is evident that systems of **landownership** were varied. While rain-fed crops were cultivated in many areas, **irrigation** was necessary in other areas. Irrigation facilities were occasionally provided by the state, but could also be arranged through local community efforts or by dominant social groups. Disputes regarding landownership and the sharing of irrigation water are described in texts. Texts such as the ***Arthaśāstra*** suggest that the state could have played an active role in organizing agricultural production: mobilizing labor, allocating resources, and claiming the final produce from a category of land designated as *sītā*, where production was managed by an officer known as the *sītādhyakṣa*. However, the degree of centralized control envisaged in this model does not seem to have been implemented in practice.

In terms of ***varṇa***, the **Dharmasūtras** and **Dharmaśāstras** recommended agriculture as an activity specific to the ***vaiśya***. However, other texts indicate that men belonging to all social categories participated in production. Specific terms used to designate cultivators include *kīnāśa* and *kuṭumbin* (Sanskrit) and *kassaka* (Pali). Texts also suggest that the rural population in many parts of the subcontinent was differentiated—with large landowners at one end of the scale, large and small peasant households constituting a heterogeneous intermediate category, and landless laborers and **slaves** at the bottom of the hierarchy. While **women** landowners were rare, they were not entirely unknown. Women contributed to agricultural production organized through households in a variety of ways—supervising and participating in labor processes such as transplantation, weeding, harvesting, threshing, and winnowing, apart from processing grain. Some texts mention taboos on women wielding the plow.

The **early medieval period** witnessed an increase in **land grants** made by the ruling elite to **religious** institutions in general and ***brāhmaṇas*** **(1)** in particular. Some historians have suggested that this led to shifts in agrarian relations. In some areas, it is likely that **tribal** social formations gave way to a more differentiated social order with the emergence of peasant communities, which were incorporated within new political formations. *See also* ATRANJIKHERA; CASTE; DAIMABAD; *DĀSA*; GANGA (2); KALIBANGAN; KAVERI RIVER; KAYATHA; MAGADHA; REVENUE SYSTEMS; VEDIC ECONOMY; *VELLĀLĀR*; VIDEGHA MĀTHAVA.

AGRONOMOI**.** Officials mentioned in **Strabo**'s (c. 64–63 BCE–24 CE) account of India, based on **Megasthenes**'s ***Indica***, as part of the bureaucracy of the **Mauryan** Empire (c. fourth–second centuries BCE). According to Strabo, their functions included measuring land, collecting taxes, supervising occupations connected with land, distributing **irrigation** water, maintaining roads, and administering justice. The term has been equated with the ***adhyakṣa*** mentioned in the ***Arthaśāstra*** and the ***rājukas*** mentioned in **Asokan inscriptions**.

AHAR. Archaeological site in Rajasthan in the Banas valley, type site of a **Chalcolithic** culture. Finds from Period I (c. 2100–1500 BCE) include wheel-made **black and red ware**, painted with white designs, generally geometrical. Some of the shapes resemble those of **Harappan pottery**. There is evidence for the use of rice. Bones of cattle, sheep, goats, and wild animals have been recovered. Houses consisted of rectangular thatched huts built on stone foundations.

Copper was used prolifically for making both **tools** and ornaments. Other finds include beads of **terracotta** and semiprecious stone. There was a hiatus before the reoccupation of the site in Period II (c. third century BCE–second century CE), which yielded evidence of mud-brick structures, millet, **iron** tools, slag, and **Indo-Greek coins**. *See also* BAGOR; BALATHAL; DANGWADA; KATRA; KAYATHA.

AHICHCHHATRA. Archaeological site in Uttar Pradesh, with evidence of occupation from c. third century BCE until the end of the first millennium CE. Distinctive archaeological features include traces of **fortifications**, which probably date to c. 100 BCE. Remains of a ***stūpa*** with a relic casket were found as well as remains of **temples**. Other finds include **Painted Grey Ware**, **Northern Black Polished Ware**, and **terracotta** figurines. Textual traditions recognized the city as the capital of northern **Pañcāla**. *See also* ACYUTA.

***AHIMSĀ*. Sanskrit** term meaning "nonviolence," which acquired centrality as a precept within traditions such as **Jainism**. Subsequently, ideas of nonviolence influenced **Buddhist** and **Brahmanical** ideas and practices as well. In effect, *ahimsā* translated into more or less stringent forms of vegetarianism, which was valorized as being both austere and pure. With a few exceptions, it did not extend to the condemnation of violence in social or political life.

AHRAURA. Archaeological site in Uttar Pradesh (c. third century BCE), find spot of a **Minor Rock Edict** of the **Mauryan** ruler **Asoka**.

AIHOLE. Site in Karnataka, an important center of **Cālukya** power (c. sixth–eighth centuries CE), find spot of more than 100 **rock-cut** and structural **temples** that were embellished with **sculpture** representing a wide variety of **Brahmanical** deities and themes from **Purāṇic** mythology. Temple building in the region continued until the 12th century.

AIHOLE INSCRIPTION. Sanskrit panegyric in ornate verse, composed by **Ravikīrti** (634–635 CE), the court poet of the **Cālukya**

ruler **Pulakeśin II**, recording the genealogy of the ruler as well as his achievements. The latter included seizing the throne from his uncle, defeating feudatory chiefs, and extending control over rulers along the western and eastern coasts. Ravikīrti also described victories over the traditional rivals of the Cālukyas, namely, the **Pallavas** of **Kanchipuram**, the **Co<u>l</u>as**, and **Pāṇḍyas**, as well as Pulakeśin's success in repelling **Harṣavardhana**, the contemporary ruler of **Kanauj**, back from the **Narmada**. Internally, Pulakeśin's kingdom consisted of three regions and 99,000 villages. Ravikīrti dated the inscription in the **Kali** era as well as the **Śaka era** and recorded that he had constructed and dedicated a **Jaina** shrine during Pulakeśin's rule.

AILA. Descendant of Ila (masculine)/Ilā (feminine), a personage mentioned in the ***Mahābhārata*** and the **Purāṇas** as one of the ancestors of the **Kurus**. She (or he) was believed to have been cursed to spend six months each year as a man and six months as a woman, and was regarded as the originator of the **Candravaṃśa**. Several **early medieval** ruling lineages claimed descent from Ila/Ilā. *See also* KHĀRAVELA.

AINKURUNŪRU. **Tamil** text (c. third century BCE–second century CE?), a collection of 500 ***akam*** or love **poems**, with 100 each set in five environments, or *tinai*, a distinctive marker of this genre of **literature**. The text is sometimes regarded as the earliest of the Tamil ***Sangam*** anthologies, and is part of the ***Eṭṭutokai***.

AITAREYA BRĀHMAṆA. **Later Vedic** ritual text (**Sanskrit**) composed c. 10th–8th centuries BCE, attributed to Mahidāsa Aitareya, dealing with a range of rituals, including those associated with **kingship**. *See also BRĀHMAṆA* (2); KINGSHIP, THEORIES OF ORIGIN; LITERATURE.

AJANTA. Site in Maharashtra, with some of the best-known **rock-cut caves**, most of which were hollowed out between the fourth to the sixth centuries CE, under the patronage of the **Vākāṭakas**. The caves include **Buddhist monasteries** and halls of worship. They were decorated with stone **sculpture**, and some of the finest wall **paintings** known from early India. Generally, the ceilings were decorated with geometric and floral motifs, whereas the walls contained paintings based on Buddhist narrative traditions, including the life of the **Buddha** and the ***Jātakas***. The paintings provide a glimpse into contemporary life, and exemplify the skill of the artists in representing the human form. Ajanta has been recognized as a World Heritage Site by the United Nations Educational, Scientific and Cultural Organization (UNESCO). *See also* BAGH; HARIṢEṆA (2).

AJĀTAŚATRU. Son and successor of **Bimbisāra**, the ruler of **Magadha** (south Bihar), c. 516–489 BCE. Traditional accounts suggest that he acquired the throne after committing parricide. He **fortified** the site of **Pāṭaligrāma**, at the confluence of the rivers Son and **Ganga (2)**, laying the foundation for the later **city** of **Pāṭaliputra**. He also acquired **Vaishali** or Vesālī to the north of the Ganga (2), and **Kāśi**, present-day Varanasi (Uttar Pradesh). Both the **Buddha** and **Mahāvīra** are recognized as his contemporaries, and the first **Buddhist Council** was probably held at **Rājagaha**, his capital. *See also* VAJJI.

AJĪTA KEŚAKAMBALIN. Materialist thinker (c. sixth century BCE), who believed that all existence was derived from four primary elements. He also argued against the belief in life after death. *See also* PHILOSOPHY.

ĀJĪVIKA. Name of a sect founded by **Makkhaliputta Gosāla**, c. sixth century BCE. In terms of precepts, there are some similarities with the contemporary doctrines of **Jainism**. The Ājīvikas were atheistic and believed that even the smallest event was predetermined. No major texts of the sect have survived, and its doctrines have been reconstructed from somewhat hostile accounts found in other, rival traditions. The **Mauryan** ruler **Asoka** donated three caves to the Ājīvikas in the **Barabar** hills. The sect survived in parts of south India until the 16th century. However, unlike **Buddhism** and Jainism, the Ājīvikas did not attain widespread popularity. *See also* DASARATHA; *DHAMMA MAHĀMATTA*; RELIGION.

AKAM*.** **Tamil** love **poems**, part of the ***Sangam anthology (c. third century BCE–second century CE?). Conventionally, *akam* poems were set in five distinctive environments: the *pālai* or arid zone, *kuriñci* or hilly tracts, *mullai* or pastoral settings, *marutam* or riverine lands, and *neytal* or the coastal region. The moods and emotions of the protagonists were synchronized with these environments in a variety of ways. *See also AINKURUNŪRU*; LITERATURE.

AKANĀNŪRU*.** **Tamil** text, one of the anthologies of the ***Eṭṭutokai, consisting of around 400 ***akam*** or love **poems**, attributed to 145 poets. *See also* LITERATURE.

AKESINES. River mentioned in Greek sources (c. fourth century BCE), identified with the river **Chenab**, one of the tributaries of the **Indus River**, forming the eastern boundary of the territory of **Poros**, one of the principal adversaries of **Alexander (of Macedon)**. The river is also identified with the **Asikinī** mentioned in the ***Ṛgveda***.

AL MASUDI. Abu al-Hasan Ali ibn al-Husayn al Masudi (896–956 CE), Arab historian, often described as the **Herodotus** of the Arabs, author of a work known as the *Muruj-adh-dhahab wa ma'adin al-jawahir* (The Meadows of Gold and the Mine of Gems), a world history consisting of 132 chapters. The work combined historical and geographical knowledge derived from earlier writings as well as information obtained during the author's extensive travels through Asia and East Africa, including Egypt. He evidently traveled through the **Indus** valley and along the west coast of the subcontinent, and his descriptions of India were based on firsthand information as well as other sources. *See also* MAHIPĀLA (1); TRAVELERS' ACCOUNTS.

ALAGANKULAN. **Archaeological** site in Tamil Nadu. Period I (c. fifth–first centuries BCE) is associated with finds of **Black and Red Ware**, **Northern Black Polished Ware**, and **rouletted ware**. Other finds include slag, **iron** artifacts, **copper coins**, glass beads, and shell bangles. Finds from Period II (c. first century BCE–third century CE) include Roman amphorae, coins, rouletted ware, and beads of semiprecious stone, glass, and shell.

ALAMGIRPUR. **Archaeological** site in western Uttar Pradesh, with two major occupational phases. Period I (c. second millennium BCE onward?) yielded evidence of **Harappan pottery**, steatite beads, faience bangles, traces of Harappan-type mud- and baked-brick structures, and **copper** artifacts. Finds from Period II (c. first millennium BCE) include **Painted Grey Ware**, **iron** and bone artifacts, and glass. There is evidence for later occupation as well.

ALEXANDER (OF CORINTH). *See* ALIKASUDARA.

ALEXANDER (OF EPIRUS). *See* ALIKASUDARA.

ALEXANDER (OF MACEDON). King (c. 356–323 BCE) who reached the northwest part of the subcontinent (c. 326 BCE) and led a campaign along the **Indus River** and its tributaries (present-day provinces of the Punjab and Sind, Pakistan). He confronted a number of local chiefs and **kings** and **tribal** oligarchies. Some rulers, such as **Ambhi** of **Taxila**, accepted his overlordship, whereas others, such as **Poros** (Greek; **Sanskrit**, Puru), offered resistance and were defeated. Alexander's victories have been attributed to the use of swift cavalry against the more unwieldy Indian **armies** that depended on the slow-moving elephant. Alexander marched up to the river **Beas**. Here his army refused to proceed further east into the realms of the **Prasii**, who were reputed to be extremely powerful. Alexander led his army down the Indus, conquering a number of principalities en route. On reaching the mouth of the river, the army was divided into three parts: Two returned along land **routes** via Iran, while the third returned by sea.

Alexander's invasion finds no mention in Indian textual traditions: Its immediate impact was possibly short-lived, as Alexander died soon after, in 323 BCE. However, his invasion evidently opened up routes of communication that were used for several centuries. Besides, a number of settlements, including some named Alexandria, were set up in the northwest, and led to more lasting if less spectacular contact between the Greeks and the local population. Some of Alexander's contemporaries as well as later Greek and Roman historians included accounts of the invasion in their works. *See also* ABASTANOI; ABHISĀRA; AGALASSOI; ARISTOBULOS; ARRIAN; CANDRAGUPTA MAURYA; DHANANANDA; NANDA; NEARCHOS; ONESICRITUS; PLUTARCH; QUINTUS CURTIUS; SELEUCOS NIKATOR.

ALIKASUDARA. **King** mentioned in **Major Rock Edict** XIII of the **Mauryan** ruler **Asoka**, as among his neighbors. Asoka claimed to have sent messengers to spread the message of ***dhamma*** in his kingdom. Alikasudara has been identified with **Alexander (of Epirus)**, 272–255 BCE, or **Alexander (of Corinth)**, r. 252–244 BCE.

ALLAHABAD PILLAR INSCRIPTION. Name assigned to an **inscription** of **Samudragupta** (c. fourth century CE), one of the most important **kings** of the **Gupta** dynasty. The inscription is on an **Asokan** pillar containing two **Minor Pillar Edicts**, one requiring that any donations made by Asoka's second queen be registered in her name and a second warning against schism in the **Buddhist *saṃgha***. The pillar was probably transported from **Kausambi** (Kosam) near Allahabad (Uttar Pradesh) to its present location by the Mughal ruler Akbar in the 15th century.

The Gupta inscription, in ornate **Sanskrit**, is partly in verse and partly in prose. It was composed by Samudragupta's court poet **Hariṣeṇa (1)** as a panegyric or ***praśasti***. It describes the king's victories over the rulers of ***āryāvarta***, or north India, and his expeditions to south India. It also suggests that neighboring rulers, including those of the northwest, northeast, and Sri Lanka, acknowledged his supremacy. The ruler's cultural accomplishments are also mentioned, as is his prowess. The inscription provides a genealogy of the dynasty. A conflict regarding Samudragupta's claims to the throne is hinted at, which was apparently resolved when he was chosen by his father, **Candragupta I**. *See also* ACYUTA; ARJUNĀYANA; DAMANA; DAVĀKA; DHANAÑJAYA; GAṆAPATI (NĀGA); HASTIVARMAN; KĀMARŪPA; KARTTRIPURA; KHARAPĀRIKA; KOṬA KULA JANA; KUBERA; MADRA; MAHENDRA; MĀLAVA; MAṆṬARĀJA; MATILA; MEGHAVARṆA; NĀGADATTA; NĀGASENA (2); NANDI; NEPĀLA; NĪLARĀJA; PIṢṬAPURA; PRĀRJUNA; RUDRADEVA; SAMATAṬA; SANAKĀNIKA; SVĀMIDATTA; TRIBES; UGRASENA; VIṢṆUGOPA; VYĀGHRARĀJĀ; YAUDHEYA.

ALLAHDINO. **Archaeological** site in Sind, Pakistan, with evidence of a planned settlement during the **Mature Harappan** (mid–third millennium BCE) phase.

ALLITROCHADES. *See* BINDUSĀRA.

ĀḺVĀR. **Tamil** term used to designate the 12 devotees of **Viṣṇu** (c. seventh–ninth centuries CE) whose devotional songs have been anthologized in the ***Nālāyira Tiviya Pirapantam***, a collection of 4,000 hymns. The Āḻvārs belonged to diverse social groups, and included one **woman, Āṇṭāḷ**. *See also* NAMMĀḺVĀR; PERIYĀḺVĀR; RELIGION; TIRUMANKAI ĀḺVĀR; VAIṢṆAVISM.

AMARAKOŚA. One of the best-known **Sanskrit** dictionaries, attributed to **Amarasiṃha** (c. fourth–fifth centuries CE), composed in verse, and more in the nature of a thesaurus of synonyms, also known as the *Nāmaliṅgānuśāsana*. *See also* LITERATURE.

AMARASIṂHA. Buddhist or **Jaina poet**, recognized as the author of the ***Amarakośa***. He is traditionally regarded as one of the nine jewels or scholars associated with king **Vikramāditya**. If the latter is identified with **Candragupta II**, Amarasiṃha may be assigned to c. fourth–fifth centuries CE. *See also* LITERATURE.

AMARAVATI. Site in Andhra Pradesh, find spot of a ***stūpa*** belonging to the **Mauryan** period (c. third century BCE), with evidence of profuse embellishments added during succeeding periods, especially during the second and third centuries CE, under the patronage of the **Sātavāhanas** and the **Ikṣvākus (2). Coins** issued by rulers of both these dynasties have been recovered from the site. **Sculptural** remains from the *stūpa*, including representations of the life of the **Buddha** and ***Jātaka*** stories, are preserved in the British Museum. Several **inscriptions** have also been recovered from the site, including a possible fragment of a Mauryan pillar inscription. The Buddhist associations of the site continued for several centuries. There is evidence for prior occupation as well, indicated by finds of **Paleolithic tools** as well as traces of **megalithic** occupation. **Pottery** recovered from the site includes **Black and Red Ware** and **Northern Black Polished Ware**.

AMBAKOT. Archaeological site in Gujarat with evidence of occupation during the **Mesolithic** phase. Finds include microliths and red ocher nodules.

AMBAPĀLĪ. A famous **courtesan**, a contemporary and follower of the **Buddha** (c. sixth century BCE), and a resident of **Vaishali**. According to Buddhist tradition, she offered hospitality to the Buddha and made gifts to the **monastic** order. She also joined the order of nuns and attained enlightenment. A poetic composition attributed to her is included in the ***Therīgāthā***. *See also* WOMEN.

AMBARI. Archaeological site in Assam. Finds include stone **sculptures** of the **goddess Śiva** and **Viṣṇu**, dating to c. seventh–eighth centuries CE. Evidence of unfinished sculptural pieces indicates that this was a workshop. Other finds include **terracotta** figurines and beads of semiprecious stone.

AMBAṢṬHA. *See* ABASTANOI.

AMBAṬṬHA. *See* ABASTANOI.

AMBHI. Ruler (c. fourth century BCE) of **Taxila** during the invasion of **Alexander (of Macedon)**. Ambhi surrendered to the latter, who in turn recognized him as the local governor. His power probably came to an end with the withdrawal of the Macedonian forces.

AMBKHERI. Archaeological site in Uttar Pradesh (c. second millennium BCE?). Finds include **Ochre-Coloured Pottery**, generally wheel-made and sometimes cord-impressed, and structural remains such as traces of a hearth and **terracotta** figurines.

AMITRACHATES. *See* BINDUSĀRA.

AMOGHAVARṢA. Rāṣṭrakūṭa ruler (r.c. 814–878 CE), known from contemporary **inscriptions** and texts, who ascended the throne at the age of 14, on his father's death. He faced revolts by feudatory chiefs, including the Western **Gaṅgas (1)**. He also came into conflict with the Eastern **Cālukyas**. He claimed to have defeated the rulers of Kerala as well as the **Pāṇḍyas**, **Coḻas**, and **Pallavas** and the rulers of **Kaliṅga**, **Magadha**, and Gujarat. Some of these claims appear exaggerated. He also entered into matrimonial alliances with several of these powers, including the feudatory chiefs. Amoghavarṣa established the Rāṣṭrakūta capital at **Mānyakheṭa**, which became a flourishing cultural center. He is recognized as the author of one of the earliest Kannada texts, a work on poetics, the *Kavirājamārga*, and a **Sanskrit** work, the *Praśnottara Ratnamālikā*. He adopted several titles, including *nṛpatuṅga* (the best of **kings**), *vīranārāyaṇa* (the valorous **Viṣṇu**), and *atiśaya dhavala* (extremely fair). It is likely that he extended patronage to both **Jainism** and **Hinduism**. Stories about his self-sacrifice were widely prevalent. The Arab traveler Sulaiman considered his realm to be one of the four most powerful kingdoms in the contemporary world.

AMRELI. Archaeological site in Gujarat, with evidence of occupation c. first century BCE onward. Finds include **Red Polished Ware**, **coins** of the western **Kṣatrapas**, and silver coins of **Kumāragupta I**.

AMRI. Pre-/early Harappan (c. mid–fourth millennium BCE onward) site in Sind, Pakistan. There is evidence for the domestication of cattle, sheep, goat, and donkey. **Architecture** includes mud-brick structures. Typical artifacts include fine **pottery**, decorated with geometric designs, occasionally bearing graffiti. There are indications of contacts with settlements in Baluchistan. The **Mature Harappan** (c. third millennium BCE) occupation of the site was unrelated to the preceding phase.

AMTALIKITA. *See* ANTIALKIDAS.

AMTEKINA. King mentioned in **Major Rock Edict** XIII of the **Mauryan** ruler **Asoka** as among his neighbors. Asoka claimed to have sent messengers to spread the message of ***dhamma*** in their lands. Amtekina is identified with Antigonos Gonatas, king of Macedonia (r. 277–239 BCE).

AMTIYAKO YONARĀJA. King mentioned in **Major Rock Edict** XIII of the **Mauryan** ruler **Asoka** as among his neighbors. Asoka claimed to have sent messengers to spread the message of ***dhamma*** in their lands. Amtiyako, identified with **Antiochos II Theos** of Syria, is also mentioned in Major Rock Edict II among the kings in whose realms Asoka made arrangements for the medical treatment of men and animals as part of his policy of *dhamma*.

ĀNANDAVARDHANA. Sanskrit author (c. ninth century CE), a contemporary of **king Avantivarman** of Kashmir. Ānandavardhana was best-known for the composition of the ***Dhvanyāloka***, a work laying down the principles of Sanskrit literary criticism. *See also* LITERATURE.

ĀNDHRA. Name assigned to the **Sātavāhana** rulers in the **Purāṇas**. Rulers of the dynasty probably acquired control over parts of the present-day province of Andhra Pradesh in the early centuries CE.

AṄGA (1). Recognized as one of the 16 ***mahājanapadas*** or major states in the sixth century BCE, with its capital at **Campā**, near Bhagalpur, present-day Bihar. **Bimbisāra**, king of **Magadha**, conquered the state c. fifth century BCE. There is **archaeological** evidence of settlement in the region from c. second millennium BCE onward.

AṄGA* (2). Sanskrit/Prakrit** term meaning "parts" or "limbs," designation for 12 canonical **Jaina** works: the ***Āyāra, ***Suyagada***, *Thāna*, *Samavāya*, *Bhagavati-Viyaha-pannatti*, ***Nāyadhammakahā***, *Uvāsagadasā*, *Antagada-dasā*, *Anuttarovaviadasā*, *Paṅhavagaranai*, *Vivāga*, and *Ditthivao*, composed in Prakrit. Of these the *Āyāra* is regarded as the oldest, followed by the *Suyagada*. The texts received their final form c. fifth century CE. Subsequently, a commentarial tradition in Prakrit and Sanskrit developed around these texts.

AṄGUTTARA NIKĀYA. **Pali** text, part of the ***Sutta Piṭaka***, compiled c. fourth century BCE. The name of the text, which deals with **Buddhist** doctrine, is derived from the fact that sections are arranged in an ascending order: Each succeeding section contains a discussion on one more theme than the preceding one. *See also* LITERATURE.

ĀṆṬĀḶ. Tamil poet and devotee of **Viṣṇu**, the only **woman** included among the 12 ***Āḻvārs***. There are two works attributed to her, the *Tiruppāvai* and the *Nācciyār Tirumoḻi*, consisting of about 30 and 143 verses respectively. These works are characterized by spiritual eroticism. Later hagiographies recognized her as a bride of the god, who met her end by merging into the image of the deity at Srirangam, Tamil Nadu. *See also* LITERATURE.

ANTALIKITA. *See* ANTIALKIDAS.

ANTIALKIDAS. Indo-Greek ruler of **Taxila** (c. second century BCE) mentioned as a ***mahārāja*** in the **Besnagar Pillar Inscription** of **Heliodoros**. The **Pali** form of his name was Amtalikita or Antalikita. Antialkidas sent Heliodoros as ambassador to the court of the king of Besnagar, ancient **Vidisha**. Antialkidas, who issued **coins** bearing his portrait, probably ruled jointly with a ruler named Lysias.

ANTICHAK. Archaeological site in Bihar, identified with **Vikramaśilā**, a **Buddhist monastery** established by the **Pāla** king **Dharmapāla**, c. ninth century CE. Structural remains include those of the monastery, a ***stūpa***, and a shrine. Other finds include **terracotta** figurines and stone and bronze **sculpture** of Buddhist deities. The monastery was destroyed in the 13th century.

ANTIGONOS GONATAS. *See* AMTEKINA.

ANTIMACHUS. Bactrian Greek ruler (185–170 BCE), who controlled parts of present-day Afghanistan and the northwestern parts of the subcontinent, known from a series of silver **coins**, containing representations of the **king** as well as legends in Greek. While some scholars consider him as the son and successor of **Euthydemos** and the brother of **Demetrios**, others suggest that he was an independent ruler. Coins indicate that he appointed his sons as coregents. He was ultimately defeated by **Eukratides**. Representations of the elephant on his coins have been regarded as indications of his support for **Buddhism**. *See also* SUGH.

ANTIOCHOS I SOTER (OF SYRIA). Son and successor (r.c. 281–261 BCE) of **Seleucos Nikator**. He sent **Deimachos** as an ambassador to **Bindusāra**, the second **Mauryan** ruler. The latter apparently requested him to send wine, figs, and a sophist. Antiochos is supposed to have replied that while the first two could be sent, the last was not on sale.

ANTIOCHOS II THEOS (OF SYRIA). Son and successor of **Antiochos I Soter** (r.c. 261–246 BCE). *See* AMTIYAKO YONARĀJA; BACTRIAN GREEK.

ANTIOCHOS III THE GREAT. Ruled between c. 223 and 187 BCE. **Bactria** became independent under **Euthydemos** during his reign. Antiochos formed an alliance with **Subhāgasena**, a **king** ruling over the Kabul valley, and received elephants from him. This suggests that the **Mauryas** had lost control over this region by the end of the third century BCE.

***ANUKRAMAṆI*.** **Sanskrit** indices, best known for the **Vedas**, organized in terms of the authors, meters, initial words, deities, and so on of Vedic hymns. The earliest known work in this category is attributed to Śaunaka (c. 600 BCE). *Anukramaṇis* as well as commentaries on them continued to be composed during subsequent periods as well. *See also* LITERATURE.

***APABHRAṂŚA*.** **Sanskrit** term, literally meaning "falling from standards or norms," used as early as c. second century BCE by **Patañjali (1)** to designate a variety of **languages**, including types of **Prakrit**, in use over a wide geographical area extending from Kashmir in the north to Maharashtra in the south. Extant literary works in Apabhraṃśa date from c. ninth century CE onward and include several **Jaina** works. These languages continued to be in use for poetic compositions until c. 1600 CE.

APARĀJITA. Last ruler of the **Pallava** dynasty, who was overthrown by the **Co<u>l</u>a** king **Āditya** (c. 880 CE).

APARĀNTAKA. Name of a region, identified with parts of present-day Gujarat and Sind.

APOLLODOTOS. **Indo-Greek** king (r.c. 175–156 BCE), known from his **coins**, son or rival of **Eukratides**. Apollodotos ruled over parts of present-day Afghanistan. Some literary traditions suggest that he killed his father.

APPAR. *See* TIRUNĀVUKKARACAR.

APSADH. **Archaeological** site in Bihar, with remains of a brick **temple** dedicated to **Viṣṇu**. According to a stone **inscription** found at the site, this was constructed by Ādityasena, a ruler belonging to the **Later Guptas** (c. seventh century CE).

ARACHOSIA. Greek name for present-day Kandahar, Afghanistan.

ARAMAIC. Name of a **script** and **language**, introduced by the **Achaemenids** (c. sixth century BCE), in the northwest of the subcontinent that continued to be in use under the **Mauryas** (c. third century BCE). *See also* ASOKAN INSCRIPTIONS; BRĀHMĪ; KHAROṢṬHĪ; PUL-I-DARUNTA; SHAR-I-KUNA.

ARAMBHA. Archaeological site in Maharashtra, with evidence of four major occupational phases. Finds associated with Period I (c. first half of the first millennium BCE?) included remains of hearths and **black and red ware**. Period II yielded **Northern Black Polished Ware, iron** equipment, and shell bangles. Period III yielded a **terracotta coin** mold, attributed to the **Śakas**, and beads of semiprecious stone. Period IV yielded a potsherd with an **inscription** in **Brāhmī**, assigned to the middle of the first millennium CE, beads, and stone **sculpture**, possibly of a **goddess**.

ARANGPUR. Archaeological site in Haryana. Finds include lower **Paleolithic tools** such as hand axes, cleavers, knives, and scrapers.

ĀRAṆYAKA**.** Literally "of the **forest**," **Sanskrit** texts (c. eighth–sixth centuries BCE) composed, preserved, and transmitted within priestly traditions. They derived their name from the fact that their contents were meant to be transmitted to a select few, in relative isolation, in forests. Their distinctive contents include reinterpretations of **sacrificial** ritual in terms of cosmic and metaphysical significance. *See also* LITERATURE.

ARCHAEOLOGICAL SURVEY OF INDIA. The Archaeological Survey of India was established in 1871. Noted directors-general included **Alexander Cunningham** and **John Marshall**. Initially, it was assumed that the Survey would be a temporary body that would be abolished once the work of survey and conservation was complete. However, by the beginning of the 20th century, the need for a permanent institution was felt, and in 1906, the Survey was constituted as a permanent entity. The Survey has continued to function as a government department after Independence (1947). At present its functions include conducting and coordinating explorations and excavations, ensuring the preservation of monuments and sites, and conducting training programs. It publishes annual reports in *Indian Archaeology—A Review*. Other publications include the series titled *Memoirs of the Archaeological Survey of India*. *See also* ARCHAEOLOGY; EPIGRAPHY.

ARCHAEOLOGY. Archaeological explorations and excavations assumed significance with the setting up of the **Asiatic Society** (1784). Until the establishment of the **Archaeological Survey of India**, archaeology remained the preserve of amateur antiquarians. Subsequently, more systematic surveys were undertaken by **Alexander Cunningham**. Initially, the focus was on surveying **early historic** sites, which were excavated using rudimentary techniques and skills, frequently causing irreparable damage to sites. The objective of such excavations was generally restricted to recovering artifacts that were thought to possess cultural value, including **sculpture**. This meant that less spectacular traces of the past were often irretrievably lost. At the same time, some investigators such as **Robert Bruce Foote** recovered traces of **prehistoric** cultures.

From the 1920s, with the discovery of the **Harappan civilization**, Harappan archaeology emerged as a major focus, and continues to dominate archaeological investigation in the subcontinent. Some of the most extensive excavations have been conducted at Harappan sites. Many of the early excavations were marred by a lack of consideration for stratigraphy, a situation that was remedied by the introduction of new methods by R. E. M. Wheeler during the 1940s.

After Independence, archaeology was recognized as a concern of both central and state governments. The post-Independence decades also witnessed the setting up of archaeology departments in a number of universities. Some of these, such as the Deccan College Post-Graduate Research Institute, Pune, Maharashtra, have conducted extensive excavations and surveys and published detailed reports of their findings. These have contributed substantially to the understanding of prehistoric and **protohistoric** cultures in the Deccan. Underwater archaeology has also been undertaken in coastal areas.

Excavations at **Mesolithic** sites such as **Adamgarh**, **Bagor**, **Bhimbetka**, and **Langhnaj** have been particularly fruitful. **Neolithic** sites at which excavations have been conducted include **Burzahom**. Excavations at **Chalcolithic** sites such as **Ahar**, **Inamgaon**, and **Narhan** have also yielded interesting evidence. Evidence of **megalithic** burials has been recovered from sites such as **Adichannallur**.

Several archaeological sites have yielded evidence of a number of occupational phases. These include **Adam**, **Atranjikhera**, **Chandraketugarh**, **Chirand**, **Daimabad**, **Dangwada**, **Eran**, **Hallur**, **Hastinapura**, **Jakhera**, **Jhusi**, **Jodhpura**, **Kausambi**, **Kayatha**, **Kolhua**, **Maheshwar**, **Maner**, **Mangalkot**, **Masaon**, **Maski**, **Mathura**, **Mayiladumparai**, **Nadner**, **Nagari**, **Nagarjunakonda**, **Sanghol**, **Sannati**, **Senuwar**, **Sodanga**, **Sonkh**, **Sonpur**, **Sunet**, **Tāmralipti**, **Taradih**, **Tharsa**, **Timbarra**, **Tripuri**, **Tumain**, **Ujjayinī**, **Utnur**, **Vaddamanu**, **Vidisha**, and **Wina**.

In spite of its potential, archaeological study has been hampered by serious problems. These include a preoccupation with vertical excavations rather than horizontal excavations or surveys. The former often yield a sequence of **pottery** types but do not permit detailed investigations of the material culture. Also, the existence of settlements as well as encroachments on and even destruction of archaeological sites pose problems, especially pertaining to the exploration of early historic and **early medieval** sites. The publication of reports has also not kept pace with investigations. *See also* BURIAL PRACTICES; CITIES; CRAFTS; DISPOSAL OF THE DEAD; EARLY HARAPPAN; GANDHARA GRAVE CULTURE; LANGUAGES; LATE HARAPPAN; MATURE HARAPPAN; MITRA, RAJENDRA LALA; ORIENTALISM; SANKALIA, HASMUKH DHIRAJLAL; TOOLS; TRADE; TRADE ROUTES.

ARCHITECTURE. The earliest traces of architecture pertain to **Mesolithic** and **Neolithic** sites, which often yield traces of huts that probably provided residential and working spaces for the early inhabitants of the subcontinent. Subsequently, there is evidence of elaborate structures associated with the **Harappan civilization** (c. 2700–1800 BCE). These include **fortification** walls, domestic architecture made of burnt brick, and buildings with specific functions such as storage spaces, **assembly** halls, and the Great Bath. There was a hiatus in this kind of construction activity until the mid–first millennium BCE, when the evidence of both burnt-brick and mud-brick structures becomes more common in the archaeological record from **early historic cities**. At the same time, wood was evidently used extensively for building. This is mentioned in early textual sources and is also suggested by the fact that early stone architecture often imitated wooden models for gateways, pillars, and railings.

Most of the architecture that has survived from this period was of **religious** origin. These include **rock-cut caves**, ***stūpas***, and **monasteries**. The first-named were most prolific along the Western Ghats, though they were constructed elsewhere as well. *Stūpas* were probably initially round mounds of earth that were encased, over the centuries, with brick and stone. While monasteries were often housed in rock-cut caves, others were built of brick (first millennium CE onward). These generally consisted of cells around a central courtyard. More or less contemporary were the earliest **temples**, also carved out or built of stone. By the mid–first millennium CE, treatises on temple architecture were written in **Sanskrit**. While actual temples did not always correspond to these, the texts represented attempts to codify architectural practices and imbue them with symbolic meaning. Secular structures, including palaces and markets, are described in Sanskrit, **Pali**, **Prakrit**, and **Tamil** textual traditions, but are less visible in the archaeological record.

Sites that have yielded traces of structural remains include **Adam**, **Adichannallur**, **Agiabir**, **Ahar**, **Alamgirpur**, **Ambkheri**, **Amri**, **Arambha**, **Arikamedu**, **Atranjikhera**, **Ayodhya**, **Bahal**, **Balakot**, **Balathal**, **Balu**, **Banahalli**, **Banavasi**, **Banawali**, **Banki**, **Bara**, **Bhagwanpura**, **Bharatpur**, **Bharuch**, **Bhorgarh**, **Birbhanpur**, **Brahmapuri**, **Brass**, **Burzahom**, **Chandoli**, **Chandraketugarh**, **Chaul**, **Chechar**, **Chirand**, **Chopani Mando**, **Dadheri**, **Daimabad**, **Damdama**, **Dangwada**, **Dharanikota**, **Dhuriapar**, **Dvarka**, **Eran**, **Gandhur**, **Ganeshwar**, **Ganwaria**, **Gilund**, **Golbai Sasan**, **Harappa**, **Hastinapura**, **Hathikera**, **Hemmige**, **Hulas Khera**, **Imlidih Khurd**, **Inamgaon**, **Jakhera**, **Jhukar**, **Jhusi**, **Kakrehta**, **Kalibangan**, **Kanchipuram**, **Kaothe**, **Kashipur**, **Katra**, **Kausambi**, **Kaveripattinam**, **Kayatha**, **Khajuri**, **Khiching**, **Khokrakot**, **Kolhua**, **Kotasur**, **Kudikadu**, **Kulli**, **Kumrahar**, **Kunal**, **Kuntasi**, **Lal Qila**, **Lothal**, **Lumbini**, **Mahagara**, **Mahasthan**, **Maheshwar**,

Mahurjhari, **Malhar**, **Maner**, **Mangalkot**, **Manjhi**, **Masaon**, **Mathura**, **Mehrgarh**, **Mitathal**, **Musanagar**, **Nadner**, **Nagara**, **Nagari**, **Nagarjunakonda**, **Nagda**, **Nagiari**, **Narhan**, **Navdatoli**, **Oriyo Timbo**, **Padri**, **Paisra**, **Paiyampalli**, **Pandu Rajar Dhibi**, **Pauni**, **Pipri**, **Pithad**, **Puduru**, **Purola**, **Rangpur**, **Ratura**, **Rehman Dheri**, **Rojdi**, **Saipai**, **Sarai Nahar Rai**, **Sekta**, **Shirkanda**, **Shri Shri Suryapahar**, **Sikligarh**, **Sisupalgarh**, **Sodanga**, **Songaon**, **Sonkh**, **Sonpur**, **Sravasti**, **Sringaverapura**, **Sugh**, **Takiaper**, **Talkad**, **Tāmralipti**, **Taradih**, **Taxila**, **Ter**, **Thanesar**, **Thotlakonda**, **Tildah**, **Tripuri**, **Tuljapur Garhi**, **Tumain**, **Ujjayinī**, **Utawad**, **Vadagokugiri**, **Vadgaon Madhavpur**, **Vadodara**, **Vaishali**, **Vidisha**, **Walki**, **Wari Bateshwar**, and **Wina**. *See also* AMARAVATI; *CAITYA*; DHOLAVIRA; EARLY MEDIEVAL PERIOD; MACKENZIE, COLIN; MAURYAN ART; MOHENJODARO.

ARIA. Greek name for present-day Herat, Afghanistan.

ARIKAMEDU. **Early historic** (c. first century BCE onward) coastal **archaeological** site in Puducherry. Finds include a structure that has been identified as a warehouse, ring wells, and rectangular tanks. There is also evidence of **textile** production, dyeing, and bead making, with finds of beads of gold, semiprecious stone, and glass. Finds of Roman amphorae, probably used to transport olive oil and wine, lamps, and glassware, indicate contact with Rome. Other **pottery** includes **Black and Red Ware**, **Arretine Ware**, **rouletted ware**, and potsherds with graffiti in the **Tamil Brāhmī script**. The site has been identified with the port of Podouke mentioned in the ***Periplus of the Erythraean Sea***.

ARISTOBULOS. Greek **architect** (d. 301 BCE) who accompanied **Alexander (of Macedon)** to the subcontinent and wrote an account of his campaigns. The account, which has not survived, was cited by later writers such as **Strabo** and **Arrian**.

ARJUNĀYANA. Community living (c. fourth century CE) in northeastern Rajasthan, mentioned in the **Allahabad Pillar Inscription** of the **Gupta** ruler **Samudragupta**. According to the inscription, it offered tribute and homage to the ruler and agreed to obey his commands.

ARMY. The army was recognized as an important component of the state by c. sixth century BCE. Even earlier, **Vedic** texts indicate that a militia was called into existence whenever **warfare** was imminent as well as for cattle raids. Many later texts refer to the four limbs or constituents of the army, which included elephants, cavalry, chariots, and infantry. The head of the army, the *senāpati*, could occasionally be a member of the royal family. Military equipment included bows and arrows, swords, javelins, and maces as well as protective equipment made of leather, cane, and metal. It is likely that the importance assigned to each wing of the army varied substantially in different regions and over time. The account of **Megasthenes** contains a description of the administration of the **Mauryan** army (c. third century BCE), which, according to him, was run by a committee of 30, divided into six boards, for the infantry, cavalry, chariots, elephants, **navy**, and commissariat, respectively. The navy seems to have been relatively insignificant, with that of the **Co̱ḻas** (c. ninth century CE onward) being somewhat exceptional.

Normative textual traditions suggest that recruitment to the army was to be structured along lines of ***varṇa***, with a preference for ***kṣatriyas***. However, texts such as the ***Arthaśāstra*** provided for a wide range of strategies of recruitment, including the employment of mercenaries and troops recruited from **tribal** or **forest** populations. It is very difficult to arrive at the exact numbers in any specific army: The figures suggested by foreign travelers or in the writings of those who used these accounts tend to be exaggerated. For instance, according to **Plutarch**, **Candragupta Maurya** had an army of 600,000 men. **Xuan Zang** credited **Harṣavardhana** (c. seventh century CE) with having 60,000 elephants and 100,000 cavalry, while **Al Masudi** (c. 10th century CE) wrote that the **Pratihāra** ruler **Mahendrapāla** had four armies of 800,000 each. *See also* ABASTANOI; AGALASSOI; ALEXANDER (OF MACEDON); BHOJA (2); DHANANANDA; KINGSHIP; MAGADHA; *MAHĀJANAPADA*; MAHIPĀLA (1); NANDA; *SAPTĀṄGA*; *SKANDHĀVĀRA*; *UTTARĀPATHA*.

ARRETINE WARE. Red glazed ware that derives its name from the place of manufacture, Arretium, present-day Arezzo, in Italy. It was often decorated by being pressed into a stamped mold, known as *Terra sigillata*. Dates for finds of the ware in **archaeological** sites on the subcontinent range between c. second century BCE and mid–first century CE. *See also* ARIKAMEDU; POTTERY.

ARRIAN. Greek historian, **philosopher**, and administrator (c. 96–180 CE), author of the *Anabasis Alexandrou*, describing the Asiatic expeditions of **Alexander (of Macedon)**. He also wrote the *Indica*, which included a description of the voyage of **Nearchos**. *See also INDICA*.

ART. The history of art in early India has been reconstructed primarily from relatively imperishable artifacts that have survived. The possibility that there was a large repertoire of art objects made of perishable materials needs to be kept in mind while assessing the significance of what is available at present. Performative traditions, referred to in texts, are also inaccessible.

It is evident that most surviving artifacts were generated by patronage from the wealthier and more powerful sections of society, including **kings**. Expressions of art produced by ordinary people, probably more ephemeral, are hardly represented. Most surviving examples of art were inspired by **religious** traditions. Virtually all the artists are anonymous. Several regional artistic styles, most evident in stone and metal **sculpture**, have been identified by art historians. These traditions were by no means isolated: There is evidence for the transmission of ideas and skills from one region to another, perhaps along the **routes** traversed by pilgrims and merchants.

The earliest examples of art belong to the **Paleolithic** period. These include engravings on ostrich shell, found at **Patne**, Maharashtra. Far more prolific are the examples of **rock art** found in sites from central and south India dating from the **Mesolithic** (10,000 BP) period onward. It is also possible to view the painted decorations on **Neolithic** and **Chalcolithic pottery**, which included a range of geometric and naturalistic motifs, as representing early artistic activity. Also associated with these and later cultures are **terracotta** figurines, many of these of females and of animals.

Some of the earliest examples of stone and metal sculpture have been recovered from excavations at **Harappan** (c. 2700–1800 BCE) sites. These include stone figurines such as that of the "priest-king," so called on account of his distinctive attire and headband, and metal figurines of which the best known is that of the "dancing girl," both marked by a high degree of artistry. Far more prolific are finds of terracotta figurines and careful representations of animals, plants, humans, and composite figures on **seals**.

New art forms emerged from the mid–first millennium BCE. Perhaps the most distinctive of these were the monolithic stone columns (mid–third century BCE), often bearing **inscriptions** of **Asoka**. These were made of sandstone found at Chunar, near **Varanasi**, Uttar Pradesh, and are distinguished by a remarkably fine polish. While the pillars are sometimes regarded as being of **Achaemenid** inspiration, the execution and the sculpture on the capitals drew on subcontinental traditions. Motifs included a variety of animal figures and floral designs.

The post-**Mauryan** phase witnessed the building of ***stūpas*** and **rock-cut caves** in several parts of the subcontinent. Many of these were embellished with some of the most remarkable examples of stone sculpture, generally in relief, at sites such as **Amaravati**, **Bharhut**, and **Sanchi**. This was also the period when images of the **Buddha** and **Bodhisattva**s and of **Jaina** ***tīrthaṅkaras*** and **Purāṇic** deities were made at centers such as **Mathura**. These were often installed in **temples** for worship. More or less contemporaneously, **Gandhara** developed as an important region for the production of Buddhist sculpture. From the second century BCE onward, rulers represented themselves and their chosen deities on **coins**. While **painting** had a long history, the best-known examples, primarily representations of Buddhist themes, come from **Ajanta** (mid–first millennium CE).

Nineteenth- and early 20th-century art historians often tried to work out a chronology of art history in terms of dynastic changes. While it is true that rulers often used visual media to project a vision of power and authority, invoking divine support or even claiming divinity, it is now evident that changes in styles of artistic expression did not always correspond with political upheavals.

Other attempts to plot artistic expression along a linear evolutionary trajectory have also proved to be futile. At another level, comparisons using Greco-Roman ideals as the yardstick, a strategy that was very popular with Western art historians in the 19th century, has been virtually abandoned following the recognition that visual media were used in a variety of ways in the subcontinent, and that these evolved through complex processes of interaction among people both within the subcontinent and beyond its frontiers. *See also* BEGRAM; COOMARASWAMY, ANANDA KENTISH; DANCE; MAURYAN ART.

***ARTHAŚĀSTRA*.** Prescriptive text in **Sanskrit**, laying down strategies for success in political matters. The text deals with details of administration, norms of justice, and foreign policy. It is characterized by a terse style and is replete with technical terminology. The authorship of the text is traditionally attributed to Cāṇakya or **Kauṭilya**, recognized as a **minister** of **Candragupta Maurya**, the founder of the **Mauryan** Empire. More recent scholarship suggests that the text was a composite work, composed and compiled between c. fourth century BCE and second century CE. *See also ADHYAKṢA*; AGRICULTURE; ARMY; CITIES; COINAGE: COURTESANS; CRAFTS; *DĀSA*; *DURGA*; ESPIONAGE SYSTEM; FOREST; FORTIFICATION; KINGSHIP; LANDOWNERSHIP; LITERATURE; MARRIAGE; NAVY; *NĪTISĀRA*; *PARIṢAD*; PASTORALISM; REVENUE SYSTEMS; ROUTES; *SAMĀHARTṚ*; *SĀMANTA*; *SANNIDHĀTṚ*; *SAPTĀṄGA*; TEXTILES; TRIBES; WARFARE.

ĀRYA*.** Term used in the ***Ṛgveda (c. second millennium BCE) and in later **Sanskrit** and **Prakrit** texts to refer to a group with distinctive social, cultural, linguistic, and ritual practices, which were regarded as prestigious and normative from the point of view of the authors of these works. The term was often used to distinguish members of the first three ***varṇas*** from the ***dāsas*** and the ***śūdras***.

ĀRYABHAṬA. Mathematician who lived in **Patna** (c. fifth century CE). Later works refer to him as Āśmaka (belonging to **Aśmaka**). He is traditionally recognized as the author of the ***Āryabhaṭīya***, in **Sanskrit**. He is credited with a range of scientific discoveries, including discovering the principles of the rotation of the earth as well as its revolution around the sun, the explanation for eclipses, the fact that planets and the moon lack original light, and the elliptical orbits of planets. *See also* ASTRONOMY; LITERATURE.

***ĀRYABHAṬĪYA*. Astronomical** text in **Sanskrit**, attributed to **Āryabhaṭa**, composed in **Kusumapura**, c. 499 CE. This is the earliest extant mathematical text attributed to an individual. *See also* LITERATURE.

ARYAN. Term derived from the **Sanskrit** word ***ārya***, used in the late 18th and early 19th century to refer to those who spoke **Indo-European languages**. The term acquired racial connotations in the 19th and 20th centuries in the context of debates on the relationship between language and race that culminated in the appropriation of the term by the Nazis. *See also ĀRYĀVARTA*; *DĀSA*.

ĀRYAŚŪRA. Author of the ***Jātakamālā*** (c. 350–400 CE), a **Buddhist** text composed in ornate **Sanskrit** prose and verse. *See also* LITERATURE.

ĀRYĀVARTA*.** **Sanskrit** term used to delimit lands where ***āryas were expected to live. While earlier texts contained lists of preferred and condemned lands, definitions of *āryāvarta* appear for the first time in the **Dharmasūtras** and **Dharmaśāstras** (c. sixth century BCE onward). It was defined in several ways: as the land between the **Ganga (2)** and the **Yamuna**, as the land where the black antelope roamed, as the land between the **Himalayas** to the north and the **Vindhyas** to the south, from the point where the **Sarasvatī** disappeared in the west, to Kālakavana (possibly in present-day Bihar) to the east. Occasionally, it was defined in social rather than spatial terms, as the land where the norms of ***varṇa*** and ***āśrama*** were observed. *See also* SAMUDRAGUPTA.

ASAṄGA. **Buddhist philosopher** (c. fifth century CE), author of the *Mahāyānasūtrālaṃkāra* and other works in **Sanskrit**, which have survived in Chinese translations. *See also* LITERATURE; VASUBANDHU; *YOGĀCĀRA*.

ASCETICISM. Ascetic traditions were significant in early India. Some scholars have attempted to trace the roots of these traditions to the **Harappan** civilization, suggesting that figures depicted on **seals** and **sculpture** represent ascetics. However, the earliest firm evidence of ascetic practices dates from **later Vedic** and subsequent textual traditions (first millennium BCE onward). In fact, historians have suggested that asceticism may have received an impetus with the growing complexity of social, economic, and political life associated with the **early historic period**.

Minimally, asceticism involved the practice of celibacy. Besides, a wide range of other practices were enjoined within specific ascetic or **renunciatory** traditions. These included rules governing attire, food, and residence as well as social intercourse in general. The more austere groups emphasized abandoning all human contact and subsisting in isolation on what was naturally available—others devised means of regulating and restricting contact with those who remained within the world.

Theoretically, ascetics could be recruited from all social groups; however, in practice men located in the lower rungs of the social hierarchy may have found it difficult to adopt these practices. References to **women** ascetics are few and far between.

Buddhism and **Jainism** (as well as other renunciatory orders) developed their own ascetic norms, recognizing these as essential for attaining enlightenment or liberation. Within the **Brahmanical** system, the attitude toward asceticism was more ambivalent: On the one hand, the power of the ascetic was acknowledged; on the other, asceticism was viewed as going against the grain of the household order, which was regarded as the foundation of society. Stories in the **Sanskrit epics** and **Purāṇas** frequently dwelt on the frailty of the ascetic. At the same time, asceticism was accommodated within the ***āśrama*** system, as a possible mode of existence during the final stage of life, open to men of the first three ***varṇas***. *See also DĀNA*; EIGHTFOLD PATH; FOREST; *KALPASŪTRA*; PĀŚUPATA; RELIGION; ŚIVA; ŚIVĀRYA; *ŚRAMAṆA*.

ASH MOUNDS. Sites (c. third millennium BCE?) such as **Utnur**, found in the southern Deccan, especially in the valley of the **Krishna River** and its tributaries. They derive their name from the fact that they consist primarily of mounds of burnt cattle dung. In some instances the ash mounds were associated with settlements, whereas in other cases they stood in isolation. It is likely that they were sites of seasonal activity, perhaps ritual in nature, indicating the presence of **pastoral** populations. *See also* BUDIHAL; FOOTE, ROBERT BRUCE; KODEKAL; KUPGAL.

ASIATIC SOCIETY. Founded by Sir **William Jones** in Calcutta (Kolkata) in 1784. Subsequently, similar societies were set up in places such as Bombay (Mumbai), Madras (Chennai), London, and Paris. The objective of the society was to study the "history, antiquities, arts, science and literature of Asia." Many of the findings of members of the society were published in a journal, *Asiatic Researches*, from 1788 until 1833. Collections of artifacts by members of the society formed the nucleus of the Indian Museum, Kolkata, which was set up in 1875. Manuscripts collected by the society were published in the *Bibliotheca Indica* series. *See also* MITRA, RAJENDRA LALA; PRINSEP, JAMES.

ASIKINĪ. *See* AKESINES.

AŚMAKA. Name of a ***mahājanapada*** (c. sixth century BCE) located on the banks of the **Godavari** in present-day Andhra Pradesh. *See also* ĀRYABHAṬA.

ASOKA. Third ruler (r.c. 273–232 BCE) of the **Mauryan** dynasty, son and successor of **Bindusāra**. Asoka's history has been reconstructed primarily on the basis of his **inscriptions**, some of which are dated in regnal years and mention contemporary rulers in West Asia and Egypt. These references have provided the basis for a relatively secure chronology. **Buddhist** tradition suggests that Asoka succeeded to the throne after a bitter struggle with his brothers. In his inscriptions, the ruler adopted the titles of *devānampiya* (beloved of the gods) and *piyadassi* (pleasing to the eye). Only a few of the **Minor Rock Edicts** carry his name, Asoka. Eight years after his coronation, Asoka undertook the conquest of **Kaliṅga**, part of present-day Orissa. According to the account of the war in **Major Rock Edict** XIII, this resulted in the death of more than 100,000 people, while more than 150,000 people were taken captive.

Thereafter Asoka decided to eschew war, adopting the policy of ***dhamma*** instead. While this change has often been idealized (and occasionally criticized) by early 20th-century scholars as an instance of pacifism, more recent studies suggest that it may have been motivated by pragmatic concerns. From this perspective, *dhamma* may have been adopted as a means of welding together a vast and disparate empire.

Asokan inscriptions mention a second queen, suggesting that he had more than one wife. Buddhist and other literary traditions mention his sons and daughter. The history of the dynasty after Asoka is obscure, and the empire disintegrated (c. 181 BCE) within 50 years of his death.

Asoka is often regarded as a unique ruler in the early Indian context. He was probably the first **king** to issue inscriptions on a systematic basis, outlining his ideas and instructions on a range of themes, including *dhamma*. Several inscriptions attest to his personal belief in Buddhism. He undertook pilgrimages to sacred places associated with the Buddha, such as **Bodh Gaya** and **Lumbini**. Buddhist tradition attributes the construction of 84,000 ***stūpas*** to the ruler. While the number is obviously mythical, the existence of Mauryan *stūpas* at sites such as **Sanchi** and **Sarnath** is corroborated by **archaeology**. He also attempted to regulate the Buddhist **monastic** order.

Asoka is also associated with some of the best-known examples of **Mauryan art**, including **sculpture**, to decorate the capitals of pillars. While some of these pillars may have predated Mauryan rule, others were probably erected during his reign. *See also* ALIKASUDARA; AMTEKINA; AMTIYAKO YONARĀJA; ASOKAN INSCRIPTIONS; *AŚOKĀVADĀNA*; BHOJA (1); BUDDHIST COUNCILS; *DHAMMA MAHĀMATTA*; *DIGVIJAYA*; DIONYSIUS; *DĪPAVAMSA*; *DIVYĀVADĀNA*; KINGSHIP; KOLHUA; MAGAS (OF CYRENE); MAHINDA; NITTUR; SLAVERY; TAXILA; TOPRA; TURAMAYA; UDEGOLAM.

ASOKAN INSCRIPTIONS. Asoka is the first ruler of early India who is known to have issued inscriptions (c. third century BCE). These are classified into four broad groups, **Major Rock Edicts**, **Minor Rock Edicts**, **Major Pillar Edicts**, and **Minor Pillar Edicts**. While most of the inscriptions were written in the **Brāhmī script**, a few from the northwest of the subcontinent were in **Kharoṣṭhī**. The bilingual inscription from Kandahar (Afghanistan) was written in the Greek and **Aramaic** scripts. The **language** in most of the inscriptions was simple **Prakrit**, while Greek and Aramaic were used in the inscription from Kandahar. The inscriptions represent a long chain of communication: from the capital, **Pāṭaliputra**, to the provincial or local officials who would have gotten the message of the ruler written and engraved on stone surfaces, which were specifically chosen to ensure that the message would last for a long time. Most of the inscriptions contain messages about Asoka's ***dhamma***, addressed to his subjects and officials as well as to his successors. In addition, they occasionally contain information about events and mention contemporary rulers as well as more or less autonomous peoples within the kingdom or along its frontiers. Some inscriptions are dated in regnal years. *See also* BHAGWANLAL INDRAJI; COḺA; JAMBUDVĪPA; KĀMBOJA; *KERALAPUTA*; LUMBINI; MAURYAN ART; *PARIṢAD*; PRINSEP, JAMES; PUL-I-DARUNTA; *RĀJUKA*; RAṬHIKA; SATIYAPUTA; SEPARATE ROCK EDICTS; SHAR-I-KUNA; *STŪPA*; SUVARṆAGIRI; TĀMBAPANNI; TRIBES; UJJAYINĪ; *YONA*.

AŚOKĀVADĀNA*.** **Buddhist Sanskrit** text, composed c. second century CE, containing legends about the **Mauryan** ruler **Asoka**. According to these legends, Asoka became an emperor because of a gift of a handful of dirt that he had made to the **Buddha** in a previous birth. The legends, which purport to be **biographical**, depict Asoka as a cruel man before his conversion to Buddhism and also record his gifts to the ***saṃgha, which evidently led to the impoverishment of the realm. While the historicity of these legends is doubtful, they are important as representing the way in which Asoka was perceived and projected within the Buddhist tradition. *See also* LITERATURE.

ĀŚRAMA*.** **Sanskrit** term to designate four modes or stages in the life of a man belonging to the first three ranks of the ***varṇa order. The four *āśramas* included ***brahmacarya***, a period meant for the observance of celibacy and the acquisition of **Vedic** learning, generally recommended for the adolescent boy; *gṛhastha*, or the state of being a householder, with obligations to marry, produce sons, and perform prescribed rituals; ***vānaprastha***, or the observance of a period of relatively less severe renunciation in the **forest**; and ***saṃnyāsa***, or complete renunciation. References to the system are found in the **Dharmasūtras** (c. fifth century BCE onward) and **Dharmaśāstras** (c. second century BCE onward). **Kings** were often described as upholding the norms of both *varṇa* and *āśrama* in **inscriptions** belonging to the **early medieval period**. However, it is difficult to determine the extent to which the system was actually followed. The term *āśrama* was also used in the sense of a hermitage. *See also* ASCETICISM; *DHARMA*; RENUNCIATORY ORDERS.

ASSEMBLIES. A variety of assemblies are mentioned in textual traditions and **inscriptions**. The ***Ṛgveda*** (c. second millennium BCE) refers to the ***sabhā***, ***samiti***, and ***vidatha***. These assemblies were centers of social, political, and ritual activities, besides serving as foci for redistributing economic resources. Some of them were open to **women**. By the first millennium BCE, assemblies lost their political importance in monarchies, although they remained centers for cultural activities. They continued to play a significant role in ***gaṇa/saṃghas***. Membership in such assemblies was restricted to men who were related through kinship ties. It is likely that these assemblies provided the model that was adopted by the **Buddhist** and **Jaina** orders.

Toward the end of the first millennium CE, village assemblies are mentioned in **Tamil inscriptions**, especially those belonging to the **Co<u>l</u>a** period. There were evidently several kinds of assemblies, including some meant exclusively for ***brāhmaṇa*** (1) landowners. Others were organizations of prosperous peasants. These assemblies organized **irrigation** works and acted as local administrative bodies, mobilizing resources and adjudicating disputes. *See also* MADURAI; *MANRAM*; *SANGAM*; UṢAVADĀTA; *VELLĀLĀR*.

AṢṬĀDHYĀYĪ. **Sanskrit** text on grammar, containing eight chapters, consisting of about 4,000 rules or ***sūtras***, attributed to **Pāṇini** (c. sixth–fifth centuries BCE). The text deals with issues of syntax, verbal forms, and rules for forming compound words. The first chapter contains meta-rules, which are applied through the rest of the text. While Pāṇini mentioned predecessors, his composition superceded their texts. Commentaries on the *Aṣṭādhyāyī* continued to be written until as late as the 16th century. *See also* LITERATURE.

ASTRONOMY. Early Indian astronomy evidently developed in a ritual context. It was used to fix the time for **Vedic** rituals and subsequently for rites of passage and for the **calendar**. The earliest phase, dated between 1000 and 400 BCE, was marked by the use of a few basic calendrical terms and the development of a rudimentary **mathematical** structure. Its use for horoscopes is dated to c. second century CE. Subsequently, early Indian astronomical ideas were substantially influenced by Babylonian and Greek ideas. *See also*

ĀRYABHAṬA; INDO-GREEK; LAGADHA; SPHUJIDHVAJA; VARĀHAMIHIRA; *YUGA*.

ASURGARH. *See* MANAMUNDA.

AŚVAGHOṢA. **Sanskrit** author (c. first century CE?). The works attributed to him include the ***Buddhacarita*** based on the life of the **Buddha**, which contributed to the development of **Mahāyāna Buddhism**, the *Saundarananda* and the *Laṅkāvatārasūtra*, a **philosophical** treatise. He was evidently well versed both in techniques of Sanskrit composition and in Buddhist doctrine. He was probably associated with the court of the **Kuṣāṇa** ruler **Kaniṣka**. *See also* LITERATURE.

***AŚVAMEDHA*.** Horse **sacrifice**, described in **later Vedic literature** (c. 10th–6th centuries BCE). The associated rituals lasted for more than a year. The sacrifice was recommended for rulers who aspired to achieve supremacy over their rivals. It also incorporated elements of fertility cults. **Inscriptions** and texts (including the **Sanskrit epics**) occasionally mention the performance of the ritual by **kings**. The **Gupta** ruler **Samudragupta** (c. fourth century CE) issued **coins** to commemorate his performance of the sacrifice. *See also DIGVIJAYA*; KINGSHIP, THEORIES OF ORIGIN; KUMĀRAGUPTA I; NĀGANIKĀ; PUṢYAMITRA ŚUṄGA.

ĀṬAVIKA RĀJĀ. **Sanskrit** term, literally meaning "**forest king**" (or chief), mentioned in the **Allahabad Pillar Inscription** of the **Gupta** ruler **Samudragupta** (c. fourth century CE). The ruler claimed to have reduced these chiefs to servitude.

ATHARVAVEDA*.** Anthology of hymns composed in **Sanskrit**, attributed to several seers and authors, compiled by priests, traditionally recognized as the latest of the four **Vedas**. It is divided into 20 sections. Many verses and hymns are common to the ***Ṛgveda. Apart from prayers to the standard Vedic gods, the *Atharvaveda* contains charms recommended as cures for disease and spells to ensure success in battle and in love. It is likely that popular practices were sanctified and codified through inclusion in this text. While the verses may have been composed fairly early, the compilation of the text may date between c. 1000 and 600 BCE. *See also ĀYURVEDA*; LITERATURE; MEDICINE.

ATRANJIKHERA. Archaeological site in Uttar Pradesh with five major occupational phases. Period I (c. first half of the second millennium BCE) yielded **Ochre-Coloured Pottery**. Finds from this phase included wattle-and-daub structures as well as evidence for the cultivation of rice, barley, and pulses. Evidence for **agriculture**, including the cultivation of a variety of crops, was found from subsequent periods as well. Other finds included cattle bone, and stone mortars and pestles. Period II (c. 1450–1200 BCE) yielded evidence for the use of **copper**. Other finds included **black and red ware**. Period III (c. 1200–600 BCE) was associated with **Painted Grey Ware**, a wide range of **iron** equipment and slag, bone **tools**, copper ornaments, and **terracotta** figurines. Period IV (c. 600–200 BCE) was associated with **Northern Black Polished Ware** and baked-brick structures. Other finds included terracotta beads, bangles and figurines, glass beads and bangles, and objects of ivory, bone, and shell. Later levels yielded **Kuṣāṇa coins** and remains of a **temple**.

ATTIRAMPAKKAM. Archaeological site in Tamil Nadu that has yielded evidence of all three phases of **Paleolithic** development as well as microliths associated with the **Mesolithic** period.

AULIKARA. Ruling lineage in central India, c. fifth century CE. **Yaśodharman** is regarded as the most important ruler of this dynasty.

AUROVILLE. Archaeological site in Puducherry, find spot of a variety of **megalithic** burials (c. first millennium BCE?), including urns, cists, and cairn circles. Other finds consist of **Black and Red Ware** and a range of **iron tools** and weapons.

AUVAIYAR. One of the best-known **Tamil women** poets, whose compositions are included in the ***Sangam*** anthologies (c. third century BCE–second century CE?) where about 60 verses are attributed to her. The name is a generic Tamil term meaning "respectable woman." The compositions attributed to her contain references to the **Coḻa**, **Cera**, and **Pāṇḍya kings** and include songs in praise of the generous donor and elegies for warriors. Later traditions occasionally described her as the sister of **Tiruvaḷḷuvār**. *See also* LITERATURE.

AVANTI. One of the 16 ***mahājanapadas*** mentioned in early **Buddhist literature** (c. sixth century BCE) with its capital at **Ujjayinī**. It included the region of Malwa, part of present-day Madhya Pradesh. *See also* DAṆḌIN; MAHESHWAR; PRADYOTA; ŚIŚUNĀGA; UDAYANA.

AVANTIVARMAN. King of Kashmir (c. 855–883 CE). He was associated with the construction of **irrigation** networks, the endowment of **temples**, and the establishment of a **city** named Avantipura. He was also recognized as a patron of scholars. *See also* ĀNANDAVARDHANA; RATNĀKARA.

AVATĀRA*. Sanskrit** term used in the **Purāṇas** (c. fourth century CE onward) to describe the incarnation and descent to earth of deities, especially **Viṣṇu**. The Purāṇas generally list 10 *avatāras* or incarnations of the deity. These include the fish, tortoise, boar, man-lion, dwarf, **Paraśurāma** (Rāma with the axe), **Rāma** (the hero of the ***Rāmāyaṇa), Balarāma, the brother of **Kṛṣṇa**, Kṛṣṇa, in some versions the **Buddha**, and Kalkin, visualized as the *avatāra* of the future. Modern scholars view the *avatāra* scheme as a means of assimilating cultic practices and beliefs that may have been the preserve of distinct peoples or regions within the **Brahmanical** pantheon. *See also* RELIGION; VAIṢṆAVISM.

***ĀYĀRA*.** The oldest of the **Jaina** canonical texts, composed in **Prakrit**, also known as the *Samayika*. It was redacted at the council of **Valabhi**, though it may have been committed to writing as early as c. 300 BCE. It was composed in a mixture of prose and verse. It contains a **biography** of **Mahāvīra** and teachings attributed to him, emphasizing renunciation, nonviolence, and the five vows. It deals with rules of conduct and consists of two sections, of which the second includes a series of appendixes to the main work.

AYODHYA. Archaeological site in Uttar Pradesh. The earliest occupational levels (c. seventh–fourth centuries BCE) yielded evidence of **Northern Black Polished Ware**. Other finds include traces of wattle-and-daub structures and **copper** and **iron** artifacts. Subsequent levels (c. fourth century BCE–fourth century CE) yielded evidence of ring wells and burnt-brick structures. Associated finds included **punch-marked** and other **coins**, **terracotta** sealings, **rouletted ware**, and **Jaina sculpture**. The settlement was probably deserted between c. 5th and 10th centuries CE and was reoccupied in the 11th century. The **city** figured in several textual traditions. Jaina tradition recognized it as the birthplace of the first and fourth ***tīrthaṅkaras***. **Buddhist** texts mentioned it as a city visited by the **Buddha** and as an important town in the ***mahājanapada*** of **Kosala**. It is mentioned as the capital of Kosala in the ***Rāmāyaṇa*** of **Vālmīki**. *See also* SĀKETA.

ĀYURVEDA*. Sanskrit** term meaning "knowledge to ensure longevity," the designation of traditions of **medical** thought codified toward the end of the first millennium BCE. The roots of *āyurveda* are traditionally traced to the ***Atharvaveda. It is likely that the system combined insights derived from popular knowledge and practice with the knowledge of specialists. Its basic premise was that health required maintaining a balance among the elements within the body, disease being the result of imbalance. Restoring the balance involved regulating diet and lifestyles as well as the use of medicines derived from plants, animals, and minerals. There was also provision for surgery. *See also CARAKA SAṂHITĀ*.

AYYAVOLE. *See* AIHOLE.

AZES II. Śaka ruler, c. first century BCE–first century CE, who ruled over parts of Afghanistan, known from his silver **coins** that contain legends in Greek and **Kharoṣṭhī** as well as representations of the **king** and images drawn from **Buddhist** and **Brahmanical** traditions. One of the most spectacular Buddhist artifacts, a sculpted golden relic casket containing coins of the ruler, was probably placed within a ***stūpa*** during his reign.

– B –

BABARKOT. Archaeological site in Gujarat with evidence of occupation during the **early historic** phase. Structural remains include traces of a **fortification** wall. Other finds include beads and bangles, evidence of millet and bones of domesticated cattle, sheep, goat, pig, and dog as well as wild animals such as boar, deer, mongoose, rat, and turtle.

BACTRIA. Ancient Greek name for part of present-day northern Afghanistan, a fertile area with several mountain ranges, located between Central Asia and the Indian subcontinent, bordering on **Gandhara**. Bactria formed part of both the **Achaemenid** Empire and of that of **Alexander (of Macedon)**. On the death of the latter, it came under the control of **Seleucos Nikator**. Several towns emerged in the region (c. fifth century BCE onward), and for centuries Greek was one of the **languages** used in the area for administrative and other purposes. *See also* ANTIOCHOS III THE GREAT; BACTRIAN GREEK.

BACTRIAN GREEK. Name assigned to ruling lineages that exercised control over northern Afghanistan and Central Asia between the third and second centuries BCE. Their histories have been reconstructed from **coins** and from Greek and Roman texts. The Bactrian kingdom was founded c. 245 BCE, when a military commander named Diodotus asserted independence from the Seleucid ruler **Antiochos II**. Bactrian rulers attempted to extend control over northern India, perhaps reaching, briefly, as far east as **Pāṭaliputra**, following the collapse of the **Mauryan** Empire. **Indo-Greek** principalities in the northwest of the subcontinent were probably the result of this eastward move. To the west, the **Parthians** and the Seleucids were their principal rivals. Bactrian Greek rulers adopted a combination of military confrontation and matrimonial alliances in their policy toward these rulers. Ultimately, the Bactrian Greek kingdom succumbed to pressures from Central Asian peoples, including the **Śakas** and the **Yuehzhi**. Bactrian Greek rulers adopted Hellenistic cultural practices in their **cities**: The town of Ai-Khanum, destroyed by invaders in 145 BCE, contained a theater and a gymnasium. The rulers were probably sympathetic toward **Buddhism**. *See also* AGATHOKLES;

ANTIMACHUS; BACTRIA; DEMETRIOS; EUKRATIDES; EUTHYDEMOS; INDO-GREEK; SILK ROUTE; TAXILA.

BADAMI. Administrative center of the **Cālukyas**, also known as Vātāpi, in Karnataka, **fortified** c. 543–44 CE, and site of some of the most distinctive **rock-cut temples** built for the worship of **Brahmanical** deities under royal patronage. These were decorated with **sculptural** representations of a variety of gods and **goddesses**. Badami was attacked by the **Pallavas** in the seventh century and lost its importance when the Cālukyas were succeeded by the **Rāṣṭrakūṭas** as the dominant ruling lineage in the region in the eighth century. *See also* NARASIMḤAVARMAN I.

BĀDARĀYANA. Philosopher, traditionally recognized as the author of the ***Brahmasūtra***, and often identified with **Vyāsa**, date uncertain.

BAGH. Site in Madhya Pradesh, with **rock-cut caves** serving as **Buddhist monasteries**, many of which were decorated with **sculpture** and **painting** dating to the **Vākāṭaka** period (c. 470–480 CE). Stylistically, there is a strong resemblance with the paintings from **Ajanta**.

BAGOR. Archaeological site in Rajasthan, with two major occupational phases. Period I, considered **Mesolithic** (c. 5500–2500 BCE), yielded several thousand microliths, generally made of quartz and chert. Faunal remains including bones of sheep, goat, cattle, deer, fish, and turtle suggest a combination of hunting, fishing, and **pastoralism** as a subsistence strategy. There are some traces of **pottery** and **copper** during the second phase of this period. The former has some parallels with that from **Kayatha** and **Ahar**. Finds of beads of agate and carnelian indicate contact with the **Harappan civilization** as well. There is evidence for **burials** within the settlement. Period II (c. 500 BCE–200 CE) yielded evidence of **iron**, pottery, and glass beads.

BAHADRABAD. Archaeological site in Uttar Pradesh, find spot of a **Copper Hoard** (c. second millennium BCE?), including rings, celts, and spearheads. Other finds include a red slipped ware, sometimes equated with **Ochre-Coloured Pottery**, although this identification is not universally accepted.

BAHAL. Archaeological site in Maharashtra, with evidence of three major occupational phases. Period I (mid–second millennium BCE?) yielded evidence of a **Chalcolithic** culture. Finds include microliths, traces of **copper**, and **pottery**. Period II (c. 600–300 BCE) yielded traces of grain, possibly rice, a range of **iron** artifacts including **tools** and weapons, **black and red ware**, and beads of semiprecious stone. Period III (c. 300 BCE–100 CE) provided evidence of **Northern Black Polished Ware**. Structural remains included ring wells. The site appears to have been abandoned as a result of floods and was reoccupied c. 1200 CE.

BAHAPUR. Archaeological site in New Delhi, find spot of a **Minor Rock Edict** of **Asoka**.

BAIRAT. Site in Rajasthan, recognized in textual traditions as the capital of the **Matsya *mahājanapada***. It is also the find spot of a **Minor Rock Edict** of **Asoka** (c. third century BCE), addressed to the **Buddhist *saṃgha***. The inscription lists a set of Buddhist texts, with the ruler exhorting monks and nuns, as well as lay men and **women**, to study and reflect on these. Other finds include remains of a Buddhist **monastery** and a shrine, possibly a ***stūpa***. Among the finds from the monastery was a hoard of **coins**, including **punch-marked** coins and **Indo-Greek** issues, and **Northern Black Polished Ware**.

BALAKOT. Archaeological site in Sind, Pakistan, with evidence for **pre-/early Harappan** and **Mature Harappan** occupation. The first phase, dated between the late fifth and the early third millennium BCE, was characterized by mud-brick **architecture**, which continued in the second phase as well. There is evidence for **agriculture** and for the domestication of animals, including cattle, sheep, and goat. **Tools** included microliths. Other finds included wheel-made **pottery**, **terracotta** figurines, and beads of semiprecious stone. There is evidence for the manufacture of shell bangles and the use of **seals** in the Mature Harappan level.

BALATHAL. Archaeological site in Rajasthan, with two occupational phases. Period I, considered **Chalcolithic** (c. 2100–1400 BCE), yielded remains of wheat, barley, rice, millets, gram, pea, and berries. Faunal remains included bones of cattle, sheep, goat, dog, deer, boar, rat, elephant, peacock, turtle, fowl, fish, and mollusks. **Pottery** included **black and red ware** similar to that found in **Ahar** and other varieties with **late Harappan** and **Kayathan** affinities. The site was reoccupied after a hiatus in the **early historic period** (c. third century BCE–third century CE). Finds from this phase included evidence of **iron** smelting and a range of iron **tools**, **copper** artifacts including **coins** and ornaments, glass bangles, beads of semiprecious stone, **terracotta** figurines, ring wells, and evidence of the use of cotton and rice.

BALI. **Sanskrit** term for tribute or tax, mentioned in textual sources, including **later Vedic literature** (c. 1000–600 BCE), and in **inscriptions** such as the **Asokan** (c. third century BCE) and later inscriptions. *See also* REVENUE SYSTEMS; RUMMINDEI.

BALU. **Archaeological** site (c. third–second millennium BCE) in Haryana. Finds include **pre-/early Harappan**, **Mature Harappan**, and **late Harappan pottery** with parallels with that from **Bara**. Structural remains include traces of a mud-brick **fortification**, a potter's kiln, and a drain. There is evidence for the cultivation of wheat and barley. Other finds include beads of **copper**, stone, **terracotta**, faience, steatite, shell, and bone.

BĀṆABHAṬṬA. **Sanskrit** author (c. seventh century CE), court poet of **Harṣavardhana**. His best-known compositions are the ***Harṣacarita***, a **biography** of his patron, and *Kādambarī*, a romance written in ornate prose. *See also* DAṆḌIN; LITERATURE.

BANAHALLI. **Archaeological** site in Karnataka. Period I (c. second millennium BCE?) is divided into two phases, **Neolithic** and **Chalcolithic**. Finds from the first phase included ground stone **tools** such as axes and saddle querns, microliths, bone tools, handmade **pottery**, and evidence for round huts. The second phase yielded small amounts of **copper**, microliths, bone tools, wheel-made pottery, a potter's kiln, and beads of semiprecious stone. Other finds included urn **burials**. Period II (c. first half of the first millennium BCE?) was associated with **megaliths**, **Black and Red Ware**, and small amounts of **iron**. Finds from period III (c. second half of the first millennium BCE?) included furnaces and slag, pointing to the local smelting of iron, and a range of tools and implements such as arrowheads, spearheads, blades, hooks, nails, and sickles. There was evidence for the manufacture of beads of carnelian, coral, and glass. Period IV, considered **early historic** (c. early centuries CE?), yielded a variety of beads and **terracotta** figurines.

BANARSIHANKALAN. Early historic (c. first millennium BCE?) **archaeological** site in Uttar Pradesh, find spot of a brick-built ***stūpa***, **terracotta** figurines, sealings, **coins**, and **Buddhist sculpture**. Finds of **pottery** include **black slipped ware** as well as **Northern Black Polished Ware**.

BANAVASI. Archaeological site in Karnataka. Period I (c. second century BCE?) yielded evidence of lead **coins**, a silver **punch-marked** coin, and **copper** coins resembling those of the **Sātavāhanas**. **Pottery** included **Red Polished Ware** and **Black and Red Ware**. Other finds included beads of **terracotta** and semiprecious stone as well as evidence for bead making. Period II, attributed more centrally to the Sātavāhanas, was marked by the construction of an enclosing wall and a **Buddhist** shrine. Traditions of pottery showed continuities with the preceding phase. There are indications of copper smelting, and the site may have housed a mint. Other finds included a lead coin of the Sātavāhana ruler **Pulumayi**, terracotta bullae with impressions of Roman emperors, ivory artifacts, objects of copper and **iron**, beads of semiprecious stone, and glass bangles and beads. Period III (c. fourth–sixth centuries CE) yielded an **inscription** of the **Kadambas**. Material remains were similar to those from the preceding period. Structures associated with this phase included a **temple**.

BANAWALI. Archaeological site in Haryana. Period I or the **pre-/early Harappan** (c. early third millennium BCE?) occupation yielded evidence of **fortification**. **Pottery** resembling types associated with **Kalibangan** was found in this and subsequent occupational levels. Other finds included **copper tools**, such as fishhooks and arrowheads, and beads of semiprecious stone. Floral remains included millets, legumes, oilseeds, barley, wheat, peas, gram, and tamarind. There is evidence for a shift to the twin-mound **architecture**, typical of the **Mature Harappan** (mid–third millennium BCE onward) phase, toward the end of this period, which is also marked by the use of Harappan-type brick, pottery, chert blades, and beads. Period II, more typically Harappan, was characterized by town planning, with evidence of a fortification wall around the settlement and a citadel in the southwest. Both burnt bricks and mud bricks were used for construction, and in the typical Harappan ratio. Other finds included pottery, weights, **seals**, sealings, figurines, ornaments, and tools. Floral remains from this phase were virtually identical with the previous phase but also included fenugreek, rice, cotton, soap nut, and dates. There is evidence for a **post-Harappan** (Period III, first half of the second millennium BCE) settlement outside the fortified area.

BANGARH. Archaeological site in West Bengal, with evidence for occupation c. second century BCE onward. There is evidence for a brick **fortification** wall. Other finds include **Northern Black Polished Ware**, **punch-marked coins**, **terracotta** plaques, and sealings with **Brāhmī inscriptions**.

BANKI. Archaeological site in Chattisgarh, with evidence of **Paleolithic** and **Mesolithic** occupations. The latter phase yielded evidence of huts, grinding stones, and microliths.

BANOTIWADI. Archaeological site in Maharashtra, find spot of **rock-cut caves** decorated with stone **sculpture**, dated between c. mid–fifth and mid–sixth centuries CE.

BARA. Archaeological site in the Punjab, with evidence of occupation, c. third millennium BCE. It is associated with a distinctive variety of wheel-made **pottery**, with a reddish brown slip, decorated with black or dark brown designs. Some of the shapes resemble those from **Harappan** sites. Structural remains include traces of mud-brick **architecture** and hearths. Other finds include bone **tools**, traces of **copper**, faience bangles, and stone mortars and pestles. Faunal remains include bones of cattle, sheep, goat, elephant, and deer. *See also* BALU; DAULATPUR; KALIBANGAN; SANGHOL.

BARABAR. Archaeological site in Bihar containing some of the earliest examples of **rock-cut caves**. These were constructed during the

Mauryan period. **Inscriptions** on the highly polished cave walls record grants made to religious sects, including the **Ājīvikas**, by the Mauryan ruler **Asoka** and his grandson **Dasaratha** (c. third century BCE).

BARBARICUM. Greek name for an **early historic** port near the mouth of the **Indus**, mentioned in the ***Periplus of the Erythraean Sea*** as a center from which cotton, silk, and semiprecious stones, including turquoise and lapis lazuli, were exported to the west.

BARYGAZA. Greek name for **Bhṛgukaccha** (present-day **Bharuch**), an **early historic** settlement on the estuary of the **Narmada**, on the Gulf of Khambat. Barygaza was one of the most important ports of the west coast, exporting ivory, semiprecious stones such as agate and carnelian, and silk and cotton **textiles**. **Archaeological** evidence indicates that it was a center for the manufacture of beads. *See also* TAGARA.

BATTLE OF THE TEN KINGS. A battle (c. late second millennium BCE?), known as the *dāśarājña* (literally, of 10 kings), mentioned in the ***Ṛgveda***, in which a ***rājā*** named Sudās, who belonged to the **Bharata (1) tribe**, was victorious over 10 *rājās* who had formed an alliance against him. The battle evidently took place on the banks of the Ravi River, a tributary of the **Indus**.

BAVIKONDA. Archaeological site (c. first millennium CE?) in Andhra Pradesh, find spot of a ***stūpa***. Other finds include votive *stūpas*, **monasteries**, and shrines. Structures that have been identified include remains of a hall that could have served as a library or a dining hall.

BAYANA. Archaeological site in Rajasthan, find spot of a hoard of nearly 2,000 gold **coins** issued by the **Gupta** rulers. These include coins of **Candragupta I**, **Samudragupta**, **Candragupta II**, Kāca, and **Kumāragupta I**. It is likely that the hoard was buried during the reign of **Skandagupta**, when there was considerable instability on account of the invasions of the **Hūṇas**.

BEAS. Tributary of the **Indus River**. It marked the easternmost limit of the advance of **Alexander (of Macedon)** (c. fourth century BCE) into the subcontinent.

BEDSA. Site in Maharashtra (early first millennium CE), with evidence of **rock-cut caves**, including a ***caitya*** and a ***vihāra***.

BEGRAM. Site in Afghanistan, identified with ancient **Kapiśa**. **Archaeological** finds include a hoard of **art** objects of Roman, Syrian, Alexandrian, Chinese, and Indic origin. The artifacts that are clearly of subcontinental origin include a cache of exquisitely carved ivory **sculptures**, dated to c. first–second centuries CE.

BELAN VALLEY. Area in Uttar Pradesh with more than 40 Lower **Paleolithic** sites, many of which were factory sites, with evidence of **tool** production. Subsequently, there were nearly 90 Middle Paleolithic sites, including several factory sites. **Neolithic** sites have also been found in the area. *See also* CHOPANI MANDO; KOLDIHWA; MAHAGARA.

BENT BAR COINS. Silver coins, generally associated with the northwest of the subcontinent, issued c. sixth century BCE onward, stamped with symbols that resemble those on **punch-marked coins**.

BESNAGAR. *See* VIDISHA.

BESNAGAR PILLAR INSCRIPTION. Prakrit inscription (c. second century BCE) found on a pillar in **Vidisha**. It is dated to the 14th regnal year of a ruler named Kāśiputra Bhāgabhadra and records the erection of the pillar by **Heliodoros**.

BHABRU. Site in Rajasthan, find spot of a **Minor Rock Edict** of **Asoka**.

BHADRABĀHU. Jaina preceptor of **Candragupta Maurya** (c. fourth–third centuries BCE), also recognized as the author of the ***Kalpasūtra***. According to Jaina tradition, he predicted a **famine** in the realm, and consequently both he and Candragupta left the capital and went to Sravana Belgola in Karnataka, where they undertook a fast unto death. This journey marks the introduction of **Jainism** into south India. *See also* DIGAMBARA; STHŪLABHADRA.

BHĀGA. **Sanskrit** word meaning "share," used to denote a tax on **agricultural** produce in the **Dharmasūtras** (c. sixth century BCE onward) and later texts and **inscriptions**. It was generally assessed at one sixth of the produce and was justified as being the wages the **king** received in lieu of the protection he offered his subjects. *See also* REVENUE SYSTEMS; RUMMINDEI.

BHAGAVAD GĪTĀ. **Sanskrit** text divided into 18 chapters, consisting of about 700 verses, possibly compiled in the early centuries of the Common Era. Composed as a dialogue between **Kṛṣṇa**, regarded as an incarnation of **Viṣṇu**, and his friend Arjuna, one of the Pāṇḍavas, the heroes of the ***Mahābhārata***, the text forms part of the **epic**. It provides a succinct summary of different **philosophical** traditions and modes of self-realization, through action, knowledge, and devotion, and is perhaps the most popular text of **Hinduism**. *See also BHAKTI*; RELIGION; ŚAṄKARĀCĀRYA; VAIṢṆAVISM.

BHĀGAVATA. Name of a **Vaiṣṇava** sect that emerged by the early centuries of the first millennium CE, with an emphasis on devotionalism, manifested through image worship. The deity was addressed as **Viṣṇu**, **Kṛṣṇa**, Nārāyaṇa, Hari, and so on. **Mathura** was a major center of this tradition, which spread to western and central India. Early expressions of the ideas of the tradition are found in the ***Bhagavad Gītā***. The beliefs and practices of this sect had similarities with those of the **Pāñcarātras**. *See also* HELIODOROS; HINDUISM; RELIGION.

BHAGIMOHARI. **Archaeological** site in Maharashtra, with evidence of **megaliths** (c. 800–400 BCE), especially stone circles. Plant remains found at the site include rice, barley, wheat, lentil, pea, gram, bean, and the Indian jujube, or *ber*. Bones of cattle, pig, horse, and birds have also been recovered. Other finds include remains of a blacksmith's kiln and a variety of **iron** equipment, including axes, hoes, and arrowheads; **Black and Red Ware**; and beads of semiprecious stone.

BHAGWANLAL INDRAJI. (1839–1888). **Archaeologist** and Indologist, noted for his significant contributions to Indian **epigraphy**. His major achievements included editing and translating **Asokan**

inscriptions and those from cave sites in western India. He also traveled extensively, collecting **manuscripts** and other artifacts. He donated his collections to various museums in India and abroad.

BHAGWANPURA. **Archaeological** site in Haryana, with evidence of a **post-Harappan** occupation (c. second millennium BCE). Associated ceramics include **Painted Grey Ware**. Other finds included **terracotta** figurines, glass bangles, bone and ivory pins, needles and styli, **copper** bangles and rods, and a **seal** with **Harappan** affinities. While most structures were small circular huts, there is evidence of a large building with as many as 13 rooms. Two **burials**, of an adult and a child, were found. These were oriented in a north–south direction, with the head facing west.

BHAJA. Site in Maharashtra, with evidence of **rock-cut caves** dated to c. first century BCE. The façade of these caves was embellished with **sculpture**. The caves included both ***caityas*** and **monasteries**.

BHAKTI. **Sanskrit** term used to designate a wide variety of theistic traditions that emerged toward the end of the first millennium BCE and developed substantially over the subsequent centuries. The basic tenets involved devotion to the point of complete surrender to a deity. The origins of *Bhakti* have been traced to some of the **Upaniṣads**. Ideas of *Bhakti* were central to some sections of the ***Bhagavad Gītā*** and found expression in texts such as the Sanskrit **epics** and the **Purāṇas**. *Bhakti* was (and remains) particularly important within certain **Vaiṣṇava** sects as well as **Śaivism** and in traditions of **goddess** worship. *See also* BHĀGAVATA; HINDUISM; MUSIC; PĀÑCARĀTRA; PROTEST MOVEMENTS; RELIGION; TEMPLES.

BHĀMAHA. **Sanskrit** author (c. sixth century CE) of the *Kāvyālaṃkāra*, a work on poetics. Later authors recognized him as an authority on the subject. *See also* LITERATURE.

BHARATA (1). Name of a **tribe** mentioned frequently in the ***Ṛgveda*** (c. second millennium BCE), also recognized as one of the ancestors of the **Kurus**, one of the two major lineages whose stories are narrated in the ***Mahābhārata***. *See also* BATTLE OF THE TEN KINGS.

BHARATA (2). Traditionally recognized as the author of the ***Nāṭyaśāstra***, a treatise in **Sanskrit** on dramaturgy, assigned in its present form to c. fifth–sixth centuries CE. *See also* DRAMA; LITERATURE.

BHĀRATAVARṢA. Sanskrit term used in the **Purāṇas** (c. fourth century CE onward) to designate the subcontinent. It was generally defined as extending from the Himavat (i.e., the **Himalayas**) in the north to the eastern, southern, and western seas.

BHARATPUR. Archaeological site in West Bengal, with evidence of four occupational phases. Finds from Period I (c. second millennium BCE) designated as **Chalcolithic** consisted of microliths, stone and bone **tools**, traces of **copper**, and **black and red ware**. Structural remains included huts and hearths. There was evidence for hunting, fishing, and **agriculture**. Period II (mid–first millennium BCE) provided evidence of the use of **iron** and **Northern Black Polished Ware**. The site was abandoned toward the end of this phase. The evidence from Period III is meager. Period IV (c. 9th–10th centuries CE) provided evidence of a brick ***stūpa*** and stone **sculpture** of the **Buddha**.

BHĀRAVI. Author (c. sixth century CE) of a **Sanskrit epic**, the *Kirātārjunīya*, based on an episode from the ***Mahābhārata***. The epic, which extends over 18 cantos, represents a conflict between the hero, Arjuna, and the god **Śiva**, who grants him a boon. It exemplifies the expression of valor as a poetic sentiment. *See also* LITERATURE.

BHARHUT. Site of a ***stūpa*** in Madhya Pradesh, built c. second century BCE. Made of brick and stone, the *stūpa* was surrounded by a circular railing with gateways, decorated with some of the earliest examples of stone relief **sculptures** representing scenes from the ***Jātakas*** and from the life of the **Buddha**. The sculptures are now preserved in the Indian Museum, Kolkata.

BHARTṚHARI. Sanskrit author (c. fifth century CE), a poet, **philosopher**, and grammarian. The major work attributed to him, the *Vākpadīya*, deals with the philosophy of **language**. He was also traditionally recognized as the author of three compilations of verses dealing with polity, erotics, and renunciation. *See also* LITERATURE.

BHARUCH. Archaeological site in Gujarat, with evidence of three occupational phases. Period I (c. mid–second millennium BCE) yielded evidence of a **Chalcolithic** culture. Period II (c. mid–first millennium BCE) provided evidence of **black and red ware** and **Northern Black Polished Ware**. Structural remains included evidence of ring wells. Other finds included beads of semiprecious stone and bangles of shell and **terracotta**. Period III (c. first–fifth centuries CE) provided evidence of a rampart. Other finds included **coins** of the **Kṣatrapas**, beads, and **sculpture**. The site remains under occupation to date. *See also* BARYGAZA.

BHARUKACCHA. Prakrit name for **Barygaza** or **Bharuch**.

BHĀSA. Sanskrit playwright (c. first–second centuries CE?), credited with the authorship of 13 plays. These include two plays based on episodes from the ***Rāmāyaṇa***, six based on episodes from the ***Mahābhārata***, and *Cārudatta*, which was later adapted and elaborated by **Śūdraka**. His best-known play is the *Svapna-vāsavadattā*, a courtly romance, set against the background of the rivalries between the rulers of two ***mahājanapadas***, **Avanti** and **Magadha**. *See also* DRAMA; LITERATURE; UDAYANA.

BHĀSKARA. Sanskrit author of a commentary, composed in **Valabhi**, c. 629 CE, on the ***Āryabhaṭīya***.

BHĀSKARAVARMAN. The most well-known ruler (c. 600–650 CE) of **Kāmarūpa** (present-day Assam), a contemporary of **Harṣavardhana**. He extended his control up to Bengal, and attended the **assemblies** organized by Harṣavardhana at **Kanauj** and **Prayāga**. The Chinese **traveler Xuan Zang** visited his court.

BHAṬṬI. Sanskrit author (c. 570–625 CE) of a long poem (in 22 cantos and 1,650 verses) known as the *Rāvanavadha* or the *Bhaṭṭikāvya*, based on the ***Rāmāyaṇa***, devised as a text to illustrate the rules of **Pāṇini**'s work on grammar. *See also* LITERATURE.

BHATTIPROLU. **Archaeological** site in Andhra Pradesh. Find spot of a ***stūpa*** (c. second century BCE–first century CE) containing an **inscribed** relic casket. The casket contained ashes, gold leaf, and **coins**.

BHAVABHŪTI. **Sanskrit** playwright (c. seventh–eighth century CE), a contemporary of **Yaśovarman**, the ruler of **Kanauj**, who was his patron. Three of his plays survive. Of these, two are based on the ***Rāmāyaṇa***, while one is a romance. *See also* DRAMA; LITERATURE; *UTTARARĀMACARITA*.

BHAWAR. **Archaeological** site in Maharashtra, with evidence of a stone circle (possibly **megalithic**) and a habitation mound. Period I (c. mid–second millennium BCE?) yielded evidence of bone **tools** that may have been used for **agricultural** activities. Period II (c. early first millennium BCE?) provided evidence of the use of **iron**. Period III, considered **Mauryan** (c. fourth–second centuries BCE), provided evidence of grinding stones and a range of iron equipment. The evidence from Period IV, assigned to the **Sātavāhanas** (c. second century BCE–second century CE), is more or less similar.

BHIMBETKA. Rock shelter site near Bhopal (Madhya Pradesh) with evidence of occupation from the Lower **Paleolithic** phase onward. There are indications of **tool** making using quartzite and sandstone. Tools included axes, cleavers, scrapers, and knives. Middle Paleolithic tools included blades and scrapers. There is evidence for occupation during the **Mesolithic** phase (c. 8000–6000 BP) as well, with finds of microliths. The walls of the rock shelters contain **paintings**, including hunting scenes and depictions of **dancing** and possibly ritual activity. The earliest of these paintings perhaps date to the Mesolithic phase. These include representations of a variety of animals such as deer, rhinoceros, elephant, and cattle. Later paintings (c. second millennium BCE onward) include scenes showing domesticated animals that are represented less realistically. Paintings attributed to the **early historic** phase (mid–first millennium BCE onward) include scenes of **warfare**. Other finds include **burials** with grave goods such as tools and coloring substances. There is evidence for contact with **Chalcolithic** cultures. **Early historic pottery**, **iron** tools, and

punch-marked coins were recovered from the topmost layers that were excavated. Bhimbetka has been recognized as a World Heritage Site by UNESCO.

BHITA. Archaeological site in Uttar Pradesh, near **Allahabad**. The settlement seems to have developed as a market. Associated finds include **Northern Black Polished Ware**, **coins** (c. first century BCE–second century CE), **terracotta** figurines, and **inscribed** sealings (c. first half of the first millennium CE).

BHITARGAON. Site of a brick **temple** (Uttar Pradesh) dated to c. fifth century CE, one of the earliest of such structures in the subcontinent. Several **terracotta sculptures** have been recovered from the site.

BHITARI. Site in Uttar Pradesh, find spot of a pillar **inscription** of the **Gupta** ruler **Skandagupta** (c. fifth century CE). The inscription, in **Sanskrit**, records the genealogy of the king and contains an account of his battles with the **Puṣyamitras** and the **Hūṇas**. Other finds include remains of a **temple** and stone **sculpture**.

BHOGAVARDHANA. Ancient name for **Bhokardan**.

BHOJA (1). Ruling lineage in Maharashtra (c. third century BCE–second century CE), mentioned in **Asokan inscriptions** as people who were incorporated within the **Mauryan** Empire. They entered into matrimonial and political alliances with the **Sātavāhanas**. *See also* KHĀRAVELA.

BHOJA (2). Pratihāra ruler (r.c. 839–892 CE), also known as Mihira Bhoja, who was successful against both the **Pālas** and the **Rāṣṭrakūṭas**. A contemporary Arab historian Sulaiman described him as the most powerful ruler in north India, with a vast **army** including cavalry and camel corps.

BHOKARDAN. Archaeological site in Maharashtra, identified with ancient **Bhogavardhana**, on the land **route** between **Ujjayinī** and **Paithan** (Pratiṣṭhāna). Major finds belong to the **Sātavāhana** period (c. second century BCE–second century CE) and include **black and**

red ware, **punch-marked coins**, and coins of the Sātavāhanas and **Nahapāṇa**. Other finds include remains of brick structures and ivory artifacts.

BHORGARH. Archaeological site in Delhi, with four occupational phases. Period I (c. second millennium BCE) yielded **late Harappan pottery**. Finds from Period II (c. first millennium BCE) included **Painted Grey Ware**. There was a hiatus between Period II and III (beginning of the first millennium CE). Finds from the latter phase included structures of burnt brick, **terracotta** figurines, **copper coins**, **iron** implements, and terracotta sealings with **Brāhmī inscriptions**. Period IV has been assigned to medieval times.

BHṚGUKACCHA. Sanskrit name for **Bharuch**.

BILSAD PILLAR INSCRIPTION. Inscription dated to the 96th year of the **Gupta era** (c. 416 CE), found in Bilsad (Uttar Pradesh), referring to the construction of a religious structure at the site during the reign of **Kumāragupta I**.

BIMBISĀRA. Recognized as the first **king** of **Magadha**, c. sixth century BCE, a contemporary of the **Buddha** and **Mahāvīra**. He set up his capital at **Rājagaha**, and extended his power through a combination of conquests and matrimonial alliances. He annexed the neighboring kingdom of **Aṅga (1)** and entered into matrimonial alliances with the ruling families of **Kosala**, **Vaishali**, and **Madra**. He established an administrative system that included central officers, judges, generals, and village headmen. He was succeeded by his son **Ajātaśatru**, a parricide. *See also* KĀŚI; PASENADI.

BINDUSĀRA. (r.c. 300–273 BCE). Son and successor of the **Maurya** ruler **Candragupta** and father of **Asoka**. Very little is known about him. He may have added a part of south India to the empire. He was also known as Amitraghāta, the slayer of foes, a name that figures as **Amitrachates** or **Allitrochades** in Greek sources. He received ambassadors from the Hellenistic kingdoms located to the northwest of the subcontinent. *See also* ANTIOCHOS I SOTER (OF SYRIA); DEIMACHOS; DIONYSIUS.

BIOGRAPHY. The writing of biographies or *caritas* was relatively rare in early Indian literary traditions. Generally, authors of biographies were more concerned with displaying their ability to use a range of poetic devices than with providing historical data. Two **Sanskrit** texts, the ***Buddhacarita*** composed by **Aśvaghoṣa** and **Bāṇabhaṭṭa**'s ***Harṣacarita***, exemplify this genre. *See also* *AŚOKĀVADĀNA*; CUNTARĀR; *KALPASŪTRA*; *LALITAVISTARA*; LITERATURE; *MAHĀVASTU*; *VINAYA PIṬAKA*.

BIRBHANPUR. Mesolithic site in West Bengal. Finds include nongeometric microliths made of chert and quartz and **tools** of fossil wood. There are traces of huts.

BISAULI. Archaeological site (c. second millennium BCE?) in Uttar Pradesh, find spot of **Ochre-Coloured Pottery** and a **copper hoard**, including anthropomorphic figures, harpoons, and celts. There is no stratigraphic connection between the two finds.

BISITUN. Also known as Behistun or Bahistan, in Iran, find spot of an **inscription** of **Darius I** dated to c. 519 BCE that lists the people of Gadara (**Gandhara**) among his subjects.

BITHUR. Archaeological site in Uttar Pradesh, find spot of **copper hoards**.

BLACK AND RED WARE. Designation of a kind of **pottery** characterized by two colors, produced by inverting and firing pots, which results in the top and the interior becoming black while the bottom and most of the exterior are red. The earliest use of this technique dates to the beginning of the second millennium BCE, and it continued to be in use for nearly two millennia. Black and red ware is found in many parts of the subcontinent, in different **archaeological** contexts, extending from Rajasthan in the west to West Bengal in the east, and from Uttar Pradesh in the north through south India. However, there are marked regional variations, and the Black and Red Ware associated with **megalithic** burials is often distinguished from other varieties. Conventionally, the lower case is adopted for the latter. Black and red ware is generally wheel-made, and common shapes include bowls and dishes.

Sites that have yielded black and red ware include **Adam**, **Agiabir**, **Ahar**, **Arambha**, **Atranjikhera**, **Bahal**, **Balathal**, **Bharatpur**, **Bharuch**, **Bhokardan**, **Campā**, **Chechar**, **Chirand**, **Dangwada**, **Datrana**, **Devangarh**, **Dharanikota**, **Dhuriapar**, **Dihar**, **Donder Khera**, **Eran**, **Erich**, **Gilaulikhera**, **Gilund**, **Golbai Sasan**, **Imlidih Khurd**, **Jakhera**, **Jaugada**, **Jhimjhimia Kalisthan**, **Jhusi**, **Jodhpura**, **Kakoria**, **Kakrehta**, **Kampil**, **Kasrawad**, **Katra**, **Khairadih**, **Khajuri**, **Koldihwa**, **Kotasur**, **Maheshwar**, **Mahisdal**, **Malhar**, **Manamunda**, **Maner**, **Mangalkot**, **Manjhi**, **Maski**, **Musanagar**, **Nadner**, **Nagara**, **Nagda**, **Narhan**, **Nasik**, **Nevasa**, **Nindaur**, **Noh**, **Oriup**, **Pandu Rajar Dhibi**, **Pauni**, **Pokharna**, **Rājagaha**, **Savalda**, **Songaon**, **Sonpur**, **Surkotada**, **Takiaper**, **Tāmralipti**, **Taradih**, **Ter**, **Timbarra**, **Tripuri**, **Tuljapur Garhi**, **Tumain**, **Ujjayinī**, **Utawad**, **Vidisha**, and **Wina**.

Sites that have yielded Black and Red Ware include **Adichannallur**, **Alagankulan**, **Amaravati**, **Arikamedu**, **Auroville**, **Banahalli**, **Banavasi**, **Bhagimohari**, **Brahmagiri**, **Chandravalli**, **Elchuru**, **Garapadu**, **Gopalapatnam**, **Hallur**, **Heggadehalli**, **Kanchipuram**, **Kaundinyapura**, **Kaveripattinam**, **Kesanapalle**, **Kodumanal**, **Korkai**, **Kunnatur**, **Machad**, **Mahurjhari**, **Mayiladumparai**, **Pachikheri**, **Paiyampalli**, **Raipur**, **Sannati**, **Shirkanda**, **Takalghat–Khapa**, **Tekkalakotta**, **Terdal**, **Tharsa**, **T. Narsipur**, **Uraiyur**, **Utnur**, **Vaddamanu**, and **Valiyapadam**. *See also* IRON AGE; NORTHERN BLACK POLISHED WARE; PAINTED GREY WARE.

BLACK SLIPPED WARE. **Pottery** found in **archaeological** sites in the northern part of the subcontinent, c. first millennium BCE. It bears a strong resemblance to the **Northern Black Polished Ware** and may have been its predecessor as well as its substitute. The fabric varies from fine to medium, and the pots were turned on a fast wheel. Common shapes include bowls, dishes, jars, and vases. Sites from where the pottery has been found include **Adam**, **Banarsihankalan**, **Dhuriapar**, **Dihar**, **Erich**, **Ganwaria**, **Garapadu**, **Imlidih Khurd**, **Jakhera**, **Jhimjhimia Kalisthan**, **Jhusi**, **Kakoria**, **Kampil**, **Kanauj**, **Katra**, **Kausambi**, **Koldihwa**, **Korkai**, **Mahisdal**, **Manjhi**, **Masaon**, **Musanagar**, **Nadner**, **Narhan**, **Noh**, **Oriup**, **Pachikheri**, **Pandu Rajar Dhibi**, **Sadhwara**, **Sanghol**, **Sannati**, **Shirkanda**, **Sunet**, **Tāmralipti**, **Vidisha**, **Wari Bateshwar**, and **Wina**. *See also* NORTHERN BLACK POLISHED WARE; PAINTED GREY WARE.

BODH GAYA. Site in Bihar where the **Buddha** is supposed to have attained enlightenment (c. sixth–fifth century BCE). The main **temple** at the site may date back to the **Kuṣāṇa** or the early **Gupta** period: It has, however, been restored several times over the centuries. A tree in the vicinity is venerated as an offshoot of the one under which the Buddha meditated. Other structural remains include votive ***stūpas*** and **monasteries**. **Northern Black Polished Ware** has also been recovered from the site. *See also* ASOKA; MEGHAVARṆA; ŚAŚĀNKA.

BODHISATTVA. Sanskrit term, meaning "one destined to become a **Buddha**." The notion developed during the early centuries of the Common Era. This was increasingly regarded as an ideal for those who followed the **Mahāyāna** form of **Buddhism**. The *bodhisattva* was distinguished by compassion for fellow beings. As such, although he was capable of attaining full Buddhahood, he refrained from doing so in order to help lesser mortals in their quest for self-realization. *See also DIVYĀVADĀNA*; GANDHARA SCHOOL OF ART; *JĀTAKA*; *VAJRAYĀNA*.

BOGAZKOY. Site in present-day Turkey also known as Boghaz Koi, find spot of an **inscription** dated to the 14th century BCE. The inscription contains the text of a treaty between the Hittites and the Mittanis and mentions a number of **Vedic** deities, including Mitra, Varuṇa, **Indra**, and the Nāsatyas. It has been used to date the development and spread of **Indo-Aryan languages**.

BOGHAZ KOI. *See* BOGAZKOY.

BRAHMACARYA*. Sanskrit** term that gained currency from c. first millennium BCE, used to designate a state of celibacy, either temporary or permanent. By the mid–first millennium BCE it was used in the **Dharmasūtras** for a mode or stage of life (āśrama***) meant for men who belonged to the first three ***varṇas***. *Brahmacarya* began with an initiatory ritual and was devoted to learning the **Vedas** from a ***brāhmaṇa*** **(1)** preceptor. The initiate or *brahmacārin* was expected to lead a carefully regulated life, offering worship to his preceptor, tending the **sacrificial** fire, and living on alms. The successful completion of *brahmacarya* was followed by a ritual bath, after which the initiate was free to return to the world and adopt a life of domesticity.

BRAHMAGIRI. Archaeological site in Karnataka, with evidence of **Mesolithic** and **Neolithic/Chalcolithic** (c. third–second millennium BCE) phases. Finds from the latter phase include stone axes, microliths, handmade **pottery**, a few **copper** and bronze objects, and traces of **burials** in urns. There is also evidence of **megalithic** and **early historic** occupations (c. first millennium BCE). The former phase yielded evidence of a wide variety of **iron** equipment and **Black and Red Ware**. Finds from the latter phase include **Russet-Coated Painted Ware**, bangles, beads of semiprecious stone, and **Roman coins**. It is also the find spot of a **Minor Rock Edict** of the **Mauryan** ruler **Asoka**. *See also* DAIMABAD; KALLUR; SUVARṆAGIRI.

BRAHMAGUPTA. Sanskrit author of a work on **astronomy**, the *Brāhmasphuṭasiddhānta*, composed in Rajasthan, c. 628 CE. *See also* LITERATURE.

BRĀHMAṆA* (1).** The first category in the fourfold ***varṇa order, commonly translated as priest. The earliest references to this category occur in the ***Ṛgveda***, c. second millennium BCE. Membership to the order was based on birth in specific clans or ***gotras***. *Brāhmaṇas* were ideally expected to fulfill certain roles, including studying and teaching the **Vedas**, officiating at **sacrifices**, and accepting gifts on ritual and other occasions as a means of livelihood. Both texts and **inscriptions** indicate that *brāhmaṇas* did not constitute a homogeneous category: There were differences in terms of the branches of learning in which they specialized as well as in terms of region and function. In some areas, especially from the mid–first millennium CE, *brāhmaṇas* received **land grants** from royal patrons and constituted a significant section of the rural elite. In other instances, ruling lineages such as the **Sātavāhanas** claimed to be *brāhmaṇas*. Prescriptive texts also recognized the possibility of *brāhmaṇa* **traders**, who were, however, prohibited from trading in certain articles, such as meat and alcoholic drinks.

While *brāhmaṇas* claimed the highest position in the *varṇa* order, there are indications that such claims were not invariably accepted.

Tensions between the ***kṣatriya*** and the *brāhmaṇa* are a recurrent theme in **later Vedic** texts (c. first millennium BCE). **Buddhist** texts contain debates on who was a "true" *brāhmaṇa*, often contesting claims to status on the basis of birth. Moreover, Buddhist and other narrative traditions occasionally satirized the *brāhmaṇa*, who was portrayed as greedy or ignorant. *See also* ASCETICISM; BUDDHA; CRAFTS; *DAKṢIṆĀ*; *DĀNA*; *DHAMMA*; *DHAMMA MAHĀMATTA*; *DHARMA*; DHARMAŚĀSTRA; DHARMASŪTRA; *ḌOMBA*; DRAMA; *DVIJA*; EARLY MEDIEVAL PERIOD; FAMILY STRUCTURE; FOREST; HINDUISM; INDO-GREEK; JANAKA; *KALI YUGA*; KANVA; KINGSHIP; KINSHIP SYSTEMS; MAJOR ROCK EDICTS; MĀNIKKAVĀCAKAR; *MANUSMṚTI*; MAUES; MAURYA; MEDICINE; PARAŚURĀMA; *PUROHITA*; *PURUṢASŪKTA*; *SABHĀ*; *SAMṢKĀRA*; ŚAṄKARĀCĀRYA; SANSKRIT; SOCIAL MOBILITY; ŚUṄGA; TANTRA; TIRUJÑĀNA CAMPANTAR; TOṆṬARAṬIPPOṬI ĀḺVĀR; UNTOUCHABILITY; UṢAVADĀTA; VADGAON MADHAVPUR; *VAIŚYA*; VAṄGA; *VARṆASAṂKARA*; VIŚVĀMITRA; WIDOWHOOD; *YONA*.

BRĀHMAṆA* (2).** Among the earliest prose works available in **Sanskrit**, part of the **later Vedic** corpus, composed between c. 10th and 6th centuries BCE. Their main focus was on explaining **sacrificial** ritual on the basis of myths, etymology, and **philosophical** speculation. They were composed and transmitted within priestly schools. The best-known works in this category are the ***Aitareya Brāhmaṇa and the ***Śatapatha Brāhmaṇa***. *See also* KINGSHIP, THEORIES OF ORIGIN; LITERATURE.

BRAHMAPURI. Archaeological site in Maharashtra (c. second century BCE–second century CE). There is evidence of baked-brick houses with stone foundations. Other finds include **Red Polished Ware**, beads of semiprecious stone and glass, **Sātavāhana coins**, and a hoard of Roman artifacts, including metal statues and vessels.

***BRAHMASŪTRA*. Sanskrit** text attributed to **Bādarāyana**, considered as the first authoritative work on **Vedānta**. It consists of four sections, with four chapters in each. The earliest extant commentary on the text is that of **Śaṅkarācārya**. *See also* PHILOSOPHY.

BRĀHMĪ. Script used to write **Prakrit**, **Sanskrit**, and **Tamil**. The name of the script is derived from **Buddhist** and **Jaina** lists, which generally describe the first script, written from left to right, as Brāhmī. The earliest evidence of the use of the script in the subcontinent is from **Asokan inscriptions** (c. mid–third century BCE). Recent finds of potsherds with graffiti from Anuradhapura, Sri Lanka, have been tentatively dated between c. sixth and fourth centuries BCE and have been used to suggest a relatively early development of the script. The origins of the script have been variously traced to **Aramaic** and, less plausibly, to the **Harappan** script. The script has been classified as consonant-syllabic, with each sign representing either a vowel or a consonant with a vowel. There are also separate signs for consonantal clusters. The earliest form included 6 signs for vowels, 32 signs for consonants, and diacritical markers for vowels. Later, more signs were added. Most of the scripts used to write Indian **languages** are derived from Brāhmī, which also spread outside the subcontinent to Tibet and Southeast Asia. *See also* TAMIL BRĀHMĪ INSCRIPTIONS.

BRASS. Archaeological site in the Punjab. Finds from the first phase (c. third–second millennium BCE) included **Harappan pottery**, pieces of faience bangles, and **terracotta** artifacts. The second phase (c. first millennium BCE) is associated with the **Painted Grey Ware**. Other finds included remains of thatched huts, beads of semiprecious stone, shell, and terracotta artifacts. The third phase (c. second century BCE–second century CE) was associated with the **Śakas** and **Kuṣāṇas**. Finds included remains of mud-brick and baked-brick structures; hearths; **iron** artifacts; terracotta figurines; beads of semiprecious stone, shell, and ivory; and **copper coins**, **seals**, and sealings with legends in **Kharoṣṭhī** and **Brāhmī**, as well as a Kharoṣṭhī **inscription**.

BṚHADĀRAṆYAKA UPANIṢAD*. One of the earliest **Upaniṣads** available at present, dating to the mid–first millennium BCE, and including discussions among **philosophers** such as **Yājñavalkya** and others. The text, in **Sanskrit**, was regarded as the concluding section of the ***Śatapatha Brāhmaṇa. It also contains genealogies or lists of teachers. *See also* GĀRGĪ; LITERATURE; MAITREYĪ.

BṚHADDEVATĀ**. Sanskrit** text (c. fifth century BCE), attributed to Śaunaka, describing **Vedic** deities and their mythology. *See also* LITERATURE; RELIGION.

BṚHADRATHA. The last ruler of the **Mauryan** dynasty (d.c. 185/181 CE). It is likely that the empire had shrunk in size by the time he assumed power. He was overthrown and killed by his general, **Puṣyamitra Śuṅga**.

BṚHASPATI SMṚTI**. Sanskrit** metrical text, one of the major **Dharmaśāstras**, attributed to Br̥haspati, composed and compiled by c. 600 CE. The text is not available at present and has been reconstructed from citations in other works. It deals at length with legal procedure and the drafting of documents. *See also* LITERATURE.

BṚHATKATHĀ**.** Literally the "big story." **Sanskrit** text, now lost, attributed to **Guṇāḍhya**, probably composed in the early centuries CE. According to tradition it was written in a **language** known as Paiśācī. Set in an urban milieu, the story inspired retellings, of which the best known is the ***Kathāsaritsāgara***. *See also* KONKU VELIR; LITERATURE; *VĀSUDEVAHINDĪ*.

BṚHATKATHĀMAÑJARI**. Sanskrit** work based on the ***Bṛhatkathā*** of **Guṇāḍhya**, composed by **Kṣemendra** (c. 1037 CE). It consists of eight chapters with about 7,500 verses. *See also* LITERATURE.

BṚHAT SAMḤITĀ**. Sanskrit** metrical work attributed to **Varāhamihira** (c. 505–587 CE), dealing with **astronomy**, astrology, and horoscopy. *See also* LITERATURE.

BUDDHA, GOTAMA. The term *Buddha* literally means "he who is awakened," although it is often translated as the enlightened one. The Buddha is recognized as the founder of **Buddhism**. Traditional dates for the Buddha suggested that he lived c. sixth century BCE, although there has been a more recent revision in favor of c. fourth century BCE. **Biographies** of the Buddha have been reconstructed using **Pali** texts that were compiled c. first century BCE. According to these traditions, the Buddha was born at **Lumbini** to a ***khattiya***

family of the **Sākya** clan and was named Siddhāttha. Gotama was his family name. He was married to his cousin Yasodharā at the age of 16 and led a life of worldly luxury until he was 29, when the sight of an old man, a sick man, a corpse, and a renouncer transformed his life. The first three served as reminders of the transience of worldly pleasures, while the last suggested a way out.

He then embarked on a quest that included meditation and severe austerities. Ultimately, he abandoned these for contemplation and attained enlightenment under a peepal tree at **Bodh Gaya**. He then proceeded to **Sarnath**, where he delivered his first sermon, including the **Four Noble Truths**, and recruited his first five disciples who formed the kernel of the **monastic** order or ***saṃgha***. He spent the next 45 years of his life wandering through present-day Uttar Pradesh and Bihar, spreading his message. His supporters included ***brāhmaṇas* (1)**, **kings**, merchants, householders, peasants, **slave** men and **women**, and **courtesans**. He breathed his last at **Kusinagara** or Kusināra, and his relics were divided among his lay supporters. These were preserved in ***stūpas***. His ideas and teachings continued to be cherished and propagated by members of the *saṃgha*. This, and the support of lay followers, including kings, enabled Buddhism to spread far beyond the subcontinent, through most of Asia. *See also* *AŚOKĀVADĀNA*; *BUDDHACARITA*; BUDDHIST COUNCILS; *DĪGHA NIKĀYA*; *DĪPAVAMSA*; *DIVYĀVADĀNA*; *GAṆA/SAṂGHA*; GANDHARA SCHOOL OF ART; *JĀTAKA*; JETAVANA; JĪVAKA KOMARABHACCA; KAPILAVASTU; *LALITAVISTARA*; *MAHĀVASTU*; MAHĀYĀNA; *MAJJHIMA NIKĀYA*; NIGALISAGAR; PALI; RUMMINDEI; *SAMYUTTA NIKĀYA*; SANCHI; SANKISSA; ŚAŚĀṄKA; SILK ROUTE; *STŪPA*; *SUTTA PIṬAKA*; *VAJRAYĀNA*; *VARṆA*; VIṢṆU.

***BUDDHACARITA*.** A **biography** of the **Buddha** (c. first century CE?) composed in ornate **Sanskrit** by **Aśvaghoṣa**. The text probably consisted of 28 cantos, of which 17 have survived. The extant text ends with the first teachings of the Buddha. *See also* LITERATURE.

BUDDHAGHOṢA. One of the greatest scholars (c. fifth century CE) and authors of noncanonical **Pali Buddhist literature**. He composed commentaries on several sections of the ***Tripiṭaka***, including the ***Jātakas***, and the *Viśuddhimagga*, a **philosophical** treatise.

BUDDHISM. Doctrine initially propounded by the **Buddha** (c. sixth century BCE), based on the **Four Noble Truths**, which advocated a way out of human suffering through the adoption of the **eightfold path**. The Buddha, ***dhamma***, and the ***saṃgha*** were recognized as the three focal points of the doctrine. Theoretically, the attainment of the ultimate goal of ***nibbāna*** was open to all aspirants, irrespective of **caste** or gender. Buddhism spread far and wide owing to royal patronage as well as the support of the laity and the efforts of monks and nuns. In the process, sectarian differences developed. These led to the emergence of **Theravāda**, **Mahāyāna**, and **Tantric** or **Vajrayāna** Buddhism. *See also* ASCETICISM; *AŚOKĀVADĀNA*; BACTRIAN GREEKS; *BRĀHMAṆA* (1); *CAITYA*; *CAKRAVARTIN*; CALENDAR; CITIES; *CŪLAVAMSA*; *DĀNA*; DEVAPĀLA; *DHAMMA*; *DHAMMA MAHĀMATTA*; *DHAMMAPADA*; DHARMAKĪRTI; DHARMAPĀLA; DINNĀGA (1); DISPOSAL OF THE DEAD; EARLY HISTORIC PERIOD; FA XIAN; *GAṆA/SAṂGHA*; GANDHARA SCHOOL OF ART; GILGIT; GODDESS CULTS; HARṢAVARDHANA; HĪNAYĀNA; HUVIṢKA; I CHING; IKṢVĀKU (2); INDO-GREEK; *JĀTAKAMĀLĀ*; *JĀTI*; JETAVANA; JĪVAKA KOMARABHACCA; KANHERI; KANIṢKA; KAPIŚA; KARLE; KHAROṢṬHĪ; *KHATTIYA*; KINGSHIP, THEORIES OF ORIGIN; KṢAHARĀTA; KUMĀRILA BHAṬṬA; KUṢĀṆA; KUSINAGARA; LALITĀDITYA MUKTĀPĪḌA; LALITAGIRI; *MAHĀJANAPADA*; *MAHĀVAMSA*; MAHINDA; *MAJJHIMADESA*; *MAṆIMEKALAI*; MATHURA; MAUES; MAURYAN ART; MEDICINE; MENANDER; MIHIRAKULA; *MILINDAPAÑHA*; MONASTERIES; NĀGANIKĀ; NĀGASENA (1); NAHAPĀṆA; NALANDA; *NĀLĀYIRA TIVIYA PIRAPANTAM*; NANAGHAT; PAHARPUR; PĀLA; PALI; PALI TEXT SOCIETY; PASENADI; PHILOSOPHY; POVERTY; PROTEST MOVEMENTS; RENUNCIATORY ORDERS; SACRIFICE; SANCHI; SANSKRIT; SĀTAVĀHANA; SLAVERY; SOCIAL MOBILITY; SRAVASTI; *STŪPA*; TAMIL BRĀHMĪ INSCRIPTIONS; *THERAGĀTHĀ*; *THERĪGĀTHĀ*; *TRIPIṬAKA*; UDAYAGIRI; UNTOUCHABILITY; UṢAVADĀTA; VAISHALI; VALABHI; *VARṆA*; VIKRAMAŚILĀ; VĪMA KADPHISES; WIDOWHOOD; XUAN ZANG; *YOGĀCĀRA*.

BUDDHIST COUNCILS. Assemblies that were convened to compile the teachings of the **Buddha** and resolve disputes within the ***saṃgha***. Histories of the councils are difficult to reconstruct as rival Buddhist schools preserved selective memories of them. The first council may have met in **Rājagaha** immediately after the death of the Buddha (c. fifth century BCE). Two of the three ***Piṭakas***, the ***Vinaya*** and the ***Sutta***, are said to have been compiled in this council, although the compilation of the former is occasionally associated with the second council. This may have been held at **Vaishali** or Vesālī, perhaps a century after the death of the Buddha (c. fourth century BCE), and was marked by a split in the *saṃgha* on issues of doctrine and discipline. A third council is associated with **Asoka** and was probably held in **Pāṭaliputra**, c. 247 BCE. Apart from handling issues of schism, the third *Piṭaka*, ***Abhidhamma***, may have been compiled at this council. A fourth (by some counts, third) council is associated with **Kaniṣka**, c. first or second century CE. This may have provided the impetus for the spread of **Mahāyāna** Buddhism. *See also DĪPAVAMSA.*

BUDDHIST HYBRID SANSKRIT. Name given to a **language** used in **Buddhist** texts composed during the early centuries of the Common Era. Its distinctive feature was the use of **Sanskrit** interspersed with **Pali** and **Prakrit** words. *See also MAHĀVASTU.*

BUDHAGUPTA. One of the last known rulers of the **Gupta** dynasty, who probably ruled during the last quarter of the fifth century CE.

BUDIHAL. Neolithic ash mound site (c. second millennium BCE?) in Karnataka, with evidence of habitation, gray and red **pottery**, and stone **tools**, including axes, hammers, querns, and blades, as well as evidence of a workshop for the production of stone artifacts. Other finds include bones of domesticated animals, especially cattle, but also sheep, goat, and pig. There are also traces of remains of plants such as the *ber* and *amla*.

BURIAL PRACTICES. Burial practices are in evidence from both **archaeological** and textual sources. Some of the earliest known instances of burials found at sites such as **Sarai Nahar Rai**, **Mahadaha**, and **Damdama** date to the **Mesolithic** phase. Generally the dead were placed in an extended position, with the head facing west. There are also instances of secondary burials, and of burials in a crouched position at sites such as **Langhnaj**. In some instances, there is evidence of burial goods, including offerings of food, ornaments, **tools**, and so on. Burials associated with the **Neolithic** phase have been found from sites in south India. In many instances, children were buried in urns.

Cemeteries have been found at several **Harappan** (c. 2700–1800 BCE) sites. These indicate a range of practices, including burial and possibly cremation. Grave goods included pots, ornaments, and tools. Some of the most elaborate burials occur in the context of the **megaliths** (c. first millennium BCE). From the second half of the first millennium BCE, the practice of burying relics of the **Buddha** or his followers in ***stūpas*** gained widespread prevalence. While the **Dharmasūtras** (mid–first millennium BCE onward) recognized cremation as an ideal mode of disposal of the dead, it is evident that burial remained in vogue for several centuries in different parts of the subcontinent.

Sites with evidence of burials include **Adam**, **Adichannallur**, **Banahalli**, **Bhagwanpura**, **Bhimbetka**, **Brahmagiri**, **Chandoli**, **Damdama**, **Gandhur**, **Hallur**, **Harappa**, **Jainal Naula**, **Kalibangan**, **Kesanapalle**, **Kodumanal**, **Korkai**, **Kunnatur**, **Ladyura**, **Lekhahia**, **Loteshwar**, **Machad**, **Mahadaha**, **Mahurjhari**, **Mayiladumparai**, **Nagarjunakonda**, **Nevasa**, **Pachikheri**, **Paiyampalli**, **Pandu Rajar Dhibi**, **Pipri**, **Raipur**, **Rakhi Garhi**, **Ramapuram**, **Sekta**, and **T. Narsipur**.

See also CEMETERY H; CHANDOLI; DISPOSAL OF THE DEAD; GANDHARA GRAVE CULTURE; HARAPPA; INAMGAON; *SATĪ*; TAKALGHAT–KHAPA.

BURZAHOM. **Neolithic** site in Kashmir (c. 2500 BCE), with evidence for the cultivation of wheat and barley and the domestication of sheep, goat, and dog. The last-named animals were occasionally buried. **Tools** were made of bone and stone. The former included harpoons, spearheads, arrow points, needles, and scrapers, while the latter consisted of axes, chisels, and grinding stones. Carnelian beads, typical of the **Harappan civilization**, have been found, indicating contact. Excavations have revealed several pits. These may have been used for storage and as dwellings, offering protection in winter. *See also* GUFKRAL; MALPUR.

– C –

CAITYA. **Prakrit/Sanskrit** term used to designate shrines, generally **Buddhist** or **Jaina**. The earliest **archaeological** remains of such shrines date from the end of the first millennium BCE onward, although it is likely that wooden prototypes existed even earlier. Generally, the *caitya* consisted of a pillared hall, with a ***stūpa*** placed in the apse, with provisions for circumambulation. While the *caitya* could be freestanding, surviving examples come from the **rock-cut caves** along the Western Ghats, with **Bhaja** and **Karle** as typical instances. *Caityas* were often built in close proximity to **monasteries**, and these were probably complementary structures. Other sites with *caityas* include **Kolhua** and **Lalitagiri**. *See also* ARCHITECTURE; CHACHEGAON; JUNNAR; RELIGION.

CAKRAVARTIN. **Sanskrit** term used to designate a ruler claiming universal sovereignty. The notion was initially developed within the **Buddhist** tradition (c. fourth century BCE) and was later adopted within the **Brahmanical** system as well. The distinctive characteristics of the *cakravartin* included bodily marks that were supposed to be auspicious, success as a conqueror with the ability to establish control over the entire realm designated as **Jambudvīpa**, and righteous rule. *See also* KINGSHIP.

CALENDAR. A variety of systems of reckoning time were in use in early India. By the end of the first millennium BCE, these were influenced by Babylonian and Greek models and were based on a combination of lunar and solar calendars. **Kings** such as **Asoka** often dated their **inscriptions** in regnal years. Others such as the **Guptas** adopted dynastic eras. Other eras used include the **Vikrama** and **Śaka** eras and the ***kali yuga***. **Jaina** and **Buddhist** traditions dated events in terms of the decease of **Mahāvīra** and the **Buddha**, respectively. *See also* LAND GRANTS.

CĀLUKYA. Ruling lineage in the western Deccan (c. sixth–eighth centuries CE), with their capital at **Badami**, Karnataka. Virtually independent branches of the lineage established control over parts of Gujarat and Andhra Pradesh. The Cālukyas consolidated their position through successes against neighboring rival powers such as the **Kadambas**. They engaged in constant **warfare** with the contemporary **Pallava** rulers in order to control the Raichur doab. They were also associated with the development of a distinctive tradition of **temple** building. Ultimately, they succumbed to the rising power of the **Rāṣṭrakūṭas**. The best-known ruler of the lineage was **Pulakeśin II**. *See also* AIHOLE; CĀLUKYA (EASTERN); COḺA; DANTIDURGA; EASTERN GAṄGA; GAṄGA (1); PATTADAKAL; RĀJARĀJA I; VIJAYĀDITYA; *YAŚASTILAKA CAMPU*; YELLESWARAM.

CĀLUKYA (EASTERN). Name of a ruling lineage (c. 7th–11th centuries CE) related to the **Cālukyas** of **Badami**. The first Eastern Cālukya ruler, Viṣṇuvardhana, was probably the brother of **Pulakeśin II**. The Eastern Cālukyas ruled from **Vengi** in Andhra Pradesh and remained an important power until the 12th century, when they merged with the **Coḷas**. Their relations with contemporary powers such as the **Rāṣṭrakūṭas** were often hostile. The administration rested on the support of feudatory chiefs. Most rulers of this lineage supported **Śaivism**. *See also* GOPALAPATNAM.

CAMPĀ. Capital of the ***mahājanapada*** of **Aṅga (1)** (c. sixth century BCE). It was one of the largest **cities** during the time of the **Buddha** and was located along riverine **trade routes** running through the **Ganga (2)** valley to the eastern sea coast. **Archaeological** excavations have revealed evidence of a **fortification** wall and moat as well as traces of a drain. Other finds include bone **tools**, **black and red ware**, **Northern Black Polished Ware**, **punch-marked** and **copper cast coins**, **terracotta** artifacts, ornaments of copper and ivory, and beads.

CĀṆAKYA. *See* KAUṬILYA.

***CAṆḌĀLA*.** **Sanskrit** term used (c. first millennium BCE onward) to designate a social category regarded as **untouchable** in the **Dharmasūtras** and **Dharmaśāstras**. The **Brahmanical** authors of these texts frequently classified all forms of contact with *caṇḍālas*, such as seeing, speaking with, and touching (especially in situations of sexual intercourse) as polluting for men who claimed high status within the **varṇa** order. *Caṇḍālas* were expected to live on the outskirts of settlements and were associated with the cremation ground. They were also expected to function as night watchmen and executioners. They evidently developed distinctive cultural and linguistic practices. Sanskrit, **Pali**, and **Prakrit** narrative traditions represent them as impoverished, marginalized people, who occasionally challenged their situation. Their condition was also noted by Chinese **travelers**, such as **Fa Xian** (c. fourth–fifth centuries CE). *See also VARṆASAMṂKARA*.

CANDRAGOMIN. **Buddhist** author (c. fifth century CE) who composed works on grammar, poetry, and healing in **Sanskrit**. *See also* LITERATURE.

CANDRAGUPTA I. Often regarded as the real founder (r.c. 319–335) of the power of the **Gupta** dynasty. He took the title of *mahārājādhirāja* (great king of kings) and married a **Licchavi** princess, **Kumāradevī**, commemorating this union by issuing a special set of **coins**. His son and successor, **Samudragupta**, was born of this union. The Gupta era (319–320 CE), mentioned in later **inscriptions**, was calculated as beginning from his reign. *See also* BAYANA.

CANDRAGUPTA II. One of the most famous rulers (r.c. 380–415 CE) of the **Gupta** dynasty, known from **inscriptions** in central India. His military exploits included victories over the **Śakas** in central and western India. His chief queen was Dhruvādevī, who may have been the widow of his brother, **Rāmagupta**. Another queen, Kuberanāgā, is mentioned by **Prabhāvatī Gupta** as her mother. Candragupta II is often identified with the legendary king **Vikramāditya**. The noted **Sanskrit** poet-playwright **Kālidāsa** may have been his contemporary. *See also* AMARASIMṂHA; BAYANA; *DEVĪCANDRAGUPTA*; KUMĀRAGUPTA I; MEHRAULI PILLAR INSCRIPTION; UDAYGIRI; VAISHALI.

CANDRAGUPTA MAURYA. The founder of the **Mauryan** Empire (r.c. 321–298 BCE), who acquired power after defeating the last ruler of the **Nanda** dynasty, with the assistance and advice of **Kauṭilya**, his **minister**. A sixth-century play, the ***Mudrārākṣasa***, described the relationship between the **king** and his minister. Candragupta rose to power after the death of **Alexander (of Macedon)**. Greek and Roman accounts suggest that the two may have met when Alexander invaded the northwestern part of the subcontinent. Alexander's successor in the region, **Seleucos Nikator**, entered into a confrontation with Candragupta. Ultimately, the conflict was resolved through a treaty, as a result of which Seleucos handed over four provinces, including parts of present-day Baluchistan and Afghanistan, to the Mauryan ruler. In return, he received 500 elephants. A matrimonial alliance also took place, presumably between a Greek princess and the Mauryan ruler or his son. Seleucos sent an ambassador, **Megasthenes**, to the Mauryan capital, **Pāṭaliputra**. His account, which survives in fragments, suggests that the Mauryan administrative apparatus was well developed and that there was a large standing **army**. According to **Jaina** tradition, Candragupta adopted **Jainism** and ended his life by fasting unto death at Sravana Belgola in Karnataka. He was succeeded by his son, **Bindusāra**. *See also* DHANANANDA; FAMINE; PUṢYAGUPTA; SANDROCOTTOS.

***CANDRAVAṂŚA*.** **Sanskrit** term, used in the **epics** and the **Purāṇas**, meaning "lunar lineage." In the **early medieval period**, several ruling lineages claimed descent from the *candravaṃśa*. *See also AILA*; MANU; SOCIAL MOBILITY.

CANDRAVARMAN. Ruler (c. fourth century CE) mentioned in the **Allahabad Pillar Inscription** in the list of the kings of ***āryāvarta*** who were uprooted by the **Gupta** ruler **Samudragupta**.

***CAṄKAM*.** *See SANGAM*.

CARAKA. Author (c. first century CE), possibly a resident of northwest India, of a **medical** treatise in **Sanskrit** known as the ***Caraka Saṃhitā***.

CARAKA SAṂHITĀ*.** **Medical** text in **Sanskrit**, attributed to **Caraka** (c. first century CE), considered as one of the basic texts of ***āyurveda. The text, written in prose in the form of a dialogue between a pupil and a teacher, consists of eight sections. The first consists of a miscellany; the second deals with symptoms of disease; the third with diagnosis, pathology, and medical etiquette; the fourth with anatomy and embryology; the fifth with senses, dreams, and foretelling death; the sixth and seventh with special and general therapies; while the last deals with theoretical issues.

CĀRVĀKA. An early **philosophical** school (c. sixth century BCE onward) that advocated materialism. Texts of the tradition have not survived, so its ideas have been reconstructed from the writings of other, often opposed schools. According to these, proponents of *cārvāka* denied the existence of the soul or of life after death and disagreed with the notion that human action could produce good or evil results in future births.

CAST COINS. Cast coins, almost always in **copper**, were issued during the second half of the first millennium BCE. The earliest varieties were uninscribed, with symbols resembling those on **punch-marked coins**. **Inscribed** coins were issued c. second century BCE onward. The most prolific of these issues were by the **Yaudheyas**, from mints at **Sunet** and **Khokrakot**. Thousands of clay molds for casting coins have been found at sites such as **Taxila**, Sunet, **Sanchi**, and **Nalanda**. Sites from which such coins have been recovered include **Chirand**, **Kayatha**, **Kumrahar**, **Lauriya Nandangarh**, **Maheshwar**, **Malhar**, **Maner**, **Mangalkot**, **Nasik**, **Nevasa**, **Noh**, **Sonkh**, and **Vidisha**. *See also* COINAGE.

CASTE. Derived from the Portuguese *castas*, c. 16th–17th centuries, and used for two overlapping social categories, ***varṇa*** and ***jāti***. The term was later adopted into other European languages as well. Castes as defined in early textual traditions, **Brahmanical** and **Buddhist**, were hierarchically ordered, with membership being determined by birth. The origins of the institution are obscure: The earliest textual reference to the four *varṇas* occurs in the latest stratum of the ***Ṛgveda*** (c. end of the second millennium BCE). Theoretically, according to Brahmanical texts such as the **Dharmasūtras** and the **Dharmaśāstras**, there were restrictions on intercaste **marriages** as well as on interdining, and social intercourse among castes was to be carefully regulated.

One of the most intriguing descriptions of castes occurs in the account of **Megasthenes**. He mentioned several social categories, including **philosophers**, **agriculturalists**, **pastoralists**, **craftsmen**, **traders**, soldiers, government officials, and councilors, a list that deviated from the standard fourfold *varṇa* order. This is one indication that in practice, social realities were fluid and complicated.

While some caste names suggest **tribal** affiliations, many correspond with occupational categories, indicating that caste identities were created through a variety of social processes. The number of groups designated as castes proliferated in **early medieval** texts. Contemporary **Purāṇic** texts (c. fourth century CE onward) almost invariably represent the breakdown of the caste system as being synonymous with chaos. This has been interpreted by present-day historians to suggest that the hierarchy as a whole as well as its specific elements may have been challenged. There were also wide regional variations in the caste system. *See also KĀYASTHA*; KINSHIP SYSTEMS; MONEY LENDING; PROTEST MOVEMENTS; ŚAIVISM; *SAMGHA*; SOCIAL MOBILITY; TRIBES.

CĀTTANĀR. Tamil author (c. sixth century CE) of the ***Maṇimekalai***. Very little is known about his personal life. *See also* LITERATURE.

***CAUPANNAMAHĀPURISACARIYAM.* Prakrit** text, composed (c. 868 CE) in a mixture of prose and verse, by an author named Sīlanka. It contains the **biographies** of 54 great men belonging to the **Jaina** tradition. *See also* LITERATURE.

CEDI (1). ***Mahājanapada*** located south of the **Yamuna**, in central India, c. sixth century BCE.

CEDI (2). Ruling lineage in Orissa c. second–first century BCE, of which **Khāravela** is the best-known **king**. *See also* SISUPALGARH.

CEMETERY H. Post-Harappan archaeological culture (c. early second millennium BCE), best known from the **pottery** painted with a range of floral and other motifs, recovered from a cemetery at **Harappa**. The **burials** consist of bones placed within large, painted urns. *See also* DAULATPUR.

CERA. Name of an **early historic** ruling lineage associated with parts of present-day Tamil Nadu and Kerala: The name of the latter is derived from that of the lineage. The history of the early rulers of this lineage has been reconstructed from ***Sangam*** **literature**, which mentions several rulers. Their capital was in **Karur**. After third century CE, there appears to have been a hiatus in the lineage, which is mentioned once more in **inscriptions** and texts dating to c. eighth century CE onward. *See also* KARIKĀḺAN; *KERALAPUTA*; NEDUNJELIYAN; PARANAR; *PATIṞṞUPATTU*.

CHACHEGAON. Early historic archaeological site in Maharashtra (c. first millennium CE?). Finds include caves meant to serve as **monasteries** for **Buddhist** monks. There are also remains of a ***caitya***.

CHALCOLITHIC. Term meaning "**copper**–stone," used to designate **archaeological** cultures where the use of copper, though documented, was relatively limited. Evidence of Chalcolithic cultures is found in several parts of the subcontinent during the second and early first millennium BCE. Some of the best-known sites are from the Deccan. Most of these sites have yielded evidence of **agriculture** and **pastoralism** and are often distinguished on the basis of distinctively decorated **pottery**. Stone **tools** formed a substantial part of the equipment. Copper artifacts generally included small tools and ornaments. Sites with evidence of Chalcolithic occupation include **Bharatpur**, **Bharuch**, **Donder Khera**, **Golbai Sasan**, **Hathikera**, **Hemmige**, **Jhusi**, **Kakrehta**, **Kesanapalle**, **Loteshwar**, **Mahisdal**, **Nasik**, **Nevasa**, **Pandu Rajar Dhibi**, **Pipri**, **Ramapuram**, **Savalda**, **Shaktari Timbo**, **Shirkanda**, **Sonpur**, **Taradih**, **Terdal**, **Tharsa**, **Tuljapur Garhi**, **Vidisha**, and **Walki**. *See also* AHAR; ART; BALATHAL; BANAHALLI; BRAHMAGIRI; CHANDOLI; DATRANA; DIHAR; DISPOSAL OF THE DEAD; ERAN; GANGA (2); GILUND; HALLUR; IRRIGATION; JORWE; KATRA; KAYATHA; KHAJURI; KOLDIHWA; KULLI; MAHESHWAR; MALWAN; NARHAN; NAVDATOLI; PREHISTORY; TRIBES; UTAWAD.

CHANDIGARH. Capital of present-day states of the Punjab and Haryana, with evidence of **Harappan pottery** (c. third millennium BCE).

CHĀNDOGYA UPANIṢAD. Among the earliest **Upaniṣads**, possibly compiled c. mid–sixth century CE. The text, in **Sanskrit**, includes discussions on rituals as well as **philosophical** speculations on the nature of the ultimate reality. Later traditions regarded it as one of the early sources of **Vedantic** ideas.

CHANDOLI. **Archaeological** site in Maharashtra, with evidence of a **Chalcolithic** settlement, mid–second millennium BCE. Finds include remains of rectangular houses with hearths. There is evidence of stone **tools**, including mortars and pestles, **copper** chisels and fish-hooks, **pottery** resembling that from **Jorwe**, beads of semiprecious stone, and ornaments of copper. There is also evidence of **burials** within the settlement.

CHANDRAKETUGARH. **Archaeological** site in West Bengal, settled c. third century BCE onward, which is one of the best-known **early historic** settlements in the region, with evidence for **fortifications**. Associated finds include **Northern Black Polished Ware**, red slipped ware, **rouletted ware**, **punch-marked coins**, **cast copper coins**, coins of the **Kuṣāṇa** and **Gupta** rulers, **seals** and sealings, **inscriptions** in **Brāhmī** and **Kharoṣṭhī**, beads of glass and semiprecious stone, ivory artifacts, and a profusion of **terracotta sculptures**, including representations of a wide range of secular and **religious** themes. There is also evidence of both burnt-brick and wattle-and-daub structures and terracotta ring wells and drains. Traces of a mud rampart have also been recovered. A brick **temple** attributed to the Gupta period (mid–first millennium CE) has also been recovered. The site continued to be occupied until the 13th century CE. Later phases yielded evidence of votive ***stūpas*** and temples.

CHANDRAVALLI. **Archaeological** site in Karnataka, with evidence of occupation c. first millennium BCE onward. The earliest levels yielded **Black and Red Ware**. Finds from Period II included **Russet-Coated Painted Ware**, **rouletted ware**, and **Sātavāhana** and **Roman coins**.

CHANHUDARO. Small **Mature Harappan** (c. third millennium BCE) settlement in Sind, Pakistan, near a point where the **Indus**

River can be crossed, with evidence for **craft** production, especially the manufacture of stone beads, weights, **seals**, and shell artifacts. There are traces of a **Late Harappan** (c. first half of the second millennium BCE) occupation related to the **Jhukar** culture.

CHARSADA. Archaeological site (c. mid–first millennium BCE onward) in the North-West Frontier Province, Pakistan, identified with ancient **Puṣkalāvatī**, referred to as Peucelaotis or Proclais in Greek sources. Finds include occupational levels associated with the **Indo-Greeks** and the **Kuṣāṇas**.

CHAUL. Archaeological site in Maharashtra, a port on the western coast, referred to in **early historic inscriptions** as Cemula. Finds include remains of an embankment, ring wells, **Sātavāhana coins**, glass beads and bangles, and Roman amphorae.

CHECHAR. Archaeological site in Bihar, with evidence of three major occupational phases. Finds associated with Period I (c. early first millennium BCE?) include **black and red ware**, bone **tools**, arrowheads, and pieces of **copper**. Period II (c. mid–first millennium BCE?) was associated with the **Northern Black Polished Ware** and **punch-marked coins**. Finds from Period III, assigned to the **Kuṣāṇa** and **Gupta** phases, included remains of a burnt-brick structure; beads of glass, ivory, and semiprecious stone; and bone artifacts.

CHENAB. Tributary of the **Indus River**. It is mentioned as the **Asikinī** in the ***Ṛgveda*** (c. second millennium BCE). *See also* AKESINES; MANDA.

CHERAMANGAD. Archaeological site in Kerala, find spot of **megalithic** (c. first millennium BCE?) **burials**. These include hood stones, umbrella stones, and stone circles. Other finds include **iron** arrowheads, knives, sickles, rods, hooks, and lamps.

CHIRAND. Archaeological site in Bihar with evidence of five major occupational phases. Period I is **Neolithic** (c. second millennium BCE). There is evidence for hunting and fishing as well as for the cultivation of rice, wheat, barley, and lentil. Domesticated animals included cattle, sheep, goat, and pig. **Tools** consisted of ground stone tools and microliths and a variety of bone tools such as chisels, picks, hammers, scrapers, needles, and arrowheads. There is evidence for the construction of huts and of hearths. Other finds included red handmade **pottery**, occasionally painted with geometric designs, and beads of semiprecious stone. There is also evidence of bone ornaments. Finds from Period II (late second–early first millennium BCE) consisted of **black and red ware**, microliths, and traces of **copper**. Period III (mid–first millennium BCE) yielded **Northern Black Polished Ware**, **iron** equipment including **agricultural** tools, **terracotta** figurines, and **punch-marked** and **cast coins**. Finds from Period IV (early first millennium CE) included traces of a **Buddhist monastery** and a hoard of **Kuṣāṇa** coins. The site was deserted and reoccupied toward the end of the first millennium CE. *See also* KHAIRADIH.

CHIRKI-ON-PRAVARA. Lower and middle **Paleolithic** site in Maharashtra, with evidence for the local manufacture of **tools** such as hand axes, cleavers, choppers, and scrapers made of quartz and chalcedony.

CHOPANI MANDO. **Archaeological** site in the **Belan valley**, Uttar Pradesh, with evidence of occupation during the upper **Paleolithic** and **Mesolithic** phases (c. 17000–7000 BCE?). Finds consisted of microliths, generally of chert. Other finds included evidence of circular huts. Subsequently, grinding stones and traces of handmade **pottery** were recovered, with evidence of hearths outside the huts. Charred rice has been recovered, along with the bones of wild cattle, sheep, and goat. There is also evidence for storage bins.

CHRISTIANITY. According to tradition, Christianity was introduced to the Malabar coastal region of Kerala by St. Thomas, c. first century CE. While the veracity of this tradition is uncertain, the existence of an old Christian community, at present known as the Syrian Christians, in the region, is undisputed. *See also* COSMAS INDIKOPLEUSTES; GONDOPHERNES.

CILAPPATIKĀRAM. *See SILAPPADIKĀRAM.*

CITIES. The earliest evidence of urban centers in the subcontinent comes from the **Harappan civilization** (c. 2700–1800 BCE), with several cities in the **Indus** valley and in regions such as Gujarat. While attempts have been made to trace connections between this phase of urbanism and the next, associated with the **early historic period**, c. mid–first millennium BCE, the similarities are general rather than specific. **Buddhist** texts recognized the existence of six major cities in north India during this period. These included **Campā**, **Sravasti**, **Kāśi**, **Kausambi**, **Sāketa**, and **Rājagaha**. **Archaeological** evidence indicates that many of these cities were **fortified**. There is also evidence for **coinage** and **craft** production. Traditionally, cities were recognized as centers of political authority. While texts such as the ***Arthaśāstra*** prescribed the laying out of planned urban centers in terms of a grid around a religiopolitical core, archaeological evidence points to more diffuse patterns of urbanism, with settlements in most cases growing organically rather than as a result of planning. Several terms were used to designate cities: these included *pura*, which often referred to a fortified settlement, *nagara*, and *nigama*, often a trading or market center.

By the end of the first millennium BCE, there is archaeological evidence of towns from other parts of the subcontinent as well, including the Deccan and the coastal areas, where several ports emerged. Some of the early urban centers probably entered into a phase of decline during the mid–first millennium CE. This is suggested by the accounts of Chinese pilgrims such as **Fa Xian** and **Xuan Zang**, and corroborated to some extent by archaeological evidence. At the same time, new towns emerged, especially in south India. Many of these grew around the nucleus of a **temple**, often built by a **king**. The temple served as a focus of religiocultural activities and often organized both **agricultural** and craft production, besides offering support to long-distance exchange. **Sanskrit**, **Prakrit**, and **Tamil** texts describe a vibrant urban milieu, dominated by an elite consisting of kings and their supporters, merchants, and bankers, with a distinctive lifestyle, including the cultivation of the **arts**. It is evident that urban populations were sharply differentiated in terms of wealth and social status: however, the existence of the urban poor is only occasionally represented in textual traditions. *See also* AYODHYA; COḺA; *DĀNA*; DRAMA; EARLY MEDIEVAL PERIOD; GANGA (2); GUILDS;

KANAUJ; KĀŚI; KAVERI RIVER; KUṢĀṆA; KUSINAGARA; MADURAI; MAHESHWAR; RĀJENDRA; SĀGALA; SĀKETA; SANKISSA; SECOND URBANIZATION; *SILAPPADIKĀRAM*; TAXILA; THANJAVUR; UJJAYINĪ; *UTTARĀPATHA*; VAISHALI; VIDISHA.

COINAGE. The earliest known coins are the **punch-marked coins**, c. sixth century BCE onward, in silver and **copper**, found almost throughout the subcontinent. These as well as some of the earliest **cast** copper **coins**, are uninscribed, although they contain symbolic representations. These were probably issued by rulers, merchant **guilds**, and local communities. Texts such as the ***Arthaśāstra*** use the terms *paṇa* or *kārṣāpaṇa* to refer to coins. It is possible that these terms were used for punch-marked coins.

Inscribed coins are available from c. second century BCE onward, the earliest being those of the **Indo-Greeks** (c. second–first century BCE). **Scripts** included Greek and **Kharoṣṭhī**, used to write Greek and **Prakrit**. These were also among the earliest coins with visual representations of the rulers. These were silver coins in two weights, the *drachm* of 4.276 grams and the *tetradrachm*, 17.106 grams. Gold coins included the *stater*, weighing 8.553 grams, and the *obol*, weighing 0.712 grams. The gold coin of the **Kuṣāṇas** (c. first century BCE–second century CE), the *dīnāra*, averaging around 8 grams, corresponded with the Roman *aureus* of Augustus in both size and weight. Apart from representations of the rulers, deities drawn from a wide range of **religious** traditions were also depicted. Hoards of imperial **Roman coins** have been recovered from south India, where they appear to have been used as bullion. Almost contemporaneously, rulers such as the **Sātavāhanas** issued coins in lead and silver. Coins were also issued by several communities, including the **Yaudheyas**. The last major issues of gold coinage are associated with the **Guptas** (c. fourth–sixth centuries CE). Subsequently, silver and copper coins continue to be found, issued by several dynasties.

The relative paucity of gold (and other) coins c. sixth century CE onward has been taken to indicate a decline in long-distance exchange, especially **trade** with the Roman Empire. However, textual and inscriptional sources continue to mention coins, and in several situations, cowries appear to have been used as a means of exchange. In south India local coinage consisted of either gold or copper, with very little silver coinage. Copper coins of the **Sālaṅkāyanas**, **Viṣṇukuṇḍins**, and early **Pallavas** have been found, while the earliest gold coins were probably those of the **Co<u>l</u>as**.

Sites from which evidence of coins and/or indications of manufacture have been recovered include **Adam**, **Agiabir**, **Ahar**, **Alagankulan**, **Amaravati**, **Amreli**, **Arambha**, **Bairat**, **Balathal**, **Banarsihankalan**, **Banavasi**, **Bayana**, **Bharuch**, **Bhattiprolu**, **Bhokardan**, **Bhorgarh**, **Brahmapuri**, **Brass**, **Campā**, **Chandraketugarh**, **Chandravalli**, **Chaul**, **Chechar**, **Chirand**, **Dangwada**, **Daulatpur**, **Dharanikota**, **Dihar**, **Elchuru**, **Eran**, **Erich**, **Ganeshwar**, **Garapadu**, **Ganwaria**, **Ghantasala**, **Gopalapatnam**, **Hasargundigi**, **Hastinapura**, **Hulas Khera**, **Jaugada**, **Jhusi**, **Jogalthembi**, **Kallur**, **Kanaganahalli**, **Kanchipuram**, **Kasrawad**, **Katra**, **Kaundinyapura**, **Kausambi**, **Kayatha**, **Khokrakot**, **Kolhua**, **Kondapur**, **Kumrahar**, **Kunnatur**, **Kusinagara**, **Lauriya Nandangarh**, **Maheshwar**, **Malhar**, **Manamunda**, **Maner**, **Mangalkot**, **Mansar**, **Masaon**, **Mathura**, **Nadner**, **Nagara**, **Nagiari**, **Nalanda**, **Narhan**, **Nasik**, **Nelakondapalli**, **Nevasa**, **Noh**, **Padri**, **Paithan**, **Pandu Rajar Dhibi**, **Pāṭalīputra**, **Pauni**, **Peddavegi**, **Piprahwa**, **Puduru**, **Purola**, **Ratura**, **Sanchi**, **Sanghol**, **Sannati**, **Sisupalgarh**, **Sodanga**, **Sonpur**, **Sonkh**, **Sopara**, **Sravasti**, **Sringaverapura**, **Sugh**, **Sunet**, **Talkad**, **Tāmralipti**, **Taradih**, **Taxila**, **Ter**, **Thanesar**, **Thotlakonda**, **Tripuri**, **Tumain**, **Ujjayinī**, **Vaddamanu**, **Vadgaon Madhavpur**, **Vaishali**, and **Vidisha**, *See also* ACYUTA; AGATHOKLES; AGNIMITRA; ANTIALKIDAS; ANTIMACHUS; APOLLODOTOS; *AŚVAMEDHA*; CITIES; DEMETRIOS; DIDDĀ; EARLY HISTORIC PERIOD; EUKRATIDES; EUTHYDEMOS; GAṆAPATI (NĀGA); GAUTAMĪPUTRA SĀTAKARṆI; GONDOPHERNES; HUVIṢKA; KANIṢKA; KOṬA KULA JANA; KUJULA KADPHISES; KUMĀRAGUPTA I; KUNINDA; MARITIME TRADE; MAUES; MENANDER; NĀGANIKĀ; NAHAPĀṆA; NAVY; NUMISMATICS; PULUMAYI II; PURI-KUṢĀṆA; RĀMAGUPTA; RĀṢṬRAKŪṬA; SACRIFICE; SĀLAṄKĀYANA; SAMUDRAGUPTA; SUGANDHĀ; TRADE; VĀSIṢṬHĪPUTRA PULUMAVI; VĪMA KADPHISES; YAJÑAŚRĪ SĀTAKARṆI.

COḺA. Name of a ruling lineage that exercised control over parts of present-day Tamil Nadu and adjoining regions c. late first millennium BCE onward. Some of the earliest references to the Coḻas are found in **Asokan inscriptions**, where they were listed among the people living beyond his frontiers. Coḻa chiefs and **kings** are also mentioned in **Tamil *Sangam* literature**. Their power centered on the fertile **Kaveri** valley. Important **cities** included the capital **Uraiyur** and the port of Puhār **(Poompuhar/Kaveripattinam)**.

Coḻa power underwent a temporary eclipse for several centuries in the first millennium CE, before being revived under **Vijayālaya** in the ninth century. The second phase of Coḻa rule is documented in **inscriptions** and texts. **Thanjavur**, and later Gangaikondacholapuram, emerged as important **cities** during this phase. The Coḻas proved to be successful in dealing with rival powers such as the **Pallavas**, **Cālukyas**, and **Pāṇḍyas**, and exercised control in the region until the 13th century. The most powerful rulers during this phase were **Rājarāja I** and **Rājendra**. This period was also marked by expeditions to Sri Lanka and Southeast Asia, for which a **navy** was created. Coḻa administration was organized around the control of several regions or *nadus*. At the local level, village **assemblies** often played a major role in administration.

Most of the Coḻa rulers were supporters of **Śaivism**. This phase of Coḻa rule is often remembered for the construction of some of the most spectacular stone **temples** in the region and for exquisite bronze **sculptures** of **Purāṇic** gods and **goddesses**. *See also* ĀDITYA; CĀLUKYA (EASTERN); COINAGE; EASTERN GAṄGA; EMPIRE; KARIKĀḺAN; MAJOR ROCK EDICTS; MARITIME TRADE; NEDUNJELIYAN; TOṆḌAI MAṆḌALAM; VIJAYĀLAYA.

COOMARASWAMY, ANANDA KENTISH. **Art** historian (1877–1947), best known for his studies on the symbolism of **Buddhist** and **Brahmanical** art, questioning the perspective that regarded Indian art as being influenced by Greek ideals and models.

COPPER. Some of the earliest and most prolific evidence of the use of copper (also alloyed with tin to make bronze) occurs in the context of the **Harappan civilization** (c. 2700–1800 BCE), where it was used to make **tools**, weapons, ornaments, vessels, and even **sculpture**. Evidence for the use of copper also occurs in **Chalcolithic** cultures. Terms used for copper in early texts such as the ***Ṛgveda*** (c. second millennium BCE) include *ayas* or metal, often qualified as *lohitāyas* (red metal) as distinct from *kṛṣṇāyas* (black metal), used to designate **iron**. Other terms include *tāmra*, part of place-names such as **Tāmralipti**. Even after the introduction and extensive use of iron from the first millennium BCE, copper continued to be used for a variety of purposes. From about the mid–first millennium BCE, copper **coins** were minted. These included **punch-marked** as well as **cast** coins. Copper coins issued by ruling lineages continued in circulation in different parts of the subcontinent for centuries. Sites that have yielded evidence of copper artifacts include **Adam**, **Adichannallur**, **Ahar**, **Alamgirpur**, **Atranjikhera**, **Ayodhya**, **Bagor**, **Balathal**, **Balu**, **Banahalli**, **Banavasi**, **Bara**, **Bhagwanpura**, **Bharatpur**, **Brahmagiri**, **Chandoli**, **Chechar**, **Chirand**, **Dadheri**, **Dangwada**, **Dat Nagar**, **Daulatpur**, **Desalpur**, **Dholavira**, **Dihar**, **Donder Khera**, **Eran**, those of the **Gandhara Grave Culture**, **Gilund**, **Golbai Sasan**, **Gudnapura**, **Hallur**, **Hastinapura**, **Hulas**, **Imlidih Khurd**, **Jakhera**, **Jhukar**, **Jodhpura**, **Kakrehta**, **Kalibangan**, **Karkabhat**, **Katra**, **Kayatha**, **Khajuri**, **Khokrakot**, **Koldihwa**, **Kondapur**, **Korkai**, **Kudikadu**, **Lal Qila**, **Lothal**, **Mahisdal**, **Manamunda**, **Mangalkot**, **Mulchera**, **Musanagar**, **Nadner**, **Nagda**, **Nagiari**, **Noh**, **Padri**, **Pandu Rajar Dhibi**, **Pauni**, **Pipri**, **Pithad**, **Raipur**, **Rajmahal**, **Rojdi**, **Sannati**, **Sekta**, **Shaktari Timbo**, **Sravasti**, **Takiaper**, **Taradih**, **Tekkalakotta**, **Tharsa**, **Timbarra**, **Tripuri**, **Tumain**, **Ujjayinī**, **Utawad**, **Vaishali**, and **Wina**. *See also* COPPER HOARDS; COPPER PLATES; GANESHWAR.

COPPER HOARDS. Name given to hoards of copper **tools** and weapons found at a number of sites in the upper and mid–**Ganga (2)** valley (c. second millennium BCE?) and in adjoining areas such as Haryana, Madhya Pradesh, Bihar, West Bengal, and Orissa. The tool types include distinctive axes, swords, anthropomorphic figures, rings, harpoons, and spearheads. Apart from the rings, the other tools were cast. Finds of copper hoards are often correlated with those of **Ochre-Coloured Pottery**. While attempts have been made to connect both tools and pottery with **Harappan** prototypes, these have not won widespread acceptance at present. *See also* BAHADRABAD; BISAULI; BITHUR; PARIAR; RAJPUR PARASU; SAIPAI.

COPPER PLATES. Copper plates were used to record **land grants**, especially from the mid–first millennium CE. Several thousands of such copper plates have been recovered from different parts of the subcontinent. These were meant to replicate palm leaves and were used to record transactions that were expected to last for a long time, ideally in perpetuity. Contemporary **Sanskrit** texts refer to these as *tāmra śāsana*, literally orders inscribed on copper. *See also* INSCRIPTIONS; SOHGAURA.

COSMAS INDIKOPLEUSTES. Greek merchant (c. sixth century CE), who later became a **Christian** monk. He traveled extensively between c. 535 and 547 CE, through the Mediterranean Sea and the Indian Ocean, including the coasts of the subcontinent and Sri Lanka. The account of his travels, *Christian Topography*, contains details about **trading** relations between the subcontinent and other lands. *See also* TRAVELERS' ACCOUNTS.

COURTESANS. While allusions to sexual promiscuity in the ***Ṛgveda*** (c. second millennium BCE) have occasionally been regarded as the precursors of institutionalized sex work, **Sanskrit**, **Prakrit**, **Pali**, and **Tamil** textual traditions indicate that courtesans were an integral part of the urban milieu during the **early historic** and **early medieval period**. Terms used to designate courtesans included *gaṇikā*, generally used for elite **women** who were expected to possess a range of accomplishments, and *veśyā*, the ordinary sex worker. Recruitment to the profession was varied: in some instances the profession was hereditary, passing from mother to daughter, while in others women were drawn in either through capture or on account of **poverty**. Attempts to regulate the profession by the state were discussed in the ***Arthaśāstra***. The ***Kāmasūtra*** included detailed discussions on possible strategies that could be adopted by the courtesan, who was also represented in a variety of literary texts, including the ***Mṛcchakaṭikam*** and the ***Silappadikāram***. *See also* AMBAPĀLĪ; BUDDHA; DĀMODARAGUPTA; MUSIC; ŚŪDRAKA.

CRAFTS. Craft traditions are in evidence in the **archaeological** record from the remote past. These included making stone **tools**, evident from the **Paleolithic** phase onward, and **pottery**, in evidence from **Neolithic** cultures. The evidence is far more prolific from the **Harappan civilization** (c. 2700–1800 BCE), where craftspersons specialized in working stone to make beads, tools, **seals**, and statues and were skilled in handling metals such as **copper**, tin, gold, and silver and materials such as shell. Skills in carpentry and weaving have also been inferred. Some historians have suggested that production of several artifacts in the Harappan civilization was probably organized through an overarching authority that procured raw materials, oversaw production, and distributed the finished product.

The ***Ṛgveda*** (c. second millennium BCE) contains references to craftsmen, including the chariot maker, and indicates that weaving was undertaken by **women**. **Prakrit** and **Pali** texts from the second half of the first millennium BCE contain references to a variety of craft groups living in urban areas as well as in villages. These included carpenters, bamboo workers, perfumers, garland makers, ivory workers, goldsmiths, jewelers, silversmiths, weavers, potters, oil-pressers, millers, and blacksmiths. Texts mention **guilds** and suggest that occupations were hereditary. Archaeological evidence from **early historic** sites also attests to the existence of craft specialists. The ***Arthaśāstra*** provided for state control of production of a variety of goods, ranging from textiles to metalworking. Whether these provisions were actually implemented is uncertain.

The social status of craft workers varied substantially. **Inscriptions** from early historic sites sometimes record gifts made to **religious** institutions by craft workers, in some instances collectively. These may indicate a relatively high social standing. At the same time, by the first millennium CE, several craft specialists including leather workers, carpenters, weavers, and blacksmiths were classified as low-status groups within the **Brahmanical** tradition. There are also indications that crafts workers were transferred to the donee when **land grants**, which became more common from the second half of the first millennium CE, were made.

Sites that have yielded evidence of craft production include **Adam**, **Adichannallur**, **Agiabir**, **Alagankulan**, **Arikamedu**, **Atranjikhera**, **Banahalli**, **Banavasi**, **Barygaza**, **Bhagimohari**, **Datrana**,

Dholavira, **Eran**, **Ganeshwar**, **Inamgaon**, **Kallur**, **Khairadih**, **Khokrakot**, **Kodumanal**, **Koldihwa**, **Kuntasi**, **Lothal**, **Mahurjhari**, **Mangalkot**, **Nageshwar**, **Nagwada**, **Nainkund**, **Narhan**, **Padri**, **Puduru**, **Shirkanda**, **Sonpur**, **Tripuri**, **Ujjayinī**, **Valmiyo Timbo**, and **Wari Bateshwar**. *See also* CASTE; CHANHUDARO; CITIES; IRON AGE; MOHENJODARO; MONASTERIES; UNTOUCHABILITY; VEDIC ECONOMY.

CŪLAVAMSA*.** Literally "Lesser Chronicle," Sinhalese **Buddhist** text composed in **Pali**, and a sequel to the ***Mahāvamsa (the "Great Chronicle"). The *Cūlavamsa* received its final form in the 19th century. The text consists of two parts, of which the first, narrating events from the fourth century to the reign of Sinhalese **king** Parākramabāhu (12th century), was probably composed by a monk named Dhammakītti. The text refers to contemporary events in the subcontinent and has been used as a source by historians. *See also* LITERATURE.

CUNNINGHAM, ALEXANDER (1814–1893). First director (1871–1885) of the **Archaeological Survey**, which was established in 1861. Cunningham undertook extensive surveys in several provinces. In many of these he tried to trace the **routes** taken by the Chinese pilgrims, especially **Xuan Zang**. The reports of these surveys were published in several volumes. He discovered a number of **early historic** sites and excavated some of the major ***stūpas***, including those at **Sanchi**. His **numismatic** and **epigraphic** studies were also important.

CUNTARĀR. **Tamil poet**, c. ninth century CE, also known as Sundaramūrti **Nāyaṉār** or Sundarār, one of the three poets whose works are included in the ***Tevāram***. He belonged to a community of **temple** priests. There are **biographic** elements in his poetry, which is devotional, invoking the god **Śiva** as a friend. He evidently visited as many as 82 **Śaiva** shrines. *See also* LITERATURE.

CYRUS. Founder of the **Achaemenid** Empire (r. 558–529 BCE), who led expeditions to the Kabul valley. He also received an emissary from a **king** of "India."

– D –

DADHERI. Archaeological site in the Punjab (c. second millennium BCE) with evidence of an overlap between **late Harappan** and **Painted Grey Ware** cultures. Apart from **pottery**, finds include evidence of mud-brick **architecture** and **copper** artifacts.

DAHIR. King (c. seventh–eighth centuries CE) of Sind in present-day Pakistan, who was defeated and killed by the Arab general **Muhammad bin Qasim** in 712.

DAIMABAD. Archaeological site in Maharashtra with evidence of three major occupational phases. Finds from Period I (c. late third millennium BCE?) include stone **tools**, gray **pottery** similar to that from **Brahmagiri**, and beads of semiprecious stone. Pottery from Period II (c. early second millennium BCE) had affinities with **Malwa ware**. Period III (mid–second millennium BCE) yielded pottery like that from **Jorwe** and **terracotta** figurines. Plant remains associated with this phase included wheat, barley, rice, millet, pea, horse gram, lentil, linseed, and *ber* or the Indian jujube. Structural remains assigned to the second millennium BCE include a possible sacrificial altar. A hoard of bronze figurines that may have **Harappan** affinities as well as **seals** have been recovered.

***DAKṢIṆĀ*. Sanskrit** term found in **Vedic literature** (c. second millennium BCE onward) and subsequently used for the **sacrificial** fees offered to ***brāhmaṇas* (1)** for the performance of rituals. *Dakṣiṇā* varied according to the magnitude of the ritual and was often of symbolic value. *Dakṣiṇā* could consist of cattle, horses, other animals, cloth, chariots, metal objects, **slave** men and **women**, and very rarely land.

***DAKṢIṆĀPATHA*.** Term, meaning "the southern path," used in **Sanskrit**, **Prakrit**, and **Pali** texts (c. mid–first millennium BCE onward) to designate **routes** leading from the **Ganga (2)** valley beyond the **Vindhyas** and the region south of the mountains. *See also* SAMUDRAGUPTA; ŚRĪ SĀTAKARṆĪ I; TRADE ROUTES.

DAMANA. Ruler (c. fourth century CE) of Eraṇḍapalla, part of present-day Andhra Pradesh, mentioned in the **Allahabad Pillar Inscription** of the **Gupta** ruler **Samudragupta** as one of those who was captured and released on condition of submission.

ḌĀMARA. Name of a socioeconomic category that exercised control over land in Kashmir. By the end of the first millennium CE *ḍāmaras* were intervening in political affairs, including questions of succession, apart from playing an important role in social and economic relations.

DAMDAMA. Mesolithic site in Uttar Pradesh, c. fourth–third millennium BCE, yielding **tools** such as microliths and grinding stones. Other remains include traces of hearths and charred animal bones and faunal remains, such as bones of cattle, sheep, goat, ass, deer, fish, and birds. There is evidence of **burials** with grave goods such as bone and ivory ornaments.

DĀMODARAGUPTA. Sanskrit poet (c. ninth century CE), **minister** of king **Jayapīḍa** of Kashmir, author of the *Kuttanīmatam*, a work dealing with the **courtesanal** tradition and providing a vivid representation of contemporary society. *See also* LITERATURE.

DĀNA. Term used in **Sanskrit**, **Prakrit**, and **Pali** texts and **inscriptions** to designate gifts, especially those made to **religious** personages and institutions. The earliest references to the term occur in the later sections of the ***Ṛgveda*** (c. late second millennium BCE) that contain verses known as the *dānastuti*, literally in praise of the gift, and by extension of the donor, composed by priests who were the recipients of these gifts.

Brahmanical, **Buddhist**, and **Jaina** traditions attempted to both encourage and regulate gift giving, evolving, by the mid–first millennium BCE, detailed rules to control the contexts and contents of such exchanges. All these traditions developed the idea that *dāna* was a means of acquiring merit. At the same time, potential donors were delimited. *Brāhmaṇas*, for instance, insisted that ***śūdras*** be kept outside the purview of such exchanges. Buddhists and Jainas took precautions to ensure that the vows of the **ascetic**, especially that of celibacy, were not violated while receiving gifts. Lists of permitted and prohibited items of gift are found in several texts.

Also debated was the relative status of donor and donee—Brahmanical texts, for instance, insisted that the recipient was superior to the donor, whereas narrative traditions often proclaimed the preeminence of the latter. From c. second century BCE onward, votive inscriptions found from several sites, including **cities**, indicate that donors sought to record their gifts, ranging from small donations to large **land grants**, permanently both for the benefit of the donee and in order to proclaim their generosity.

DANCE. Some of the earliest representations of scenes of dancing occur in cave **paintings** found in **Mesolithic** rock shelters. Subsequently, finds of **sculpture** and representations on **seals** from the **Harappan civilization** (c. 2700–1800 BCE) have been taken to represent dancers. Textual references to dancing occasionally occur in **Vedic** and later **literature**. Dancers, as also other professional entertainers, both men and **women**, were viewed with disfavor in the **Dharmasūtras** and the **Dharmaśāstras** (mid–first millennium BCE onward). However, other texts such as the ***Nāṭyaśāstra*** attempted to codify performative traditions, including dance. In the course of the first millennium CE other traditions, including those of devotional **religion**, visualized deities such as **Śiva** in the role of cosmic dancer. *See also* ART.

DAṆḌA. **Sanskrit** term meaning "stick," which gained currency from c. sixth century BCE onward, used in the sense of coercive force, punishment, and, by extension, justice. The ideal **king** was expected to wield the *daṇḍa*.

DAṆḌIN. Sanskrit poet (c. eighth century CE?) who lived at the court of the **Pallava** ruler **Narasimhavarman II**. His best-known compositions include the *Kāvyādarśa*, a work on poetics; the ***Daśakumāracarita***, an anthology of stories; and the *Avantisundarī*, a work modeled on the compositions of **Bāṇabhaṭṭa** describing the wedding of the princess of **Avanti** to a prince of **Mālava** named Rājavāhana. *See also* LITERATURE.

DANGWADA. Archaeological site in Madhya Pradesh with several occupational phases dating from the end of the third millennium BCE to the medieval period. The finds from Period I have parallels with the **Kayatha** culture. Finds from Period II (early second millennium BCE) include white-painted **black and red ware** like that from **Ahar** and **terracotta** figurines. Period III (mid–second millennium BCE) yielded **pottery** resembling that from **Malwa**. Other finds included microliths, grinding stones, and storage jars with traces of grain. Period IV (early first millennium BCE) yielded black and red ware, **iron** artifacts, and shell ornaments. Finds from Period V (second half of the first millennium BCE) included iron and **copper** artifacts, **punch-marked coins**, **Northern Black Polished Ware**, and ring wells. Finds from Period VI and VII (early first millennium CE) included gold, silver, and ivory artifacts, beads of semiprecious stone, and terracotta **seals** with **inscriptions** in **Brāhmī**. Finds from Period VIII (mid–first millennium CE) included terracotta sealings.

DANTIDURGA. Founder (c. eighth century CE) of the **Rāṣṭrakūṭa** power. He established himself after defeating the last known ruler of the **Cālukyas** of **Badami**.

DAOJALI HADING. Archaeological site in Assam. Finds include **Neolithic** polished stone **tools** and querns and handmade **pottery**. The dating of the finds is uncertain.

DARIUS I. The third ruler of the **Achaemenid** dynasty (r. 523–486 BCE). The people of Gadara (**Gandhara**) are listed among his subjects in the **Bisitun inscription**, while the Hidus (**Hindus**, people of the **Indus** valley) are mentioned in inscriptions found at **Persepolis**, **Hamadan**, and **Naqsh-i-Rustum**. Darius's conquests in the region are also mentioned by **Herodotus**. *See also* XERXES.

DĀSA*.** People mentioned in the ***Ṛgveda (c. second millennium BCE), where they were generally represented as enemies of the **Aryans**. While the difference between the Aryans and the Dāsa was often regarded as racial in the 19th and 20th centuries, the terms probably designated groups that had different cultural (including ritual) practices and spoke different **languages**. The interaction between the

Dāsa and the Ārya included open hostility as well as assimilation. The term acquired connotations of **slavery**, which have persisted to the present. References to the use of *dāsas* for household and **agricultural** work are frequent in **Buddhist literature** from the mid–first millennium BCE onward. Details on recruitment of slaves were laid down in texts such as the ***Arthaśāstra***. These included those born into slavery, the children of slaves, and prisoners of war in addition to those who were sold into slavery. The regular use of the feminine form *dāsī* points to the existence of **women** slaves.

***DAŚAKUMĀRACARITA*.** **Sanskrit** prose text attributed to **Daṇḍin** (c. seventh century CE?). It describes the adventures of 10 princes who decide to go their own ways and reassemble at **Ujjayinī**. The text consists of 14 chapters, of which chapters 6 to 13 constitute the core. In spite of its title, there are 8 stories rather than 10. It provides a realistic representation of contemporary society. *See also* LITERATURE.

DAŚAPURA. **City** in Malwa, identical with present-day Mandasor. *See also* SOCIAL MOBILITY; YAŚODHARMAN.

***DĀŚARĀJÑA*.** *See* BATTLE OF THE TEN KINGS.

DASARATHA. Grandson (c. third century BCE) of the **Mauryan** ruler **Asoka**. Like his grandfather, he adopted the title of *devānāmpiya* or "beloved of the gods." **Inscriptions** indicate that he was a patron of the **Ājīvikas**. He donated caves for their residence in the **Nagarjuni Hills** (present-day Bihar). *See also* BARABAR.

DAT NAGAR. **Archaeological** site in Himachal Pradesh, with evidence of an urban settlement dating to the **Kuṣāṇa** period (c. early first millennium BCE). Finds include **copper** and **terracotta** artifacts, stone **sculpture**, **coins**, **iron** equipment, beads of carnelian, and bangles.

DATRANA. **Archaeological** site in Gujarat, with evidence of two phases of occupation. Finds from **Mesolithic** (Period I) levels include microliths made of chert and jasper. Finds from **Chalcolithic** levels (Period II, c. second millennium BCE) consisted of stone blade **tools**, possibly manufactured locally; beads of semiprecious stone; evidence for bead making, including stone drills; animals bones, such as those of cattle, sheep, goat, antelope, and pig; **black and red ware**; and **late Harappan pottery**.

DAULATPUR. Archaeological site in Haryana, with evidence of occupation c. second millennium BCE onward. The earliest phase, identified as **late Harappan**, yielded **pottery** that has parallels with that from **Bara** and **Cemetery H**. Other finds included **copper tools** and ornaments and **terracotta** figurines. Finds that may be attributed to the first millennium BCE include **Painted Grey Ware**, copper **coins**, and sealings.

DAVĀKA. Kingdom (c. fourth century CE), probably in eastern Assam, mentioned in the **Allahabad Pillar Inscription** of **Samudragupta**, according to which the ruler of the kingdom paid tribute and homage and agreed to follow the orders of the **Gupta** king.

DEIMACHOS. Greek ambassador (c. third century BCE) sent by the **king** of Syria to the court of the **Mauryan** ruler **Bindusāra**.

DEMETRIOS. Bactrian Greek ruler (c. third–second century BCE), the son of **Euthydemos** and the son-in-law of Antiochos, **king** of Syria. He extended control over parts of Afghanistan and the northwestern part of the subcontinent by c. 190 BCE, but was overthrown by **Eukratides**. Silver **coins** issued by Demetrios, with Greek and **Kharoṣṭhī** legends and representations of elephants, have been recovered from **Taxila**, which may have served as his capital.

DEOGARH. Site of the *Daśāvatara* (10 incarnations of **Viṣṇu**) **temple** (Uttar Pradesh) dated to c. sixth century CE. The temple is noteworthy for its **sculpture**, including scenes from the ***Rāmāyaṇa*** and from legends about **Kṛṣṇa**.

DESALPUR. Archaeological site in Gujarat with evidence of a **Harappan** settlement (c. third–early second millennium BCE) with traces of **fortification** walls. Other finds include Harappan **pottery**, **seals**, **terracotta** figurines, beads, **copper tools**, and ornaments.

DEVANGARH. Archaeological site in Jharkhand, possibly **early historic** (c. mid–first millennium BCE?), with evidence of **fortifications** and finds of **black and red ware** and **Northern Black Polished Ware**.

DEVANIMORI. Archaeological site in Gujarat, presently submerged under water. The site was occupied in the **early historic period** (c. first half of the first millennium BCE). Finds include **Red Polished Ware**, Roman amphorae, and an **inscribed** relic casket. Structural remains include a ***stūpa***, a **Buddhist** shrine, and **monastery**.

DEVAPĀLA. Pāla ruler (r.c. 810–850), son and successor of **Dharmapāla**. In the panegyrics included in **inscriptions**, he is credited with the conquest of distant lands, including **Kāmboja** in the northwest, and victories over the **Hūṇas**, **Drāviḍas**, and **Pratihāras**. He also claimed to have conquered **Prāgjyotiṣa** and Utkala (part of present-day Orissa), extending his control from the **Himalayas** to the **Vindhyas** and from the eastern to the western seas. In the absence of corroborative evidence, historians consider these claims to be exaggerated. Devapāla was a patron of **Buddhism** and offered support to the monastery at **Nalanda**.

DEVARDHI GANI. Jaina teacher (c. fifth–sixth centuries CE) at **Valabhi** who presided over a council of teachers who compiled the texts regarded as canonical within the **Śvetāmbara** tradition. Two works are attributed to him: the *Nāndisūtra*, a eulogy of the major teachers including the 24 ***tīrthaṅkaras***; and the *Anuyogadvārasūtra*, an account of the major tenets of Jainism.

***DEVĪCANDRAGUPTA*. Sanskrit** play attributed to **Viśākhadatta** (c. sixth century CE). The fragmentary version of the play available at present describes how **Candragupta II** married Dhruvādevī, his brother's widow. It also suggests that Candragupta defeated the **Hūṇas** after killing his brother, who had surrendered to them. *See also* LITERATURE.

DEVĪMĀHĀTMYA*. Sanskrit poem**, consisting of around 700 verses, also known as the ***Durgāsaptaśati, composed c. fourth–sixth centuries

CE, and incorporated within the *Mārkaṇḍeya* ***Purāṇa***. The theme of the poem is the victory of the **goddess** over demons, and its compilation may represent an attempt to synthesize different cults of the goddess. *See also* LITERATURE.

DHAMMA*.** Term used in **Asokan inscriptions** (c. third century BCE) to designate a set of norms and practices prescribed by the ruler for his subjects. These included an emphasis on general qualities such as compassion; generosity; truthfulness; purity; gentleness; obedience toward parents and elders, including teachers; respect toward ***brāhmaṇas* (1)** and ***śramaṇas; kindness toward **slaves** and servants; and abstention from violence. The practice of *dhamma* was expected to lead to benefits in both this world and the next.

Historians have speculated about the reasons that led to the promulgation of *dhamma*. Some have pointed to similarities between *dhamma* and **Buddhism**. Others argue that the precepts of *dhamma* were fairly general and were not specifically Buddhist. *Dhamma* has also been viewed as an expression of state ideology and a means of holding together a heterogeneous **empire**, with diverse populations, by developing a code for social interaction. To some extent this is corroborated by the use of the phrase *dhamma vijaya*, or the conquest by or for *dhamma*, used by Asoka in contrast to the notion of ***digvijaya*** enunciated in theories of **kingship**. *See also* MAJOR PILLAR EDICTS; MAJOR ROCK EDICTS.

***DHAMMA MAHĀMATTA*.** A special category of officials appointed by the **Mauryan** emperor **Asoka**. The functions of the *dhamma mahāmatta* are elucidated in the seventh **Major Pillar Edict**. They were expected to establish contact with both renouncers and householders and to maintain links with various sects. Groups specifically enumerated include the **Buddhists**, ***brāhmaṇas* (1)**, **Ājīvikas**, and **Jainas**. The *dhamma mahāmattas* were also in charge of gifts made by members of the royal household. *See also* RENUNCIATORY ORDERS.

DHAMMAPADA*.** **Pali** text, recognized as part of the ***Sutta Piṭaka, an anthology of about 400 verses drawn from **Buddhist** sources, which perhaps received its final form c. first century BCE. The distinctive feature of the text is its simplicity, evident in both style and content. *See also* LITERATURE.

DHANANANDA. The last ruler (c. fourth century BCE) of the **Nanda** dynasty of **Magadha**, a contemporary of **Alexander (of Macedon)**. Greek sources mention his names as Agrammes or Xandrames. They describe his vast wealth, the extent of his territory, and his **army**, which evidently included 20,000 cavalry, 200,000 infantry, 2,000 chariots, and 3,000 elephants. He was evidently an oppressive ruler, who was defeated and killed (c. 322–321 BCE) by **Candragupta Maurya**, the founder of the Mauryan dynasty, with the help and advice of **Kauṭilya**.

DHANAÑJAYA. Ruler (c. fourth century CE) of Kusthalapura, possibly in present-day Tamil Nadu. He is mentioned in the **Allahabad Pillar Inscription** of the **Gupta** ruler **Samudragupta** as one of those who was captured but subsequently released on condition of submission to the **king**.

DHANSURA. Archaeological site in Gujarat, with evidence of two occupational phases associated with **Mesolithic** cultures. Finds from Period I included nongeometric microliths, saddle querns, cattle bones, and human skeletal remains. Geometric microliths and finds of charred bones of animals and birds characterized Period II.

DHĀNYAKAṬAKA. Literally "paddy town," a center of **Sātavāhana** power, identified with **Dharanikota**.

DHARANIKOTA. Archaeological site in Andhra Pradesh, near **Amaravati**, with evidence of two occupational phases (c. 400 BCE–400 CE). Structural remains from Period I included traces of a wharf. **Black and Red Ware** and **Northern Black Polished Ware** were also recovered from this period. Other finds included glass ornaments. Finds from Period II included **rouletted ware** and **Sātavāhana coins**. *See also* DHĀNYAKAṬAKA.

DHARMA*. Sanskrit** term with a complex set of meanings, including notions of righteousness and social norms. The latter were expected to vary according to ***varṇa, ***āśrama***, and gender. The ideal **king**

was expected to uphold the norms of *dharma* in both general and specific ways. The term gained currency from c. sixth century BCE onward, and several texts, known as the **Dharmasūtras** and the **Dharmaśāstras**, were devoted to elucidating the content and modes of enforcing *dharma*. Authored by ***brāhmaṇas*** **(1)**, the texts also recognized situations where norms could be difficult to uphold, and provided for alternatives. All texts on *dharma* recognized the **Vedas** as authoritative. *See also JĀTI*; *KARMA*; *PURUṢĀRTHA*; VIṢṆU.

DHARMAKATHĀ**.** **Prakrit** term used to designate a category of **literature**, generally within the **Jaina** tradition, where narratives were used to convey **religious** messages. While the tradition claimed that these stories, often derived from folk tales, dated back to c. second–third centuries CE, surviving works belong to c. eighth century CE. These include the ***Samaraicchakahā*** attributed to **Haribhadra Sūrī** and the ***Kuvalayamālā*** of **Udyotana Sūri**.

DHARMAKĪRTI. Buddhist author (c. seventh century CE) of a **Sanskrit** text on logic, the *Pramāṇavārttikā*. He was also recognized as a poet and a **philosopher**. *See also* LITERATURE; *YOGĀCĀRA*.

DHARMAPĀLA. The second major ruler (r.c. 770–810 CE) of the **Pāla** dynasty. He came into conflict with the contemporary **Rāṣṭrakūṭa** and **Pratihāra** rulers. Although he had some initial successes and even managed to install his protégée Cakrāyudha in **Kanauj**, these victories were short-lived. Claims in **inscriptions** that he exercised control over several **kingdoms** in north and central India appear to have been poetic exaggerations. Inscriptions also record that he was well versed in the *śāstras* and ensured that the norms regarding ***varṇa*** were followed. He was a supporter of **Buddhism**, and the **monastery** at **Vikramaśilā** was probably founded during his reign. He was succeeded by his son Devapāla. *See also* PAHARPUR.

DHARMAŚĀSTRA. Sanskrit term used to designate a category of texts composed c. second century BCE onward. These works, generally in verse, laid down social norms as defined by ***brāhmaṇas*** **(1)**. The best-known work in this category is the ***Manusmṛti***. Several commentaries on specific *dharmaśāstras* were composed over the centuries, and these were often used to define and codify **Hindu** law in the colonial period and subsequently. *See also* *ĀRYĀVARTA*; *ĀŚRAMA*; *BṚHASPATI SMṚTI*; DANCE; DHARMASŪTRA; DISPOSAL OF THE DEAD; *GOTRA*; GUILDS; INHERITANCE LAWS; IRRIGATION; *JĀTI*; KANE, PANDURANG VAMAN; *KĀTYĀYANASMṚTI*; KINSHIP SYSTEMS; *KṢATRIYA*; LAND GRANTS; LANDOWNERSHIP; LITERATURE; MARRIAGE; MONEY LENDING; *NĀRADA SMṚTI*; *NIŚĀDA*; REVENUE SYSTEMS; *SAMṆYĀSA*; SOCIAL MOBILITY; *STRĪDHANA*; *ŚŪDRA*; *SŪTA*; UNTOUCHABILITY; *VAIŚYA*; *VARṆA*; *VARṆASAMṆKARA*; WIDOWHOOD; WOMEN; *YĀJÑAVALKYASMṚTI*.

DHARMASŪTRA. **Sanskrit** term used to designate prose works, composed c. sixth–second centuries BCE. Four major authors are recognized: Gautama, Baudhāyana, Vasisṭha, and Āpastamba. The texts, recognized as part of the ***Vedāṅgas***, laid down social norms as defined by the ***brāhmaṇas* (1)**. These included prescriptions for what were considered as ideal situations as well as provisions for handling what were regarded as social crises from the perspective of the *brāhmaṇa* authors. The later **Dharmaśāstras** elaborated on these concerns. *See also* *ĀRYĀVARTA*; *ĀŚRAMA*; DANCE; DISPOSAL OF THE DEAD; *GOTRA*; *GṚHAPATI*; INHERITANCE LAWS; IRRIGATION; *JĀTI*; KINSHIP SYSTEMS; *KṢATRIYA*; LAND GRANTS; LANDOWNERSHIP; LITERATURE; MARRIAGE; MONEY LENDING; *NIŚĀDA*; REVENUE SYSTEMS; *SAMṆYĀSA*; SOCIAL MOBILITY; *ŚŪDRA*; UNTOUCHABILITY; *VAIŚYA*; *VARṆA*; *VARṆASAMṆKARA*; WIDOWHOOD; WOMEN.

***DHARMOPADEŚAMĀLĀVIVARAṆA*.** **Prakrit** work composed by a **Jaina** author Jayasimha Sūri, c. ninth century CE, comprising didactic narratives that provide insight into contemporary social and cultural practices. *See also* LITERATURE.

DHAULI. Site in Orissa, ancient Tosali. Find spot of a set of the **Major Rock Edicts** of **Asoka**, and of an elephant sculpted on the rock surface that is regarded as one of the best examples of **Mauryan sculpture**. Copies of the **Separate Rock Edicts** have also been found here. *See also* MAURYAN ART.

DHOLAVIRA. Mature Harappan site (c. 2700–1800 BCE) in Kutch, Gujarat. Its distinctive features include evidence of stone **architecture**, **fortifications** with gateways, a unique citadel, and reservoirs. There are indications of the manufacture of metal and shell artifacts and of bead making. A large **inscription** was recovered from the site. Other finds included typical Harappan **pottery**, stone blades, beads of semiprecious stones, including two hoards of more than 800 beads, more than a hundred **seals**, sealings, weights, **copper tools**, and **terracotta** artifacts, including figurines. The site was probably abandoned after the Mature Harappan phase.

DHURIAPAR. Archaeological site in Uttar Pradesh, with four occupational phases. Period I (c. 1300–600 BCE) was associated with finds of **black and red ware**, **black slipped ware**, bone artifacts, and **terracotta** beads. Period II (c. 600–200 BCE) yielded **Northern Black Polished Ware**. Finds from Period III (c. 200 BCE–500 CE) have been assigned to the **Kuṣāṇa** and **Gupta** periods, included **iron** objects and bangles of terracotta and glass. The last phase, Period IV (c. 900–1500 CE), was associated with the remains of a burnt-brick wall.

***DHVANYĀLOKA*. Sanskrit** text on poetics, comprising verses and commentary, authored by **Ānandavardhana** during the reign of king **Avantivarman** (855–884 CE) of Kashmir. *See also* LITERATURE.

DIDDĀ. Literally elder sister, a name bestowed on her by her subjects, was the wife of a ruler of Kashmir named Kṣemagupta. She exercised influence during his reign as well as those of her son and grandson, ultimately ascending the throne as an independent queen (c. 980/1 to 1003 CE). Her name figures on **coins** and in **inscriptions**; she was also remembered as a ruler who undertook building activities on a large scale. She appointed her nephew as her successor. *See also* KINGSHIP; WOMEN.

DIDWANA. Lower **Paleolithic** (c. 400,000 years BP) site in Rajasthan, with evidence of occupation up to the **Mesolithic** phase. Dates for the Middle Paleolithic phase range around c. 150,000 BP. Finds include blade and flake **tools**, hand axes, and microliths.

DIGAMBARA. Sanskrit/Prakrit term meaning "sky-clad," used for one of the two major sects that emerged within **Jainism**. The distinctive features of this tradition include an insistence on giving up clothes, considered symbolic of property. According to later tradition, the split between the Digambaras and the **Śvetāmbaras** developed c. early third century BCE, when a section of the community led by **Bhadrabāhu** that migrated to Karnataka because of a **famine** in the north retained the ancient practice of abandoning the use of clothes whereas those who remained in the north under the leadership of **Sthūlabhadra** adopted the use of white clothes, arguing that these were necessary in a situation of social crisis. The Digambaras believe that **women** are incapable of attaining *mokṣa* or liberation unless they are reborn as men. Besides, they believe that the Jaina canonical texts were lost, c. second century BCE. The Digamabaras were particularly influential in south India. *See also* KUNDAKUNDA; *MAHĀPURĀṆA*; *YAŚASTILAKA CAMPU*.

DĪGHA NIKĀYA*. Pali** text, part of the ***Sutta Piṭaka, compiled c. fourth century BCE. The name of the text is derived from the fact that it is an anthology of some of the longest discourses attributed to the **Buddha**. It includes the *Mahāparinibbāna Sutta*, describing the last journey and death of the Buddha. *See also* KINGSHIP, THEORIES OF ORIGIN.

DIGVIJAYA*. Sanskrit** term meaning "conquest of the directions." Some of the earliest references to the concept occur in the context of the ***aśvamedha **sacrifice** (early first millennium BCE). It is evident that the **Mauryan** emperor **Asoka** developed his ideal of ***dhamma*** *vijaya* as a contrast to that of *digvijaya* associated with earlier and contemporary notions of **kingship**. However, *digvijaya* retained its significance as an ideal, and several kings, including the **Gupta** ruler **Samudragupta**, claimed to have successfully realized this goal. Such achievements were often commemorated in **inscriptions**. *See also* LALITĀDITYA MUKTĀPĪḌA.

DIHAR. Archaeological site in West Bengal, with evidence of two major occupational phases. Period I (c. late second millennium–early first millennium BCE?) is considered **Chalcolithic**. Finds include a wide variety of bone **tools**, microliths, **black and red ware**, **black slipped ware**, **copper** ornaments, and traces of huts. Finds from

Period II (**early historic**, mid–first millennium BCE onward) consisted of **iron** artifacts, silver **punch-marked** and **cast** copper **coins**, **terracotta** figurines, and beads of semiprecious stone.

DINNĀGA (1). Buddhist logician (c. fifth century CE), belonging to the **Sarvāstivādin** tradition, author of a **Sanskrit** text, the *Pramāṇasamuccaya*, in which he refuted the arguments of the ***Nyāya sūtras***. *See also* LITERATURE; *YOGĀCĀRA*.

DINNĀGA (2). Sanskrit playwright (c. sixth–seventh century CE) who composed a play, the *Kundamālā*, based on the last section of the ***Rāmāyaṇa***, dealing with the banishment of Sītā, the birth of her children, and her reconciliation with **Rāma**. *See also* LITERATURE.

DIODORUS SICULUS. Greek historian (c. first century BCE–first century CE) who traveled through Europe and Asia and compiled the *Bibliotheca Historica*, in 40 parts, providing a historical account from the remote past to the time of Julius Caesar. His work included quotations from earlier texts that are now lost. *See also INDICA*; TRAVELERS' ACCOUNTS.

DIONYSIUS. Greek envoy, sent (c. third century BCE) by **Ptolemy Philadelphus** of Egypt, to the court of either of the **Mauryan** rulers, **Bindusāra** or **Asoka**, at **Pāṭaliputra**.

DĪPAVAMSA*.** The earliest **Pali** chronicle available from Sri Lanka, compiled c. fourth century CE. It consists of verse interspersed with prose. It contains an account, not necessarily historically accurate, of the **Buddha**'s visit to Sri Lanka, the **Buddhist Councils**, the reign of **Asoka**, and the visit of the latter's son, **Mahinda**, to the island. It also chronicles the compilation of the ***Tripiṭaka during the reign of the Sinhalese **king** Vattha gāmini. *See also* LITERATURE.

DISPOSAL OF THE DEAD. Archaeological evidence indicates that **burial** was among the earliest modes of disposal of the dead practiced in the subcontinent. Burials have been found from **Mesolithic** sites such as **Sarai Nahar Rai**, **Langhnaj**, **Bagor**, and **Lekhahia**. Several **Harappan** sites have yielded evidence of cemeteries located outside the settlement, with indications of cremation, fractional burials, and full burials. Burials are also in evidence at **Neolithic** sites such as **Burzahom** and **Brahmagiri** and at **Chalcolithic** sites such as **Daimabad** and **Inamgaon**.

The ***Ṛgveda*** contains hymns that were used during rituals associated with the dead. Later texts, including the **Gṛhyasūtras**, **Dharmasūtras**, and **Dharmaśāstras** laid down the ritual for cremation. Death was supposed to lead to a period of ritual impurity, which affected all those who were close to the deceased. The termination of this inauspicious phase was marked by the *śrāddha*, literally a ritual in which respects were offered to the departed soul, who was also assimilated to the category of deceased paternal ancestors. Participants in the ritual included close kinsmen, especially those who shared a common patrilineage. Variations were introduced based on ***varṇa***. Men and **women** who had violated social norms were denied access to the ritual. The norms laid down in the texts were probably followed by some but not all sections of society.

Variant practices are indicated by finds of **megaliths** in the Deccan and in south India. Another significant alternative was provided by the **Buddhist** practice of burying relics from the human body (among other things) in certain ***stūpas***. *See also SATĪ.*

***DIVYĀVADĀNA*.** **Sanskrit** anthology of stories in prose and verse dealing with the life of the **Buddha** and **Bodhisattvas**, compiled c. third–fourth centuries CE. Although it contains references to figures like **Asoka**, it is not particularly reliable for the reconstruction of historical events. *See also* LITERATURE.

ḌOMBA*.** Social category associated with handling the dead, often regarded as **untouchable** or low by ***brāhmaṇas **(1)**. By the 10th century, some *ḍombas*, who included entertainers, evidently occupied significant positions in the royal court in Kashmir, with their **womenfolk** gaining the status of wives of the **king**.

DONDER KHERA. **Archaeological** site in Rajasthan. The earliest occupation (c. second millennium BCE?) was **Chalcolithic**, with finds of **black and red ware**. Finds from the second phase (c. first millennium BCE) included **Painted Grey Ware** and **copper**, **iron**, and

terracotta artifacts. **Sculptures** of **Brahmanical** and **Jaina** deities were also recovered from the site.

DRAMA. Theatrical performance in early India is best known from **Sanskrit** plays composed by playwrights such as **Bhāsa**, **Śūdraka**, **Kālidāsa**, and **Bhavabhūti**. It is possible that performative traditions emerged from ritual contexts: Certain **Vedic sacrifices**, for instance, included dialogues to be chanted by the priests and other participants. Most of the extant plays draw on themes from the Sanskrit **epics** and the **Purāṇas**, which were often adapted to focus on themes of love and valor, two of the major preoccupations of royalty. It is likely that these were meant to be performed at the royal court or for audiences that included the urban elite. Virtually all plays had a happy ending, and most plays included a stock character known as the *vidūṣaka*, a ***brāhmaṇa*** **(1)** who acted as a foil to the royal hero and generally provided comic relief.

Dialogue in Sanskrit was reserved for elite men: **Women**, men of "low" status, and the *vidūṣaka* were expected to converse in various forms of **Prakrit**. By c. sixth century CE, an attempt was made to codify dramatic praxis in the ***Nāṭyaśāstra*** attributed to **Bharata (2)**. This laid down norms of performance, the social categories involved, **language** to be used, structure and themes of plays, and the kinds of gesture, **music**, costumes, and so on that were to be used. The extent to which these norms were actually followed is uncertain, as extant plays do not always conform to these prescriptions. It is also likely that there were popular performative traditions that were not codified or committed to writing. *See also* HARṢAVARDHANA; INDO-GREEK; LITERATURE.

DRĀVIḌA. Term used in **Prakrit** and **Sanskrit inscriptions** and texts (c. second century BCE onward) to designate peoples in south India in general and the **Tamil** region in particular. *See also* DEVAPĀLA.

DRAVIDIAN. Term used by Robert Caldwell in 1856 to designate **languages** spoken in south India, including **Tamil**, Malayalam, Telugu, and Kannada, suggesting that these were different from the **Indo-Aryan** languages. At present, pockets of Dravidian-language speakers are found in other parts of the subcontinent, and it is likely that this was true in the past as well.

DURGA. **Sanskrit** term, literally meaning "difficult to access," used in the ***Arthaśāstra*** (c. fourth century BCE onward) and other texts dealing with statecraft to designate a fortified settlement. *See also* FORTIFICATION.

DURGĀSAPTAŚATI. **Sanskrit** text consisting of 700 verses in praise of the **goddess**. *See also DEVĪMĀHĀTMYA.*

DVARAKA. Archaeological site in Gujarat. Excavations have provided evidence of three occupational phases. Finds from Period I (c. second century BCE) include **pottery**, especially red ware. Period II (c. first–fourth centuries CE) yielded evidence of amphorae. Period III (c. seventh–eighth centuries CE) was associated with remains of stone structures. Offshore explorations suggest that there may have been a settlement from c. 2000 BCE onward. Textual traditions including the ***Mahābhārata*** and the **Purāṇas** associate the site with **Kṛṣṇa**. *See also* YĀDAVA.

DVIJA. **Sanskrit** term, meaning "twice-born," used c. mid–first millennium BCE onward to designate men belonging to the first three ***varṇas*** who had performed the rites of initiation necessary for the pursuit of **Vedic** studies. In later textual traditions (c. first millennium CE), the term became virtually synonymous with ***brāhmaṇa*** **(1)**.

– E –

EARLY HARAPPAN. Name given to **archaeological** cultures (c. late fourth–early third millennium BCE) found in the **Indus** valley and adjoining regions, including the **Ghaggar–Hakra** valley, and Baluchistan (Pakistan). Each of these cultures was characterized by a distinctive ceramic tradition. Subsistence strategies were based on a combination of **agriculture** and **pastoralism**. There are signs of contact among these cultures. What distinguishes them from **Mature**

Harappan settlements is the absence of evidence for social differentiation, sophisticated **craft** specialization, writing, and public **architecture** (apart from rudimentary **fortifications**). Many of these sites were abandoned, others show signs of disruption, whereas yet others were resettled during the Mature Harappan phase. *See also* AMRI; BALAKOT; BALU; BANAWALI; HARAPPAN CIVILIZATION; KALIBANGAN; KOT DIJI; KURUKṢETRA; MITATHAL; NAL; RAKHI GARHI; REHMAN DHERI; ROHRI; SANGHOL; SISWAL; SOTHI; WARFARE.

EARLY HISTORIC PERIOD. Term used to designate developments in the subcontinent c. sixth century BCE onward, distinguished by the emergence of **cities**; growing use of **iron** equipment; use of **punch-marked** and other **coins** for exchange; growth of long-distance **trade**; intensification of **agriculture** in the major river valleys; social stratification in both urban and rural areas; the emergence of chiefdoms, **kingdoms**, and oligarchies in several areas; and the first documented **empire**, with its nucleus in **Magadha**. The history of this period has been reconstructed using texts and (c. third century BCE onward) **Brāhmī** and **Kharoṣṭhī inscriptions**, pointing to the revival of traditions of writing, which had disappeared with the collapse of the **Harappan civilization**. Archaeologically, sites that yield **Northern Black Polished Ware** and associated finds are often designated as early historic.

While some scholars suggest that there were continuities between Harappan and early historic cities, the differences in terms of environmental conditions, technology, as well as in the **script** are marked: These indicate that early historic developments originated in a context that was different from that of the Harappan civilization. Other developments associated with this phase include **philosophical** speculation and the growth of **Buddhism** and **Jainism**. The beginnings of **Prakrit** and **Tamil** literary traditions also date to this period. Developments in **architecture** include the earliest examples of ***stūpas*** and **rock-cut caves**. **Sculpture** includes some of the earliest stone images and reliefs and **terracotta** figurines. The terminal point of the early historic period is variously dated between the early and mid–first millennium CE. *See also* ARCHAEOLOGY; ARIKAMEDU; ASCETICISM; *ĀŚRAMA*; BABARKOT; BALATHAL; BANAHALLI; BANARSIHANKALAN;

BARYGAZA; BHIMBETKA; BRAHMAGIRI; CERA; CHACHEGAON; CHANDRAKETUGARH; CHAUL; CITIES; COURTESANS; CRAFTS; CUNNINGHAM, ALEXANDER; DEVANIMORI; DIHAR; EARLY MEDIEVAL PERIOD; ERAN; FORTIFICATION; KALYAN; KĀŚI; KODUMANAL; LAND GRANTS; MADURAI; MAHASTHAN; MANSAR; MARITIME TRADE; MAURYAN ART; SĀKETA; SANGHOL; SANKISSA; SEALS; SLAVERY; SRAVASTI; SRINGAVERAPURA; SUGH; TAGARA; TAXILA; TEXTILES; TRANSPORT, MODES OF; TRIBES; UJJAYINĪ; WARI BATESHWAR.

EARLY MEDIEVAL PERIOD. Term used to designate developments in the subcontinent c. early to mid–first millennium CE onward. According to some historians this was a phase of urban decay, accompanied by if not the result of the decline in long-distance **trade**. However, it is evident that while some **early historic cities** were abandoned or relatively less prosperous than before, urban centers emerged in other parts of the subcontinent, often around the nucleus of a market, **temple**, or political center. There are also indications that overseas contacts, including trade, continued, even though their specific nature may have changed. This period was also marked by the proliferation of **land grants**, generally made by the ruling elite to ***brāhmaṇas*** **(1)**. While some scholars have often viewed land grants and the rights conferred on the donee as exemplifying the weakening if not collapse of centralized political structures, others suggest that such grants were a means of agrarian expansion, especially into areas that were **forested**, with **tribal** populations, who were now often integrated within the ***varṇa–jāti*** system. Other developments include the increasing visibility of **Purāṇic** traditions, where the worship of local and regional deities was often integrated with that of **Viṣṇu**, **Śiva**, and the **goddess**. In terms of **architecture** this period is characterized by the emergence of structural temples, often embellished with **sculptures** of gods and goddesses. Taken together, these developments crystallized in the course of the second millennium CE in the emergence of regions—defined in terms of distinct sociocultural and linguistic features. Many of these regional identities continue to date. *See also* AGRICULTURE; ARCHAEOLOGY; *ĀŚRAMA*; CANDRAVAMṢA; CASTE; COURTESANS;

IKṢVĀKU (1); KINGSHIP; *MAHĀRĀJA*; MANU; PROTEST MOVEMENTS; RENUNCIATORY ORDERS; *SABHĀ*; ŚAIVISM; *SĀMANTA*; *SKANDHĀVĀRA*; SOCIAL MOBILITY; *ŚŪDRA*; TANTRA; YĀDAVA.

EASTERN GAṄGA. Name of a ruling lineage that acquired power in parts of present-day Orissa from c. eighth century CE. Rulers of this dynasty entered into matrimonial alliances with contemporary **Coḻa** and **Cālukya** rulers, although this did not prevent conflicts between them. The dynasty grew in strength from the 11th century. While its power declined in the 13th century, references to rulers of the lineage occur as late as the 15th century.

EIGHTFOLD PATH. Often regarded as a middle path between the extremes of **asceticism** and worldly existence, the path was recommended in early **Buddhism** (c. sixth century BCE) as a means of overcoming desire. It was regarded as the fourth of the **Four Noble Truths** and included the cultivation of right views, aspirations, speech, conduct, livelihood, effort, mindfulness, and meditation. Those following the path were assured of attaining ***nibbāna***.

ELCHURU. Archaeological site in Andhra Pradesh. There is evidence of a **Neolithic** occupation, with finds of handmade **pottery**, and remains of sheep, goat, cattle, and deer. Other finds include a **burial** from a circular hut, with grave goods including pottery and grinding stones. The **early historic** levels at the site have yielded lead **coins** of the **Sātavāhanas**, a range of wheel-made pottery including **Black and Red Ware**, shell and ivory bangles (the former probably manufactured locally), and beads of semiprecious stone.

ELEPHANTA. Island off the coast of Maharashtra, site of **rock-cut caves**, dating from c. sixth century CE onward. Within these caves are some of the most spectacular examples of stone **sculptures** pertaining to **Śaiva** themes. The site is among those recognized as a World Heritage Site by UNESCO.

ELLORA. Site in Maharashtra, with some of the most spectacular examples of **rock-cut architecture**, c. 7th–10th century CE. These include **Buddhist monasteries** planned, in one instance, as a three-story structure, lavishly decorated with **sculpture**. Other structures include the Kailasanatha **temple**, a spectacular **Śaiva** shrine, a free-standing structure carved out of a single rock, under the patronage of the **Rāṣṭrakūṭa** rulers, decorated with sculpture depicting scenes from **Purāṇic** mythology. There are several **Jaina** temples and monasteries as well, some of which contain traces of **painting**. Ellora has been recognized as a World Heritage Site by UNESCO.

EMPIRE. The terminology used in early texts and **inscriptions** does not differentiate between empires and other states. However, since the 19th century, modern historians have classified certain political formations as empires. This classification rests on a consideration of specific features such as the diversity of territories over which control was exercised, the complexity of the administrative and military apparatus, and indications of an imperial ideology exemplified in visual and textual traditions. There is at present no consensus about which polities meet these criteria. Generally, historians acknowledge that the **Mauryan** state was an empire. Other polities that are often but not always classified in the same category include those of the **Sātavāhanas**, **Kuṣāṇas**, **Guptas**, and **Coḻas**. *See also DHAMMA*; EARLY HISTORIC PERIOD; KINGSHIP.

EPIC. Genre of **literature**, term used by modern historians to designate some texts composed in early India, distinguished on account of their length as well as content, with a focus on themes of heroism. The four works that are usually so classified include the **Sanskrit** ***Mahābhārata*** and ***Rāmāyaṇa*** and the **Tamil** ***Silappadikāram*** and ***Maṇimekalai***. This classification was not recognized within indigenous literary traditions, where, for instance, the *Mahābhārata* was described as an ***itihāsa*** while the *Rāmāyaṇa* was considered as a *mahākāvya* or great **poem**. *See also CANDRAVAMŚA*; DRAMA; FOREST; GAṄGA (1); ILANKO AṬIKAḶ; MANU; SOCIAL MOBILITY; *ŚŪDRA*; SWAMINATHA IYER, U. V.; *VARṆA*; VASIṢṬHA; VIŚVĀMITRA; WARFARE; YĀDAVA.

EPIGRAPHY. Epigraphic studies began from the end of the 18th century. A major landmark was the decipherment of the **Brāhmī** and

Kharoṣṭhī scripts during the 1830s, with **James Prinsep** playing a major role in both these processes. Texts and translations of **inscriptions** were published in several journals and serial publications, including the *Journal of the Asiatic Society of Bengal*, the *Journal of the Bombay Branch of the Royal Asiatic Society*, and *Indian Antiquary*. The Department of Epigraphy, Government of India, was set up in 1883 under J. F. Fleet. With the publication of the *Epigraphia Indica* since 1888, inscriptions have been made available to scholars on a systematic basis. From 1890, a new series titled *South Indian Inscriptions* was published. Inscriptions have also been collated in special volumes in the *Corpus Inscriptionum Indicarum* series. Noted epigraphists in the 19th century included Bhau Daji, **Bhagwanlal Indraji**, R. G. Bhandarkar, **Alexander Cunningham**, Georg Buhler, G. S. Ojha, and E. Hultzsch. In the 20th century, the contributions of **Dinesh Chandra Sircar** and V. V. Mirashi were particularly significant. At present, the epigraphic branch of the **Archaeological Survey of India** is located in Mysore, Karnataka. Recent decades have seen collections of inscriptions published for individual states. However, publication and translation have not kept pace with new discoveries. *See also* ORIENTALISM.

ERAN. Archaeological site in Madhya Pradesh, with indications of occupation from the **Chalcolithic** period onward. Finds from the earliest period (IA) include stone **tools** such as microliths, animal bones, white-painted **black and red ware**, **pottery** with parallels with **Malwa** ware, **terracotta** figurines, and remains of a hearth. Period IB provides evidence of pottery with parallels with **Kayatha**, **Neolithic** ground stone axes, terracotta figurines, and traces of **copper** and bones. Other finds include evidence of bead making. Period II, assigned to the **early historic period** (c. 700 BCE–100 CE), has yielded evidence of **Northern Black Polished Ware**, **punch-marked coins**, an **inscription** in **Mauryan Brāhmī**, black and red ware, copper rings, pins, spearheads, **iron** chisels, arrowheads, swords and daggers, terracotta animal figurines, mortars and pestles, bone points, beads of semiprecious stone, and shell bangles. There is evidence for a mud-brick **fortification** wall. While a date as early as the Chalcolithic phase has been suggested for the structure, there is as yet no consensus on this issue. Period III (c. first–sixth centuries CE) has yielded **Red Polished Ware**, iron tools, shell and glass bangles, a stone image of a ***tīrthaṅkara***, a hoard of more than 3,000 punch-marked coins, coins of **Rāmagupta**, **Nāga** coins, and terracotta **seals**. Eran is also the find spot of inscriptions pertaining to the **Gupta** period and of **sculpture**, including a colossal image of **Viṣṇu** represented as a boar. The site was abandoned and then reoccupied in the 14th century. *See also SATĪ.*

ERICH. Archaeological site in Uttar Pradesh with four occupational phases. The first phase (Period I), dated to the period before c. sixth century BCE, is characterized by finds of **black slipped ware** and **black and red ware**. Finds from Period II (c. 600–200 BCE) include **Northern Black Polished Ware**, **iron** objects, traces of structures, **terracotta** beads, glass bangles, and **copper coins**. Period III (c. 200 BCE–300 CE) revealed evidence of a **monastic** establishment, terracotta sealings, and artifacts of bone, copper, and iron. Period IV (c. 300–600 CE) has been described as the **Gupta** phase at the site.

ERRAGUDI. Site in Andhra Pradesh, also known as Yerragudi, where a set of the **Major** and **Minor Rock Edicts** (c. third century BCE) of the **Mauryan** ruler **Asoka** has been found.

ESPIONAGE SYSTEM. While it is likely that most rulers employed spies, the institution is discussed at length in the ***Arthaśāstra***, attributed to **Kauṭilya**, the **minister** of **Candragupta Maurya** (c. fourth century BCE). According to the text, spies could be recruited from virtually any social category and could include both men and **women**. The functions suggested for spies included eliciting and shaping public opinion both within the realm and outside. They were also expected to carry out assassinations of those designated as the **king**'s enemies.

EṬṬUTOKAI. Anthology of eight collections of **poems**, the ***Ainkurunūru***, ***Kuruntokai***, ***Naṟṟinai***, ***Akanānūru***, ***Kalittokai***, ***Patiṟṟupattu***, ***Puranānūru***, and ***Paripāṭal***, part of the **Tamil *Sangam*** corpus. The first five deal with themes of love, the next two contain descriptions of heroic activities, while the last contains both kinds of works. The compilation in its final form probably dates to c. third century CE. *See also* LITERATURE; NAKKĪRAR.

EUKRATIDES. One of the last important **Bactrian Greek** rulers (c. 170–145 BCE), among the earliest to issue gold **coins**. Some of his coins, in silver and **copper**, carry Greek and **Prakrit** legends, the latter written in **Kharoṣṭhī**. It is likely that Eukratides overthrew the Euthydemids and advanced into the subcontinent to the **Indus River**. However, his control over the area was short-lived, as he was assassinated while returning after this victory. *See also* DEMETRIOS.

EUTHYDEMOS. Bactrian Greek ruler (c. 235–200 BCE), known from his silver **coins**. He came into conflict with the Seleucids to the west and the **Indo-Greek** rulers to the east. *See also* DEMETRIOS; EUKRATIDES.

– F –

FA HIEN. *See* FA XIAN.

FA XIAN. Chinese **Buddhist** pilgrim (whose name was earlier spelled as Fa Hien) who came to the subcontinent c. 399–415 CE. He came along the land **route**, entering the subcontinent from the northwest, then traveled through the **Ganga (2)** valley, and finally left for China along the sea route from east India through Southeast Asia. His major objective was to visit the principal sites associated with **Buddhism**, descriptions of which form a substantial part of his account. He also provided details about social practices, including the prevalence of **untouchability**. *See also* TRAVELERS' ACCOUNTS.

FAMILY STRUCTURE. Attempts to reconstruct family structures in early India have been made by historians, sociologists, and anthropologists, drawing on textual and **inscriptional** evidence. The ***Rgveda*** (c. second millennium BCE) suggests that while patriliny was prevalent, there was more than one form of household organization: Some households were headed by men, but others were jointly controlled by husband and wife. By the mid–first millennium BCE, **Pali** and **Prakrit** works indicate that among the elite (political, social, and economic) the former pattern had acquired widespread prevalence. The access to resources exercised by family members was regulated by the male head of the household, who was expected to ensure the well-being of those under his control. Generally, the male head represented the household on ritual and social occasions as well.

Brahmanical texts known as the **Gṛhyasūtras**, composed in **Sanskrit**, attempted to regulate life within the household. However, the norms elucidated in these texts were probably not uniformly followed. The household organization of nonelite groups, including the "lower castes," is far less visible in textual accounts and may have varied from the Brahmanical norm. There is evidence for regional variation as well, with indications that matrilineal descent was often recorded, especially in the Deccan and the rest of south India. *See also* INHERITANCE LAWS; MARRIAGE; WOMEN.

FAMINE. Famine is hinted at in some of the earliest texts, where, in the ***Ṛgveda*** (c. second millennium BCE), drought is described as a demon, with deities being invoked for its destruction. By the mid–first millennium BCE and subsequently, **Buddhist** and **Jaina** texts dealing with rules about alms giving contain discussions about situations of scarcity. A **Mauryan inscription** from **Sohgaura** also alludes to such a situation and measures to deal with it, and according to Jaina tradition **Candragupta Maurya** abdicated his throne and went to Karnataka with his preceptor when his realm faced a famine. It is possible that some of the measures for **irrigation** envisaged in texts and inscriptions were meant to mitigate the possibilities of food shortage. Storage facilities, found at **archaeological** sites, may have been used to stock grain to tide over such eventualities.

FOOTE, ROBERT BRUCE. Geologist (d. 1912), who in the course of his surveys (between 1863 and 1884) in south India and Gujarat discovered some of the earliest evidence of stone **tools**. He located more than 400 **prehistoric** sites during the course of his tours. These included **Paleolithic**, **Neolithic**, and **ash mound** sites. His catalogs and notes were published posthumously (1914, 1916) and formed the earliest systematic documentation of prehistoric finds in the subcontinent.

FOREST. Clearing of forested land for **agriculture** was a long-term process discernible at different points of time in different parts of the subcontinent. While its beginnings may be traced to the **Neolithic**, initial clearings were probably meant to be temporary rather than permanent. There is no way of assessing the extent of forest cover, and while several **archaeological** sites have yielded evidence of wild plant remains, this is as yet not sufficient to provide an understanding of the nature of forest cover in different parts of the subcontinent.

Forests find mention in a variety of textual traditions, **Sanskrit**, **Prakrit**, **Pali**, and **Tamil**. Some of the earliest accounts are found in **later Vedic** texts (early first millennium BCE), which include legends about clearing forests by burning them down. Most of the textual descriptions of forests were produced by outsiders, to whom forest dwellers appeared as enigmatic beings, who were often represented as barely human. Both the major Sanskrit **epics** contain elaborate descriptions of the sojourn of the protagonists through forested terrain. These and other accounts suggest that **ascetics** in general and ***brāhmaṇas* (1)** in particular often set up hermitages in the forest—while these were meant to be retreats from the world, they also served as spaces from which the forest could be explored and brought within the control of settled populations. In Tamil ***Sangam* literature**, the forest was represented as one of five environmental types, each associated with distinct modes of livelihood and emotional expression.

From the point of view of the state, the forest was regarded as a resource. Texts such as the ***Arthaśāstra*** suggested that ideally the state was expected to assert a monopoly over forests, especially those that were rich in timber and elephant herds. Other texts describe the exploits of **kings** during the royal hunt. Archaeological sites that have yielded evidence of wild animals include **Adamgarh**, **Ahar**, **Babarkot**, **Bagor**, **Balathal**, **Bara**, **Campā**, **Chopani Mando**, **Ganeshwar**, **Gufkral**, **Imlidih Khurd**, **Langhnaj**, **Mahadaha**, and **Narhan**. *See also* *ĀRAṆYAKA*; ĀṬAVIKA RĀJĀ; EARLY MEDIEVAL PERIOD; MAGADHA; *MULLAIPPĀṬṬU*; *NIŚĀDA*; PROTEST MOVEMENTS; PULINDA; REVENUE SYSTEMS; TRIBES; *VĀNAPRASTHA*.

FORTIFICATION. **Archaeological** evidence indicates that several of the major **Harappan** settlements were fortified (c. third millennium BCE). It is evident that fortification, known by the **Sanskrit** term

durga, was regarded as an essential feature of most urban centers by c. sixth century BCE. Texts such as the ***Arthaśāstra*** laid down norms for the construction of the ideal **city**. This was to be surrounded by a moat and walls, which were to be surmounted by watchtowers. **Megasthenes** described the **Mauryan** capital of **Pāṭaliputra** as being surrounded by a wooden palisade with 64 gates, surmounted by 570 towers. Traces of fortifications have been discovered from surveys and excavations at several **early historic** cities, including **Ahichchhatra**, **Chandraketugarh**, **Eran**, **Kausambi**, **Mahasthan**, **Mathura**, **Rājagaha**, **Sisupalgarh**, **Sravasti**, **Ter**, **Ujjayinī**, and **Vidisha**. Other sites with evidence of fortifications include **Babarkot**, **Balu**, **Banawali**, **Bangarh**, **Desalpur**, **Devangarh**, **Dholavira**, **Harappa**, **Jaugada**, **Kalibangan**, **Katra**, **Kuntasi**, **Nagara**, **Nindaur**, **Rakhi Garhi**, **Rehman Dheri**, **Rojdi**, **Surkotada**, **Sutkagendor**, **Vadagokugiri**, and **Valmiyo Timbo**. *See also* EARLY HARAPPAN; *MAHĀJANAPADA*; *SAPTĀṄGA*.

FOUR NOBLE TRUTHS. The cornerstone of early **Buddhism** (c. sixth century BCE), consisting of the following beliefs: that human existence was full of suffering, that suffering was caused by desire, that desire could be eliminated, and that the **eightfold path** was a means of attaining this end.

– G –

GAṆA/SAṂGHA. Form of government found in some ***mahājanapadas*** (c. sixth century BCE) and later states as well. Its distinctive feature was the absence of monarchy. The ruling class, often identified as ***kṣatriyas***, included, in some cases, several thousand men, who often constituted a militia. It is likely that resources such as arable land were collectively owned by these elites and were cultivated by **slaves** and hired laborers. **Assemblies** were a regular feature, and decisions were usually arrived at through consensus, although voting was known as well. It is possible that the *gaṇa/saṃgha* provided the model for **monastic** orders within **Jainism** and **Buddhism**. Both the **Mahāvīra** and the **Buddha** belonged to the ruling elites of these states. Important *gaṇa/saṃghas* included the **Vajji** confederacy.

Gaṇa/saṃghas were found in north Bihar and adjoining areas, and in the northwest, in regions such as the Punjab. The last of the *gaṇa/saṃghas* probably collapsed with the establishment of the **Gupta** Empire. *See also* KINGSHIP.

GAṆAPATI (NĀGA). Ruler (c. fourth century CE) mentioned in the **Allahabad Pillar Inscription** of the **Gupta** ruler **Samudragupta** among those who were uprooted by him in ***āryāvarta***. He is also known from **coins** found in the **Ganga (2)–Yamuna** doab and central India.

GANDHARA. Region in present-day Pakistan, recognized as a ***mahājanapada*** (c. sixth century BCE) in **Buddhist** tradition. Important **cities** in the region included **Taxila** and **Puṣkalāvatī**. *See also* ACHAEMENID; DARIUS I; MANUSCRIPTS; MENANDER.

GANDHARA GRAVE CULTURE. Archaeological culture found in the Swat valley, in present-day Pakistan, dating between c. 1600 and 500 BCE. The earliest sites have yielded **pottery** that has parallels with Central Asia and Iran, **copper** artifacts, and **terracotta** figurines. Other finds from later levels (c. 900 BCE onward) include **iron** artifacts. **Burials** associated with the culture were diverse: While some of the dead were buried in graves made of stone slabs, there were instances of fractional and postcremational burials in urns as well. Burials of horses with a variety of equipment as well as indications of contact with Iran and Central Asia have sometimes been taken as an indication that those associated with the culture spoke **Indo-Aryan languages**.

GANDHARA SCHOOL OF ART. Tradition of **sculpture** that flourished in the northwestern part of the subcontinent during the early centuries of the Common Era, attaining its fullest expression under the **Kuṣāṇa** rulers. Although secular scenes and people were depicted, the surviving examples of sculpture are predominantly **Buddhist**, including some of the earliest anthropomorphic representations of the **Buddha** and **Bodhisattvas** and depictions of stories from the ***Jātakas***. The sculptors often adopted Hellenistic motifs. These are apparent in the ways in which clothes, hairstyles, and even facial features were represented. Examples of such sculpture have been recovered from the northwestern part of the subcontinent, Afghanistan, and Central Asia. The tradition evidently declined by c. mid–first millennium CE. *See also* INDO-GREEK; KANIṢKA.

GANDHUR. Archaeological site in Andhra Pradesh, with evidence of a **Neolithic** settlement (c. second millennium BCE?). Finds include structural remains, pits, microliths, animal bones, especially cattle, and **burials**.

GANESHWAR. Archaeological site in Rajasthan. Phase I is identified as **Mesolithic** (c. 3800 BCE). Finds from this level consisted of microliths, with evidence of the local manufacture of **tools**. Phase II (c. 2800 BCE) yielded **copper** tools and weapons, such as arrowheads, spearheads, and chisels, as well as copper ornaments. Other finds included handmade and wheel-made **pottery** resembling that associated with the **Sothi** culture. There is evidence for stone huts with circular floors. Faunal remains included bones of domesticated cattle, sheep, goat, pig, dog, ass, camel as well as deer, rabbit, wolf, and fish. Phase III (c. 2000 BCE) is marked by the profuse use of copper, with several thousand artifacts found from sites located near the copper mines. More than 80 sites with similar cultural patterns have been found in adjoining districts. It is likely that these settlements were developed to take advantage of the proximity to sources of copper ores in the Aravalli Mountains. The site was reoccupied during the second half of the first millennium BCE, with evidence of the use of **iron** blades, lances, spearheads, daggers, knives, sickles, axes, and nails. Remains of furnaces, slag, iron ore, bellows, and other equipment associated with blacksmiths suggest local production of iron equipment. Other finds include **punch-marked coins** and remains of a **monastery**.

GAṄGA (1). Also known as the **Western Gaṅgas**, name of a ruling lineage that exercised control over southern Karnataka between the 4th and 10th centuries CE. For most of this period they were feudatories, first of the **Cālukyas** and later of the **Rāṣṭrakūṭas**, and had matrimonial alliances with both these dynasties. They evidently joined the Cālukyas in their wars with the **Pallavas**. The best-known ruler of the

Western Gaṅgas was Durvinīta (c. sixth century CE). Panegyrics in his **inscriptions** describe him as equal to **Manu** and the heroes of **Sanskrit epics**, versed in ***āyurveda***, **music**, **dance**, and both Sanskrit and Kannada. Bilingual inscriptions indicate that the Gaṅgas encouraged the use of both **languages**. The last Gaṅga ruler was overthrown by **Rājarāja Co<u>l</u>a**. The **temples** and the **sculpture** of this period suggest that the rulers offered support to both **Jainism** and **Śaivism**.

GANGA (2). Also known as the Ganges, one of the major rivers of the subcontinent, which rises in the **Himalayas** and flows in a southeasterly direction toward the Bay of Bengal. There is evidence of **Mesolithic**, **Neolithic**, and **Chalcolithic** cultures along the river valley. By the mid–first millennium BCE, several **cities** (many of which continue to be settled to date) and states emerged along the banks of the river, which served for centuries as a major artery of riverine and overland communication **routes**. The fertile soil of the flood plains of the river has been exploited for **agriculture** for centuries. *See also* GANGARIDAI; MADHYADEŚA; MAGADHA; *MAJJHIMADESA*; SECOND URBANIZATION; *UTTARĀPATHA*; YAMUNA.

GANGARIDAI. Kingdom, perhaps located near the delta of the **Ganga (2)**, mentioned by Greek and Roman authors (c. first century CE).

GANGES. *See* GANGA (2).

GANWARIA. Archaeological site in Bihar that has been identified with **Kapilavastu** on the basis of finds of **inscribed terracotta** sealings. Period I (c. eighth–sixth centuries BCE) yielded **black slipped ware**. Finds from Period II (c. sixth–second centuries BCE) included **Northern Black Polished Ware**, terracotta figurines, and **punch-marked coins**. Period III (c. second–first centuries BCE) yielded remains of mud-brick structures. Finds from period IV (c. first–fourth centuries CE) included **Buddhist** shrines, stone and terracotta **sculpture**, beads of terracotta and semiprecious stone, two hoards of coins, and coins of the **Kuṣāṇas**.

GANWERIWALA. Large, unexcavated **Harappan** (c. third millennium BCE?) site in the **Ghaggar–Hakra** valley, Pakistan. There are indications that it conforms to the typical twin-mound pattern discernible at sites such as **Mohenjodaro**.

GARAPADU. **Archaeological** site in Andhra Pradesh, with evidence of **Neolithic** (c. second millennium BCE?), **megalithic** (c. first millennium BCE?), and **early historic** (c. second century BCE onward?) occupations. Finds from the first phase include remains of animal bones as well as bone implements, stone axes, microliths, steatite beads, and handmade **pottery**. Finds from megalithic levels consisted of **Black and Red Ware**, **iron** artifacts, and beads of semiprecious stone. The early historic levels yielded **black slipped ware**, bangles of shell and glass, and lead **coins**.

GĀRGASAMḤITĀ. **Sanskrit** work on divination, composed c. first century BCE–first century CE, structured as a dialogue. It describes procedures of divination based on the observation of celestial phenomena, animals, bird calls, and so on. Divination was used to predict rainfall and the outcome of military expeditions, among other things. *See also* LITERATURE.

GĀRGĪ. **Woman philosopher** (c. sixth century BCE), mentioned in the ***Bṛhadāraṇyaka Upaniṣad***. The text records discussions in which she participated. On one occasion she acted as a judge in a dispute between rival philosophers. On another occasion she posed questions about the nature of the ultimate reality, and was evidently silenced by **Yājñavalkya**, a contemporary male philosopher.

GĀTHĀSAPTAŚATI. *See SATTASAĪ.*

GAUḌA. Name used in **Sanskrit** texts for a part of West Bengal, which emerged as a significant political unit c. mid–first millennium CE onward, especially under **Śaśāṅka**. *See also* VĀKPATI; YAŚOVARMAN.

GAUḌAPĀDA. **Sanskrit** author (c. eighth century CE), often regarded as the preceptor of **Śaṅkarācārya**. He is recognized as the author of the *Māṇḍukya kārikā*, a commentary on the *Māṇḍukya* ***Upaniṣad***. The work shows traces of **Buddhist** influence.

GAUḌAVĀHO. *See* VĀKPATI.

GAUTAMA. Traditionally recognized as the author (c. fifth century BCE?) of the ***Nyāya sūtra*** in **Sanskrit**.

GAUTAMĪ BALAŚRĪ. *See* GOTAMĪ BALAŚRĪ.

GAUTAMĪPUTRA SĀTAKARṆI. Sātavāhana ruler (c. 80–104 CE), known from **inscriptions**, especially those of his mother, **Gotamī Balaśrī**. These contain panegyrics of the ruler, who is described as controlling parts of present-day Gujarat, Rajasthan, Madhya Pradesh, and Maharashtra and as being victorious over *khattiyas* (***kṣatriyas***) in general and the **Śakas**, ***Yavanas***, and Pahlavas (**Parthians**) in particular. He is also depicted as a just ruler who upheld the norms of the ***varṇa*** order and as the epitome of physical, moral, and cultural excellence. He issued silver, bronze, and lead **coins**. *See also* JOGALTHEMBI; NAHAPĀṆA; PULUMAYI II; VĀSIṢṬHĪPUTRA PULUMAVI.

GAVIMATH. Site in Karnataka. Find spot of a **Minor Rock Edict** (c. third century BCE) of the **Mauryan** ruler **Asoka**.

GHAGGAR–HAKRA. Nonperennial river system, flowing through Haryana and the Cholistan desert of Pakistan. It is possible that the drainage flowed into the Rann of Kutch in the third millennium BCE. Surface surveys of the river valley have revealed dense clusters of settlement during the **pre-** and **protohistoric** phases, including the **Harappan** phase. It is likely that the river regime underwent changes and that the region experienced desiccation subsequently. The Ghaggar is sometimes identified with the **Sarasvatī** mentioned in the ***Ṛgveda***, although this identification is by no means universally accepted. *See also* GANWERIWALA; INDUS SARASVATI CIVILIZATION; KALIBANGAN.

GHANTASALA. Archaeological site in Andhra Pradesh, with three occupational phases. Finds from Period I (c. first–third centuries CE) include **rouletted ware**, a **Brāhmī inscription** on a potsherd, and **copper coins** of the **Sātavāhanas**. Finds from Period II

(c. third–sixth centuries CE), associated with the **Ikṣvākus (2)**, included a brick structure that may have been part of a shrine. Period III was dated to c. sixth–seventh centuries CE.

GHAṬOTKACA. Recognized in genealogies of the **Guptas** as the second ruler of the dynasty (c. fourth century CE).

GILAULIKHERA. Archaeological site in Madhya Pradesh, with four occupational phases. Period I (c. mid–second to mid–first millennium BCE) yielded **pottery** similar to that from **Malwa**, **black and red ware**, **Northern Black Polished Ware**, and **iron** and **terracotta** artifacts. Period II (c. fourth–first centuries BCE) was associated with similar finds. Finds from Period III (c. first century BCE–second century CE) consisted of iron artifacts and terracotta **seals**. Period IV (c. second–sixth centuries CE) yielded glass and ivory artifacts.

GILGIT. Region in north Pakistan, an important node along the **Silk Route**, associated with finds of some of the earliest surviving **manuscripts** in the subcontinent, written on birch bark. The manuscripts, dating to the mid–first millennium CE, consist primarily of **Buddhist** texts written in **Sanskrit**.

GILUND. Archaeological site in Rajasthan, with evidence of two occupational phases. Period I (c. second millennium BCE), considered **Chalcolithic**, provided evidence of mud-brick structures. Other finds included microliths, a range of **copper tools**, white-painted **black and red ware**, **terracotta** figurines, and beads of semiprecious stone. Period II provided evidence of a settlement dated to c. first millennium BCE.

GIRNAR. Site in Gujarat, locally regarded as a sacred mountain, with a natural rock at the entrance to a valley. Find spot of a set of the **Major Rock Edicts** of **Asoka**. *See also* JUNAGADH; TUṢĀSPA.

GODAVARI. River originating near **Nasik**, Maharashtra, and flowing southeastward into the Bay of Bengal. Several **archaeological** sites, **prehistoric**, **protohistoric**, and **early historic**, have been located along the river and its tributaries. The Godavari valley probably formed the nucleus of the **Sātavāhana** state. *See also* AŚMAKA.

GODDESS CULTS. The existence of goddess cults has been traced back to the **Mesolithic** phase on the basis of finds, at some sites, of stones smeared with red ocher, often regarded as symbolic of the goddess in later cultic practice. Goddess worship has also been inferred from finds of **terracotta** female figurines from **Neolithic** and **Harappan** sites. However, in the absence of corroborative textual evidence, these projections remain somewhat speculative.

In the ***Ṛgveda*** (c. second millennium BCE), and the **later Vedic** tradition (early first millennium BCE) references to goddesses are few and far between. It is from the late first millennium BCE to early first millennium CE that goddesses gain greater visibility in both visual and textual representations. **Sculptures** of goddess-like figures occur at sites of ***stūpas*** such as **Sanchi**, suggesting that these deities may have been incorporated within popular **Buddhism**. By the mid–first millennium CE, the goddess was represented in **temples** and in textual traditions as an independent figure and increasingly as the consort of **Purāṇic** deities such as **Śiva** and **Viṣṇu**.

Historians of religion have sometimes suggested that the multiplicity of representations and names of the goddess mask the notion of one universal feminine principle identified as a mother goddess. While this is plausible, it is also likely that distinct regional traditions as well as variations among the social groups who invoked the goddess may account for these differences. *See also* ADITI; *BHAKTI*; *DEVĪMĀHĀTMYA*; EARLY MEDIEVAL PERIOD; RELIGION; ŚAṄKARĀCĀRYA; *SATĪ*; *SILAPPADIKĀRAM*; ŚIVA; WOMEN.

GOLBAI SASAN. **Archaeological** site in Orissa, with two occupational phases. Finds associated with Period I (c. second millennium BCE?), considered **Neolithic**, included handmade **pottery** and pieces of bone. Period II consisted of two subphases. Finds from the first, **Chalcolithic** subphase (c. first millennium BCE?) included **copper tools** and ornaments, ground stone axes, saddle querns, a wide variety of bone tools, **terracotta** spindle whorls, **black and red ware**, and remains of circular huts. The second subphase yielded **iron** equipment. Throughout, there were finds of animal bones, especially of cattle, goat, deer, and elephant. There was also evidence for the cultivation of rice and pulses.

GONDOPHERNES. Parthian ruler (c. first century CE), who ruled over the northwestern part of the subcontinent, known from a **Prakrit inscription**, written in **Kharoṣṭhī**, found from **Takht-i-Bahi** and from **coins**. According to tradition, St. Thomas is supposed to have brought knowledge of **Christianity** to the subcontinent during his reign. *See also* SANGHOL.

GOP. Site of an early stone **temple** in Gujarat, dated to the period of **Maitraka** rule, c. sixth century CE.

GOPAGIRI. Ancient name of present-day Gwalior (Uttar Pradesh), find spot of **inscriptions** and **temples** dating c. eighth century CE onward.

GOPALAPATNAM. Archaeological site in Andhra Pradesh, occupied between c. first and fourth centuries CE. Finds include remains of a **monastery**, votive ***stūpas***, **rouletted ware**, **Black and Red Ware**, and beads of **terracotta** and semiprecious stones. Other finds include **coins** of the Eastern **Cālukyas** and some **Brāhmī inscriptions**.

GORAJ. Archaeological site in Gujarat, find spot of a brick **temple**, with plaques of **Viṣṇu**, **Śiva**, and other **Purāṇic** deities (c. 2nd–14th century CE).

GOTAMĪ BALAŚRĪ. Mother of the **Sātavāhana** ruler **Gautamīputra Sātakarṇi** (c. first–second centuries CE). She recorded the achievements of her son in an **inscription** at **Nasik**. This describes her as being generous, compassionate, truthful, and self-controlled and records the gift of a cave to members of the **Buddhist *saṃgha***.

GOTRA*.** A system of claiming descent from priestly clans mentioned in the ***Ṛgveda (c. second millennium BCE). *Gotra* identities were important in the ritual context. Later, in the **Dharmasūtras** and **Dharmaśāstras** (c. sixth century BCE onward), *gotras* were used to define exogamous **marriage** groups. On marriage, **women** were expected to affiliate to the *gotra* of their husband, giving up their natal affiliations. However, several **inscriptions** of ruling lineages from the Deccan indicate that this was not always observed. While *gotra* identities were particularly important for ***brāhmaṇas* (1)**, they were also occasionally extended to ***kṣatriyas*** and ***vaiśyas*** as well. Members of a *gotra* could exercise claims to **inheritance** in the absence of more immediate heirs. *See also* VASIṢṬHA; VIŚVĀMITRA.

GRAHAVARMAN. Maukhari ruler (c. sixth–seventh centuries CE), brother-in-law of **Harṣavardhana**, who was killed (606 CE) in combat with the combined forces of **Śaśāṅka**, the ruler of Bengal, and the contemporary **later Gupta** ruler.

GRĀMAṆĪ*. Sanskrit** term, literally "leader of a village," used to designate the village headman in **later Vedic literature** (c. mid–first millennium BCE). The *grāmaṇī* was often a ***vaiśya, who was expected to help the ***rājā*** in mobilizing resources from the village. It is likely that the position became hereditary in the course of time.

GṚHAPATI*. Sanskrit** term used to designate the male head of the household. While the earliest usage occurs in the ***Ṛgveda (c. second millennium BCE), the term became more common in the first millennium BCE. Texts such as the **Dharmasūtras** and the **Gṛhyasūtras** indicate that the *gṛhapati* was expected to function as the head of the household on ritual occasions. He also exercised control over the resources and residents, being expected to ensure the well-being of the latter. By the mid–first millennium BCE and later, the *gṛhapati* or *gahapati* (**Pali**) is also mentioned in **Buddhist** texts, where the term was often used to denote a peasant and was occasionally extended to large landowners or prosperous heads of households in urban centers. *See also VARṆA*.

GṚHYASŪTRA. Sanskrit prose ritual texts, part of the ***Vedāṅgas***, composed c. sixth–fourth centuries BCE, laying down procedures for the performance of domestic rituals, including rites of passage. *See also* DISPOSAL OF THE DEAD; FAMILY STRUCTURE; *GṚHAPATI*; *SAṂSKĀRA*.

GUDIMALLAM. Site in Andhra Pradesh, find spot of one of the earliest **Śaiva sculptures**, dated to c. first century BCE, combining a representation of the deity in an anthropomorphic and *linga* (phallic) form.

GUDNAPURA. Archaeological site in Karnataka, with evidence of a brick-built **temple** consisting of a central shrine, pavilion, surrounding wall, and platform attributed to the **Kadamba** ruler Ravivarman (r. 485–519 CE). An **inscription** of the ruler has also been recovered from the site. Other finds consist of stone **sculptures** of **Jaina** ***tīrthaṅkaras***. A range of artifacts including a **copper** casket containing semiprecious stones, ornaments of copper and silver, copper ingots, **iron** nails, **terracotta** figurines, and glass bangles have also been found at the site.

GUFKRAL. Neolithic (c. mid–third millennium BCE) site in Kashmir, with evidence for the cultivation of wheat, barley, lentils, peas, and of domesticated sheep and goat. There are also indications of hunting deer, bear, wild sheep, goat, and cattle. It is likely that this settlement preceded the better-known occupation at **Burzahom**. *See also* MALPUR.

GUILDS. Textual evidence points to the existence of guilds (**Sanskrit** ***śreṇi***) from the mid–first millennium BCE in north India. These included associations of both merchants and **craftsmen**. It is likely that membership of these organizations was hereditary. Toward the end of the first millennium BCE and subsequently, **inscriptions** from western India indicate that guilds sometimes functioned as banks, accepting deposits and using the interest for specific purposes. There are also indications (c. mid–first millennium CE) that heads of guilds played an important role in the local administration of **cities**. Texts such as the **Dharmaśāstras** occasionally recognized the rights of guilds to frame their own regulations. *See also* COINAGE; *MAṆIGRĀMAM*; MONEY LENDING; SEALS; SOCIAL MOBILITY; TEXTILES.

GUJJARA. Site in Uttar Pradesh, find spot of a **Minor Rock Edict** (c. third century BCE) of the **Mauryan** ruler **Asoka**.

GUMLA. Archaeological site in the Gomal valley, North-West Frontier Province, Pakistan. The earliest occupational levels provided evidence for microliths and bones of domesticated cattle. Subsequent levels yielded **pottery** having parallels with cultures in Baluchistan and **Kot Diji**. There is evidence that the site was occupied during the **Mature Harappan** phase (c. 2700–1800 BCE) as well.

GUṆĀḌHYA. Author (c. first century CE?) of the ***Bṛhatkathā***, a work that is no longer available, in Paiśācī, a form of **Prakrit**. *See also* KONKU VELIR; LITERATURE.

GUPTA. Ruling dynasty that established control over north India (c. fourth–sixth centuries CE). The origins of the dynasty are obscure, but it is likely that **Magadha** with its capital at **Pāṭaliputra** or eastern Uttar Pradesh was the seat of power, from where the rulers expanded their dominions through conquest and matrimonial alliances. The history of the dynasty has been reconstructed from **inscriptions**, many of which are dated in the Gupta era, beginning c. 319–320 CE, **coins**, and textual sources. The Gupta administration was perhaps less centralized than that of the **Mauryas**. It is also evident that the process of making **land grants** gained momentum during this period. The Gupta rulers patronized **Sanskrit**. Some of the earliest extant **temples** in north India were constructed during this period for the worship of **Purāṇic** deities, who were represented in **sculpture**. *See also* BAYANA; BUDHAGUPTA; CANDRAGUPTA I; CANDRAGUPTA II; EMPIRE; ERAN; *GAṆA/SAṂGHA*; GHAṬOTKACA; HŪṆA; IRON PILLAR; KĀLIDĀSA; KĀMANDAKA; KARDAMAKA; KINGSHIP; KUMĀRAGUPTA I; KUṢĀṆA; *MAHĀRĀJA*; MAITRAKA; MEHRAULI PILLAR INSCRIPTION; NACHNA KUTHARA; NALANDA; NARASIṂHAGUPTA BĀLĀDITYA; PUṆḌRA; RĀMAGUPTA; SAMUDRAGUPTA; SANCHI; SKANDAGUPTA; ŚRĪ GUPTA; UJJAYINĪ; VAISHALI; VĀKĀṬAKA.

GURJARA PRATIHĀRA. *See* PRATIHĀRA.

– H –

HĀLA. Sātavāhana ruler (c. first century CE), recognized as the compiler and author of the ***Sattasaī***. *See also* LITERATURE.

HALLUR. Archaeological site in Karnataka with evidence of two occupational phases. The earliest levels of Period I are considered **Neolithic**, while the later phases are **Chalcolithic**. Finds from Period

I included ground stone axes, traces of **copper**, and gray **pottery**. Faunal remains consisted of bones of cattle, sheep, goat, and deer. Plant remains included millet and rice. Toward the end of this phase, bean, gram, and *ber*, or the Indian jujube, were also recovered. Period II was **megalithic** (c. first millennium BCE), providing evidence of **burials**, **Black and Red Ware**, a wide range of **iron tools** and weapons, **terracotta** artifacts, and beads of semiprecious stone.

HAMADAN. Find spot of an **inscription** (c. sixth–fifth centuries BCE) of **Darius I** in Iran that mentions the Hindus among his subjects.

HARAPPA. Type site of the **Harappan civilization**, in the Punjab, Pakistan, on the Ravi, a tributary of the **Indus**. The site was badly vandalized during the 19th century, when its bricks were robbed to construct railway lines. The lowest excavated levels at the site, which contain evidence of the earliest occupation, have yielded **pottery** similar to that found from **Kot Diji**. Other finds include **terracotta** bangles and figurines, beads of semiprecious stone, and steatite. The next phase was marked by the beginning of mud-brick **fortification** and traces of town planning. The **Mature Harappan** (c. 2700–1800 BCE) phase at the site witnessed the construction of a walled citadel mound, with an elaborate, possibly ceremonial, entrance to the west. A structure identified as a granary has been located outside the walled area. Related structures include platforms, possibly for pounding grain, and 14 small houses that have often been identified as workers' quarters. Cemeteries were found on the outskirts of the settlement. These included one that was Harappan and another, identified as **Cemetery H**, with distinctive pottery and **burial practices**. *See also* MARSHALL, JOHN HUBERT.

HARAPPAN CIVILIZATION. Bronze Age civilization, first discovered at **Harappa**, Pakistan. At least three phases are recognized in the history of the civilization. These include the **Early/pre-Harappan** phase, the **Mature Harappan** phase (c. 2700–1800 BCE), and the **Late/post-Harappan** (c. 1800 BCE). The Harappan civilization is also occasionally referred to as the **Indus Valley Civilization** or the **Indus Sarasvati Civilization**. To date, more than 1,000 Harappan sites have been identified, distributed over an area of 1 million square kilometers, extending from Afghanistan to western Uttar Pradesh, and from Kashmir to the coastal areas of Maharashtra. Of these, about 100 sites have been excavated.

There were continuities with pre-/early Harappan archaeological cultures in the region in terms of subsistence strategies. Major crops included wheat, barley, pulses, peas, linseed, mustard, and cotton. Sites in Gujarat have yielded evidence for the cultivation of rice and millets. Domesticated animals included cattle, sheep, and goat. There was also evidence of hunting and fishing.

Many of the sites provided evidence for walled settlements. In several cases, the western part of the settlement, often described as a citadel, was both higher and smaller, and included public buildings. Brick size was standardized, and there is evidence for the use of baked brick at several sites. Systematically laid out drains and streets suggest town planning.

Typical artifacts found at Harappan sites include square or rectangular **seals**, generally made of steatite, containing visual representations as well as writing in a **script** that has not been deciphered to date. Other distinctive stone artifacts consist of beads of semiprecious stones, especially carnelian, and cubical stone weights crafted with remarkable precision. **Pottery** is distinctive as well. While pots were generally undecorated, those that were painted contained depictions of plants, animals, and geometric motifs in black on a red background. **Copper**, bronze, silver, and gold artifacts point to well-developed metallurgy.

There are also indications of long-distance exchange within the subcontinent, where Harappan beads have been recovered from sites such as **Burzahom** and **Kayatha**. Other regions with which there was contact include the copper-yielding areas of Rajasthan and the gold mines of Karnataka. Beyond the subcontinent, Harappan pottery, some bearing graffiti marks, has been found at Oman. Besides, Mesopotamian sites have yielded evidence of **seals** and beads. **Meluhha**, a region mentioned in Mesopotamian texts, was probably identical with the Indus valley.

While the ways in which **craft** production and long-distance exchange were organized are difficult to reconstruct with certainty, it is evident that the economy of the civilization was complex. The existence of statelike political structures has been inferred on the basis of the high degree of standardization in the production of a range of goods, evident in the archaeological record.

Efforts have also been made to reconstruct **religious** beliefs and practices. Some structures, such as the Great Bath at **Mohenjodaro** and the fire altars at **Kalibangan**, may have had ritual functions. The imagery on seals was probably derived from myths. One type of seal, depicting a figure seated cross-legged and surrounded by animals, has often been thought to represent **Śiva**. Some highly polished stones have also been regarded as symbols of the phallic form of the deity. However, attempts to connect Harappan religious beliefs with either the **Vedic** or the **Purāṇic** traditions are somewhat speculative and not entirely convincing.

By the early second millennium BCE, virtually all the urban centers were in a state of decline. This has variously been attributed to environmental degradation and natural calamities such as floods and earthquakes. It is also possible that the breakdown of political institutions and the complex economic networks with which they were inextricably connected may explain the collapse. *See also* ASCETICISM; BAGOR; BURIAL PRACTICES; CHANDIGARH; CITIES; CRAFTS; DAIMABAD; DANCE; DESALPUR; DISPOSAL OF THE DEAD; EARLY HISTORIC PERIOD; FORTIFICATION; GANWERIWALA; GHAGGAR–HAKRA; GODDESS CULTS; HULAS; IRRIGATION; KOTLA NIHANG KHAN; KULLI; KUNAL; LANGUAGES; LOTESHWAR; MANDA; MARITIME TRADE; MATHEMATICS; NAGWADA; PADRI; PROTOHISTORY; RANGPUR; ROPAR; ROUTES; SACRIFICE; SECOND URBANIZATION; SHAKTARI TIMBO; SHORTUG(H)AI; SURKOTADA; TERRACOTTA; TEXTILES; TRADE; TRADE ROUTES; TRANSPORT, MODES OF.

HARIBHADRA SŪRĪ. Jaina author (c. eighth century CE), belonging to the **Śvetāmbara** tradition, who wrote in both **Sanskrit** and **Prakrit**. About 50 works attributed to him are available at present. His major compositions include the ***Samaraicchakahā*** and the *Dhūrta kathā*, a compilation of stories about scoundrels. *See also* LITERATURE.

HARIṢEṆA (1). Court **poet** of the **Gupta** ruler **Samudragupta** (c. fourth century CE) and author of the **Allahabad Pillar Inscription**.

He was also designated as the *mahādaṇḍanāyaka* (**judicial** officer), *sāndhivigrahika* (**minister** of war and peace), and *kumārāmātya* (minister) of the ruler.

HARIṢEṆA (2). Vākāṭaka ruler (r.c. 460–478). Many of the caves at **Ajanta** were excavated during his reign.

HARIVAMŚA*. Sanskrit** text, an appendix (c. first century CE?) of the ***Mahābhārata attributed to **Vyāsa**. The text consists of more than 16,000 verses arranged in three sections. The first deals with the creation and previous incarnations of the deity, the second with the present incarnation as **Kṛṣṇa**, while the third contains **Purāṇic** narratives. *See also* LITERATURE.

***HARṢACARITA*.** A **biography** of **Harṣavardhana** composed by **Bāṇabhaṭṭa** (c. seventh century CE) in ornate **Sanskrit** prose. The text consists of eight sections, of which the first few are autobiographical. It includes an account of the ruler's ancestry, his early life, and culminates with his accession to the throne. *See also* LITERATURE; *SATĪ*.

HARṢAVARDHANA. Ruler (r. 606–647) belonging to the Vardhana lineage of **Thanesar**, who established control over north India. The Chinese pilgrim **Xuan Zang** visited his court and left a detailed account of the **king** and his kingdom. His court **poet Bāṇabhaṭṭa** composed a **biography**, the ***Harṣacarita***. He is also known from contemporary **inscriptions**. His sister, **Rājyaśrī**, was married to the **Maukhari** ruler **Grahavarman**. On the latter's death, Harṣa acquired control over his territories and made **Kanauj** the center of his power. Although Harṣa was fairly successful in north India, he was defeated by the **Cālukya** ruler **Pulakeśin II** when he attempted to cross the **Narmada**. Harṣa probably supported both **Buddhism** and **Śaivism**. He is considered to be the author of three **Sanskrit** plays, the *Ratnāvali*, *Priyadarśikā*, and *Nāgānandā*. *See also* BHĀSKARAVARMAN; DRAMA; NALANDA; PRABHĀKARAVARDHANA; PUṢYABHŪTI; RĀJYAVARDHANA.

HASARGUNDIGI. Archaeological site (c. early first millennium CE) in Karnataka, with evidence of a burnt-brick ***stūpa***, decorated with ornamental panels and surrounded by a limestone railing. Other finds include **Sātavāhana coins**, **terracotta** figurines, and shell bangles.

HASTINAPURA. Archaeological site on the **Ganga (2)**, in western Uttar Pradesh, identified with the capital of the **Kurus**, the protagonists of the ***Mahābhārata***. Excavations at the site have provided evidence of four occupational phases. Period I (c. second millennium BCE) yielded **Ochre-Coloured Pottery**. Finds from Period II (c. first half of the first millennium BCE) included **Painted Grey Ware**. There is evidence for the cultivation of rice and the rearing of cattle, sheep, pig, and horse. Other finds consisted of bone, **copper** and **iron tools**, and weapons, glass bangles, beads of semiprecious stone, and **terracotta** figurines. There is also evidence of flooding (c. eighth century BCE). Period III (c. second half of the first millennium BCE) provided evidence of both mud-brick and baked-brick structures and ring wells. Other finds included **Northern Black Polished Ware** and **punch-marked coins**. Period IV (c. first–third centuries CE) yielded terracotta plaques and **Kuṣāṇa** coins. Subsequently, there was a hiatus in occupation until the 11th century CE.

HASTIVARMAN. Ruler of Vengi in Andhra Pradesh, c. fourth century CE, listed in the **Allahabad Pillar Inscription** among those defeated by the **Gupta** ruler **Samudragupta**, but subsequently reinstated on condition of submission.

HATHIGUMPHA. Cave site in Orissa. Find spot of an **inscription** of **Khāravela**, c. second century BCE. The inscription, which is damaged, provides a year-by-year account of his achievements and records the dedication of a set of caves to the **Jaina monastic** order. *See also* UDAYAGIRI.

HATHIKERA. Archaeological site in West Bengal, with two phases of occupation. The **Chalcolithic** phase, Period I (c. second millennium BCE?) yielded bones of cattle and pig and traces of wattle-and-daub structures. There is evidence for the use of **iron** in Period II (c. first millennium BCE?), with finds such as sickles, slag, and pieces of metal.

HATHNORA. Site in the **Narmada** valley, Madhya Pradesh, from which hominid fossil remains were recovered. The identification of the remains within existing taxonomies of hominids and the stratigraphic location of the finds remain somewhat uncertain at present.

HEGGADEHALLI. Megalithic site in Karnataka (c. 50 BCE), with hundreds of graves including stone circles, cairns, and cists, some of which have been excavated. Associated finds include **Black and Red Ware** and **iron tools** and weapons.

HELIODOROS. A resident of **Taxila**, who was sent as an ambassador by the **Indo-Greek** ruler **Antialkidas**, or Antalikita, to the ruler of **Vidisha**, Kāśīputra Bhogabhadra, c. 140–130 BCE. He erected a stone pillar surmounted by the *garuḍa*, a mythical bird, regarded as the mount of **Viṣṇu**. The pillar contains a **Prakrit inscription**, proclaiming his faith in the **Bhāgavata** sect of **Vaiṣṇavism**.

HEMMIGE. Archaeological site in Karnataka with traces of three cultural phases. The first phase, considered **Paleolithic**, provided evidence of **tools** made of stone and fossil wood. Finds from the **Neolithic–Chalcolithic** (c. second millennium BCE?) phase included remains of huts and **pottery**. **Megaliths** (c. first millennium BCE) were also found at the site.

HERO STONE. Tamil *virakkal*, mentioned in the ***Sangam*** **literature** (c. third century BCE–second century CE?), stone memorials generally erected in honor of men who had died in battle. Actual examples of such stones have been found dating to the early first millennium CE, and are more prolific c. sixth century CE onward. The memorial often included representations of the scene of death as well as **inscriptions**. While hero stones have been found in several parts of the subcontinent, they are particularly abundant in peninsular India.

HERODOTUS. Greek writer (c. 484–430 BCE?) often regarded as the "Father of History" for his work dealing with the war between the Greeks and Persians. Herodotus was widely traveled; however, while he may have visited Babylon, it is unlikely that he traveled further east. Herodotus's description of India, by which he meant the northwestern part of the subcontinent, included within the Persian Empire in the fifth century BCE, was based on secondhand sources. It contains myths about the people and the land as well as more accurate information about the contribution in terms of men and money made by the Indians to the Persian war effort. *See also* TRAVELERS' ACCOUNTS.

HIMALAYA. Sanskrit term meaning "the abode of snow," name given to the range of mountains, among the largest in the world, which forms the northern frontier of the subcontinent. The mountains include some of the highest in the world. There has been a two-way traffic across the mountain ranges for millennia—with **traders**, pilgrims, and **pastoral** peoples negotiating the passes interspersed through the length of the range. Most of the major rivers that flow through the northern part of the subcontinent originate in the Himalayas. These include the **Indus**, **Ganga (2)**, and their major tributaries, many of which are perennial. *See also* DEVAPĀLA; *UTTARĀPATHA*.

HĪNAYĀNA. Sanskrit term meaning "the lesser vehicle," used c. early centuries of the first millennium CE onward, name assigned to **Buddhist** schools that emphasized the quest for individual enlightenment and self-realization as opposed to the **Mahāyāna** tradition with its belief in the role of **Bodhisattvas** in helping those in the quest of enlightenment.

HINDU. Term of Persian origin, derived from the name of the **Indus River**, initially used to refer to people living on the banks of the river and the lands to the east. It was adopted by the Arabs toward the end of the first millennium CE, and in the course of the second millennium, acquired connotations of people with cultural and **religious** practices that were different from those who professed Islam, including an acceptance of the ***varṇa*** order and image worship. *See also* DHARMAŚĀSTRA; HINDUISM; *YĀJÑAVALKYASMṚTI*.

HINDUISM. Name given by 19th-century Western scholars to a set of beliefs and practices prevalent in the subcontinent. These included diverse, occasionally conflicting theistic traditions focused on the major **Purāṇic** and **Tantric** deities and their incarnations, manifested in a range of devotional cults with varied practices that evolved over centuries through a process of interaction between **Brahmanical** and local or regional traditions. Histories of individual sects and of the entire complex of beliefs have been reconstructed primarily on the basis of **Sanskrit** texts composed and compiled by ***brāhmaṇas* (1)** and to a lesser extent through an analysis of **inscriptions**, **sculpture**, iconography, and **architecture**, especially that of **temples**.

These indicate that the support for specific sects varied over time—depending, for instance, on the availability of royal patronage and the support of influential social categories, including peasants, merchants, and **craftsmen**. Although the principal **Vedic** deities such as **Agni**, **Indra**, and **Soma** were relegated to the background by the first millennium CE, as was the practice of **sacrifice**, which was only occasionally revived, many, though not all of the relatively new traditions, explicitly acknowledged the authority of the Vedas. Although some sects developed critiques of the ***varṇa*** system, most Hindu sects accepted it. *See also BHAGAVAD GĪTĀ*; BHĀGAVATA; *BHAKTI*; MATHURA; MATURE HARAPPAN; RELIGION; ŚAIVISM; ŚIVA; VAIṢṆAVISM.

HIPPALUS. Greek sailor (c. first century CE) credited with the "discovery" of the monsoon winds. While the idea of the discovery has been contested by recent scholarship, it is evident that knowledge of the direction of the winds speeded up voyages from Africa and Arabia to the subcontinent through the Arabian Sea instead of along the longer coastal **route** and provided a stimulus to long-distance **trade**.

HIRAPUR KHADAN. Archaeological site in Madhya Pradesh, with evidence of lower **Paleolithic**, middle Paleolithic, and **Mesolithic tools**. Finds include choppers, hand axes, cleavers, scrapers, points, borers, and microliths.

HIUEN TSANG. *See* XUAN ZANG.

HULAS. Archaeological site (c. 2000 BCE) in western Uttar Pradesh. Finds include a **Harappan** sealing; **terracotta** objects; beads of faience, carnelian, and agate; bangles of **copper** and faience; and remains of rice, barley, wheat, millet, lentil, pea, gram, cotton, almond, and walnut.

HULAS KHERA. Archaeological site in Uttar Pradesh with evidence for occupation between c. 700 BCE and 500 CE. There is evidence for rice, barley, wheat, millet, pea, gram, and *ber*, or the Indian jujube. Structural remains include baked-brick houses ascribed to the **Kuṣāṇa** phase (c. first century BCE–first century CE). Associated finds consisted of a **seal** with a **Brāhmī inscription**, **terracotta** figurines, **copper** Kuṣāṇa **coins**, glass beads, bone arrowheads and awls, **iron** spearheads and axes, and storage jars. Finds associated with the **Gupta** period included terracotta figurines and a sealing.

HŪṆA. Central Asian people, often identified with the Hephthalites or White Huns, who reached the northwestern frontiers of the subcontinent c. fifth century CE. They were confronted by the **Gupta** rulers, especially **Skandagupta**. Subsequently, they succeeded in establishing control over the northwestern parts of the subcontinent and emerged as military elites in several localities. *See also* BAYANA; DEVAPĀLA; *DEVĪCANDRAGUPTA*; KUMĀRAGUPTA I; KUṢĀṆA; MIHIRAKULA; SODANGA; TORAMĀṆA; YAŚODHARMAN.

HUNSGI-BAICHBAL. Tributaries of the **Krishna River**, in present-day Karnataka. About 120 lower **Paleolithic** (c. 350,000 BP) sites have been found in the valley, suggesting more or less continuous occupation. **Tools** include hand axes, cleavers, choppers, knives, and scrapers, made from locally available stone such as granite, limestone, and quartzite. There are indications that the population was seasonally mobile, with a clustering of settlements around water sources during the hot arid season and dispersal during the rainy season. At some sites, there is evidence of stone boulders that were probably arranged to support structures meant to provide shelter.

HUVIṢKA. Kuṣāṇa ruler (c. second century CE), successor of **Kaniṣka**, best known from his gold **coins** depicting a wide range of deities, **Buddhist**, **Brahmanical** (especially **Śaiva**), and others worshipped in West and Central Asia. **Mathura** was an important political center during his reign. He is often identified with Huṣka, mentioned in the ***Rājataraṅgiṇī*** as the founder of a **city** in Kashmir named Huṣkapura after him.

– I –

I CHING. Chinese **Buddhist** monk (635–713) whose name was earlier spelled as I Tsing, who left China in 671, and came to India to study the rules of the Buddhist **monastic** order. He arrived at the port of **Tāmralipti** in 673, from where he went to the monastery of **Nalanda**, where he spent 10 years. He collected more than 400 **Sanskrit** texts and returned to China via Sumatra in 695. He translated 56 works from Sanskrit into Chinese and left an account of his stay in India, including details of the monastic discipline, or ***vinaya***, as practiced in India. *See also* TRAVELERS' ACCOUNTS.

I TSING. *See* I CHING.

IKṢVĀKU (1). Lineage of the hero of the ***Rāmāyaṇa***, regarded as the ruling family of **Kosala**, also identified as the **solar dynasty**, from which several ruling lineages claimed descent during the **early medieval period**. *See also* MANU.

IKṢVĀKU (2). Ruling dynasty (c. second–fourth centuries CE) that emerged in Andhra Pradesh after the decline of the **Sātavāhanas**, who were initially their overlords. While the **kings** were supporters of **Vaiṣṇavism**, **women** belonging to the lineage were patrons of **Buddhism**. Some of the best-known ***stūpas*** in the region were either constructed or embellished during this period. Sites yielding evidence of occupation during this period include **Amaravati** and **Nelakondapalli**. *See also* GHANTASALA; NAGARJUNAKONDA; SĀLAṄKĀYANA; VADDAMANU; YELLESWARAM.

ILANKO AṬIKAḶ. Author (c. second–third century CE?) of the **Tamil epic**, the ***Silappadikāram***. He was influenced by **Jainism** as well as **Śaivism**. *See also* LITERATURE.

IMLIDIH KHURD. Archaeological site in Uttar Pradesh with evidence of two occupational phases. Period I, assigned to the mid–second millennium BCE, provided evidence of animal bones, including those of domesticated cattle, sheep, goat, and pig and of wild animals such as deer, hog, and wolf. Plant remains consisted of traces of rice, wheat, barley, millet, lentil, peas, gram, and sesame and fruits such as *ber*, *amla*, and grape. Other finds included handmade **pottery**, remains of huts and hearths, beads, and bone equipment. Period II (c. 1300–800 BCE) has parallels with **Narhan**. Animal remains consisted of those found in the first phase and horse bones. This phase also yielded white-painted **black and red ware**, **black slipped ware**, **terracotta** beads, **copper** weapons and ornaments, and bone points. The topmost layers provided evidence of **Northern Black Polished Ware**.

INAMGAON. **Archaeological** site in Maharashtra, with evidence of three occupational phases. Period I (c. 1600–1400 BCE) yielded remains of domestic **architecture** including storage bins and hearths. There was evidence for **agriculture**; the rearing of cattle, sheep, goat, and pig; hunting; and fishing. Other finds consisted of stone **tools** and red **pottery** painted with black designs. There was evidence for **burials** within the settlement. Period II (c. 1400–1000 BCE) yielded signs of settlement planning, with areas reserved for potters and smiths as well as a granary. There were also traces of an embankment and a channel that may have been used for **irrigation**. Other finds included an elaborate burial, thought to be that of a chief. There was evidence of wheat, rice, barley, and lentil. The pottery in this phase had parallels with **Jorwe**. **Terracotta** figurines were also recovered. Period III (c. 1000–700 BCE) was identified as a phase of decline, when the settlement size shrank, associated with a phase of aridity, and sheep and goat **pastoralism** probably became the dominant subsistence strategy.

INDICA. Greek text, now lost, composed (c. fourth–third centuries CE) by **Megasthenes**, the ambassador sent to the **Mauryan** court by **Seleucos Nikator**. The text was cited by later authors such as **Arrian**, **Diodorus**, and **Strabo** and has been partially reconstructed from the fragments that survived as quotations. It evidently included detailed descriptions of the Mauryan administrative system, the organization of the **army**, the **king**'s daily routine, and contemporary society.

Owing to the inaccuracies and exaggerations in the text, the author has sometimes been considered unduly credulous; nevertheless, the account remains a valuable source for reconstructing the history of the Mauryan Empire. More recent historiography has contextualized the author's tendency to project the subcontinent as a utopia within contemporary Greek intellectual discourse, which may explain the narrative strategies and devices he adopted.

INDO-ARYAN. Name assigned by philologists in the 19th century to **languages** that emerged in the subcontinent, including and derived from **Sanskrit**. The ***Ṛgveda*** (c. second millennium BCE) is regarded as the earliest text composed in an Indo-Aryan language. *See also* BOGAZKOY; DRAVIDIAN; GANDHARA GRAVE CULTURE.

INDO-EUROPEAN. Name given to a family of **languages** by Thomas Young in 1813. These included languages derived from **Sanskrit**, Persian, and most non-Slavic European languages such as Latin, French, English, and German. It was demonstrated that these languages shared a common vocabulary as well as other linguistic features. The historical relationship among the peoples speaking these languages and whether they had shared a common homeland became issues of intense—often highly politicized—debates in the 19th and 20th centuries. *See also* ARYAN; INDO-IRANIAN.

INDO-GREEK. Term used to describe several ruling dynasties, possibly related to as well as rivals of the **Bactrian Greeks**, which controlled the northwest of the subcontinent c. second century BCE onward, until they were displaced by the **Śakas** and **Kuṣāṇas**. The best-known Indo-Greek ruler was **Menander**. Important **cities** within the domains of these rulers included **Taxila**, **Puṣkalāvatī**, and **Sāgala**. It is likely that control over **routes** of long-distance communication and **trade** contributed to the prosperity of these **kingdoms**. One of the distinctive features of Indo-Greek rule was the issue of **coins** with both Greek and **Prakrit** legends, the latter generally written in the **Kharoṣṭhī script**. A variety of deities and symbols drawn from the Greek pantheon and cultural traditions and from **Zoroastrian**, **Buddhist**, and **Brahmanical** traditions were represented on these coins. It is likely that Indo-Greek rulers contributed to the development of the **architecture** of ***stūpas*** in the region. They may have also laid the foundation for the development of the **Gandhara school of art**, and the growth of **Mahāyāna** Buddhism. It is from this period onward that Greek influence is discernible in Indian treatises on **medicine**, **astronomy**, and **drama**. *See also* ANTIALKIDAS; APOLLODOTOS; CHARSADA; EUTHYDEMOS; KUJULA KADPHISES; KUNINDA; MAUES; SILK ROUTE.

INDO-IRANIAN. Name assigned in the 19th century to the branch of the **Indo-European language** family used in Iran (including Old Persian) and languages derived from **Sanskrit** used in the subcontinent. These languages probably became distinct by c. 2000 BCE.

INDOS. Greek name for the **Indus River**, derived from the **Sanskrit** name for the river, **Sindhu** (used in the ***Ṛgveda*** and later texts), and by extension, the name of the land to the east of the river. The present name *India* is derived from this root.

INDRA. One of the principal deities of the ***Ṛgveda*** (c. second millennium BCE), generally represented as a warrior and as a generous patron of his supporters. He was associated with the chariot, and conceptualized as being armed with a thunderbolt. Offerings to Indra included the sacred drink **Soma**. *See also* HINDUISM; RELIGION.

INDRAPRASTHA. Capital of the Pāṇḍavas, the heroes of the ***Mahābhārata***, usually identified with a **Painted Grey Ware** site in present-day Delhi. *See also* KURU.

INDUS RIVER. Major river rising in the Tibetan plateau and flowing through the **Himalayas** in a southwesterly direction to the Arabian Sea. The earliest civilization (**Harappan**) of the subcontinent flourished on the banks of the Indus and its tributaries. The river finds mention in **Sanskrit** literature as **Sindhu**, also a generic term meaning "river," from which the province of Sind (present-day Pakistan) gets its name. It was the first major river system encountered by travelers and invaders, including the Persians and the Greeks, who entered the subcontinent through the passes along the northwestern mountain systems and referred to the people they met as Indians. *See also* CHENAB; HINDU; INDOS; JHELUM; MELUHHA; MOHENJODARO; SAUVĪRA; SILK ROUTE.

INDUS SARASVATI CIVILIZATION. Name used for the **Harappan civilization** in some recent scholarship. The justification for the nomenclature rests on identifying the **Ghaggar–Hakra** with the river **Sarasvatī** mentioned in the ***Ṛgveda***. There is a dense cluster of **pre-/early Harappan** and **Mature Harappan** sites along the river valley. However, there are several sites in other regions as well. Besides, the suggested equation between **Vedic** literature and the Harappan civilization has been widely questioned. As such, the nomenclature of Harappan is considered more acceptable.

INDUS VALLEY CIVILIZATION. Name used for the **Harappan civilization**, especially in earlier writings, when most of the known sites were discovered along the **Indus River** and its tributaries. However, subsequent discoveries have indicated a much wider geographical extent. Hence, the nomenclature usually adopted at present is Harappan civilization, derived from the type site of **Harappa**, where evidence of the civilization was first identified.

INHERITANCE LAWS. Some of the earliest codifications of inheritance laws occur in the **Dharmasūtras** (mid–first millennium BCE onward) and the later **Dharmaśāstras**. According to these **Brahmanical** texts, inheritance was determined on the basis of gender, with **women** being either excluded or granted residual rights in the absence of other heirs. The only exception to this was in the case of ***strīdhana***. Birth in the first three ***varṇas*** was also considered important, with the ***śūdra*** being denied access to resources. Among sons, the eldest was often accorded a special share. Inheritance could be settled either during the lifetime of the father, if he so desired, or after his death. Disputes regarding inheritance could be resolved by taking recourse to the **judicial** system. It is likely that the impact of these norms was often limited, with customary practices and regional traditions shaping actual transactions. *See also* FAMILY STRUCTURE; *GOTRA*; *YĀJÑAVALKYASMṚTI*.

INSCRIPTIONS. Inscriptions constitute one of the most important sources for reconstructing early Indian history. These are found on a variety of surfaces, including stone, and metal, especially **copper plates**. Other metallic surfaces that were inscribed include gold, silver, and brass. The inscription on the **iron pillar** at Mehrauli, New

Delhi, is exceptional. Inscriptions are also found on potsherds and on **terracotta** artifacts, especially **seals** and sealings.

The most commonly used **script** in **early historic** inscriptions was **Brāhmī**. Paleographic studies have traced the evolution of the script from **Asokan** Brāhmī to several later variants. Other scripts in use, especially in the northwest, included **Kharoṣṭhī**, **Aramaic**, and Greek. The earliest inscriptions in the subcontinent were in **Prakrit**, with the use of Greek and Aramaic being confined to the northwest. The earliest **Sanskrit** inscriptions date to c. first century BCE, which was also the period from which **Tamil** inscriptions have been found. From the second half of the first millennium CE, there is evidence of bilingual inscriptions (in Sanskrit and regional **languages** such as Tamil, Telugu, and Kannada) especially in south India. Prakrit ceased to be an inscriptional language around the same time.

While most inscriptions were in prose, there were several inscriptions in verse as well as a combination of prose and verse. Inscriptions varied considerably in length—some consisting of not more than a couple of words, whereas others ran into several lines. Some inscriptions contained dates in regnal years or one of the several eras that were in use in early India. Others have been dated on the basis of paleography.

In terms of contents, inscriptions are often classified as votive or panegyric. However, these are not watertight categories, and there is often an overlap—votive inscriptions often included praise of the donor and/or donee. Another category that overlaps is memorial inscriptions, often part of **hero stones**. Besides, some of the major inscriptions, such as those of Asoka, do not fall into either category. In some instances, **sculpture** or images were accompanied by label inscriptions. Votive inscriptions recorded grants of **architectural** features such as pillars or pavement slabs or sculptural elements, including images; they also recorded the construction and donation of more substantial structures, such as **temples** and caves, or the development of public works such as **irrigation** facilities. While many votive inscriptions were short, others, especially **land grants** that were recorded on copper plates, tended to be long, including genealogies of the donor and donee and details of the land that was donated.

Inscriptions have been used to reconstruct political history, including genealogies of ruling lineages. They also generally provide relatively secure chronologies and details of administrative structures. Land grant inscriptions, in particular, have been used to reconstruct economic processes and the histories of social groups and **religious** sects. Several inscriptions have been studied as literary works and thus constitute a resource for reconstructing cultural history as well. Besides, where label inscriptions are available with sculpture or **paintings**, these are often used to date the visual material. The place-names mentioned in inscriptions and their find spots are often used to reconstruct historical geography.

Sites that have yielded inscriptions include **Adichannallur**, **Amaravati**, **Apsadh**, **Arambha**, **Arikamedu**, **Banavasi**, **Bangarh**, **Barabar**, **Bhita**, **Bhorgarh**, **Bogazkoy**, **Brass**, **Chandraketugarh**, **Dangwada**, **Devanimori**, **Dholavira**, **Eran**, **Ghantasala**, **Gopagiri**, **Gopalapatnam**, **Gudnapura**, **Hamadan**, **Hulas Khera**, **Jetavana**, **Junnar**, **Kanaganahalli**, **Kanheri**, **Karle**, **Kasrawad**, **Kausambi**, **Khajuri**, **Khandagiri**, **Kodumanal**, **Korkai**, **Kumrahar**, **Kusinagara**, **Lalitagiri**, **Mahasthan**, **Malhar**, **Mandhal**, **Mayiladumparai**, **Nagara**, **Nagari**, **Nanaghat**, **Naqsh-i-Rustum**, **Nasik**, **Padri**, **Pauni**, **Pavurallakonda**, **Pehoa**, **Persepolis**, **Rabatak**, **Sanchi**, **Sanghol**, **Sarnath**, **Surkh Kotal**, **Thanesar**, **Thanjavur**, **Thotlakonda**, **Udaygiri**, **Ujjayinī**, **Uraiyur**, **Vaddamanu**, **Vadgaon Madhavpur**, and **Vidisha**. *See also* AIHOLE INSCRIPTION; ALLAHABAD PILLAR INSCRIPTION; ASOKAN INSCRIPTIONS; COINAGE; CO<u>L</u>A; CRAFTS; *DĀNA*; DEVAPĀLA; DHARMAPĀLA; DHOLAVIRA; *DIGVIJAYA*; EPIGRAPHY; GAUTAMĪPUTRA SĀTAKARṆI; GONDOPHERNES; GUILDS; GUPTA; HARṢAVARDHANA; HATHIGUMPHA; HELIODOROS; HINDUISM; *JĀTAKA*; KINSHIP SYSTEMS; LANDOWNERSHIP; MACKENZIE, COLIN; NUMISMATICS; *PRAŚASTI*; PRATIHĀRA; PROTEST MOVEMENTS; SACRIFICE; SĀTAVĀHANA; SOCIAL MOBILITY; SOHGAURA; *ŚŪDRA*; TAMIL BRĀHMĪ INSCRIPTIONS; *VAIŚYA*; *VĀJAPEYA*; VIṢṆUKUṆḌIN; WARFARE; WOMEN; YAŚODHARMAN.

IRON AGE. The earliest instances of the use of iron in the subcontinent may date to c. second half of the second millennium BCE. However, it is only in the first millennium BCE that the use of iron for making a range of **tools** and weapons became far more prolific. Unambiguous textual references to the metal also date to the first millennium BCE. In the northwest, iron equipment was found in sites of the **Gandhara Grave Culture**, and date to c. 900–800 BCE. Finds of iron associated with **Painted Grey Ware** levels in the **Ganga (2)** valley pertain to the same period. Iron artifacts were also found in association with **megaliths**, both in central and south India. Related finds include **Black and Red Ware**. In most of these regions, iron ores are available locally. The earliest finds consisted of small hunting and fishing tools. Subsequently, weapons and tools for **agriculture** and **craft** production became more important. The proliferation of the use of iron is associated with the **Northern Black Polished Ware** phase, c. 600 BCE onward. The most spectacular use of iron is seen in the **Iron Pillar** at Mehrauli. Sites that have yielded evidence of iron artifacts include **Adam**, **Adichannallur**, **Agiabir**, **Ahar**, **Alagankulan**, **Alamgirpur**, **Arambha**, **Atranjikhera**, **Ayodhya**, **Bagor**, **Bahal**, **Balathal**, **Banahalli**, **Banavasi**, **Bhagimohari**, **Bharatpur**, **Bhawar**, **Bhimbetka**, **Bhorgarh**, **Brahmagiri**, **Brass**, **Cheramangad**, **Chirand**, **Dangwada**, **Dat Nagar**, **Dhuriapar**, **Dihar**, **Donder Khera**, **Eran**, **Erich**, sites of the **Gandhara Grave Culture**, **Ganeshwar**, **Garapadu**, **Gilaulikhera**, **Golbai Sasan**, **Gudnapura**, **Hallur**, **Hastinapura**, **Hathikera**, **Heggadehalli**, **Hulas Khera**, **Jainal Naula**, **Jakhera**, **Jaugada**, **Jhimjhimia Kalisthan**, **Jhusi**, **Jodhpura**, **Kakrehta**, **Kallur**, **Karkabhat**, **Katra**, **Kausambi**, **Kayatha**, **Khairadih**, **Khajuri**, **Khokrakot**, **Kodumanal**, **Koldihwa**, **Korkai**, **Kotasur**, **Kudikadu**, **Kunnatur**, **Ladyura**, **Lalitagiri**, **Lauriya Nandangarh**, **Machad**, **Maheshwar**, **Mahisdal**, **Mahurjhari**, **Manamunda**, **Mangalkot**, **Maski**, **Mayiladumparai**, **Mulchera**, **Musanagar**, **Nadner**, **Nagara**, **Nagda**, **Nainkund**, **Nalanda**, **Narhan**, **Nasik**, **Noh**, **Pachikheri**, **Paiyampalli**, **Pandu Rajar Dhibi**, **Pauni**, **Puduru**, **Raipur**, **Rajmahal**, **Sanghol**, **Satdhara**, **Sekta**, **Shirkanda**, **Sisupalgarh**, **Sodanga**, **Sonpur**, **Sravasti**, **Sugh**, **Takalghat–Khapa**, **Takiaper**, **Talkad**, **Taradih**, **Tharsa**, **Thotlakonda**, **Timbarra**, **T. Narsipur**, **Tripuri**, **Tumain**, **Udayagiri**, **Ujjayinī**, **Utnur**, **Vaddamanu**, **Vaishali**, **Valiyapadam**, **Vidisha**, and **Wari Bateshwar**. *See also* COPPER; EARLY HISTORIC PERIOD; MAGADHA; TRADE; VEDIC ECONOMY; *YUGA*.

IRON PILLAR. Fourth century CE pillar at **Mehrauli**, New Delhi, more than seven meters in length, and with a diameter of more than four meters at its base. It is estimated to weigh more than 6,000 kilograms. It retains its anticorrosive properties to date. The pillar bears an **inscription** mentioning a king named Candra, which is in all likelihood a reference to one of the rulers of the **Gupta** dynasty. *See also* IRON AGE; MEHRAULI PILLAR INSCRIPTION.

IRRIGATION. Given the rainfall regime of the subcontinent, irrigation was important for **agriculture** in several areas. Traces of embankments, suggesting an attempt to regulate the flow of water, have been found in some **Neolithic** and **Chalcolithic** sites. It is also likely that some form of irrigation was used in the **Harappan civilization** (c. 2700–1800 BCE), although the exact mechanisms remain open to debate. From the mid–first millennium BCE, **Sanskrit**, **Pali**, and **Prakrit** texts mention wells and canals, and the **Dharmasūtras** and **Dharmaśāstras** contain provisions for regulating disputes regarding the sharing of irrigation water. From the second half of the first millennium CE, there are **inscriptional** references to the construction of tanks to store rainwater, especially in peninsular India. *See also* AGRICULTURE; FAMINE; INAMGAON; JUNAGADH ROCK INSCRIPTION; KULLI; *MAṆIGRĀMAM*; SKANDAGUPTA.

ĪŚVARAKṚṢṆA. Author (c. third century CE) of the *Sāṃkhyakārikā*, a **Sanskrit** text consisting of 72 verses, one of the oldest available works dealing with the ***Sāṃkhya*** system of **philosophy**. *See also* LITERATURE.

ITIHĀSA*.** **Sanskrit** term meaning "so it was," often taken to mean history, used to designate a genre of **literature** exemplified by the ***Mahābhārata.

– J –

JADIVASAHA. *See* YATIVṚṢABHA.

JAGGAYYAPETA. **Archaeological** site in Andhra Pradesh, with evidence of ***stūpas*** and **sculpture** dated to c. first century BCE.

JAIMINI. Recognized as the author of the ***Mīmāṃsā sūtra***, a compilation of around 2,500 aphorisms, grouped in 12 chapters, dealing with the **sacrificial** tradition. The text, in **Sanskrit**, is dated between c. 200 BCE and 200 CE. Several commentaries, including that of **Śabarasvāmin**, were written on the text. *See also* LITERATURE.

JAINAL NAULA. Archaeological site in Uttarakhand (c. first millennium BCE?) with evidence of **megalithic** urn and cist **burials**. Other finds include **iron** pins, nail, and a sickle and **Painted Grey Ware**.

JAINISM. Religious tradition that gained importance from c. sixth century BCE. The best-known teacher of the Jaina tradition was **Mahāvīra**. The basic tenets included nonviolence, truthfulness, abstaining from stealing, celibacy, and renouncing all worldly possessions, including clothes. The Jainas held that souls were present in all beings, whether animate or inanimate, and taught that the soul could be freed from the bondage of ***karma*** through the practice of austerities, final liberation being contingent on the complete renunciation of worldly existence. The emphasis on nonviolence meant that the tradition remained beyond the reach of peasants. It attained its greatest popularity among merchants. Jaina teachers used the **language** of the people for purposes of communication. Most of the early Jaina works were in **Prakrit**; later works (from c. seventh–eighth centuries CE onward) were in **Sanskrit**.

Jainism spread from Bihar to other parts of north India, including **Mathura**, and to Orissa by the turn of the millennium. The sectarian divide between the **Digambaras** and **Śvetāmbaras** crystallized by c. first century CE. Subsequently, Jainism spread to areas such as Gujarat and Rajasthan (where the tradition has a large number of adherents to date), Karnataka, Tamil Nadu, and other parts of the Deccan. During the course of the second millennium CE, the influence of Jainism declined in many areas in the face of competition from **Vaiṣṇavism** and **Śaivism**. *See also ĀCĀRAṄGA SŪTRA*; *AHIMSĀ*; *AṄGA* (2); *APABHRAṂŚA*; ASCETICISM; *ĀYĀRA*; BHADRABĀHU; *CAITYA*; CALENDAR; CANDRAGUPTA MAURYA; *DĀNA*; DEVARDHI GANI; *DHAMMA MAHĀMATTA*; *DHARMAKATHĀ*; *DHARMOPADEŚAMĀLĀVIVARAṆA*; EARLY HISTORIC PERIOD; ELLORA;

GAṆA/SAṂGHA; GAṄGA (1); GUDNAPURA; HARIBHADRA SŪRĪ; HATHIGUMPHA; ILANKO AṬIKAḶ; *KALPASŪTRA*; KHANDAGIRI; KHĀRAVELA; KINGSHIP, THEORIES OF ORIGIN; KONKU VELIR; KUMĀRILA BHAṬṬA; *KUVALAYAMĀLĀ*; MADURAI; *MAHĀJANAPADA*; MAHENDRAVARMAN I; *MAJJHIMADESA*; MĀNYAKHEṬA; MATHURA; MONASTERIES; *NĀLĀYIRA TIVIYA PIRAPANTAM*; *NĀYADHAMMAKAHĀ*; *NIRYUKTI*; PĀRŚVA; *PAUMACARIYA*; PHILOSOPHY; PROTEST MOVEMENTS; RĀṢṬRAKŪṬA; RENUNCIATORY ORDERS; ṚṢABHA; SACRIFICE; *SAMARAICCHAKAHĀ*; *SAMAYASĀRA*; SAṂGHADASAGANI (2); *SILAPPADIKĀRAM*; ŚIVĀRYA; SOCIAL MOBILITY; STHŪLABHADRA; *STŪPA*; *SUYAGADA*; TALKAD; TAMIL BRĀHMĪ INSCRIPTIONS; *TĪRTHAṄKARA*; TIRUJÑĀNA CAMPANTAR; TIRUNĀVUKKARACAR; TIRUTTAKKA TEVAR; TIRUVAḶḶUVĀR; TOLKĀPPIYAR; TOṆṬARAṬIPPOṬI ĀḺVĀR; UDAYAGIRI; UDYOTANA SŪRI; UNTOUCHABILITY; *UPADESAMĀLĀ*; VADODARA; VAISHALI; VALABHI; VIMALASŪRI; WIDOWHOOD; *YAŚASTILAKA CAMPU*.

JAKHERA. **Archaeological** site in Uttar Pradesh, with four occupational phases. Period I (c. second millennium BCE?) yielded **Ochre-Coloured Pottery**. Finds from Period II (c. late second–early first millennium BCE?) included **black and red ware** and **black slipped ware**. Finds from Period III (c. early to mid–first millennium BCE) consisted of **Painted Grey Ware**, remains of round huts, **iron** arrowheads, hoes, nails, sickles, hooks, knives, spearheads, slag, mortars and pestles of stone, **tools** of bone and antler, beads of glass and semiprecious stone, **copper** and gold ornaments, and **terracotta** figurines. Period IV (mid–first millennium BCE) provided evidence of **Northern Black Polished Ware**.

JAMBUDVĪPA. **Sanskrit/Prakrit** term, meaning "the island where the *jambu* (a kind of tree) grows," used to designate the subcontinent. Some of the earliest instances of the use of the term occur in **Asokan inscriptions** (c. third century BCE). The usage of the term became more common in the first millennium CE, especially in **Purāṇic** texts. *See also CAKRAVARTIN.*

***JANA*.** **Sanskrit** term occurring frequently in **Vedic literature** (c. second millennium BCE onward), used to refer to a people, **tribe**, or community. *See also JANAPADA*.

JANAKA. **Sanskrit** term meaning "father," used as a proper name for a ruler of **Videha**, identified as the father of Sītā in the ***Rāmāyaṇa***. Janaka is also mentioned as a **philosopher-king**, who participated in discussions with ***brāhmaṇas*** **(1)**, some of which were recorded in the **Upaniṣads** (c. sixth century BCE). It is uncertain whether Janaka is a proper name or a generic term.

JANAPADA*.** **Sanskrit** term meaning "the place where the ***jana sets its foot," used to designate territories that were often named after the ruling lineages of the people who settled in the region. References to *janapadas* became relatively common from the first millennium BCE onward. In subsequent texts and **inscriptions**, the term was often used to designate specific administrative units or the countryside, as distinct from the *pura* or the **fortified city**. *See also* ADAM; MADRA; *MAHĀJANAPADA*.

***JĀTAKA*.** **Pali** texts that received their final form in the fifth century CE. The *Jātakas* contain stories about **Bodhisattvas**, that is, the **Buddha** in his previous births. Many of these stories, which number more than 500, were probably derived from folk traditions. Each *Jātaka* contains a set of verses, which were regarded as canonical within the Buddhist tradition. Visual representations, and **inscriptions** mentioning specific stories, are found as early as the second century BCE from sites such as **Bharhut**. The former are also found at **Sanchi** and **Ajanta**, an indication of the long-drawn process of compilation and transmission. *See also* BUDDHAGHOṢA; GANDHARA SCHOOL OF ART; *KHUDDAKA NIKĀYA*; KINGSHIP; LITERATURE.

***JĀTAKAMĀLĀ*.** **Sanskrit Buddhist** text attributed to **Āryaśūra** (c. fourth century CE). It includes 34 didactic stories that have parallels in other Buddhist **literature,** including the **Pali** canon. *See also* LITERATURE.

***JĀTI*.** **Sanskrit** term used (c. first millennium BCE onward) to define social categories. *Jāti* affiliation was determined on the basis of birth.

Generally, members of a *jāti* shared a common occupation, and were bound by ties of **marriage** and commensality. These formed part of *jāti* ***dharma***, which was recognized, but not codified within the **Dharmasūtras** and **Dharmaśāstras**. *Jāti* and ***varṇa*** were often used synonymously. However, while the number of *varṇas* was fixed at four, there was no fixity about the number of *jātis*. Although *jātis* were often ranked hierarchically, the exact position of specific *jātis* could vary over time and space, subject as it was to complex negotiations. **Buddhist** texts recognized distinctions between high and low *jātis*, suggesting that this form of stratification had a fairly widespread prevalence. *See also* CASTE; EARLY MEDIEVAL PERIOD; *VARṆASAMṆKARA*.

JATINGA RAMESVARAM. **Archaeological** site in Karnataka, find spot of a **Minor Rock Edict** (c. third century BCE) of the **Mauryan** ruler **Asoka**.

JAUGADA. **Archaeological** site in Orissa, where a set of the **Major Rock Edicts** (c. third century BCE) of the **Mauryan** ruler **Asoka** has been found. Copies of the **Separate Rock Edicts** have also been found here. Excavations at the site have yielded traces of **fortifications**, **black and red ware**, **iron** artifacts, and **Puri–Kuṣāṇa coins**.

JAYAPĪḌA. **King** (c. ninth century CE) of Kashmir. According to the ***Rājataraṅgiṇī***, he embarked on a series of conquests in north India, with mixed results. He was a patron of **Sanskrit literature**. *See also* DĀMODARAGUPTA.

JETAVANA. Literally the grove of Jeta, located on the outskirts of **Sravasti**, one of the most famous **monasteries** according to **Buddhist** tradition. According to traditional accounts, the grove was purchased by Anāthapiṇḍika, a merchant who was a lay follower of the **Buddha**, by covering the entire area (with one small exception) with **coins**. He then donated it to the Buddha, who is believed to have spent several rainy seasons in this particular retreat. Chinese Buddhist pilgrims who visited the site during the first millennium CE left descriptions of it in their accounts. **Archaeological** explorations and excavations at the site since the 19th century have revealed remains of monasteries and ***stūpas*** and finds of **sculpture** and **inscriptions**. Most of the finds date to the first millennium CE.

JHELUM. A major tributary of the **Indus River** flowing through Kashmir and the Punjab.

JHIMJHIMIA KALISTHAN. Archaeological site in Bihar, with evidence of three occupational phases. Finds associated with Period I (c. first millennium BCE?) included **black and red ware** and **iron** artifacts. Period II (late first millennium BCE?) was marked by finds of **Northern Black Polished Ware**, **black slipped ware**, beads of semiprecious stone, and bone arrowheads. Period III has been assigned to the **Śuṅga–Kuṣāṇa** phase.

JHUKAR. Late/post-Harappan (early second millennium BCE) **archaeological** culture in Sind, Pakistan, identified from the type site of Jhukar and from sites such as **Mohenjodaro** and **Chanhudaro**. Its typical features include relatively poorly built houses, uninscribed **seals** that may have served as amulets, distinctive **pottery**, and **copper** and bronze artifacts, including pins, that suggest contacts with Central Asia.

JHUSI. Archaeological site in Uttar Pradesh, with evidence of four occupational phases. The first period (c. early first millennium BCE?) is marked by a **Chalcolithic** culture. **Pottery** includes **black slipped ware**, **black and red ware**, and **Northern Black Polished Ware**. In the second period (c. latter half of the first millennium BCE?), there is evidence of ring wells, and structures of both baked brick and wattle-and-daub. Other finds consist of Northern Black Polished Ware, **punch-marked coins**, cast **copper** coins, **terracotta** figurines, beads, **seals** and sealings, **iron** artifacts, bone points, and beads of semiprecious stone. There is also evidence of animal bones with cut marks, indicating that they were used as food. Period III is attributed to the **Śaka–Kuṣāṇa** phase (late first millennium BCE–early first millennium CE). Pottery includes **Red Polished Ware** and black and red ware. This period also yielded terracotta seals, figurines, and ornaments; copper and iron artifacts; and bone and shell objects. Period IV has been assigned to the **Gupta** period (c. fourth–sixth centuries CE).

JĪVAKA KOMARABHACCA. Physician, reputedly a contemporary of the **Buddha** (c. sixth century BCE). Stories regarding his skill were narrated within the **Buddhist** tradition. He was also known for his generosity, treating the Buddha, and members of the **monastic** order, free of cost, besides donating his mango grove, known as the Jīvakārāma, at **Rājagaha**, to the Buddhist ***saṃgha***.

JÑĀNASAMBANDAR. *See* TIRUJÑĀNA CAMPANTAR.

JÑĀTRIKA. Clan belonging to the **Vajji** confederacy, to which **Mahāvīra**, the most important teacher of **Jainism**, belonged.

JODHPURA. Archaeological site in Rajasthan, with evidence of three occupational phases. Period I (c. early second millennium BCE) yielded **Ochre-Coloured Pottery**, **copper** and **terracotta** artifacts, and stone beads. Finds from Period II (late second–early first millennium BCE) included **black and red ware**. Finds from Period III (early first millennium BCE) consisted of **Painted Grey Ware** and **iron** and bone **tools**.

JOGALTHEMBI. Archaeological site in Maharashtra, find spot of a hoard of several thousand **coins** issued by the **Śaka** ruler **Nahapāṇa**, which were restruck by the **Sātavāhana king Gautamīputra**.

JONES, WILLIAM (1748–1794). A judge of the Supreme Court at Calcutta (Kolkata) and founder of the **Asiatic Society**, he translated **Sanskrit** works into English, most notably the ***Abhijñāna Śākuntalam*** of **Kālidāsa**. He was among the first to draw attention to the linguistic affinities between Sanskrit, Persian, Greek, Latin, German, and Celtic as well as to similarities in the early myths and legends preserved in these **languages**. Much of Jones's work was structured within a Biblical framework of the unity of the human race. *See also* SANDROCOTTOS.

JORWE. Archaeological site in Maharashtra with evidence of a **Chalcolithic** culture (c. 1400–700 BCE), characterized by a distinctive **pottery** known as the Jorwe Ware. This is distinguished by its fine fabric, dull red slip, and black painted designs, which were generally geometric. Occasionally, there were potters' marks and graffiti. Common shapes included bowls and vases. It is likely that this tradition developed from the **Malwa Ware**. Other finds included stone **tools** and beads of semiprecious stone. *See also* CHANDOLI; DAIMABAD; INAMGAON; MAHESHWAR; NASIK; NEVASA; SONGAON; TULJAPUR GARHI.

JUDICIAL SYSTEM. Details of the judicial system and processes can be gleaned from textual traditions c. sixth century BCE onward. **Asokan inscriptions** provide insight into the system established and maintained by the **Mauryas**. Texts such as the **Dharmasūtras** and **Dharmaśāstras** attempted to define the scope and function of judicial institutions. Theoretically, the king was regarded as the head of the system, but there are references to local, autonomous courts as well. Judges could include ***brāhmaṇas*** **(1)** as well as prosperous members of the local elite. Scribes were also employed to record proceedings. Several categories of witnesses were recognized. Those who were thought to be incapable of acting as witnesses included **women**, minors, the disabled, debtors, and those who had renounced the world. The texts suggest that in many cases the ***varṇa*** of both the plaintiff and the accused were taken into consideration, and punishments could vary according to their status. A range of punishments was recommended, including fines, debt bondage in case of inability to pay fines, imprisonment, and the death penalty. *Brāhmaṇas* were generally considered exempt from the severest forms of punishments such as the death penalty, which was to be replaced by banishment. In some cases, penances were prescribed instead of punishment. It is unlikely that the system was uniform throughout the country. **Early medieval** texts recognized the scope for institutions such as **guilds**, and other associations such as **monastic** orders to frame and implement their own rules. *See also* INHERITANCE LAWS; LAND GRANTS; MAJOR PILLAR EDICTS; *PARIṢAD*; *RĀJUKA*.

JUNAGADH. Site in Gujarat, also known as **Girnar**, find spot of natural rock with three major **inscriptions**, including a set of the **Major Rock Edicts** of **Asoka**, an inscription of the **Śaka** ruler **Rudradāman**, and one of the **Gupta** king **Skandagupta**. There are traces of an earthen embankment near the site, which may have been part of the **irrigation** works mentioned in the inscriptions.

JUNAGADH ROCK INSCRIPTION. Name assigned to the **inscription** of the **Śaka** ruler **Rudradāman** found at **Junagadh**. One of the earliest known **Sanskrit** inscriptions, it is dated to c. 150 CE. It records the initial construction (c. third century BCE?) of an **irrigation** system comprising a lake, embankments, and channels under the initiative of the local governor appointed by the **Mauryan** rulers. This was damaged in a storm. Rudradāman evidently undertook repair works, and claimed that this was done without imposing any financial burden on his subjects. The inscription is an early instance of a ***praśasti***, and includes poetic, and somewhat exaggerated, descriptions of the ruler's genealogy, his learning and accomplishments, and his victories in battle. *See also* TUṢĀSPA.

JUNNAR. Archaeological site in Maharashtra, located near **Nanaghat**, with evidence of more than 100 **rock-cut caves** excavated between c. second century BCE and third century CE. Most of the caves were meant to serve as **monasteries** and ***caityas*** for **Buddhist** monks, although there are indications of **Jaina** establishments as well. **Inscriptions** indicate that the donors of these structures included members of the ruling elite and ordinary people and ***yavanas***.

– K –

KACCANA. Author (c. seventh century CE) of a grammar on **Pali**, known as the *Kaccana-vyākaraṇa*. *See also* LITERATURE.

KADAMBA. Ruling lineage (c. fourth–sixth centuries CE), which established control over parts of present-day Karnataka. The kings of this lineage engaged in a long-drawn rivalry with the **Pallavas**. *See also* BANAVASI; CĀLUKYA; GUDNAPURA; MAYŪRAŚARMAN; SANNATI; VĀKĀṬAKA.

KADPHISES I. *See* KUJULA KADPHISES.

KAHAUM PILLAR INSCRIPTION. Inscribed pillar found at Kahaum, a site in Uttar Pradesh. The **inscription**, dated to the **Gupta**

period (c. 460 CE), records the dedication of five images of **Jaina** saints and mentions the reigning king, **Skandagupta**.

KĀKA. Community living (c. fourth century CE) in central India, mentioned in the **Allahabad Pillar Inscription** of the **Gupta** ruler **Samudragupta** as among those who offered homage and tribute, and agreed to obey his commands.

KĀKAVARṆA. *See* KĀLĀŚOKA.

KAKORIA. Archaeological site in Uttar Pradesh (c. first millennium BCE?) with evidence of **megalithic burials** including cairn circles and cists. Associated **pottery** consisted of **black and red ware**, **black slipped ware**, and red ware. Other finds included microliths. Remains of habitations were also found.

KAKREHTA. Archaeological site in Madhya Pradesh, with evidence of five occupational phases. Period I, considered to be **Mesolithic**, yielded stone **tools**. Period II (c. second half of the second millennium BCE–early first millennium BCE) saw a **Chalcolithic** occupation. Finds included microliths, traces of **copper**, and **black and red ware**. Period III (mid–first millennium BCE?) witnessed the introduction of **iron**. Period IV was associated with finds of **Northern Black Polished Ware**. Finds from Period V (end of the first millennium BCE?) included the same **pottery**, glass bangles, and ring wells.

KALABHRA. A people or ruling lineage in the Tamil region (c. sixth century CE), known only from the **inscriptions** of the **Pallavas** and **Cālukyas**, who claimed to have overthrown them. It is possible that they were patrons of **Buddhism**. *See also* SIMHAVIṢṆU.

KALACURI. Name of several ruling lineages, not necessarily related to each other, that exercised power over different parts of the subcontinent at different points of time. One of the branches, associated with central and western India, was powerful from the sixth to the eighth century CE. Another, associated with **Tripuri** (Madhya Pradesh) was powerful between the 8th and 11th century. Both these lineages are known from **coins** and **inscriptions**, the latter including those of their rivals such as the **Cālukyas**, **Rāṣṭrakūtas**, **Pālas**, and **Pratihāras**. A third lineage of the same name exercised power in Karnataka in the 12th century. *See also* MAHIPĀLA (2).

KĀLĀŚOKA. Also known as Kākavarṇa, ruler of **Magadha** (c. fifth century BCE). **Pāṭaliputra** finally became the capital of the state during his rule. The second **Buddhist Council** at **Vaishali** was also held during this period.

KALHAṆA. Author (12th century CE) of the ***Rājataraṅgiṇī***, a history of Kashmir. A ***brāhmaṇa*** **(1)** and the son of an ex-**minister**, Kalhaṇa visualized his work as a poem, and attempted to judge past and contemporary rulers impartially. He evidently consulted a variety of sources, including **inscriptions**, royal orders, and earlier texts that have unfortunately not survived. *See also* LALITĀDITYA MUKTĀPĪḌA; LITERATURE.

KALI YUGA*.** The last of four ages that constitute a cycle of human existence according to the **Purāṇic** tradition (c. fourth century CE onward). Astronomical calculations made from the middle of the first millennium of the Common Era were projected backward to suggest that this age, which is supposed to continue to the present, began from 3102 BCE. The *Kali yuga* was generally portrayed in the Purāṇas as a time of decline from the point of view of the dominant social groups, a time when social norms were violated, and the privileges of the ***brāhmaṇas (1) were called into question. *See also* *KALPA* (2); *YUGA*.

KALIBANGAN. Pre-/early Harappan site (c. early third millennium BCE) in the **Ghaggar** valley (Rajasthan), named after the black **terracotta** bangles found on the surface. Two major occupational phases have been identified. Period I yielded traces of a plowed field and structural remains, including mud-brick **architecture**, with ovens and storage pits. There are also indications of mud-brick **fortification**. Other finds consisted of microliths, beads of semiprecious stones, and bangles of terracotta, shell, and **copper**. These levels were also characterized by a distinctive bichrome painted **pottery**, with black and white designs painted on a red surface. Painted motifs included geometric designs and floral and faunal patterns. This is often divided into several subcategories on the basis of fabric. The pottery has parallels with **Bara** ware. The site was reoccupied in Period II after a break, in the **Mature Harappan phase** (mid–third millennium BCE onward). Architecturally, this phase was characterized by the construction of a fortified small, high mound to the west, the typical citadel of Harappan settlements. The lower mound to the east was also fortified. Besides, there is evidence for well-laid-out streets. However, drains were apparently local rather than part of a centralized network. Habitation extended beyond the fortified area as well. Most houses were of mud brick, and many of them had wells. The use of baked brick was relatively restricted. Other finds associated with the latter phase include fire altars and a cemetery. *See also* BANAWALI; KUNAL; MITATHAL; SOTHI.

KĀLIDĀSA. Sanskrit poet and **dramatist** (c. fourth–fifth centuries CE), a contemporary and possibly a court poet of the **Gupta** rulers. He may have been a native of **Ujjayinī**. He is generally considered as one of the most versatile authors. His compositions include three long poems: *Meghadūta*, a lyrical monologue; *Raghuvaṃśa*, based on the ***Rāmāyaṇa***; and *Kumārasambhava*, based on myths about **Śiva** and Pārvatī. His plays, which deal with romances about **kings**, include the *Mālavikāgnimitram*, *Vikramorvaśīyam*, and ***Abhijñāna Śākuntalam***. The last was among the first Sanskrit works to be translated into European languages, and was widely acclaimed in the 19th century. *See also* DRAMA; JONES, WILLIAM; LITERATURE.

KALIṄGA. Part of present-day Orissa. The **Maurya** ruler **Asoka** conquered Kaliṅga (c. 260 BCE). The destruction that ensued on account of this conquest apparently filled him with remorse, and consequently he decided to give up **warfare** as an instrument of state policy. *See also* KHĀRAVELA; MAHĀPADMA NANDA; MAJOR ROCK EDICTS; NANDA; RĀJARĀJA I; SLAVERY.

KALITTOKAI. Anthology of **Tamil poems**, part of the ***Sangam*** collection (c. third century BCE–second century CE?) containing 150 poems in the *kali* meter, dealing with the theme of love, included in the ***Eṭṭutokai***. The anthology is divided into five parts, each attributed to a single poet.

KALLUR. **Archaeological** site in Karnataka, with evidence of two occupational phases. Period I (c. second millennium BCE?) yielded microliths and ground stone axes, having parallels with finds from **Brahmagiri** and **Maski**. Period II (c. first millennium CE) yielded evidence of **Russet-Coated Painted Ware**, **iron** working, beads of semiprecious stone, shell bangles, and **Sātavāhana coins**.

KALPA **(1).** Name assigned to a category of normative texts composed in **Sanskrit**, c. first millennium BCE, recognized as part of the ***Vedāṅgas***. *Kalpa* texts included the **Śrautasūtras**, **Gṛhyasūtras**, **Dharmasūtras**, and **Śulbasūtras**.

KALPA **(2).** A measure of time, frequently mentioned in the **Purāṇas**, consisting of 4,320,000,000 human years. Each *kalpa* was visualized as consisting of several *mahāyugas* or great ages, each subdivided into four *yugas* or ages, known as the *kṛta*, *tretā*, *dvāpara*, and *kali*, followed by *sandhis* or periods of transition, after which the next cycle of *mahāyugas* is supposed to start afresh. The present epoch is conceived of as being part of a ***Kali yuga***, beginning from c. 3102 BCE.

KALPASŪTRA**.** **Jaina** canonical text composed in **Prakrit** and attributed to **Bhadrabāhu** (c. fourth–third century BCE). It consists of three sections: one containing **biographies** of the ***tīrthaṅkaras*** including **Mahāvīra**, the second including a list of religious leaders, and the third containing rules for **ascetics**, with a focus on those meant for the rainy season. *See also* LITERATURE.

KALSI. Site near Dehradun, Uttarakhand, find spot of a set of **Major Rock Edicts** of **Asoka**, written in the **Brāhmī script**.

KALYAN. An **early historic** sea port on the west coast, in present-day Maharashtra, with evidence of contact with contemporary inland sites.

KĀMANDAKA. Author of the ***Nītisāra***, perhaps composed during the **Gupta** period, c. sixth century CE. *See also* LITERATURE.

KĀMARŪPA. Kingdom (c. fourth century CE), part of the Brahmaputra valley in present-day Assam, mentioned in the **Allahabad Pillar Inscription** of the **Gupta** ruler **Samudragupta**, according to which the unnamed ruler of the state offered tribute and homage to the **king**, and agreed to obey his commands. One of the best-known rulers of the region was **Bhāskaravarman**.

KĀMASŪTRA. **Sanskrit** text on erotics, attributed to **Vātsyāyana**, dated to c. second–fourth centuries CE. The text consists of seven sections, focusing on the ordering of sexual relations within the household, classification of sexual acts, possibilities of adultery, sex work, and recipes for aphrodisiacs. The intended audience was probably urban elite men. Most of the text consists of terse prose sentences, some couched in highly technical language. *See also* COURTESANS; LITERATURE.

KĀMBOJA. People mentioned in **Asokan inscriptions** (c. third century BCE) as living in the northwest, possibly in the region around Kabul, Afghanistan. *See also* DEVAPĀLA.

KAMPAN. Author (c. ninth century CE) of the ***Rāmāvatāram***, a version of the ***Rāmāyaṇa*** in **Tamil**. *See also* LITERATURE.

KAMPIL. **Archaeological** site in Uttar Pradesh, identified with **Kāmpilya**. Excavations have yielded traces of settlement c. first millennium BCE onward. Finds include **Painted Grey Ware**, **black slipped ware**, **black and red ware**, and **terracotta** figurines.

KĀMPILYA. City mentioned in the ***Mahābhārata***, generally identified with the site of **Kampil**. Textual traditions describe it as the capital of the ***mahājanapada*** of **Pañcāla**.

KAṆĀDA. Author (c. first century CE?) of the ***Vaiśeṣika sūtra*** in **Sanskrit**. *See also* LITERATURE.

KANAGANAHALLI. **Mesolithic** and **early historic** (c. first century BCE–first century CE) site in Karnataka with evidence of a brick ***stūpa***, with a carved limestone railing. Other finds include **sculpture**

of the **Buddha** in limestone, **terracotta** figurines, **inscriptions**, **Northern Black Polished Ware**, and lead **coins** of the **Sātavāhanas**.

KANAUJ. Archaeological site in Uttar Pradesh, identified with ancient **Kānyakubja**. The site was occupied from the first millennium BCE onward. Finds include **Painted Grey Ware**, **black slipped ware**, and **Northern Black Polished Ware**. Other finds consisted of **terracotta** figurines and plaques, and **sculptures** of **Purāṇic** deities, dating to c. seventh–eighth centuries CE. Located on the **Ganga (2)**, the **city** emerged as a major political and cultural center during the second half of the first millennium CE and was the capital of the **Maukhari** rulers. Subsequently, **Harṣvardhana** (c. seventh century) and the **Pratihāras** exercised control over the city. *See also* DHARMAPĀLA; MAHENDRAPĀLA; PĀLA; YAŚOVARMAN.

KANCHIPURAM. Archaeological site in Tamil Nadu, recognized as the capital of the **Pallavas**. There is evidence of occupation from the second half of the first millennium BCE onward. Finds include **Black and Red Ware**, **rouletted ware**, amphorae, **terracotta** figurines, **Sātavāhana coins**, and remains of **Buddhist** structures. *See also* TOṆḌAI MAṆḌALAM; VIṢṆUGOPA.

KANDHAR. Archaeological site in Maharashtra, with evidence of a stone structure that may have been a **temple**, possibly a **Śaiva** shrine, built by the **Rāṣṭrakūṭa** ruler Kṛṣṇa III in the 10th century CE.

KANE, PANDURANG VAMAN. (1880–1972). Author of the monumental *History of the Dharmasastras* in five volumes, the first edition of which was published between 1930 and 1962. It is an encyclopedic work based on **Sanskrit** texts and commentaries (from c. sixth century BCE to c. 1800 CE) dealing with legal, social, and ritual norms and practices. Kane also edited several Sanskrit texts and authored a work on Sanskrit poetics.

KANHERI. Buddhist rock-cut cave site in Maharashtra (c. second century CE). Two **inscriptions** of the **Sātavāhana** ruler **Yajñaśrī Sātakarṇi** have been found on the wall of a cave. The site witnessed a resurgence of activity during the fifth–sixth centuries CE, with a total of more than 100 caves being excavated in the area. Many of the caves were embellished with **sculpture**.

KANIṢKA. The most important of the **Kuṣāṇa** rulers (c. early second century CE?). His dominions extended from Varanasi in the east to Central Asia. Important **cities** within his kingdom included **Mathura** and Peshawar (Pakistan). According to the ***Rājataraṅgiṇī***, he founded a city named Kaniṣkapura in Kashmir. Kaniṣka is known as a patron of **Buddhism**. One of the largest ***stūpas*** was built in Peshawar during his reign. This was also the time when the tradition of **sculpture** associated with the **Gandhara school of art** flourished. Buddhist tradition suggests that he may have convened the fourth **Buddhist Council** in Kashmir. The iconography on his **coins** includes representations of **Brahmanical**, Buddhist, Greek, and Iranian deities. The royal titles adopted by him may have been influenced by Chinese traditions. Earlier attempts to correlate the era associated with him with the **Śaka era** have been called into question on the basis of **inscriptional** evidence. He was succeeded by **Huviṣka**. *See also* AGESILAOS; AŚVAGHOṢA; NĀGĀRJUNA; RABATAK INSCRIPTION; SHAJI-KI-DHERI.

KANVA. **Brahmanical** ruling lineage of **Magadha** (c. first century BCE), mentioned in the **Purāṇas**, which state that the founder of the lineage, Vāsudeva, killed his **Śuṅga** overlord to gain power. *See also* KINGSHIP.

KĀNYAKUBJA. **Sanskrit** name of present-day **Kanauj**.

KAOTHE. **Archaeological** site in Maharashtra, with evidence of a **Neolithic** occupation (c. 2000–1800 BCE). Finds include evidence of circular pit dwellings, traces of millet and sesame, bone **tools**, remains of the buffalo, and **pottery** resembling **Savalda Ware**.

KAPILA. A **philosopher** (c. first millennium BCE?), traditionally recognized as an authority on ***Sāṃkhya*** philosophy. His compositions, if any, are not available at present.

KAPILAR. One of the best-known **poets** of the **Tamil *Sangam*** anthologies, which contain more than 200 compositions attributed to him. One of his compositions, the *Kuriñcipāṭṭu*, about a romance between a young woman and a hunter, forms part of the ***Pattupāṭṭu***. *See also* LITERATURE.

KAPILAVASTU. Chief city of the **Sākyas**, c. sixth century BCE, often identified with **Piprahwa** in eastern Uttar Pradesh, on the basis of **seals** belonging to a **monastery** of the **Kuṣāṇa** period, which refer to the site as Kapilavastu. *See also* GANWARIA.

KAPIŚA. Region mentioned in early Indian texts, part of present-day Afghanistan, on the **Silk Route**, an area where **Buddhism** spread c. late first millennium BCE–early first millennium CE.

KĀRAIKKĀL AMMAIYĀR. Tamil woman poet (c. sixth century CE), originally named Punītavatī, a devotee of **Śiva** who composed more than 100 verses in praise of the deity.

KARDAMAKA. Name of a ruling lineage, a branch of the **Śakas**, who controlled parts of central and western India between c. second and fourth century CE, known from their **coins** and **inscriptions**. The best-known ruler of this lineage was **Rudradāman**. The Kardamakas were probably the Śakas who were overthrown by the **Guptas**.

KARIKĀḺAN. One of the best-known rulers among the early **Coḻas** (c. second century CE). He is credited with defeating his rivals among the **Pāṇḍyas** and **Ceras**, and promoting the extension of **agriculture** and long-distance **trade**. *See also PAṬṬINAPPĀLAI*.

KARKABHAT. Archaeological site in Chattisgarh, with evidence of **megalithic** stone circles (c. first half of the first millennium BCE). Associated finds include **iron** spearheads, daggers, arrowheads, and spikes; **copper** and gold ornaments; red **pottery**; and a sculptured menhir. The absence of skeletal remains may indicate the prevalence of cremation rather than **burial**.

KARLE. Archaeological site in the Western Ghats, Maharashtra, with one of the largest **rock-cut caves** (c. second century CE) dedicated to the **Buddhist** order. The façade is decorated with **sculpture**, and there are signs of wooden embellishment as well. **Inscriptions** mentioning **Śaka** and **Sātavāhana** rulers have been found on the walls of the cave, which also contains a ***stūpa*** that was the focus of worship. *See also CAITYA*; NAHAPĀṆA.

KARMA*. Sanskrit** term meaning "action," used c. mid–first millennium BCE onward within several **philosophical** traditions to suggest that present human existence is the result of past actions. The theory was used both to justify existing social inequalities by explaining these as the outcome of previous actions and to suggest that the individual could change his or her fate by acting according to ***dharma. *See also* BUDDHISM; JAINISM; POVERTY; SOCIAL MOBILITY; UPANIṢAD.

KARTTRIPURA. Kingdom (c. fourth century CE), possibly in present-day Uttarakhand, mentioned in the **Allahabad Pillar Inscription** of the **Gupta** ruler **Samudragupta**. According to the inscription, the unnamed king of this state offered tribute and homage and agreed to follow the commands of the Gupta **king**.

KARUR. City mentioned in **Tamil *Sangam*** literature as the capital of the **Ceras**. *See also* KODUMANAL.

KASHIPUR. Archaeological site in Uttarakhand. Finds consist of **Painted Grey Ware** (c. first millennium BCE?) and remains of a brick structure, possibly a **temple**, dating to the mid–first millennium CE as well as **terracotta** figurines that have been assigned to c. 9th–10th centuries CE.

KĀŚI. Name of a ***mahājanapada*** (c. sixth century BCE), including parts of eastern Uttar Pradesh. Its capital, of the same name, situated at the confluence of the **Ganga (2)** with two smaller streams, was one of the most important **cities** during the **early historic period**. The state was absorbed into the *mahājanapada* of **Kosala**. When a Kosalan princess was married to the **Magadhan** ruler **Bimbisāra**, the city itself was gifted to the bridegroom. *See also* TEXTILES.

KASIA. Archaeological site in Uttar Pradesh, identified with ancient Kusinārā (**Kusinagara**), the site of the great decease of the **Buddha**.

Finds include ***stūpas*** and **monasteries** dating to the first millennium CE.

KASRAWAD. Archaeological site in Madhya Pradesh. Finds include remains of several baked-brick ***stūpas***, silver and **copper punch-marked coins**, **pottery**, including **Northern Black Polished Ware** and **black and red ware**, **terracotta** artifacts, and **inscriptions** dated to c. second century BCE. The site was evidently deserted subsequently.

KATHĀSARITSĀGARA*. Sanskrit** anthology of stories, based on the ***Bṛhatkathā of **Guṇāḍhya**, compiled by **Somadeva** between c. 1063 and 1082 CE. It is divided into eight chapters and includes more than 300 stories woven into the framing narrative. *See also* LITERATURE.

KATRA. Archaeological site in Madhya Pradesh with evidence of three occupational phases. The first period (**Neolithic–Chalcolithic**) is subdivided into two subphases. Period I A (c. 1800–1700 BCE) yielded evidence of handmade pots and white-painted **black and red ware** having parallels with **pottery** from **Ahar**. Other finds included stone blades, grinding **tools**, and remains of huts. In the next phase (Period I B, c. 1700–1500 BCE), parallels with the pottery from Ahar continued. Additionally, **Malwa**-type pots were also found. Other finds consisted of beads of steatite and other stones and **terracotta** that have parallels with **Nagda** and **Navdatoli**. Finds from Period II (c. 1500–1200 BCE) included pots with parallels to the Malwa tradition, stone blades, grinding tools, and beads of terracotta and **copper**. There was a hiatus between Periods II and III. The latter (c. 750–300 BCE) provided evidence of **black slipped ware**, black and red ware, **Northern Black Polished Ware**, bone tools, **iron** nails and spearheads, copper rings, a **punch-marked coin**, and shell and glass bangles. A **fortification** wall was also associated with this period.

KĀTYĀYANA. Sanskrit author (c. third century BCE) of a commentary on **Pāṇini**'s ***Aṣṭādhyāyī***, who attempted to incorporate new material and analyses. The work is no longer available as an independent text, but survives in citations in **Patañjali**'s ***Mahābhāṣya***. *See also* LITERATURE.

KĀTYĀYANASMṚTI. **Sanskrit** metrical work, attributed to Kātyāyana, composed and compiled by c. 600 CE, one of the major **Dharmaśāstras**. The complete text is no longer available, but nearly 1,000 verses have been collated from other texts. These suggest that the text dealt with legal procedure. *See also* LITERATURE.

KAUNDINYAPURA. Archaeological site in Maharashtra with evidence of three occupational phases. Period I (c. eighth–sixth centuries BCE) provided evidence of **megaliths** and **Black and Red Ware**. Period II (mid–first millennium BCE) yielded **Northern Black Polished Ware** and **punch-marked coins**. Finds from Period III (c. 150 BCE–200 CE) included **Red Polished Ware**, beads of semiprecious stone, and **Sātavāhana** coins.

KAUSAMBI. Archaeological site near Allahabad (Uttar Pradesh), also known as Kosam, with evidence of continuous occupation from c. eighth century BCE to c. sixth century CE. There is evidence of four occupational phases. Evidence from Period I was relatively scanty. Finds from Periods II and III included **Painted Grey Ware**, **black slipped ware**, and **Northern Black Polished Ware**. Period IV has been assigned to the first millennium CE. Structural remains associated with Periods III and IV consisted of burnt-brick **architecture** and ring wells, remains of a **monastic** complex that has been identified from **inscriptions** as the Ghoṣitārāma, a monastery mentioned in early **Buddhist** texts, ***stūpas***, and a structure that has been designated as a palace. Besides, there is evidence of a **fortification** wall and moat, whose dates have not been satisfactorily established. Other finds consisted of an inscribed **Asokan** pillar. **Coins**, including **punch-marked** coins and those of the **Kuṣāṇas** and several other ruling lineages, have also been recovered. The site has also yielded **seals** and sealings; **terracotta** figurines; artifacts of ivory, horn, and bone; beads of semiprecious stone; and **iron** equipment. *See also UTTARĀPATHA*; VATSA.

KAUṬILYA. Political thinker (c. fourth century BCE), also recognized as the chief **minister** of **Candragupta Maurya**. According to some traditions, the latter owed his success to the guidance offered by the former. Kauṭilya is traditionally regarded as the author

The Great Stupa at Sanchi. Courtesy of the American Institute of Indian Studies.

One of the earliest rock-cut caves (c. third century BCE), donated by the Mauryan emperor Asoka to the sect of the Ājīvikas.

A rock-cut Jaina monastery in Orissa, c. first century BCE.

Part of the Buddhist monastery at Nalanda, one of the most important centers of education in the subcontinent, mid–first millennium CE onward.

One of the earliest rock-cut temples at Mahabalipuram, Tamil Nadu, mid–first millennium CE.

A sculptural representation of an urban scene from Sanchi, Madhya Pradesh, c. second century BCE.

An early votive inscription from Karle, Maharashtra, written in Prakrit, using the Brāhmī script, c. first century CE.

One of several vibrant representations of animals in early Indian sculpture, from Bharhut, c. second century BCE.

A representation of the Buddha from Sarnath, Uttar Pradesh, mid–first millennium CE.

Colossal sculpture of Śiva, Elephanta Caves, Maharashtra, c. mid–first millennium CE.

The goddess Durgā, depicted as killing the buffalo demon, c. mid–first millennium CE, Aihole, Karnataka.

of the ***Arthaśāstra***. *See also* DHANANANDA; LITERATURE; *MUDRĀRĀKṢASA*.

KAVERI RIVER. River in peninsular India that rises in the west and flows through the present-day states of Karnataka and Tamil Nadu into the Bay of Bengal. The Kaveri delta has always been important for settled **agriculture**. Some of the earliest **cities** and kingdoms in the region developed along the Kaveri valley. *See also* COḺA.

KAVERIPATTINAM. Archaeological site in Tamil Nadu, recognized in **Tamil** textual traditions as the chief port of the **Coḻas**, located near the point where the **Kaveri River** meets the Bay of Bengal. **Archaeological** evidence includes remains of a wharf, a water tank, and a **Buddhist monastery**. Other finds consisted of **Black and Red Ware**, **rouletted ware**, and beads of semiprecious stone. *See also* *PAṬṬINAPPĀLAI*; POOMPUHAR.

***KĀYASTHA*. Sanskrit** term used to designate an occupational category of scribes, which crystallized into a **caste** by the mid–first millennium CE. Closely associated with the administration in regions such as Kashmir and Bengal, the *kāyastha* was occasionally regarded as a symbol of oppression in a society where literacy was the monopoly of the privileged few.

KAYATHA. Archaeological site in Madhya Pradesh, with four occupational phases, type site of a **Chalcolithic** culture associated with the spread of **agriculture** in the region, dated to c. 2300–1800 BCE (Period I), characterized by a distinctive **pottery** with a brown slip and geometric designs painted in dark red or violet. Pots with incised designs are also common. Other finds included cast **copper** axes and copper bangles. Also noteworthy are finds of beads of steatite and necklaces of semiprecious stones, which were probably of **Harappan** origin. Period II (c. 1700–1500 BCE) yielded white-painted **black and red ware** showing parallels with **Ahar**. Other finds included **terracotta** bull figurines. Period III (c. 1500–1200 BCE) yielded pottery similar to the **Malwa ware**. Period IV (mid–first millennium BCE) provided evidence of **iron**, **Painted Grey Ware**, **Northern Black Polished Ware**, beads of semiprecious stone, copper ornaments, terracotta figurines, and **cast** copper **coins**. Period V (mid–first millennium CE) provided evidence of baked-brick houses and **sculpture**, including images of the **Buddha**. The site remained under occupation until the medieval period. *See also* BAGOR; BALATHAL; DANGWADA; ERAN.

***KERALAPUTA*.** Literally the sons of Kerala, the name of a people residing outside the frontiers of the **Mauryan** Empire, mentioned in **Asokan inscriptions**, and identified with the **Ceras** who controlled parts of present-day Tamil Nadu and Kerala.

KESANAPALLE. Archaeological site in Andhra Pradesh with evidence of two occupational phases. Period I (c. eighth–fifth centuries BCE), designated as **Chalcolithic**, yielded **Black and Red Ware**, and remains of cattle, sheep, goat, pig, and deer. Finds from Period II (c. fifth century BCE–first century CE) included **megalithic** cist **burials**, **Northern Black Polished Ware**, and **rouletted ware**.

KHAIRADIH. Archaeological site in Uttar Pradesh, with three occupational phases. Period I (c. 1000 BCE) yielded **black and red ware** similar to that found at **Chirand**, bone **tools**, and beads of semiprecious stone. Finds from Period II (c. fourth–second centuries BCE) consisted of **terracotta** figurines, beads of semiprecious stone, and spindle whorls. Other finds included evidence of a blacksmith's workshop, with furnaces and slag, indicating the local manufacture of **iron** artifacts. The finds from Period III (c. second century BCE–second century CE) were more or less similar.

KHAJURI. Archaeological site in Uttar Pradesh, with two occupational phases. Finds from Period I, designated as **Chalcolithic** (c. second millennium BCE?), included microliths, bone **tools**, wheel-made **pottery**, and wattle-and-daub structures. There is evidence of **agriculture**, hunting, and fishing. Faunal remains consisted of bones of cattle, sheep, goat, deer, and fish. Other finds included **copper** artifacts, beads of semiprecious stone, and traces of **iron** slag found toward the end of this phase. Period II (c. first millennium BCE?) yielded iron tools and weapons, **black and red ware**, animal bones, remains of rice, copper ornaments, and beads of semiprecious stone.

KHANDAGIRI. Site in Orissa, with evidence for **Jaina rock-cut caves**, c. first century BCE, some of which contain **sculpture** and **inscriptions**. *See also* KHĀRAVELA.

KHARAPĀRIKA. Community living (c. fourth century CE) in central India, mentioned in the **Allahabad Pillar Inscription** of the **Gupta** ruler **Samudragupta** as among those who offered tribute and homage and agreed to obey the commands of the ruler.

KHĀRAVELA. Ruler of Orissa, c. second century BCE, known from the **Hathigumpha inscription**. The inscription, in **Prakrit**, chronicles his achievements. It describes him as an **Aila**, as a ***mahārāja***, and the lord of **Kaliṅga**, a descendant of Mahāmeghavāhana, who is otherwise unknown, and as belonging to the ruling lineage of the **Cedis (2)**. The inscription, which is in the nature of a panegyric, describes him as endowed with auspicious signs, with his fame spreading in the four directions. He is also represented as being well-versed in law, accountancy, and writing. The inscription provides a chronicle of his reign, mentioning his victories over rulers in western and central India, including the **Sātavāhanas**, **Raṭhikas**, and **Bhojas (1)**, and his successes in north India against the ruler of **Rājagaha** and **Magadha** and the Greeks. He also claimed victory over the chiefs of the **Tamil** lands and possibly acquired booty, including horses, elephants, jewels, and pearls from the **Pāṇḍya** ruler. The inscription lists his various endowments, including tanks, cisterns, and a canal, and his patronage of cultural activities. Finally it documents his gifts to the **Jaina monastic** order. *See also* SĀTAKARṆĪ II; UDAYAGIRI.

KHAROṢṬHĪ. **Script** used to write **Prakrit** in the northwest part of the subcontinent, attested for the first time in **Asokan inscriptions** (c. mid–third century BCE) in **Shahbazgarhi** and **Mansehra**. It was written from right to left and was probably derived from **Aramaic**. The name of the script is derived from **Buddhist** and **Jaina** lists. Examples of the script have been found from Afghanistan and Central Asia, where it was in use until the mid–third century CE. Most Kharoṣṭhī inscriptions are associated with Buddhist artifacts such as relic caskets, structural remains of **monasteries**, and images. It was also used in the writing of **manuscripts**. **Coins** bearing Kharoṣṭhī inscriptions have also been found from the northwestern part of the subcontinent. *See also* KUJULA KADPHISES; KUṢĀṆA.

KHATTIYA**.** **Pali/Prakrit** term, the equivalent of the **Sanskrit** ***kṣatriya***, used in **Buddhist** texts (c. sixth century BCE onward) to designate the ruling elite. In Buddhist references to the ***varṇa*** order, the *khattiya* was placed first, even before the ***brāhmaṇa*** **(1)**. *See also VARṆA.*

KHICHING. **Archaeological** site in Orissa, with evidence of a **monastery**, ***stūpa***, **sculptures** of **Jaina** and **Purāṇic** deities including **Viṣṇu** and **Śiva**, and remains of a **Śaiva temple** dating to c. ninth century CE.

KHOKRAKOT. **Archaeological** site in Haryana. Finds from Period I (c. first half of the first millennium BCE?) included **Painted Grey Ware**, bone **tools**, an **iron** sickle, and **terracotta** figurines. Period II (mid/late first millennium BCE?) was associated with **Northern Black Polished Ware**, iron artifacts and slag, beads of semiprecious stone, and terracotta figurines. Period III A (c. second–first centuries BCE) yielded evidence of burnt-brick **architecture**. Other finds consisted of red ware, iron slag, **copper** nails, **coins**, **seals**, terracotta figurines, and bangles of copper and shell. Finds from Period III B included grinding stones, iron slag, artifacts such as nails, fishhooks and rings, a gold ring, copper coins of the **Kuṣāṇas**, terracotta human and animal figurines, and shell bangles. The material remains from Period III C were poor. A brick **temple** dating to the **Gupta** period was found in Period IV. *See also* CAST COINS.

KHUDDAKA NIKĀYA**.** Anthology of **Pali** texts, part of the ***Sutta Piṭaka***. These texts were probably added on to the **Buddhist** canon over a long period of time, c. fourth century BCE onward. Among the texts included in the *Khuddaka Nikāya* are the ***Dhammapada***, ***Theragāthā***, ***Therīgāthā***, and the ***Jātakas***. *See also* LITERATURE.

KINGSHIP. The use of the **Sanskrit** term ***rājā*** from the ***Ṛgveda*** (c. second millennium BCE) onward points to the existence of chiefs or kings. While *rājā* remained the basic title of rulership, used by kings such as **Asoka**, later rulers often adopted more grandiose titles such as ***mahārāja*** or *mahārājādhirāja*. Ideally, **Brahmanical** sources suggest that the *rājā* was expected to be a ***kṣatriya***, but textual traditions and **inscriptions** indicate that several ruling lineages were of non-*kṣatriya* origin. These included the **Mauryas**, **Śuṅgas**, **Kanvas**, **Sātavāhanas**, and **Guptas**.

Kingship was expected to be hereditary, but primogeniture was by no means automatically recognized. However, succession was by and large confined to men, either sons or brothers, and occasionally other kinsmen. **Women** had no legitimate claims to the throne, and the few who claimed power, such as **Diddā** in Kashmir, were regarded with disfavor by the ***brāhmaṇas* (1)**. Other women, such as **Prabhāvatī Gupta**, functioned as regents. Generally, royal women were expected to remain within the *antaḥpura* or the inner apartments of the palace.

Literary descriptions suggest that that king's palace was luxurious, with a variety of people including priests, scholars, and musicians. While this was the king's residence, he also traveled in order to hunt, on pilgrimages, and to wage war.

Brahmanical sources suggest that priests were expected to play a crucial role in the state. This stemmed from their ability to perform rituals for the success of the king and the well-being of his subjects. It is also likely that they had administrative and advisory roles. Brahmanical texts laid down the rights and duties of the king. The former included the right to taxation. Resources that were mobilized as taxes, or as tribute from **warfare**, were often used to maintain the **army**, in supporting a luxurious lifestyle that was commented on by foreign travelers such as **Megasthenes**, and on a range of activities that can broadly be defined as welfare works. Duties that were specified for the king included maintaining the systems of ***varṇa*** and ***āśrama***, which were regarded as components of the notion of ***dharma***. While many of these ideas were reiterated in **early historic** and **early medieval** royal **inscriptions**, it is uncertain how far they were implemented in practice. The ruler was also expected to administer ***daṇḍa*** or justice, which very often involved protecting property and familial norms. In this context, the ruler was occasionally visualized in paternalistic terms.

Narrative traditions such as the ***Jātakas*** recognized the possibility of wicked or oppressive kings, and suggested ways and means of removing them. Normative texts such as the ***Arthaśāstra*** also cautioned rulers against excesses, warning them of dire consequences. It is likely that in practice kings may have adopted policies and strategies that were shaped as much if not more by considerations of expediency as by the precepts elucidated in normative texts. *See also ABHIṢEKA*; ARMY; ART; ASOKA; *AŚVAMEDHA*; ĀṬAVIKA RĀJĀ; BIMBISĀRA; BUDDHA; *CAKRAVARTIN*; CALENDAR; CITIES; COḺA; *DHAMMA*; *DIGVIJAYA*; *ḌOMBA*; DRAMA; EARLY HISTORIC PERIOD; EMPIRE; ESPIONAGE SYSTEM; FOREST; *GAṆA/SAṂGHA*; HARṢAVARDHANA; IKṢVĀKU (2); INDO-GREEK; JANAKA; JAYAPĪḌA; KĀLIDĀSA; KHĀRAVELA; KINGSHIP, THEORIES OF ORIGIN; KOSALA; LALITĀDITYA MUKTĀPĪḌA; LAND GRANTS; LANDOWNERSHIP; MAHĀPADMANANDA; MAMALLAPURAM; MANU; *MANUSMṚTI*; MINISTERS; MONASTERIES; *NĀRADA SMṚTI*; *PARIṢAD*; *PURANĀNURU*; *RĀJANYA*; *RĀJASŪYA*; RĀMA; RENUNCIATORY ORDERS; REVENUE SYSTEMS; *SABHĀ*; *SAṂGHA*; *SAMITI*; *SAPTĀNGA*; *SILAPPADIKĀRAM*; *SKANDHĀVĀRA*; TRIBES; UDAYANA; UPANIṢAD; *VĀJAPEYA*; VIKRAMĀDITYA; *YĀJÑAVALKYASMṚTI*; *YAJURVEDA*.

KINGSHIP, THEORIES OF ORIGIN. Some of the earliest speculations on the origins of the institution occur in myths found in **later Vedic literature** (c. 10th–6th centuries BCE), especially in ***Brāhmaṇas* (2)**, such as the ***Aitareya Brāhmaṇa*** and the ***Śatapatha Brāhmaṇa***. Possibilities explored include suggestions that a leader in war was elected as ***rājā*** by the gods. Alternatives included gods (and by extension men) who became *rājā* through divine support, won through the performance of **sacrifices** such as the ***aśvamedha***, ***rājasūya***, and ***vājapeya***. Implicit in such speculation was the notion of divine origin. It is likely that these ideas developed in the region of the **Kuru** and **Pañcāla**, associated with the **Ganga (2)–Yamuna** doab. Notions of divine origin were explicitly and implicitly reiterated through the centuries and are found in **inscriptions** and visual media that frequently equated rulers with deities.

Buddhist and **Jaina** theories were somewhat different and suggested a contractual element. These accounts, found in texts such as the ***Dīgha Nikāya***, envisaged an initial condition of primeval bliss, without economic, social, and political differences, and consequently, no need for mechanisms of governance. Such mechanisms were thought to have emerged when, through a process of inevitable decay, human existence was no longer harmonious. Men were then supposed to have felt the need for social regulation, and chose a man whose duty it was to enforce norms in return for a share of the produce of the fields. He was known as *Mahāsammata* (the Great Chosen One) and as *rājā* (one who pleases his subjects).

KINSHIP SYSTEMS. A variety of textual and **inscriptional** evidence has been used by social historians to reconstruct histories of kinship. The ***Ṛgveda***, the earliest text available at present (c. second millennium BCE) indicates the existence of both patriliny and patriarchy. Somewhat later, by the mid–first millennium BCE, the **Dharmasūtras** and **Dharmaśāstras** valorized *kanyādāna*, literally the gifting of the daughter, and kin/clan exogamy, as the ideal. Inscriptions from the Deccan and south India (c. second century BCE onward) indicate that matrilineal affiliation was recognized among several ruling lineages including that of the **Sātavāhanas**, which may have practised cross-kin **marriage**. It is likely that there were variations in kinship systems in different regions of the subcontinent (as at present) as well as among different **castes** and classes. It is possible that patriliny was most important for the propertied classes and for social categories such as the ***brāhmaṇa* (1)** that emphasized ritual purity.

KODEKAL. Archaeological site in Andhra Pradesh with evidence of a **Neolithic** culture (c. 2300–1800 BCE). Finds include an **ash mound**; bones of cattle, goat, dog, ass, and deer; and red and gray **pottery**.

KODUMANAL. Archaeological site in Tamil Nadu with evidence of occupation during the **megalithic** and **early historic periods**. It was located on the route from **Karur**, the **Cera** capital, to **Muziris**. The megalithic phase (c. 250 BCE–100 CE) has yielded evidence of a habitation-cum-**burial** site, with more than 150 burials. Grave goods consisted of **Black and Red Ware**; **Red Polished Ware**; **iron** swords, arrowheads, axes, equipment for horses, and knives; beads of semiprecious stone; and gold and silver ornaments. Other finds included **terracotta** and glass objects. The early historic phase (c. 100–250 CE) yielded beads of semiprecious stone. The site is mentioned in ***Sangam* literature** as a center for bead making. Furnaces provide evidence for iron smelting. Other noteworthy finds include potsherds **inscribed** with personal names.

KOLDIHWA. Archaeological site in the **Belan valley**, Uttar Pradesh, with evidence of three major occupational phases. Period I, considered **Neolithic**, yielded evidence of ground stone **tools**, microliths, and handmade **pottery**. The dating of the Neolithic levels is not firmly established at present. Finds from Period II (c. 1400 BCE–600 BCE?), regarded as **Chalcolithic**, included **black and red ware**, **black slipped ware**, traces of **copper**, bone tools, mortars and pestles, and rice. Finds from Period III (mid–first millennium BCE) consisted of evidence for the cultivation of wheat and pulses and for the manufacture of **iron** equipment.

KOLHUA. Archaeological site in Bihar with three major phases of occupation. Period I (c. third–first centuries BCE) has provided evidence of **Northern Black Polished Ware**, a silver **punch-marked coin**, **terracotta** human and animal figurines, and beads of semiprecious stone. Other finds include remains of an **Asokan** pillar, remains of a ***stūpa***, a ***caitya***, and **sculpture**. Period II is attributed to the **Śuṅga-Kuṣāṇa** phase (c. first century BCE–second/third century CE). This was marked by the establishment of a **monastery** that lasted for several centuries. Other remains include traces of a brick-lined tank. The last phase (Period III) is attributed to the **Gupta**/post-Gupta phase (c. fourth–seventh centuries CE). This phase yielded terracotta **seals**.

KONDAPUR. Archaeological site in Andhra Pradesh, with evidence of occupation between c. first century BCE and second century CE. Finds included remains of a brick ***stūpa***; **Red Polished Ware**; **rouletted ware**; **Sātavāhana** and **Roman coins**; **terracotta** figurines; bangles of shell, **copper**, glass, terracotta, and ivory; and beads of terracotta, shell, and semiprecious stone.

KONKU VELIR. Tamil author with **Jaina** affiliations (c. eighth century CE), who composed the ***Perunkatai***, a long **poem** about the adventures of the **Vatsa** prince Utayanan (**Udayana**), evidently based on the ***Bṛhatkathā*** of **Guṇāḍhya**. *See also* LITERATURE.

KORKAI. Archaeological site in Tamil Nadu, identified as the major port of the **Pāṇḍyas**, mentioned in early **Tamil** literature. Finds include **megalithic burials**, ring wells, **Black and Red Ware**, **black slipped ware**, **rouletted ware**, potsherds with **Brāhmī inscriptions**, and **iron** and **copper** artifacts.

KOSALA. Name of a ***mahājanapada***, including parts of eastern Uttar Pradesh. According to the ***Rāmāyaṇa***, its chief **city** was **Ayodhya**. However, **Buddhist** tradition regarded **Sravasti** as the chief city. The **kings** of Kosala were engaged in constant conflict with the rulers of **Magadha**, who proved victorious. Kosala ceased to exist as an independent state by the fourth century BCE. *See also* IKṢVĀKU (1); KĀŚI; PASENADI; SĀKYA; VIḌŪḌABHA.

KOSAM. *See* KAUSAMBI.

KOSAMBI, DAMODAR DHARMANANDA. (1907–1966). Noted scholar, a famous mathematician, **numismatist**, **Sanskritist**, and one of the pioneers of Marxist historiography in the subcontinent. His major works include *An Introduction to the Study of Indian History* (1957) and *Culture and Civilization of Ancient India in Historical Outline* (1965).

KOT DIJI. Pre-/early Harappan site in Sind (c. 3500–2800 BCE), characterized by fine **pottery**, reoccupied during the **Mature Harappan** phase. There are traces of burning and destruction prior to the reoccupation. *See also* GUMLA; HARAPPA; REHMAN DHERI.

KOṬA KULA JANA. People mentioned (c. fourth century CE) in the **Allahabad Pillar Inscription** of the **Gupta** ruler **Samudragupta** as among those who were uprooted by him in ***āryāvarta***. **Coins** attributed to these people have been found from present-day Haryana.

KOTASUR. Archaeological site in West Bengal, with four occupational phases. Finds associated with Period I (c. sixth century BCE?) include **black and red ware**, **Northern Black Polished Ware**, **ter-**

racotta beads, and **iron** artifacts. Period II yielded terracotta figurines including those assigned to the **Śuṅga** period (c. second century BCE). Period III was associated with burnt-brick walls (c. first–third centuries CE?). Period IV was assigned to the fourth–eighth centuries CE. There is also evidence of **fortification**.

KOTLA NIHANG KHAN. **Archaeological** site in the Punjab. Finds consist of **Harappan** artifacts such as **pottery**, weights, bricks, bangles, and figurines. There is evidence of later occupation as well.

KRISHNA RIVER. Name of a river in peninsular India, flowing from west to east through the present-day states of Karnataka and Andhra Pradesh into the Bay of Bengal. Several **archaeological** sites, ranging from the **Paleolithic** to the **early medieval periods**, have been found along the river and its tributaries.

KṚṢṆA. Name of one of the major protagonists in the ***Mahābhārata***, the mainstay of the Pāṇḍavas, identified in sections of the ***Bhagavad Gītā*** as well as in the **Purāṇas** as an ***avatāra*** of **Viṣṇu**. *See also* DEOGARH; DVARAKA; *HARIVAMṢA*; PASTORALISM; YĀDAVA.

KṢAHARĀTA. Name of a ruling lineage of the **Śakas** known from both **coins** and **inscriptions**, which exercised control over parts of present-day Maharashtra and Gujarat, including coastal areas, during the second century CE. The Kṣaharātas supported both **Buddhist** and **Brahmanical** practices. The best-known ruler of this lineage was **Nahapāṇa**.

KṢATRAPA*.** **Sanskritized** form of ***satrap, a term of Persian origin, meaning "governor" or "viceroy," adopted by **Śaka** rulers of northern and western India c. early first millennium CE onward. *See also* LAND GRANTS; *MAHĀKṢATRAPA*; MANSAR; SPHUJIDHVAJA.

KṢATRIYA*.** **Sanskrit** term for men belonging to the second category of the fourfold ***varṇa order, increasingly used from the mid–first millennium BCE onward. According to the **Dharmasūtras** and the **Dharmaśāstras**, the duties of the *kṣatriyas* included protecting the people, collecting taxes and tribute, and administering justice. They were also expected to study the **Vedas**, make gifts to ***brāhmaṇas* (1)**, and perform **sacrifices**, rights that were common to the first three *varṇas*. Ruling lineages generally, though not invariably, claimed *kṣatriya* status. Both the **Buddha** and the **Mahāvīra** were recognized as *kṣatriyas*. *See also GAṆA/SAMGHA*; GAUTAMĪPUTRA SĀTAKARṆI; *GOTRA*; *KHATTIYA*; KINGSHIP; KURU; MALLA; MARRIAGE; NANDA; PARAŚURĀMA; *RĀJANYA*; *RĀJASŪYA*; SOCIAL MOBILITY; VAJJI; VIŚVĀMITRA; WARFARE; YAUDHEYA; *YAVANA*.

KṢEMENDRA. Sanskrit author (c. 10th–11th centuries) who lived in Kashmir. The compositions attributed to him include the ***Bṛhatkathāmañjari*** and a satirical work known as the *Narmamālā*. *See also* LITERATURE.

KUBERA. Ruler (c. fourth century CE) of Devarāṣṭra, possibly in present-day Andhra Pradesh, mentioned in the **Allahabad Pillar Inscription** of the **Gupta** ruler **Samudragupta** as one of those who was captured but released on condition of submission.

KUCHAI. Archaeological site in Orissa, with evidence of a **Neolithic** settlement (c. second millennium BCE?). Finds include ground stone axes, microliths, and **pottery**.

KUDIKADU. Archaeological site, coastal Tamil Nadu, with evidence of occupation between c. first century BCE and second century CE. Finds include **rouletted ware**, pieces of imitation and original amphorae, **iron** artifacts, beads of glass and semiprecious stone, **terracotta** human figurines, and **copper** ornaments. There are remains of a burnt-brick structure, which was possibly part of a bead-making workshop.

KUJULA KADPHISES. Earliest known **Kuṣāṇa** ruler in the subcontinent, also designated as Kadphises I (c. first half of the first century CE), mentioned in Chinese chronicles, which indicate that he extended control from Afghanistan to the northwestern part of the subcontinent. His **coins**, which show **Indo-Greek** influence, contain legends in the **Kharoṣṭhī script**. *See also* VĪMA KADPHISES.

KULLI. Archaeological site in Baluchistan (Pakistan), type site of a **Chalcolithic** culture (c. 2500–200 BCE), with several settlements in the region. The best-known settlement of this culture is Nindowari. Subsistence strategies involved a combination of **agriculture** (wheat and barley) and **pastoralism**. There is evidence of embankments that were probably constructed to meet the requirements of **irrigation**. Houses were built of stone. The wheel-made **pottery** is distinctive, decorated with floral and faunal motifs interspersed with geometric designs painted in black on a buff surface. Other finds include **terracotta** figurines. There is evidence of contact with both the contemporary **Harappan** and the Mesopotamian civilizations.

KUMĀRADEVĪ. Princess belonging to the **Licchavi** lineage, married to the first major **Gupta** ruler, **Candragupta I** (c. fourth century CE). While the alliance strengthened the power of the Guptas, the Licchavis are not heard of subsequently.

KUMĀRAGUPTA I. Son and successor (r.c. 415–454) of the **Gupta** ruler **Candragupta II**, known from the **Bilsad Pillar Inscription** and several **copper plate land grant** records found from Bengal. He issued a wide variety of gold and silver **coins**. The **Hūṇas** attacked the kingdom during his reign, but he was evidently successful in meeting this challenge. He is known to have performed the ***aśvamedha*** **sacrifice**. *See also* BAYANA; PUṢYAMITRA.

KUMĀRILA BHAṬṬA. Philosopher c. seventh–eighth centuries CE, exponent of the ***mīmāṃsā*** school of thought and author of the *Mīmāṃsāśloka vārttikā* in **Sanskrit**. He opposed both **Buddhism** and **Jainism**, and upheld the validity of **sacrificial** rituals. *See also* LITERATURE; PRABHĀKARA.

KUMRAHAR. Archaeological site in present-day **Patna**, Bihar. Excavated remains include traces of a hall with stone pillars, attributed to the **Mauryan** period (c. fourth–second century BCE). Excavations have yielded evidence of five subsequent occupational phases. Finds from Period I (c. 150 BCE), included **pottery** and **cast** and **punch-marked coins**. Period II (c. 150 BCE–100 CE) yielded **terracotta** figurines attributed to the **Śuṅga** period. Finds from Period

III (c. 100–300 CE) consisted of **Kuṣāṇa** coins, figurines, **inscribed** sealings, and remains of a ***stūpa***. Period IV (c. 300–450 CE) yielded coins of **Candragupta II** and remains of a **monastery**. Finds from the last archaeological phase, Period V (c. 450–600 CE), included inscribed potsherds and sealings. The site was abandoned and subsequently reoccupied in the 17th century.

KUNAL. Archaeological site in Haryana, with evidence of **pre-/early Harappan** and **Harappan** (c. third millennium BCE) occupational phases. Finds associated with the first phase included remains of huts and hearths, evidence of **agriculture** and domesticated animals, stone blades, bone **tools**, **copper** arrowheads and fishhooks, and handmade **pottery**. During the second phase, there was evidence for mud-brick **architecture**. Finds of pottery suggest parallels with **Kalibangan**. Other finds consisted of beads of semiprecious stone. Finds from the third phase included bricks of Harappan proportion; **seals** with geometric motifs; copper ornaments and tools; a hoard of gold and silver ornaments, including bangles, amulets, and crowns; and several thousand beads of semiprecious stones, including those of lapis lazuli, agate, faience, and carnelian. Plant remains point to the cultivation of wheat, barley, pea, lentil, sesame, and rice.

KUNDAKUNDA. Digambara Jaina teacher (c. second century CE) of Andhra Pradesh, author of several works in **Prakrit**, including the *Aṣṭapahuda*, ***Samayasāra***, and the *Niyamasāra* dealing with **monastic** discipline, *Pravacanasāra* dealing with **philosophy**, and the *Pañcāstikāyasāra* dealing with metaphysics. *See also* LITERATURE.

KUNINDA. State in the central **Himalayas**, between the **Yamuna** and the **Beas**, best-known from issues of silver **coins** (c. first century BCE–third century CE) that show **Indo-Greek** influence. Legends on the coins were in **Prakrit**, written using both the **Brāhmī** and the **Kharoṣṭhī scripts**. *See also* PUROLA; SANGHOL.

KUNNATUR. Archaeological site in Tamil Nadu with evidence of **megalithic burials** (c. first millennium BCE) including cairns and cists. Other finds consisted of **Black and Red Ware**, **iron** equipment, **copper coins**, **terracotta** figurines, beads, and glass bangles.

KUNTASI. Archaeological site in Gujarat, with evidence of two occupational phases, **Mature Harappan** (c. 2300–1900 BCE) and **Late Harappan** (c. 1900–1700 BCE). During the first period, there was evidence of a citadel mound, protected by a double **fortification** wall of rubble set in mud masonry, a **pottery** kiln, and furnaces that were probably part of a workshop. There were also traces of structures used for storage. Other finds included Harappan pottery, beads of gold and carnelian, microbeads of steatite, and weights. This may have been a center for procuring and processing raw materials.

KUPGAL. Archaeological site in Karnataka, with evidence of a **Neolithic** culture (c. second millennium BCE?). Finds included microliths, evidence for the manufacture of stone **tools**, rock bruisings representing human and animal figures, potsherds, and **ash mounds**.

KURNOOL. District in Andhra Pradesh with Upper **Paleolithic** (c. 19,000–16,000 BP) cave sites, with evidence of stone and bone **tools**. The latter included scrapers, chisels, and shouldered points. *See also* MUCHCHTLA CHINTAMANI GAVI.

KURU. Name of a ***kṣatriya*** lineage, and by extension, of the land where members of the lineage settled, identified with the **Ganga (2)–Yamuna** doab, with major settlements at **Hastinapura** and **Indraprastha**. The Kurus rose to importance during the first half of the first millennium BCE. They were mentioned in **later Vedic** literature, where their ritual practices were praised. They were the main lineage described in the ***Mahābhārata***. They evidently declined in importance during the **early historic period**. *See also* AILA; BHARATA; KINGSHIP, THEORIES OF ORIGIN.

KURUKṢETRA. Archaeological site in Haryana, often identified as the site of the war depicted in the ***Mahābhārata***. There is evidence of a **pre-/early Harappan** occupation showing similarities with **Siswal** (c. third millennium BCE). Other finds consisted of Harappan type **pottery**, **Painted Grey Ware** (c. early first millennium BCE), and evidence for occupation during the **early historic** and **early medieval periods**.

KURUNTOKAI. Anthology of **Tamil poems**, part of the ***Eṭṭutokai*** or ***Sangam*** (c. third century BCE–second century CE?) **literature**, containing more than 400 love poems attributed to about 200 different poets.

KUṢĀṆA. Ruling lineage of Central Asian origin that entered the subcontinent c. first century CE, after being pushed out by the Xiongnu, a nomadic pastoral group. In the subcontinent, the Kuṣāṇas displaced the **Indo-Greeks** and the **Śakas**. At the height of their power, their empire extended from Central Asia, through Afghanistan, to parts of the **Ganga (2)** valley. Important **cities** under their control included **Kapiśa**, Peshawar, **Taxila**, and **Mathura**. The Kuṣāṇas probably derived their power from control of **trade** along the **Silk Route**. Their **coins**, inspired by Indo-Greek models, indicate that they extended support to a variety of **religious** traditions: **Buddhism**, **Zoroastrianism**, **Śaivism**, and Hellenistic. Legends on the coins were in Greek and **Kharoṣṭhī**.

The earliest known Kuṣāṇa ruler was **Kujula Kadphises** and the best-known Kuṣāṇa ruler was **Kaniṣka**. The Kuṣāṇas were among the earliest rulers to use grand titles such as ***mahārāja*** and *rājātirāja* (king of kings). They were perhaps inspired by Persian models. They also adopted the title of *devaputra* or son of the gods, perhaps in imitation of contemporary Chinese rulers. Their claims to divinity are evident from their coins and from the shrines erected to house images at Mat near Mathura and **Surkh Kotal** in Afghanistan. After the third century CE, Kuṣāṇa power was undermined by the emergence of the Sasanian Empire in the west and the **Gupta** Empire to the east. Mention of the Kuṣāṇas occurs until the sixth century, when the last vestiges of their power were wiped out by the **Hūṇas**. *See also* BRASS; CHARSADA; DAT NAGAR; EMPIRE; GANDHARA SCHOOL OF ART; HUVIṢKA; SAMUDRAGUPTA; SANGHOL; SURKH KOTAL; TAKHT-I-BAHI; VĀSUDEVA; VĪMA KADPHISES; YUEHZHI.

KUSINAGARA. Also known as Kusinārā, **early historic city** (c. sixth century BCE) in the ***mahājanapada*** of **Malla**, in present-day Uttar Pradesh. According to **Buddhist** tradition, it was the site of the great decease of the **Buddha**. **Archaeological** remains include a ***stūpa*** that may date to the time of **Asoka**. A relic casket containing precious stones and a gold **coin** of **Kumāragupta I** was found at the site. Other finds include Buddhist **sculpture**. **Inscriptions** dating to the mid–first millennium CE mention the existence of eight **monasteries** in the area, which remained in occupation until the 10th–11th centuries CE. *See also* KASIA.

KUSINĀRA. *See* KUSINAGARA.

KUSUMAPURA. Sanskrit term meaning "city of flowers" used in texts as a name for **Pāṭaliputra**. *See also ĀRYABHAṬĪYA*.

***KUVALAYAMĀLĀ*. Prakrit** text composed c. eighth century CE by **Udyotana Sūri**, a **Jaina** author, an example of the use of narratives for didactic purposes. The text provides valuable linguistic and cultural evidence about western India. *See also* LITERATURE.

– L –

LADYURA. Archaeological site in Uttarakhand, find spot of **megalithic burials**, **iron** artifacts, and **pottery**, dating to c. second–first centuries BCE.

LAGADHA. Sanskrit author (c. 400 BCE) of a text on **astronomy**, a recension of the *jyotiṣa* ***vedāṅga***, consisting of 36 verses. He referred to 27 asterisms but did not mention the planets or the zodiac signs. *See also* LITERATURE.

LAL QILA. Archaeological site in Uttar Pradesh with evidence of **Ochre-Coloured Pottery** (c. first half of the second millennium BCE), mud-brick structures, **copper** artifacts, **terracotta** figurines, and beads. There is evidence for the cultivation of rice and wheat, and for domesticated cattle.

LALITĀDITYA MUKTĀPĪḌA. King of Kashmir (c. 724–760), belonging to the Kārkoṭa dynasty, described in **Kalhaṇa**'s chronicle.

He is credited with defeating **Yaśovarman**, the ruler of **Kanauj**. This was recognized as part of a campaign of "world conquest" or ***digvijaya***. He was associated with the construction of several shrines, both **Buddhist** and **Vaiṣṇava**. He was also recognized as laying down the norms for governance in the region. Among the other events of his reign was the dispatch of an embassy to China. *See also* MARTAND.

LALITAGIRI. Archaeological site in Orissa. Finds included **Northern Black Polished Ware**; **inscriptions** dated to c. second, third, and sixth centuries CE; remains of ***stūpas***; an apsidal brick structure, possibly a ***caitya***; stone **sculptures**, including an image of the **Buddha** and **Purāṇic** deities; carved pillars; **terracotta** plaques; votive *stūpas*; terracotta **seals** and sealings; and relic caskets of gold and silver. Other finds consisted of **iron** sickles and spearheads. There is also evidence of a **monastery**. Some stone images of the Buddha found at the site may date to c. 11th–12th centuries CE.

LALITAVISTARA*.** A **biography** of the **Buddha** composed in **Buddhist Hybrid Sanskrit** by an anonymous author (c. third–fifth centuries CE?). It is likely that the sculptures on the famous ***stūpa at Borobudur (Indonesia, c. ninth century CE) were inspired by the text. *See also* LITERATURE.

LALMAI HILLS. Region in present-day Bangladesh, with evidence of fossil wood **tools**, attributed to the Upper **Paleolithic** phase. Tool types included hand axes, blades, burins, knives, and points.

LAND GRANTS. The gifting of land was recommended in prescriptive **Sanskrit** texts such as the **Dharmasūtras** and the **Dharmaśāstras** from the **early historic period** onward. However, the earliest **inscriptional** evidence indicative of the prevalence of the practice dates to the first centuries of the Common Era and is associated with the western **Kṣatrapas** and the **Sātavāhanas**.

Land grants became much more common from the second half of the first millennium CE. Many of these grants were recorded on **copper plates**, and several thousands of these have been recovered. These recorded donations made by **kings** and other functionaries.

Some grants were made by elite **women** as well. The inscriptions, in Sanskrit and other regional **languages**, generally included a eulogy of the donor. The place of issue and the date, often an auspicious occasion according to the **religious calendar**, were also usually mentioned. The details of the grant, including the qualities of the donee(s), were often elaborated. Besides, instructions were issued to local functionaries and the residents of the area where the land was granted.

Grants could consist of entire villages or of delimited fields. In many cases, the boundaries were laid down. Many of these grants were made in perpetuity, and the donee, more often than not a religious functionary (generally a ***brāhmaṇa* (1)**), received rights to collect taxes and tribute and to exercise **judicial** and/or police functions over the inhabitants.

The significance of land grants has been the subject of historiographical debates for decades. On the one hand are scholars who argue that land grants were symptomatic of the fragmentation of political authority, often equated with the feudalization of the socioeconomic order. Others suggest that land grants served as a mechanism for integrating relatively less stratified populations within new regional polities. Recent regional studies indicate that the implications of such grants varied considerably over space and time. *See also AGRAHĀRA*; CRAFTS; *DĀNA*; EARLY MEDIEVAL PERIOD; GUPTA; INSCRIPTIONS; LANDOWNERSHIP; MAITRAKA; MINISTERS; MONASTERIES; REVENUE SYSTEMS; TEMPLES; THANJAVUR.

LANDOWNERSHIP. The question of landownership was discussed in **Sanskrit** texts such as the **Dharmasūtras**, **Dharmaśāstras**, and the ***Arthaśāstra*** c. sixth century BCE onward. These texts indicate that a variety of practices were prevalent. While the **king** was occasionally represented as the owner of the realm, this claim did not translate into an absolute ownership of land. In some areas, land was probably regarded as a resource to be used by the entire community, and even when individual ownership was recognized, kinsmen and neighbors often had a claim when the owner wished to dispose of his property. While small landowners cultivated their fields with the help of household labor, large landowners depended on sharecroppers and landless laborers. By the mid–first millennium CE, and in some cases even earlier, texts recognized the possibility of buying, selling, mortgaging, and renting land, laying down norms to regulate conflicts relating to these transactions, which are documented in **inscriptions** as well. Although exceptional, there is evidence for **women** landowners. *See also* AGRICULTURE.

LANGHNAJ. Archaeological site in Gujarat, with evidence of a **Mesolithic** occupation (c. 2000 BCE?). There is evidence for hunting and fishing. Animal remains included bones of deer, wolf, and rat. There were indications of the use of fire. **Tools** consisted of microliths that were probably locally manufactured. Traces of **pottery** and metal indicate contact with neighboring cultures. There is evidence for **burials**, where the dead were oriented in an east–west direction.

LANGUAGES. Evidence for languages in use in early India comes from texts and **inscriptions**. While the latter are fairly securely dated, dates for the former are far more difficult to arrive at, as surviving **manuscripts** are almost invariably late. The earliest deciphered inscriptions (c. third century BCE), those of **Asoka**, were in **Prakrit**. His inscriptions also indicate that Greek and **Aramaic** were in use in the northwestern part of the subcontinent. **Sanskrit** inscriptions are widely available from c. early first millennium CE, and **Tamil** was used extensively in inscriptions from the second half of the first millennium CE.

A variety of texts have survived in Sanskrit, Prakrit, **Pali**, and Tamil. Some of these, such as the ***Ṛgveda*** in Sanskrit, may have been composed as early as the second millennium BCE. By the first millennium CE, Sanskrit emerged as the dominant language for court poetry, apart from being used for **Brahmanical** rituals. At the same time, it is likely that other languages, including those belonging to the Tibeto-Burman and Austro-Asiatic language families and **Dravidian** languages other than Tamil, were in use, as their influence can occasionally be detected in texts.

Attempts have also been made to equate language-speaking groups with **archaeological** cultures. These have generally focused on trying to identify speakers of **Indo-Aryan** languages in the archaeological record. Such attempts are based on recovering data on material culture from the *Ṛgveda* and matching these with archaeological evidence. Most of these attempts have proved problematic, given the nature of the text, which focuses on the relatively narrow domain of rituals rather than on the entire spectrum of material and social existence. While some scholars argue that the language used on **Harappan seals** was an early form of Sanskrit, others suggest that it may have been proto-Dravidian. It is unlikely that the matter will be satisfactorily resolved until the **script** is deciphered. *See also APABHRAMṢA*; ARYAN; BHARTṚHARI; BUDDHIST HYBRID SANSKRIT; *DĀSA*; DRAMA; GAṄGA (1); INDO-EUROPEAN; INDO-IRANIAN; JAINISM; JONES, WILLIAM; *MLECCHA*; PĀṆINI.

LATE HARAPPAN. The late Harappan or the **post-Harappan** phase (c. early second millennium BCE) was characterized by a decline of the major urban centers of the **Harappan civilization**. It was also marked by the disappearance of certain features considered typical of the civilization—inscribed **seals**, standardized weights, certain distinctive **crafts** including the manufacture of beads, the use of standardized bricks for construction, and uniform **pottery**. Several reasons have been suggested for this change. These include floods and changes in the course of the rivers along which sites were located. Other possibilities include environmental degradation. It is also evident that long-distance **trade** networks collapsed.

The phase was marked by distinctive regional developments. For instance, small-scale nonurban settlements proliferated in some areas, such as the Punjab, Haryana, and Gujarat, while most settlements were deserted in areas such as Sind. While there were continuities in subsistence strategies between the new **archaeological** cultures and the Harappan civilization, the decorations on pottery and metal working were often distinctive, in some instances suggesting a resurgence of local traditions that had been incorporated within the Harappan network. In other instances, there is evidence of contact with regions to the west, including Iran and Afghanistan. *See also* BALATHAL; BALU; BHORGARH; CHANHUDARO; DADHERI; DATRANA; DAULATPUR; JHUKAR; KUNTASI; LOTHAL; MALWAN; NAGIARI; PITHAD; RAKHI GARHI; RANGPUR; ROJDI; SANGHOL; SUNET; VALMIYO TIMBO.

LATER GUPTA. Name assigned by historians to a ruling lineage that controlled parts of present-day Bihar, Bengal, and possibly central

India during the seventh and eighth centuries CE. Their links, if any, with the **Gupta** rulers is uncertain. *See also* GRAHAVARMAN.

LATER VEDA. Term used by modern scholars to designate **Vedic** texts, apart from the ***Ṛgveda***, which were composed and compiled c. first half of the first millennium BCE. These include the ***Yajur-***, ***Sāma-***, and ***Atharvaveda***, the **Brāhmaṇas (2)**, and the **Upaniṣads**. *See also* KURU; LITERATURE; *RATNIN*; SACRIFICE; *VĀJAPEYA*; VEDIC ECONOMY.

LAURIYA ARARAJ. Archaeological site in Bihar. Finds include an **Asokan** pillar inscribed with a set of the **Major Pillar Edicts**.

LAURIYA NANDANGARH. Archaeological site in Bihar. Finds include an **Asokan** pillar (*in situ*) inscribed with a set of the **Major Pillar Edicts**, and a ***stūpa***. The site was occupied between c. third century BCE and sixth–seventh centuries CE. Associated finds consisted of **iron** artifacts, **punch-marked** and **cast coins**, **terracotta** figurines, sealings, and remains of a birch bark **manuscript**.

LEKHAHIA. Archaeological site in Uttar Pradesh, with evidence of a **Mesolithic** occupation (c. third millennium BCE?). Finds included microliths, rock **paintings**, and **burials** oriented in an east–west direction.

LICCHAVI. One of the leading clans of the **Vajji** confederacy, which continued to play an important role in the political affairs of north India for nearly a millennium (c. sixth century BCE onward). The mother of the **Gupta** ruler **Samudragupta** was a Licchavi. *See also* CANDRAGUPTA I; KUMĀRADEVĪ; MAHĀVĪRA; VAISHALI.

LITERATURE. A wide range of texts in **Sanskrit**, **Prakrit**, **Pali**, and **Tamil** is available for early India. There is evidence for a variety of literary genres—**drama**, **poems**, **epics**, and poetic **biographies**. Other categories of literature include ritual texts containing prayers, prescriptions, and myths (mainly in Sanskrit, especially the **Vedas** and **Purāṇas**) in verse as well as prose and the ***śāstras***, codifying and laying down norms on a variety of subjects—ritual, social life, grammar, **music**, poetics, and the sciences (composed in Sanskrit).

Prakrit works include a vast corpus associated with **Jainism**, comprising both canonical and noncanonical works, extremely rich in terms of their narrative content. While early **Buddhist** compositions that have survived were in Pali, later works were in Sanskrit. Many of the latter, lost for centuries, have been reconstructed from Tibetan and Chinese translations. Tamil works include ***Sangam*** literature as well as the devotional compositions attributed to the ***ālvārs*** and ***nāyanārs***.

While texts were occasionally attributed to specific authors, several major works (including the Sanskrit epics and Purāṇas) were probably composed and compiled over centuries. The authors of Sanskrit texts were generally ***brāhmaṇas* (1)**. Buddhist and Jaina texts were compiled and preserved within the **monastic** order, recruits for which were drawn from fairly diverse social backgrounds. Those who composed in Tamil also belonged to a wide range of social categories. Compositions attributed to **women**, although relatively rare, are found in all the major **languages**.

Although levels of literacy were probably low, texts such as the Purāṇas and the epics were meant to be recited, and would thus have been accessible to large sections of the population. This was also true of Prakrit, Pali, and Tamil narratives and poems. It is also likely that many narratives incorporated stories that were in circulation through other modes—oral communication, visual representations in **sculpture** and **painting**, and the performing arts.

For authors and works on aesthetics, *see also* ABHINAVAGUPTA; ĀNANDAVARDHANA; *DHVANYĀLOKA*. For biographies and their authors, *see also* AŚVAGHOṢA; BĀṆABHAṬṬA; *BUDDHACARITA*; *CAUPANNAMAHĀPURIṢACARIYAM*; *HARṢACARITA*; *LALITAVISTARA*; *MAHĀVASTU*. For chronicles, *see also* *DĪPAVAMSA*; *MAHĀVAMSA*; *RĀJATARAṄGIṆĪ*. For dictionaries and their authors, *see also* *AMARAKOŚA*; AMARASIṂHA; *PAIALACCHINĀMAMĀLĀ*; *PINKALANTAI*; *TIVĀKARAM*. For epics and their authors, *see also* CĀTTANĀR; ILANKO AṬIKAḶ; *MAHĀBHĀRATA*; *MAṆIMEKALAI*; *RĀMĀYAṆA*; *SILAPPADIKĀRAM*; VĀLMĪKI; VYĀSA. For compositions based on the epics and their authors, *see also* BHĀRAVI; DINNĀGA (2); KAMPAN; *PAUMACARIYA*; *RĀMĀVATĀRAM*; *SETUBANDHA*; VIMALASŪRI. For authors and compositions on grammar and language, *see also* *AṢṬĀDHYĀYĪ*; BHARTṚHARI; BHAṬṬI; CANDRAGOMIN; KĀTYĀYANA; *MAHĀBHĀṢYA*;

PĀṆINI; PATAÑJALI (1); *TOLKĀPPIYAM*; TOLKĀPPIYAR; VARARUCI; YĀSKA. For narratives and their authors, *see also* ĀRYAŚŪRA; *BṚHATKATHĀ*; *BṚHATKATHĀMAÑJARI*; *DAŚAKUMĀRACARITA*; *DHARMAKATHĀ*; *DHARMOPAD/EŚAMĀLĀVIVARAṆ*; GUṆĀḌHYA; HARIBHADRA SŪRĪ; *KATHĀSARITSĀGARA*; KONKU VELIR; KṢEMENDRA; *KUVALAYAMĀLĀ*; *NĀYADHAMMAKAHĀ*; *PAÑCATANTRA*; *PERUNKATAI*; SAṂGHADASAGANI (1); SOMADEVA; UDYOTANA SŪRI; *VĀSUDEVAHINDĪ*; VIṢṆUŚARMAN. For philosophers and philosophical treatises, *see also* ASAṄGA; BĀDARĀYANA; *BRAHMASŪTRA*; DHARMAKĪRTI; DINNĀGA (1); GAUḌAPĀDA; GAUTAMA; ĪŚVARAKṚṢṆA; JAIMINI; KAṆĀDA; KUMĀRILA BHAṬṬA; *NYĀYA SŪTRA*; PATAÑJALI (2); PRABHĀKARA; ŚABARASVĀMIN; *SAMAYASĀRA*; ŚAṄKARĀCĀRYA; VĀCASPATI MIŚRA; *VAIŚEṢIKA SŪTRA*; VASUBANDHU; *YOGASŪTRA*. For plays, playwrights, and dramaturgical compositions and authors, *see also ABHIJÑĀNA ŚĀKUNTALAM*; BHARATA (2); BHĀSA; BHAVABHŪTI; *DEVĪCANDRAGUPTA*; HARṢAVARDHANA; KĀLIDĀSA; MAHENDRAVARMAN I; *MṚCCHAKAṬIKAM*; *MUDRĀRĀKṢASA*; *NĀṬYAŚĀSTRA*; ŚŪDRAKA; *UTTARARĀMACARITA*; VIŚĀKHADATTA. For prescriptive texts and authors, *see also ARTHAŚĀSTRA*; *BṚHASPATI SMṚTI*; DHARMAŚĀSTRA; DHARMASŪTRA; KĀMANDAKA; *KĀMASŪTRA*; *KĀTYĀYANASMṚTI*; KAUṬILYA; MANU; *MANUSMṚTI*; MEDHĀTITHI; *NĀRADA SMṚTI*; *NĪTISĀRA*; VĀTSYĀYANA; *VEDĀṄGA*; *YĀJÑAVALKYASMṚTI*. For poetic compositions, poetics, and authors, *see also AINKURUNŪRU*; *AKAM*; *AKANĀNŪRU*; ĀṆṬĀL; AUVAIYAR; BHĀMAHA; DAṆḌIN; *EṬṬUTOKAI*; HĀLA; KALHAṆA; KĀLIDĀSA; KAPILAR; MĀGHA; *MALAIPATUKATAM*; MĀNIKKAVĀCAKAR; *MULLAIPPĀṬṬU*; NAKKĪRAR; *NAṞṞINAI*; PARANAR; *PARIPĀṬAL*; *PATIṞṞUPATTU*; *PAṬṬINAPPĀLAI*; *PATTUPĀṬṬU*; *PURANĀNURU*; RĀJAŚEKHARA; *SANGAM*; *SATTASAĪ*; *SIRIPANAṞṞUPPATAI*; *TIRUMURUKĀṞṞUPPAṬAI*; TIRUTTAKKA TEVAR; VĀKPATI. For religious literature and authors of religious texts, *see also ABHIDHAMMA PIṬAKA*; *ĀGAMA*; *AITAREYA BRĀHMAṆA*; *AṄGA* (2); *AṄGUTTARA NIKĀYA*; *ANUKRAMAṆI*; *ĀRAṆYAKA*; *AŚOKĀVADĀNA*; *ATHARVAVEDA*; *ĀYĀRA*; BHADRABĀHU;

BHAGAVAD GĪTĀ; *BRĀHMAṆA* (2); *BṚHADĀRAṆYAKA UPANIṢAD*; *BṚHADDEVATĀ*; BUDDHAGHOṢA; *DEVĪMĀHĀTMYA*; *DHAMMAPADA*; *DIVYĀVADĀNA*; *HARIVAṂŚA*; *JĀTAKA*; *JĀTAKAMĀLĀ*; *KALPASŪTRA*; *KHUDDAKA NIKĀYA*; KUNDAKUNDA; LATER VEDA; *MAHĀPURĀṆA*; *MAJJHIMA NIKĀYA*; *MILINDAPAÑHA*; *NĀLĀYIRA TIVIYA PIRAPANTAM*; NAMMĀḺVĀR; *NIRYUKTI*; PERIYĀḺVĀR; PURĀṆA; RATNĀKARA; *ṚGVEDA*; *SAMARAICCHAKAHĀ*; *SĀMAVEDA*; SAṂGHADASAGANI (2); *SAMYUTTA NIKĀYA*; *ŚATAPATHA BRĀHMAṆA*; ŚIVĀRYA; ŚRAUTASŪTRA; *SUYAGADA*; *TEVĀRAM*; *THERAGĀTHĀ*; *THERĪGĀTHĀ*; TIRUJÑĀNA CAMPANTAR; *TIRUKKURAL*; TIRUMANKAI ĀḺVĀR; TIRUMULAR; TIRUNĀVUKKARACAR; *TIRUVĀCAKAM*; TIRUVAḶḶUVĀR; *UPADESAMĀLĀ*; *VINAYA PIṬAKA*; *VIṢṆUDHARMOTTARA PURĀṆA*; *YAJURVEDA*; *YAŚASTILAKA CAMPU*; *ZEND AVESTA*. For scientific, medical, and astrological treatises and authors, *see also* ĀRYABHAṬA; *ĀRYABHAṬĪYA*; BHĀSKARA; BRAHMAGUPTA; *BṚHAT SAṂHITĀ*; CARAKA; *CARAKA SAṂHITĀ*; *GĀRGASAṂHITĀ*; LAGADHA; PATAÑJALI (2); SPHUJIDHVAJA; ŚULBASŪTRA; SUŚRUTA; *SUŚRUTA SAṂHITĀ*; VARĀHAMIHIRA; YATIVṚṢABHA.

LOKĀYĀTA. **Sanskrit** term, literally "that which is prevalent among the people," used to designate (c. mid–first millennium BCE onward) a **philosophical** system based on empirical observation and a rejection of the authority of the **Vedas**. Original texts of the school are no longer available, and it has been reconstructed from representations in opposing traditions. These often portray Lokāyāta thought as hedonistic, and as prescribing instantaneous gratification of the senses.

LOTESHWAR. **Archaeological** site in Gujarat, with two occupational phases. Period I is **Mesolithic**, with evidence of microliths and **burials**. Period II is **Chalcolithic**, with indications of contact with **Harappan** settlements, evident in finds of microbeads of steatite and beads of semiprecious stone.

LOTHAL. Small **Mature Harappan** (c. mid–third millennium BCE onward) settlement near the Gulf of Khambat, Gujarat. Significant structures include a possible dockyard, a warehouse, a workshop for manufacturing stone beads, evidence of shellworking, and a cemetery. There are also traces of a drainage system and possible fire altars. Other finds include **seals** and several sealings. One seal is of a type known from the Persian Gulf, and is indicative of long-distance maritime exchange networks. Other finds consist of typical **pottery**, **copper** and gold artifacts, weights, and **terracotta** figurines. There is also evidence of a **late Harappan** occupation. *See also* TRADE.

LUMBINI. Also known as Lummini, birthplace of the **Buddha**, located in Nepal. Finds from the site include an **Asokan** pillar, with an **inscription** (mid–third century BCE) recording the ruler's pilgrimage to the site and the tax exemptions that he granted to mark the occasion. There are also remains of **monasteries** and ***stūpas***, some of which date to the first millennium CE. Other structures include a water tank and a **temple** to the local **goddess**. Lumbini was declared a World Heritage Site by UNESCO in 1997. *See also* RUMMINDEI.

LUMMINI. *See* LUMBINI.

LUNAR DYNASTY. *See* CANDRAVAṂŚA.

LUSTROUS RED WARE. Type of **pottery** found from the western parts of the subcontinent c. 1100–800 BCE. It gets its name from the burnishing of the surface that makes it shine. It was often painted in black. Designs include representations of animals, especially deer, and geometric motifs. Typical shapes include bowls. *See also* MALWAN; ORIYO TIMBO; RANGPUR.

– M –

MACHAD. **Archaeological** site in Kerala, find spot of **megalithic burials** (c. first millennium BCE?). Other finds include **Black and Red Ware**, a wide range of **iron** equipment, and beads of semiprecious stone.

MACKENZIE, COLIN (1753–1821). Engineer with the British East India Company, the first surveyor general of India, who collected more than 8,000 **inscriptions** and prepared 2,000 drawings of **architectural** remains in south India.

MADHYADEŚA. Sanskrit term, literally "the central land," used c. second half of the first millennium BCE onward, to designate the area including the **Ganga (2)–Yamuna** doab and the mid–Ganga valley, regarded as the heartland of **Brahmanical** culture. *See also MAJJHIMADESA*.

MADRA. Name of a ***janapada***, roughly corresponding with the region of central Punjab. It attained importance during the first millennium BCE. Its chief city was Sākala (**Sāgala**, identified with Sialkot). The Mādrakas or people of Madra are mentioned (c. fourth century CE) in the **Allahabad Pillar Inscription** of the **Gupta** ruler **Samudragupta** among those who offered tribute and homage and agreed to obey the commands of the **king**.

MADURAI. Early historic city in present-day Tamil Nadu, recognized in tradition as the center where poetic compositions were recited in **assemblies** known as ***Sangam*** (hence the name of these anthologies of **Tamil literature**). It was also recognized as the capital of the **Pāṇḍyas**. It was evidently an important center for **Jainism** in the first millennium CE. *See also SILAPPADIKĀRAM*; TEXTILES.

MAGADHA. The most important of the ***mahājanapadas*** that emerged c. sixth century BCE, located in south Bihar, with the **Ganga (2)** forming its northern boundary. The first capital of the state was **Rājagaha**. Later, the capital was shifted to **Pāṭaliputra**. Magadha benefited from its location along **routes** of communication and was richly endowed with fertile **agricultural** land. Besides, the **forests** to the south abounded in elephants, which were an important component of the **army**. To the south were also some of the richest **iron** ore deposits in the subcontinent, in present-day Jharkhand. The rulers of Magadha exploited these natural advantages and adopted a variety of strategies, including marital alliances, **warfare**, and sowing dissension among their rivals, to expand their sphere of influence. As a result, most of the other *mahājanapadas* in north India were brought within the Magadhan Empire over a period of 200 years. Magadha also formed the nucleus of the **Mauryan** Empire (c. fourth–third century BCE). In the second century BCE, **Khāravela**, the ruler of **Kaliṅga**, claimed to have defeated the contemporary ruler of Magadha. *See also* AJĀTAŚATRU; BIMBISĀRA; DHANANANDA; EARLY HISTORIC PERIOD; GUPTA; KĀLĀŚOKA; KANVA; KĀŚI; KHĀRAVELA; KOSALA; MAHĀPADMA NANDA; MALLA; NANDA; PASENADI; ŚIŚUNĀGA; UDAYIN; VAJJI.

MAGAS (OF CYRENE). Ruler (r.c. 300–250) mentioned as a contemporary of **Asoka** in **Major Rock Edict XIII** (c. third century BCE).

MĀGHA. Sanskrit author (c. seventh century CE) of the *Śiśupālavadha*, an ornate poetical composition in 20 sections based on an episode from the ***Mahābhārata***. *See also* LITERATURE.

MAHABALIPURAM. *See* MAMALLAPURAM.

MAHĀBHĀRATA*. Sanskrit epic** that attained its present length (approximately 100,000 verses spread over 18 sections) over a period of several centuries. Terminal dates for the composition are c. fourth–fifth centuries CE. The authorship of the text is attributed to **Vyāsa**, literally the arranger. The narrative revolves around the land between the **Ganga (2)** and the **Yamuna**, and describes the struggle for succession between cousins, the Kauravas and Pāṇḍavas, both part of the **Kuru** lineage, which culminated in a war in which the latter were victorious. The historicity of the narrative remains uncertain. There are several didactic sections, of which the *Śānti Parvan* and the ***Bhagavad Gītā are among the best known. Some sections of the text have parallels in the ***Manusmṛti***. *See also ABHIJÑĀNA ŚĀKUNTALAM*; BHĀRAVI; BHĀSA; DVARAKA; *HARIVAMŚA*; INDRAPRASTHA; *ITIHĀSA*; KĀMPILYA; KṚṢṆA; KURUKṢETRA; LITERATURE; MĀGHA; MARRIAGE; PĀÑCARĀTRA; PARAŚURĀMA; *RĀJASŪYA*; *SATĪ*; *SŪTA*.

MAHĀBHĀṢYA*. Sanskrit** commentary on **Pāṇini**'s grammar, attributed to **Patañjali (1)** composed c. 150 BCE. The text is composed in a dialogic style and deals with about 1,700 of the ***sūtras of the original. *See also* KĀTYĀYANA; LITERATURE.

MAHADAHA. Mesolithic site in Uttar Pradesh (c. sixth millennium BCE), with evidence of a variety of bone and antler **tools**, including arrowheads, points, blades, knives, chisels, scrapers, and saws. Stone tools included microliths made of chert, chalcedony, quartz, crystal, and agate. Animal remains included bones of wild cattle, deer, pig, and turtle. There is evidence of bone ornaments as well. **Burials** were oriented in an east–west direction. Grave goods included bone tools and ornaments, microliths, shell, and animal bones.

MAHAGARA. Archaeological site in the **Belan valley**, Uttar Pradesh, with evidence of **Mesolithic** (c. 11,000–8000 BCE?) and **Neolithic** (c. 7000 BCE?) phases. The latter has yielded evidence of mud huts and a structure that has been identified as a cattle pen. There are indications of the domestication of cattle, sheep, and goat. **Tools** consisted of ground stone tools, microliths, and bone arrowheads. Other finds included **pottery**. The presence of rice husk in the pottery indicates cultivation. While dates as early as the seventh millennium BCE have been suggested for these finds, this is not as yet established beyond doubt.

MAHĀJANAPADA. Name given to a type of state that developed in the north and parts of central India, c. sixth century BCE onward. *Mahājanapadas* included both monarchies and oligarchies. What distinguished them from earlier states, known as ***janapadas***, was a capital, often **fortified**, and more or less institutionalized means of resource mobilization. Some *mahājanapadas* had standing **armies**. Information on the earliest *mahājanapadas* comes from **Buddhist** and **Jaina** sources. *See also* AṄGA; AŚMAKA; AVANTI; CEDI (1); *GAṆA/SAṂGHA*; GANDHARA; KĀŚI; KOSALA; MAGADHA; MALLA; MATSYA; PAÑCĀLA; SECOND URBANIZATION; ŚŪRASENA; VAJJI; VATSA; VIDEHA.

MAHĀKṢATRAPA. **Sanskrit** term, literally "great ***kṣatrapa***," used by the **Śaka** rulers and their subordinates, c. early first millennium BCE.

MAHANADI. River that rises in Chhatisgarh and flows through Orissa, draining into the Bay of Bengal. Its delta formed the nucleus of early **kingdoms** in the region. *See also* MAHENDRA.

MAHĀPADMA NANDA. King of **Magadha** (c. fourth century BCE), associated with a policy of expansion. He may have extended control up to **Kaliṅga**, part of present-day Orissa.

MAHĀPURĀṆA*. Sanskrit** hagiographic **poem**, also known as the *Triśaṣṭi-lakṣaṇa-mahāpurāṇa saṃgraha*, composed by a **Digambara Jaina** monk named Jinasena in the ninth century CE. The text describes the lives of the 24 ***tīrthaṅkaras, focusing in particular on the first *tīrthaṅkara*, **Ṛṣabha**. *See also* LITERATURE.

***MAHĀRĀJA*. Sanskrit** term meaning "great **king**," which became a part of royal titles in the post-**Mauryan** period (c. second century BCE onward). The title was used by the **Kuṣāṇas** among others. By the **early medieval period**, it was used for vassals of important rulers such as the **Guptas**, who themselves adopted the grandiose title of *mahārājādhirāja*, that is, overlord of *mahārājas*. *See also* KHĀRAVELA.

MAHĀSAṂGHIKA. Theravāda Buddhist school that emerged c. fourth century BCE onward. Initially, its differences from other schools were in terms of the rules of monastic discipline. In the course of the next two centuries, the Mahāsaṃghikas split into several sects, some of which developed into the **Mahāyāna** tradition by c. first century CE.

MAHASTHAN. Early historic (c. fifth century BCE onward) **archaeological** site in Bangladesh, with traces of a mud rampart. **Pottery** includes **Northern Black Polished Ware**. Among other finds is an **inscription** in **Mauryan Brāhmī** and a **temple** that has been attributed to the **Gupta** period. There is evidence for **fortification** during the **Pāla** period. *See also* PUṆḌRA.

***MAHĀVAMSA*.** Sinhalese **Buddhist** chronicle, composed c. fifth–sixth century CE, in **Pali**, attributed to a monk named Mahānāma. The text contains a history of Buddhism (c. sixth century BCE–fourth century CE), including details of political history. *See also CŪLAVAMSA*; LITERATURE.

***MAHĀVASTU*.** **Biography** of the **Buddha** composed in **Buddhist Hybrid Sanskrit**, by an anonymous author (c. third–fifth centuries CE?). *See also* LITERATURE.

MAHĀVĪRA. Literally, the great hero, the most renowned teacher of **Jainism** (c. sixth century BCE). According to Jaina tradition, Mahāvīra, initially known as Vardhamāna, was born in the **Jñātrika** clan of the **Licchavis**. His father, Siddhārtha, was probably a chief of the clan, and a **kṣatriya**. Vardhamāna was married at the age of 28, but renounced the world soon after. He attained enlightenment after practicing severe austerities for 12 years, after which he was known as Mahāvīra, Jina (the conqueror), and **Tīrthaṅkara** (one who helps others to cross through the stream of worldly existence). Mahāvīra taught his doctrine for about 30 years, traveling through present-day Bihar and Uttar Pradesh. He also established orders for monks and nuns. He passed away in **Pava**, in present-day Bihar. *See also ĀYĀRA*; *GAṆA/SAMṂGHA*; *KALPASŪTRA*; *NĀYADHAMMAKAHĀ*; PĀRŚVA.

MAHĀYĀNA. **Sanskrit** term, literally "the great vehicle," major **Buddhist** tradition that emerged around the beginning of the first millennium CE in the northwestern part of the subcontinent. Its distinctive features included belief in the **Bodhisattva**, beings capable of attaining liberation, who remained in the world to ensure the welfare of lesser mortals, thus exemplifying the quality of compassion. The tradition developed theistic elements, including the worship of the **Buddha** and other divinities in anthropomorphic form. In terms of **philosophy** it was associated with the notion of *śūnya* or void. By the end of the first millennium CE, Mahāyāna Buddhism had spread along the **Silk Route** to Central Asia, China, Korea, and Japan. *See also* BUDDHIST COUNCILS; HĪNAYĀNA; INDO-GREEK; MAHĀSAMṂGHIKA; NĀGĀRJUNA; THERAVĀDA; VASUBANDHU.

MAHENDRA (SON OF ASOKA). *See* MAHINDA.

MAHENDRA. Ruler (c. fourth century CE) of a region designated as southern **Kosala** (perhaps part of the valley of the **Mahanadi** River in present-day Chattisgarh and Orissa), listed in the **Allahabad Pillar Inscription** of the **Gupta** ruler **Samudragupta** and mentioned among those who were captured and released on condition of submission to the Gupta **king**.

MAHENDRAPĀLA. Pratihāra ruler (r.c. 892–908), often considered one of the most powerful rulers of the lineage, who succeeded in extending his dominions up to Bengal in the east. **Inscriptions** indicate that he exercised control over **Kanauj**, and over Gujarat and the Punjab as well. His court poet was **Rājaśekhara**.

MAHENDRAVARMAN I. Pallava ruler (r. 590–630), famed for his military exploits as well as for his patronage of the arts. Initially, he was probably a supporter of **Jainism**, but later he switched allegiance to **Śaivism**. Some of the earliest Pallava **rock-cut temples** have been attributed to his reign. He is also recognized as the author of a **Sanskrit** play, the *Mattavilāsa prahasanam*, a farce on a variety of **religious** sects. *See also* LITERATURE; NARASIMHAVARMAN I; TIRUNĀVUKKARACAR.

MAHESHWAR. Archaeological site in Madhya Pradesh, identified with **Māhiṣmatī**, mentioned as a **city** of **Avanti** in early **Buddhist** tradition. There is evidence for several occupational levels at the site and the twin settlement of **Navdatoli**. The earliest levels yielded a range of middle **Paleolithic tools**. The site witnessed a substantial **Chalcolithic** occupation during the second millennium BCE. There was evidence of **agriculture**, **pastoralism**, and hunting, with finds of wheat, rice, pulses, oilseeds, and bones of cattle, pig, and deer. Associated **pottery** included painted **black and red ware**, **Malwa ware**, and **Jorwe ware**. There were traces of mud-brick **architecture**. Tools consisted of microliths and **copper** equipment. The site was reoccupied in the mid–first millennium BCE after a flood. Finds from this level included **Northern Black Polished Ware**, **iron** equipment, bangles of glass, and **punch-marked** and **cast coins**. Subsequently, there was evidence for **Red Polished Ware**.

MAHINDA. Son of **Asoka** (c. third century BCE), also known as Mahendra, mentioned in Sinhalese chronicles, according to which he was sent by his father to spread the message of **Buddhism** to Sri Lanka. *See also DĪPAVAMSA*.

MAHIPĀLA (1). Pratihāra ruler (r. 912–930). **Al Masudi**, who visited his court, described his power, wealth, and **army**. His court poet **Rājaśekhara** attributed conquests beyond the **Vindhyas** to his patron, but these accounts are probably exaggerated.

MAHIPĀLA (2). Pāla ruler (c. 995–1043 CE), known from **inscriptions**, who apparently succeeded in restoring Pāla control over parts of Bengal and Bihar, overcoming the threats posed by the Caṇḍelas and **Kalacuris**. His name is associated with several towns and tanks in the region. It is likely that he embellished the settlement at **Paharpur** with **monasteries**, ***stūpas***, and a **temple**. He was remembered in folksongs as a popular ruler.

MAHISDAL. Archaeological site in West Bengal, with evidence of two occupational phases. Period I (c. 1300–700 BCE) has been designated as **Chalcolithic**. Finds included **black and red ware**, traces of **copper**, microliths, bone **tools**, and beads of semiprecious stone. Period II (c. 700 BCE onward) yielded evidence of the use of **iron** and **black slipped ware**.

MĀHIṢMATĪ. Early historic city, mentioned in textual traditions including the ***Mahābhārata***, identified with **Maheshwar**.

MAHURJHARI. Archaeological site in Maharashtra, with evidence of **megalithic burials** including stone cairns (c. first millennium BCE). Associated finds included **Black and Red Ware**, **iron** equipment, gold ornaments, beads, and horse burials. Subsequently, there was evidence for the manufacture of beads of semiprecious stone, dating to the **early historic period** (c. second half of the first millennium BCE). Other finds consisted of baked-brick structures. An **inscribed seal** (c. mid–first millennium CE) was also recovered from the site.

MAITRAKA. Ruling lineage in Gujarat, initially feudatories of the **Guptas**, who came to power at the beginning of the sixth century CE, known from their **land grant inscriptions**. The dynasty ruled for about 250 years from their capital at **Valabhi**. *See also* GOP.

MAITREYĪ. **Woman philosopher** (c. sixth century BCE) mentioned in the ***Bṛhadāraṇyaka Upaniṣad***, which records a dialogue between her and her husband, the sage **Yājñavalkya**. The latter was supposed to have imparted philosophical knowledge to her, on her request, before he abandoned the life of a householder.

MAJJHIMA NIKĀYA**.** **Pali** text, part of the ***Sutta Piṭaka***, compiled c. fourth century BCE, which derives its name from the fact that it is an anthology of about 150 middle-length discourses attributed to the **Buddha**. *See also* LITERATURE.

MAJJHIMADESA**.** **Prakrit/Pali** term, meaning "central lands," used in **Jaina** and **Buddhist** texts (c. sixth century BCE onward) to designate the mid–**Ganga (2)** valley and adjoining regions to the east. The nucleus of this territory was further east than that of the ***madhyadeśa*** mentioned in **Sanskrit** texts.

MAJOR PILLAR EDICTS. A set of **inscriptions** of the **Mauryan** ruler **Asoka** (c. third century BCE), dated to the 26th year of the ruler's reign, found engraved on stone pillars in Bihar, Haryana, and Uttar Pradesh. Two of the pillars were transported to Delhi by Sultan Firoz Shah Tughlaq in the 14th century. As in the case of his other inscriptions, there is a preoccupation with enunciating the principles of ***dhamma***. The first three edicts contain general statements on the theme. The fourth edict contains detailed instructions for the ***rājukas***. It also includes a set of provisions for mitigating the harshness of the **judicial** system, providing, among other things, for a reprieve of three days for those sentenced to death. The fifth edict contains a long list of animals, birds, and aquatic creatures, and mentions restrictions on killing and/or castrating them. The sixth edict is general in nature. The seventh edict occurs only on the Delhi–Topra Pillar. It refers to the functions of the *rājukas* and ***dhamma mahāmattas*** and mentions activities undertaken by the ruler such as planting trees and digging wells. *See also* LAURIYA ARARAJ; LAURIYA NANDANGARH; MEERUT; RAMPURWA; TOPRA.

MAJOR ROCK EDICTS. Inscriptions of the **Mauryan** ruler **Asoka** (c. third century BCE), some of which are dated in regnal years, found generally along the frontiers of his **kingdom**. The best known among these is Edict XIII, which expressed the remorse of the ruler after the conquest of **Kaliṅga** during the eighth year of his reign. This victory was followed by the capture of 150,000 people and the killing of 100,000, while many more died. The inscription also mentioned several independent rulers to the west. These references have been used to determine the chronology of the Mauryas. The inscription also referred to peoples living both within and outside the realm, especially to the south, including the **Co<u>l</u>as** and **Pāṇḍyas** as well as those of Sri Lanka. (The Co<u>l</u>as, Pāṇḍyas, and ruling lineages in Kerala and western India were also mentioned in the second rock edict.) The ruler claimed to have spread the message of ***dhamma*** among all these peoples (including those in the western kingdoms). This particular edict is missing from the sets found in Orissa, where it was replaced by two **Separate Rock Edicts**.

The other edicts elucidated the principles of Asoka's *dhamma*. These included restrictions on social gatherings and abstinence from eating meat (Edict I). Edict II described measures taken to provide medical facilities to humans and animals and arrangements for the well-being of travelers. Edict III recommended practices such as honoring one's parents; making gifts to friends, kinsfolk, ***brāhmaṇas* (1)**, and renouncers; and practicing moderation. It also stated that periodic tours were to be undertaken by designated officials. Edict IV mentioned, among other things, that spectacular displays were organized to convey the message of *dhamma* to his subjects. Edict V announced the creation of a special category of officials known as the ***dhamma mahāmatta***, for the propagation of *dhamma*. Edict VI proclaimed that the ruler was accessible to reporters at all times and places. Edict VIII mentioned that the ruler had replaced pleasure trips with journeys to spread *dhamma*. Edict IX condemned the performance of rituals and advocated the practice of *dhamma*, including kindness toward servants and **slaves**, as an alternative. Edict XII laid down the means of ensuring harmonious relations among people belonging to different sects. Edict XIV laid down the principles underlying the composition and dissemination of the message of *dhamma*. The other edicts reiterated some of these messages and ideas.

All the Major Rock Edicts were in **Prakrit**, and most of them were written in the **Brāhmī script**. The only exceptions were those found in the North-West Frontier Province (Pakistan), written in **Kharoṣṭhī**. An abbreviated version of the edicts, in Greek and **Aramaic**, was found in Afghanistan. *See also* DHAULI; ERRAGUDI; GIRNAR; JAUGADA; KALSI; MAGAS (OF CYRENE); MANSEHRA; SHAHBAZGARHI; SOPARA; TURAMAYA.

MAKKHALIPUTTA GOSĀLA. Philosopher, recognized as the founder of the **Ājīvika** tradition (c. sixth century BCE), which was characterized by a belief in determinism and a consequent denial of free will.

MALAIPATUKATAM*. Tamil poem**, part of the ***Pattupāṭṭu of the ***Sangam*** anthology (c. third century BCE–second century CE?), attributed to the poet Perunkaucikan. The composition included descriptions of the realm of his patron, hill **tribes**, and information about **music**. *See also* LITERATURE.

MĀLAVA. Community, possibly **pastoral**, that moved from the northwest part of the subcontinent to Rajasthan and central India. The Mālavas are mentioned (c. fourth century CE) in the **Allahabad Pillar Inscription** of **Samudragupta** among those who offered tribute and homage and agreed to obey the commands of the **king**. *See also* DAṆḌIN; SEALS.

MALHAR. Archaeological site in Chattisgarh, with evidence of five occupational phases. Finds from Period I (c. first half of the first millennium BCE) included remains of a baked-brick wall. Period II (second half of the first millennium BCE) yielded evidence of a mud rampart, **black and red ware**, **Northern Black Polished Ware**, **punch-marked** and **cast coins** as well as issues attributed to the **Sātavāhanas**, and **terracotta** sealings with **Brāhmī inscriptions**. Finds from Period III (mid–first millennium CE) consisted of remains of a **temple** and other **Buddhist** structures. There were no substantial remains for the next two phases, although the site continued to be occupied until the beginning of the second millennium CE.

MALKHED. *See* MĀNYAKHEṬA.

MALLA. ***Mahājanapada*** (c. sixth century BCE) in north Bihar, with two principal **cities**, **Kusinagara** and **Pava**. It consisted of a confederacy of ruling ***kṣatriya*** lineages. It was absorbed into the **Magadhan** Empire by the fourth century BCE.

MALPUR. Archaeological site in Kashmir, with evidence of a **Neolithic** (c. third millennium BCE) culture similar to that at **Burzahom** and **Gufkral**. Finds included a range of stone **tools**, grinding stones, and handmade **pottery**.

MALWA WARE. Name assigned to **pottery** made on a slow wheel, and used in central India, c. 1600–1200 BCE. Distinctive features include a coarse fabric; red, orange, or pink color; and painted designs consisting of both geometric and naturalistic motifs. Typical shapes include a channel-spouted bowl and other types of bowls and vases. *See also* DAIMABAD; DANGWADA; ERAN; JORWE; KATRA; KAYATHA; MAHESHWAR; SONGAON; TULJAPUR GARHI.

MALWAN. Archaeological site in Gujarat, with evidence of a **late Harappan** and **post-Harappan Chalcolithic** settlement (c. second millennium BCE). Finds included stone **tools**; **terracotta** figurines; bones of cattle, sheep, goat, dog, horse, pig, and deer; and **Lustrous Red Ware**.

MAMALLAPURAM. Coastal **archaeological** site in Tamil Nadu, also known as Mahabalipuram, an important sea port from the beginning of the Common Era. It attained its greatest importance under the **Pallava** ruler **Narasiṃhavarman I** (c. seventh century CE). Its distinctive features include **rock-cut** monolithic stone **temples** and other temples, of which the most famous is the **Shore temple**. Many of the structures and rock surfaces were embellished with some of the finest examples of stone **sculpture** derived from **Purāṇic** themes. These sculptures were probably intended to project the power of the **king**, who was often implicitly equated with the deities who were represented. The site is recognized as a World Heritage Site by UNESCO.

MANAMUNDA. Archaeological site in Orissa also known as Asurgarh, with evidence of two occupational phases. Period I A (c. fourth century BCE) yielded microliths and **copper** artifacts. Finds from Period I B included a **punch-marked coin** and **iron** artifacts such as knives, daggers, and spearheads. Other finds consisted of charred rice and **black and red ware**. Period II is dated to c. second–third centuries CE.

MANDA. Archaeological site on the **Chenab** River in Kashmir, with three occupational phases. Period I (c. third millennium BCE) yielded evidence of **Harappan pottery**, potsherds with graffiti, and a Harappan **seal**. Period II was designated as **early historic** (mid–first millennium BCE onward), while Period III was associated with the **Kuṣāṇas** (early first millennium CE).

MANDASOR. *See* DAŚAPURA.

MANDHAL. Archaeological site in Maharashtra with evidence of occupation from the early centuries CE. Structural remains include three **temples** belonging to the mid–first millennium CE. Other finds include a **copper plate land grant inscription** of the **Vākāṭakas**.

MANER. Archaeological site in Bihar, with evidence of occupation from the end of the second millennium BCE onward. Four occupational phases have been identified. The first (Period I) was **Neolithic**, with evidence of microliths, bone points, **pottery**, and **terracotta** spindle whorls. Period II was identified as **Chalcolithic**. Finds included microliths and stone blades and flakes. Pottery consisted of **black and red ware**. Other finds consisted of bone points and terracotta beads and **copper** artifacts similar to those associated with copper **hoards**. The third phase (Period III, c. mid–first millennium BCE) was characterized by finds of **Northern Black Polished Ware**; terracotta ring wells; **iron** artifacts, including spearheads; bone points; **cast** copper **coins**; and terracotta and stone beads and sealings. There was an occupational hiatus before Period IV, assigned to the **Pāla** period (c. eighth century CE onward). Finds from this phase included iron nails, bone points, terracotta and stone beads, terracotta animal and human figurines, and structural remains.

MANGALKOT. Archaeological site in West Bengal. The occupation is divided into seven periods, with evidence of overlaps and disturbed layers. Finds in Period I (**Chalcolithic**) included bone **tools** and microliths; bones of cattle, tortoise, and fish; impressions of husk on **pottery**, indicating the cultivation of rice; handmade pottery; and **black and red ware**. Period II, dated to c. 1500–700 BCE, yielded bone tools; **iron** daggers, sickles, and slag; **copper** fishhooks and rings; evidence of wattle-and-daub structures and hearths; antlers; tortoise shell; beads of semiprecious stone; and black and red ware. Period III, dated between c. 700 and 400 BCE, is defined as transitional. Finds from Period IV (c. fourth–first centuries BCE) consisted of **punch-marked** and copper **cast coins**, **Northern Black Polished Ware**, **terracotta** figurines, a copper bowl, and beads of semiprecious stone and glass. Period V, associated with the **Śuṅga-Kuṣāṇa** phase (c. second century BCE–second century CE), yielded iron nails, storage jars, **rouletted ware**, terracotta figurines, copper artifacts, beads of semiprecious stone, burnt-brick structures, and ring wells. Finds from Period VI (c. third–fifth centuries CE) consisted of inscribed **seals** and sealings, copper cast coins, and unfinished as well as finished beads of semiprecious stone, suggestive of local manufacture. The occupational layers in Period VII were disturbed. There is evidence of a **temple** and stone **sculptures** that probably date to the **early medieval period**.

MANIGARA. Paleolithic site in Uttar Pradesh, find spot of more than 200 stone artifacts including pebble **tools**, cleavers, and scrapers of quartzite.

***MAṆIGRĀMAM*. Guild** of merchants in south India, active from the end of the first millennium CE to the mid–second millennium CE. There is **inscriptional** evidence to suggest that members of this association were closely connected with **temple** administration and **irrigation** works. They were also involved in overseas **trade**.

MĀNIKKAVĀCAKAR. Tamil Śaiva poet (c. ninth century CE), whose devotional poems were anthologized in the ***Tiruvācakam***, literally sacred chant. Hagiographical traditions suggest that he was a ***brāhmaṇa* (1)** by birth and that he constructed a Śaiva shrine at Tirupenturai, Tamil Nadu. He is supposed to have embarked on a pilgrimage of Śaiva **temples**, ultimately passing away at Chidambaram. *See also* LITERATURE.

***MAṆIMEKALAI*. Tamil Buddhist epic**, composed by **Cāttanār**, c. sixth century CE, named after the chief protagonist, Maṇimekalai, the heroine who renounces worldly pleasures in favor of a life of meditation and compassion. The text enunciates Buddhist **philosophy**, ethics, and principles. *See also* LITERATURE.

MANJHI. Archaeological site in Bihar, with three occupational phases. Period I (c. 1000–500 BCE) provided evidence of **black slipped ware** and **black and red ware**, besides remains of wattle-and-daub structures. Period II (c. 500 BCE onward) yielded evidence of burnt-brick structures, town planning, ring wells, traces of a road, and **Northern Black Polished Ware**. Plant remains included wheat, barley, rice, gram, lentil, millet, grape, pea, and sesame. Period III (c. second–third centuries CE) yielded **terracotta** figurines and a sealing.

MANRAM*.** Village **assembly**, mentioned in **Tamil *Sangam texts (c. third century BCE–second century CE?), usually associated with shrines or sacred trees as well as a center for social activities.

MANSAR. Early historic (c. late first millennium BCE) **archaeological** site in Maharashtra. Finds included a structure tentatively identified as a **monastery**. There is evidence of a low wall and a circumambulatory path and images of deities. Other finds consisted of silver portrait **coins**, coin molds attributed to the **Kṣatrapas**, and **copper** coins attributed to the **Vākāṭakas** (mid–first millennium CE). **Iron** nails, chains, needles, hoes, axes, rods, chisels, and hooks; ornaments of copper, silver, glass, and shell; and **terracotta** plaques have also been found.

MANSEHRA. Archaeological site in Pakistan (North-West Frontier Province), find spot of a set of the **Major Rock Edicts** of **Asoka**. These were inscribed in **Kharoṣṭhī**.

MAṆṬARĀJA. Ruler (c. fourth century CE) of an unidentified region called Kaurāla, mentioned in the **Allahabad Pillar Inscription** of the **Gupta** ruler **Samudragupta**, one of those who was captured and released when he submitted to the latter.

MANU. Conceptualized in the **Sanskrit epic** and **Purāṇic** traditions (dated in their final forms to c. fourth–fifth centuries CE) as the primeval man, and, by extension as the first **king** of the human race. His children included a son, **Ikṣvāku (1)**, and an androgynous being known as Ila (masculine)/Ilā (feminine) who spent half his existence as a man and half as a **woman**. Ikṣvāku was regarded as the progenitor of the **Sūryavaṃśa** or solar lineage, Ila of the **Candravaṃśa** or lunar lineage. From the **early medieval period** onward, most ruling lineages in north and central India claimed affiliation with one or other of these two lineages. *See also* AILA; *MANUSMṚTI*.

MANUSCRIPTS. While there is evidence for a vast and complex textual tradition in early India, surviving manuscripts from the period are few and far between. **Sanskrit** birch bark **Buddhist** manuscripts recovered from **Gilgit** and **Gandhara**, written in **Kharoṣṭhī**, dating to the early centuries of the Common Era, are somewhat exceptional finds. Palm leaves were also used as a writing surface. Most texts in Sanskrit and **Prakrit** survive in copies that were made during the second millennium in a variety of regional scripts derived from **Brāhmī**. **Pali** manuscripts from Sri Lanka have also proved extremely valuable.

Many manuscripts were initially prepared and preserved in **monasteries**, Buddhist, **Jaina**, and **Brahmanical**. From the late 18th century, manuscripts were collected and sent to European libraries and museums, where catalogs were prepared and texts were both edited and translated. The 19th and 20th centuries have witnessed manuscript collections being developed in Indian museums and universities, including Oriental institutes at Vadodara, Pune, and Chennai. At present, the government of India has launched a program for collecting, preserving, and digitizing manuscripts under the aegis of the National Mission for Manuscripts, established in 2003. *See also* LANGUAGES; MITRA, RAJENDRA LALA; ORIENTALISM; SWAMINATHA IYER, U. V.

MANUSMṚTI. **Sanskrit** text, one of the most important **Dharmaśāstras**, also known as the *Mānavadharmaśāstra*, attributed to **Manu**, composed and compiled c. 200 BCE–100 CE. It consists of approximately 2,700 verses, arranged in 12 books or sections. These deal with cosmogonic and **philosophical** ideas, rules, and rituals to be observed by the ***brāhmaṇa*** **(1)** householder in particular; relations among the ***varṇas*** and between the sexes; and functions of the **king**, including legal procedures. Several commentaries were written on the text in the first and second millennia. The work was among the first Sanskrit texts to be translated into English and was regarded as a model for modern legal provisions during colonial rule in the 19th and 20th centuries. More recently, its provisions have been contested on the grounds that these are both casteist and sexist. *See also MAHĀBHĀRATA*; MEDHĀTITHI; *YAVANA*.

MĀNYAKHEṬA. Present-day Malkhed (Karnataka), the capital of the **Rāṣṭrakūṭas** between the 8th and 10th centuries CE. It was also an important **Jaina** center.

MARITIME TRADE. The earliest definitive evidence for maritime trade occurs in the context of the **Harappan civilization** (c. 2700–1800 BCE). There are indications that sea **routes** from the coasts of Sind and Gujarat to the Persian Gulf were in use, with contact with Oman, Bahrain, and Mesopotamia. It is possible that **copper** was obtained from Oman. Mesopotamian texts refer to a region known as **Meluhha**, which has often been identified with the **Indus valley**.

From the **early historic period**, there is evidence for the existence of coastal port towns along both the eastern and western coasts. Some of the former and several of the latter find mention in the ***Periplus of the Erythraean Sea***, which lists imports and exports from each of these centers. This indicates that various kinds of **textiles**, spices, especially pepper, and medicinal herbs were the principal exports. Imports included a range of prestige goods. **Pali**, **Prakrit**, **Sanskrit**, and **Tamil** texts also refer to overseas voyages undertaken by merchants from the subcontinent. These voyages were recognized as both risky and highly profitable. Finds of hoards of **Roman coins** from peninsular India also bear testimony to overseas contacts through the

Arabian Sea to East Africa and Aden. Besides, there are indications of contact through the Bay of Bengal with Southeast and East Asia. Visual representations of ships in **sculpture** and **painting** indicate well-developed traditions of shipbuilding.

While some historians suggest that there was a decline in overseas trade with the west following the collapse of the Western Roman Empire, others argue that trade with East Africa and Byzantium continued. Contact with the east was also sustained.

The concerns of maritime trade often influenced political developments: It is evident that the rivalry between the **Śakas** and the **Sātavāhanas** was partly owing to attempts to monopolize control over ports on the west coast. It is also apparent that the **Co<u>l</u>as** adopted expansionist policies in order to control the routes of communication along the Bay of Bengal.

The presence of merchants from distant lands is occasionally documented in **inscriptions**, which refer to the ***yavana*** and to Arab merchants, whose presence became increasingly important in ports along the west coast during the first millennium CE. *See also MAṆIGRĀMAM*; PĀṆḌYA; TRADE.

MARRIAGE. Marriage was recognized as the most important rite of passage for **women**, and one of the most important ones for men within the **Brahmanical** tradition. The **Dharmasūtras** and **Dharmaśāstras** (c. sixth century BCE onward) list six to eight different forms of marriage. These included relatively prestigious forms, where the daughter was conferred as a gift to the groom by her father, and what were viewed as less respectable forms, including marriages that involved the payment of bride price, marriages where men and women chose their partners, and unions that followed rape and/or abduction. Ideally, marriage partners were expected to belong to the same ***varṇa***. While unions between men of higher status with women of lower status were occasionally accommodated, the reverse was viewed with disfavor.

Normative texts indicate a preference for marriage where priests were present, and the ritual was conducted around the **sacrificial** fire. There was an emphasis on exogamy, although the practice of endogamy was recognized in south India. There was also an attempt to keep the age of marriage for women as close to puberty as possible, although narrative texts suggest that marriage between older men and women was by no means uncommon. It is evident that marital practices varied according to social status and region. One of the major variants was the *svayamvara*, recognized as a practice among ***kṣatriyas***, where the groom was selected after a contest, often involving a test of prowess. The recognized objectives of marriage included the continuation of the Brahmanical ritual tradition and producing progeny, especially sons.

While divorce was not viewed favorably within the normative Brahmanical tradition, there are indications that it was possible. Women could be abandoned on a variety of counts—including insubordination, not producing the desired offspring, and so on. Occasionally, texts such as the ***Arthaśāstra*** included provisions allowing women who were deserted to remarry. It is possible that these provisions were more common in customary practice that was not codified. The remarriage of **widows**, too, was viewed with disfavor within the Brahmanical tradition, although it may have been prevalent among some sections of society. Widowers, on the other hand, were generally encouraged to remarry in order to continue their ritual practices as well as their lineages.

Polygyny was permitted, and narratives suggest that it was fairly common among the ruling elite. Some prescriptive texts provide for men of "higher" *varṇas* to acquire wives from "lower" *varṇas*. Polyandry was relatively rare but was occasionally documented. The most spectacular instance is from the ***Mahābhārata***, where the Pāṇḍavas are represented as sharing a common wife, Draupadī. *See also* FAMILY STRUCTURE; *GOTRA*; *JĀTI*; KINSHIP SYSTEMS; *SAMṢKĀRA*; SAMUDRAGUPTA; UNTOUCHABILITY; *VARṆASAMṢKARA*.

MARSHALL, JOHN HUBERT. Director general of the **Archaeological Survey** of India (1902–1934). He was one of the earliest professionally trained archaeologists, with training in excavations conducted in Greece, Turkey, and Crete, to join the Archaeological Survey. He prepared a manual on conservation that continues to be used at present. He is best known for his supervision of the excavations at **Mohenjodaro** and **Harappa**. His publications include *Mohenjodaro and the Indus Civilization*. He was also associated with the excavations at the **early historic** site of **Taxila**. Marshall left India after his retirement in 1934.

MARTAND. Archaeological site of a Sun **temple**, now in ruins, in Kashmir, built in the eighth century CE by **King Lalitāditya**.

MASAON. Archaeological site in Uttar Pradesh with evidence of four occupational phases. Structural remains from Period I (c. 600–300 BCE) included baked-brick **architecture** and ring wells. Other finds consisted of **Northern Black Polished Ware**, **black slipped ware**, **punch-marked coins**, and **terracotta** figurines. Finds associated with Period II (c. 200 BCE–50 CE) were more or less identical. Period III (c. 100–250 CE) yielded **Kuṣāṇa** coins, **seals**, and sealings. Seals, sealings, and figurines were also found in Period IV (c. 250–600 CE).

MASKI. Archaeological site in Karnataka, with evidence of three occupational phases. Period I, considered **Neolithic–Chalcolithic** (c. second millennium BCE?), yielded evidence of cattle, sheep, and goat rearing and the cultivation of millets. Other finds included stone blades, ground stone axes, microliths, **pottery**, and traces of **copper**. Finds associated with Period II (c. first millennium BCE) consisted of **megaliths**, **Black and Red Ware**, and **iron** artifacts. Period III (c. first–third centuries CE) provided evidence of **Russet-Coated Painted Ware**, **rouletted ware**, and **terracotta** figurines. Maski is also the find spot of a **Minor Rock Edict** of **Asoka**, one of the few mentioning the personal name of the ruler. *See also* KALLUR; TERDAL.

MATHEMATICS. The earliest indications of precise mathematical calculations are available from the **Harappan civilization** (c. 2700–1800 BCE), where finds of weights and measuring scales indicate the application of mathematical principles. Subsequently, the **Śulbasūtras**, **later Vedic** texts (c. first half of the first millennium BCE), suggest familiarity with geometric principles. By the first millennium CE, a system of writing numerals was developed, evident in **inscriptions**. This culminated in the use of a symbol for zero, and the working out of a place-value system. The Arabs adopted this system, which subsequently spread to Europe. This facilitated calculations. Mathematics was often used for **astronomical** and astrological calculations. Among the best-known mathematician-astronomers are **Āryabhaṭa** and **Varāhamihira**. *See also* YATIVṚṢABHA.

MATHURA. Ancient settlement on the **Yamuna**. It was recognized as the capital of the **Śūrasena** ***mahājanapada*** in early textual traditions. **Archaeological** evidence indicates that the site was settled since c. eighth century BCE. It became an important urban center c. fifth century BCE onward, owing its prosperity to its strategic location along **routes** of communication between north and south India as well as east and west India. Its political importance continued during the rule of the **Śakas** and **Kuṣāṇas**. It was also a center for a variety of **religious** traditions, including **Buddhism**, **Jainism**, and **Brahmanical Hinduism**. Structural finds include remains of Buddhist and Jaina ***stūpas*** and a **fortification** wall. A **temple**, apparently meant for the worship of Kuṣāṇa rulers, has been found in the vicinity of the city. Mathura was noted for a distinctive **sculptural** tradition, including some of the earliest anthropomorphic representations of the **Buddha** and the **Mahāvira** in sandstone. The settlement declined in importance from c. fifth century CE.

Excavations have yielded evidence of five occupational phases. Finds from Period I (c. sixth–fourth centuries BCE) include **Painted Grey Ware** and traces of mud-brick **architecture**. Period II (c. fourth–second centuries BCE) yielded **Northern Black Polished Ware**, **punch-marked coins**, **terracotta** figurines, and beads of semiprecious stone. Finds from Period III (c. second–first centuries BCE) consisted of terracotta plaques, **seals**, and sealings. Period IV (c. first–third centuries CE) witnessed the construction of *stūpas*. The earliest stone sculpture also dates to this period. Many of these traditions continued during Period V (c. fourth–sixth centuries CE). *See also* BHĀGAVATA; SANGHOL; SECOND URBANIZATION; SONKH; *UTTARĀPATHA*; YĀDAVA.

MATILA. Ruler (c. fourth century CE) mentioned in the **Allahabad Pillar Inscription** of the **Gupta** ruler **Samudragupta** as one of the kings of ***āryāvarta*** whom he had uprooted. Matila may have controlled a part of the **Ganga (2)–Yamuna** doab.

MATSYA. Name of a ***mahājanapada***, including parts of present-day Rajasthan. Its capital was **Bairat**. It attained importance in the sixth century BCE.

MATURE HARAPPAN. Phase of the **Harappan civilization** (c. 2700–1800 BCE), with evidence of settlements in Sind, the Punjab, and Baluchistan (Pakistan); northwest India, including the Punjab, Haryana, Rajasthan, and Gujarat; and Afghanistan. Subsistence strategies show a broad similarity with **early/pre-Harappan archaeological** cultures. There is evidence for the cultivation of wheat and barley, with some amount of rice and millets. Other crops include peas, lentil, cotton, and sesame. Domesticated animals consisted of cattle, sheep, and goat.

The major settlements were planned urban centers, with drainage systems, baked-brick **architecture**, and streets oriented along a grid pattern. Several Mature Harappan sites contain citadels: a section of the settlement that was often **fortified**, and built on raised platforms, with distinctive buildings. Other unique features include **pottery**. In terms of painted varieties, the diagnostic ware is one with black designs, generally naturalistic, on a red background. Common motifs consist of the pipal leaf and the peacock, while unique forms include perforated jars, scored goblets, and dish-on-stand. While **copper** and bronze artifacts, including **tools**, weapons, utensils, and jewelry, have been recovered, stone tools, especially blades, were also in use. **Crafts** comprised metalworking and bead making (especially using steatite and carnelian), besides producing seals. There is evidence for the use of steatite stamp **seals** with short **inscriptions**, a standardized system of weights, and a **script** that has not been deciphered. While most of the inscriptions are on steatite seals, inscriptions have also been found on metal surfaces and terracotta, shell, and ivory objects.

Harappan seals have been found in Mesopotamian sites such as Ur and Kish, pointing to the existence of long-distance exchange networks. Other indications of contact are provided by finds of Harappan pottery at sites in Oman and Bahrain. Weights corresponding to the Harappan standard have also been found from these regions. Harappan pottery has been recovered from the site of Ra's al-Junayz on the Arabian coast.

While the archaeological record points to the existence of social differences, there have been debates on the political structure. One possibility, suggested by the uniformity in town planning and craft production, is that there was a centralized polity. The other suggestion that has been advanced is of a looser confederacy of provinces or regions. This is based on the evidence of variations within the overarching uniformity.

Attempts to reconstruct Harappan **religious** beliefs and practices have been somewhat speculative in the absence of textual evidence. The visual imagery, including figurines and representations of female figures on seals, has been interpreted as an indication of the existence of a cult(s) of the mother **goddess**. Architectural features such as the Great Bath and wells have been interpreted as signs of the importance assigned to water in rituals. The possibility of the worship of trees, as also of certain sacred animals, has also been recognized. Some sites have provided evidence for fire altars. Some of these elements resurface in later **Hinduism**; however, at present it is difficult to trace a continuous historical tradition from the Harappan evidence to later times. *See also* ART; CHANHUDARO; DHOLAVIRA; GUMLA; HARAPPA; KALIBANGAN; KOT DIJI; KUNTASI; LOTHAL; MITATHAL; MOHENJODARO; NAGESHWAR; RAKHI GARHI; ROHRI; ROJDI; SUTKAGENDOR; TRADE; VALMIYO TIMBO; WARFARE.

MAUES. The earliest known **Śaka** ruler in the subcontinent (c. 80–60 BCE) who evidently overcame the **Indo-Greeks** in the northwest and ruled from **Taxila**. Maues is known primarily from his **coins**, which were modeled on those of the Indo-Greeks, with legends in Greek and **Kharoṣṭhī**. Representations on the coins include symbols drawn from **Buddhist** and **Brahmanical** traditions.

MAUKHARI. Ruling dynasty in north India, c. sixth century CE, with their capital at **Kanauj**. *See also* GRAHAVARMAN; HARṢAVARDHANA; NALANDA.

MAURYA. Name of a ruling lineage that established one of the earliest **empires** in the subcontinent (c. fourth–second centuries BCE). The best-known rulers of the dynasty are **Candragupta**, the founder, and his grandson **Asoka**. The nucleus of the empire was **Magadha**, with its capital at **Pāṭaliputra**. The empire stretched from Afghanistan in the west to Bengal in the east, and included most of Karnataka and Andhra Pradesh. At its height, the empire encompassed at least four provinces apart from the core area, with **Taxila**, **Ujjayinī**, **Suvarṇagiri**, and Tosali (**Dhauli**) as the four provincial capitals.

Details of Mauryan administration have been reconstructed on the basis of the account of **Megasthenes**, the ***Arthaśāstra***, and the evidence of Asokan **inscriptions**. While the *Arthaśāstra* describes a highly and uniformly centralized polity, it is likely that in practice administrative policies were more flexible, varying from region to region and supported by a fairly complex bureaucratic structure and a standing **army**. Resources were mobilized through taxes imposed on **agriculture**, **trade**, **craft** production, and **pastoralism**.

Jaina tradition recognizes Candragupta as a patron of Jainism. While Asoka adopted **Buddhism**, he also propagated a more eclectic set of beliefs and practices, designated as ***dhamma***.

The collapse of the Mauryan Empire was occasionally attributed to a **Brahmanical** reaction. However, the evidence for such a reaction is rather thin. It is possible that both the bureaucratic and the military structures were overstretched with the attempt to control an extremely diverse territory. What is also evident is that the collapse was accompanied by the emergence of vibrant regional polities in several parts of the subcontinent. *See also* ACHAEMENID; BINDUSĀRA; BṚHADRATHA; DASARATHA; *DHAMMA MAHĀMATTA*; FORTIFICATION; GUPTA; *INDICA*; JUNAGADH ROCK INSCRIPTION; *KERALAPUTA*; KINGSHIP; KUMRAHAR; MAHASTHAN; MAURYAN ART; *MUDRĀRĀKṢASA*; NAVY; PUNCH-MARKED COINS; PUṆḌRA; SISUPALGARH; SLAVERY; SOHGAURA; SUBHĀGASENA; *ŚŪDRA*; ŚUṄGA; TUṢĀSPA.

MAURYAN ART. Mauryan art provides some of the earliest examples of stone carving in the **early historic period**. Distinctive artifacts include polished stone pillars, generally made from sandstone quarried from Chunar, Uttar Pradesh. These pillars consisted of monoliths that were transported to the sites where they were erected. While it is possible that some of these pillars predate Mauryan rule, others were probably erected during the reign of **Asoka**. Many of these pillars bear Asokan **inscriptions**. Generally, the top of the pillar was decorated with an elaborate capital, which includes some of the finest specimens of early stone **sculpture**. Best known are the four lions surmounting the pillar at **Sarnath**, now adopted by the government of India as its national emblem; and a bull, from the pillar at **Rampurwa**, Bihar. In **Dhauli**, Orissa, the natural rock surface was carved to produce a magnificent elephant. It is possible that the representation of animals was inspired by **Buddhist** tradition, where many of the animals depicted were regarded as symbolic of the Buddha and/or stages in his life.

Mauryan **architecture** is represented by remains of a pillared hall at **Pāṭalīputra** and by a series of **rock-cut caves** in the **Barabar** and **Nagarjuni hills**, Bihar, distinguished by finely polished walls. While Asoka is credited with the construction of several ***stūpas*** according to Buddhist tradition, most surviving examples, such as the *stūpa* at **Sanchi**, were subsequently rebuilt and embellished. *See also* SATDHARA; SIKLIGARH; SODANGA; VAISHALI.

MAX MULLER, FRIEDRICH (1823–1900). One of the most influential linguists and **Sanskrit** scholars of the 19th century, he published an edition of the ***Ṛgveda*** along with the 14th-century commentary of Sāyana in six volumes between 1849 and 1875. In 1866, he was appointed professor of comparative philology at Oxford. Between 1876 and 1900, he edited the *Sacred Books of the East*, in 51 volumes. An ardent Indophile who had never visited India, he attempted to steer clear of a racist understanding of Indian history, even as he occasionally romanticized the past.

MAYILADUMPARAI. **Archaeological** site in Tamil Nadu, with evidence of four occupational phases. Period I, possibly **Mesolithic** (c. 10,000–3,000 BCE), yielded microliths. Period II (c. 3000–1000 BCE) was **Neolithic**. Finds from this phase included ground stone axes and **pottery**. Period III (c. 1000–300 BCE) was associated with **megaliths**, with finds of more than 1,000 **burials**, including cairns and cists. Grave goods consisted of **Black and Red Ware** and a wide range of **iron** artifacts. Period IV, considered **early historic** (c. 300 BCE–300 CE), yielded potsherds **inscribed** in **Tamil Brāhmī** and **rock paintings** depicting scenes of **warfare**.

MAYŪRAŚARMAN. Best-known ruler (r.c. 345–360 CE) of the **Kadambas**. He was successful in his attacks on the **Pallavas** and commemorated his victories by performing **Vedic sacrifices**.

MAYURBHANJ. District in Orissa, with evidence of lower **Paleolithic** sites. Finds included pebble **tools** and hand axes made of quartzite.

MEDHĀTITHI. Sanskrit writer, who lived in Kashmir c. ninth century CE, author of the *Manubhāṣya*, a commentary on the ***Manusmṛti***. *See also* LITERATURE.

MEDICINE. Some of the earliest textual references to diseases and possible cures come from the ***Atharvaveda*** (c. first half of the first millennium BCE). The text describes a range of pathological symptoms and prescribes cures such as medication, chants, and spells. Subsequently, c. mid–first millennium BCE onward, healing traditions evidently crystallized around **renunciatory** institutions, including **Buddhist monasteries**. Buddhist texts detail medical symptoms and their treatment along lines that later developed into the system of ***āyurveda***, best exemplified in the works of **Caraka** and **Suśruta**. While physicians are mentioned in texts, the attitude toward this social category was somewhat ambivalent within the **Brahmanical** tradition. *See also* INDO-GREEK.

MEERUT. Settlement in Uttar Pradesh. Find spot of an **Asokan** pillar inscribed with a set of the **Major Pillar Edicts** that was transported to Delhi in the 14th century by Sultan Firoz Shah Tughlaq.

MEGALITH. Burial sites (c. 1000 BCE to the early centuries of the Common Era) found throughout peninsular India and in Kashmir and Ladakh, often, though not always, marked by the use of large blocks of stone. It is likely that the megaliths found in Karnataka and Andhra Pradesh were earlier than those found in Tamil Nadu and Kerala. In some cases, stone slabs were used to construct underground burial chambers, in other instances, single stones, or groups of stones were arranged on the surface to indicate burial sites. Typologies of megaliths have been developed to distinguish between dolmens, cairns, urn burials, and the use of hood stones or cap stones. In most instances, there is evidence of multiple, fragmentary burials, often after the exposure of bones.

Grave goods include a wide range of **iron** equipment and **Black and Red Ware** vessels. However, other kinds of **pottery** are known as well. These include gray wares, black wares, red wares, and **black slipped ware**. Other metal objects were of **copper**, bronze, and gold. Some megaliths did not contain skeletal remains and were probably part of a different tradition.

Related habitation sites have provided evidence of **pastoralism**. Domesticated animals include cattle, sheep, goat, pig, horse, ass, and dog. In some instances, horse bones are present in burials. Evidence of cultivated plants consisted of wheat, barley, millet, pulses. More than 2,000 megalithic sites have been identified to date. These include **Adichannalur**, **Amaravati**, **Auroville**, **Banahalli**, **Bhagimohari**, **Bhawar**, **Brahmagiri**, **Cheramangad**, **Garapadu**, **Hallur**, **Heggadehalli**, **Hemmige**, **Jainal Naula**, **Kakoria**, **Karkabhat**, **Kaundinyapura**, **Kesanapalle**, **Kodumanal**, **Korkai**, **Kunnatur**, **Ladyura**, **Machad**, **Mahurjhari**, **Maski**, **Mayiladumparai**, **Nagarjunakonda**, **Nainkund**, **Nittur**, **Pachikheri**, **Paiyampalli**, **Raipur**, **Sanganakallu**, **Shirkanda**, **Takalghat–Khapa**, **Terdal**, **Tharsa**, **T. Narsipur**, **Valiyapadam**, and **Yelleswaram**. *See also* DISPOSAL OF THE DEAD; TAMIL.

MEGASTHENES. Greek ambassador, sent to the court of **Candragupta Maurya** by **Seleucos Nikator** (c. fourth century BCE), who left an account of his experiences. The original work, titled ***Indica***, was lost, but Megasthenes was cited by later Greek writers, and his account has been reconstructed from these citations. He evidently described the capital, the palace, the **king**'s daily routine, the administrative system, and the **caste** system. While earlier historians often considered his writing at face value, more recent scholarship has tended to evaluate it in terms of the context in which he wrote, which may account for a tendency to exaggerate and occasionally valorize the practices he witnessed. *See also AGRONOMOI*; ARMY; CASTE; FORTIFICATION; NAVY; PĀṬALIPUTRA; SLAVERY; STRABO.

MEGHAVARṆA. Ruler of Sri Lanka, mentioned in the **Allahabad Pillar Inscription** of **Samudragupta** as one of those who accepted the overlordship of the **Gupta king**. According to Chinese sources, he sent an embassy with gifts for the contemporary Indian ruler in order to get permission to erect a shrine at **Bodh Gaya**.

MEHRAULI PILLAR INSCRIPTION. Undated inscription found on an **iron pillar** at Mehrauli, New Delhi. The inscription has been assigned to the **Gupta** period (c. fourth–sixth century CE) on paleographic grounds. The text is a posthumous panegyric in praise of a ruler named Candra, variously identified as **Candragupta II** or **Samudragupta**. It mentions victories against the **Vaṅgas** and over peoples in the **Indus** valley. It also states that his fame spread to the southern (Indian) ocean. The pillar itself is described as being erected in honor of the god **Viṣṇu**.

MEHRGARH. Neolithic (c. 8000–5000 BCE) site in the Bolan valley, Baluchistan (Pakistan), with evidence of mud-brick **architecture**, including special storage structures. There is evidence for the cultivation of barley and wheat. Domesticated animals included sheep, goat, and cattle. Other finds consisted of stone **tools**, baskets, shell bangles, and clay figurines. Handmade **pottery** is found in the later phases. There was a separate cemetery, with grave goods such as animals and pots, tools, and ornaments. Finds of beads of lapis lazuli and turquoise indicate contact with Afghanistan and Baluchistan, while the use of shell suggests contact with coastal settlements.

MELUHHA. Region mentioned in Mesopotamian cuneiform texts (c. third millennium BCE onward), generally identified with the **Indus** valley and the area of the **Harappan civilization**. The identification is corroborated by finds of Harappan artifacts, including typical beads and **seals**, from contemporary **archaeological** sites in Iraq. It is likely that contact between Mesopotamia and Meluhha was established through both overland and sea **routes**. Mesopotamian texts mention the ships of Meluhha as well as the goods obtained from the region. These included ivory, wood, gold, lapis lazuli, and carnelian. *See also* MARITIME TRADE.

MENANDER. One of the best-known **Indo-Greek** rulers (r.c. 155–130 BCE), known as Milinda in **Pali** texts, who controlled **Gandhāra**

and the Punjab, with **Taxila** and **Sāgala** (present-day Sialkot in Pakistan) as major centers of power. Some texts suggest that he may have led an expedition up to the mid–**Ganga (2)** valley. However, the effects, if any, of this conquest, were short-lived. Menander is also recognized as a patron of **Buddhism**, with the ***Milindapañha*** recording his conversion after a long dialogue with **Nāgasena (1)**. Menander's **coins** contain legends in both Greek and **Kharoṣṭhī**. *See also* SUGH.

MESOLITHIC. Archaeological category, often regarded as a transitional phase between the **Paleolithic** and the **Neolithic**. While the Mesolithic phase probably began c. 10,000 BP, Mesolithic cultures survived in different parts of the subcontinent until the beginning of the Common Era. A larger number of sites, including cave sites, which are relatively better preserved, have been recovered from this period in comparison to the preceding Paleolithic phase. Distinctive **tools** associated with this phase include microliths, small stone tools, often less than a centimeter in length, usually made of chert, chalcedony, jasper, and agate. They are often classified into nongeometric and geometric varieties. While it was assumed that the geometric varieties are more evolved and consequently later, this may not hold true in all instances. Microliths were often used as arrowheads. They were also hafted onto handles to produce composite tools such as sickles. The use of microliths continued well beyond the Mesolithic phase. Other tools include hammer stones and grinding equipment as well as bone tools.

In some instances, Mesolithic communities were in contact with **agricultural** and metal-using communities and adopted the use of artifacts such as **pots** and the limited use of metals. The evidence of both domesticated and wild animals from certain sites indicates the coexistence of and interaction between hunting and **pastoral**/agro-pastoral populations. Some sites have yielded evidence of **burials** as well. Some of the earliest examples of **painting** in rock shelters belong to this phase. Sites yielding evidence of this phase include **Adamgarh**, **Ambakot**, **Attirampakkam**, **Bagor**, **Banki**, **Bhimbetka**, **Birbhanpur**, **Brahmagiri**, **Chopani Mando**, **Damdama**, **Datrana**, **Dhansura**, **Didwana**, **Ganeshwar**, **Hirapur Khadan**, **Kakrehta**, **Kanaganahalli**, **Langhnaj**, **Lekhahia**, **Loteshwar**, **Mahadaha**,

Mahagara, **Pachikheri**, **Paisra**, **Pithad**, **Rangpur**, **Sannati**, **Santhli**, **Sarai Nahar Rai**, **Shaktari Timbo**, **Vanpasari**, and **Vidisha**. *See also* ART; BURIAL PRACTICES; DANCE; GANGA (2); GODDESS CULT; NARMADA; PREHISTORY; ROCK ART.

MIHIRA BHOJA. *See* BHOJA (2).

MIHIRAKULA. Son and successor of the **Hūṇa** ruler **Toramāṇa**, c. sixth century CE, mentioned in both the ***Rājataraṅgiṇī*** and in **Xuan Zang**'s account, where he is described as a persecutor of **Buddhists**. He was probably defeated by the **Gupta** ruler **Narasiṃhagupta** and by **Yaśodharman**, the ruler of Mandasor (**Daśapura**).

MILINDA. *See* MENANDER.

MILINDAPAÑHA. **Pali** text, literally the questions of Milinda, or **Menander**, the best-known of the **Indo-Greek kings**. The questions were addressed to a **Buddhist** monk named **Nāgasena (1)**. The text received its final form c. fifth century CE. *See also* LITERATURE; SĀGALA.

MĪMĀṂSĀ. **Sanskrit** term meaning "investigation" or "enquiry," name of a school of **philosophy** that emerged toward the end of the first millennium BCE and provided an exegesis on **Vedic** rituals, often referred to as the *pūrva* (earlier) *mīmāṃsā* as opposed to the *uttara* (later) *mīmāṃsā* or ***vedānta***. The ideas developed within this tradition influenced other discourses such as grammar. *See also* JAIMINI; KUMĀRILA BHAṬṬA; PRABHĀKARA; ŚABARASVĀMIN.

MINISTERS. A variety of generic terms were used to designate ministers in early Indian texts and inscriptions. The former included the **Sanskrit** *mantrin* or *amātya* (**Pali** *amacca*). The position of such ministers could occasionally be hereditary. Principal ministers included the ***purohita***. According to the ***Arthaśāstra***, ministers were paid cash salaries. However, later texts indicate that they could receive **land grants** as well. Their main function appears to have been advisory and supervisory. There is occasional mention of a council of ministers, the ***pariṣad***. *See also* CANDRAGUPTA

MAURYA; DĀMODARAGUPTA; HARIṢEṆA (1); KAUṬILYA; *MUDRĀRĀKṢASA*; *SAPTĀṄGA*.

MINOR PILLAR EDICTS. Name assigned to **Asokan inscriptions** (c. third century BCE) engraved on pillars, found at **Rummindei**, **Nigalisagar**, **Allahabad**–Kosam, **Sanchi**, and **Sarnath**. Most of these dealt explicitly with the concerns of the ruler as a **Buddhist**. *See also* ALLAHABAD PILLAR INSCRIPTION; KAUSAMBI; RUMMINDEI.

MINOR ROCK EDICTS. Name assigned to a set of two **Asokan inscriptions** (c. third century BCE), written in the **Brāhmī script**, in **Prakrit**. The contents of the Minor Rock Edicts are less standardized than those of the **Major Rock Edicts**. They mention that although Asoka had adopted **Buddhism**, he was not particularly zealous initially. However, with the passage of time he became more determined to ensure that gods and men could mingle together, and that his message would be widely disseminated. Officials and social categories that were expected to participate in the endeavor were also listed. The edicts are widely distributed and have been found at several sites in Madhya Pradesh, Delhi, Uttar Pradesh, Bihar, and Andhra Pradesh, with a major cluster in Karnataka. *See also* AHRAURA; BAHAPUR; BAIRAT; BHABRU; BRAHMAGIRI; ERRAGUDI; GAVIMATH; GUJJARA; JATINGA RAMESVARAM; MASKI; NITTUR; PALKIGUNDU; PANGURARIA; RAJULA MANDAGIRI; SAHASRAM; SIDDAPUR; SRINIVASPURI; UDEGOLAM.

MITATHAL. Archaeological site in Haryana, with evidence of two occupational phases. Period I, defined as **pre-/early Harappan** (c. first half of the third millennium BCE), yielded evidence of mudbrick **architecture** and **pottery** having parallels with **Siswal** and **Kalibangan**. Period II (mid–third millennium BCE onward) provided evidence of a **Mature Harappan** settlement, with the typical twin mound pattern and evidence of Harappan pottery in addition to the earlier wares. Other finds included stone weights, **terracotta** figurines, and beads of semiprecious stone.

MITHILA. The capital of **Videha**, a ***mahājanapada*** mentioned in the **Sanskrit epics**, in present-day Bihar.

MITRA, RAJENDRA LALA. Indologist (1822–1891), closely associated with the **Asiatic Society** of Bengal. He edited and published numerous **Sanskrit** texts and **inscriptions**, prepared catalogs of Sanskrit **manuscripts**, and was known for his knowledge of several European and Indian **languages**. He also undertook surveys of the **archaeological** remains of Orissa and explored the site of **Bodh Gaya**.

***MLECCHA*. Sanskrit** term used (c. first millennium BCE onward) to designate people who did not speak Sanskrit and were hence considered outsiders. It was occasionally used for people such as the Greeks, who did not belong to the subcontinent. *See also* SKANDAGUPTA.

MOHENJODARO. One of the most important **Mature Harappan** settlements, more than 200 hectares in size, in Sind, Pakistan, located close to the **Indus River**. The location of the settlement in close proximity to a fertile alluvial plain was also important in terms of riverine and land **routes** of communication. The site consists of a relatively small, high citadel mound to the west and a low sprawling mound to the east. The lowest levels of the settlement have not been reached, as they are submerged under rising subsoil water. Both mounds, which rest on mud-brick platforms, have been excavated.

Structures on the citadel mound include the Great Bath, an artificial tank, with evidence of waterproofing, more than 14 m long and about 7 m wide, with a depth of around 2.4 m, with steps leading down to it from the narrower sides. There were rooms all around the tank, including one with a well, which probably provided water to fill the tank. An elaborate drain carried away water from the bath. The entire structure is one of the few freestanding buildings on the citadel mound. Other structures include a storage space, often classified as a granary. This consists of a row of platforms that were probably surmounted by a wooden superstructure. There is also evidence of a pillared hall.

The typical **architecture** of the lower city consisted of large residential houses, with wells, bathrooms, and an elaborate network of drains. In most instances, rooms were built around a courtyard. There is also evidence of streets laid out approximately in a grid pattern. There is evidence for a wide range of **craft** production, including the manufacture of **seals**, beads of semiprecious stone, metallurgy, **pottery**, and ivory and shell working. Some of the best examples of **sculpture** from the civilization have been recovered from the site. Given the wide range of activities evidenced in the archaeological record, it is likely that the city was an administrative center as well as a center for craft production. It has been recognized as a World Heritage Site by UNESCO. *See also* HARAPPAN CIVILIZATION; JHUKAR; MARSHALL, JOHN HUBERT.

MONASTERIES. The tradition of living in monasteries emerged with the growth of **renunciatory orders**, c. mid–first millennium BCE onward. The best-known monastic institutions were those of the **Buddhists** and **Jainas**, both of whom laid down elaborate rules to regulate life within the monastery. Initially, monasteries were envisaged as temporary residences during the rainy season. However, by the time of **Asoka**, there is evidence of some of the earliest **rock-cut caves**, which were meant to serve as more permanent residences.

By the first millennium CE, there is evidence for freestanding monasteries, built of brick. These usually comprised a shrine and a central courtyard, with cells for residence on all sides. Remains of monasteries have been found from several **archaeological** sites. Construction of these structures, as of the rock-cut caves, was financed by lay supporters, **kings**, merchants, **craftsmen**, and ordinary men and **women**. Some of the largest monasteries, such as that at **Nalanda**, were maintained by **land grants**.

Apart from serving as shelters where renouncers could meditate, monasteries also emerged as important **religious** and educational institutions and often housed libraries. Sites with remains of monasteries include **Adurru**, **Ajanta**, **Antichak**, **Bagh**, **Bairat**, **Bavikonda**, **Bodh Gaya**, **Chachegaon**, **Chirand**, **Devanimori**, **Ellora**, **Erich**, **Ganeshwar**, **Gopalapatnam**, **Junnar**, **Kasia**, **Kausambi**, **Kaveripattinam**, **Khiching**, **Kolhua**, **Kumrahar**, **Kusinagara**, **Lalitagiri**, **Lumbini**, **Mansar**, **Nagarjunakonda**, **Nelakondapalli**, **Paharpur**, **Panguraria**, **Pāṭaliputra**, **Pavurallakonda**, **Piprahwa**, **Pitalkhora**, **Sanchi**, **Sanghol**, **Sankissa**, **Sarnath**, **Shaji-ki-dheri**, **Sirpur**, **Sravasti**, **Takht-i-Bahi**, **Taradih**, **Taxila**, **Thotlakonda**, **Tripuri**, **Udayagiri**, and **Vaddamanu**. *See also* ASOKA; ASSEMBLIES; BAGH; *GAṆA/SAṂGHA*; JETAVANA; JĪVAKA KOMARABHACCA; JUDICIAL

SYSTEM; MANUSCRIPTS; MEDICINE; PĀLA; PĀŚUPATA; *SAṂGHA*; ŚAṄKARĀCĀRYA; SEALS; UDAYAGIRI; *VIHĀRA*; VIKRAMAŚILĀ.

MONEY LENDING. Money lending is documented in the **Dharmasūtras** and **Dharmaśāstras** (c. mid–first millennium BCE), which attempted to regulate the practice. It is also mentioned in literary narratives. Normative texts recognized money lending as a legitimate occupation for the ***vaiśya***. Rates of interest were expected to vary according to the ***varṇa*** of the debtor, as also the kind of risk involved. In case of failure to repay the loan, the debtor, especially if he belonged to the "lower" **castes**, could be subjected to debt bondage. From the early centuries of the first millennium CE, **inscriptions** indicate that donors often deposited money with **guilds** in order to support **religious** institutions out of interest.

MONUMENTS. Among the earliest monuments that have survived are those belonging to the **Harappan civilization** (c. 2700–1800 BCE), at sites such as **Mohenjodaro**. Subsequently, monuments belonging to the **Mauryan** period (c. fourth–second centuries BCE) have been recovered. Most surviving monuments belong to the first millennium CE. These include ***stūpas***, **rock-cut caves**, freestanding **monasteries**, and **temples**. Virtually no secular monuments have survived for this period.

***MṚCCHAKAṬIKAM*.** **Sanskrit** play, composed by **Śūdraka**, generally attributed to the early centuries of the Common Era. The play is set in **Ujjayinī** and deals with the romance between a **courtesan** named Vasantasenā and an impoverished merchant named Cārudatta. It contains vivid representations of urban life in early India. *See also* LITERATURE.

MUCHCHTLA CHINTAMANI GAVI. Upper **Paleolithic** cave site, part of the **Kurnool caves** in Andhra Pradesh, with evidence of a fireplace, one of the earliest instances of its kind in the subcontinent.

***MUDRĀRĀKṢASA*.** **Sanskrit** play authored by **Viśākhadatta** (c. sixth century CE?), set in the **Mauryan** period, describing the strategies employed by **Kauṭilya** (Cāṇakya) to win over a rival **minister** to the side of **Candragupta Maurya**. *See also* LITERATURE.

MUHAMMAD BIN QASIM. Arab general who conquered Sind with the support of the contemporary caliph, Al Hajjaj, in 712, defeating and killing the local ruler, **Dahir**.

MULCHERA. Archaeological site in Maharashtra, with remains of a **temple** dated to the late **Sātavāhana**–early **Vākāṭaka** period (c. second–fourth century CE). Other artifacts include **iron** nails and **copper** objects used during worship.

MULLAIPPĀṬṬU*. Tamil poem**, part of the ***Pattupāṭṭu, of the ***Sangam*** anthology (c. third century BCE–second century CE?), attributed to a poet named Napputanār, dealing with the *mullai* or **forest** region, and combining descriptions of love and **warfare**. *See also* LITERATURE.

MUSANAGAR. Archaeological site in Uttar Pradesh, with five major occupational phases. Period I (c. early first millennium BCE?) yielded handmade as well as wheel-made **pottery**. The latter included **black and red ware** and **black slipped ware**. Remains of wattle-and-daub structures were also found. **Tools** included bone points. Period II (mid–first millennium BCE?) yielded, additionally, **Painted Grey Ware**, while finds from Period III (second half of the first millennium BCE?) included **Northern Black Polished Ware**, **terracotta** figurines, and structures of burnt brick. Finds from Period IV (c. first millennium CE?) included **iron** tools and **copper** artifacts. The finds from the last phase (Period V) were more or less identical.

MUSIC. The earliest text pointing to the development of music is the ***Sāmaveda*** (c. early first millennium BCE), providing for the chanting of **Vedic** mantras by specially trained priests, a practice that continues to date. Other texts such as the ***Nāṭyaśāstra*** contain descriptions of a wide range of string, percussion, and wind instruments, many of which are depicted in **sculpture** and **painting** as well. Texts and visual representations point to the presence of both men and **women** performers. Apart from ritual uses, music was an integral part of urban culture, with **courtesans** in particular being expected to cultivate the requisite skills. Occasionally, rulers such as **Samudragupta** were represented as musicians.

Musical performers evidently came from varied social backgrounds—while some were regarded as part of the urban elite, others, including itinerant performers, were often treated with scant respect.

From the second half of the first millennium CE, if not earlier, devotional songs were recognized as an integral part of traditions of ***Bhakti***. *See also MALAIPATUKATAM*.

MUZIRIS. Port in Kerala, mentioned in the ***Periplus of the Erythraean Sea***, as one of the major centers for the export of pepper, now identified with the site of Pattanam, which has yielded evidence of Roman amphorae, **pottery** of West Asian origin, and **rouletted ware**. *See also* KODUMANAL.

– N –

NACHNA KUTHARA. Archaeological site in Madhya Pradesh, find spot of a two-storeyed **temple** probably dedicated to **Śiva**, attributed to the **Gupta** period (c. fifth–sixth centuries CE). This is one of the earliest examples of a structural temple with an enclosed circumambulatory path. The doorway, which faces west, was decorated with **sculptured** panels.

NADNER. Archaeological site in Madhya Pradesh, 35 km from **Pangurariа**, with six occupational phases. Period I is associated with **Mesolithic tools** including scrapers, borers, flakes, and blades. Period II, assigned to c. 700–500 BCE, yielded **iron** sickles, crucibles, **copper** artifacts, shell and **terracotta** ornaments, beads, and **black and red ware**. Period III, divided into two phases, is dated between c. 500 and 300 BCE. Finds in the first phase include **Northern Black Polished Ware** (which continued in the next phase as well as in Period IV), evidence for wattle-and-daub structures, and shell bangles. Finds in the second phase consisted of iron chisels, nails, sickles, arrowheads, and slag. Other finds included **punch-marked coins**

(which continued through Period V), beads of semiprecious stone, stone **sculpture**, and ring wells. Period IV (c. 300–200 BCE) yielded black and red ware, **black slipped ware**, inscribed coins, terracotta figurines, remains of wattle-and-daub structures, and bone points. Period V (c. 200 BCE–200 CE) is associated with copper coins of the **Sātavāhanas**, iron arrowheads, beads, and terracotta figurines. Structural remains consisted of a drain of baked brick. Period VI (c. 9th–10th centuries CE) is associated with remains of **Brahmanical** and **Jaina temples**.

NĀGA. Sanskrit term meaning "serpent" or "elephant," used for several ruling lineages in north and central India. It was also used to refer to mythical beings. **Samudragupta** claimed to have defeated Nāga chiefs in north India (c. fourth century CE). *See also* ERAN; GAṆAPATI (NĀGA).

NĀGABHAṬA I. First important ruler (r. 730–756 CE) of the **Pratihāras** of **Kanauj**. His territories included parts of present-day Rajasthan, Gujarat, and Malwa.

NĀGABHAṬA II. Pratihāra ruler (r.c. 793–833) who succeeded in regaining control over **Kanauj**, which had been lost to the **Pālas**, and was also successful against the **Rāṣṭrakūṭas**.

NĀGADATTA. Ruler (c. fourth century CE) mentioned in the **Allahabad Pillar Inscription** of the **Gupta** ruler **Samudragupta** among the **kings** of ***āryāvarta*** who were uprooted.

NĀGANIKĀ. Wife of the **Sātavāhana** ruler **Śrī Sātakarṇī**; I (c. second century BCE), known from her votive **inscriptions**—which also record the genealogy of the dynasty, indicating that she belonged to a *mahārathi* (a powerful local lineage) family—and from **coins**. She made donations to **Buddhist** institutions and participated in the performance of the ***aśvamedha*** **sacrifice** by her husband. *See also* WOMEN.

NAGARA. Archaeological site in Gujarat, with evidence of three occupational phases. Period I (mid–first millennium BCE) yielded traces of an earthen embankment; bones of cattle, sheep, goat, pig, ass, and camel; **iron** artifacts; and **black and red ware**. Finds from Period II (c. third century BCE–first century CE) included **Northern Black Polished Ware**, **punch-marked coins**, and **terracotta** figurines. Finds from Period III (c. first–ninth centuries CE) consisted of coins issued by the **Kṣatrapas**, **inscribed seals**, Roman amphorae, **Red Polished Ware**, beads of semiprecious stone, and glass bangles.

NAGARI. Archaeological site in Rajasthan, identified with Mādhyamikā, the capital of the ***janapada*** of the Śibis. Finds included **Northern Black Polished Ware** (c. 400 BCE) and **Red Polished Ware**. Other finds consisted of **terracotta** figurines, **punch-marked coins**, and issues attributed to the **Kṣatrapas** and the Śibi *janapada*. There are traces of a **fortification** wall dating to the mid–first millennium CE. An **inscription** dated to the fifth century CE records the construction of a **temple** dedicated to **Viṣṇu** and the performance of **sacrifices** such as the ***aśvamedha*** and ***vājapeya***.

NĀGĀRJUNA. Mahāyāna Buddhist philosopher (c. first century CE), best known as the exponent of the theory of *śūnyavāda* or essencelessness. He may have been a contemporary of the **Kuṣāṇa king Kaṇiṣka**. While his ideas appeared nihilistic, he and his followers conceded that human existence was real, although qualified, and recognized the possibility of attaining *nirvāṇa* (***nibbāna***) in the present. This philosophical tradition was known as *mādhyamika* (intermediate or middle) as opposed to the **Theravāda** tradition on the one hand and the **Yogācāra** school of thought on the other.

NAGARJUNAKONDA. Archaeological site in Andhra Pradesh, now submerged under water, with evidence of several occupational phases. The earliest evidence is **Paleolithic**, with a wide range of stone **tools**. This was followed by a **Mesolithic** occupation. Finds from this period included microliths. Subsequently, there is evidence of a **Neolithic** settlement dated to c. 2500 BCE. Finds from this phase consisted of stone tools, **pottery**, pit dwellings, and **burials**. **Megalithic** remains (c. first millennium BCE) were also recovered from the site. Subsequently a large **Buddhist *stūpa*** with elaborate **sculptural** embellishments, including narratives from the ***Jātakas*** as well as symbolic and anthropomorphic representations of the Buddha, was built. There is evidence for smaller *stūpas*, many built on the spoke-wheel pattern. Several **monasteries** were constructed during the rule of the **Ikṣvākus (2)** (c. second–fourth centuries CE). Some of the *stūpas* yielded relics. Other structures associated with this phase consist of ramparts, tanks, wells, and an amphitheater. There is also evidence of **Brahmanical temples**, including those meant for the worship of **Śiva** and the mother **goddess**. Shrines continued to be built at the site until c. seventh century CE.

NAGARJUNI HILLS. Site of **Mauryan rock-cut caves** in Bihar, dedicated to the **Ājīvikas**. *See also* DASARATHA.

NĀGASENA (1). A **Buddhist** teacher (c. second century BCE?), protagonist of the ***Milindapañha***, a **Pali** text written as a dialogue between him and Milinda or **Menander**.

NĀGASENA (2). One of the rulers of ***āryāvarta*** (c. fourth century CE) mentioned in the **Allahabad Pillar Inscription** as among those who were uprooted by the **Gupta** ruler **Samudragupta**.

NAGDA. Archaeological site in Madhya Pradesh, with evidence of three occupational phases. Period I (c. second millennium BCE?), considered **Chalcolithic**, yielded microliths, traces of **copper**, painted **pottery**, **terracotta** figurines, and evidence of a rampart. Period II (c. first half of the first millennium BCE?) provided evidence of **iron** tools and weapons and **black and red ware**. Finds from Period III (c. 500–200 BCE) included **Northern Black Polished Ware**, iron equipment, and bone and ivory artifacts. *See also* KATRA.

NAGESHWAR. A **Mature Harappan** (c. second half of the third millennium BCE) site in Gujarat, with evidence of shellworking. Artifacts manufactured from conch shell at the site consisted of bangles, beads, and inlay work. Other finds included stone blades and weights, and **terracotta** figurines. Faunal remains such as bones of cattle, goat, sheep, deer, and fish were also found.

NAGIARI. Archaeological site in the Punjab, occupied from the **late Harappan** (Period I A, c. second millennium BCE) period onward. Finds associated with the second phase (Period I B, c. 12th–6th centuries BCE) included thatched huts, storage bins, animal bones, charred wheat and rice, **copper** artifacts, **terracotta** figurines, beads of semiprecious stone, **Painted Grey Ware**, and gray ware. The site was subsequently abandoned, and reoccupied c. first century BCE–first century CE (Period II, the **Kuṣāṇa** phase), associated with finds of copper **coins**. A further phase of abandonment was followed by another occupation, c. 1300–1600 CE (Period III).

NAGWADA. **Archaeological** site (c. mid third–early second millennium BCE) in Gujarat. Finds consisted of **Harappan**-type **pottery**, ornaments and beads of semiprecious stone, bangles, shell inlay, stone weights, chert drills, and sealings. There is evidence for the local manufacture of beads and shell bangles. Faunal remains include those of domesticated camel, cattle, sheep, goat, and pig. *See also* SANTHLI; SHAKTARI TIMBO.

NAHAPĀṆA. **Śaka** ruler (c. 119–124 CE) of the **Kṣaharāta** branch, who exercised control over Gujarat and parts of Maharashtra, known from **coins** and **inscriptions** and mentioned in the ***Periplus of the Erythraean Sea***. He was defeated by the **Sātavāhana** ruler **Gautamīputra Sātakarṇi**, who overstruck his silver coins. His inscriptions, as well as those of his son-in-law **Uṣavadāta**, indicate that he made grants to **Buddhist** institutions in **Karle** and **Nasik**. *See also* JOGALTHEMBI.

NAINKUND. **Megalithic** (c. first millennium BCE?) site in Maharashtra, with evidence for a furnace for producing **iron**.

NAKKĪRAR. **Tamil poet**, two of whose compositions, the *Netunalvātai* and the *Tirumurukāṟṟuppaṭai*, are included in the ***Pattupāṭṭu***, part of the ***Sangam*** anthology (c. third century BCE–second century CE?). The first work describes a queen who mourns for her husband who is absent in the battlefield, while the second is composed in praise of the deity Murukan. Some of Nakkīrar's compositions are also included in the ***Eṭṭutokai***. *See also* LITERATURE.

NAL. **Early/pre-Harappan archaeological** culture (c. third millennium BCE) in Baluchistan, distinguished by its typical **pottery**, characterized by designs painted in black and polychrome varieties.

NALANDA. Site in Bihar with **Buddhist monasteries** and ***stūpas***, dated to the **Gupta**/post-Gupta period (c. sixth–eighth century onward). It was recognized as one of the most important centers of Buddhist learning, sustained by royal patronage, including that of the Gupta rulers, and was visited by the Chinese Buddhist pilgrims **Xuan Zang** and **I Ching** in the seventh century CE. According to Xuan Zang, the establishment was supported with the revenues of 100 villages and housed 10,000 students. It was patronized by the **Pālas**, and some of the best examples of Pāla period **sculpture** in stone and metal have been recovered from the site. These include more than 500 bronzes of deities of the **Vajrayāna** pantheon. Other finds include **seals** of the Guptas, **Maukharis**, **Harṣavardhana**, and officials of the monastery; **coins** of the Gupta rulers; a variety of **iron** equipment including **agricultural tools**; bronze vessels; and bone and ivory artifacts. The site was abandoned after the 13th century. *See also* CAST COINS; DEVAPĀLA.

NĀLĀYIRA TIVIYA PIRAPANTAM. An anthology of 4,000 hymns in **Tamil**, attributed to 12 **Vaiṣṇava** saints (c. sixth–ninth century CE). The compositions include devotional works marked by mystic eroticism as well as others highlighting sectarian differences between the **Buddhists** and **Jainas**. *See also* LITERATURE; NAMMĀḺVĀR; PERIYĀḺVĀR; TIRUMANKAI ĀḺVĀR.

NAMMĀḺVĀR. Tamil saint (c. ninth century CE) who belonged to the ***veḷḷāḷār*** community, the most prolific of the ***āḻvārs***, whose compositions were anthologized in the ***Nālāyira Tiviya Pirapantam***. His writings are characterized by simplicity of language and the use of erotic imagery.

NANAGHAT. Site in the Western Ghats, Maharashtra, near a pass leading into the Deccan plateau, find spot of **inscriptions** of the **Sātavāhanas** and several **rock-cut caves** donated to **Buddhist** institutions. Some of these caves contained **sculpture** representing the rulers and their families. *See also* JUNNAR.

NANDA. Name of a ruling lineage of obscure origin that attained power in **Magadha**, c. fifth–fourth centuries BCE. The genealogy and names of Nanda rulers are recorded in the **Purāṇas** as well as in **Buddhist** and

Jaina texts. According to the Purāṇas the Nandas were not ***kṣatriyas***: In fact, the destruction of several *kṣatriya* lineages is attributed to them. Their control extended over most of north India and possibly **Kaliṅga** as well. According to Greek accounts, they maintained a huge standing **army**. **Alexander (of Macedon)** is supposed to have retreated from the banks of the **Beas** as his soldiers were unwilling to encounter this force. Texts also describe the Nanda rulers as extremely wealthy, on account of having mobilized resources through taxation. The last Nanda ruler was overthrown by **Candragupta Maurya**. *See also* DHANANANDA; MAHĀPADMA NANDA; ŚIŚUNĀGA.

NANDI. Ruler (c. fourth century CE), perhaps belonging to a **Nāga** clan, mentioned in the **Allahabad Pillar Inscription** of the **Gupta** ruler **Samudragupta** as one of those who was uprooted in ***āryāvarta***.

NAQSH-I-RUSTUM. Site of the tomb of **Darius I**, in Iran, with an **inscription** listing the Hidus among his subjects.

***NĀRADA SMṚTI*.** **Sanskrit** metrical work, attributed to Nārada, a legendary sage, that was composed and compiled by c. 600 CE and is one of the major **Dharmaśāstras**. Apart from sections on legal procedure, it contains a discussion on the duties of the **king**. *See also* LITERATURE.

NARASIMḤAGUPTA BĀLĀDITYA. **Gupta** ruler, c. sixth century CE, who succeeded in defeating the **Hūṇa** ruler **Mihirakula**.

NARASIMḤAVARMAN I. Also known as Mahāmalla (r. 630–668), son and successor of the **Pallava king Mahendravarman I**. He defeated the **Cālukya** ruler **Pulakeśin II** and attacked his capital **Badami**, taking the title of *vātāpikoṇḍa* to commemorate this exploit. He also sent naval expeditions to Sri Lanka. Much of the building activity at **Mamallapuram** is associated with his reign. The Chinese pilgrim **Xuan Zang** visited **Kanchipuram** during his reign.

NARASIMḤAVARMAN II. Also known as Rājasimḥa or the royal lion, **Pallava king** (r. 700–728) whose rule was peaceful. He sent embassies to China, perhaps in order to safeguard maritime **trade**

routes. Several **temples** including the **Shore Temple** at **Mamallapuram** and the Kailasanatha temple at **Kanchipuram** were built during his reign. He was a patron of **poets** such as **Daṇḍin**.

NARHAN. Archaeological site in Uttar Pradesh with four occupational phases. Period I (c. 1300–800 BCE), considered **Chalcolithic**, yielded evidence for the cultivation of wheat, barley, rice, millet, gram, pea, and lentil as well as oilseeds such as sesame, mustard, and linseed. Fruit remains included *ber* or the Indian jujube, grape, date, jackfruit, and mango. Other plant remains consisted of acacia, mulberry, basil, sal, tamarind, tamarisk, teak, and bamboo. Animal bones included those of cattle, sheep, goat, deer, and horse. **Tools** were generally made of stone and bone. Typical **pottery** consisted of white painted **black and red ware**. There was also evidence of wattle-and-daub structures, hearths, and potters' kilns. Period II was characterized by finds of **black slipped ware**. Most of the plant remains of the preceding period were found in this phase as well, with the addition of others such as safflower, *sissoo*, *amla*, and *jamun*. **Iron** equipment was also recovered from these levels. Finds from Period III (c. 600–200 BCE) consisted of **Northern Black Polished Ware**, traces of mud-brick **architecture**, **terracotta** figurines, and **copper coins**. Plant remains included pine and sandalwood, which were not available locally, in addition to those found earlier, which would have been available locally. Period IV (c. 200 BCE–200 CE?) provided evidence of burnt-brick structures and ring wells. *See also* AGIABIR; IMLIDIH KHURD; WINA.

NARMADA. River running through central India and draining into the Arabian Sea. The river valley is noted for finds of **Paleolithic tools** and fossil remains. Several **Mesolithic** and **early historic** sites were located along or near its banks. *See also* BARYGAZA; HATHNORA; NAVDATOLI.

NAṞṞIṆAI. Anthology of **Tamil** love **poems**, part of the ***Eṭṭutokai*** collection of ***Sangam*** **literature** (c. third century BCE–second century CE?).

NASIK. Archaeological site in the Western Ghats, on the **Godavari** in Maharashtra, with evidence of four occupational phases. Period I

(c. second millennium BCE?) designated as **Chalcolithic**, provided evidence of microliths and **pottery** resembling **Jorwe ware**. Period II (c. fifth century BCE–first century CE) yielded a variety of **iron** equipment, bone points, **Northern Black Polished Ware**, **black and red ware**, and **terracotta** artifacts. Finds from Periods III and IV (c. first–third centuries CE) included **cast coins**, **Russet-Coated Painted Ware**, **Red Polished Ware**, and Roman pottery. Several **inscriptions**, including some issued by the **Sātavāhanas** and **Śakas**, were found in neighboring caves. *See also* GOTAMĪ BALAŚRĪ; NAHAPĀṆA; YAJÑAŚRĪ SĀTAKARṆI.

***NĀṬYAŚĀSTRA*.** **Sanskrit** work on **drama**, attributed to **Bharata (2)**, which probably received its final form c. fifth–sixth centuries CE. The work deals with origin myths, the construction of theaters, *rasas* or sentiments that are to be expressed, costumes, gestures, the use of **dance** and **music**, the structure of plays, and the attributes of actors as well as **language**—including the use of Sanskrit and varieties of **Prakrit** to indicate the social status of the characters. *See also* ABHINAVAGUPTA; LITERATURE.

NAVDATOLI. **Archaeological** site on the south bank of the **Narmada**, Madhya Pradesh, at a point where the river can be crossed. Finds included a variety of **Paleolithic tools**. The major occupation was **Chalcolithic** (c. 2000–1300 BCE). Crops consisted of wheat, barley, rice, and pulses. There is evidence for the consumption of beef, pork, and fish. Finds of **copper** tools were scarce. Stone tools were far more plentiful, and several thousand such tools, including blades, knives, and points, have been found. A wide range of painted ceramics has been recovered from the site. Channel-spouted bowls found from the site have some resemblance to similar pots in Iran. Other finds include evidence of circular and rectangular thatched huts. One structure has been identified as an altar, possibly used for ritual purposes. The site was reoccupied in the **early historic period**. Finds from this phase include remains of a ***stūpa***. *See also* KATRA; MAHESHWAR.

NAVY. The earliest definitive references to a navy occur in the context of the **Mauryan Empire** (c. fourth–second century BCE).

Megasthenes refers to a board for managing the navy, while the ***Arthaśāstra*** mentions an officer known as the *navādhyakṣa*, literally the superintendent of boats or ships, who probably combined civil functions such as collecting customs dues with military responsibilities. Given the long coastline of the subcontinent and the use of maritime **routes** for communication and commerce, states in peninsular India maintained navies. Ships are represented on the coins of the **Sātavāhana** ruler **Pulumayi II**. The **Pallavas** probably used their naval power to attack Sri Lanka, while the **Co̲las** used their navy to control routes to Southeast Asia as well. Navies were probably used both against rival rulers and pirates. *See also* MARITIME TRADE.

***NĀYADHAMMAKAHĀ*.** **Prakrit** work, one of the **Jaina** canonical texts, containing stories and parables narrated by **Mahāvīra**, compiled c. 100 BCE. *See also* LITERATURE.

NĀYA̲N̲ĀR*.** **Tamil** term used for 63 devotees of **Śiva**, whose hagiographies were compiled in the *Periyapurāṇam* attributed to Cekkilār and compiled in the 12th century. Some of the compositions attributed to them were anthologized in the ***Tevāram. These included the works of **Tirujñāna Campantar**, **Tirunāvukkaracar**, and **Cuntarār**.

NEARCHOS. (c. 360–300 BCE), a companion of **Alexander (of Macedon)**, who accompanied him on his expedition to the subcontinent. Nearchos was appointed as admiral and led the fleet down the **Indus** through the Arabian Sea to the Persian Gulf during the retreat of the Greek forces. His account of this voyage was preserved by **Arrian**.

NEDUNJELIYAN. **Pāṇḍya** ruler (c. third century CE), mentioned in the ***Sangam*** anthologies as a great conqueror, who defeated his contemporary **Co̲la** and **Cera** counterparts.

NELAKONDAPALLI. **Early historic** (early first millennium CE?) **archaeological** site in Andhra Pradesh, also known as Nellakondapally, with remains of a ***stūpa*** and a **monastic** complex. Other finds included coins of the **Ikṣvākus** and the **Viṣṇukuṇḍins**, beads of semiprecious stone, red ware, **terracotta** figurines, and shell artifacts.

NELLAKONDAPALLY. *See* NELAKONDAPALLI.

NEOLITHIC. The Neolithic in the subcontinent, marking the beginning of the domestication of plants and animals, shows significant regional variations. The earliest evidence is from **Mehrgarh**. Other important sites include **Burzahom**. While sites in the northwest provide evidence for the cultivation of wheat and barley, those in central India, such as **Mahagara** and other sites in the **Belan valley**, have yielded evidence of the domestication of rice. The southern Neolithic sites have yielded evidence of a variety of pulses and millets. Domesticated animals included sheep, goat, and cattle. Cattle were particularly important in the Neolithic sites in the south. Typically, the Neolithic is associated with ground stone **tools**. However, a number of sites provide evidence for other kinds of tools, including microliths and bone tools. Handmade **pottery** has been found from most sites, although some have yielded evidence of preceramic/aceramic levels as well.

Dates for the Neolithic vary substantially. The beginnings of the Neolithic in Mehrgarh are dated to c. 8000 BCE, the sites in the Deccan are dated to the beginning of the third millennium BCE, those in Bihar to the second millennium BCE, while those in the northeast may be as late as the first millennium BCE. Sites from which evidence of Neolithic cultures have been recovered include **Banahalli**, **Brahmagiri**, **Budihal**, **Chirand**, **Daojali Hading**, **Elchuru**, **Eran**, **Gandhur**, **Garapadu**, **Golbai Sasan**, **Gufkral**, **Hallur**, **Hemmige**, **Kaothe**, **Katra**, **Kodekal**, **Koldihwa**, **Kuchai**, **Kupgal**, **Malpur**, **Nittur**, **Paiyampalli**, **Piklihal**, **Pynthorlangtein**, **Sanganakallu**, **Tāmralipti**, **Taradih**, **Tekkalakotta**, **T. Narsipur**, **Utnur**, and **Watgal**. *See also* ART; BURIAL PRACTICES; FOOTE, ROBERT BRUCE; GANGA (2); GODDESS CULTS; IRRIGATION; MESOLITHIC; PREHISTORY; TEXTILES; TRIBES.

NEPĀLA. Kingdom (c. fourth century CE), identified with present-day Nepal. According to the **Allahabad Pillar Inscription** of the **Gupta** ruler **Samudragupta**, the unnamed **king** of this region offered tribute and homage and agreed to obey the commands of the Gupta ruler.

NEVASA. Archaeological site on the Pravara, a tributary of the **Godavari** in Maharashtra, with evidence of five occupational phases.

Periods I and II have yielded a wide range of lower (c. 350,000 BP) and middle **Paleolithic tools**. Finds from Period III, designated as **Chalcolithic** (c. second millennium BCE), included hearths, storage jars, **pottery** resembling **Jorwe ware**, microliths, ground stone axes, **copper** tools and ornaments, and more than 100 **burials** of children. Finds from Period IV (mid–first millennium BCE to early first millennium CE) included **Northern Black Polished Ware**, **black and red ware**, **Russet-Coated Painted Ware**, a wide range of copper and **iron** equipment, bone tools, **terracotta** figurines, and **punch-marked**, **cast copper**, and **Sātavāhana coins**. Finds from Period V include Roman amphorae, **Red Polished Ware**, **rouletted ware**, and **Roman coins**. The site was abandoned c. 2nd century CE and was reoccupied in the 14th century.

***NIBBĀNA*.** **Prakrit/Pali** term meaning "extinction," used in **Buddhist** texts to describe the ultimate goal of extinguishing desires and attaining enlightenment. *See also* EIGHTFOLD PATH; NĀGĀRJUNA.

NIGALISAGAR. **Archaeological** site in Bihar, find spot of an **Asokan Pillar** with a **Minor Pillar Edict**, mentioning that Asoka enlarged a *thuba* (***stūpa***) in honor of a **Buddha** named Konakamana, evidently a personage different from Gautama Buddha.

NIGHAṆṬU*.** **Sanskrit** text, glossary of **Vedic** terms (c. first half of the first millennium BCE) that probably existed prior to the composition of the ***Nirukta attributed to **Yāska**. The extant text consists of five chapters, of which the first three list synonyms, the fourth deals with rare forms and homonyms, while the fifth deals with names of deities.

NĪLARĀJA. Ruler (c. fourth century CE) of an unidentified region known as Avamukta, possibly in Andhra Pradesh, mentioned in the **Allahabad Pillar Inscription** of the **Gupta** ruler **Samudragupta** as one of those who was captured but released on condition of submission.

NINDAUR. **Early historic** (c. mid–first millennium BCE?) **archaeological** site in Bihar, with evidence of **fortifications** and finds of **black and red ware** and **Northern Black Polished Ware**.

NIRUKTA. **Sanskrit** text attributed to **Yāska** (c. eighth–sixth century BCE), a commentary on the ***Nighaṇṭu***. The text, which consists of 12 chapters, survives in two versions.

NIRYUKTI. **Prakrit** commentaries on the **Jaina** canonical texts, composed in the form of mnemonic verses. The earliest of these date to c. sixth century CE. *See also* LITERATURE.

NIŚĀDA. **Sanskrit** term used (c. first millennium BCE onward) to designate a social category that was considered low and often **untouchable** from the perspective of the **Brahmanical** authors of the **Dharmasūtras** and **Dharmaśāstras**. *Niśādas* were often associated with the **forest**, and may have been hunters.

NĪTISĀRA. **Sanskrit** text on law and social norms, attributed to **Kāmandaka**, dated to c. sixth century CE. It consists of 20 sections and appears to be an abridged version of the ***Arthaśāstra***. *See also* LITERATURE.

NITTUR. Archaeological site in Karnataka. Finds include **Paleolithic tools**, **Neolithic** ground stone axes, **megalithic** stone circles (c. first millennium BCE). It is also the find spot of a **Minor Rock Edict** of **Asoka** mentioning the ruler's personal name.

NOH. Archaeological site in Rajasthan, with evidence of five occupational phases. Period I (c. second millennium BCE?) yielded **Ochre-Coloured Pottery**. Finds from Period II (latter half of the second millennium BCE?) included **black and red ware**. Period III (first half of the first millennium BCE?) yielded **Painted Grey Ware**, **black slipped ware**, **iron** and **copper** artifacts, and traces of rice. Finds from Period IV (second half of the first millennium BCE) included **Northern Black Polished Ware**, **cast copper coins**, and **terracotta** figurines. Finds from Period V (c. second century BCE–third century CE) included terracotta artifacts and coins.

NORTHERN BLACK POLISHED WARE. Distinctive **pottery**, found from **archaeological** sites belonging to the second half of the first millennium BCE. It declined in popularity subsequently. While the greatest concentration of this variety of pottery is in the mid–**Ganga (2)** valley (parts of present-day Uttar Pradesh and Bihar), it is found widely distributed throughout other parts of the subcontinent, including sites such as **Taxila** in the northwest, and several sites in the south. It was made on a fast wheel, had a thin fabric and a glossy surface, and was generally black, although other shades are known. It was usually undecorated. Common shapes include dishes and bowls. It was found in association with other types of pottery, including the **Painted Gray Ware**, **black and red ware**, **black slipped ware**, and plain gray and red wares. Sites that have yielded Northern Black Polished Ware include **Adam**, **Agiabir**, **Ahichchhatra**, **Alagankulan**, **Amaravati**, **Arambha**, **Atranjikhera**, **Ayodhya**, **Bahal**, **Bairat**, **Banarsihankalan**, **Bangarh**, **Bharatpur**, **Bharuch**, **Bhita**, **Bodh Gaya**, **Campā**, **Chandraketugarh**, **Chechar**, **Dangwada**, **Devangarh**, **Dharanikota**, **Dhuriapar**, **Eran**, **Erich**, **Ganwaria**, **Gilaulikhera**, **Hastinapura**, **Imlidih Khurd**, **Jakhera**, **Jhimjhimia Kalisthan**, **Jhusi**, **Kakrehta**, **Kanaganahalli**, **Kanauj**, **Kasrawad**, **Katra**, **Kaundinyapura**, **Kausambi**, **Kayatha**, **Kesanapalle**, **Khokrakot**, **Kolhua**, **Kotasur**, **Lalitagiri**, **Mahasthan**, **Maheshwar**, **Malhar**, **Maner**, **Mangalkot**, **Manjhi**, **Masaon**, **Mathura**, **Musanagar**, **Nadner**, **Nagara**, **Nagari**, **Nagda**, **Narhan**, **Nasik**, **Nevasa**, **Nindaur**, **Noh**, **Oriup**, **Pandu Rajar Dhibi**, **Pauni**, **Pokharna**, **Rājagaha**, **Rajmahal**, **Sadhwara**, **Sarnath**, **Satdhara**, **Sodanga**, **Sonkh**, **Sonpur**, **Sravasti**, **Sringaverapura**, **Sugh**, **Takiaper**, **Tāmralipti**, **Taradih**, **Taxila**, **Ter**, **Tildah**, **Timbarra**, **Tripuri**, **Tumain**, **Ujjayinī**, **Vaishali**, **Vidisha**, and **Wari Bateshwar**. *See also* EARLY HISTORIC PERIOD; IRON AGE; PUNCH-MARKED COINS; TRADE.

NUMISMATICS. Numismatics developed in India in the late 18th–early 19th centuries under the aegis, initially, of the **Asiatic Society** and scholars such as **James Prinsep** and **Alexander Cunningham**. **Coins** were studied for their **inscriptions**: Finds of coins with both Greek and **Kharoṣṭhī** legends provided the basis for some of the earliest decipherments. Since then, numismatic studies have focused on a variety of issues. Coins have been used to reconstruct dynastic histories, as for instance in the case of the **Indo-Greeks**. The imagery on coins has also been studied to reconstruct **religious** beliefs and practices and to examine questions of visual symbolism. Metallurgic studies and analyses of techniques of manufacture have been undertaken. There have also been studies on the economic significance of the circulation of coins. Numismatic publications include the *Journal of the Numismatic Society of India*, published by Banaras Hindu University, Varanasi, and the *Numismatic Digest*, published by the Indian Institute of Research in Numismatic Studies, Nasik. *See also* ORIENTALISM.

NYĀYA*. Philosophical** tradition that emphasized logic and observation as a means of attaining knowledge, developed c. early first millennium CE. Its influence extended to other disciplines such as linguistics. The texts pertaining to the tradition include the ***Nyāya sūtra attributed to **Gautama** and the ***Vaiśeṣika sūtra*** attributed to **Kaṇāda**. *See also* VĀCASPATI MIŚRA; *VAIŚEṢIKA*.

NYĀYA SŪTRA*.** Text in **Sanskrit**, attributed to **Gautama** (c. fifth century BCE?). It was regarded as a foundational text for the ***nyāya school of thought. It consisted of five chapters containing more than 500 *sūtras*, laying down the basis of logic and proof. Over the centuries, a rich commentarial tradition developed around the text. *See also* DINNĀGA (1); LITERATURE.

– O –

OCHRE-COLOURED POTTERY. Ceramic type (c. first half of the first millennium BCE) often found in association with **copper hoards**, especially from **archaeological** sites in Uttar Pradesh and adjoining provinces. The ceramic consists of thick as well as thin fabrics. Shapes include vases, basins, dish-on-stand, and storage jars. Some pots were decorated with painting and incised designs. The **pottery** is wheel thrown. Find spots of the pottery include **Ambkheri**, **Ahichchhatra**, **Atranjikhera**, **Bahadrabad**, **Bisauli**, **Hastinapura**, **Jakhera**, **Jodhpura**, **Lal Qila**, **Noh**, **Rajpur Parasu**, **Sadhwara**, and **Saipai**.

ONESICRITUS. Greek author, contemporary and **biographer** of **Alexander (of Macedon)**, who accompanied him on his expedition to the subcontinent.

ORIENTALISM. Term used for the perspective adopted by western scholars who examined "the east," including India, in the colonial context. The perspective was characterized by a tendency to view the east as the opposite or the "other" of the west and led to a certain degree of stereotyping—in the context of India, for instance, people were often projected as more spiritual or more sensual than their western counterparts as well as less rational beings living in a stagnant social order. There was also a tendency to focus on the elements of Indian civilization that were thought to be relatively exotic. Even within the postcolonial context, Orientalist ideas have proved influential.

In spite of the limitations of Orientalism, scholars working within an Orientalist framework laid the foundations of several disciplines that contributed to an understanding of early Indian history, including philology, **epigraphy**, **numismatics**, and **archaeology**, besides painstakingly collecting, editing, translating, and publishing **manuscripts** in a variety of **languages**.

ORIUP. **Archaeological** site in Bihar, with evidence of three occupational phases. Finds from Period I (early first millennium BCE?) included **black and red ware**, **black slipped ware**, and **Northern Black Polished Ware**. Other finds included bone **tools**, microliths, and beads of semiprecious stone. The **pottery** associated with Period II (late first millennium BCE?) was similar. Associated finds included **terracotta** figurines and artifacts of ivory, glass, and stone. Period III was assigned to the **Pāla** period (c. eighth century CE).

ORIYO TIMBO. **Archaeological** site (c. second millennium BCE) in Gujarat, with evidence of **Lustrous Red Ware**, hearths, and storage pits.

OSIAN. Site in Rajasthan, a center of **Pratihāra** power, with several **Brahmanical** and **Jaina temples** built between the 8th and 11th centuries CE.

OZENE. Name used in the ***Periplus of the Erythraean Sea*** for **Ujjayinī**.

– P –

PACHIKHERI. Archaeological site in Maharashtra, with evidence of four occupational phases. Finds from Period I, considered **Mesolithic** (c. third–second millennium BCE?), included nongeometric microliths. Period II (c. first millennium BCE?) provided evidence of **megalithic burials**, **iron** equipment, and **pottery**, including **black slipped ware** and **Black and Red Ware**. Finds from Period III, regarded as **Mauryan** (c. fourth–second century BCE), included iron equipment and animal, especially cattle, bones. Period IV, assigned to the **Sātavāhana** phase (c. second century BCE–second century CE), yielded iron **tools**, grinding stones, and beads of semiprecious stones. There is evidence for occupation during the medieval period as well.

PADRI. Archaeological site in Gujarat, with evidence of occupation during the **Harappan** and **early historic** phases. Finds associated with Period I (c. third millennium BCE) include Harappan **pottery** and traces of mud-brick **architecture**. There were also signs of **copper** working and finds of copper **tools**, and evidence for the manufacture of stone tools. Period II (c. first century BCE–first century CE) was associated with a burnt-brick structure, **inscriptions** and **coins** of the **Kṣatrapas**, and finds of **terracotta** plaques and figurines.

PAHARPUR. Archaeological site in Bangladesh, with several **Buddhist monuments** including ***stūpas***, **monasteries**, and a **temple** to the **goddess** Tārā. Most of these buildings were constructed in the eighth century, during the reign of the **Pāla** ruler **Dharmapāla**. Other finds include stone **sculpture** and **terracotta** plaques and figurines representing a variety of **Brahmanical** and Buddhist deities. The site remained in occupation until the 12th century CE. It has been recognized as a World Heritage Site by UNESCO. *See also* MAHIPĀLA (2).

PAHLAVA. *See* PARTHIAN.

PAIALACCHINĀMAMĀLĀ. **Prakrit** lexical work attributed to Dhanapāla (c. 10th century CE), consisting of 275 verses listing about 1,000 words. It includes both homonyms and synonyms. *See also* LITERATURE.

PAINTED GREY WARE. Pottery (c. first half of the first millennium BCE) found in the mid–**Ganga** (2) valley and adjoining regions. It usually constituted a small proportion of pottery assemblages, which included **black and red ware**, **black slipped ware**, and other plain gray and red wares, often used to make storage jars. The Painted Grey Ware was distinguished by its thin fabric, and was made using a fast wheel. Common shapes included bowls and dishes. Designs, generally geometric, were painted in black. Sites that have yielded Painted Grey Ware include **Ahichchhatra**, **Atranjikhera**, **Alamgirpur**, **Bhagwanpura**, **Bhorgarh**, **Brass**, **Dadheri**, **Daulatpur**, **Donder Khera**, **Hastinapura**, **Indraprastha**, **Jainal Naula**, **Jakhera**, **Jodhpura**, **Kampil**, **Kanauj**, **Kashipur**, **Kausambi**, **Kayatha**, **Khokrakot**, **Kurukṣetra**, **Mathura**, **Musanagar**, **Nagiari**, **Noh**, **Purola**, **Sadhwara**, **Sanghol**, **Sonkh**, **Sravasti**, **Sugh**, **Sunet**, **Thanesar**, **Ujjayinī**, and **Vidisha**. *See also* IRON AGE; NORTHERN BLACK POLISHED WARE.

PAINTING. Traditions of painting in the subcontinent have been traced back to **Mesolithic** sites such as **Adamgarh** and **Bhimbetka**. Subsequently, painted decoration is in evidence on **pottery** found from several **Neolithic** and **Chalcolithic** sites. Other paintings that have survived are from cave sites such as **Ajanta** and **Bagh**. **Sanskrit** textual traditions described painting as an accomplishment expected of urbane **women** and men. However, examples of such paintings have not survived. *See also* DANCE; MAYILADUMPARAI; ROCK ART; TEXTILES.

PAISRA. Archaeological site in Bihar with evidence of occupation during the **Paleolithic** and **Mesolithic** (c. 6000 BCE) periods. Finds from the first phase included hand axes, cleavers, and evidence for a workshop to manufacture stone **tools**. Finds from the second phase consisted of microliths and traces of hearths.

PAITHAN. Archaeological site in Maharashtra, identified with Pratiṣṭhāna, the capital of the **Sātavāhanas** (c. second century BCE–

second century CE), mentioned in **Jaina**, **Buddhist**, and **Brahmanical literature**. It is referred to in the ***Periplus of the Erythraean Sea*** as Paethana, a source from which onyx was procured. Finds include **punch-marked**, **Roman**, and Sātavāhana **coins**.

PAIYAMPALLI. Archaeological site in Tamil Nadu, with evidence of two occupational phases, with an overlap. Period I (first half of the second millennium BCE) was **Neolithic**, with evidence for ground stone **tools** and bone implements and for pit dwellings. There was evidence for both **agriculture** and **pastoralism**. Domesticated animals included cattle, sheep, goat, and pig, with indications of deer being hunted. These subsistence strategies continued in the second period as well. Other finds included **terracotta** figurines. Finds from Period II (late second–early first millennium BCE) consisted of **megalithic** stone circles containing **burials** with a range of **iron** tools and weapons. This phase also yielded **Black and Red Ware** and beads of semiprecious stone.

PĀLA. Ruling lineage that controlled parts of Bengal and Bihar from the 8th to the 11th century CE. Information about the dynasty, whose origins are obscure, is available from **inscriptions** and textual traditions. The founder of the dynasty was Gopāla. **Dharmapāla**, **Devapāla**, and **Mahipāla (2)** were among the more important rulers. The Pālas were engaged in a struggle for the control of **Kanauj**, the other contenders being the **Pratihāras** and **Rāṣṭrakūṭas**. The Pālas were patrons of **Buddhism** and built new **monasteries** besides extending patronage to existing institutions such as **Nalanda**. Many of these structures were embellished with stone and metal **sculptures** of **Brahmanical** and Buddhist deities, including **goddesses**, pointing to the growing influence of **Tantric** traditions. This was also the period when Buddhism spread from eastern India to Tibet and parts of Southeast Asia. *See also* BHOJA (2); KALACURI; RĀJENDRA; TĀMRALIPTI; TARADIH; *VAJRAYĀNA*.

PALEOLITHIC. Earliest **archaeological** phase in human history, identified on the basis of finds of stone artifacts, conventionally divided into three subphases—Lower, Middle, and Upper Paleolithic.

In the context of the subcontinent, the Lower Paleolithic corresponds with the geological phase of the Middle Pleistocene. Artifacts belonging to this phase have been recovered from geological strata associated with the erosion or deposition layers of river valleys as well as in the form of surface finds. Some of the largest numbers of surface finds have been recovered from the western Malwa plateau region (Madhya Pradesh), from the **Belan valley**, and the **Hunsgi-Baichbal** region. Important sites include **Didwana** and **Bhimbetka**.

Chronologies for this phase remain somewhat tentative, but suggested dates range between 200,000 and 150,000 years BP. Typical stone **tool** types include pebble tools and core tools, generally made of quartzite.

The Middle Paleolithic is distinguished by tools such as scrapers, points, and borers made of chert, chalcedony, agate, and jasper. Approximate chronologies for this phase range from 150,000 to 40,000 years BP.

Upper Paleolithic tools consist of blades, scrapers, knives, burins, and points. Materials for making tools included quartzites, limestone, chert, chalcedony, agate, and jasper. There is evidence for bone tools from the **Kurnool** caves. Evidence of grinding stones suggests the use of plant foods, while stone net-sinkers point to fishing. Other finds associated with this phase include ostrich eggshell beads and bone figurines. The tentative dates for this phase range between 40,000 and 10,000 years BP.

Other sites from which evidence of the Paleolithic period have been found include **Amaravati**, **Arangpur**, **Attirampakkam**, **Banki**, **Chirki-on-Pravara**, **Chopani Mando**, **Hemmige**, **Hirapur Khadan**, **Lalmai Hills**, **Maheshwar**, **Manigara**, **Mayurbhanj**, **Muchchtla Chintamani Gavi**, **Navdatoli**, **Nittur**, **Paisra**, **Patne**, **Riwat**, **Rohri**, **Sanghao**, and the **Soan valley**. *See also* ART; FOOTE, ROBERT BRUCE; MESOLITHIC; NARMADA; PREHISTORY.

PALI. Term meaning "text," especially sacred text, used by extension to designate the **language** of texts of the **Theravāda Buddhist** tradition. According to Buddhist tradition, the language was Māgadhī, probably a form of **Prakrit** spoken in central or eastern India, used by the **Buddha** to spread his message. Pali texts include works on Buddhist **religion** and **philosophy**. Several genres are recognized.

These include the *sutta*, or teachings of the Buddha, in prose, *geyya*, a mixture of prose and verse, *veyyākaraṇa* or expositions, *gāthā* or verse, *udāna* or ecstatic utterances, *itivuttaka* or brief sayings, the ***Jātakas***, *abbhutadharma* or descriptions of supernatural power and *vedalla*, or dialogue texts. Both the canonical texts and commentaries were preserved in Sri Lanka. *See also ABHIDHAMMA PIṬAKA*; *AṄGUTTARA NIKĀYA*; *CŪLAVAMSA*; *DHAMMAPADA*; *DĪGHA NIKĀYA*; *DĪPAVAMSA*; KACCANA; *KHUDDAKA NIKĀYA*; LITERATURE; *MAHĀVAMSA*; *MAJJHIMA NIKĀYA*; MANUSCRIPTS; *MILINDAPAÑHA*; PALI TEXT SOCIETY; *SAMYUTTA NIKĀYA*; *SUTTA PIṬAKA*; *THERAGĀTHĀ*; *THERĪGĀTHĀ*; *TRIPIṬAKA*; *VINAYA PIṬAKA*.

PALIBOTHRA. Ancient Indian **city** on the banks of the **Ganga (2)**, mentioned by **Pliny**, identified with **Pāṭaliputra**. *See also* PRASII.

PALI TEXT SOCIETY. Founded in London in 1881, with the objective of publishing texts on early **Buddhism**, the Society has published several volumes of **Pali** canonical texts, commentaries, and English translations.

PALKIGUNDU. Archaeological site in Karnataka. Find spot of a **Minor Rock Edict** of **Asoka**.

PALLAVA. Ruling dynasty in the Tamil region, perhaps originally subordinate to the **Sātavāhanas**. The earliest evidence of rulers belonging to this lineage date from c. third century CE. However, it is difficult to trace a continuous dynastic history. The Pallavas consolidated power by the end of the sixth century, after defeating the **Kalabhras**. They established control over parts of Andhra Pradesh and Tamil Nadu, with **Kanchipuram** as their capital. Important rulers included **Mahendravarman** and **Narasiṃhavarman I**. Contemporary rival powers included the **Cālukyas** and the **Pāṇḍyas**. Internecine **warfare** weakened all three powers and led to the rise of the **Colas**. **Inscriptional** evidence, which includes votive inscriptions in both **Prakrit** and **Sanskrit**, indicates that the rulers granted land, with tax exemptions, to ***brāhmaṇas* (1)**. They worshipped deities such as **Śiva** and **Viṣṇu** and performed **Vedic sacrifices**.

Some of the earliest **rock-cut** and structural **temples** were built under their patronage at sites such as **Mamallapuram**. *See also* APARĀJITA; BADAMI; COINAGE; GAṄGA (1); KADAMBA; LAND GRANTS; MAYŪRAŚARMAN; NARASIMHAVARMAN II; NAVY; SĀLAṄKĀYANA; SIMHAVIṢṆU; TALKAD; TOṆḌAI MAṆḌALAM; URAIYUR; VIJAYĀDITYA; VIṢṆUGOPA.

PAÑCĀLA. Name of a ***mahājanapada***, situated in western Uttar Pradesh. It acquired importance from the first half of the first millennium BCE. Important **cities** included **Kāmpilya** and **Ahichchhatra**. *See also* KINGSHIP, THEORIES OF ORIGIN.

PĀÑCARĀTRA. A **Sanskrit** term, literally "five nights," name of a **Vaiṣṇava** sect that gained popularity from the early centuries of the first millennium CE onward. Several texts, including the ***āgamas*** and the ***Mahābhārata***, contain descriptions of the beliefs and practices of this tradition, which involved worship of the chosen deity in **temples**, emphasizing devotion or ***Bhakti***, and an acceptance of the social order. *See also* BHĀGAVATA.

PAÑCATANTRA. Compilation of **Sanskrit** stories (c. fourth–fifth centuries CE) in prose and verse, attributed to Viṣṇuśarman, ostensibly composed for the education of princes. The work is divided into five sections and includes animal fables that attained widespread popularity and were disseminated in other countries as well. *See also* LITERATURE.

PANDU RAJAR DHIBI. Archaeological site in West Bengal, with evidence of five occupational phases. Finds from Period I (c. 1600–1400 BCE) included handmade **pottery** and implements of bone, stone, and fossil wood. Also found were remains of rice, traces of huts, and **burials** within the settlement. Period II, considered **Chalcolithic** (c. 1400–900 BCE), yielded **black and red ware**, **copper** artifacts, **terracotta** figurines, beads of semiprecious stone, and bones of deer and cattle. Finds from Period III (c. 900–600 BCE) were more or less identical, with the addition of **iron** equipment and **black slipped ware**. The material culture of Period IV (c. 600–300 BCE) was similar. Period V (c. 200 BCE–200 CE) witnessed the introduction of **Northern Black Polished Ware**. The settlement continued to be occupied until the sixth century CE. Significant finds included **coins** of the **Kuṣāṇas** and **Guptas**.

PĀṆḌYA. Ruling lineage in south India, mentioned in **Asokan inscriptions** (c. third century BCE). The Pāṇḍyas also figure in **Tamil *Sangam* literature**, where their capital, **Madurai**, was recognized as the place where literary **assemblies** were held. Names of rulers occur in some of the compositions, but with few details. The lineage apparently lost its importance when the **Kalabhras** were active in the region, but it regained power subsequently. With the rise of the **Co<u>l</u>as**, the Pāṇḍyas were reduced to a position of subordination. However, the period from the 11th century onward witnessed a revival of their power, which culminated in the 13th century.

Pāṅḍya rulers are mentioned in Roman and Chinese accounts. It is likely that the rulers attempted to control **maritime trade routes**, both western and eastern. *See also* KARIKĀ<u>L</u>AN; KHĀRAVELA; KORKAI; MAJOR ROCK EDICTS; NEDUNJELIYAN; RĀJARĀJA I; TIRUJÑĀNA CAMPANTAR; URAIYUR.

PANGURARIA. Archaeological site in Madhya Pradesh, find spot of a **Minor Rock Edict** of **Asoka** (c. third century BCE). The site has remains of several **monasteries** and ***stūpas***.

PĀṆINI. Sanskrit grammarian (c. fifth–fourth century BCE) who lived in Śalātura in **Gandhāra**, author of the ***Aṣṭādhyāyī***. Pāṇini used the Sanskrit term *bhāṣā*, meaning "**language**," to refer to the Sanskrit analyzed in his work as distinct from *chandas*, or **Vedic** Sanskrit. *See also* KĀTYĀYANA; LITERATURE; *MAHĀBHĀṢYA*.

PARANAR. Tamil poet whose works are included in several of the ***Sangam*** anthologies (c. third century BCE–second century CE?). He composed poems on the themes of love and war as well as in praise of his patron, the **Cera king** Cenkuṭṭuvan. *See also* LITERATURE.

PARAŚURĀMA. Legendary figure, mentioned in the ***Rāmāyaṇa*** and the ***Mahābhārata***, where he is described as a ***brāhmaṇa* (1)** who destroyed ***kṣatriyas***. He was regarded as an ***avatāra*** of **Viṣṇu** in the **Purāṇic** tradition.

PARIAR. Archaeological site in Uttar Pradesh, find spot of **copper hoards** (c. second millennium BCE?).

PARIPĀṬAL. Anthology of **Tamil poems**, part of the ***Eṭṭutokai*** corpus of ***Sangam*** literature (compiled between c. third century BCE and second century CE?). The anthology includes the work of 13 poets on a variety of sacred and secular themes. *See also* LITERATURE.

PARIṢAD. **Sanskrit** term used to designate councils, c. first millennium BCE onward. Membership of such councils was probably restricted to men belonging to the first two ***varṇas***. In some cases the councils acted as advisory bodies for the **king**; in other instances they served as **judicial** bodies. The *parisa* mentioned in **Asokan inscriptions** may have been identical with the *pariṣad*. The ***Arthaśāstra*** mentions a council known as the *mantri pariṣad*, literally the council of **ministers** or advisors.

PĀRŚVA. Jaina *tīrthaṅkara* (c. eighth century BCE?), regarded as the predecessor of **Mahāvīra** according to the Jaina tradition. He is associated with laying down most of the basic tenets of the faith.

PARTHIAN. People of Iranian origin, who entered northwest India c. first century CE and exercised control over parts of this region until they in turn were ousted by the **Śakas**. They were referred to as Pahlavas in **Sanskrit** textual traditions. *See also* BACTRIAN GREEK; GONDOPHERNES; SILK ROUTE.

PASENADI. King of **Kosala** (c. sixth century BCE), mentioned in **Buddhist** sources as a contemporary of the **Buddha** and **Bimbisāra**. He followed a policy of expansion and forged marital ties with the ruler of **Magadha** as well as with the **Sākyas**. One of his wives, Mallikā, was sympathetic toward Buddhism. *See also* VIḌŪḌABHA.

PASTORALISM. Pastoralism was an important component of subsistence strategies in the early Indian context. The earliest evidence for pastoralism comes from **Neolithic** sites, many of which have yielded remains of bones of domesticated animals, especially cattle, sheep, and goat. Pastoralism was evidently important in the

Harappan civilization, where pastoral groups may have been involved in the transport of goods over long distances. The ***Ṛgveda*** also provides evidence of pastoralism—the vocabulary of the text draws substantially on pastoral imagery. Pastoral groups are mentioned in later textual traditions as well—in **Sanskrit**, **Pali**, **Prakrit**, and **Tamil**.

Texts such as the ***Arthaśāstra*** indicate that pastoral people could be recruited for the **army**, and were expected to pay taxes. There are indications that the cultural practices of pastoral groups were adopted and adapted within the **Brahmanical** belief system—the most outstanding instance being that of **Kṛṣṇa**, who was frequently conceptualized as a cowherd deity. Archaeological sites that have yielded evidence of domesticated animals include **Adamgarh**, **Ahar**, **Amri**, **Atranjikhera**, **Babarkot**, **Bagor**, **Balakot**, **Balathal**, **Bara**, **Bhagimohari**, **Budihal**, **Burzahom**, **Chirand**, **Damdama**, **Datrana**, **Gandhur**, **Ganeshwar**, **Golbai Sasan**, **Gufkral**, **Gumla**, **Hallur**, **Hastinapura**, **Hathikera**, **Imlidih Khurd**, **Inamgaon**, **Kesanapalle**, **Khajuri**, **Kodekal**, **Lal Qila**, **Mahagara**, **Maheshwar**, **Mangalkot**, **Maski**, **Mehrgarh**, **Nagara**, **Nageshwar**, **Nagwada**, **Narhan**, **Pachikheri**, **Paiyampalli**, **Pandu Rajar Dhibi**, **Rehman Dheri**, **Rojdi**, **Saipai**, **Shaktari Timbo**, **Shirkanda**, **Sugh**, **Takalghat–Khapa**, **Tekkalakotta**, and **Wina**. *See also* ASH MOUNDS; CASTE; MĀLAVA; MEGALITH; *VAIŚYA*; *VARṆA*; VEDIC ECONOMY.

PĀŚUPATA. A **Śaiva** sect that gained popularity from the early centuries of the first millennium CE onward, emphasizing monism and focusing on the devotional worship of **Śiva** as *paśupati* or the lord of creatures or souls. The Pāśupatas advocated **asceticism**. Pāśupata **monasteries** or *maṭhas*, many established with royal patronage, flourished in several parts of the subcontinent.

PATALENE. Name used in Greek accounts to designate the region of the delta of the **Indus**.

PĀṬALIGRĀMA. The site that later developed into the city of **Pāṭaliputra**. The foundations of the settlement were laid by **Ajātaśatru** (c. sixth–fifth centuries BCE).

PĀṬALIPUTRA. Capital (c. fifth century BCE onward) of the ***mahājanapada*** of **Magadha**, identified with **Patna** in present-day Bihar, strategically located at the confluence of the **Ganga (2)**, Punpun, Gandak, and Son Rivers. A description of the **city** is provided in **Megasthenes**'s ***Indica***. This suggests that the city was surrounded by a moat and a rampart with 64 gates and more than 500 towers. Extensive excavations have proved difficult owing to existing settlements. However, **archaeological** excavations have provided evidence of a pillared hall attributed to the **Mauryas**. Other structures include remains of a wooden palisade and traces of **Buddhist monasteries**. According to Buddhist tradition, the third **Buddhist Council** was held here. Four major occupational phases have been identified in excavations at the site. Finds from Period I (c. sixth–second centuries BCE) include **punch-marked coins**. Period II (c. second century BCE–second century CE) provided evidence of **terracotta** figurines. Period III (c. second–fourth centuries CE) yielded **Kuṣāṇa** coins, remains of a ***stūpa***, and sealings. Finds from Period IV (c. fourth century CE onward) were relatively insignificant.

Megasthenes's account also contains details about the administration of the city, which, according to him, was run by a board consisting of 30 members, divided into six committees. These were meant to regulate craft production, ensure the well-being of foreigners, record births and deaths, supervise weights and measures, oversee sales, and collect taxes on transactions, respectively. *See also* AJĀTAŚATRU; GUPTA; KĀLĀŚOKA; KUSUMAPURA; PALIBOTHRA; PĀṬALIGRĀMA; SECOND URBANIZATION; UDAYIN; *UTTARĀPATHA*.

PATAÑJALI (1). Sanskrit grammarian (c. second century BCE), author of the ***Mahābhāṣya***, a commentary on **Pāṇiṇi**'s ***Aṣṭādhyāyī***. *See also* LITERATURE.

PATAÑJALI (2). Philosopher and author of the ***Yogasūtra*** (c. second century BCE–second century CE?), regarded as the fundamental text of ***yoga***. *See also* LITERATURE.

PATIRṚṚUPATTU*.** Anthology of **Tamil poems** that forms part of the ***Eṭṭutokai corpus of ***Sangam* literature** (c. third century BCE–second century CE?). It originally consisted of 100 poems divided into sets of 10, each composed by a single poet in praise of the valor and benevolence of a **Cera king**, who seems to have generously rewarded the composer.

PATNA. Capital of Bihar, identified with ancient **Pāṭaliputra**, the capital of **Magadha**, by a geographer named James Rennell in the 18th century. *See also* ĀRYABHAṬA; KUMRAHAR.

PATNE. Paleolithic site in Maharashtra. The Upper Paleolithic levels at the site have yielded evidence of beads made of ostrich eggshell as well as specimens of engraved ostrich shell, probably the earliest instance of a work of **art**.

PATTADAKAL. Site in Karnataka, find spot of **Cālukya temples**, of which the best known is one dedicated to Virūpākṣa, a form of **Śiva**. The temple was built by Lokamahādevī, the wife of the reigning **king** Vikramāditya II (r. 733–744 CE). It was decorated with some of the finest examples of stone **sculpture** derived from **Purāṇic** themes. Pattadakal was declared a World Heritage Site by UNESCO in 1987.

PAṬṬINAPPĀLAI. **Tamil** composition, attributed to Ruttiran Kaṇṇanār, part of the ***Pattupāṭṭu*** corpus of ***Sangam*** **literature** (c. third century BCE–second century CE?). The **poem** was composed in praise of the **Coḻa king Karikāḻan** and contains a vivid description of the **city** of **Kaveripattinam**. *See also* LITERATURE.

PATTUPĀṬṬU. One of the two major anthologies of **Tamil *Sangam* literature** (compiled c. third century BCE–second century CE?). The corpus includes the ***Tirumurukāṟṟuppaṭai***, *Porunarāṟṟuppaṭai*, *Cirupāṇāṟṟuppaṭai*, *Perumpāṇāṟṟuppaṭai*, ***Mullaippāṭṭu***, *Maturaikkāñci*, *Neṭunalvāṭai*, *Kuriñcipāṭṭu*, ***Paṭṭinappālai***, and ***Malaipatukatam***. Texts that are classified as *āṟṟuppaṭai* include prayers for help. Most of the anthologies deal with themes of love and war and include vivid descriptions of nature and everyday life. *See also* KAPILAR; LITERATURE; NAKKĪRAR.

PAUMACARIYA. **Prakrit** work attributed to Vimalasūri (c. third–fifth century CE?). The text, which consists of more than 8,000 verses, is a **Jaina** version of the ***Rāmāyaṇa***. *See also* LITERATURE.

PAUNI. Archaeological site in Maharashtra, with evidence of four occupational phases. Finds from Period I, defined as pre-**Mauryan** (c. sixth–fourth centuries BCE), included **black and red ware** and beads of semiprecious stone. Period II, assigned to the Mauryan period (c. fourth–second centuries BCE), yielded **Northern Black Polished Ware**, **copper** ornaments, beads of semiprecious stone, ivory artifacts, and remains of a rampart. Finds from Period III (c. second–first centuries BCE) consisted of **terracotta** figurines and artifacts similar to those of the previous phase. Period IV (c. first century BCE–second century CE) yielded traces of stone and brick structures, **iron** artifacts, **coins**, and an **inscribed seal**. The site continued to be occupied until the middle of the first millennium CE.

PAVA. City (in Uttar Pradesh) in the ***mahājanapada*** of **Malla**, regarded as the spot where **Mahāvīra** breathed his last.

PAVURALLAKONDA. Archaeological site in Andhra Pradesh. Finds include a **Brāhmī inscription** dated to c. second century BCE, and remains of a **monastery** and votive ***stūpas***.

PEDDAVEGI. Archaeological site in Andhra Pradesh. The earliest levels are associated with the **Sālaṅkāyanas** (c. fourth–fifth centuries CE), followed by the **Viṣṇukuṇḍins** (c. fifth–sixth centuries CE) and the eastern **Cālukyas** (c. sixth–seventh centuries CE). Structural remains include those of a **temple** evidently built by reusing parts of a **Buddhist** ***stūpa*** and shrine. **Terracotta** figurines, shell bangles, beads of semiprecious stone, stone plaques with images of **Purāṇic** deities, and **copper coins** of the Viṣṇukuṇḍins were also found at the site.

PEHOA. Site in Haryana, near Thanesar, known as Pṛthudaka in early textual traditions, an important node along the **trade route** linking the subcontinent with West and Central Asia, and mentioned as the site of a regular fair for buying and selling horses in a ninth-century **inscription**.

***PERIPLUS OF THE ERYTHRAEAN SEA*.** Greek text composed by an anonymous sailor (c. 75 CE), describing ports along the western and eastern coast of the subcontinent and listing their imports and exports. *See also* ARIKAMEDU; BARBARICUM; BARYGAZA; MARITIME TRADE; MUZIRIS; NAHAPĀṆA; OZENE; PAITHAN; TAGARA; TEXTILES.

PERIYĀḺVĀR. Tamil Vaiṣṇava saint (c. seventh century CE), recognized as one of the 12 ***āḻvārs***. More than 400 compositions in the ***Nālāyira Tiviya Pirapantam*** are attributed to him. *See also* LITERATURE.

PERSEPOLIS. One of the most important political centers of the **Achaemenid** Empire. The **inscription** of **Darius I** from Persepolis, carved between c. 518 and 515 BCE, mentions the Hindus among his subjects. Inscribed clay tablets found here point to the exchange of letters between the ruler and his representative in the Indian province. Inscriptions of later rulers, **Xerxes** and Artaxerxes, list the Indian provinces among their dominions.

PERUNKATAI*. Tamil** text, attributed to **Konku Velir** (c. eighth century CE), based on a **Sanskrit** work authored by a **Jaina king** (c. sixth century CE). This in turn was derived from the ***Bṛhatkathā of **Guṇāḍhya**. However, in the Tamil version the central figure is a king named Utayanan, and not Narasiṃhavāhana, the hero of the original text. The narrative culminates in the renunciation of the world by the hero. *See also* LITERATURE.

PESHAWAR. City in Pakistan, located near the Khyber Pass, on one of the major **routes** linking the subcontinent to Central Asia, identified with Puruṣapura or **Puṣkalāvatī**. *See also* SHAJI-KI-DHERI.

PHILOSOPHY. Several philosophical traditions are documented from the mid–first millennium BCE onward. These included **Buddhism**, **Jainism**, and **Brahmanical** philosophies and a range of other traditions. Brahmanical texts classified philosophical schools into two broad categories: *nāstika*, including those of the Buddhists and Jainas who denied the authority of the **Vedas**; and *āstika*, those who recognized the sanctity of the Vedas. The latter included ***Sāṃkhya***, ***Yoga***, ***Vedānta***, ***Mīmāṃsā***, ***Nyāya***, and ***Vaiśeṣika***. Philosophical texts, generally written in **Sanskrit**, were characterized by certain distinctive features. The earliest texts were ***sūtras***. These were followed by commentaries, often composed in the form of disputation texts, where the perspective of the opponent was first expounded and then refuted. Most texts composed in the first millennium CE were commentaries on earlier works rather than original compositions. Subsequently, versified summaries of philosophical tenets were compiled in texts known as *kārikās* and *vārttikās*. In some instances, these modes of composition continued until the end of the 17th century. *See also* AJĪTA KEŚAKAMBALIN; BHARTṚHARI; *BRĀHMAṆA* (2); *BRAHMASŪTRA*; *CĀRVĀKA*; CASTE; *CHĀNDOGYA UPANIṢAD*; EARLY HISTORIC PERIOD; GĀRGĪ; ĪŚVARAKṚṢṆA; JANAKA; KAPILA; *KARMA*; KUMĀRILA BHAṬṬA; LOKĀYĀTA; MAHĀYĀNA; MAITREYĪ; MAKKHALIPUTTA GOSĀLA; *MAṆIMEKALAI*; *MANUSMṚTI*; NĀGĀRJUNA; PATAÑJALI (2); PRABHĀKARA; PROTEST MOVEMENTS; ŚABARASVĀMIN; SACRIFICE; *SAMAYASĀRA*; ŚAṄKARĀCĀRYA; *SUYAGADA*; TANTRA; UPANIṢAD; VASUBANDHU; YĀJÑAVALKYA; *YOGĀCĀRA*.

PIKLIHAL. Neolithic (c. third–second millennium BCE) site in Karnataka, with evidence of cattle rearing and cultivation. Other finds include handmade **pottery** and traces of **painting** on rock surfaces.

***PINKALANTAI*. Tamil** dictionary, authored by Pinkalar in the 10th century CE. It consists of 10 sections, dealing with 14,700 words. *See also* LITERATURE.

PIPRAHWA. Archaeological site in eastern Uttar Pradesh, often identified with **Kapilavastu**. Finds include a ***stūpa*** dated to c. third–second centuries BCE, a relic casket, **punch-marked coins**, and remains of **monasteries**. **Inscribed seals** belonging to the **Kuṣāṇa** period refer to the site as Kapilavastu. *See also* GANWARIA.

PIPRI. Archaeological site in Madhya Pradesh, with evidence of a **Chalcolithic** culture (c. second millennium BCE?). There is evidence of circular dwelling pits, hearths, and animal **burials**. **Pottery** is handmade, with black designs including geometric, human, and animal motifs painted on a red surface. Other finds include microliths and other stone **tools**, probably made locally, beads of semiprecious stone, and shell artifacts. Metal objects include **copper** fishhooks.

PIṢṬAPURA. Region, possibly in present-day Andhra Pradesh. The **Allahabad Pillar Inscription** states that the ruler (c. fourth century CE) of this area, whose name is not known, was among those who were captured by the **Gupta king Samudragupta** and released on condition of submission.

PIṬAKA*.** **Pali** term, meaning "basket," used to describe the three anthologies of texts, ***Abhidhamma, ***Sutta***, and ***Vinaya***, considered canonical within early **Buddhist** tradition. *See also* BUDDHIST COUNCILS.

PITALKHORA. Site in Maharashtra, with evidence of **rock-cut caves**, dated to c. first century BCE. The structures include both shrines and **monasteries**. Other finds include stone **sculpture**.

PITHAD. **Archaeological** site in Gujarat with two occupational phases. Period I is **Mesolithic**. Finds include microliths and ostrich eggshell. Period II has been designated as **Late Harappan**. Finds include remains of a rubble wall, **pottery** that has parallels with **Rojdi**, beads of semiprecious stone, **copper** and bronze artifacts, and bone, horn, and antlers.

PLINY. (b. 23 CE, d. 79 CE). Roman administrator and author. His major work was the *Historia Naturalis*, which described Indo-Roman **trade** among other things. Pliny complained that there was a drain of wealth to India, as goods from the subcontinent were in great demand among the Roman elite. *See also* PALIBOTHRA.

PLUTARCH. Greek **philosopher**, **biographer**, and essayist (b. 46 CE, d. 120/127 CE). His best-known work is the *Bioi Paralleloi*, a study of 50 important Greeks and Romans, including **Alexander (of Macedon)**.

POETRY AND POETS. The earliest examples of poetry available in the subcontinent are the hymns of the ***Ṛgveda*** (c. second millennium BCE), in **Sanskrit**. By the end of the first millennium BCE, there is evidence for poetic compositions in **Pali**, **Prakrit**, and **Tamil**, the last-named providing some of the earliest examples of secular poetry. A wide variety of texts consisted of metrical compositions. These included the **epics**, **Dharmaśāstras**, and **Purāṇas**. Poems also formed an integral part of plays. **Inscriptions**, especially panegyrics, were occasionally composed in a poetic style. *See also AINKURUNŪRU*; *AKAM*; *AKANĀNŪRU*; AMARASIMHA; ĀṆṬĀL; BĀṆABHAṬṬA; CUNTARĀR; DĀMODARAGUPTA; *DEVĪMĀHĀTMYA*; *EṬṬUTOKAI*; HARIṢEṆA (1); KĀLIDĀSA; *KALITTOKAI*; KAPILAR; KĀRAIKKĀL AMMAIYĀR; KONKU VELIR; *KURUNTOKAI*; *MAHĀPURĀṆA*; *MALAIPATUKATAM*; MĀNIKKAVĀCAKAR; *MULLAIPPĀṬṬU*; NAKKĪRAR; *NARṚINAI*; PARANAR; *PARIPĀṬAL*; *PATIRṚUPATTU*; *PAṬṬINAPPĀLAI*; *PATTUPĀṬṬU*; *PRAŚASTI*; *PURANĀNURU*; RĀJAŚEKHARA; RAVIKĪRTI; SAMUDRAGUPTA; *SANGAM*; *SILAPPADIKĀRAM*; *SIRIPANARṚUPPATAI*; *THERAGĀTHĀ*; *THERĪGĀTHĀ*; TIRUJÑĀNA CAMPANTAR; *TIRUKKURAḺ*; TIRUMANKAI ĀḺVĀR; TIRUMULAR; *TIRUMURUKĀRṚUPPAṬAI*; TIRUNĀVUKKARACAR; TIRUTTAKKA TEVAR; *TIRUVĀCAKAM*; *TOLKĀPPIYAM*; VĀKPATI.

POKHARNA. Early historic (mid–first millennium BCE?) **archaeological** site in West Bengal. Finds include **black and red ware** and **Northern Black Polished Ware**.

POOMPUHAR. Coastal **archaeological** site in Tamil Nadu, identified with **Kaveripattinam** or Puhār. *See also SILAPPADIKĀRAM*.

POROS. (Greek name of Puru.) Ruler of a small state on the **Jhelum**, a contemporary of **Alexander (of Macedon)**. According to Greek accounts, he refused to surrender to Alexander. In the ensuing battle (c. 326 BCE) the elephants in the **army** of Poros proved ineffectual against the Macedonian force. Alexander spared the life of the defeated **king**. Subsequently, the Macedonian army refused to proceed further east, and Alexander was forced to retreat.

POST-HARAPPAN. Name assigned to **archaeological** cultures found in the area of the **Harappan civilization** during the first half of the second millennium BCE. *See also* BHAGWANPURA; CEMETERY H; JHUKAR; LATE HARAPPAN.

POTTERY. Pottery is among the most commonly found **archaeological** materials from sites in the subcontinent and is frequently used as a marker to differentiate between phases of cultural development. The earliest pottery, found from **Neolithic** sites, was generally corded, handmade, with evidence of the use of rice husk and straw as binding material. Shapes include bowls, storage jars, vases, basins, and so on, sometimes decorated with **painted** or incised designs. Variations in the designs on pottery and in the fabric and shape have been used to distinguish among **Chalcolithic** cultures that shared a common subsistence base. Some of these cultures were contemporaneous with the **Harappan civilization**, whose pottery was distinctive in terms of decoration, shapes, and standardization.

While archaeological sites are often classified on the basis of typologies derived from pottery, such as **Painted Grey Ware**, **Black and Red Ware**, **Northern Black Polished Ware**, etc. the evidence from virtually every site indicates that a wide range of different kinds of pottery was in use simultaneously. In fact, the diagnostic pottery types are often present only in small quantities.

Finds of Roman pots, including amphorae, as well as local imitations of Roman pottery provide evidence of connections with the West and the importance of long-distance exchange. *See also* ARRETINE WARE; ART; BLACK SLIPPED WARE; CEMETERY H; JORWE; KALIBANGAN; KAYATHA; KULLI; LUSTROUS RED WARE; MALWA WARE; MEGALITH; MUZIRIS; OCHRE-COLOURED POTTERY; RED POLISHED WARE; ROULETTED WARE; RUSSET-COATED PAINTED WARE; NAL; SAVALDA WARE; SEKTA; SOTHI.

POVERTY. Perhaps the earliest instance of social differentiation, evident in the **archaeological** record, is from the **Harappan civilization**, where some structures in **Harappa** have been identified as workmen's quarters. Narrative traditions from the mid–first millennium BCE in **Pali** and **Prakrit**, and slightly later in **Tamil** and **Sanskrit**, recognized the existence of impoverished people, including landless laborers, **slaves**, captives, and those subject to debt-bondage.

While some traditions such as **Buddhism** advocated compassion and charity as modes of alleviating poverty, others regarded poverty as the outcome of past ***karma***. *See also* COURTESANS.

PRABHĀKARA. ***Mīmāṃsā*** **philosopher** (c. eighth century CE), disciple and critic of **Kumārila**, and author of the *Bṛhatī*, a commentary in **Sanskrit** on the *Śabara bhāṣya* composed by **Śabarasvāmin** on the work of **Jaimini**. *See also* LITERATURE.

PRABHĀKARAVARDHANA. Ruler, belonging to the **Puṣyabhūti** lineage of **Thanesar** (c. sixth century CE). His daughter **Rājyaśrī** was married to the **Maukhari** ruler **Grahavarman**. Prabhākaravardhana was succeeded by his younger son, **Harṣavardhana**.

PRABHĀVATĪ GUPTA. Daughter (c. fourth–fifth centuries CE) of the **Gupta** ruler **Candragupta II**, and wife of the **Vākāṭaka** ruler **Rudrasena II**. One of the few **women** known to have exercised political power, she acted as a regent for her sons for about 15 years, during which period she made **land grants** in favor of **Vaiṣṇava** institutions and teachers. *See also* KINGSHIP; PRAVARASENA II.

PRADYOTA. **King** of **Avanti** (c. sixth century BCE) whose daughter married his rival, **Udayana**. He also waged war against the contemporary rulers of **Magadha** and **Taxila**.

PRĀGJYOTIṢA. Name used in **Sanskrit** texts and **inscriptions** (c. mid–first millennium CE onward) to designate present-day Assam. *See also* DEVAPĀLA.

PRAKRIT. Term derived from the **Sanskrit** word *prakṛti*, meaning "natural," used to designate several **languages** and dialects. Prakrit was used in **inscriptions** (c. third century BCE–fifth century CE), being gradually replaced by Sanskrit and regional languages. It was also a language of literary composition, including **poems**, **epics**, and other narratives, especially within the **Jaina** tradition. *See also* *APABHRAṂŚA*; ASOKAN INSCRIPTIONS; *ĀYĀRA*; *CAUPANNAMAHĀPURIṢACARIYA*; *DHARMAKATHĀ*; *DHARMOPADEŚAMĀLĀVIVARAṆA*; DRAMA; EARLY HIS-

TORIC PERIOD; *KALPASŪTRA*; KHAROṢṬHĪ; KUNDAKUNDA; *KUVALAYAMĀLĀ*; MANUSCRIPTS; *NĀYADHAMMAKAHĀ*; *NIRYUKTI*; *PAIALACCHINĀMAMĀLĀ*; PALI; *PAUMACARIYA*; *SAMARAICCHAKAHĀ*; *SAMAYASĀRA*; SAMGHADASAGANI (1); SAMGHADASAGANI (2); *SATTASAĪ*; *SETUBANDHA*; ŚIVĀRYA; *SUYAGADA*; UDYOTANA SŪRI; *UPADESAMĀLĀ*; *VĀSUDEVAHINDĪ*; VIMALASŪRI; YATIVṚṢABHA.

PRĀRJUNA. Community living in central India (c. fourth century CE), mentioned in the **Allahabad Pillar Inscription** of the **Gupta** ruler **Samudragupta** among the peoples who offered him tribute and homage and agreed to obey his orders.

PRAŚASTI. **Sanskrit** term meaning "praise," used to designate a genre of eulogistic **inscriptions**, generally composed by court poets in ornate prose or **poetry** in praise of rulers, c. first millennium CE onward. *Praśastis* contained the genealogy of the ruler or patron, a description of his physical attributes including comparisons with Sanskrit **epic** heroes, an account of his achievements, especially his military victories, besides descriptions of his social and cultural accomplishments and piety. While somewhat stereotypical, they provide insight into the ideals of courtly culture. *See also* ALLAHABAD PILLAR INSCRIPTION; JUNAGADH ROCK INSCRIPTION.

PRASENAJIT. *See* PASENADI.

PRASII. Name used by Greek and Roman authors (c. first century BCE–first century CE) to describe a **kingdom** in eastern India, with its capital at **Palibothra**, identified with **Pāṭaliputra**.

PRATIHĀRA. Name of at least two ruling lineages that dominated north and central India (c. sixth century CE onward). The origins of the **Pratihāras** (occasionally referred to in **inscriptions** as the Gurjara Pratihāras) are obscure. The earliest ruler of the western branch, where **Osian** was an important center, was Haricandra. The other branch was initially associated with **Ujjayinī** and later with **Kanauj**. Rulers of this lineage, which was powerful between the 8th and 10th centuries CE, extended loose control from Gujarat in the west to Bihar in the east. Their power was contested by the **Rāṣṭrakūṭas** and the **Pālas**. By the 10th century, the power of the Pratihāras was eclipsed by that of their feudatories such as the Paramāras, Caṇḍelas, and **Kalacuris**. One of the last known rulers of the lineage, Rājyapāla, was defeated by Mahmud of Ghazni in 1018. *See also* BHOJA (2); DEVAPĀLA; DHARMAPĀLA; MAHENDRAPĀLA; MAHIPĀLA (1); NĀGABHAṬA I; NĀGABHAṬA II.

PRATIṢṬHĀNA. *See* PAITHAN.

PRAVARASENA I. Vākāṭaka ruler (c. 280–340 CE), who extended control over parts of the Deccan, and performed a series of **Vedic sacrifices**.

PRAVARASENA II. Vākāṭaka ruler (c. 420–452 CE), son of **Prabhāvatī Gupta**, known from his **inscriptions** recording **land grants** to ***brāhmaṇas* (1)**. It is likely that he founded the city of Pravarapura, possibly present-day Paunar in Maharashtra. He built a **temple** in honor of **Rāma**, conceptualized as an ***avatāra*** of **Viṣṇu**. Stone **sculptures**, perhaps meant to decorate this temple, have been recovered. Pravarasena is regarded as the author of a **Prakrit** text, the ***Setubandha***.

PRAYĀGA. Ancient name of **Allahabad**, a **city** located close to the confluence of the **Ganga (2)** and the **Yamuna**. The ancient settlement of **Kausambi** is near Allahabad.

PRE-HARAPPAN. *See* EARLY HARAPPAN.

PREHISTORY. Term used to designate those periods for which written sources are not available, including the **Paleolithic**, **Mesolithic**, **Neolithic**, and in some instances the **Chalcolithic** phases of early Indian history. With the realization of the limitations of written sources in terms of their perspectives and subject matter, historians are increasingly reluctant to operate with a sharp divide between history and prehistory. *See also* FOOTE, ROBERT BRUCE.

PRINSEP, JAMES. Official (1800–1840) in charge of mints of the British East India Company, who came to India in 1819. He was the secretary of the **Asiatic Society** between 1832 and 1838 and made substantial contributions to the development of **numismatics** and **epigraphy**. His major achievement was the decipherment of **Asokan inscriptions** in 1837.

PROSTITUTION. *See* COURTESANS.

PROTEST MOVEMENTS. Attempts to find instances of protest movements in early India have focused on two categories of evidence, both implicit rather than explicit. One consists of **philosophical** and religious traditions, such as those of the sixth century BCE, including, but not confined to, **Buddhism** and **Jainism**, which developed critiques of the ***varṇa***-based **Brahmanical** order. Later traditions of ***Bhakti*** also suggested that **caste** affiliations were irrelevant in the devotional mode of worship. However, while criticizing the criteria for determining caste and the relevance of the system, none of these traditions questioned its existence or suggested its complete abolition.

Textual references to peasants abandoning their lands and moving into **forested** areas, presumably to escape from the oppression of local landed intermediaries and/or the state, have also been interpreted as proof of protest or resistance, corroborated by the fact that some **early medieval inscriptions** included provisions insisting that cultivators remain attached to the land, suggesting that they may have attempted to flee from villages if they faced too many demands on their resources. While not spectacular, such protests were obviously a threat to the financial stability of the state and local landed intermediaries. *See also* REVENUE SYSTEMS.

PROTOHISTORY. Name assigned by historians and archaeologists to the phase of history for which written sources are available but not entirely accessible. Generally, the **Harappan civilization** (c. 2700–1800 BCE) is classified as protohistoric as the **script** has not yet been deciphered. The **Vedic** evidence (c. second to early first millennium BCE) is also often considered protohistoric as the chronology of the texts remains somewhat uncertain, and the texts do not present a direct historical narrative. **Archaeological** cultures that were more or less contemporary with the Harappan civilization and the Vedic texts are also occasionally classified as protohistoric, on the assumption that they were in contact with literate societies.

PṚTHUDAKA. *See* PEHOA.

PTOLEMY. Geographer, **astronomer**, and **mathematician** (c. 90–168 CE), who probably lived in Alexandria, Egypt, and wrote in Greek. His work on geography, the *Geographia*, contains a description of the subcontinent based on contemporary Hellenistic sources.

PTOLEMY PHILADELPHUS. Ruler of Egypt (r. 281–246 BCE) who sent an ambassador, **Dionysius**, to the court of the contemporary **Mauryan king**. *See also* TURAMAYA.

PUDURU. Early historic site in Andhra Pradesh. Finds include **terracotta** ring wells, Mediterranean amphorae, **rouletted ware**, **coins** dated to c. second–third centuries CE, beads of semiprecious stone, and large quantities of **iron** slag, indicating local manufacture. There is also evidence of bead making.

PUHĀR. *See* POOMPUHAR.

PULAKEŚIN II. Cālukya ruler (r. 609–642 CE), best known from a eulogistic **inscription** that described his military successes over rivals within the **kingdom** as well as against external enemies. His most celebrated exploit was his victory over **Harṣavardhana**, in a battle fought on the banks of the **Narmada**. He also fought battles with the traditional rivals of the Cālukyas, the **Pallavas**, and probably met his end while defending his capital from an attack by the Pallava ruler **Narasiṃhavarman I**. *See also* CĀLUKYA (EASTERN).

PUL-I-DARUNTA. Site in the Lamghan valley, Afghanistan. Find spot of an **Asokan inscription** (c. third century BCE) in **Aramaic**.

PULINDA. Name used in **Sanskrit** and other textual traditions (c. mid–first millennium BCE onward) to designate **tribal** groups living in **forests**, who were occasionally expected to provide military support to rulers.

PULUMAYI II. Son and successor (c. second century CE) of the **Sātavāhana** ruler **Gautamīputra Sātakarṇi**. Pulumayi ruled for 24 years. His **coins**, some of which depict ships, have been found in the eastern Deccan, suggesting that he lost control over the western provinces of the **kingdom**. *See also* NAVY.

PUNCH-MARKED COINS. Earliest (c. sixth century BCE onward) **coins** minted in the subcontinent, generally of silver or **copper**, identified with the *kārṣāpaṇa* mentioned in textual sources. These are small and thin coins in a variety of shapes—round, square, rectangular, oblong, and oval. Weights for silver coins are around 3.564 grams, while those for copper coins are around 9.460 grams, multiples of the *rati*, a seed used for weighing precious metal, averaging 0.12 grams. The coins were not inscribed, but were stamped with symbols. Several hundred symbols have been identified. These have often been taken to be identification marks of ruling lineages and/or merchant or banking groups. In **archaeological** contexts, these coins usually occur with **Northern Black Polished Ware** and have been found from several sites throughout the subcontinent. The issue seems to have stopped c. second century BCE (with the end of the **Mauryan** Empire) although the coins remained in circulation for several centuries.

Find spots of punch-marked coins include **Adam**, **Ayodhya**, **Bairat**, **Banavasi**, **Bangarh**, **Bhimbetka**, **Bhokardan**, **Campā**, **Chandraketugarh**, **Chechar**, **Chirand**, **Dangwada**, **Dihar**, **Eran**, **Ganeshwar**, **Ganwaria**, **Hastinapura**, **Jhusi**, **Kasrawad**, **Katra**, **Kaundinyapura**, **Kausambi**, **Kolhua**, **Kumrahar**, **Lauriya Nandangarh**, **Maheshwar**, **Malhar**, **Manamunda**, **Mangalkot**, **Masaon**, **Mathura**, **Nadner**, **Nagara**, **Nagari**, **Nevasa**, **Paithan**, **Pāṭaliputra**, **Piprahwa**, **Sonkh**, **Sonpur**, **Sravasti**, **Sugh**, **Taxila**, **Tripuri**, **Tumain**, **Vaddamanu**, **Vadgaon Madhavpur**, **Vaishali**, and **Vidisha**.

See also BENT BAR COINS; CAST COINS; COINAGE, EARLY HISTORIC PERIOD; TRADE.

PUṆḌRA. Name of a region, part of present-day West Bengal and Bangladesh, mentioned in the ***Aitareya Brāhmaṇa*** and subsequent texts and **inscriptions**. **Mahasthan**, identified from an inscription assignable to the **Mauryan** period as Puṇḍranagara, probably constituted the nucleus of the region, which extended from the **Ganga (2)** in the west to the Karatoya River in the east and the Padma River in the south, with the foothills of the **Himalayas** constituting the northern frontier. Inscriptions belonging to the **Gupta** period described Puṇḍravardhana as a *bhukti* or administrative unit. The frontiers of Puṇḍra expanded to the east, west, and south to incorporate neighboring areas. It remained an important region along **routes** to the northeast and China throughout the first millennium CE.

PURĀṆA. **Sanskrit** texts, generally in simple verse, literally dealing with that which is old. This genre of text is mentioned in the ***Atharvaveda***, the **Dharmasūtras**, and the ***Arthaśāstra***. Traditionally, there were supposed to be 18 Purāṇas, although the list was not standardized. The earliest compositions include the *Brahmāṇḍa*, *Matsya*, *Viṣṇu*, *Bhāgavata* and *Mārkaṇḍeya Purāṇa*. Most of these were probably composed between c. 300 and 1000 CE, although some sections of specific texts may be older.

The Purāṇas were expected to have five components: a description of primary creation, secondary creation, genealogies, and accounts of cosmic cycles and of ruling lineages. These elements are by no means uniformly present in all texts. The Purāṇas laid down modes of worship for deities such as **Viṣṇu**, **Śiva**, and the **goddess**, and the texts were accessible to **women** and ***śūdras***, who could listen to their recitation.

The composition and dissemination of the Purāṇas has often been viewed as an attempt to integrate a variety of regional and local traditions within an overarching **Brahmanical** framework. Many of the Purāṇas were composed in regions other than the **Ganga (2)** valley. The genealogies in the Purāṇas have occasionally been used to reconstruct dynastic history. *See also AVATĀRA*; *BHAKTI*; *CANDRAVAMṢA*; *DEVĪMĀHĀTMYA*; DRAMA; DVARAKA; EARLY MEDIEVAL PERIOD; *HARIVAMṢA*; JAMBUDVĪPA; *KALI YUGA*; *KALPA* (2); KANVA; KṚṢṆA; LITERATURE; MANU; NANDA; PURĀṆIC RELIGION; SĀTAVĀHANA; *SŪTA*;

TEMPLES; VAIṢṆAVISM; VĀKĀṬAKA; *VARṆA*; VASIṢṬHA; *VIṢṆUDHARMOTTARA PURĀṆA*; VIŚVĀMITRA; VYĀSA.

PURANĀNURU*.** Anthology of **Tamil poems**, part of the ***Eṭṭutokai collection within the ***Sangam*** corpus. It consists of 400 poems on the theme of **warfare** (composed c. third century BCE–second century CE?). The **poets** included men and **women**, **kings**, priests, merchants, potters, hunters, and so on. *See also* LITERATURE; YĀDAVA.

PURĀṆIC RELIGION. Purāṇic **religion**, best understood from the **Purāṇas**, compiled mid–first millennium CE onward, is often distinguished from **Vedic** religion. While the Purānas acknowledged the sanctity of the Vedas, the pantheon that was considered significant was distinctive, emphasizing the worship of **Viṣṇu**, **Śiva**, and the **goddess**, each conceptualized in a variety of forms. In terms of ritual praxis, the focus was on image worship in **temples**. Purāṇic religion is often regarded as a continually evolving amalgam of local, regional, and subcontinental traditions. *See also* ELLORA; HARAPPAN CIVILIZATION; HINDUISM; MAMALLAPURAM; PARAŚURĀMA; PATTADAKAL; SOCIAL MOBILITY; TRIBES; UDAYGIRI; VADAGOKUGIRI.

PURI-KUṢĀṆA. Name assigned to a variety of **copper coins**, imitations of those of the **Kuṣāṇas**, found from several sites in Orissa including **Sisupalgarh**, dating to c. second–fourth centuries CE. *See also* JAUGADA.

PUROHITA*.** **Sanskrit** term meaning "one who leads," used for the chief priest associated with the performance of **sacrifices**. The term occurs as early as the ***Ṛgveda (c. second millennium BCE). The *purohita* was often one of the closest advisors of the ***rājā***, especially in the case of rulers who attempted to govern in accordance with **Brahmanical** norms. *See also* MINISTERS; *RATNIN*.

PUROLA. Archaeological site in Uttarakhand. Finds include **Painted Grey Ware** (c. first millennium BCE), skeletal remains of the domesticated horse, and a brick structure that may have served as a **sacrificial** altar. Other finds include **copper coins** of the **Kunindas** (c. first century BCE–second century CE).

PURU. *See* POROS.

PURUṢAPURA. Sanskrit name, used in **early historic** texts, for present-day **Peshawar**.

PURUṢĀRTHA*.** Term used in **Sanskrit** texts (c. mid–first millennium BCE onward) to refer to the four goals that a man was expected to attain. These included ***dharma; *artha*, or material prosperity; *kāma*, or the fulfillment of sensual desires; and *mokṣa*, or liberation.

PURUṢASŪKTA*.** Name of a cosmogonic hymn in the last *maṇḍala* or section of the ***Ṛgveda. The hymn describes the creation of the universe from the sacrifices of *puruṣa* or the primeval man. The world that was created was visualized as including the social order consisting of the four ***varṇas***, with the ***brāhmaṇa* (1)** at the apex of the hierarchy. The text thus provides one of the earliest references to this fourfold classification of society.

PUṢKALĀVATĪ. Sanskrit term meaning "full of lotuses," name of a city in **Gandhara**, identified with either **Charsada** or **Peshawar**. *See also* INDO-GREEK.

PUṢYABHŪTI. Ruling lineage, c. sixth–seventh centuries CE, associated with **Thanesar**. **Harṣavardhana** is the best-known ruler of this dynasty.

PUṢYAGUPTA. A provincial governor of **Candragupta Maurya**, described as a ***vaiśya*** in the **Junagadh Rock Inscription** of **Rudradaman**. According to the inscription, he constructed a lake known as the Sudarśana (literally pleasant to look at) in the region.

PUṢYAMITRA. Name of a lineage that was powerful in central India during the fifth century CE and posed a challenge to the power of the **Gupta** rulers, including **Kumāragupta** and **Skandagupta**.

PUṢYAMITRA ŚUṄGA. General of the last **Mauryan** ruler, **Bṛhadratha**, who killed the latter and assumed power (c. 185–151 BCE). He is credited with the performance of the ***aśvamedha*** **sacri-**

fice. **Buddhism** flourished during his reign, and **Vidisha** emerged as a major political and cultural center.

PYNTHORLANGTEIN. Archaeological site in Meghalaya, with evidence of occupation during the **Neolithic** phase (date uncertain). There is evidence of the local manufacture of stone **tools**, including adzes, axes, chisels, points, blades, scrapers, and so on.

– Q –

QUINTUS CURTIUS. Roman historian (c. first century BCE–first century CE), author of a **biography** of **Alexander (of Macedon)** that has survived in parts.

– R –

RABATAK INSCRIPTION. Inscription in Bactrian, written in the Greek **script**, found in Rabatak, near **Surkh Kotal** in Afghanistan, atttributed to the **Kuṣāṇa** ruler **Kaniṣka**. The inscription records the construction of a shrine and the making of images of several deities and Kuṣāṇa **kings**. It also contains a genealogy of Kaniṣka and mentions several **cities** that were under his control, including **Sāketa**, **Kausambi**, **Pāṭaliputra**, **Campā**, and **Ujjayinī**.

RAIPUR. Archaeological site in Maharashtra, with evidence of **megalithic** cairn **burials** (c. first millennium BCE?). Other finds include **iron** equipment such as knives, chisels, daggers, and ladles, **copper** ornaments, and **Black and Red Ware**.

RĀJĀ*. Sanskrit** term used for rulers, which occurs as early as the ***Ṛgveda (c. second millennium BCE). Initially, the term evidently had connotations of chiefship rather than **kingship**, with the *rājā* being described as the recipient of tribute rather than regular taxes, and as a patron of **sacrifices**. The earliest **epigraphic** use of the term occurs in **Asokan inscriptions** (c. third century BCE). Later rulers often adopted more grandiose titles such as ***mahārāja*** (literally, great king). *See also GRĀMAṆĪ*; KINGSHIP, THEORIES OF ORIGIN; *PUROHITA*; *RĀJANYA*; *RATNIN*; *SABHĀ*; *SAMITI*.

RĀJAGAHA. Archaeological site in Bihar, the first capital of the ***mahājanapada*** of **Magadha** (c. sixth century BCE). It was located amid hills, and was thus naturally protected. It is recognized in **Buddhist** tradition as the venue of the first **Buddhist Council**. Archaeological remains include traces of stone and earth **fortifications** and finds of **black and red ware** and **Northern Black Polished Ware**. *See also* JĪVAKA KOMARABHACCA; KHĀRAVELA; UDAYIN.

RĀJAGṚHA. *See* RĀJAGAHA.

RĀJANYA*. Sanskrit** term used in the early and **later Vedic** texts (c. second–first millennium BCE) for men belonging to the second ***varṇa. The term is suggestive of close connections with the ***rājā*** or **king**. It was more or less synonymous with, and later generally replaced by, the term ***kṣatriya***.

RĀJARĀJA I. Often regarded as the most powerful ruler (r. 985–1014 CE) of the **Co<u>l</u>a** dynasty and credited with a wide range of military exploits, including leading an expedition to Sri Lanka. His other victories, recorded in **inscriptions**, were over the traditional rivals of the Co<u>l</u>as, the **Cālukyas** and **Pāṇḍyas**. He also led expeditions against the rulers of **Kaliṅga**. He embellished his capital, **Thanjavur**, with the Bṛhadīśvara **temple** (also known as the Rājarājeśvara temple, named after him), built in honor of his chosen deity, **Śiva**. *See also* GAṄGA (1); RĀJENDRA; *TEVĀRAM*.

RĀJAŚEKHARA. Court **poet** (c. 9th–10th centuries CE) of the **Pratihāra** rulers **Mahendrapāla** and **Mahipāla (1)**. His major works include the *Kāvyamīmāṃsā*, a work on poetics in **Sanskrit**, and the *Karpūramañjari*, a **Prakrit** play about the romance between a **king** and a princess. *See also* LITERATURE.

RĀJASŪYA*. Sacrifice**, described in the **later Vedic** texts (c. 1000–600 BCE), prescribed for a ***kṣatriya who wished to be proclaimed as **king**. The ritual could last for a year and included several events such as rites to ensure the prosperity of the realm, rituals performed in the homes of the supporters of the sacrificer, contests in which he was expected to be victorious, sprinkling the sacrificer with sanctified waters, and proclamations of his change of status by the priest. The performance of the ritual is described in the ***Mahābhārata*** and is also documented in **inscriptions**. *See also* KINGSHIP, THEORIES OF ORIGIN; *RATNIN*.

***RĀJATARAṄGIṆĪ*.** Literally the river of kings, **Sanskrit** text composed by **Kalhaṇa** in the 12th century, containing an account of rulers of Kashmir from the beginning of creation to the author's times. His account included cosmogonic myths and purported to narrate a continuous history of **kings** from the remote past to his own times. The narrative gains in accuracy and realism from the seventh century CE onward, while the earlier period is described through a mixture of myth, folk traditions, and historical data. *See also* JAYAPĪḌA; LITERATURE; MIHIRAKULA.

RĀJENDRA. One of the best-known rulers (r.c. 1014–1044 CE) of the **Coḻa** dynasty, son and successor of **Rājarāja I**, credited with several military exploits, described in contemporary **inscriptions**. He waged wars against the **Cālukyas** and **Pāṇḍyas**, traditional rivals of the Coḻas. He also led expeditions against the rulers of **Kaliṅga**, and went as far north as the **Ganga (2)** valley, attacking the **kingdom** of the **Pālas**. He celebrated this expedition by founding a new **city**, Gangaikkondacholapuram, with a central **temple** dedicated to **Śiva**. He also carried on campaigns and led naval expeditions against contemporary rulers of Sri Lanka and several states in Southeast Asia. It is likely that he had diplomatic relations with the Chinese emperor. From 1018, his son and successor, Rājātirāja, acted as his coregent.

RAJGHAT. Site near **Varanasi** (Uttar Pradesh) with evidence for occupation c. eighth century BCE onward.

RAJGIR. *See* RĀJAGAHA.

RAJMAHAL. Archaeological site in Bihar, with three major occupational phases. Period I (mid–first millennium BCE?) is associated with **Northern Black Polished Ware**. Other finds consisted of **iron**

chisels, nails, and slag; **copper** rods and wires; bone arrowheads; stone pestles; beads of semiprecious stone; and figurines. Finds from Period II (c. second century BCE–second century CE) included **terracotta** figurines. Period III has been assigned to medieval times.

RAJPUR PARASU. Archaeological site (c. second millennium BCE?) in Uttar Pradesh, find spot of **copper hoards** and **Ochre-Coloured Pottery**. The copper artifacts included axes, bars, and harpoons.

RĀJUKA*.** Term used in **Asokan inscriptions** to designate a category of officials, occasionally considered the equivalent of the ***agronomoi mentioned by **Megasthenes**. Asokan inscriptions indicate that they played a crucial role in provincial administration and were expected to undertake periodic tours of inspection and ensure the implementation of **judicial** norms. *See also* MAJOR PILLAR EDICTS.

RAJULA MANDAGIRI. Archaeological site in Andhra Pradesh. Find spot of a **Minor Rock Edict** of **Asoka** (c. third century BCE).

RĀJYAŚRĪ. Sister of **Harṣavardhana** and wife of the **Maukhari** ruler **Grahavarman** (c. late sixth–early seventh centuries CE). According to the ***Harṣacarita***, Rājyaśrī attempted to commit ***satī*** after the death of her husband but was saved by her brother, who took over Grahavarman's **kingdom** and integrated it within his own realm. *See also* WOMEN.

RĀJYAVARDHANA. Elder brother of **Harṣavardhana**, who died fighting against **Śaśāṅka** and the contemporary **later Gupta** ruler in defense of **Grahavarman** (c. early seventh century CE).

RAKHI GARHI. Site in Haryana (c. third millennium BCE onward?) with **pre-/early**, **Mature**, and **late Harappan** occupational levels. The site has yielded evidence of **pottery**, **terracotta** figurines, bronze artifacts, **seals**, weights, and beads of semiprecious stone. Other finds include traces of **fortification**, fire altars, and a cemetery.

RĀMA. Chief protagonist of the ***Rāmāyaṇa***, represented as an ideal **king** and identified as an ***avatāra*** of **Viṣṇu**.

RĀMAGUPTA. Gupta ruler (c. fourth century CE), known from the **coins** he issued. According to tradition he signed a "dishonorable" agreement with his enemies, the **Śakas**, and was possibly deposed and killed by his brother and successor, **Candragupta II**. *See also* ERAN.

RAMAPURAM. Archaeological site in Andhra Pradesh, with evidence of a **Chalcolithic** settlement (c. second millennium BCE?). Finds included saddle-querns, beads of semiprecious stone, **terracotta** figurines, and traces of **burials** within residential structures.

RĀMĀVATĀRAM*. Tamil** version of the ***Rāmāyaṇa, composed by **Kampan** (c. ninth century CE), containing about 10,000 verses. This version is characterized by an explicit deification of the hero. *See also* LITERATURE.

***RĀMĀYAṆA*. Sanskrit epic**, which received its final form around the middle of the first millennium CE. Its composition is attributed to the sage **Vālmīki**. The text, consisting of about 24,000 verses in seven sections, narrates the story of **Rāma**, a prince of **Ayodhya**, and his wife, Sītā. Major episodes include his exile from the **kingdom**, his adventures in the **forest** leading to the abduction of his wife by the demon king Rāvaṇa, his victory over the latter, and his triumphant return to his capital. The story was represented in **sculpture** as well. It is evident that the kernel of the story may have been known several centuries ago. Other versions are found within the **Buddhist** and **Jaina** traditions. *See also AVATĀRA*; BHĀSA; BHAṬṬI; BHAVABHŪTI; DEOGARH; DINNĀGA (2); IKṢVĀKU (1); JANAKA; KĀLIDĀSA; KOSALA; LITERATURE; PARAŚURĀMA; *PAUMACARIYA*; *RĀMĀVATĀRAM*; *SETUBANDHA*; *UTTARARĀMACARITA*; VIMALASŪRI.

RAMPURWA. Archaeological site in Bihar, find spot of an **Asokan** (c. third century BCE) pillar inscribed with a set of the **Major Pillar Edicts**. This was surmounted by a bull capital, which is regarded as one of the finest specimens of **Mauryan sculpture**. *See also* MAURYAN ART.

RANGPUR. Archaeological site in Gujarat with evidence of a **Mesolithic** occupation. There is also evidence of a **Harappan** (c. third millennium BCE) settlement with civic **architecture** such as streets and drains. Other finds consisted of beads, weights, and **pottery** of both Harappan and local varieties. There is evidence for **late/post-Harappan** (c. second–early first millennium BCE) levels as well. These are distinguished by finds of **Lustrous Red Ware**.

RĀṢṬRAKŪṬA. Ruling lineage in the western Deccan (c. 8th–10th centuries CE), with their capital at **Mānyakheṭa**. The history of the Rāṣṭrakūṭas has been reconstructed on the basis of **inscriptions**, **coins**, and texts in **Sanskrit**, **Prakrit**, Arabic, and Kannada. **Amoghavarṣa** was among the more powerful rulers of the lineage. At the height of their power, the Rāṣṭrakūṭas controlled parts of southern, western, and central India, competing with the **Pratihāras** and the **Pālas** for control over **Kanauj**. The Rāṣṭrakūṭas exercised control over ports along the western coast. Revenues for the state were derived from taxes on **agriculture**, **trade**, and **craft** production. Rāṣṭrakūṭa rulers encouraged the use of both Sanskrit and Kannada, and supported the worship of **Brahmanical** deities, besides offering patronage to **Jaina** institutions. Some of the most famous **temples**, including the Kailasanatha temple at **Ellora**, were constructed during this period. *See also* BHOJA (2); CĀLUKYA; CĀLUKYA, EASTERN; DANTIDURGA; DHARMAPĀLA; GANGA (1); KALACURI; KANDHAR.

RAṬHIKA. Ruling lineages in Maharashtra (c. third century BCE–second century CE), mentioned in **Asokan inscriptions** as people who were incorporated within the **Mauryan** Empire. They entered into matrimonial and political alliances with the **Sātavāhanas**. *See also* KHĀRAVELA.

RATNĀKARA. Sanskrit author (c. ninth century CE) of a text known as the *Haravijaya*, recounting the exploits of the god **Śiva**. He was associated with the court of Jayāditya and **Avantivarman**, **kings** of Kashmir. *See also* LITERATURE.

RATNIN*.** **Sanskrit** term meaning "one who bears jewels," used in **later Vedic literature** (c. first half of the first millennium BCE) to refer to a category of supporters of the ***rājā, including the ***purohita***, charioteer, general, as well as wives of the ruler. The number of *ratnins* mentioned in texts varied from 10 to 12. The *ratnins* had ritual, social, and political roles that were highlighted during the performance of **sacrifices** such as the ***rājasūya***.

RATURA. **Archaeological** site in Uttarakhand. Period I (c. second century BCE–second century CE) is associated with finds of **pottery**, **iron** equipment including arrowheads and nails, carnelian beads, glass bangles, and "**tribal**" **copper coins**. There was a hiatus between Period I and II. The latter (c. 8th–12th centuries CE) witnessed the construction of stone walls at the site.

RAVIKĪRTI. Court **poet** (c. seventh century CE) of the **Cālukyan** ruler **Pulakeśin II**, and author of the **Aihole Inscription**.

RED POLISHED WARE. **Pottery** made of well-levigated clay, covered with a red slip, generally found in **archaeological** sites in Gujarat, c. first century BCE–fifth century CE. Typical shapes include jars and bowls. Find spots of the ware include **Amreli**, **Banavasi**, **Brahmapuri**, **Devanimori**, **Eran**, **Jhusi**, **Kaundinyapura**, **Kodumanal**, **Kondapur**, **Maheshwar**, **Nagara**, **Nagari**, **Nasik**, **Nevasa**, **Sanchi**, **Sannati**, **Sodanga**, **Sugh**, **Tāmralipti**, **Ter**, **Timbarra**, **Tripuri**, **Tumain**, **Vadgaon Madhavpur**, and **Vadodara**.

REHMAN DHERI. **Archaeological** site in the North-West Frontier Province, Pakistan, with evidence of a **pre-/early Harappan** occupation, dated between c. 3400 BCE and 2100 BCE. There is evidence for the cultivation of wheat and barley and for the domestication of cattle, sheep, and goat. **Architectural** structures include mud-brick **fortification**. The **pottery** has parallels with **Kot Diji**. Unique features include the use of graffiti on pots.

RELIGION. There is evidence for a wide range of religious beliefs and practices in early India. While attempts have been made to interpret **archaeological** artifacts, including stones smeared with red ocher, figurines, and rock **paintings** found in **Paleolithic**, **Mesolithic**, **Neolithic**, and **Chalcolithic** contexts as expressions of religious ideas, such interpretations remain somewhat speculative in the absence of textual corroboration. Reconstructions of **Harappan** religious beliefs are also tentative.

The early **Vedic** tradition (c. second millennium BCE) indicates the prevalence of a **sacrificial** cult in the northwest of the subcontinent, centering on worship of deities such as **Agni**, **Indra**, and **Soma**. **Goddesses** were relatively insignificant within this tradition. By the early first millennium BCE, **later Vedic** texts indicate that the sacrificial cult had become more elaborate and had spread to the mid–**Ganga (2)** valley, culminating in elaborate rituals meant to legitimize the acquisition of power by **kings** in the ***janapadas***.

The mid–first millennium BCE witnessed critiques of the sacrificial cult, evident in a variety of **philosophical** traditions, including **Buddhism** and **Jainism**. By the end of the first millennium, there is evidence for the growth of theistic tendencies within these traditions as well as those that culminated in **Purāṇic** beliefs and practices. This period also witnessed the development of ***Bhakti*** or devotionalism as a mode of worship, a tendency that was strengthened from the second half of the first millennium CE. While the **Brahmanical** tradition laid emphasis on the role of a specialized priesthood, others such as Buddhism and Jainism accorded the highest respect to those who renounced worldly life.

Norms governing Brahmanical religious praxis including rites of passage were codified in **Sanskrit** texts. Religious ideas, beliefs, and experiences were also expressed in Sanskrit, **Prakrit**, **Pali**, and **Tamil** compositions. Some of these were reflected in **architecture** as well, especially as manifested in the construction of ***stūpas*** and **temples**. While **terracotta** figurines and **sculpture** recovered from several sites have often been interpreted as having ritual functions, the use of images for worship is conclusively documented from the end of the first millennium BCE.

It is also evident that while some popular religious beliefs and practices were occasionally represented in textual and visual media, most were not systematically recorded. It is likely that some of these traditions went into the making of **Tantric** beliefs and practices, which became increasingly influential from the second half of the first millennium CE onward. *See also ĀGAMA*; ĀJĪVIKA; *ĀḺVĀR*; ART; ASCETICISM; BUDDHISM; *CAITYA*; COINAGE; *DĀNA*; DANCE; HINDUISM; INSCRIPTIONS; JAINISM; LAND GRANTS; LITERATURE; MATURE HARAPPAN; MONASTERIES; RENUNCIATORY ORDERS; VAIṢṆAVISM; ZOROASTRIANISM.

RENUNCIATORY ORDERS. These constituted an important component of the social universe in early India. The best known of such orders were those of the **Buddhists** and **Jainas**, which were founded during the **early historic period** (c. sixth century BCE onward), and the **Brahmanical** ascetic orders, which emerged during the **early medieval period** (c. fourth century CE onward). Members of these orders generally observed celibacy and lived in isolation or in communities of their own. They also adopted distinctive norms regarding food and clothing. Special rites of initiation, often accompanied by a period of apprenticeship, marked the entry of new recruits into the order. While there was an inherent element of misogyny in most renunciatory traditions, **women** were permitted entry, with restrictions, within both the Buddhist and the Jaina orders.

Occasionally, **kings** intervened to regulate the affairs of these orders. **Asoka**, for instance, issued proclamations for the Buddhist ***saṃgha***. By the early medieval period, there are indications that the state recognized the rights of these institutions to conduct their own affairs. Although there were restrictions on acquiring property, most orders tended to accumulate resources as a result of the donations made by lay patrons. The latter included kings, merchants, householders, and **guilds** of **craftsmen** among others. Attitudes toward renouncers were often characterized by ambivalence. On the one hand, they were respected and revered. On the other hand, they were viewed as men and women who had abdicated their social responsibilities. The fraudulent ascetic was also a stock figure in literary texts. *See also* ASCETICISM; MONASTERIES; RELIGION; ROCK-CUT CAVES; *SAṂNYĀSA*; SLAVERY; *VINAYA PIṬAKA*.

REVENUE SYSTEMS. The evidence for revenue systems in early India comes from texts and **inscriptions**. The early and **later Vedic** texts (c. second millennium BCE onward) indicate that chiefs initially mobilized resources in the form of gifts and booty. By the mid–first millennium BCE, more or less regular systems of tax collection were apparently in place in several ***janapadas*** in north India. These were described in texts such as the **Dharmasūtras** and **Dharmaśāstras**. The basic tax was described as the *ṣaḍ-bhāga*, literally the sixth portion. Ideally, tax was expected to be one sixth of the **agricultural** produce, although texts such as the ***Arthaśāstra*** suggest that taxes could be raised further if necessary. The text also laid down a variety of taxes on a range of economic activities, including **craft** production, **trade**, and **pastoralism**, specifying that taxes could be collected in cash, kind, or even in the form of labor, and describing the revenue network from the village to the center. **Land grant** inscriptions from the first millennium CE often mention taxes and dues on all kinds of local produce, water resources, plants, and trees and on resources such as minerals from the soil, often varying from region to region. Usually the right to collect these dues was transferred to the donee.

Prescriptive texts justified the collection of revenue by the state using one of two popular arguments. The first suggested that revenue constituted the wages of the **king** for the service he rendered in protecting his subjects. The second line of reasoning was that the king was the owner of the realm: Revenue was thus the equivalent of rent that his subjects paid for the use of the resources of the realm.

Prescriptive texts often warned against excessive revenue demands, which were viewed as being counterproductive. Narrative traditions in **Sanskrit**, **Pali,** and **Prakrit** refer to oppressive kings and tax collectors, and describe the responses of subjects to them. These ranged from open hostility and violence to more passive strategies of abandoning settlements and fleeing to the **forests**. *See also AGRAHĀRA*; *BALI*; *BHĀGA*; PROTEST MOVEMENTS.

***ṚGVEDA*.** Anthology of hymns in **Vedic Sanskrit**, attributed to seers, probably composed and compiled during the second millennium BCE, in the region drained by the **Indus** and its tributaries. It is divided into 10 sections or books. Books 2 to 7, also known as the "Family Books" because their composers were related to select priestly lineages, constitute the core. Only one recension of the text is available at present. The principal deities invoked include **Agni**, or the god of fire; **Indra**, a warrior god; and **Soma**, a deified plant. The text was (and continues to be) transmitted orally. The best-known commentary on the text is that of Sāyana (c. 14th century CE). *See also GOTRA*; LITERATURE; MAX MULLER, FRIEDRICH; PASTORALISM; *SĀMAVEDA*; TAMIL; VASIṢṬHA; *VEDA*; VEDIC

ECONOMY; *VIDATHA*; *VIŚ*; VIṢṆU; VIŚVĀMITRA; WARFARE; WOMEN; *ZEND AVESTA*.

RIWAT. Paleolithic site near Rawalpindi (Pakistan), from where stone **tools** dated to 1.9 million years BP have been recovered.

ROCK ART. The earliest instances of **painting** in rock shelters and caves dates to the **Mesolithic** phase (c. 10,000 BP onward). Several thousand painted surfaces have been found in sites in Madhya Pradesh, such as **Bhimbetka**, and in other parts of central India. The earliest paintings are in shades of red. Most of the colors used were derived from minerals. The paintings include depictions of wild animals, marked by realism and dynamism. Representations of people are far more schematic. They occur in hunting scenes, scenes of **dancing**, as well as in depictions of routine activities. Present-day speculations on the objectives of these paintings range from suggestions that they were part of ritual or magical activities to more mundane ideas that they may represent attempts to depict daily life.

ROCK-CUT CAVES. These form a distinctive element in early Indian **architecture**. Some of the earliest examples dating to the **Mauryan** period (c. fourth–third centuries BCE) replicated wooden models. Most of these caves were dedicated to **renunciatory** groups and provided wanderers with shelter during the rainy season. Some of the most spectacular instances of rock-cut caves are found in sites from the Western Ghats, where they were hollowed out from c. second century BCE onward. Some of these served as shrines (***caityas***), whereas others served as **monasteries**. Early examples of rock-cut caves that functioned as **Brahmanical** shrines have been found from **Udaygiri**, Madhya Pradesh (c. fifth century CE). In some instances, as at **Ellora**, the rock-cut cave evolved into the freestanding **temple**, carved out of a monolith. *See also* AIHOLE; AJANTA; BAGH; BANOTIWADI; BARABAR; BEDSA; BHAJA; EARLY HISTORIC PERIOD; ELEPHANTA; ELLORA; JUNNAR; KANHERI; KARLE; KHANDAGIRI; MAHENDRAVARMAN I; MAURYAN ART; NAGARJUNI HILLS; NANAGHAT; PITALKHORA; *SAṂGHA*; SĀTAVĀHANA; TAMIL BRĀHMĪ INSCRIPTIONS; VETALWADI.

ROHRI. Site on the **Indus River** in Sind (Pakistan), with evidence of stone **tool** manufacture dating to the **Paleolithic** period (c. 500,000 BP). Stone from the site was also used during the **Early** and **Mature Harappan** (c. third–second millennium BCE) phases.

ROJDI. Mature Harappan (c. third–second millennium BCE) settlement in Gujarat, characterized by stone **architecture**, including remains of **fortification**. There is evidence of the cultivation of millets. Domesticated animals included cattle, sheep, and goat. There are indications of rearing chicken as well as of hunting. Other finds consisted of **copper tools**, carnelian, shell and **terracotta** beads, spindle whorls, and **late Harappan pottery**. *See also* PITHAD.

ROMAN COINS. Roman **coins**, especially those belonging to the first century CE, have been found from a number of sites in south India. These include silver *denarii* and gold *aurei*, the latter being particularly plentiful. These finds have been interpreted as bullion transferred to the subcontinent to meet the requirements of **trade**. Within the subcontinent, the coins evidently no longer circulated as currency and were used as jewelry in several instances. Sites that have yielded Roman coins include **Brahmagiri**, **Chandravalli**, **Kondapur**, **Nevasa**, **Paithan**, **Sisupalgarh**, **Thotlakonda**, **Ujjayinī**, and **Vadgaon Madhavpur**.

ROPAR. Harappan site (c. third millennium BCE) in the Punjab, located at a node of communication between the plains and the **Himalayas** on the Sutlej River, a tributary of the **Indus River**. Finds consisted of **seals**, sealings, blades, faience objects, and **terracotta** wheels and carts. **Pottery** includes Harappan as well as non-Harappan types.

ROULETTED WARE. Designation of **pottery**, generally dishes decorated with two or three concentric bands, thought to be produced by a roulette. Finds of this type of pottery date between c. first and second centuries CE. While some of the pottery could be of Mediterranean origin, local manufacture is also likely. Sites from which rouletted ware has been found include **Alagankulan**, **Arikamedu**, **Ayodhya**, **Chandraketugarh**, **Chandravalli**, **Dharanikota**, **Ghantasala**, **Gopalapatnam**, **Kanchipuram**, **Kaveripattinam**, **Kesanapalle**, **Kondapur**,

Korkai, **Kudikadu**, **Mangalkot**, **Maski**, **Muziris**, **Nevasa**, **Puduru**, **Sannati**, **Sisupalgarh**, **Tāmralipti**, and **Wari Bateshwar**.

ROUTES. A number of routes criss-crossed the subcontinent and were evidently in use since ancient times. These included routes along the river valleys, both major and minor, that were used for both land and river traffic. Maritime routes connecting coastal ports and harbors with one another as well as with overseas **trading** centers were also in existence from the time of the **Harappan civilization** if not earlier. Overland routes through passes were in use, connecting the subcontinent with Afghanistan, Iran, Central Asia, and Tibet. Two routes (with branches) are mentioned in texts such as the ***Arthaśāstra***. These are the ***uttarāpatha*** or northern route and the ***dakṣiṇāpatha*** or southern route. Most of these routes were apparently unusable during the rainy season, when, however, sailors took advantage of the monsoon winds to make swift maritime crossings. *See also* ALEXANDER (OF MACEDON); CUNNINGHAM, ALEXANDER; FA XIAN; GANGA (2); HIPPALUS; INDO-GREEK; MAGADHA; MARITIME TRADE; MATHURA; MELUHHA; MOHENJODARO; NARASIṂHAVARMAN II; NAVY; PĀṆḌYA; PEHOA; PESHAWAR; PUṆḌRA; SILK ROUTE; TAXILA; WARFARE; YAJÑAŚRĪ SĀTAKARṆI.

ṚṢABHA. The first ***tīrthaṅkara*** recognized in **Jaina** tradition. *See also MAHĀPURĀṆA*.

RUDRADĀMAN. **Śaka** ruler (c. second century CE), known from the **Junagadh Rock Inscription**. He is represented in the inscription as an accomplished man, distinguished and learned, with a full treasury. It is likely that he was successful in wresting control over parts of western and central India from the **Sātavāhanas**. He adopted the title of *mahākṣatrapa*. *See also* KARDAMAKA; TUṢĀSPA.

RUDRADEVA. Ruler (c. fourth century CE) mentioned in the **Allahabad Pillar Inscription** as one of the **kings** belonging to ***āryāvarta*** who was uprooted by the **Gupta** ruler **Samudragupta**.

RUDRASENA II. **Vākāṭaka** ruler, c. 390 CE, who was married to **Prabhāvatī Gupta**, the daughter of **Candragupta II** of the **Gupta**

dynasty. Rudrasena died after a short reign of five years and his **widow** assumed control as regent.

RUMMINDEI. Archaeological site in Nepal. Find spot of a **Minor Pillar Edict** of **Asoka** (c. third century BCE). The inscription records the ruler's visit to the site, mentioned as **Lummini**. The visit is dated to the 20th year of Asoka's reign. The inscription describes the site as the birthplace of the **Buddha** and mentions the erection of the pillar and the construction of stone structures. It also records certain tax exemptions granted to the village—it was exempted from ***bali***, and the ***bhāga*** was reduced to one eighth.

RUPNATH. Site in Madhya Pradesh, find spot of a **Minor Rock Edict** of **Asoka**.

RUSSET-COATED PAINTED WARE. Pottery, generally painted with linear designs, that gets its name from the use of an ocher slip. It is found in two fabrics, fine and coarse. Typical shapes include bowls and vases. **Archaeological** finds of the pottery date between c. third century BCE and third–fourth century CE. Sites that have yielded this pottery include **Brahmagiri**, **Chandravalli**, **Kallur**, **Maski**, **Nasik**, **Nevasa**, **Sannati**, **Uraiyur**, **Utnur**, and **Vadgaon Madhavpur**.

– S –

ŚABARASVĀMIN. Author (c. second–fourth centuries CE?) of a commentary in **Sanskrit** known as the *Śabara bhāṣya*, on **Jaimini**'s text on ***mīmāṃsā***. The text was significant for its attempts to define sources of knowledge in terms of perception, inference, and testimony. *See also* PRABHĀKARA.

SABHĀ*. Sanskrit** term meaning "**assembly**," used in the ***Ṛgveda (c. second millennium BCE) and subsequently. Initially the *sabhā* was an assembly associated with the ***rājā***, and often had connotations of a royal court. Membership of the *sabhā* was probably somewhat more exclusive than that of the ***samiti***. While members of the *sabhā* acted as advisors of the *rājā*, their effective political powers were probably limited. The *sabhā* was also the setting for literary discussions and cultural performances. Subsequently, the meaning of the term was extended to include assemblies for such activities, in which the urban elite participated, with or without the presence of the **king**. In the **early medieval** context in south India, the term *sabhā* was used to designate a village assembly consisting of ***brāhmaṇas*** **(1)**.

SACRIFICE. While structures identified as fire altars have been found at some **Harappan** sites, the best-known traditions of sacrifice in the subcontinent are described in the **Vedas**. The ***Ṛgveda*** (c. second millennium BCE) contains chants that were meant to be used in the sacrifice, where offerings of ghee, grain, and in some instances animals, were made in specially kindled sacrificial fires to deities, generally by specialist priests. Many of these offerings were meant to ensure the birth of sons, longevity, victory in battle, access to cattle (the major form of wealth), and prosperity. The **later Vedic** texts, including the **Śrautasūtras** (early and mid–first millennium BCE) laid down the rules governing the sacrifice in great detail, classifying sacrifices into routine, daily, fortnightly, and seasonal rituals and more elaborate ceremonies that could last for more than a year, meant to be performed by those who aspired to chiefly or royal status. The social categories that could be present at sacrifices, as well as the roles assigned to them, were carefully regulated. In this context, the sacrifice was often conceptualized as a cosmogonic event, associated typically with the creator god, Prajāpati.

From the mid–first millennium BCE, there appears to have been a reaction against the performance of sacrifices, most explicit in critiques developed within **Buddhism** and **Jainism**. Even within the **Brahmanical** tradition, **philosophers** suggested that the sacrifice was meant to be symbolic rather than actual. While sacrifices continued to be performed, and were sometimes recorded in **inscriptions** and commemorative **coins**, alternative modes of worship evidently became more popular in the first millennium CE. *See also ĀRAṆYAKA*; *AŚVAMEDHA*; *BRĀHMAṆA* (1); *BRĀHMAṆA* (2); *DAKṢIṆĀ*; DRAMA; HINDUISM; JAIMINI; KINGSHIP, THEORIES OF ORIGIN; *KṢATRIYA*; KUMĀRILA BHAṬṬA; MARRIAGE; MAYŪRAŚARMAN; PALLAVA; PRAVARASENA I; *PUROHITA*; *RĀJĀ*; *RĀJASŪYA*; RELIGION;

SAMSKĀRA; *ŚATAPATHA BRĀHMAṆA*; ŚRĪ SĀTAKARṆĪ I; *ŚŪDRA*; ŚULBASŪTRA; VADGAON MADHAVPUR; *VAIŚYA*; *VĀJAPEYA*; *VIDATHA*; VIDEGHA MĀTHAVA; VIṢṆUKUṆḌIN; WOMEN; *YAJURVEDA*.

SADHWARA. **Archaeological** site (c. first millennium BCE?) in Uttar Pradesh, with evidence of **Ochre-Coloured Pottery**, **Painted Grey Ware**, **black and red ware**, and **Northern Black Polished Ware**. Other finds include beads of semiprecious stones.

SĀGALA. **City** mentioned in the ***Milindapañha***, identified with Sialkot, Pakistan. The text describes the city as very well laid out and prosperous, with flourishing markets in cloth, precious stones, and other valuables. *See also* INDO-GREEK; MADRA; MENANDER.

SAHASRAM. **Archaeological** site in Bihar. Find spot of a **Minor Rock Edict** of **Asoka**.

SAHET MAHET. *See* SRAVASTI.

SAIPAI. **Archaeological** site in Uttar Pradesh with evidence of **copper hoards** and **Ochre-Coloured Pottery**. Associated finds consisted of grinding stones, stone blades, cattle bones, and evidence for huts.

ŚAIVISM. Strand of **Hinduism** that became particularly important c. first millennium CE onward, and continues to flourish to date. While its roots are often traced to the worship of the minor **Vedic** deity Rudra, it is evident that it developed well beyond these early traces. Emphasis was laid on the worship of **Śiva**, visualized in both iconic and aniconic modes (including worship of phallic emblems). Regional sects of Śaivism emerged in several parts of the subcontinent. One of the most significant of these developed in Kashmir (c. ninth century CE onward), emphasizing the possibility of the devotee achieving union with the deity, transcending social barriers of **caste**. It also recognized possibilities of liberation even for the nonrenunciate householder.

Several **early medieval** ruling lineages, such as the **Co<u>l</u>as**, emerged as patrons of Śaivism. *See also BHAKTI*; CĀLUKYA (EASTERN); CRAFTS; CUNTARĀR; ELEPHANTA; ELLORA; GAṄGA (1);

GUDIMALLAM; HARṢAVARDHANA; HINDUISM; HUVIṢKA; ILANKO AṬIKAḶ; JAINISM; KANDHAR; KUṢĀṆA; MAHENDRAVARMAN I; MĀNIKKAVĀCAKAR; PĀŚUPATA; RELIGION; THANJAVUR; TIRUJÑĀNA CAMPANTAR; TIRUMANKAI ĀḺVĀR; TIRUNĀVUKKARACAR; VĪMA KADPHISES.

ŚAKA. People of Central Asian origin, occasionally referred to as Scythians, who occupied the northwestern parts of the subcontinent c. first century BCE, and then extended control over parts of northern, central, and western India. One of their major centers of power was at **Mathura**. In western India, they came into conflict with the **Sātavāhanas**. Śaka power survived until the fifth century CE, when the last of the Śaka rulers was overthrown by **Candragupta II** of the **Gupta** dynasty. *See also* ABHĪRA; AZES II; BACTRIAN GREEK; GAUTAMĪPUTRA SĀTAKARṆI; INDO-GREEK; JOGALTHEMBI; KARDAMAKA; KṢAHARĀTA; *KṢATRAPA*; KUṢĀṆA; *MAHĀKṢATRAPA*; MARITIME TRADE; MAUES; NAHAPĀṆA; NASIK; PARTHIAN; RĀMAGUPTA; RUDRADĀMAN; SAMUDRAGUPTA; SILK ROUTE; UṢAVADĀTA.

ŚAKA ERA. Era commencing from 78 CE and in use to date. While the era was often associated with **Kaniṣka**, recent research indicates that any connection between this ruler and the era is unlikely. As of now, the exact ruler or event from which this era dates remains uncertain.

SĀKALA. *See* SĀGALA.

SĀKETA. **City** mentioned in **early historic** textual traditions in **Sanskrit**, **Pali**, and **Prakrit**, occasionally identified with **Ayodhya**.

SĀKYA. Clan or **tribe** living in present-day north Bihar, c. sixth century BCE. The **Buddha** was born into this clan. Their chief city was **Kapilavastu**. By the fifth century BCE, the tribe was assimilated within the **kingdom** of **Kosala**. *See also* PASENADI; VIḌŪḌABHA.

SĀLAṄKĀYANA. Name of a ruling lineage that succeeded the **Ikṣvākus (2)** in Andhra Pradesh, c. fourth–fifth centuries CE, known from **inscriptions** and **coins**. Members of the lineage may have been vassals of the **Pallavas**.

SAMĀHARTṚ**.** **Sanskrit** term used in the ***Arthaśāstra*** to designate an official in charge of the royal exchequer.

SĀMANTA**.** **Sanskrit** term used in the ***Arthaśāstra*** and in later texts and **inscriptions**. While the initial meaning of the term was a neighboring chief or ruler who exercised control over or near the frontiers of the realm, it was later used to designate a category of feudatories who offered military support and homage to rulers, receiving gifts that were often a marker of status as well as entering into marital alliances with their acknowledged superior. In spite of their apparently subordinate status, *sāmantas* were often virtually autonomous for all practical purposes. Mention of this category is especially frequent in the **early medieval period**.

SAMARAICCHAKAHĀ**.** **Prakrit** narrative, containing a mixture of prose and verse, attributed to **Haribhadra Sūrī** (c. eighth century CE). The work traces the lives of its protagonists through nine births, and enunciates **Jaina** ethics. The style is lucid, and the representations vivid. *See also* LITERATURE.

SAMATAṬA. Name of the southeastern part of present-day Bangladesh. Its ruler (unnamed) was designated as a neighboring **king** in the **Allahabad Pillar Inscription** of the **Gupta** ruler **Samudragupta** (c. fourth century CE) and was described as one among those who offered to pay tribute and homage, apart from obeying his commands.

SĀMAVEDA**.** A collection of hymns, mainly collated from the ***Ṛgveda***, especially from Books 8 and 9, probably compiled c. first half of the first millennium BCE. It was compiled for the use of priests who were expected to chant the hymns according to prescribed melodies. Three recensions of the text survive at present. *See also* MUSIC; *VEDA*.

SAMAYASĀRA**.** **Prakrit** work attributed to **Kundakunda** (c. second century CE), also known as the *Samayapahuda*, a **Jaina philosophical** treatise dealing with the nature of the self.

SĀMAYIKĀ. *See ĀYĀRA.*

SAMṂGHA. **Buddhist monastic** order, which originated during the lifetime of the **Buddha** (c. fifth century BCE). Entry into the order was open to all irrespective of **caste** and social standing. However, **slaves**, debtors, and royal servants had to obtain permission from their masters, creditors, and the **king**, respectively, before joining the order.

The order of nuns was evidently established after that of the monks, and was governed by eight special rules (in addition to the ***Vinaya Piṭaka***), which ensured the subordination of nuns to monks. **Women** had to take the permission of their parents or husband before renouncing the world.

Both monks and nuns were expected to observe celibacy and depend on alms obtained during the daily begging round for subsistence. The rest of the day was to be spent in meditation and listening to discourses. The basic equipment of the renouncer was simple, consisting of a set of robes, an alms bowl, and other necessities.

There was no centralized authority within the *saṃgha*, and the only hierarchy recognized was in terms of seniority. Those living together were expected to meet fortnightly to listen to the *Vinaya Piṭaka* and to confess any violations they committed.

Initially, those who joined the *saṃgha* were expected to wander from place to place throughout the year, choosing a residence only during the rainy season, when travel was difficult. By the second century BCE, these temporary shelters developed into permanent structures—**rock-cut caves** as well as brick and stone buildings, the latter generally consisting of cells built around a central courtyard.

The orders were sustained for centuries by donations made by the laity, both men and women. However, the donations made to the order of the nuns were relatively less substantial, and this may account for the disappearance of the order by the end of the first millennium CE. The order of the monks was more prosperous and lasted longer. The *saṃgha* preserved Buddhist textual traditions, and monasteries were often centers of learning, where a wide range of disciplines were taught. *See also AŚOKĀVADĀNA*; BUDDHIST COUNCILS; JĪVAKA KOMARABHACCA; RENUNCIATORY ORDERS; SANCHI.

SAMṆGHADASAGANI (1). Author (c. fifth century CE) of the first part of the *Vasudevahindī*, a **Prakrit** anthology of tales, probably drawn from folk narratives, combining elements of entertainment and education. *See also* LITERATURE.

SAMṆGHADASAGANI (2). Prakrit author (c. eighth century CE), also known as Kṣamaśramaṇa, a contemporary of **Haribhadra Sūrī**. The works attributed to him include the *Bṛhatkalpa bhāṣya* and the *Pañcakalpabhāṣya*, consisting of several thousand verses dealing with the daily discipline of **Jaina** monks and nuns. *See also* LITERATURE.

SAMITI*. Sanskrit** term meaning "**assembly**," used in the ***Ṛgveda (c. second millennium BCE). The *samiti* was evidently a popular assembly, with wider representation than in the ***sabhā***; both assemblies were associated with the ***rājā***. While the word continued to be used subsequently, the assembly appears to have lost its political significance with the consolidation of political power in the hands of **kings**.

***SĀMṆKHYA*.** One of the six schools of **philosophy** recognized in the **Sanskritic** tradition, which emerged between c. fourth century BCE and first century CE. **Kapila** was recognized as the major proponent of this school of thought. The name *sāṃkhya* is derived from the notion of counting, and one of the distinctive features of the tradition was the attempt to conceptualize reality through a process of enumeration. The school was characterized by an emphasis on dualism—visualized in terms of *prakṛti*, conceived of as an active feminine principle, and *puruṣa*, the male principle. The school exerted considerable influence on other systems of thought. *See also* ĪŚVARAKṚṢṆA; TANTRA; VĀCASPATI MIŚRA.

SAMṆYĀSA*. Sanskrit** term used to designate a state of renunciation, which gained currency from the mid–first millennium BCE. **Dharmasūtras** and especially **Dharmaśāstras** laid down rituals to mark entry into what was often regarded as the last stage in the life of a man belonging to the first three ***varṇas. These rituals included the performance of a mock funeral, after which the renouncer abandoned both his household and the ritual fire. *See also* RENUNCIATORY ORDERS.

SAMṢKĀRA. Term used to designate rites of passage, which were codified in the **Gṛhyasūtras** (c. sixth century BCE onward). These included a cluster of rituals associated with conception and birth, meant to ensure the birth of a boy, initiation into **Vedic** learning, and **marriage**. Ideally, these rituals required the presence of a ***brāhmaṇa*** **(1)**, the use of *mantras* or Vedic chants, and the kindling of the **sacrificial** fire. The earliest texts indicate that ***śūdras*** were denied access to these rituals. Besides, when rituals apart from marriage were performed for **women**, these were done without the use of *mantras*. The extent to which these Brahmanical norms were adopted by other sections of society is uncertain.

SAMUDRAGUPTA. One of the best-known rulers of the **Gupta** dynasty (r.c. 335–376 CE), whose exploits were documented in the **Allahabad Pillar Inscription** composed by his court poet **Hariṣeṇa (1)**. This suggests that he was chosen as successor by his father, **Candragupta I**. He was also known as *Licchavidauhitra*, that is, the grandson of the **Licchavis**, indicating the importance of the matrimonial alliance between the Guptas and the Licchavis. Samudragupta embarked on a series of conquests. He followed a policy of uprooting rulers (and presumably annexing their kingdoms) in the region designated as ***āryāvarta***. Elsewhere, in the south (***dakṣiṇāpatha***), he adopted a policy of capturing and subsequently releasing rulers who submitted to him. The inscription suggests that a number of kings and peoples who lived along the frontiers of his domains submitted to him, offering to pay tribute, obey his commands, and render homage. Besides, the **Kuṣāṇas**, **Śakas**, and the ruler of Simhala or Sri Lanka apparently offered respect, gave their daughters in **marriage** to the king, and requested from him permission to use his **seal** in their kingdoms. He performed the ***aśvamedha*** **sacrifice** to commemorate his victories, issuing a set of commemorative **coins** to mark the occasion. The inscription and coins indicate that he was also a **poet** and a **musician**. *See also* ABHĪRA; ĀṬAVIKA RĀJĀ; ACYUTA; ARJUNĀYANA; BAYANA; CANDRAVARMAN; DAMANA; DAVĀKA; DHANAÑJAYA; *DIGVIJAYA*; GAṆAPATI (NĀGA); HASTIVARMAN; KĀKA;

KĀMARŪPA; KARTTRIPURA; KHARAPĀRIKA; KOṬA KULA JANA; KUBERA; LICCHAVI; MADRA; MAHENDRA; MĀLAVA; MAṆṬARĀJA; MATILA; MEGHAVARṆA; MEHRAULI PILLAR INSCRIPTION; NĀGA; NĀGADATTA; NĀGASENA (2); NANDI; NEPĀLA; NĪLARĀJA; PIṢṬAPURA; PRĀRJUNA; RUDRADEVA; SAMATAṬA; SANAKĀNIKA; SVĀMIDATTA; TRIBES; UGRASENA; VIṢṆUGOPA; VYĀGHRARĀJĀ; YAUDHEYA.

SAMYUTTA NIKĀYA**.** **Pali** text, part of the ***Sutta Piṭaka***, compiled c. fourth century BCE. It derives its name from the fact that it records more than 50 discussions generated when the **Buddha** met people who were identified as important within the tradition. *See also* LITERATURE.

SANAKĀNIKA. Community living (c. fourth century CE) in central India, mentioned in the **Allahabad Pillar Inscription** of the **Gupta** ruler **Samudragupta** as among those who offered tribute and homage and agreed to obey his commands.

SANCHI. Site in Madhya Pradesh, near **Vidisha**, containing some of the best-preserved ***stūpas*** in the subcontinent. An **Asokan** pillar inscribed with a **Minor Pillar Edict** warning against schism in the **Buddhist** *saṃgha* and associated **archaeological** finds indicate that the construction of the largest *stūpa* was probably undertaken during the **Mauryan** period (c. third century BCE). It was enlarged in the second century BCE, and ornamental gateways were added in the first century BCE. **Inscribed** caskets indicate that the *stūpas* contained relics of the **Buddha** and his disciples. A number of **monasteries** form part of the complex. Several hundred votive inscriptions have been recovered from the site. The site is best known for its elaborate **sculpture**, including visual representations of the ***Jātakas***, on the railings and gateways associated with the *stūpas*. New monuments, including a **temple**, were constructed at the site during the **Gupta** period (c. fifth century CE), and existing structures were embellished with new sculptural forms, including representations of the Buddha. Other finds include **coins** of the **Kṣatrapas**, **terracotta** figurines, and **Red Polished Ware**. Sanchi has been recognized as a World Heritage Site by UNESCO. *See also* CAST COINS.

SANDROCOTTOS. Ruler mentioned in Greek sources, and identified with the **Mauryan** ruler **Candragupta** by **William Jones**.

***SANGAM*.** Name given to an **assembly** of **Tamil poets** who met in **Madurai** (c. third century BCE–second century CE?). By extension, the works that were compiled as a result are often known as *Sangam* **literature**. Eight anthologies are recognized, comprising more than 2,000 poems attributed to more than 400 **poets**, including a handful of **women**. *See also AINKURUNŪRU*; *AKAM*; AUVAIYAR; CERA; COḺA; *EṬṬUTOKAI*; FOREST; HERO STONE; *KALITTOKAI*; KAPILAR; KODUMANAL; *KURUNTOKAI*; *MULLAIPPĀṬṬU*; PĀṆḌYA; PARANAR; *PATIṞṞUPATTU*; *PAṬṬINAPPĀLAI*; *PATTUPĀṬṬU*; *PURANĀNURU*; *SIRIPANAṞṞUPPATAI*; SWAMINATHA IYER, U. V.; WARFARE.

SANGANAKALLU. Archaeological site in Karnataka with evidence of a **Neolithic** culture (c. third millennium BCE) and **megalithic** burials (c. first millennium BCE).

SANGHAO. Middle and Upper **Paleolithic** cave site near Peshawar, North-West Frontier Province, Pakistan. Finds include scrapers, blades, points, and burins.

SANGHOL. Archaeological site in the Punjab, with four occupational phases. Period I (c. third millennium BCE) had parallels with the **pre-/early Harappan** culture of **Bara** with evidence of **terracotta** and faience beads and bangles, beads of semiprecious stone, and terracotta figurines. The next phase contained evidence of an overlap with the **late Harappan**. This was followed by Period II (c. early first millennium BCE?) associated with finds of **Painted Grey Ware**, **black slipped ware**, beads, and glass bangles. There is also evidence of an **early historic** occupation (Periods III and IV), with a pre-**Kuṣāṇa** (c. second–first century BCE) and a Kuṣāṇa phase. Finds from the former level consisted of beads of semiprecious stones and bone points, **copper coins** of **Gondophernes**, and **seals** and sealings with **Brāhmī** and **Kharoṣṭhī** legends. Other finds included evidence of a mint and coin molds of the **Kunindas**, as well as fire altars. Burnt-brick structures were in evidence in the latter phase. An elaborate structure, identified as a palace, has been found. The site also yielded copper and gold coins of **Vīma Kadphises** and **Vāsudeva**, **iron** artifacts, terracotta figurines, shell bangles that may have been locally manufactured, bone and ivory artifacts, and seals and sealings, dating to the fourth–fifth centuries CE. There was evidence of a **monastic** complex and a hoard of coins dating to c. sixth century CE. Plant remains included barley, wheat, rice, millet, lentil, pea, pulses, linseed, sesame, mustard, cotton, horse gram, hyacinth bean, fenugreek, coriander, cumin, black pepper, grape, almond, walnut, date, soap nut, poppy, acacia, jasmine, fig, *amla*, custard apple, and *ber* or the Indian jujube. An intriguing find from the site was the remains of a ***stūpa*** railing consisting of more than 100 sculpted sandstone pillars that was systematically dismantled and buried. Stylistically, the **sculpture**, which included representations of **women** and vegetation, suggests affinities with **Kuṣāṇa** traditions (c. first–second centuries CE) of **Mathura**. Other finds include a relic casket with a Kharoṣṭhī **inscription**.

SANKALIA, HASMUKH DHIRAJLAL (1908–1989). Architect of modern Indian **archaeology**, best known for his pioneering work on Indian **prehistory**. He was associated with the Deccan College, Pune, training several generations of archaeologists. He conducted major explorations and excavations at **Neolithic** and **Chalcolithic** sites in Gujarat, Rajasthan, Maharashtra, and Madhya Pradesh. His interests extended to historical geography, **art**, **architecture**, and iconography and the correlation of textual and archaeological evidence.

ŚAṄKARĀCĀRYA. One of the best-known proponents of monist **philosophy**, ***advaita***, author in **Sanskrit** (c. eighth century CE) of commentaries on the major **Upaniṣads**, the ***Bhagavad Gītā***, and the ***Brahmasūtra***. Several devotional hymns and verses in praise of **Śiva** and the **goddess** are also attributed to him. Hagiographies suggest that he was born in Kerala and traveled throughout the subcontinent, engaging in philosophical disputations in which he was victorious. He is also associated with the setting up of four **Brahmanical monastic** establishments (*maṭhas*) at Sringeri (Karnataka), Dwaraka (Gujarat), Puri (Orissa), and Badrinath (Uttarakhand). *See also* GAUḌAPĀDA; LITERATURE.

SANKISSA. Early historic city mentioned in **Buddhist** texts, recognized as the site of a miracle performed by the **Buddha** that was often represented in **sculpture**. The city has been identified with a site of the same name near **Sravasti**, which has yielded remains of **monasteries** and ***stūpas***.

SANNATI. Archaeological site in Karnataka where a set of the **Separate Rock Edicts** of **Asoka** (c. third century BCE) has been found. The earliest occupational phase was **Mesolithic**, characterized by finds of nongeometric microliths. The second period was marked by the use of **black slipped ware** and **Black and Red Ware** (c. first millennium BCE). The subsequent occupation is divided into two phases. The first phase was marked by finds of Black and Red Ware and beads of **terracotta** and semiprecious stones. The second phase yielded black slipped ware, **Red Polished Ware**, **Russet-Coated Painted Ware**, and **rouletted ware**. Other finds included beads of semiprecious stones, lead or potin **coins** typical of the **Sātavāhanas**, beads, bangles, **copper** artifacts, and the remains of a ***stūpa***. There is also evidence of a **temple** belonging to the **Kadambas**.

SANNIDHĀTṚ*. Sanskrit** term used in the ***Arthaśāstra to designate the treasurer.

SANSKRIT. Language used to compose a wide range of texts. The earliest examples are ritual texts in **Vedic** Sanskrit (c. second millennium BCE). Later works were composed in classical Sanskrit, which reached its apogee in the first millennium CE. Works composed in Sanskrit include ritual and legal texts, the **Purāṇas**, ***śāstras*** including works on grammar, scientific treatises such as works on **astronomy**, **mathematics**, **medicine**, **epics**, **poems**, narratives, plays, **biographies**, treatises on poetics and **philosophy**, apart from commentaries. While many of these works were **Brahmanical**, several **Buddhist** works were also composed in Sanskrit from c. first millennium CE onward. The earliest **inscriptions** in Sanskrit also date to the same period. *See also ABHIJÑĀNA ŚĀKUNTALAM*; *AITAREYA BRĀHMAṆA*; *AMARAKOŚA*; *ANUKRAMAṆI*; *ĀRAṆYAKA*; *ARTHAŚĀSTRA*; *ĀRYABHAṬĪYA*; *AŚOKĀVADĀNA*; *AṢṬĀDHYĀYĪ*; *ATHARVAVEDA*; *BHAGAVAD GĪTĀ*; *BRĀHMAṆA* (2); *BRAHMASŪTRA*; *BṚHADĀRAṆYAKA UPANIṢAD*;

BṚHADDEVATĀ; *BṚHASPATI SMṚTI*; *BṚHATKATHĀMAÑJARI*; *BṚHAT SAMḤITĀ*; *BUDDHACARITA*; BUDDHIST HYBRID SANSKRIT; *CARAKA SAMḤITĀ*; *CHĀNDOGYA UPANIṢAD*; *DAŚAKUMĀRACARITA*; *DEVĪCANDRAGUPTA*; *DEVĪMĀHĀTMYA*; DHARMAŚĀSTRA; DHARMASŪTRA; *DHVANYĀLOKA*; *DIVYĀVADĀNA*; DRAMA; *GĀRGASAMḤITĀ*; GṚHYASŪTRA; GUPTA; *HARIVAMḤŚA*; *HARṢACARITA*; *JĀTAKAMĀLĀ*; *KĀMASŪTRA*; *KATHĀSARITSĀGARA*; *KĀTYĀYANASMṚTI*; LATER VEDA; LITERATURE; *MAHĀBHĀRATA*; *MAHĀBHĀṢYA*; *MAHĀPURĀṆA*; MANUSCRIPTS; *MANUSMṚTI*; MAX MULLER, FRIEDRICH; *MṚCCHAKAṬIKAM*; *MUDRĀRĀKṢASA*; *NĀRADA SMṚTI*; *NĀṬYAŚĀSTRA*; *NIGHAṆṬU*; *NIRUKTA*; *NĪTISĀRA*; *NYĀYA SŪTRA*; *PAÑCATANTRA*; *RĀJATARAṄGIṆĪ*; *RĀMĀYAṆA*; *ṚGVEDA*; *SĀMAVEDA*; *ŚATAPATHA BRĀHMAṆA*; ŚRAUTASŪTRA; ŚULBASŪTRA; *SUŚRUTA SAMḤITĀ*; UPANIṢAD; *UTTARARĀMACARITA*; *VAIŚEṢIKA SŪTRA*; *VEDA*; *VEDĀṄGA*; XUAN ZANG; *YĀJÑAVALKYASMṚTI*; *YAJURVEDA*; *YAŚASTILAKA CAMPU*; YĀSKA; *YOGASŪTRA*; *ZEND AVESTA*.

SANTHLI. Archaeological site in Gujarat, with two occupational phases. Period I, designated as **Mesolithic**, has yielded finds of geometric and nongeometric microliths and skeletal remains of cattle (probably wild), sheep, goat, deer, pig, and fish. Finds from Period II, characterized as **Chalcolithic** (c. second millennium BCE), consisted of **pottery** similar to that from **Nagwada** and stone and shell ornaments.

SAPTĀṄGA*. Sanskrit** word meaning "seven limbs," used in texts on polity such as the ***Arthaśāstra (c. fourth century BCE onward). The term was used to designate seven elements, regarded as essential components of the state. These were the **king**, **ministers**, the ally, treasury, **army**, the **fortified** settlement, and the populated countryside. The textual tradition incorporated debates on the relative importance of these constituents of the state.

SARAI NAHAR RAI. Mesolithic site (c. 10,000–9,000 BCE) in Uttar Pradesh, with evidence of geometric microliths; bones of bison, rhinoceros, fish, and deer; and tortoise shells. Structural remains include traces of a prepared floor that may have been part of a dwelling place. There is evidence for **burials** within the habitation area, with the bodies oriented in an east–west direction with grave goods such as microliths and shells.

SARASVATĪ. Name of a river, mentioned in the ***Ṛgveda*** and later texts, occasionally identified with the **Ghaggar–Hakra**. *See also* INDUS SARASVATI CIVILIZATION; VIDEGHA MĀTHAVA.

SARNATH. Site near **Varanasi** (Uttar Pradesh) recognized as the place where the **Buddha** taught for the first time. **Archaeological** finds include **Northern Black Polished Ware**, remains of ***stūpas*** and **monasteries**, and several **inscriptions**, indicating that the site continued to be occupied until c. 12th century CE. Other finds consisted of an **Asokan** pillar inscribed with a **Minor Pillar Edict** exhorting Buddhist monks and nuns to avoid schism. The pillar was surmounted by a lion capital that has been adopted as the national emblem of India.

SĀRTHAVĀHA. **Sanskrit** term used c. late first millennium BCE onward to designate the leader of a **trading** caravan. The *satthavāha* (**Pali** and **Prakrit**) also figured in narratives and was mentioned in **inscriptions** that indicate that he was generally regarded as a respected and powerful member of urban society.

SARVĀSTIVĀDA. Major school within **Theravāda Buddhism** that developed c. second century BCE onward. Its distinctive feature was the belief in the existence of everything, past, present, and future, even though the manifestations were subject to change. *See also* DINNĀGA (1); VASUBANDHU.

ŚAŚĀṄKA. Ruler of Bengal (**Gauḍa**) in the seventh century CE, who killed **Grahavarman**, the **Maukhari** ruler of **Kanauj**. In turn, Śaśāṅka's ally Devagupta was killed by **Rājyavardhana**, who belonged to the ruling lineage of **Thanesar** and was the brother-in-law of Grahavarman. Finally, Śaśāṅka met his end in battle with **Harṣavardhana**, the younger brother of Rājyavardhana. According to **Xuan Zang**, Śaśāṅka was opposed to **Buddhism** and uprooted the Bodhi tree at **Bodh Gaya**.

ŚĀSTRA*.** **Sanskrit** term, used from the late first millennium BCE onward to designate texts that were regarded as authoritative or normative in a wide range of subjects, including the ***puruṣārthas.

SĀTAKARṆĪ. Title used by **Sātavāhana** rulers, occasionally interpreted as a reference to a clan totem.

SĀTAKARṆĪ II. **Sātavāhana** ruler (c. second century BCE), who reigned for 56 years, probably a contemporary of **Khāravela**. He may have added parts of Madhya Pradesh to his **kingdom**.

***ŚATAPATHA BRĀHMAṆA*.** Ritual text (**Sanskrit**) composed c. eighth–sixth centuries BCE. It derives its name from a recension that contains 100 (*śata*) chapters. It deals with a wide range of rituals including royal **sacrifices** and the *agnicayana*, a special ritual for constructing a sacrificial altar. Those cited as authorities include **Yājñavalkya** and Śāṇḍilya. *See also BRĀHMAṆA* (2); KINGSHIP, THEORIES OF ORIGIN; LITERATURE; VIDEGHA MĀTHAVA.

SĀTAVĀHANA. Ruling lineage, also known as the **Āndhras**, in western and central India (c. third century BCE–second century CE), known from **Prakrit inscriptions** found from sites such as **Nasik**, **Karle**, and **Nanaghat**, **coins** and textual traditions, including the **Purāṇas**. The last-named texts mention 30 **kings** of the dynasty, some of whom are also known from inscriptions and coins. However, some of the rulers mentioned in coins do not figure in the Purāṇic lists. The origins of the lineage are obscure, although some rulers claimed to be ***brāhmaṇas*** **(1)**.

Sātavāhana rulers evidently derived resources from the control of **trade routes**, including maritime routes through the Arabian Sea and the Bay of Bengal. Inscriptions refer to the rulers as lords of the three oceans, and ships are represented on their coins. Control over trade routes was often contested, and there is evidence of conflicts with the **Śakas** of western India. The most successful Sātavāhana ruler was **Gautamīputra**.

The Sātavāhanas ruled with the help of local lineages such as those of the **Raṭhikas** and **Bhojas (1)**. Other officials mentioned in inscriptions include the *mahāsenāpati* or the great general. There are indications of marital relations among these categories, which constituted the ruling elite. Rulers were often identified through the use of metronymics.

Some of the earliest evidence of **land grants** occurs in Sātavāhana inscriptions. These were generally made to **Buddhist** institutions. Several **rock-cut caves** in the Western Ghats and adjoining areas were excavated during their rule. Pratiṣṭhāna (present-day **Paithan**, in Maharashtra), the center of their power, remained a flourishing **city** until c. third century CE. *See also* ADAM; AMARAVATI; BANAVASI; BHAWAR; BHOKARDAN; CHAUL; DHĀNYAKAṬAKA; EMPIRE; GODAVARI; HĀLA; IKṢVĀKU (2); JOGALTHEMBI; KHĀRAVELA; KINSHIP SYSTEMS; MARITIME TRADE; NAHAPĀṆA; NASIK; PALLAVA; PULUMAYI II; RUDRADĀMAN; SĀTAKARṆĪ; SĀTAKARṆĪ II; SIMUKA; ŚRĪ SĀTAKARṆĪ I; VĀSIṢṬHĪPUTRA PULUMAVI; YAJÑAŚRĪ SĀTAKARṆI.

SATDHARA. Archaeological site in Madhya Pradesh, find spot of several ***stūpas*** that may date to the **Mauryan** period (c. fourth–second centuries BCE). Other finds included **Northern Black Polished Ware** and **iron** artifacts.

SATĪ*.** Term derived from the **Sanskrit** root *sat* meaning "goodness," also the name of a **goddess**, recognized as a form of the goddess Durgā. The term has been used to designate wives who followed their husband onto the funeral pyre, thus epitomizing the ideal of wifely devotion. Allusions to funerary practices in the ***Ṛgveda (c. end of the second millennium BCE) indicate that the **widow** was expected to lie on the funeral pyre with her deceased husband, but was then recalled to the world of the living. Instances of the practice are rare in the **early historic period**, although it is mentioned in some of the accounts of the invasion of **Alexander (of Macedon)**. However, textual references to the practice are found in the Sanskrit **epics**, especially the ***Mahābhārata***. An **inscription** from **Eran**, c. 510 CE, is one of the earliest documents recording the practice. It is also mentioned in the ***Harṣacarita***. Validation of the practice in prescriptive **literature** dates from the eighth century CE. At the same time, there was criticism of the practice, especially within **Tantricism**. *See also* BURIAL PRACTICES; DISPOSAL OF THE DEAD; RĀJYAŚRĪ; WOMEN.

SATIYAPUTA. People mentioned in **Asokan inscriptions** as living along the southern frontiers of Asoka's realm.

SATRAP. A term used to designate provincial governors in the **Achaemenid** Empire, and used subsequently by rulers and their subordinates in the northwestern part of the subcontinent. *See also KṢATRAPA*.

***SATTASAĪ*.** An anthology of approximately 700 erotic verses in **Prakrit** attributed to **Hāla**. Some of these verses may have been derived from folk traditions. *See also* LITERATURE.

SAUVĪRA. Name of a state in the northwestern part of the subcontinent, generally mentioned in conjunction with **Sindhu** or the **Indus** valley in the ***Mahābhārata*** and in **early historic** texts and **inscriptions**.

SAVALDA. Archaeological site in Maharashtra, recognized as the type site for **Savalda ware**. Two occupational phases (c. second–early first millennium BCE) have been identified. Period I, considered **Chalcolithic**, yielded the typical **pottery** and stone blades. Finds from Period II consisted of **black and red ware**. *See also* KAOTHE.

SAVALDA WARE. Pottery (c. second millennium BCE) made on a slow wheel, of medium to coarse fabric, with a reddish slip, generally painted with geometric or naturalistic designs in black. Common shapes include jars, dishes, bowls, and vases. *See also* SAVALDA; TERDAL.

SCRIPTS. The earliest known examples of writing occur on the **Harappan seals** (c. 2700 BCE–1800 BCE). The script has not been satisfactorily deciphered as yet. Decipherment of the script has been hampered by the absence of long **inscriptions** as well as the absence of bilingual inscriptions. A further problem has been posed by the uncertainty about the **language** in which they were written. Approximately 400 signs have been identified in the script. It is likely that the script was written from right to left.

The subsequent evidence for writing comes from the **Asokan inscriptions** (c. third century BCE), which were written in **Brāhmī**, **Kharoṣṭhī**, **Aramaic**, and Greek. While some attempts have been made to trace connections between the Harappan script and Brāhmī, these have not been substantiated at present. It is likely that both Brāhmī, which was written from left to right, and Kharoṣṭhī, which was written from right to left, were derived from West Asian scripts. *See also* EARLY HISTORIC PERIOD.

SCULPTURE. Remains of sculpture have been recovered from several **archaeological** sites. These include **Aihole**, **Ajanta**, **Amaravati**, **Ambari**, **Antichak**, **Arambha**, **Ayodhya**, **Badami**, **Bagh**, **Banarsihankalan**, **Banotiwadi**, **Begram**, **Bhaja**, **Bharatpur**, **Bharhut**, **Bharuch**, **Bhitari**, **Dat Nagar**, **Deogarh**, **Donder Khera**, **Elephanta**, **Ellora**, **Eran**, **Ganwaria**, **Gudimallam**, **Gudnapura**, **Jaggayyapeta**, **Jetavana**, **Kanaganahalli**, **Kanauj**, **Kanheri**, **Karle**, **Kayatha**, **Khajuri**, **Khandagiri**, **Khiching**, **Kolhua**, **Kusinagara**, **Lalitagiri**, **Mangalkot**, **Mathura**, **Nadner**, **Nagarjunakonda**, **Nalanda**, **Nanaghat**, **Paharpur**, **Pattadakal**, **Peddavegi**, **Pitalkhora**, **Sanchi**, **Sanghol**, **Sirpur**, **Surkh Kotal**, **Talkad**, **Tāmralipti**, **Taradih**, **Taxila**, **Ter**, **Thanesar**, **Thotlakonda**, **Tumain**, **Udayagiri**, **Udaygiri**, **Ujjayinī**, and **Vadodara**. Sculpture in stone and metal has survived best in the archaeological records. **Terracotta** figurines are also extremely prolific.

Some of the earliest examples of sculpture have been recovered from **Neolithic** sites. **Harappan** sculpture (c. 2700–1800 BCE) is remarkable for its naturalistic representations of both humans and animals. In the **early historic period**, sculpture was associated with urban life. It was used to embellish religious monuments, including **Buddhist** ***stūpas***. Traditions of sculptural representation also emerged within **Jainism** and **Brahmanical Hinduism**. **Mathura** and **Taxila** were recognized as major centers for the production of stone sculpture. It is also likely that terracotta figurines recovered from several early historic sites were produced to cater to the demands of urban elites.

During the **early medieval period**, sculpture was increasingly used to embellish **temples**, such as those at Aihole and **Mamallapuram**. Sculptural representations included those of **Purāṇic** deities and of narrative scenes drawn from the **Sanskrit epics**. Ruling lineages such as the **Coḻas** and **Pālas** patronized bronze sculpture.

Appreciation of the aesthetic qualities of early Indian sculpture have varied sharply over the past two centuries. On the one hand, the earliest art historians, working within the colonial context, were often unable to understand the significance of the symbolism associated with these visual traditions. On the other hand, Indian nationalist historians generally argued that these traditions projected spiritual ideals, and occasionally did not acknowledge the sensuous quality of these representations. More recently, attempts have been made to contextualize these art forms in order to arrive at an understanding of their significance. *See also* ART; GANDHARA SCHOOL OF ART; MAURYAN ART; TEXTILES; WARFARE.

SCYTHIAN. *See* ŚAKA.

SEALS. Seals have been recovered from a variety of **archaeological** contexts. The best known are the **Harappan** seals (c. 2700 BCE–1800 BCE). These were usually made of steatite, and generally contain depictions of animals, mythical and real, as well as more complex representations, perhaps derived from narratives. The commonest representations are of a single-horned animal, often called the unicorn. Other animals shown include the bull, rhinoceros, elephant, and tiger. They also contain writing in a **script** that is as yet undeciphered.

Seals of clay, stone, **copper**, bronze, silver, bone, and ivory have been recovered from sites belonging to the **early historic** phase (c. sixth century BCE onward). These include royal seals as well as those of administrative officials and offices. Other seals and sealings were used by **guilds** of bankers, **traders**, and artisans; **temples**; and **monasteries**. Generally, the name of the owner, genealogical information, and official designations were recorded on seals. In some instances, as at **Nalanda**, **Buddhist** prayers were inscribed on seals. Seals belonging to groups such as the **Mālavas** and **Yaudheyas** have also been recovered.

Find spots of seals include **Balakot**, **Banawali**, **Bhagwanpura**, **Brass**, **Chandraketugarh**, **Chanhudaro**, **Daimabad**, **Dangwada**, **Desalpur**, **Dholavira**, **Eran**, **Gilaulikhera**, **Hulas Khera**, **Jhukar**, **Jhusi**, **Kapilavastu**, **Kausambi**, **Khokrakot**, **Kolhua**, **Kunal**, **Lalitagiri**, **Lothal**, **Mahurjhari**, **Manda**, **Mangalkot**, **Masaon**, **Mathura**, **Nagara**, **Nalanda**, **Pauni**, **Piprahwa**, **Rakhi Garhi**, **Ropar**, **Sanghol**, **Sirpur**, **Sodanga**, **Sonkh**, **Sunet**, **Surkotada**, **Takiaper**, **Taradih**, **Thanesar**, **Udayagiri**, **Ujjayinī**, **Vadodara**, **Vaishali**, and **Vidisha**.

Find spots of sealings include **Adam**, **Ayodhya**, **Banarsihankalan**, Banawali, **Bangarh**, **Bhita**, **Bhorgarh**, Brass, Chandraketugarh, Dangwada, **Daulatpur**, Dholavira, **Erich**, **Ganwaria**, **Hulas**, Hulas Khera, Jhusi, Kausambi, **Kumrahar**, Lalitagiri, Lothal, **Malhar**, **Maner**, Mangalkot, **Manjhi**, Masaon, Mathura, **Nagwada**, **Pāṭaliputra**, Ropar, Sanghol, **Sonpur**, **Sravasti**, **Sringaverapura**, Sunet, Taradih, Thanesar, **Tripuri**, Udayagiri, Ujjayinī, and Vaishali. *See also* SAMUDRAGUPTA; SCRIPTS; TERRACOTTA; TOOLS; TRADE ROUTES.

SECOND URBANIZATION. Often used to designate the emergence of urban centers in the **Ganga (2)** valley during the sixth century BCE, as distinct from the first urbanization, associated with the **Harappan civilization**. Many of the urban centers that emerged during this phase, such as **Pāṭaliputra** and **Mathura**, survive to the present day. Most of these centers were the capitals of ***mahājanapadas***, and many of them were **fortified**. **Archaeological** evidence indicates that these **cities** developed out of a process of organic growth and were consequently not planned in the way Harappan settlements were. Textual traditions, especially **Buddhist** and **Jaina**, suggest that these cities were often centers of **craft** production, with busy markets. Many of them were located along **routes** of long-distance communication connecting different parts of the subcontinent as well as the world beyond. **Religious** institutions were often clustered in and around these centers.

SEKTA. **Archaeological** site in Manipur with evidence of wattle-and-daub structures and urn **burials** (c. first century BCE–second century CE?). Other finds included handmade and wheel-made **pottery**, beads of semiprecious stone, **copper** ornaments, and **iron** equipment such as arrowheads, spearheads, knives, daggers, and so on. *See also* VADAGOKUGIRI.

SELEUCOS NIKATOR. General and successor of **Alexander (of Macedon)**, who took charge of the provinces bordering the Indian subcontinent as well as parts of West Asia (c. 323 BCE). He came into conflict with **Candragupta Maurya** (c. 305 BCE) and was possibly defeated. As part of the negotiations that followed, he gave four provinces to the Mauryan ruler, entered into a matrimonial alliance with him, and received 500 elephants in exchange. He also sent **Megasthenes** as his ambassador to the Mauryan court. *See also* ANTIOCHOS I SOTER (OF SYRIA).

SENUWAR. **Archaeological** site in Bihar. The first period (I) was **Neolithic** (c. 2000–1400 BCE) with evidence for the cultivation of rice, barley, millet, peas, and lentil. There was also evidence of *mahua*, *sal*, acacia, bamboo, *siris*, jujube, and other trees. **Tools** consisted of microliths and ground stone tools such as pestles and querns as well as equipment made of bone. Other finds included **pottery**, both handmade and wheel-made. There was evidence for the construction of huts. In the subsequent period II (**Chalcolithic**) dated to the second half of the second millennium BCE, there is evidence for the cultivation of beans, sesame, safflower, and linseed. There were also remains of deodar, jackfruit, and mango trees. Metal equipment included **copper** fishhooks and needles. Other finds consisted of ground stone tools, unfinished as well as finished bone tools, including chisels and points, and unfinished as well as finished beads of agate and carnelian, and **black and red ware**. There was evidence of wattle-and-daub structures. Animal remains from the first two periods included cattle, horse/ass, sheep, goat, pig, cat, dog, deer, rat, turtle, and so on. Period III (c. second half of the first millennium BCE?) yielded evidence of **Northern Black Polished Ware** and **iron** artifacts. There are also indications of the construction of a rampart. Finds from period IV, attributed to the **Kuṣāṇa** period, included iron tools and **terracotta** figurines.

SEPARATE ROCK EDICTS. **Asokan inscriptions** (c. third century BCE) found at **Dhauli** and **Jaugada**, Orissa, and at **Sannati**, Karnataka. In Orissa, these edicts were inserted in place of **Major Rock Edict** XIII. The inscriptions mention Tosali (present-day **Dhauli**), Ujjeni (**Ujjayinī**), and Takhasilā (**Taxila**) as administrative centers of the **Mauryan** Empire, from which officials were instructed to go on periodic tours of inspection to ensure the implementation of **judicial** reforms. The edicts elucidate Asoka's paternalistic attitude toward his subjects and neighboring peoples. The occasions on which the inscriptions were to be read out are also mentioned.

***SEṬṬHI*.** **Pali/Prakrit** term used (mid–first millennium BCE onward) to designate a wealthy man, a merchant-cum-banker, who often played an important role in urban life.

SETUBANDHA*.** **Prakrit epic**, attributed to the **Vākāṭaka** ruler **Pravarasena II** (c. 410–440 CE). It consists of 15 cantos including about 1,300 verses. It deals with an episode from the ***Rāmāyaṇa, the crossing of the ocean by **Rāma**. *See also* LITERATURE.

SHAHBAZGARHI. Site in the North-West Frontier Province (Pakistan) where a set of the **Major Rock Edicts** of **Asoka** has been found. These were inscribed in the **Kharoṣṭhī script**.

SHAJI-KI-DHERI. **Archaeological** site near Peshawar, North-West Frontier Province, Pakistan. Finds include the remains of a ***stūpa*** with an **inscribed** relic casket mentioning a **monastery** constructed by the **Kuṣāṇa king Kaniṣka** (c. second century CE).

SHAKTARI TIMBO. **Archaeological** site in Gujarat, with evidence of three major occupational phases. The first, associated with the **Mesolithic** (c. fourth–third millennium BCE?) was characterized by finds of microliths. The second or **Chalcolithic** (c. third–second millennium BCE) phase yielded evidence of **copper** fishhooks and other equipment, **pottery** resembling that from **Nagwada**, traces of **Harappan** pottery, stone blades, beads of semiprecious stone, spindle whorls, and bones of cattle, sheep, goat, and deer. The occupation from c. fifth to sixth centuries CE yielded beads and pottery.

SHAR-I-KUNA. Site in Kandahar (Afghanistan). Find spot of a bilingual **Asokan inscription**, in Greek and **Aramaic**.

SHIKARPUR. *See* VALMIYO TIMBO.

SHIRKANDA. **Archaeological** site in Maharashtra, with evidence of **Chalcolithic** and **megalithic** cultures (c. second–first millennium BCE?). Finds include remains of circular huts and animal bones including cattle, sheep, and goat, bone **tools**, remains of furnaces, slag and **iron** tools, **Black and Red Ware**, **black slipped ware**, and ornaments of glass, shell, and **terracotta**.

SHORE TEMPLE. One of the best-known **temples** built during the reign of the **Pallava king Narasiṃhavarman II** (c. first half of the eighth century CE) at **Mamallapuram**, Tamil Nadu. The temple, built of stone, included shrines for the worship of both **Viṣṇu** and **Śiva**. Some of the earliest extant examples of towers or *śikharas* surmount these shrines.

SHORTUG(H)AI. Harappan site (c. third millennium BCE) in present-day Afghanistan, located close to sources of lapis lazuli.

SHRI SHRI SURYAPAHAR. Archaeological site in Assam, with remains of brick structures dating to c. sixth–ninth centuries CE. Other antiquities included **terracotta** images, molded tiles, and plaques.

SHYAMSUNDAR TILA. Archaeological site in Tripura, find spot of a ***stūpa*** and **terracotta** plaques with **Buddhist** imagery (c. 9th–10th centuries CE).

SIDDAPUR. Site in Karnataka. Find spot of a **Minor Rock Edict** of **Asoka**.

SIDDHĀTTHA. *See* BUDDHA.

SIKLIGARH. Archaeological site in Bihar with evidence of a **Mauryan** stone pillar (c. third century BCE?) and a mud rampart.

SILAPPADIKĀRAM. **Tamil poem**, often considered as an **epic**, attributed to a **Jaina** monk named **Ilanko Aṭikaḷ**. Various dates have been assigned to the text, ranging from the 2nd to the 12th centuries CE. The text narrates the travails of a merchant of Puhār (**Poompuhar**) who falls in love with a **courtesan**, abandoning his chaste wife. Ultimately, he returns to the latter, but is falsely charged with theft and sentenced to death. His wife invokes her chastity to wreak havoc on the unjust **king** and the **city** of **Madurai**. Subsequently, she is worshipped as a **goddess**. The work is in three parts, divided into 30 sections. The parts are named after the capital cities of the three major kingdoms of the region. The text provides a vivid description of urban life and arts. *See also* LITERATURE.

SILK ROUTE. Name assigned to several **routes**, mainly overland but some maritime, that connected China with West Asia and the Mediterranean and flourished throughout the first millennium CE. The routes derive their name from the fact that one of the major goods transported from east to west was silk, manufactured in China, although other goods were carried as well. No single trading group had control over the entire stretch of this vast network of routes. Ruling elites situated along the route attempted to control traffic and reap the benefits of this risky but lucrative **trade** network. Among ruling lineages linked with the subcontinent, the **Bactrian Greeks**, **Indo-Greeks**, **Parthians**, **Śakas**, and **Kuṣāṇas** opened up routes from Central Asia to West Asia through the northwestern part of the subcontinent. In the case of the last two groups, it is likely that routes down the **Indus** and through the Arabian Sea were exploited as well. Maritime routes from China were linked with ports along both the eastern and the western coasts of the peninsula. The overland Silk Route in particular was also used by **Buddhist** teachers to spread the faith to Central Asia and beyond. *See also* GILGIT; KAPIŚA; MAHĀYĀNA; MARITIME TRADE; TRADE ROUTES; VĪMA KADPHISES.

SIMḤAVIṢṆU. **Pallava** ruler (r. 560–580) who revived the fortunes of the lineage after the **Kalabhra** interlude in the history of south India.

SIMUKA. First known ruler of the **Sātavāhanas** (c. 230 BCE), mentioned in the **Purāṇas**. **Jaina** accounts state that he ruled for 23 years. He was evidently dethroned and killed.

SINDHU. Term used in the ***Ṛgveda*** (c. second millennium BCE) and subsequently to refer to both water bodies in general and to the **Indus River**. In the **early historic period** it was used to designate the Indus valley as a sociopolitical unit. *See also* INDOS.

SIRCAR, DINESH CHANDRA (1907–1984). One of the best-known **epigraphists** of the 20th century, Sircar deciphered, edited, and published several **inscriptions**. He taught for many years at the

University of Calcutta and served as government epigraphist. His major publications include *Select Inscriptions* (two volumes), *Indian Epigraphy*, and *Indian Epigraphical Glossary*. He also contributed to the reconstruction of dynastic histories as well as to the debates on social, economic, **religious**, and cultural history.

SIRIPANAṞṞUPPATAI. **Tamil** work composed by Nallur Nattattanar, one of the ten idylls of the **Sangam** anthology. The text consists of about 270 lines in praise of the generous patron, aimed at ensuring more gifts in the future. *See also* LITERATURE.

SIRPUR. Archaeological site in Madhya Pradesh, with evidence of three occupational phases from the mid–first millennium CE to the early centuries of the second millennium. Finds include remains of two large **Buddhist monasteries** and a **temple**. The monastery remained in occupation until the 11th century. Other finds consisted of stone and metal **sculpture** of the **Buddha** as well as **inscribed seals**. Later finds included sculpture of deities from the **Śaiva** pantheon.

ŚIŚUNĀGA. Ruler of **Magadha** (c. fifth century BCE) who defeated the contemporary ruler of **Avanti**. The ruling lineage he established was succeeded by that of the **Nandas**.

SISUPALGARH. Archaeological site in Orissa, dated to c. third century BCE, which may have been the provincial capital of the **Mauryas** or the capital of the local **Cedi** rulers. It was abandoned by c. fourth century CE. Excavations have revealed evidence of extensive ramparts around the settlement, which is about 1 sq km, with symmetrical entrances and a central hall. Other finds included both **Roman** and Indian **coins**, **pottery** including **rouletted ware**, beads of semiprecious stone, **iron tools** and weapons, and **terracotta** artifacts. *See also* PURI-KUṢĀṆA.

SISWAL. Archaeological site in Haryana, with evidence (c. third millennium BCE) of **pre-/early Harappan pottery**. *See also* KURUKṢETRA; MITATHAL.

ŚIVA. One of the principal deities in the **Hindu** pantheon, described in several major **Purāṇas**. Attempts have been made to connect the deity with Rudra, mentioned in the ***Ṛgveda*** (c. second millennium BCE). However, the worship of Śiva attained importance in the post-Vedic period (c. late first millennium BCE onward). The deity was visualized as an **ascetic**, and was often worshipped in phallic form. Later traditions connected him with gods such as Skanda and Gaṇeśa, both of whom were identified as his sons. He was also associated with the **goddess**, who, in the form of Pārvatī (the goddess of the mountains), was recognized as his consort. From the second half of the first millennium CE, shrines to worship the deity, who was the focus of a variety of devotional cults, were constructed in several parts of the country. *See also* CUNTARĀR; DANCE; EARLY MEDIEVAL PERIOD; HARAPPAN CIVILIZATION; KĀLIDĀSA; KĀRAIKKĀL AMMAIYĀR; NACHNA KUTHARA; *NĀYAṈĀR*; PALLAVA; PĀŚUPATA; PATTADAKAL; RĀJARĀJA I; RĀJENDRA; RATNĀKARA; RELIGION; ŚAIVISM; ŚAṄKARĀCĀRYA; SHORE TEMPLE; TIRUMULAR.

ŚIVĀRYA. Jaina teacher who flourished c. second century CE, author of a **Prakrit** work, the *Bhagavatiarādhanā*, dealing with the practice of **asceticism**. *See also* LITERATURE.

SKANDAGUPTA. One of the last major rulers of the **Gupta** dynasty (r.c. 455–467), known from an **inscription** found at **Junagadh**, which included a panegyric of the ruler. The inscription describes him as being chosen by the **goddess** of fortune, which has been interpreted as a reference to a possible struggle for succession. He was credited with control of the entire earth extending up to the four oceans and with repelling the advances of the ***mlecchas***. The inscription records the repair (c. 456–57 CE) of the **irrigation** work at the site by Parṇadatta, an official who was also eulogized. Another undated inscription at **Bhitari** mentions Skandagupta's victory over the **Hūṇas**. *See also* BAYANA; KAHAUM PILLAR INSCRIPTION; PUṢYAMITRA.

***SKANDHĀVĀRA*. Sanskrit** term for **army** camps marked by the presence of the **king** when he embarked on military campaigns, mentioned in **early medieval** texts and **inscriptions**. The *skandhāvāra* often functioned as a mobile capital, from where the king issued orders and administered justice. *See also* WARFARE.

SLAVERY. The existence of slavery has been documented from a variety of textual traditions. The ***Ṛgveda*** contains references to ***dāsa*** and *dāsī*, men and **women** who were regarded as a form of property and gifted on ritual and other occasions. Subsequently, prescriptive and narrative texts from the **early historic period** onward refer to servile populations. Slaves were used as domestic labor and were occasionally employed in **agriculture** as well. Their dependence on their masters is evident from the fact that they had to get the permission of their owners before joining **renunciatory orders** such as **Buddhism**. Textual traditions also suggest that slave women could be expected to render sexual services. These were sometimes used by the women and their kinfolk as strategies of upward **social mobility**.

Megasthenes, who visited the subcontinent during the **Mauryan** period, noted that chattel slavery was unknown in India. This was probably because the forms and scale of slavery were different from those in contemporary Greece. Some historians have suggested that the existence of the ***śūdra varṇa***, whose members were ideally supposed to serve those belonging to the first three *varṇas*, obviated the need for large-scale chattel slavery.

The Mauryan emperor **Asoka** advised masters to be gentle toward their slaves. At the same time, it is evident that large numbers of people were captured and enslaved after his victory in the war in **Kaliṅga**.

There are no references to slave revolts in textual traditions. However, narratives occasionally contain stories about disobedient slaves, which may indicate some amount of everyday resistance. *See also* TRADE.

SOAN VALLEY. Area in the Siwalik Hills, Pakistan, from where Lower **Paleolithic** pebble **tools** as well as Middle and Upper Paleolithic tools have been recovered.

SOCIAL MOBILITY. The question of social mobility in early India has aroused considerable interest in recent decades. Nineteenth- and early-20th-century reconstructions of social history were often based on an acceptance of **Sanskrit** prescriptive texts, the **Dharmasūtras** and **Dharmaśāstras**, at face value. These suggested that the fourfold ***varṇa*** order was generally prevalent and became more rigid with the passage of time. Subsequently, examination of **Buddhist** and **Jaina** texts in **Pali** and **Prakrit**, as well as the evidence from **inscriptions**, has indicated a more complex scenario. It is evident that the *varṇa* order did not prevail throughout the subcontinent. Besides, many of the social categories mentioned in texts and inscriptions did not fit within the fourfold *varṇa* order. Social status, moreover, was not determined only on the basis of birth, as envisaged in the *varṅa* order, but could vary according to context, thus providing for mobility. It is also likely that social boundaries were less rigid in urban centers. A rare inscription, found at Mandasor (**Daśapura**), describes how a **guild** of silk weavers moved from Gujarat to this **city** and adopted a wide range of new professions. Within narrative traditions, the perceived discrepancies between ascribed and attained status were often explained or justified in terms of the theory of ***karma***.

Social mobility has often been conceptualized in terms of Brahmanization and/or kṣatriyization, involving the adoption of the values, norms, and practices of ***brāhmaṇas* (1)** and ***kṣatriyas***, respectively, by those who aspired to higher status. Such modes of upward mobility are evident in the case of a number of **early medieval** ruling lineages that claimed descent from lunar (***candravaṃśa***) or **solar** dynasties mentioned in the Sanskrit **epics**, often reinforcing this by seeking divine support through the invocation of **Purāṇic** deities. *See also* SLAVERY; UNTOUCHABILITY.

SODANGA. Archaeological site in Madhya Pradesh, with evidence of four occupational phases. Period I (c. 600 BCE–200 BCE) yielded traces of a stone wall. Other finds included a stone elephant that may be **Mauryan**, and a lotus capital, possibly from a Mauryan pillar. Period II (c. 200 BCE–75 CE) is attributed to the **Śuṅga–Kuṣāṇa–Sātavāhana** phase. Finds consisted of **Northern Black Polished Ware** and **terracotta** figurines. Period III (c. 76–300 CE) is designated as the **Kṣatrapa–Sātavāhana** phase. Finds included **coins**, inscribed **seals**, **iron** and shell artifacts, and **Red Polished Ware**. Period IV (c. 300–600 CE) was associated with the **Guptas**, **Aulikaras**, and **Hūṇas**. Finds from this phase included iron and shell objects. This period yielded evidence of a layer of ash, which has been interpreted as an indication of the destruction of the settlement by the Hūṇas.

SOHGAURA. Archaeological site in Uttar Pradesh, find spot of a **copper plate** containing a **Mauryan inscription** in **Prakrit**, written in the **Brāhmī script**. The inscription refers to the construction of granaries to store grain that would be available in case of a **famine**.

SOLAR DYNASTY. Designation of the **Ikṣvākus (1)**, who were regarded as descendants of the sun, described in ancient texts as the **Sūryavaṃśa**. In the **early medieval period**, several ruling lineages in different parts of the subcontinent claimed descent from this dynasty. *See also* SOCIAL MOBILITY.

SOMA. A plant mentioned in **Vedic literature** (c. second millennium BCE), worshipped as a deity, with several hymns addressed to it (collated in the ninth section of the ***Ṛgveda***) and used to prepare a juice that was offered to the gods and consumed on ritual occasions. In later tradition, Soma was one of the names of the moon. *See also* HINDUISM.

SOMADEVA. Author (c. 11th century CE) of the ***Kathāsaritsāgara***, who lived in Kashmir. The text was apparently composed for Sūryamatī, the wife of the contemporary ruler. Although Somadeva was a worshipper of **Śiva**, the text displays **Buddhist** influence as well. *See also* LITERATURE.

SONGAON. Archaeological site in Maharashtra, with evidence of three occupational phases. Period I (c. second millennium BCE) yielded traces of handmade **pottery** and pit dwellings. Pottery from Period II (second half of the second millennium BCE) had parallels with that from **Malwa** and **Jorwe**. Other finds included traces of charred wheat. Period III, assigned to the first half of the first millennium BCE, yielded **black and red ware**.

SONKH. Archaeological site in Uttar Pradesh, near **Mathura**, with five occupational phases. Finds from Period I (c. first half of the first millennium BCE) included wattle-and-daub structures and **Painted Grey Ware**. Period II (c. 400–200 BCE) yielded **Northern Black Polished Ware**, **punch-marked** and **cast coins**, and **terracotta** figurines. Finds from Period III (c. second–first centuries BCE) consisted of local coins and structural remains of mud-brick as well as burnt-brick ring wells and a **temple**. Period IV (c. first–third centuries CE) yielded **Kṣatrapa** and **Kuṣāṇa** coins and **seals**.

The site was evidently destroyed during Period V (c. fourth–seventh centuries CE).

SONPUR. Archaeological site in Bihar with evidence for three occupational phases. Period I, identified as **Chalcolithic** (c. 1100–650 BCE), provided evidence of wattle-and-daub structures, handmade **pottery** and **black and red ware**, bone **tools**, microliths, rice husk, beads of **terracotta** and semiprecious stone, and **iron** ore and slag. Period II (c. 650–200 BCE) yielded a wide variety of iron equipment, **copper** ornaments, **punch-marked** and other **coins**, terracotta figurines, **Northern Black Polished Ware**, and ring wells. Finds from Period III (c. 200 BCE–200 CE) included bone and ivory artifacts, sealings, and red pottery.

SOPARA. Coastal site in Maharashtra, known in ancient texts as Sūrpāraka, find spot of a fragment of the **Major Rock Edicts** VIII and IX of **Asoka**. Other finds include remains of a **Buddhist *stūpa***, **Sātavāhana coins** dated to the second century CE, and remains of a **temple**. Sopara has occasionally been identified with Ophir mentioned in Biblical texts.

SOTHI. Archaeological site in Rajasthan, associated with a type of **pottery** that is generally identified as **pre-/early Harappan**. The pottery and other aspects of material culture have similarities with those from **Kalibangan**. *See also* GANESHWAR.

SPHUJIDHVAJA. Sanskrit author of a work on **astronomy**/astrology, the *Yavana jātaka* (c. 269–70 CE), based on the translation of a Greek work from Alexandria. It deals with birth horoscopes, military astrology, and astronomy during the reign of the western **Kṣatrapa** ruler Rudrasena II. *See also* LITERATURE.

***ŚRAMAṆA*. Sanskrit** term (**Pali/Prakrit** *samana*), literally "one who strives," used to designate **ascetics** from mid–first millennium BCE onward. *See also DHAMMA*; *YONA*.

ŚRAUTASŪTRA. Category of **Sanskrit** prose texts, recognized as part of the **Vedāṅgas**, composed between c. 800 and 400 BCE. The texts deal with major **sacrificial** rituals, laying down the sequence and modes of performance, and were meant to be used as manuals by priests. *See also* LITERATURE.

SRAVASTI. Early historic city, mentioned in **Buddhist** and other textual traditions as one of the important cities in the ***mahājanapada*** of **Kosala**, identified with the **archaeological** site of Sahet Mahet in Uttar Pradesh, on the banks of the Rapti River, a tributary of the **Ganga (2)**. Excavations have yielded evidence of four occupational phases. Finds from Period I (c. first half of the first millennium BCE) included **Painted Grey Ware** and traces of **Northern Black Polished Ware**, which became more common in the subsequent period. Other artifacts consisted of beads of glass and semiprecious stone, ivory objects, and **copper** ornaments. Period II (mid–first millennium BCE onward) provided evidence of **fortifications** and ring wells. Other finds included **iron** equipment, **punch-marked** and other **coins**, sealings, and **terracotta** figurines. Period III (c. first century BCE–first century CE) was associated with structural remains, including those of a tank built of burnt brick, a ***stūpa***, and a **monastery** that was repeatedly rebuilt until the **early medieval period**. The site was also occupied during the early to post-**Gupta** period (Period IV, c. third–seventh centuries CE), when a shrine was added to the monastery. Other finds consisted of a variety of iron equipment and slag; fragments of glass and shell bangles; beads of semiprecious stone; terracotta figurines, including a head of the **Buddha**; and terracotta sealings inscribed in Gupta-period **Brāhmī**. There is evidence for occupation in the post-Gupta period as well, until c. 12th century CE. The site was identified on the basis of a 12th-century copper **plate** grant that mentioned the city and **Jetavana**, a Buddhist monastery mentioned frequently in textual traditions. *See also* SANKISSA.

ŚREṆI. **Sanskrit** term used (c. mid–first millennium BCE onward) to refer to **guilds**. The functions of *śreṇis*, which could be associations of merchants or **craftsmen**, included fixing wages, organizing production, and mediating in disputes. The *śreṇi* was headed by an "elder" who occasionally played an important role in civic administration. Members sometimes made grants collectively to **religious** institutions. *Śreṇis* also functioned as trustees of religious endowments and acted as banks.

ŚRĪ GUPTA. Recognized in genealogies of the **Gupta** rulers as the first ruler of the dynasty (c. third–fourth century CE).

ŚRĪ SĀTAKARṆĪ I. Sātavāhana ruler, c. second century BCE. According to a **Nanaghat inscription**, he performed the horse **sacrifice** and made lavish gifts to the sacrificial priests. He is also described as the lord of **Dakṣiṇāpatha**. *See also* NĀGANIKĀ.

SRINGAVERAPURA. Archaeological site near Allahabad, Uttar Pradesh, with evidence of **Northern Black Polished Ware**. Structural remains include a tank attributed to the **early historic** phase (c. mid–first millennium BCE?). Other finds consisted of **terracotta** figurines, a sealing **inscribed** in **Brāhmī**, and **coins** dating from the **Kuṣāṇa** to the **Gupta** periods (late first millennium BCE to mid–first millennium CE).

SRINIVASPURI. Part of New Delhi, find spot of a **Minor Rock Edict** of **Asoka**.

STHĀNĪŚVARA. Present-day **Thanesar** in Haryana.

STHŪLABHADRA. Jaina monk (c. fourth century BCE). According to the Jaina tradition, he remained behind in north India when **Candragupta Maurya** and **Bhadrabāhu** left for south India toward the end of the former's rule. He is credited with introducing the use of clothes, which was subsequently adopted by the **Śvetāmbara** sect of the Jainas. *See also* DIGAMBARA.

STRABO. Greek geographer and historian (b. 64/63 BCE, d. 24 CE), author of a historical work in 43 parts that is no longer extant. His work on geography was in 17 parts, of which all except the seventh have survived. Six parts relate to Asia, and it is in these that excerpts from **Megasthenes**'s ***Indica*** are found. *See also AGRONOMOI*.

***STRĪDHANA*. Sanskrit** term, literally "the wealth of a **woman**," used in the **Dharmaśāstras** (late first millennium BCE onward), to designate the resources that married women could claim. These included movable property such as jewelry, clothes, and utensils.

The husband's claim to *strīdhana* was restricted, and on the woman's death this wealth was expected to pass on to her children. *See also* INHERITANCE LAWS.

***STŪPA*.** **Sanskrit** word meaning "mound," name generally given to **Buddhist** monuments (although there were some **Jaina** *stūpas* as well). *Stūpas* were meant to preserve the memory of the **Buddha**, and symbolized his presence. *Stūpas* have been found almost throughout the subcontinent, with the exception of the northeast, and Kerala. Traditions of *stūpa* building spread through Central Asia to China, Korea, and Japan as well as to Sri Lanka and Southeast Asia.

The earliest *stūpas* were probably earthen mounds. Later, these were encased with brick and, in many instances, stone. The mound contained a shaft, within which relics were placed, often in carefully prepared caskets. Relics could include corporal remains (such as the teeth, or bone fragments) of the Buddha or of important monks or articles that had been used by them. Some *stūpas* were commemorative of events and did not contain relics. A ceremonial umbrella (a symbol of royalty) and railings were often placed at the apex of the mound. The central mound was often surrounded by a circumambulatory path, with railings and gateways.

Some of the earliest extant *stūpas* date to the **Mauryan** period (c. third century CE) although **Asokan inscriptions** and Buddhist tradition suggest that the practice of constructing these mounds began earlier. While some of the earliest examples were roughly hemispherical, *stūpas* were built in a variety of shapes and sizes. Many *stūpas*, such as the great *stūpa* at **Sanchi**, continued to be embellished for centuries. Decorations on railings, pillars, and gateways include some of the best examples of stone **sculpture** known from early India. The construction and embellishment of these monuments was sustained by royal patrons as well as through donations made by monks, nuns, and lay supporters drawn from a wide range of social categories.

Sites with remains of *stūpas* include **Adam**, **Adurru**, **Ahichchhatra**, **Amaravati**, **Antichak**, **Banarsihankalan**, **Bavikonda**, **Bharatpur**, **Bharhut**, **Bhattiprolu**, **Bodh Gaya**, **Chandraketugarh**, **Devanimori**, **Gopalapatnam**, **Hasargundigi**, **Jaggayyapeta**, **Jetavana**, **Kanaganahalli**, **Karle**, **Kasia**, **Kasrawad**, **Kausambi**, **Khiching**, **Kolhua**, **Kondapur**, **Kumrahar**, **Kusinagara**, **Lalitagiri**, **Lauriya**

Nandangarh, **Lumbini**, **Mathura**, **Nagarjunakonda**, **Nalanda**, **Navdatoli**, **Nelakondapalli**, **Paharpur**, **Panguraria**, **Pāṭaliputra**, **Pavurallakonda**, **Peddavegi**, **Piprahwa**, **Sanghol**, **Sankissa**, **Sannati**, **Sarnath**, **Satdhara**, **Shaji-ki-dheri**, **Shyamsundar Tila**, **Sopara**, **Sravasti**, **Takht-i-Bahi**, **Taradih**, **Taxila**, **Ter**, **Thotlakonda**, **Tumain**, **Ujjayinī**, **Vadagokugiri**, **Vadamanu**, and **Vaishali**. *See also CAITYA*; CUNNINGHAM, ALEXANDER; DISPOSAL OF THE DEAD; EARLY HISTORIC PERIOD; IKṢVĀKU (2); INDO-GREEK; KANIṢKA.

SUBHĀGASENA. Ruler in the northwestern part of the subcontinent (late third–early second centuries BCE), who may have established an independent **kingdom** in the region, breaking away from **Mauryan** control. *See also* ANTIOCHOS III THE GREAT.

ŚŪDRA**.** **Sanskrit** term used (c. first millennium BCE onward) to designate the fourth category in the fourfold ***varṇa*** order. The **Dharmasūtras** and the early **Dharmaśāstras** prescribed servitude as the sole legitimate duty of this category. The texts also excluded *śūdras* (as well as **women**) from the exercise of ritual rights, including performing **sacrifices** and learning the **Vedas**. However, by the **early medieval period**, *śūdras* and women were given access to texts such as the Sanskrit **epics** and the **Purāṇas**. The latter texts occasionally described certain ruling lineages, such as the **Mauryas**, as being of *śūdra* origin, and there are other indications to suggest that *śūdras* may have had access to material resources. As in the case of the ***vaiśya***, the term *śūdra* is rarely used as a marker of identity in **inscriptions**. *See also DĀNA*; INHERITANCE LAWS; *SAMṢKĀRA*; SLAVERY; UNTOUCHABILITY; *VARṆASAMṢKARA*.

ŚŪDRAKA. **Sanskrit** playwright (c. early centuries CE?), author of the ***Mṛcchakaṭikam***. He is represented in the prologue of the text as being versed in the ***Ṛgveda***, ***Sāmaveda***, in **mathematics**, **courtesanal** lore, and in elephant lore. *See also* DRAMA; LITERATURE.

SUGANDHĀ. One of the queens to rule in Kashmir (904–906 CE), Sugandhā began as the guardian of her minor son, but soon exercised power independently, issuing **coins** in her own name. She was ousted from power, and was killed in 914 when she attempted to stage a comeback. *See also* WOMEN.

SUGH. Archaeological site in Haryana, with evidence of two occupational phases, both **early historic**. Period I (c. fifth–first centuries BCE) provided evidence of **Painted Grey Ware**, **Northern Black Polished Ware**, ring wells, **iron tools**, **punch-marked copper** and silver **coins**, coins of **Menander** and **Antimachus**, **terracotta** figurines, and beads of semiprecious stone and glass. Bones of cattle, horse, sheep, goat, and pig have been recovered. Finds from Period II (c. first century BCE–third century CE) are similar, apart from traces of mud-brick and burnt-brick structures. **Pottery** included red ware and **Red Polished Ware**.

ŚULBASŪTRA. Sanskrit prose ritual texts, part of the **later Vedic** corpus, dealing with the construction of the **sacrificial** altar, dated to c. mid–first millennium BCE, which indicate the development and application of geometrical principles. *See also* LITERATURE; MATHEMATICS; *VEDĀṄGA*.

SUNDARĀR. *See* CUNTARĀR.

SUNET. Archaeological site in the Punjab with six occupational phases. Period I (c. 1800–1400 BCE) has been designated as **Late Harappan**. Period II (c. 1000–600 BCE) is associated with finds of **Painted Grey Ware**. Period III (c. 600–200 BCE) yielded **black slipped ware**. Other finds included a **terracotta seal**. Period IV (c. 200 BCE–300 CE) was assigned to the **Śaka–Kuṣāṇa** period. Finds consisted of Kuṣāṇa **coins** and a hoard of 30,000 coins of the **Yaudheyas**. Finds of coin molds of the latter indicate that the site may have housed a mint. Period V (c. 300–600 CE) was associated with the **Guptas**. Finds from this period included seals and sealings. Period VI (c. 600–800 CE) was designated as **early medieval**. *See also* CAST COINS.

ŚUṄGA. Ruling dynasty of ***brāhmaṇa* (1)** origin, which established control over north and parts of central India (c. 181 BCE–73 BCE). According to tradition, the first ruler of this dynasty, **Puṣyamitra**, overthrew and killed the last **Mauryan** ruler. *See also* AGNIMITRA; KANVA; KINGSHIP.

ŚŪRASENA. ***Mahājanapada*** (c. sixth century BCE), with its capital at **Mathura**.

SURKH KOTAL. Archaeological site in Afghanistan, find spot of a **temple** and **sculptures** of **Kuṣāṇa kings** as well as **inscriptions**. *See also* RABATAK INSCRIPTION.

SURKOTADA. A **fortified Harappan** settlement (c. second half of the third millennium BCE) in Gujarat. Finds include Harappan **seals** and **pottery**. There is evidence for **black and red ware** from later (c. second millennium BCE) occupational levels at the site.

SŪRPĀRAKA. Ancient name of present-day **Sopara**.

SŪRYAVAMṢ́A. Sanskrit term meaning "**solar** lineage," adopted by several **early medieval** dynasties. *See also* MANU.

SUŚRUTA. Author (c. sixth century BCE?) of a **medical** text in **Sanskrit**, the ***Suśruta Saṃhitā***, one of the earliest attempts to codify surgical knowledge. *See also* LITERATURE.

***SUŚRUTA SAṂHITĀ*. Sanskrit medical** text attributed to **Suśruta**, compiled c. early first millennium CE. The text consists of two parts, discussing surgical instruments and surgical procedures, respectively, the latter being classified into eight categories. The text is suggestive of the importance assigned to practical experience in the field. *See also* LITERATURE.

SŪTA*. Sanskrit** term used in **later Vedic** texts (c. 1000–500 BCE) to designate the charioteer or bard associated with the chief or **king**. The *sūta* accompanied his patron on his campaigns, and was expected to compose and sing his praises on ritual and other occasions. Traditionally, some of the narratives incorporated in the ***Mahābhārata and the **Purāṇas** are recognized as being derived from the stories preserved by the *sūta*. The *sūta* seems to have lost social standing during the **early historic period**, when the **Dharmaśāstras** generally classify them among the "low-born."

SUTKAGENDOR. Fortified Mature Harappan (c. third millennium BCE) settlement near the Makran coast, Pakistan, which may have been used as a halting station for vessels plying between the Harappan civilization and Mesopotamia.

SŪTRA. **Sanskrit** term meaning "thread," used, c. mid–first millennium BCE onward, for a category of prescriptive or normative texts dealing with a wide range of subjects. *Sūtras* were generally composed in terse prose and consisted of formulaic sentences. *See also* LITERATURE.

SŪTRAKṚTĀṄGA. *See SUYAGADA.*

SUTTA PIṬAKA. **Pali** text consisting of five sections: the ***Dīgha Nikāya***, ***Majjhima Nikāya***, ***Samyutta Nikāya***, ***Aṅguttara Nikāya***, and ***Khuddaka Nikāya***, compiled, according to early **Buddhist** tradition, during the first **Buddhist Council**. Many of the texts in the first four anthologies are attributed to the **Buddha** and may date between c. fourth and third centuries BCE. These include discussions on a range of doctrines pertaining to early Buddhism. The compilation of these texts is attributed to Ānanda, often recognized as the chief disciple of the Buddha. *See also DHAMMAPADA*; LITERATURE.

SUVARṆAGIRI. **City** mentioned in **Asokan inscriptions** as the capital of the southern part of the **Mauryan** Empire, often identified with **Brahmagiri**.

SUYAGADA. **Prakrit Jaina** text, also known as the *Sūtrakṛtāṅga*, perhaps compiled c. first millennium CE, recognized as the second of the ***aṅgas***. Part of the text was composed in the form of a dialogue between a monk and his disciple. The text consists of two parts, dealing with Jaina doctrine, the norms monks were expected to observe, and critiques of other contemporary **religious** and **philosophical** traditions. *See also* LITERATURE.

SVĀMIDATTA. Ruler (c. fourth century CE) of a region known as Koṭṭūra, possibly in present-day Orissa, mentioned in the **Allahabad Pillar Inscription** of the **Gupta** ruler **Samudragupta** as one of those who was captured and then released when he submitted to the Gupta **king**.

ŚVETĀMBARA. Jaina sect, so-called because of their adoption of white clothes in contrast to the **Digambaras**. The latter held that the canonical tradition was lost, while the former recognized the existence of canonical texts, the 12 ***aṅgas***. Unlike the Digambaras, the Śvetāmbaras believed that **women** could attain liberation. These sectarian differences probably crystallized toward the end of the first millennium BCE. *See also* DEVARDHI GANI; HARIBHADRA SŪRĪ; STHŪLABHADRA.

SWAMINATHA IYER, U. V. (b. 1855–d. 1942). Tamil scholar who systematically collected **manuscripts** relating to ancient and medieval Tamil **literature** and brought to light several texts including the Tamil **epics**, and the corpus of ***Sangam*** literature. He edited and published many of these works, laying the foundation for subsequent studies in Tamil language and literature. His writings, including an unfinished autobiography, are available in eight volumes.

– T –

T. NARSIPUR. Archaeological site in Karnataka with two occupational phases. Period I is **Neolithic** (c. second millennium BCE?) with evidence of ground stone axes, handmade **pottery**, and **burials**. Period II is **megalithic** (c. first millennium BCE), with evidence of **Black and Red Ware** and **iron** equipment.

TAGARA. Early historic city mentioned in textual traditions, identified with **Ter**. According to the ***Periplus of the Erythraean Sea***, **textiles** were sent from Tagara to the port of **Barygaza**.

TAKALGHAT–KHAPA. Twin **megalithic** (c. first millennium BCE) sites in Maharashtra. Finds included **Black and Red Ware**; a variety of **iron** equipment; bones of cattle, pig, and horse; and **burials** of horses with the dead, at Khapa. Other finds consisted of beads of semiprecious stone and glass.

TAKHT-I-BAHI. Archaeological site in the North-West Frontier Province, Pakistan, with evidence of **monasteries** and ***stūpas*** dated to the **Kuṣāṇa** period (c. early first millennium CE), recognized as a World Heritage Site by UNESCO. *See also* GONDOPHERNES.

TAKIAPER. **Archaeological** site in Uttar Pradesh. Two occupational phases have been identified. Period I (c. mid–first millennium BCE) yielded **black and red ware** and **Northern Black Polished Ware**, **copper** and **iron** artifacts, animal bones, and **terracotta** figurines. Finds from Period II (c. early centuries CE) included traces of stone **architecture** and a **seal**.

TAKṢAŚILĀ. See TAXILA.

TALKAD. **Archaeological** site in Karnataka, with evidence of occupation during the **early historic** (c. early first millennium BCE) and **early medieval periods**. Finds from the first phase included **pottery**, **iron** artifacts, **terracotta** figurines, beads of semiprecious stone, and ivory and shell objects. There is evidence of a brick structure, possibly a **Jaina** shrine (c. seventh–eighth centuries CE), a terracotta **coin** mold, and stone **sculpture** that has affinities with **Pallava** styles.

TĀMBAPANNI. Name for Sri Lanka, used in **Asokan inscriptions** (c. mid–third century BCE.

TAMIL. One of the oldest **languages** of the subcontinent, belonging to the **Dravidian** family. Tamil loan words have been identified in the ***Ṛgveda***. It is also likely that some of the **megalithic** cultures of south India were associated with peoples using the language. The earliest Tamil texts available at present are those of the ***Sangam*** anthologies (c. third century BCE onward). *See also AINKURUNŪRU*; *AKAM*; *AKANĀNŪRU*; CUNTARĀR; *DRĀVIḌA*; EARLY HISTORIC PERIOD; *EṬṬUTOKAI*; INSCRIPTIONS; *KALITTOKAI*; KONKU VELIR; *KURUNTOKAI*; *MALAIPATUKATAM*; MĀNIKKAVĀCAKAR; *MAṆIMEKALAI*; *MULLAIPPĀṬṬU*; *NĀLĀYIRA TIVIYA PIRAPANTAM*; *NAṞṞINAI*; *PARIPĀṬAL*; *PATIṞṞUPATTU*; *PAṬṬINAPPĀLAI*; *PATTUPĀṬṬU*; *PERUNKATAI*; *PINKALANTAI*; *PURANĀNURU*; *RĀMĀVATĀRAM*; *SILAPPADIKĀRAM*; *SIRIPANAṞṞUPPATAI*; SWAMINATHA IYER, U. V.; TAMIL BRĀHMĪ INSCRIPTIONS; *TEVĀRAM*; TIRUJÑĀNA

CAMPANTAR; *TIRUKKURAḶ*; TIRUMANKAI ĀḺVĀR; TIRUMULAR; *TIRUMURUKĀṞṞUPPAṬAI*; TIRUNĀVUKKARACAR; TIRUTTAKKA TEVAR; *TIRUVĀCAKAM*; TIRUVAḶḶUVĀR; *TIVĀKARAM*; *TOLKĀPPIYAM*.

TAMIL BRĀHMĪ INSCRIPTIONS. Name assigned to **inscriptions** found in **rock-cut** and natural caves, located along **trade routes**, among the oldest known inscriptions in **Tamil**, written in the **Brāhmī script**, which was modified to take into account the phonetic specificities of the **language**. Most of these are short votive inscriptions, which date to the late first millennium BCE–early first millennium CE and record grants to **Jaina** and, in some instances, **Buddhist** monks.

TAMLUK. *See* TĀMRALIPTI.

TĀMRALIPTI. Archaeological site in West Bengal identified with present-day Tamluk, with evidence of five occupational phases. Period I has been designated as **Neolithic** (c. second millennium BCE?). Period II (c. fourth–second centuries BCE) was associated with **black and red ware**, **black slipped ware**, **Northern Black Polished Ware**, **coins**, and **terracotta** figurines. Finds from Period III included **rouletted ware**, **Red Polished Ware**, and remains of a brick tank and ring wells. Period IV yielded **sculpture** belonging to the **Gupta** (mid–first millennium CE) age. The last period, V, has been assigned to the **Pāla** (late first millennium CE) phase. *See also* COPPER.

TANTRA. Systems of **religious** thought and practice that were codified from the **early medieval period** onward. In terms of **philosophy**, some of the principles were derived from **Sāṃkhya** and recognized the importance of the feminine principle in creation. Initiation into the tradition by gurus, who could be men or **women** belonging to the "lower" social orders, was considered essential. There was an emphasis on ritual praxis, including, in some instances, symbolic or actual sexual intercourse, which was regarded as liberating if undertaken in the proper context. Tantric beliefs and practices influenced both **Brahmanical** traditions and **Buddhism** and were prevalent in several parts of the subcontinent. *See also* PĀLA; TRIBES; *VAJRAYĀNA*.

TANTRICISM. Name assigned by modern scholars and historians of **religion** (c. 19th century onward) to beliefs and practices derived from ***tantra***. *See also* HINDUISM; *SATĪ*; UDAYAGIRI.

TAPTI. River rising in Madhya Pradesh, central India, and flowing westward through Maharashtra and Gujarat into the Arabian Sea.

TARADIH. Archaeological site in Bihar with evidence of occupation c. second millennium BCE onward. The earliest levels (Period I) yielded evidence of a **Neolithic** settlement. Finds included handmade **pottery**, hearths, ground stone **tools**, such as pestles, and bone tools, including points and arrows. The subsequent **Chalcolithic** levels (Period II) yielded **black and red ware**, grinding stones, bone arrowheads, **copper** ornaments and tools, microbeads of steatite, other stone beads, and **terracotta** figurines. **Iron**-bearing levels (Period III, c. first millennium BCE) provided evidence of tools, including nails and knives. Traces of paddy husk were also found. Later levels (Period IV, mid–first millennium BCE) yielded **Northern Black Polished Ware**, iron tools and slag, sealings, **cast** copper **coins**, and shell bangles. There is also evidence of burnt-brick structures. Finds from the subsequent level (V), assigned to the **Kuṣāṇa** period (c. first century BCE–first century CE), included red pottery, glass beads, and traces of a burnt-brick structure. Period VI, assigned to the **Gupta** period (c. fourth–sixth centuries CE), provided evidence of a **monastery**, iron artifacts, including needles, and bone ornaments. Other finds included votive ***stūpas***, stone **sculpture** of the **Buddha**, terracotta **seals**, sealings, and figurines. There were also traces of a rampart. The last phase was associated with a monastery, *stūpa*, votive *stūpas*, seals, and sealings of the **Pāla** period (c. 8th–11th centuries CE).

TAXATION. *See* REVENUE SYSTEMS.

TAXILA. Early historic (c. sixth century BCE onward) **city** in the Punjab, Pakistan, mentioned in Greek texts, including accounts of the invasion of **Alexander (of Macedon)**, known in early **Sanskrit** sources as Takṣaśilā. The site consists of three principal mounds, those of Bhir, Sirkap, and Sirsukh. The earliest evidence of occupation is from the Bhir Mound. Early levels yielded **pottery** resembling the **Northern Black Polished Ware** and **punch-marked coins**. There were traces of wells and drains. Other remains included those of ***stūpas***, of which the most prominent is the Dharmarājika, possibly built by **Asoka**, and **monasteries**. Asokan **inscriptions** indicate that Taxila was a provincial capital under the **Mauryas**. The city was described as an important center of learning in **Buddhist** texts. While the Bhir Mound was a relatively unplanned settlement, Sirkap, which was probably built by the **Bactrian Greeks**, was a planned settlement. Structural remains from Sirkap included an apsidal Buddhist shrine. Other finds consisted of coins, **sculpture**, gold and silver jewelry, pearls, amethysts, coral, and so on. Sirsukh, which was settled during the **Kuṣāṇa** period, has not been systematically explored. Taxila evidently owed its importance to its crucial location along the ***uttarāpatha***, one of the major **routes** running through north India and linking with Afghanistan and Central Asia. Taxila has been recognized as a World Heritage Site by UNESCO. *See also* CAST COINS; DEMETRIOS; GANDHĀRA; HELIODOROS; INDO-GREEK; MARSHALL, JOHN HUBERT; MAUES; MENANDER.

TEKKALAKOTTA. Archaeological site in Karnataka, with evidence of **Neolithic** and later occupations. The first phase (c. second millennium BCE) yielded microliths, ground stone axes, bone **tools**, beads of semiprecious stone, ornaments of gold and **copper**, and handmade **pottery**. Animal remains included bones of cattle, sheep, mollusks, rodents, and tortoise. The second phase (c. first millennium BCE) provided evidence of **Black and Red Ware**.

TEMPLES. While shrines are referred to in early textual traditions (c. mid–first millennium BCE onward), definite structural remains of temples have been identified from the first millennium CE. Temples generally consisted of a central shrine known as the *garbhagṛha*, which housed the image of the principal deity. The entrance to the shrine was often decorated with **sculpture** depicting auspicious symbols or minor deities who were visualized as gatekeepers. Some of the earliest temples, such as those at **Deogarh**, were made of brick and stone. While temples in north India were freestanding structures, traditions of constructing **rock-cut** temples emerged in the Deccan and elsewhere in peninsular

India. **Inscriptions** found in or near temples or on the walls indicate that rulers and feudatories often provided the resources for temple construction and **land grants** for their maintenance. Temples became centers of devotional cults, associated with traditions of ***Bhakti***.

By the sixth century CE, temples began acquiring a tower, known as the *śikhara*, constructed over the central shrine. Later, pavilions, porches, and entrances were added on. The Kailasanatha temple at **Kanchipuram**, attributed to the **Pallava** ruler **Narasiṃhavarman II** (c. eighth century CE), displays some of the typical **architectural** features of later south Indian temples. These include an enclosure wall, gateways, a pillared hall, and towers over the central shrine. The walls of many of these shrines were decorated with elaborate sculpture, depicting scenes from the **Purāṇas**. Several regions evolved distinctive styles of temple construction, which were further elaborated in the course of the late first and second millennia CE.

Sites with remains of temples include **Ahichchhatra**, **Aihole**, **Apsadh**, **Atranjikhera**, **Badami**, **Banavasi**, **Bhitargaon**, **Bhitari**, **Bodh Gaya**, **Chandraketugarh**, **Ellora**, **Gop**, **Gopagiri**, **Goraj**, **Gudnapura**, **Kandhar**, **Kashipur**, **Khiching**, **Khokrakot**, **Lumbini**, **Mahasthan**, **Malhar**, **Mamallapuram**, **Mandhal**, **Mangalkot**, **Martand**, **Mathura**, **Mulchera**, **Nachna Kuthara**, **Nadner**, **Nagarjunakonda**, **Osian**, **Paharpur**, **Pattadakal**, **Peddavegi**, **Sanchi**, **Sannati**, **Sirpur**, **Sonkh**, **Sopara**, **Sugh**, **Surkh Kotal**, **Takiaper**, **Thanjavur**, **Ujjayinī**, **Vadagokugiri**, and **Vidisha**. *See also* CITIES; COḺA; EARLY MEDIEVAL PERIOD; GAṄGA (1); GODDESS CULTS; GUPTA; HINDUISM; *MAṆIGRĀMAM*; MĀNIKKAVĀCAKAR; PĀÑCARĀTRA; PURĀṆIC RELIGION; RĀJARĀJA I; RĀJENDRA; RĀṢṬRAKŪṬA; SEALS; VAIṢṆAVISM; VIJAYĀDITYA; WARFARE.

TER. **Archaeological** site in Maharashtra, identified with **Tagara**, mentioned in early Indian as well as Greco-Roman texts. Excavations have yielded remains of a ***stūpa*** built along a spoke-wheel plan. Other structures included remains of a brick-built tank (c. first century CE). There is also evidence of a **fortification** wall. Associated **pottery** consisted of **Northern Black Polished Ware**, **Red Polished Ware**, and **black and red ware**. **Coins**, including those of the **Sātavāhanas** and **Kṣatrapas**, have been recovered from the site. Other finds consisted of beads of semiprecious stone, shell bangles, bone and ivory pieces, stone **sculpture**, **terracotta** figurines, clay bullae of Roman origin, and glass bottles.

TERDAL. Archaeological site in Karnataka with evidence of two occupational phases. Period I, considered **Chalcolithic** (c. second millennium BCE), provided evidence of ground stone axes and microliths. **Pottery** included gray ware similar to that from **Maski** and other varieties resembling **Savalda Ware**. Period II (c. 1200–700 BCE) provided evidence of **megalithic burials** and **Black and Red Ware**.

TERRACOTTA. Terracotta artifacts are among the most common finds at **archaeological** sites. These include figurines of animals such as the bull, **women**, and less frequently men. While some of these may have been toys, others probably had decorative or ritual uses. Finds from **Harappan** sites include terracotta cakes, often of a roughly triangular shape. The use to which these cakes were put is uncertain. Terracotta ring wells have been frequently found at **early historic** sites. It is likely that these were meant for disposing of refuse and/or were used for sanitation. Other terracotta artifacts include spindle whorls. Several sites have yielded finely produced terracotta plaques, decorated with **sculpture**, the exact significance of which remains uncertain. Terracotta beads and bangles have also been found. It is possible that these were used by ordinary people as substitutes for the more expensive gold, silver, or stone jewelry that may have been worn by the elite. Terracotta **seals** and sealings, generally containing **inscriptions** in **Brāhmī**, have been recovered from several early historic and **early medieval** sites.

Sites that have yielded terracotta artifacts including figurines are **Adam**, **Adichannallur**, **Agiabir**, **Ahar**, **Ahichchhatra**, **Ambari**, **Ambkheri**, **Antichak**, **Atranjikhera**, **Ayodhya**, **Balakot**, **Balathal**, **Balu**, **Banahalli**, **Banarsihankalan**, **Banavasi**, **Bangarh**, **Bhagwanpura**, **Bharuch**, **Bhita**, **Bhitargaon**, **Bhorgarh**, **Brass**, **Campā**, **Chandraketugarh**, **Chirand**, **Daimabad**, **Dangwada**, **Dat Nagar**, **Daulatpur**, **Desalpur**, **Dholavira**, **Dhuriapar**, **Dihar**, **Donder Khera**, **Eran**, **Erich**, sites of the **Gandhara Grave Culture**, **Ganwaria**, **Gilaulikhera**, **Gilund**, **Golbai Sasan**, **Gopalapatnam**, **Gudnapura**, **Hallur**, **Harappa**, **Hasargundigi**, **Hastinapura**, **Hulas**, **Hulas Khera**, **Imlidih Khurd**, **Inamgaon**, **Jakhera**, **Jhusi**, **Jodh-**

pura, **Kalibangan**, **Kampil**, **Kanaganahalli**, **Kanauj**, **Kanchipuram**, **Kashipur**, **Kasrawad**, **Katra**, **Kausambi**, **Kayatha**, **Khairadih**, **Khokrakot**, **Kodumanal**, **Kolhua**, **Kondapur**, **Kotasur**, **Kudikadu**, **Kulli**, **Kumrahar**, **Kunnatur**, **Lalitagiri**, **Lal Qila**, **Lauriya Nandangarh**, **Lothal**, **Malhar**, **Maner**, **Mangalkot**, **Manjhi**, **Mansar**, **Masaon**, **Maski**, **Mathura**, **Mitathal**, **Musanagar**, **Nadner**, **Nagara**, **Nagari**, **Nagda**, **Nageshwar**, **Nagiari**, **Narhan**, **Nasik**, **Nelakondapalli**, **Nevasa**, **Noh**, **Oriup**, **Padri**, **Paharpur**, **Paiyampalli**, **Pandu Rajar Dhibi**, **Pāṭaliputra**, **Pauni**, **Peddavegi**, **Rajmahal**, **Rakhi Garhi**, **Ramapuram**, **Rojdi**, **Ropar**, **Sanchi**, **Sanghol**, **Sannati**, **Shirkanda**, **Shri Shri Suryapahar**, **Shyamsundar Tila**, **Sisupalgarh**, **Sodanga**, **Sonkh**, **Sonpur**, **Sravasti**, **Sringaverapura**, **Sunet**, **Talkad**, **Tāmralipti**, **Taradih**, **Ter**, **Tharsa**, **Timbarra**, **Tripuri**, **Udayagiri**, **Uraiyur**, **Utawad**, **Vadagokugiri**, **Vadgaon Madhavpur**, **Vadodara**, **Vaishali**, **Valmiyo Timbo**, and **Wina**.

TEVĀRAM. **Tamil** text, literally meaning "in praise of the lord," containing the compositions of **Tirunāvukkaracar**, **Tirujñāna Campantar**, and **Cuntarār**, all part of the **Nāyanār** tradition. According to tradition, the text was compiled during the reign of **Rājarāja Coḻa** (c. 10th–11th centuries CE). *See also* LITERATURE.

TEXTILES. The evidence for the cultivation of plant fibers such as cotton is found from **Neolithic** sites in the northwest of the subcontinent and from **Harappan** sites. **Terracotta** spindle whorls found at several **early historic** sites point to a well-developed system of textile production. Representations of textiles in **sculpture** and **painting** indicate that cloth was sometimes decorated with designs that may have been printed, painted, woven, or embroidered. Texts such as the ***Arthaśāstra*** discuss aspects of textile production, including the use of **women** laborers. It is likely that production was organized at several levels, ranging from the household at one end of the spectrum to workshops controlled by the state, as suggested by the *Arthaśāstra*. Other sources, such as the ***Periplus of the Erythraean Sea***, provide evidence of the demand for a wide variety of cotton textiles produced in the subcontinent. Weavers' **guilds** find mention in **inscriptions**. Recognized centers of textile production included **Kāśi** in the north and **Tagara** and **Madurai** in the south. *See also* ARIKAMEDU; BARYGAZA; TRADE; URAIYUR; VAṄGA.

THANESAR. Archaeological site in Haryana, identified as Sthānīśvara, mentioned in **Sanskrit** literature. Finds include **Painted Grey Ware** (c. first millennium BCE). The major occupation dates from the **Kuṣāṇa** (c. first century BCE–third century CE) period onward. Finds from Kuṣāṇa levels consisted of **terracotta** sealings, figurines, and plaques; red ware; beads of semiprecious stone; ivory and shell bangles; and **copper coins**. Traces of a mud rampart have also been assigned to this period. Subsequent levels, assigned to the **Gupta** period (c. fourth–sixth centuries CE), have yielded stone **sculpture** including images of **Viṣṇu** and other **Brahmanical** deities. Other finds consisted of beads of semiprecious stone, terracotta figurines and sealings, and structural remains. The city emerged as a major political center of north India c. sixth–seventh centuries CE, when it was associated with rulers such as **Harṣavardhana**. In fact, a local mound is named Harsh ka Tila after him. Finds from this phase included remains of a massive brick building, stone **inscriptions**, beads of semiprecious stone, terracotta **seals** and molds, shell and ivory bangles, coins, and terracotta figurines.

THANJAVUR. Capital of the **Co<u>l</u>as**, in present-day Tamil Nadu. The Co<u>l</u>a **king Rājarāja I** constructed the famous Bṛhadīśvara **temple** (also known as the Rājarājeśvara temple after him), one of the best-known **Śaiva** shrines, in the **city**. This became the nucleus of the settlement, with **traders** and **craftspersons** clustering around the neighborhood of the shrine. **Inscriptions** indicate that the temple was supported through **land grants**. *See also* VIJAYĀLAYA.

THARSA. Archaeological site in Maharashtra, with evidence of four occupational phases. Period I (c. first millennium BCE) has been characterized as **Chalcolithic** or **megalithic**. Finds included **Black and Red Ware**, **terracotta** spindle whorls, bone artifacts, grinding stones, and **copper** ornaments. Period II, associated with the **Sātavāhana** phase (c. second century BCE–second century CE), provided evidence for the use of **iron**, **pottery**, beads of semiprecious stone, and terracotta figurines. Finds from Period III, associated with the **Vākātakas** (c.

fourth–sixth centuries CE), consisted of beads, glass bangles, and terracotta figurines. Period IV has been assigned to the medieval period.

THERAGĀTHĀ*.** **Pali** text, part of the ***Tripiṭaka, and of the ***Khuddaka Nikāya***, compiled c. first century BCE. It includes **poems** attributed to 264 **Buddhist** monks, recounting their experiences of attaining liberation. *See also* LITERATURE.

THERAVĀDA. Literally the path or tradition of the elders, name of one of the earliest sects within **Buddhism** (c. sixth century BCE onward), which emphasized the quest for individual enlightenment and was often defined in opposition to the **Mahāyāna** school of thought. The Theravāda tradition remains influential in Sri Lanka and Southeast Asia. *See also* MAHĀSAMGHIKA; NĀGĀRJUNA; PALI; *SARVĀSTIVĀDA*.

THERĪGĀTHĀ*.** **Pali** text, part of the ***Tripiṭaka and the ***Khuddaka Nikāya***, compiled c. first century BCE. It consists of an anthology of more than 70 hymns attributed to **Buddhist** nuns, who recounted their experiences of attaining liberation. *See also* LITERATURE.

THOTLAKONDA. **Archaeological** site in coastal Andhra Pradesh, overlooking the Bay of Bengal, with evidence of occupation between c. second century BCE and second century CE. Finds include a ***stūpa***, a pillared hall, a ***caitya***, **monasteries**, and **rock-cut** cisterns. There are also **sculptural** remains and **inscriptions**. Other finds consisted of votive *stūpas*, **coins** of the **Sātavāhanas** and the Roman emperor Tiberius, amphorae, and **iron** nails.

TILDAH. **Early historic** (c. mid–first millennium BCE?) **archaeological** site in West Bengal, with traces of a mud rampart and evidence of **Northern Black Polished Ware**.

TIMBARRA. **Archaeological** site in Gujarat with evidence of three occupational phases. Finds from Period I (c. mid–first millennium BCE) consisted of **black and red ware**, **Northern Black Polished Ware**, **iron** artifacts, and **terracotta** figurines. Period II (c. first–third centuries CE) yielded **Red Polished Ware** and **copper** artifacts and beads. Period III (c. 600–1000 CE) yielded iron artifacts.

***TĪRTHAṄKARA*. Sanskrit/Prakrit** term meaning "someone who is capable of leading people across the stream (of worldly existence)," a title used to designate **Jaina** teachers, c. mid–first millennium BCE onward. *See also KALPASŪTRA*; *MAHĀPURĀṆA*; MAHĀVĪRA; PĀRŚVA; ṚṢABHA.

TIRUJÑĀNA CAMPANTAR. Tamil Śaiva poet, also known as Jñānasambandar, c. seventh century CE, born of ***brāhmaṇa* (1)** parents. He is supposed to have visited more than 200 shrines and challenged **Jaina** influence by establishing **Śaivism** in the **Pāṇḍya kingdom**. More than 4,000 compositions attributed to him have survived to date. His devotional **poetry** is characterized by spiritual eroticism. *See also NĀYAṈĀR*; *TEVĀRAM*; TIRUNĀVUKKARACAR.

***TIRUKKURAḶ*. Tamil** composition attributed to **Tiruvaḷḷuvār** (c. sixth century CE). It consists of more than 1,300 couplets meant to serve as a guide to a virtuous life. The message is universalistic. As many as 10 commentaries were composed on the work. *See also* LITERATURE.

TIRUMANKAI ĀḺVĀR. Tamil poet and saint (c. seventh century CE), recognized as one of the ***āḻvārs***, author of a large number of compositions found in the ***Nālāyira Tiviya Pirapantam***. His works are sectarian, marked by anti-**Śaivite** sentiment, and are remarkable for both scholarship and spiritual eroticism. *See also* LITERATURE.

TIRUMULAR. Tamil poet (c. sixth century CE), who composed more than 3,000 verses in praise of **Śiva**. *See also* LITERATURE.

TIRUMURUKĀṞṞUPPAṬAI*. Tamil** (c. seventh–eighth centuries CE) composition, one of the **poems** of the ***Pattupāṭṭu. It belongs to a genre of songs addressed to a patron, and meant to invoke generosity. In this case, the composition, running to about 300 lines, is addressed to the deity Murukaṉ. *See also* LITERATURE.

TIRUNĀVUKKARACAR. Tamil poet (c. 610–691 CE) who belonged to a ***vellālār*** family. He initially supported **Jainism** but later adopted **Śaivism**. He visualized himself as a servant of the deity. He visited more than 100 Śaivite shrines. More than 3,000 of his compositions, primarily devotional poems, survive. His compositions are marked by a spirit of humility. The name Appar, meaning "father," was given to him by **Tirujñāna Campantar**. He is credited with winning the **Pallava** ruler **Mahendravarman** to Śaivism. His compositions were included in the ***Tevāram***. *See also* LITERATURE; *NĀYAṈĀR*.

TIRUTTAKKA TEVAR. Tamil Jaina poet (c. ninth century CE). Jaina legends recognize him as a member of the **Co̱la** royal family, who joined the Jaina monastic order. He is regarded as the author of a love poem, which depicts how the hero acquired eight wives. *See also* LITERATURE.

***TIRUVĀCAKAM.* Tamil** (c. ninth century CE) anthology of **poems**, attributed to **Mānikkavācakar**. The anthology includes about 650 verses that are marked by a high devotional quality. *See also* LITERATURE.

TIRUVAḶḶUVĀR. Tamil author, c. sixth century CE, composer of the ***Tirukkuraḷ***. He was probably a **Jaina**, a weaver or a herald. *See also* AUVAIYAR; LITERATURE.

***TIVĀKARAM.* Tamil** dictionary, compiled c. ninth century CE by Tivākarar. The text lists about 9,500 words and consists of 12 sections, most of which deal with synonyms, while the 11th section deals with homonyms. *See also* LITERATURE.

TOLKĀPPIYAM. The earliest available **Tamil** work on grammar (c. fifth century CE?). It discusses the structure of the **language**, including nouns, verbs, and morphology. It also contains a section on **poetry**, prosody, and rhetoric. *See also* LITERATURE; TOLKĀPPIYAR.

TOLKĀPPIYAR. Author of the ***Tolkāppiyam*** (c. fifth century CE?) who may have been a **Jaina**. *See also* LITERATURE.

TOṆḌAI MAṆḌALAM. Name of a region, part of present-day Tamil Nadu, centering around **Kanchipuram**. Both the **Pallavas** and the **Co̱las** attempted to assert control over this area.

TOṆṬARAṬIPPOṬI ĀḺVĀR. Tamil Vaiṣṇava saint (c. seventh century CE). According to tradition he belonged to a ***brāhmaṇa* (1)** family. His name means "dust on the feet of the devotees" (of the lord, i.e., Viṣṇu). His compositions are marked by an anti-**Jaina** sentiment.

TOOLS. Tools are among the most common finds at **archaeological** sites. These range from the earliest stone tools that date back to the **Paleolithic** period and were used for digging and cutting, chopping, scraping, skinning, and preparing plant and animal produce for consumption. Subsequently, in the **Mesolithic** period, microliths may have served as arrowheads, and ground stone equipment, including mortars, pestles, axes, and hoes, is often regarded as evidence of a growing dependence on **agricultural** production and the processing of grain and other plant produce for food during the **Neolithic** phase. Both stone and metal equipment were invaluable for **craft** production—some of the fine **Harappan** beads and **seals** were manufactured using a variety of materials, while carpentry, including the manufacture of carts, chariots, and boats, was facilitated by the use of **iron** equipment.

Most of the earliest tools were made through flaking pebbles and shaping them into a suitable artifact. Virtually nothing is known about the ways in which tool making was organized. Sites that have yielded Paleolithic tools include **Amaravati**, **Arangpur**, **Attirampakkam**, **Banki**, sites in the **Belan Valley**, **Bhimbetka**, **Chirki-on-Pravara**, **Didwana**, **Hemmige**, **Hirapur Khadan**, sites along the **Hunsgi-Baichbal**, **Kurnool**, **Maheshwar**, **Manigara**, sites in **Mayurbhanj**, **Nagarjunakonda**, sites along the **Narmada** valley, **Navdatoli**, **Nevasa**, **Paisra**, **Riwat**, **Rohri**, and **Sanghao**. Some sites such as **Birbhanpur**, Hemmige, **Lalmai Hills**, and **Pandu Rajar Dhibi** have yielded wooden tools, including those made of fossil wood.

The subsequent Mesolithic phase is associated with microliths, tiny stone tools that could have been used as arrowheads and as parts of composite tools such as sickles and saws. Microliths have been found from several sites: **Adam**, **Adamgarh**, **Ambakot**, Attirampakkam, **Bagor**, **Bahal**, **Balakot**, **Banahalli**, Banki, **Bharatpur**, Bhimbetka, Birbhanpur, **Brahmagiri**, **Chirand**, **Chopani Mando**, **Damdama**, **Dangwada**, **Datrana**, **Dhansura**, Didwana, **Dihar**, **Eran**, **Gandhur**, **Ganeshwar**, **Gilund**, **Gumla**, Hirapur Khadan, **Kakoria**, **Kakrehta**,

Kalibangan, **Kallur**, **Kuchai**, **Kupgal**, **Langhnaj**, **Loteshwar**, **Mahadaha**, **Mahagara**, **Mahisdal**, **Manamunda**, **Mangalkot**, **Maski**, **Mayiladumparai**, Nagarjunakonda, **Nagda**, **Nasik**, Nevasa, **Oriup**, **Pachikheri**, Paisra, **Pipri**, **Pithad**, **Sannati**, **Santhli**, **Sarai Nahar Rai**, **Shaktari Timbo**, **Sonpur**, **Tekkalakotta**, **Tripuri**, **Utawad**, **Vadodara**, **Vanpasari**, **Vidisha**, and **Watgal**.

Ground stone tools—including polished axes, mortars, and pestles, often regarded as equipment typical of societies that depend on domesticated plants as a source of food—are regarded as characteristically Neolithic. Sites that have yielded these tools include Banahalli, Chirand, **Daojali Hading**, Eran, **Garapadu**, **Golbai Sasan**, **Hallur**, Kallur, **Koldihwa**, Kuchai, Mahagara, **Malpur**, Maski, Mayiladumparai, **Mehrgarh**, **Paiyampalli**, **Taradih**, Tekkalakotta, and **T. Narsipur**.

Sites that have yielded other stone tools include **Atranjikhera**, **Banawali**, Banki, **Bara**, Bharatpur, **Bhawar**, Brahmagiri, Budihal, **Burzahom**, **Chandoli**, Chopani Mando, **Daimabad**, Damdama, Dangwada, Datrana, Eran, **Inamgaon**, **Jakhera**, **Jorwe**, **Katra**, **Kunal**, Kupgal, **Nadner**, **Nageshwar**, **Narhan**, Navdatoli, Nevasa, Pachikheri, **Padri**, Pandu Rajar Dhibi, Pipri, **Pynthorlangtein**, **Rajmahal**, **Ramapuram**, Rohri, Saipai, **Savalda**, **Tharsa**, **Utawad**, **Valmiyo Timbo**, Vanpasari, and Watgal.

Apart from stone, animal bones were also often worked into tools. Sites that have yielded bone tools include Adam, **Alamgirpur**, Atranjikhera, Banahalli, **Bara**, Bharatpur, Bhawar, Burzahom, **Campā**, **Chechar**, Chirand, Dihar, Garapadu, Golbai Sasan, **Hastinapura**, **Hulas Khera**, Jakhera, **Jhimjhimia Kalisthan**, **Jodhpura**, **Kaothe**, Katra, **Khairadih**, **Khajuri**, **Khokrakot**, Koldihwa, Kunal, Kurnool, Mahadaha, Mahagara, **Mahisdal**, Maner, Mangalkot, Maski, **Musanagar**, Nadner, Narhan, Nasik, Nevasa, Oriup, Paiyampalli, Pandu Rajar Dhibi, Rajmahal, **Shirkanda**, Sonpur, Taradih, Tekkalakotta, **Walki**, and **Wina**.

From the end of the fourth millennium BCE, there is evidence for the use of **copper** and, somewhat later, bronze. Sites that have yielded copper tools include **Ahar**, Alamgirpur, Atranjikhera, Banawali, Chandoli, **Desalpur**, Ganeshwar, Gilund, Golbai Sasan, Hastinapura, **Kayatha**, Kunal, Maheshwar, Mangalkot, Maski, Musanagar, Navdatoli, Nevasa, Padri, Pandu Rajar Dhibi, Pipri, Rajmahal, **Rajpur Parasu**, **Rojdi**, Taradih, and Valmiyo Timbo. It must be noted that the use of metal tools, including saws, chisels, knives, axes, needles, razors, drills, and so on, did not mean that stone and bone equipment was no longer produced. In fact, these materials continued to be in use for millennia.

The earliest evidence for the manufacture and use of iron tools dates to the end of the second millennium BCE–beginning of the first millennium BCE. Sites that have yielded iron tools include Adam, **Adichannallur**, **Agiabir**, Ahar, **Alagankulan**, Alamgirpur, **Arambha**, Atranjikhera, **Auroville**, Bahal, Banahalli, Bhawar, Bhimbetka, Brahmagiri, **Cheramangad**, Chirand, Dangwada, Dihar, Eran, Ganeshwar, Garapadu, Golbai Sasan, Hallur, Hastinapura, **Heggadehalli**, Hulas Khera, Jakhera, Jhimjhimia Kalisthan, Jodhpura, Kallur, Katra, Khajuri, Khokrakot, **Kodumanal**, **Lalitagiri**, Manamunda, Maner, Mangalkot, **Mansar**, Maski, Mayiladumparai, Musanagar, Nadner, Nagda, **Nalanda**, Narhan, Nasik, Nevasa, Pachikheri, Paiyampalli, Pandu Rajar Dhibi, **Raipur**, Rajmahal, **Ratura**, **Sekta**, **Sisupalgarh**, **Sugh**, Taradih, **Udayagiri**, **Valiyapadam**, and Wina.

TOPRA. Site in Haryana. Find spot of an **Asokan** pillar containing a set of the **Major Pillar Edicts**.

TORAMĀṆA. Hūṇa ruler who ruled over parts of central India during the late fifth–early sixth centuries CE. *See also* MIHIRAKULA.

TOSALI. *See* DHAULI.

TRADE. Long-distance exchange was an important element in the economy of the subcontinent from early times. The **archaeological** evidence from the **Harappan civilization** indicates that resources such as timber, metal, and semiprecious stones were procured from long distances along land, riverine, and sea **routes**, although the manner in which these resources were procured remains a matter of speculation.

From the **early historic period**, textual sources within the subcontinent as well as Greek and Roman accounts and archaeological evidence are indicative of trade both within the subcontinent and outside through a number of routes of communication. Finds of **Northern Black Polished Ware** and **punch-marked coins** from several sites within the subcontinent have been interpreted as evidence of trading networks. Greek and Roman sources refer to a wide range of produce obtained from the subcontinent, including spices, especially pepper (obtained from south India), perfumes, **textiles**, sugar, rice, ivory, **iron** and steel artifacts, dyestuffs, and exotic animals and birds that were in demand in the West. Roman coins, **pottery**, glassware, wine, and **slaves** were received in return. Silks and porcelain were probably imported from China, and the northwest of the subcontinent was incorporated within the **Silk Route** for several centuries.

While there have been suggestions that long-distance trade with the West declined with the collapse of the Western Roman Empire, recent studies indicate that the situation was more complex, and trade with other regions (including the Eastern Roman Empire and Southeast Asia) continued to flourish.

While some of the overseas trade was under the control of the Arabs, texts and **inscriptions** as well as **sculpture** and **painting** represent Indian mercantile traditions. Traders who controlled these networks of communication were often both wealthy and powerful. Terms used to designate traders or merchants include ***seṭṭhi* (Pali/Prakrit)** and *vanik* **(Sanskrit)**. *See also* BARBARICUM; BARYGAZA; CASTE; COSMAS INDIKOPLEUSTES; EARLY MEDIEVAL PERIOD; HIPPALUS; INDO-GREEK; KUṢĀṆA; MARITIME TRADE; PLINY; ROMAN COINS; *SĀRTHAVĀHA*; SEALS; TRADE ROUTES; TRANSPORT; *UTTARĀPATHA*; *VAIŚYA*; *VARṆA*; WARI BATESHWAR.

TRADE ROUTES. Ancient **trade** routes have been reconstructed with the help of both textual and **archaeological** evidence. The latter is particularly valuable for the period prior to the mid–first millennium BCE. Trade routes in the **Harappan civilization** have been reconstructed on the basis of finds of raw materials such as metals and stones and finished goods such as **seals** and beads, which point to the existence of routes connecting the heartland of the civilization with areas to the west as well as to other regions in the subcontinent.

From the mid–first millennium BCE onward, texts refer to two major clusters of routes, known as the ***uttarāpatha*** and the ***dakṣiṇāpatha*** (literally the northern and southern paths, respectively). Passes along the Western Ghats assumed importance along routes linking the Deccan Plateau to the western coast. Several sea routes emanated from ports along both the eastern and the western coasts. From the beginning of the first millennium CE, a major branch of the **Silk Route** passed through the western part of the subcontinent. *See also* MARITIME TRADE; SĀTAVĀHANA; TAMIL BRĀHMĪ INSCRIPTIONS.

TRANSPORT, MODES OF. A wide variety of modes of transport were in use in early India. These ranged from the use of human power and pack animals to bullock carts and boats. Visual representations available from the **Harappan civilization** point to the use of carts and boats. Early **Vedic** texts mention the use of the horse-drawn chariot. From the **early historic period** onward elephants were also used, especially by **kings**. *See also* TRADE.

TRAVELERS' ACCOUNTS. Travelers' accounts available in Greek, Chinese, and Arabic have often been used as a source for reconstructing early Indian history. Accounts in Greek include those written by men who accompanied **Alexander (of Macedon)** as well as the work of **Megasthenes**. Later writers in Greek and Latin frequently drew on these works.

The accounts in Chinese were written by **Buddhist** pilgrims who came to the subcontinent to learn about the precepts and practice of Buddhism and to collect texts, which they then translated into Chinese. Accounts in Arabic were written by scholars who were part of a wider universe of learning, located between East and West Asia on the one hand and Europe and North Africa on the other.

Nineteenth- and early 20th-century historians frequently treated these accounts at face value and tapped them for information. Subsequently, scholars have examined the intellectual and social contexts in which these narratives were written and circulated to arrive at a more nuanced understanding of their contents. The question of the possible informants of these travelers has also been explored. *See also* AL MASUDI; AMOGHAVARṢA; ARMY; COSMAS INDIKOPLEUSTES; DIODORUS SICULUS; FA XIAN; HERODOTUS; I CHING; XUAN ZANG.

TRIBES. Historians and anthropologists have classified certain groups of peoples in early India as tribes. The term is generally used for preliterate peoples, who used natural resources collectively and had distinctive social, cultural, and **religious** beliefs and practices. Tribal societies have been envisaged as relatively egalitarian in comparison to **caste** society. From this perspective, many of the **Neolithic** and **Chalcolithic** cultures evident in the **archaeological** record have been regarded as exemplifying the material culture of tribal societies.

Terms in texts, such as the words ***jana*** and ***viś*** used in the ***Ṛgveda*** (c. second millennium BCE), have often been interpreted as meaning "tribe" or "clan." In the **early historic period**, texts such as the ***Arthaśāstra*** elucidate policies that were meant to be adopted toward **forest** peoples, often regarded as synonymous with tribal populations. These indicate that they could be part of militias that were mobilized. **Asokan inscriptions** contain a message of firmness toward and a veiled threat of the use of force against such peoples. **Kings** or chiefs of forest peoples also figure in the **Allahabad Pillar Inscription** of **Samudragupta**, listed among those who were subjugated.

It is likely that the relationships between tribal groups and those who controlled kingdoms associated with stratified societies were complex and varied over time and space. There were networks of economic exchange, based on the demand for forest produce including animals, birds, timber, plant produce, and minerals. Tribal populations may have become increasingly differentiated as a result of contacts with kingdoms, and in some areas, tribal chiefs may have become kings in their own right.

In terms of religious beliefs, tribal cults were often assimilated within **Brahmanical** belief systems. These developments may have shaped both **Purāṇic** and **Tantric** traditions. *See also* ABASTANOI; ABHĪRA; AGRICULTURE; ARMY; BHARATA; EARLY MEDIEVAL PERIOD; *MALAIPATUKATAM*; PULINDA; SĀKYA.

TRIPIṬAKA**.** **Pali** term meaning "three baskets" used to refer to the anthologies of early **Buddhist** canonical works. The *Tripiṭaka* comprised the ***Abhidhamma***, ***Sutta***, and ***Vinaya***. *See also* BUDDHAGHOṢA; *DĪPAVAMSA*; *THERAGĀTHĀ*; *THERĪGĀTHĀ*.

TRIPURI. Archaeological site in Madhya Pradesh, with several occupational phases. The earliest occupation, Period I (first half of the first millennium BCE), provided evidence of microliths and **pottery**.

Period II (mid–first millennium BCE) yielded **iron** and **copper** artifacts, **Northern Black Polished Ware**, **black and red ware**, beads of semiprecious stone, and **terracotta** objects. Period III (c. 300–100 BCE) provided evidence for ring wells, **Red Polished Ware**, **punch-marked coins**, and local issues and coins attributed to the **Sātavāhanas**. Period IV (c. 100 BCE–200 CE) was associated with remains of **Buddhist monasteries** and sealings of local rulers. Period V (c. 200–400 CE) yielded evidence of metalworking and a hoard of beads of semiprecious stones. *See also* KALACURI.

TULJAPUR GARHI. **Archaeological** site in Maharashtra with two occupational phases, both **Chalcolithic** (c. second millennium BCE?). Period I had parallels with **Malwa** culture, while Period II had parallels with **Jorwe**. Finds consisted of traces of round huts, **black and red ware**, and beads of semiprecious stone. Plant remains included rice, millet, wheat, barley, gram, lentil, pea, and *babul*.

TUMAIN. **Archaeological** site in Madhya Pradesh, with four occupational phases. Period I (c. fifth–second century BCE) provided evidence of **copper**, **iron**, and bone artifacts. Other finds included **Northern Black Polished Ware**, **black and red ware**, and **punch-marked coins**. Structural remains consisted of three ***stūpas***. Period II (c. second century BCE–first century CE) yielded, in addition to these artifacts, traces of baked-brick structures and ring wells. Period III (c. first–fifth centuries CE) yielded **Red Polished Ware**. Period IV (c. 6th–12th centuries CE) provided evidence of **sculpture** of **Purāṇic** deities and a hoard of more than 600 silver coins of the Indo-Sasanian variety.

TURAMAYA. Ruler mentioned in **Major Rock Edict** XIII of the **Mauryan king Asoka**, who claimed to have sent emissaries to preach ***dhamma*** to his realm. Turamaya has been identified with the contemporary ruler of Egypt, **Ptolemy Philadelphus**.

TUṢĀSPA. Name of one of the governors of the **Mauryas**, who was in charge of the area around **Girnar** (c. third century BCE). His name is Iranian, and he is described as a ***yavana rājā*** in the **Junagadh Rock Inscription** of **Rudradāman**, which mentions that he was responsible for the initial construction of the Sudarśana Lake.

– U –

UDAYAGIRI. Archaeological site in Orissa, with evidence of **Jaina** caves, dated to c. first century BCE. These include the **Hathigumpha** cave that contains the **inscription** of **Khāravela**. Other finds consisted of remains of a large **monastic** complex, with a stone gateway, and rooms on all four sides of an open courtyard, with stone **sculptures** of the **Buddha** and Buddhist divinities, dated to c. seventh–eighth centuries CE. The iconography is suggestive of **Tantric** influences. **Terracotta seals** and sealings mention Śrī Mādhavapura Mahāvihāra, probably the name of the establishment. Other finds included terracotta plaques with Buddhist motifs, and **iron** artifacts such as nails, arrowheads, knives, and spearheads. *See also* CEDI.

UDAYANA. King of **Vatsa** (c. sixth century BCE), and hero of several romantic works, including the *Svapna Vāsavadattā* attributed to **Bhāsa**. These refer to his wives and lovers, of whom Vāsavadattā, the daughter of the king of **Avanti**, was the best known. While these works also ascribe a series of military exploits to the ruler, the historicity of these descriptions is doubtful. *See also* KONKU VELIR.

UDAYGIRI. Rock-cut cave site in Madhya Pradesh, containing **sculptural** representations of **Purāṇic** deities, including those of the **goddess** Gaṇeśa, and forms of **Viṣṇu**, including an image of the deity as a boar, **Śaiva** images, as well as **inscriptions** pertaining to the reign of the **Gupta** ruler **Candragupta II** (c. fifth century CE).

UDAYIN. Ruler (c. fifth century BCE), of **Magadha**, who transferred the capital of the state from **Rājagaha** to **Pāṭalīputra**.

UDEGOLAM. Site in Karnataka. Find spot of a **Minor Rock Edict** of **Asoka**, mentioning the personal name of the ruler.

UDYOTANA SŪRI. Jaina author (c. eighth century CE) of a **Prakrit** text in prose and verse, the ***Kuvalayamālā***, consisting of stories about a hero named Kuvalayacandra. This was part of the genre known as ***Dharmakathā***. *See also* LITERATURE.

UGRASENA. Ruler (c. fourth century CE) of Pallaka (a state to the south of the **Krishna River**, Andhra Pradesh). He is mentioned in the **Allahabad Pillar Inscription** of the **Gupta** ruler **Samudragupta** among those **kings** who were captured and reinstated when they submitted to him.

UJJAYINĪ. One of the most important **early historic cities**, located in present-day Madhya Pradesh, known from **archaeological** evidence and from **inscriptional** and textual references. The earliest archaeological levels (Period I, c. first half of the first millennium BCE) have yielded evidence of the use of **iron** to manufacture a wide range of artifacts. Other finds included **black and red ware** and **Painted Grey Ware**. Some architectural features such as traces of a moat and mud-brick **fortifications** have also been ascribed to this phase. Period II (mid–first millennium BCE to c. 200 BCE) yielded **Northern Black Polished Ware**. Structural remains consisted of traces of a rampart and ring wells and remains of a massive brick ***stūpa*** and a tank. **Coins**, copper, and a wide range of iron equipment, artifacts of ivory and bone, **seals**, and **terracotta** figurines were also found. Period III (c. 200 BCE–1300 CE) was divided into three subphases. Finds consisted of beads of semiprecious stone, glass bangles, stone **sculpture** of **Purāṇic** deities, coins of the **Kṣatrapas** and **Kuṣāṇas**, a mold for **Roman coins**, and inscribed sealings.

According to an **Asokan** inscription, Ujjayinī was a provincial capital of the **Mauryas**. It also figures in the works of **Kālidāsa** and was evidently an important political and cultural center under the **Gupta** rulers (c. fourth–sixth centuries CE). *See also MṚCCHAKAṬIKAM*; VIKRAMĀDITYA.

UNTOUCHABILITY. The earliest indications of the designation of social groups as untouchable occur in **later Vedic** texts (c. first half of the first millennium BCE onward), where the presence of certain categories, including menstruating **women**, specific occupational groups, and ***śūdras***, was considered inauspicious on ritual occasions. Anything touched or even seen by them had to be discarded or ritually purified, while conversation with them had to be avoided.

Subsequently, the **Dharmasūtras** and **Dharmaśāstras** elaborated on these principles, extending them to prohibitions on **marriage** and sharing food, with severe punishments and penances prescribed for ***brāhmaṇas* (1)** who violated these norms. Simultaneously, lists of those classified as untouchable were drawn up. These lists grew more elaborate with the passage of time. They included those who followed occupations such as hunting, handling the dead, leather-working, and other **crafts**. The low status ascribed to them was often justified by claiming that they were the offspring of hypergamous marriages between women and men of the four primary ***varṇas*** as well as further permutations and combinations of their offspring, all considered violations of the norms of *varṇa*.

The practice of untouchability is attested to in **Buddhist** and **Jaina** narrative **literature** as well, which suggest that elite groups often adopted and enforced these norms, insisting that categories such as the ***caṇḍāla*** reside outside the settlement. At the same time, some narratives represented situations of contesting and reversing the social hierarchies represented within the Brahmanical order. **Travelers' accounts** occasionally provide graphic descriptions of untouchability in daily social interaction. *See also ḌOMBA*; *NIŚĀDA*; SOCIAL MOBILITY.

***UPADESAMĀLĀ*.** **Prakrit** text (literally the "garland of instructions") also known as *Uvaesamālā*, attributed to the **Jaina** author Dharmadāsa Gani (c. fourth–fifth centuries CE). The work contains stories about great men. It also includes more than 500 verses in simple language, aimed at teaching the tenets of Jainism, besides tales of animals and birds. Several commentaries were written on the text. *See also* LITERATURE.

UPANIṢAD. A category of **Sanskrit** texts, the earliest of which are dated to c. sixth century BCE. The ***Chāndogya*** and the ***Bṛhadāraṇyaka*** are among the best-known works in this genre. They contain some of the earliest detailed **philosophical** speculations regarding the nature of the ultimate reality, often visualized as a universal soul, of which the individual soul was a specific manifestation. They also included critiques of ritualism and an emphasis on acquiring knowledge as a means of self-realization. Some of the earliest discussions on the theory of transmigration or ***karma*** can be found in these texts, which were often composed as dialogues. The protagonists included priests, chiefs or **kings**, a handful of **women**, and, occasionally, men of relatively low social standing. The school of philosophy associated with ***Vedānta*** traced its origins to these texts. The later Upaniṣads contained theistic ideas as well. *See also BHAKTI*; JANAKA; LATER VEDA; LITERATURE; ŚAṄKARĀCĀRYA; YĀJÑAVALKYA.

URAIYUR. Archaeological site in Tamil Nadu, recognized as the capital of the early **Co̱las**. Textual traditions describe it as an important center of **textile** production. During the seventh and eighth centuries, the **Pallava** and **Pāṇḍya** rulers fought for its control. Subsequently it was incorporated within the **early medieval** Co̱la state.

Excavations have yielded evidence of two occupational phases. Finds from Period I (c. first–fourth centuries CE) included **Black and Red Ware**, **Russet-Coated Painted Ware**, **inscribed** potsherds, beads of glass, **terracotta**, and semiprecious stone. Other finds consisted of a dyeing vat and bone points. Period II (c. 5th–10th centuries CE) yielded glass beads and bangles and terracotta figurines.

UṢAVADĀTA. Śaka ruler (c. second century CE), known from **inscriptions** at **Nasik**. He was the son-in-law of **Nahapāṇa**. The inscriptions record his gifts of gold, cattle, villages, coconut trees, and wives to ***brāhmaṇas* (1)** and the arrangements he made for rest houses, ferries, drinking water, and **assemblies**. He also granted land for the maintenance of the **Buddhist monastic** order.

UTAWAD. Archaeological site in Madhya Pradesh, with evidence of a **Chalcolithic** culture (c. second millennium BCE?). There are remains of dwelling pits, fireplaces, and storage bins and evidence for butchering of animals. Stone **tools** included locally manufactured microliths, generally of chalcedony, besides scrapers, choppers, flakes, and grinding stones. Other finds consisted of white-painted **black and red ware**, **copper** artifacts such as fishhooks and rings, beads of steatite and shell, and **terracotta** objects.

UTNUR. Archaeological site in Karnataka with evidence of three occupational phases. Periods I and II (c. third–second millennium BCE) were **Neolithic**, with evidence of **ash mounds** produced by burning cattle dung. Other finds included gray **pottery**. The site was abandoned and reoccupied in Period III (mid–first millennium BCE onward). Evidence from this level consisted of **iron** equipment, **Black and Red Ware**, and **Russet-Coated Painted Ware**.

UTTARĀPATHA. Literally the "northern path," term used in **Sanskrit**, **Prakrit**, and **Pali** works to designate **routes** that ran along the **Ganga (2)** valley extending from the eastern coast to **Taxila** and beyond in the northwest. Important **cities** along these routes that were used by **traders**, pilgrims, and **armies** included **Pāṭaliputra**, **Kausambi**, and **Mathura**. Branches of the route extended to the foothills of the **Himalayas** in the north and the **Vindhyas** to the south. *See also* TRADE ROUTES.

UTTARARĀMACARITA. **Sanskrit** play attributed to **Bhavabhūti** (c. seventh–eighth centuries CE). The play depicts a sequel to the main events of the ***Rāmāyaṇa***, leading to reconciliation between **Rāma** and Sītā. *See also* LITERATURE.

UVAESAMĀLĀ. *See UPADESAMĀLĀ.*

– V –

VĀCASPATI MIŚRA. **Sanskrit** author (c. ninth century CE) of two major commentaries on the ***nyāya*** system of thought. Of these compositions, the *Nyāya-vārttikā-tātparya-ṭīkā* is the best known. He is also recognized as the author of commentaries on texts relating to the ***Vedānta***, ***sāṃkhya***, and ***yoga*** traditions. *See also* LITERATURE.

VADAGOKUGIRI. **Archaeological** site in Meghalaya, find spot of a ***stūpa*** made of mud and brick, two groups of **temples** dated to c. 9th–10th centuries CE, as well as traces of **fortification**. Other finds include **pottery** similar to that found at **Sekta** and **terracotta** tiles with representations of **Purāṇic** deities.

VADDAMANU. **Archaeological** site in Andhra Pradesh, with four occupational phases: Period I (c. 200 BCE–100 CE), Period II (c. 100–250 CE), Period III (c. 250–500 CE), and Period IV (c. 500–600 CE). Finds include pillars, railings, **Black and Red Ware**, **punch-**

marked coins, and coins issued by the **Sātavāhanas**. The major finds are associated with Period III, which yielded red slipped ware, **iron** artifacts, **Brāhmī inscriptions**, **coins** of the **Ikṣvākus**, and evidence of a **Buddhist monastery** and ***stūpa***.

VADGAON MADHAVPUR. Archaeological site in Karnataka, with evidence of three occupational phases. Period I (c. third–second centuries BCE) was not associated with any major finds. Finds from Period II (c. second century BCE–first century CE) consisted of an **inscribed** pillar describing a **sacrifice** performed by a ***brāhmaṇa*** **(1)**. Period III (c. first–second centuries CE) provided evidence of a baked-brick structure, including a shrine, **Red Polished Ware**, **Russet-Coated Painted Ware**, **terracotta** figurines, **punch-marked coins**, **Sātavāhana** and **Roman** coins, and a hoard of uninscribed coins.

VADODARA. Archaeological site in Gujarat, with three distinct occupational phases. Period I yielded microliths. Period II (c. late first millennium BCE) yielded **Red Polished Ware**, traces of baked-brick structures, **terracotta seals**, and Roman bronze vessels. Finds from Period III (c. 6th–10th centuries CE) included a hoard of bronze **Jaina sculptures**.

VAIŚEṢIKA**.** School of **philosophy** related to ***nyāya***. According to tradition, its founder was **Kaṇāda** (c. first century CE?), who composed the ***Vaiśeṣika sūtra***.

VAIŚEṢIKA SŪTRA**. Sanskrit** text (c. first century CE?) attributed to **Kaṇāda**. Divided into 10 chapters, the text elaborates on an atomistic theory of matter. Several commentaries were written on the text, of which one of the earliest was the *Praśastapāda* (c. fifth century CE). *See also* LITERATURE.

VAISHALI. Archaeological site in Bihar, mentioned in a range of textual traditions, especially **Buddhist** and **Jaina** (c. sixth century BCE onward), which recognized it as the capital of the **Licchavis**. It was also recognized as the site of the second **Buddhist Council**. Archaeological finds include remains of a ***stūpa***, which contained a casket with shell, beads, gold artifacts, a **copper punch-marked coin**, and a tank that may have been used for ritual bathing. Other finds consisted of an uninscribed stone column with a lion capital, which may have been a **Mauryan** pillar. There is also evidence of a mud rampart, built between c. fourth and second centuries BCE. Associated finds included **Northern Black Polished Ware**, **terracotta** figurines, and beads of semiprecious stone. There is a well that has been assigned to the **Kuṣāṇa** period, which also yielded **seals** and sealings, **iron** rings, and artifacts of copper, bone, and ivory. Other finds consisted of seals belonging to the **Gupta** period (c. fourth–sixth centuries CE), which mentioned the name of the **city** as well as the designations of officials associated with the local administration. One of the seals mentioned Dhruvasvāminī, the wife of **Candragupta II**. *See also* VAJJI.

VAIṢṆAVISM. **Religious** tradition that gained importance from the first millennium CE, although some scholars trace its roots to a few references to **Viṣṇu** in early and **later Vedic** texts. Vaiṣṇavism was a theistic tradition, within which several sects emerged. A core belief was that the deity was incarnated in a variety of forms, the ***avatāras***. The emphasis was on devotional worship within **temples**. Textual traditions associated with Vaiṣṇavism were compiled during the course of the first millennium and were incorporated in the **Purāṇas**. Other significant compositions include those of the ***Āḻvārs***. Vaiṣnavism continues to be an extremely significant strand within present-day **Hinduism**. *See also BHAGAVAD GĪTĀ*; BHĀGAVATA; *BHAKTI*; HELIODOROS; IKṢVĀKU (2); JAINISM; LALITĀDITYA MUKTĀPĪḌA; *NĀLĀYIRA TIVIYA PIRAPANTAM*; PĀÑCARĀTRA; PERIYĀḺVĀR; TOṆṬARAṬIPPOṬI ĀḺVĀR; *VIṢṆUDHARMOTTARA PURĀṆA*.

VAIŚYA*.** **Sanskrit** term, derived from the word ***viś, used (c. first millennium BCE onward) to designate men belonging to the third category of the fourfold ***varṇa*** order. The duties assigned to the *vaiśya* were laid down in the **Dharmasūtras** and the **Dharmaśāstras** and included engaging in **agriculture**, **pastoralism**, **trade**, and **money lending**. They were also expected to perform **Vedic sacrifices**, study the Vedas, and make gifts to ***brāhmaṇas* (1)**, ritual rights that they shared with members of the first two *varṇas*. While the category of *vaiśya* was recognized in prescriptive texts, it was rarely used in **in-**

scriptions, even when men identified themselves in terms of their occupations. *See also GOTRA*; *GRĀMAṆĪ*; PUṢYAGUPTA; *ŚŪDRA*.

***VĀJAPEYA*.** **Sacrifice** described in **later Vedic** texts, recommended for a **king** who wished to claim overlordship over others. A salient feature of the ritual was a chariot race, in which the sacrificer was expected to emerge victorious. **Inscriptions** of the **early historic** and the **early medieval periods** indicate that the ritual was performed by rulers. *See also* KINGSHIP, THEORIES OF ORIGIN.

VAJJI. ***Mahājanapada*** (c. sixth century BCE) situated to the north of Bihar, bordering Nepal. Its distinctive feature was an oligarchic/democratic form of government, involving the participation of men belonging to ***kṣatriya*** lineages. Chief among these lineages were the **Licchavis** and **Jñātrikas**. The chief city of the state, **Vaishali**, or Vesālī, was one of the most important urban centers of the time. The Vajji confederacy was destroyed (c. fifth century BCE) by **Ajātaśatru**, the **king** of **Magadha**, and its territories incorporated within the nascent Magadhan Empire. However, individual lineages such as the Licchavi survived for several centuries. *See also GAṆA/SAMṂGHA*.

***VAJRAYĀNA*.** A **Tantric** form of **Buddhism** that emphasized the importance of the female principle or *śakti*, associated with the **Buddha** and **Bodhisattvas**. Like many forms of Tantricism, it incorporated sexual intercourse within ritual practice. It gained popularity under the **Pāla** rulers of eastern India, c. ninth century CE onward, with the **monastery** at **Vikramaśilā** as a major center. This form of Buddhism spread to Tibet as well. *See also* NALANDA.

VĀKĀṬAKA. Ruling lineage of Madhya Pradesh, c. fourth–fifth centuries CE. Members of the lineage established matrimonial ties with the **Guptas**, **Viṣṇukuṇḍins**, and **Kadambas**. According to the **Purāṇas**, the founder of the dynasty was **Vindhyaśakti**. Some of the major **paintings** and **sculpture** in the caves of **Ajanta** were executed during their rule. *See also* BAGH; HARIṢEṆA (2); MANDHAL; PRABHĀVATĪ GUPTA; PRAVARASENA I; RUDRASENA II; VINDHYAŚAKTI.

VĀKPATI. Court **poet** (c. eighth century CE) of **Yaśovarman**, and author of the **Prakrit** poem *Gauḍavāho* describing the life and achievements of his patron, including his conquest of **Gauḍa**, a kingdom in Bengal. *See also* LITERATURE.

VALABHI. Site in Gujarat, where the texts of **Jainism** received their final shape, c. fifth century CE, also the capital of the **Maitrakas**. It was an important sea port and a flourishing **Buddhist** center. *See also* DEVARDHI GANI.

VALIYAPADAM. Archaeological site (c. first millennium BCE?) in Kerala, with evidence of **megaliths**, **Black and Red Ware**, and **iron** equipment including knives, axes, and daggers.

VĀLMĪKI. Recognized as the author of the **Sanskrit** ***Rāmāyaṇa***, which attained its present form c. fifth century CE. Very little is available by way of secure biographical details. The text itself indicates that the author possessed considerable poetic skills. *See also* LITERATURE.

VALMIYO TIMBO. Archaeological site (c. third–second millennium BCE) in Gujarat, also known as Shikarpur. The **pottery** shows affiliations with **Mature Harappan** and **Late Harappan** ceramics. Other finds include beads of semiprecious stone, especially microbeads of steatite, chert blades, drills, querns, **copper** chisels, and **terracotta** figurines and ornaments. Finds of fragmentary conch shells and shell bangles indicate that this may have been a site for the manufacture of shell goods. There is also evidence of a mud-brick **fortification** around the settlement. Plant remains include evidence of wheat and millet and of trees such as *ber*, *sal*, and silk cotton.

VĀNAPRASTHA. **Sanskrit** term used c. mid–first millennium BCE onward to designate the third phase or ***āśrama*** in the life of a man belonging to the first three ***varṇas***. This was meant to be a period of retirement from the world, ideally to be spent in a **forest**, but not in a state of complete renunciation.

VAṄGA. Name assigned in **Sanskrit** texts to a region in eastern India, possibly part of present-day Bangladesh, including the deltaic region.

References in **later Vedic** texts (first half of the first millennium BCE) suggest that **Brahmanical** norms were not prevalent in the area. Later texts such as the ***Arthaśāstra*** mention it as important for **textile** production. It was also occasionally mentioned in **inscriptions** such as the **Mehrauli Pillar Inscription**.

VANPASARI. Archaeological site in Andhra Pradesh, with evidence of occupation during the **Mesolithic** phase. Finds include stone **tools** made of chert and quartz, such as blades, burins, scrapers, flakes, microliths, saddle querns, and bones of small animals.

VARĀHAMIHIRA. Sanskrit author of the ***Bṛhat saṃhitā***, the *Pañcasiddhāntika* and the *Bṛhajjātaka*, a work dealing with horoscopy, c. sixth century CE. *See also* LITERATURE; MATHEMATICS.

VARANASI. Present-day name of ancient **Kāśi**. *See also* RAJGHAT; SARNATH.

VARARUCI. Author (c. sixth century CE?) of the *Prākṛtaprakāśa*, a work on **Prakrit** grammar consisting of 12 chapters. *See also* LITERATURE.

VARDHAMĀNA. *See* MAHĀVĪRA.

VARṆA*. Sanskrit** term used for a fourfold classification of society into ***brāhmaṇa* (1)**, ***kṣatriya, ***vaiśya***, and ***śūdra***, often approximately translated as priest, warrior, ordinary people, and laborers. The earliest reference to this classification is found in the ***Puruṣasūkta***, a hymn (c. 1000 BCE?) in the ***Ṛgveda***, in one of the first attempts to accord divine sanction to the fourfold order. Later texts such as the **Dharmasūtras** and the **Dharmaśāstras** (c. sixth century BCE onward) laid down the functions of these social categories. The Sanskrit **epics** and **Purāṇas** contain narratives about conflicts between *brāhmaṇas* and *kṣatriyas*. While these accord victory to the *brāhmaṇa*, it is evident that the relative importance of the priest and the warrior was contested. *Varṇa* figured in non-Brahmanical texts as well.

When *varṇa* categories were enumerated in early **Buddhist** literature, the ***khattiya*** (**Pali** term for *kṣatriya*) was placed at the head of the list, with the **Buddha** being recognized as a *khattiya*. It was also recognized that these social divisions were irrelevant once a person renounced the world. Buddhist texts mention other hierarchies, defined as "high" and "low" apart from those based on *varṇa*. "High" families or *kulas* included those of the *khattiya*, *bambhana* (*brāhmaṇa*), and *gahapati* (Sanskrit ***gṛhapati***). "Low" *kulas* included the ***caṇḍāla*** and ***niṣāda***. Occupations were also similarly categorized. Professions that involved writing and accountancy were considered "high." "Low" professions were those that involved manual labor. **Agriculture**, **pastoralism**, and **trade** were also regarded as prestigious occupations. *See also ĀŚRAMA*; CASTE; *DHARMA*; DHARMAPĀLA; DISPOSAL OF THE DEAD; *DVIJA*; EARLY MEDIEVAL PERIOD; GAUTAMĪPUTRA SĀTAKARṆI; HINDUISM; INHERITANCE LAWS; *JĀTI*; JUDICIAL SYSTEM; KINGSHIP; *MANUSMṚTI*; MARRIAGE; MONEY LENDING; *PARIṢAD*; PROTEST MOVEMENTS; *SAṂNYĀSA*; SLAVERY; SOCIAL MOBILITY; UNTOUCHABILITY; *VĀNAPRASTHA*; *VARṆASAṂKARA*; *YAVANA*.

VARṆASAṂKARA*.** **Sanskrit** term used (c. mid–first millennium BCE onward) for real and/or hypothetical **marriages** or sexual unions between men and **women** belonging to different ***varṇas. The **Dharmasūtras** and **Dharmaśāstras** contained lists of offspring produced from such unions, which grew longer with the passage of time. From the **Brahmanical** perspective, hypergamous unions were regarded as somewhat less problematic than hypogamous unions. It is likely that the theory of *varṇasaṃkara* was evolved to incorporate social groups within the *varṇa* and ***jāti*** framework. At the same time, it was used to order these groups hierarchically. For instance, the ***caṇḍāla***, who was ranked lowest, was represented as the offspring of unions between *brāhmaṇa* women and ***śūdra*** men.

VASIṢṬHA. Name of a sage mentioned in the ***Ṛgveda***, which contains several compositions attributed to him and other members of his clan. Later tradition recognized him as the founder of a ***gotra***. **Sanskrit epic** and **Purāṇic** traditions contained stories of his conflict with and victory over **Viśvāmitra**.

VĀSIṢṬHĪPUTRA PULUMAVI. Son and successor of **Gautamīputra Sātakarṇi** (r.c. 130–159), known from **inscriptions** and **coins**. These indicate an attempt to extend **Sātavāhana** control over the eastern Deccan.

VASUBANDHU. Brother of **Asaṅga** (c. fifth century CE), author of the *Abhidharmakośa*, a major work of **Sarvāstivādin philosophy** in **Sanskrit**. He later turned toward the **Mahāyāna** tradition, perhaps under the influence of his brother. *See also* LITERATURE; *YOGĀCĀRA*.

VĀSUDEVA. Kuṣāṇa ruler, mid–third century CE, who was defeated by the contemporary Sasanian ruler of Persia, Shahpur I. Vāsudeva probably ruled over parts of northwestern India. *See also* SANGHOL.

VĀSUDEVAHINDĪ*. Prakrit** narrative (c. second century CE) about the wanderings of Vāsudeva, the father of **Kṛṣṇa**, modeled on the ***Bṛhatkathā of **Guṇāḍhya** and possibly composed by Saṃghadāsa Gani Vācaka. *See also* LITERATURE.

VĀTĀPI. *See* BADAMI.

VATSA. ***Mahājanapada*** (c. sixth century BCE) south of the **Ganga (2)**, with its capital at **Kausambi**. The most famous ruler of this state was **Udayana**. *See also* KONKU VELIR.

VĀTSYĀYANA. Sanskrit author, recognized as the author of the ***Kāmasūtra***. Very little is known about him. The text indicates that he was familiar with the ***Manusmṛti*** and the ***Arthaśāstra***. *See also* LITERATURE.

VEDA*. Sanskrit** term meaning "knowledge," used for sacred texts consisting of chants and prayers. These were composed in Vedic Sanskrit, which differs from classical Sanskrit in terms of both vocabulary and grammatical structure. Three or four texts were recognized as constituting the core of Vedic **literature**. These included the ***Ṛgveda, ***Sāmaveda***, ***Yajurveda***, and ***Atharvaveda***. The composition and compilation of these texts, which were orally transmitted through priestly lineages, dates from c. mid–second millennium BCE to the mid–first millennium BCE. Subsequently, ancilliary texts, the ***vedāṅgas***, were included in the corpus. Later **Brahmanical** tradition recognized the Vedas as authoritative in all matters pertaining to ***dharma***. *See also ANUKRAMAṆĪ*; *BRĀHMAṆA* (1); *BRĀHMAṆA* (2); *BṚHADDEVATĀ*; DANCE; *DVIJA*; HARAPPAN CIVILIZATION; HINDUISM; INDUS SARASVATI CIVILIZATION; *JANA*; *KṢATRIYA*; LATER VEDA; LOKĀYĀTA; *MĪMĀṂSĀ*; *NIGHAṆṬU*; PROTOHISTORY; PURĀṆIC RELIGION; SACRIFICE; ŚAIVISM; *SAMṢKĀRA*; *ŚŪDRA*; *VEDĀNTA*; VYĀSA; XERXES; YĀSKA.

VEDĀṄGA. Literally "limbs of the **Vedas**," prose works composed in **Sanskrit** c. sixth–second centuries BCE, including works on grammar, prosody, etymology, phonetics, and astrology. The sixth category, known as ***kalpa* (1)**, included four subgroups—the **Śrautasūtras**, laying down the procedure for major **sacrificial** rituals; the **Gṛhyasūtras**, dealing with domestic rituals, including rites of passage; the **Dharmasūtras**, dealing with social norms; and the **Śulbasūtras**, laying down rules for the measurement and construction of sacrificial altars, including the earliest codification of the application of geometric principles. The texts were composed and taught within priestly schools and are generally characterized by a terse style. *See also* LAGADHA; LITERATURE; YĀSKA.

VEDĀNTA. Literally the culmination of **Vedic** thought, derived from the **Upaniṣads** and the **Vedas**, one of the most influential schools of **philosophy**, which advocated monism, the existence of a single reality, the perception of which was thought to be obscured by an illusory world. The best-known proponent of *Vedānta* was **Śaṅkarācāraya** (c. eighth century CE). *See also CHĀNDOGYA UPANIṢAD*; *MĪMĀṂSĀ*; VĀCASPATI MIŚRA.

VEDIC ECONOMY. Scholars examining **Vedic literature** (c. second–first millennium BCE) suggest that early Vedic texts such as the ***Rgveda*** (which pertains to the northwestern part of the subcontinent) contain evidence of **pastoralism**, with cattle being particularly important. Other animals mentioned include the horse, sheep, and goat. Evidence for **agriculture**, though present, is relatively limited: The *Ṛgveda* contains reference to *yava*, a generic term used for grain and for barley in particular. **Crafts** such as weaving and carpentry (especially the manufacture of wooden chariots) were evidently well developed. While metals were known, the use of **iron** is somewhat uncertain.

Later Vedic texts (c. first half of the first millennium BCE) focus on the region of the **Ganga (2)–Yamuna** doab and adjoining areas. While pastoralism remained important, agriculture assumed greater significance, with texts mentioning several varieties of crops grown in different seasons. Another major development was the use of iron, referred to as the black metal in contrast to **copper**–bronze, often described as the red metal.

VELLĀLĀR. **Tamil** term used to designate peasants. The category was internally differentiated and included both large landholders and small cultivators. The *vellālār* often played an important role in **assemblies** that were responsible for local administration. *See also* NAMMĀḺVĀR; TIRUNĀVUKKARACAR.

VENGI. Region in Andhra Pradesh, extending approximately from the **Godavari** to the **Krishna**. From the seventh century CE onward, this region emerged as the nucleus of an important **kingdom** under the control of the **Eastern Cālukyas**.

VESĀLĪ. **Pali/Prakrit** name for **Vaishali**.

VETALWADI. **Archaeological** site in Maharashtra, find spot of an early example of a **rock-cut cave** (c. first century CE?).

VIDARBHA. Region in central India, mentioned in the **Sanskrit epics** and the **Purāṇas**.

VIDATHA. Name of an **assembly** mentioned in the ***Ṛgveda***. Activities associated with the *vidatha* included the performance of **sacrifices** and the distribution of booty. It is likely that both men and **women** participated in these assemblies.

VIDEGHA MĀTHAVA. Chief/**king** mentioned in the ***Śatapatha Brāhmaṇa***. He evidently migrated from the **Sarasvatī** to the Sadānīrā (identified with the Rapti, a tributary of the **Ganga (2)**), and was credited with the introduction of the **Vedic sacrificial** cult, settled **agriculture**, and the **Brahmanical** social order in **Videha** (c. seventh century BCE?).

VIDEHA. Name of a ***mahājanapada*** located in north Bihar. *See also* JANAKA; MITHILA; VIDEGHA MĀTHAVA.

VIDIŚĀ. *See* VIDISHA.

VIDISHA. **Archaeological** site in Madhya Pradesh, identical with Vidiśā mentioned in **Sanskrit** texts and **inscriptions** and also known as Besnagar. Period I was a **Mesolithic** phase, which yielded geometric and nongeometric microliths. Period II, designated as **Chalcolithic**, dated to c. second millennium BCE. There were traces of **Painted Grey Ware** toward the end of this phase (c. 900 BCE). Finds from Period III (c. first millennium BCE) included **black and red ware**, **black slipped ware**, and **Northern Black Polished Ware**. Associated finds consisted of ring wells, drains, **iron** artifacts, **punch-marked** and **cast coins**, **inscribed seals**, and traces of wheat. The inscription of **Heliodoros** belonged to the same period. Structural remains included traces of a **temple** and **fortifications**. The site continued to be occupied until the middle of the first millennium CE. Textual and inscriptional evidence indicates that it was a flourishing urban center throughout most of this period. *See also* PUṢYAMITRA ŚUNGA; SANCHI.

VIḌŪḌABHA. Son and successor of **Pasenadi**, the **king** of **Kosala** (c. sixth century BCE). **Buddhist** tradition mentions his attack on the **Sākyas**.

VIHĀRA. Term used to designate **Buddhist monasteries** in **Prakrit**, **Pali**, and **Sanskrit** texts and **inscriptions**, c. late first millennium BCE onward.

VIJAYĀDITYA. **Cālukya** ruler (r. 696–733), whose rule was marked by relative peace, apart from conflicts with the **Pallavas**. This was also a period when several **temples** were built under royal patronage.

VIJAYĀLAYA. Coḻa ruler (r.c. 841–871), known from **inscriptions**, who established control over **Thanjavur**.

VIKRAMA ERA. Name of an era, still in use, beginning from c. 58 to 57 BCE. It is uncertain who started the era and why.

VIKRAMĀDITYA. Sanskrit term meaning "the sun of valor," name of a legendary **king** mentioned in several narrative traditions, also a title adopted by rulers, of whom the best known is **Candragupta II**. Vikramāditya was often associated with **Ujjayinī**.

VIKRAMAŚILĀ. Monastic establishment, mentioned in Tibetan sources as a center of **Tantric Buddhism**, identified with **Antichak**. *See also* DHARMAPĀLA; *VAJRAYĀNA*.

VĪMA KADPHISES. Son and successor of the **Kuṣāṇa** ruler **Kujula Kadphises** (c. first century CE). Vīma Kadphises exercised control over Afghanistan and the northwestern parts of the subcontinent. He is known from his gold **coins**, which followed Roman standards and were probably used for long-distance exchange along the **Silk Route**. The imagery on the coins indicates support for both **Buddhism** and **Śaivism**. *See also* SANGHOL.

VIMALASŪRI. Prakrit author of the ***Paumacariya***, a **Jaina** version of the ***Rāmāyaṇa***. This version was set in urban centers, and **Rāma** was visualized not as an incarnation of **Viṣṇu** but as a Jaina saint. *See also* LITERATURE.

***VINAYA PIṬAKA*. Pali** text, recognized as part of **Buddhist** canonical **literature**, compiled during the first **Buddhist Council** (c. fifth century BCE). The compilation is traditionally attributed to Upāli, a barber who was also one of the principal disciples of the **Buddha**. The text consists of three sections of which the first, the *Sutta vibhaṅga*, contains rules for monks and nuns. The second section, known as the *Mahāvagga*, contains a **biography** of the Buddha as well as special rules for the order, while the third section, the *Parivāra*, consists of appendixes to the main text. *See also* LITERATURE; *SAṂGHA*.

VINDHYAS. Mountain range running from west to east, often regarded as a frontier between the **Ganga (2)** valley and peninsular India. Some early **Sanskrit** texts describe it as the southern limit of ***āryāvarta***. *See also* AGASTYA; DEVAPĀLA; MAHIPĀLA (1); *UTTARĀPATHA*.

VINDHYAŚAKTI. Ruler (c. third century CE), recognized as the founder of the **Vākāṭaka** lineage in the **Purāṇas**.

VIŚ*.** **Sanskrit** term used in the ***Ṛgveda (c. second millennium BCE) and in **later Vedic** texts to refer to communities, **tribes**, and clans. Subsequently, the usage of the term became relatively rare. The word ***vaiśya*** is derived from the term *viś*.

VIŚĀKHADATTA. **Sanskrit** playwright (c. sixth century CE), author of the ***Mudrārākṣasa*** and the ***Devīcandragupta***. *See also* LITERATURE.

VIṢṆU. One of the major deities in the **Purāṇic** pantheon. The earliest references to Viṣṇu are found in the ***Ṛgveda***, but the worship of the deity gained popularity in the first millennium CE. The deity was visualized as the preserver of the world. The notion of incarnation was central to the theology that developed, with the theory that the deity descended on earth for the protection of ***dharma*** or righteousness. Ten ***avatāras*** or incarnations of the deity were recognized. These included Varāha or the boar, a deity popular in central India; **Kṛṣṇa**, popular in parts of northern and central India; **Rāma**; and, in some versions, the **Buddha**. Different forms of **Vaiṣṇavism** attained importance in several parts of the subcontinent in the course of the first and second millennium CE. The worship of Viṣṇu and Vaiṣṇavite deities continues to be popular to date. *See also* DEOGARH; EARLY MEDIEVAL PERIOD; ERAN; GODDESS CULTS; HELIODOROS; MEHRAULI PILLAR INSCRIPTION; PALLAVA; PARAŚURĀMA; RELIGION; SHORE TEMPLE; *VIṢṆUDHARMOTTARA PURĀṆA*.

***VIṢṆUDHARMOTTARA PURĀṆA*.** A **Sanskrit** text, one of the important **Purāṇas** within the **Vaiṣṇava** tradition, compiled c. 400–1000

CE, consisting of three parts. The first part deals with cosmogonies, myths about **Viṣṇu**, and legends about rulers belonging to the **solar** and **lunar** dynasties. The second part deals with the duties of the **king** and the norms governing ***varṇa*** and ***āśrama***. The third part contains discussions on a variety of subjects such as **art**, culture, **religion**, **philosophy**, **music**, and so on. *See also* LITERATURE.

VIṢṆUGOPA. Ruler of **Kanchipuram** c. fourth century CE, possibly belonging to the **Pallava** dynasty, mentioned in the **Allahabad Pillar Inscription** as one of those who was captured by the **Gupta** ruler **Samudragupta** but subsequently released when he submitted to the **king**.

VIṢṆUKUṆḌIN. Ruling lineage in Andhra Pradesh, c. fifth–sixth centuries CE. **Inscriptions** mention that the rulers performed **Vedic sacrifices**. *See also* NELAKONDAPALLI; VĀKĀṬAKA.

VIṢṆUŚARMAN. Author of the ***Pañcatantra*** (c. fourth–fifth centuries CE). *See also* LITERATURE.

VIŚVĀMITRA. Sage mentioned in the ***Ṛgveda*** (c. second millennium BCE), recognized as the founder of a ***gotra*** and the composer of several hymns. According to narratives preserved in the **Sanskrit epics** and the **Purāṇas**, he was a ***kṣatriya*** who aspired to the status of a ***brāhmaṇa* (1)**. Accounts of his conflicts with **Vasiṣṭha** are also preserved in these stories. *See also* SOCIAL MOBILITY.

VYĀGHRARĀJĀ. Ruler (c. fourth century CE) of a region known as Mahākāntāra (literally the great wilderness), identified with parts of central India. He is mentioned in the **Allahabad Pillar Inscription** of **Samudragupta** among rulers who were captured but subsequently released on condition of submission to the **Gupta king**.

VYĀSA. Literally, one who spreads, also known as Vedavyāsa and Kṛṣṇadvaipāyana, traditionally recognized as the author (as well as one of the protagonists) of the **Sanskrit *Mahābhārata***, the **Purāṇas**, and Upapurāṇas and the compiler of the **Vedas**. It is possible that the term was generic rather than specific. *See also HARIVAMṢA*; LITERATURE.

– W –

WALKI. Archaeological site in Maharashtra, a **Chalcolithic** settlement that was probably seasonally occupied c. 13th century BCE. Finds include remains of circular huts, with evidence of storage space and fire pits, threshing floors, animal sheds, and bone **tools**.

WARFARE. Evidence for warfare has been reconstructed from **archaeological**, **inscriptional**, and textual sources. The presence of walled settlements in the **pre-/early Harappan** and **Mature Harappan** contexts has often been regarded as indicating tension if not conflict and the need to ensure protection for the population. Clay balls found at these sites may have been used as sling balls for attack. Subsequently, texts such as the ***Ṛgveda*** (c. second millennium BCE) contain prayers for victory in wars that were fought to acquire cattle, prisoners (who were possibly enslaved), and access to resources such as land and water. By the mid–first millennium BCE, if not earlier, ***kṣatriya*** warriors and war leaders figure in **Sanskrit**, **Pali**, and **Prakrit** texts. Somewhat later, warrior chiefs were glorified in the **Tamil *Sangam*** anthologies. Texts such as the ***Arthaśāstra*** contain detailed discussions on strategies of warfare. The **Mauryan** emperor **Asoka** claimed to have eschewed warfare after the conquest of **Kaliṅga**, where large numbers of people were killed and captured.

Inscriptions from the **early historic** and **early medieval period** indicate that warfare remained an important component of state policies. While wars were occasionally waged to acquire territory and/or control over **routes** of communication, they were often in the nature of plundering raids. The successful warrior was frequently compared with **epic** heroes, and scenes of war, drawn from myths and legends, were occasionally represented in **sculpture** used to decorate **temple** walls. *See also* ARMY; HERO STONE; KINGSHIP; MAGADHA; *MULLAIPPĀṬṬU*; NAVY; *PURANĀNURU*; *SKANDHĀVĀRA*.

WARI BATESHWAR. Early historic (c. sixth–fifth centuries BCE?) **archaeological** site in present-day Bangladesh, with traces of a mud rampart, possibly an important center for **trade** with Rome and Southeast Asia, with connections with inland areas through the Brahmaputra valley. Finds of **pottery** included **black slipped ware**,

Northern Black Polished Ware, **rouletted ware**, and red ware. There is evidence of **iron** working as well. Other local manufactures included beads of semiprecious stone and glass.

WATGAL. Archaeological site in Karnataka, with evidence of **Neolithic** occupation. All the levels have yielded evidence of chipped stone blades and microliths made of chert and chalcedony. Other finds included grinding stones and beads of steatite and shell. The first level, dated to c. 3000 BCE, was aceramic. The second level was dated between c. 2700 and 2000 BCE, the third level between c. 2000 and 1000 BCE, and the fourth level to the period after 1000 BCE.

WESTERN GAṄGA. *See* GAṄGA (1).

WIDOWHOOD. Discussions on widowhood occur systematically in textual traditions from c. mid–first millennium BCE, when a distinctive lifestyle for widows, characterized by austerity, was laid down in the **Dharmasūtras** and the **Dharmaśāstras**. These prescriptions became more elaborate during the first millennium CE. The widow was expected to follow them on the assumption that she was responsible for her husband's death and consequently had to perform a lifelong penance.

The extent to which these prescriptions were implemented has been a matter of debate. It is possible that these norms were more prevalent among ***brāhmaṇas*** **(1)** and other social categories that aspired to high status. Provisions were made, although with a certain degree of reluctance, for childless widows to beget children for their husbands' lineage. This practice, known as *niyoga*, was carefully regulated by senior men within the family who chose the partner with whom the widow was expected to cohabit. ***Satī***, or the immolation of the widow on the funeral pyre of her husband, was known, but generally not recommended in most of the early texts.

Narrative traditions occasionally represented widows as wielding power in the family. Other representations were more ambivalent, depicting widows as **women** whose sexuality, if uncontrolled, could pose a challenge to the existing social order. There are indications that widows may have found refuge within the **Buddhist**, **Jaina**, and other **renunciatiory orders**. *See also* MARRIAGE.

WINA. Archaeological site in Uttar Pradesh with four phases of occupation. Period I (consisting of two subphases) yielded cord-impressed **pottery** from the earliest levels (c. 1600–1300 BCE). Pottery from the second subphase had parallels with that from **Narhan**. Other varieties found included white-painted **black and red ware** and **black slipped ware**. Associated finds consisted of wattle-and-daub huts with ovens and storage pits, bone points, and beads of **terracotta** and semiprecious stone. This phase provided evidence of rice, barley, wheat, pulses, pea, gram, mustard, and sesame. Animal bones were also recovered. Period II (c. first millennium BCE?) yielded **iron** and bone **tools**, black slipped ware, and beads. Finds from Period III (late first millennium BCE-early first millennium CE) included pottery ascribed to the **Śaka–Kuṣāṇa** phase, terracotta figurines, and **copper**, iron, and bone artifacts. Period IV was assigned to the **Gupta** period (mid–first millennium CE).

WOMEN. Documenting the presence of women in early India has acquired considerable importance in recent decades. These studies are primarily based on **inscriptional** and textual sources and suffer from a bias in favor of literate, elite categories of women. There have been relatively few attempts to use **archaeological** evidence for such reconstructions. The ***Ṛgveda*** (c. second millennium BCE) mentions a handful of women seers and **poets** in a long list of men. Subsequently, **later Vedic** texts indicate attempts to regulate the role and presence of women in the **sacrifice**, where they were generally assigned subordinate roles. From the mid–first millennium BCE, texts such as the **Dharmasūtras** and **Dharmaśāstras** laid down provisions for extending the regulation of women's lives to other spheres as well—access to property was restricted, the ideal of early **marriage** was propagated, and attempts were made to ensure that women remained chaste.

The extent to which these provisions were followed has been the matter of some debate and discussion. It is likely that these were perhaps enforced most strictly on women who belonged to elite groups. At the same time, inscriptions and narrative texts suggest that such women had access to property and often disposed of this on their own. It is also evident that women participated in a wide range of productive activities, including **agriculture** and **craft** production. **Renunciatory orders** also provided space for women who wished to opt out of the household existence that was regarded as the norm. *See also* AMBAPĀLĪ; ĀṆṬĀḶ; ASCETI-

CISM; ASSEMBLIES; AUVAIYAR; BUDDHA; COURTESANS; DANCE; *DĀSA*; DIDDĀ; DIGAMBARA; DISPOSAL OF THE DEAD; *ḌOMBA*; DRAMA; ESPIONAGE SYSTEM; FAMILY STRUCTURE; GĀRGĪ; GODDESS CULTS; *GOTRA*; IKṢVĀKU (2); INHERITANCE LAWS; JUDICIAL SYSTEM; KĀRAIKKĀL AMMAIYĀR; KINGSHIP; KUMĀRADEVĪ; LAND GRANTS; LANDOWNERSHIP; MAITREYĪ; MANU; MONASTERIES; MUSIC; NĀGANIKĀ; PRABHĀVATĪ GUPTA; PURĀṆA; *PURANĀNURU*; RĀJYAŚRĪ; *RATNIN*; *SAṂGHA*; *SAṂSKĀRA*; *SANGAM*; SANGHOL; *SATĪ*; SLAVERY; *STRĪDHANA*; *ŚŪDRA*; SUGANDHĀ; ŚVETĀMBARA; TANTRA; TERRACOTTA; TEXTILES; *THERĪGĀTHĀ*; UNTOUCHABILITY; UPANIṢAD; *VARṆASAṂKARA*; *VIDATHA*; WIDOWHOOD; *YĀJÑAVALKYASMṚTI*.

– X –

XERXES. Achaemenid ruler (c. 485–465 BCE), son and successor of **Darius I**. His **inscriptions** mention Gadaara and Hindu among his territories as well as a conflict with the worshippers of the *daivas* (*devas*, gods in the **Vedic** tradition). *See also* HERODOTUS.

XUAN ZANG. Chinese **Buddhist** pilgrim (whose name was earlier spelled as Hiuen Tsang) who visited the subcontinent between c. 630 and 644 CE. He left a detailed account known as the *Si yu ki* or "Record of the Western Kingdom," describing his travels and including an account of the state of Buddhism and of the court of **Harṣavardhana**, where he stayed for several years. He also studied at **Nalanda**. He translated several Buddhist works from **Sanskrit** into Chinese. *See also* BHĀSKARAVARMAN; CUNNINGHAM, ALEXANDER; MIHIRAKULA; NARASIṂHAVARMAN I; TRAVELERS' ACCOUNTS.

– Y –

YĀDAVA. Ruling lineage associated with **Mathura** and **Dvaraka** in the **Sanskrit epic** and **Purāṇic** traditions. According to these traditions, **Kṛṣṇa** was associated with this lineage. Several **early medieval** and later ruling lineages in different parts of the subcontinent claimed affinity with the Yādavas.

YAJÑAŚRĪ SĀTAKARṆI. One of the last major rulers of the **Sātavāhana** dynasty (r.c. 170–99 CE). His **coins** have been found throughout the Deccan. Some have representations of ships, which may suggest control over maritime **routes**. His **inscriptions** have been found in **Kanheri** and **Nasik**.

YĀJÑAVALKYA. Philosopher (c. sixth century BCE?) associated with the **Upaniṣadic** tradition, sometimes regarded as one of the earliest proponents of idealistic monism. His dialogues with his wives and other contemporaries are recorded in the Upaniṣads. *See also* GĀRGĪ; MAITREYĪ; *ŚATAPATHA BRĀHMAṆA*.

***YĀJÑAVALKYASMṚTI*. Sanskrit** metrical text composed c. 200–400 CE, recognized as one of the principal **Dharmaśāstras**, attributed to Yājñavalkya, not identical with the philosopher of the same name. It consists of three sections, one dealing with rituals and the duties of the householder, a second with titles of law, and a third with penances. The themes addressed include sources of law, rules regarding **women**, **inheritance**, and the duties of **kings**. Several important commentaries on this text were composed during the first and second millennia. Two of these, the *Mitākṣarā*, attributed to Vijñāneśvara, and the *Dāyabhāga*, attributed to Jīmūtavāhana (both c. 11th and 12th centuries CE), have remained influential in discussions of **Hindu** law to date. *See also* LITERATURE.

***YAJURVEDA*.** An anthology of ritual formulas and instructions for priests, arranged according to **sacrificial** requirements, compiled c. first half of the first millennium BCE. It contains some of the earliest examples of **Sanskrit** prose. It deals with routine daily, fortnightly, and seasonal sacrifices as well as special rituals to proclaim the authority of **kings**. The text was transmitted through two distinct modes, known as the Black and the White traditions respectively. In the former, exegetical statements were interspersed with the ritual formulations, whereas these were treated separately in the latter. *See also* LITERATURE; *VEDA*.

YAMUNA. Tributary of the **Ganga (2)**, a river rising in the **Himalayas** and joining with the Ganga at Allahabad. Some important ***janapadas*** and ***mahājanapadas*** were located in the Ganga–Yamuna doab, as were **early historic cities** such as **Mathura**. *See also* MADHYADEŚA.

YAŚASTILAKA CAMPU. **Sanskrit** text, attributed to Somaprabhu Sūri (c. 10th century CE), a **Jaina** scholar of the **Digambara** sect, composed under the patronage of a feudatory of the contemporary **Cālukya** ruler, Arikesarin III. The composition combined prose and verse and dealt with **Yaśodharman**, the ruler of **Avanti**, describing his conversion to Jainism. *See also* LITERATURE.

YĀSKA. Traditionally recognized as the author of the ***Nirukta***, a work on **Sanskrit** etymology, composed c. eighth–sixth centuries BCE. The text includes lists of synonyms and homonyms and a section discussing the etymology of the names of **Vedic** deities, who were classified as celestial, atmospheric, and terrestrial. The work was recognized as a ***vedāṅga***. *See also* LITERATURE; *NIGHAṆṬU*.

YAŚODHARMAN. Ruler (c. sixth century CE) of Malwa, central India, known from the Mandasor (**Daśapura**) pillar **inscription**. He is credited with victories over the **Hūṇas**, who were led by **Mihirakula**. The inscription, which is eulogistic, describes him as ruling over the entire land from the Brahmaputra River in the east to the western seas, and from the **Himalayas** to Mahendragiri in south India. These claims are not corroborated by other sources. *See also* AULIKARA; *YAŚASTILAKA CAMPU*.

YAŚOVARMAN. Ruler (c. 725–752) of **Kanauj**. He came into conflict with the contemporary rulers of Kashmir and **Gauḍa**. He was a patron of **poets** including **Vākpati** and **Bhavabhūti**. The former composed a **Prakrit** eulogy, describing the victories of his patron, including the defeat of the **king** of Gauḍa. *See also* LALITĀDITYA MUKTĀPĪḌA.

YATIVṚṢABHA. Also known as Jadivasaha, author (c. fifth century CE) of **Prakrit** texts on cosmography and **mathematics** that have parallels with ancient Greek and Chinese works. *See also* LITERATURE.

YAUDHEYA. Community settled in northwestern India, along the Sutlej valley, known primarily from their **coins**. The ruling lineage claimed ***kṣatriya*** status. They are mentioned (c. fourth century CE) in the **Allahabad Pillar Inscription** in the list of people who offered tribute and homage and agreed to obey the orders of the **Gupta** ruler **Samudragupta**. *See also* CAST COINS; SEALS; SUNET.

YAVANA*.** Term used in **Sanskrit** (c. second half of the first millennium BCE onward) to designate "outsiders" or "foreigners," especially those present in the northwestern part of the subcontinent. It was probably derived from the name of the Greek city-state of Ionia, in present-day Turkey, and was used initially for the Greeks. It was later extended to categories such as the Arabs and Turks. **Dharmaśāstras** such as the ***Manusmṛti described the *yavanas* as degenerate ***kṣatriyas***, thus accommodating them within the framework of the ***varṇa*** order. *See also* GAUTAMĪPUTRA SĀTAKARṆI; JUNNAR; MARITIME TRADE; TUṢĀSPA; *YONA*.

YELLESWARAM. **Archaeological** site in Andhra Pradesh, now submerged in the **Krishna**, with evidence of three occupational phases. Period I (c. first millennium BCE) yielded **megaliths**. Period II (c. third century CE) provided evidence of a pillared hall and a shrine, attributable to the **Ikṣvāku (2)** period. Period III (c. second millennium CE) was associated with a later **Cālukyan** occupation.

YERRAGUDI. *See* ERRAGUDI.

YOGA*.** **Sanskrit** term meaning "union," used to refer to one of the six major systems of early Indian **philosophy**. **Patañjali** (2) (probably a different person from the grammarian of the same name) was recognized as the chief proponent of the system, and the author or compiler of a text known as the ***Yogasūtra (c. second century BCE–second century CE?). The system emphasized a range of physical and mental exercises, which were meant to ensure self-discipline as a prerequisite to the attainment of knowledge of the ultimate reality. *See also* VĀCASPATI MIŚRA.

***YOGĀCĀRA*.** **Buddhist philosophical** tradition that emphasized idealism. The earliest known text of the school is the *Mahāyānasūtrālaṃkāra* attributed to **Asaṅga** (c. fifth century CE). Others who contributed to the tradition included **Vasubandhu**, **Dinnāga (1)**, and **Dharmakīrti**. *See also* NĀGĀRJUNA.

YOGASŪTRA*.** **Sanskrit** text (compiled c. second century CE?) attributed to **Patañjali (2)**, enunciating the practice of ***yoga. The text consists of four sections dealing with the aims and means of meditation as well as supernatural powers and liberation. A commentary, known as the *Vyāsabhāṣya*, was written on the text in the fourth century. *See also* LITERATURE.

YONA*.** **Prakrit** term (derived from Ionian) used in **Asokan inscriptions** (c. third century BCE) to refer to people in the northwest of the subcontinent, possibly of Greek origin. The Yonas are represented as a people with a distinct social order, where the categories of the ***brāhmaṇa (1) and ***śramaṇa*** did not exist. *See also YAVANA*.

YUEHZHI. Nomadic people originally living in northwest China who moved to Central Asia c. second century BCE. The **Kuṣāṇas** were a branch of these people, who reached the subcontinent, c. first century BCE. *See also* BACTRIAN GREEK.

YUGA*.** Notion of time found in **astronomical** and other texts. The *yuga* consisted of a cycle, whose beginning and end were marked by a conjunction of planets. The *mahāyuga* or great cycle consisted of 4,320,000 solar years. This in turn was divided into four subsets: the *kṛta yuga* or golden age, lasting for 1,728,000 years; the *tretā* or silver age of 1,296,000 years; the *dvāpara*, lasting for 864,000 years; and the ***kali or **iron** age, lasting for 432,000 years. The present *kali yuga* is supposed to have commenced in 3102 BCE. Apart from distinctive time spans, each successive age is supposed to be marked by moral and material decline in comparison with the preceding phase.

– Z –

ZEND AVESTA. One of the major texts of **Zoroastrianism**, compiled over several centuries (c. early first millennium BCE onward). Its core component includes *gāthās* or verses in praise of several deities. These have parallels with the ***Ṛgveda*** in terms of both content and **language**, the latter showing parallels with **Vedic Sanskrit**. At the same time, there are instances of reversals of meanings as well. For instance, the term *ahura* (Sanskrit *asura*) had positive connotations in the *Avesta*, whereas it was invested with a certain degree of ambiguity in Vedic texts and almost invariably had a negative connotation in later Sanskrit **literature**.

ZOROASTRIANISM. Ancient **religious** tradition of Persia (Iran) associated with Zarathustra. The religion included rituals involving the use of fire. Zoroastrian influence was evident in the northwest of the subcontinent from the end of the first millennium BCE. Zoroastrians migrated from Iran and settled along the west coast of the subcontinent from c. eighth century CE onward. *See also* INDO-GREEK; KUṢĀṆA; *ZEND AVESTA*.

Bibliography

CONTENTS

INTRODUCTION

There is a vast and steadily growing body of literature on early Indian history. However, the foci of scholarly interest as well as the methodologies of analyses have shifted over the decades. Some of the earliest scholarship (often available in reprinted editions) focused on dynastic history, concentrating in particular on the Mauryas and the Guptas.

Subsequently, other dynasties received attention. Within the subcontinent, the concern with dynastic history was often part of assertions of national identity.

Although histories of ruling lineages continue to be written, the post-Independence era has witnessed a broadening of historical investigations to include issues related to economic and social history. The latter has proved to be particularly challenging, given the absence of historical records produced by marginalized social groups. It is in this context that historians have devised strategies of reading texts produced by dominant ruling elites against the grain.

Early Indian architecture, sculpture, painting, and literary traditions have attracted attention since the late 18th century. Some of the earliest works were characterized by a fascination for the exotic. More recently, cultural production has been contextualized in more meaningful ways. Similar trends are apparent in studies on early Indian religious traditions as well.

The bibliography is divided into thematic sections. Although many of the works listed deal with more than one theme, each text has been listed under the thematic heading that seemed most appropriate in order to avoid repetition. The interested reader may therefore find it worthwhile to consult more than one section.

A. L. Basham's *The Wonder That Was India*, first published in 1954, remains one of the most accessible introductions to early Indian history. A more provocative and stimulating entry point is provided by D. D. Kosambi's *An Introduction to the Study of Indian History* (first published in 1956), one of the first major explorations of the past from a Marxist perspective. R. S. Sharma (2005) provides a lucid narrative of the period from a more or less identical position. The reader who wishes to pursue these themes further will find Romila Thapar's *Early India* (2002) as well as Brajadulal Chattopadhyaya's *The Making of Early India* (1994) valuable. For a wide range of papers, many of which summarize recent research findings on a variety of themes, see Olivelle (2006). Upinder Singh's *A History of Ancient and Early Medieval India* (2008) provides a useful summary of the present state of knowledge about the subject.

Several works summarize archaeological findings: Of these, the essays edited by F. R. Allchin (1995) in the anthology titled *The Archaeology of Early Historical South Asia* are thought-provoking. The more advanced reader may wish to consult Dilip K. Chakrabarti's *Oxford Companion to Indian Archaeology* (2006).

Historical geography has unfortunately not been a fashionable theme in recent decades. Those interested in historical geography will find Brajadulal Chattopadhyaya's *A Survey of the Historical Geography of Ancient India* useful. Y. Subbarayalu's *Political Geography of the Chola Country* (1973) remains unsurpassed in terms of detailed scholarship.

Readers interested in surveys of historiography will find the volume titled *Recent Perspectives of Early Indian History*, edited by Romila Thapar (1995), helpful. More recently, Nayanjot Lahiri (*Finding Forgotten Cities*, 2005) and Upinder Singh (*The Discovery of Ancient India*, 2004) have provided lively accounts of the history of archaeology in the subcontinent.

Some of the journals and serials listed in the bibliography are/were exclusively devoted to articles on early Indian history/archaeology. The others frequently/occasionally contain material on the subject. Two series of texts, the *Sacred Books of the East* and *Ancient Indian Tradition and Mythology*, contain translations of early Indian religious literature. The first series (in 50 volumes) includes texts from other parts of Asia as well. The latter series (in which 68 volumes have been published to date) consists of translations from selected Purāṇas.

There have been some attempts to produce multivolume histories of India. Of these, the *History and Culture of the Indian People* series, written from a broadly nationalist perspective, has been completed. Other series include *A People's History of India*, written explicitly for the lay reader, *Comprehensive History of India*, and the *History of Science, Philosophy and Culture in Indian Civilization*. The first and the last are ongoing projects, with several volumes relating to early India already published.

Interested readers can consult a variety of reference works, including encyclopedias, dictionaries, indexes, bibliographies, and atlases. Some of the works listed, such as the *Vedic Bibliography* (Dandekar, 1946 onward), deal with a wide variety of subjects apart from those indicated in the title. The use of the Sanskrit term *kosa* in the title of a book indicates that it is an encyclopedia/dictionary.

Several secondary works are available summarizing and analyzing archaeological evidence relating to prehistoric and protohistoric cultures, the Harappan civilization, and other themes. K. Paddayya's study of a Paleolithic culture of Karnataka (*The Acheulian Culture of the Hunsgi Valley (Peninsular India): A Settlement System Perspective*, 1982) remains a classic, as does M. K. Dhavalikar's discussion of a Chalcolithic society of Maharashtra (*The First Farmers of the Deccan*, 1988). Zarine Cooper's exploration of the Andaman Islands (*Archaeology and History: Early Settlements in the Andaman Islands*, 2002) is an insightful study of a relatively less well-known area.

The scholarship on the Harappan civilization is perhaps one of the most rapidly growing areas today. Shereen Ratnagar's *Understanding Harappa* (2001) provides a brilliant introduction to the issues, problems, and possibilities of this scholarship. Those looking for more details on recent archaeological work in the subcontinent can consult the four-volume series titled *Indian Archaeology in Retrospect* edited by S. Settar and R. Korisettar (2002).

The two volumes of inscriptions edited and anthologized by D. C. Sircar (*Select Inscriptions Bearing on Indian History and Civilisation*, 1965, 1983) remain invaluable as an introduction to the epigraphic sources used to reconstruct early Indian history. Richard Salomon's more recent study, *Indian Epigraphy: A Guide to the Study of Inscriptions in Sanskrit, Prakrit and Other Indo-Aryan Languages* (1998), is useful for those interested in the contexts and contents of early inscriptions. For a stimulating analysis of numismatic data, see John Deyell, *Living without Silver* (1990).

Hemchandra Raychaudhuri's *Political History of Ancient India from the Accession of Parikshit to the Extinction of the Gupta Dynasty*, with a commentary by B. N. Mukherjee (1996), provides insights into the painstaking strategies used to reconstruct dynastic histories in the early 20th century and subsequently. K. A. Nilakanta Sastri's reconstruction of the dynastic history of the Co̱las (1975) is also a classic study in the same mold. For an example of the ways in which subsequent scholarship both draws on and qualifies our understanding of political ideas and institutions, see James Heitzman, *Gifts of Power: Lordship in an Early Indian State* (2002).

Several histories of specific regions of the subcontinent have been published. While some of these deal with political or dynastic histories, others explore economic, social, and cultural trends. A classic in this category is the *History of the Bengali People*, by Niharranjan Ray, originally written in Bengali but now available in an abridged English translation (1994).

For an overview of some of the themes in economic history that have attracted scholarly attention, the reader may consult *Economy and Society in Early India: Issues and Paradigms*, by D. N. Jha (1980). Those interested in agrarian relations will find *Land System and Rural Society* edited by Bhairabi Prasad Sahu (1997) useful. Ranabir Chakravarti's *Trade and Traders in Early Indian Society* (2007) provides a valuable introduction to discussion on exchange, commerce, and related issues.

Several themes have figured in recent discussions on social history. On the caste system, Louis Dumont's *Homo Hierarchicus* (1980), originally published in French, has been extensively critiqued for a somewhat uncritical acceptance of the Brahmanical model. Historians such as Uma Chakravarti (*Everyday Lives, Everyday Histories: Beyond the Kings and Brahmanas of 'Ancient' India*, 2006) and Aloka Parasher-Sen (*Subordinate and Marginal Groups in Early India*, 2004), have drawn attention to marginalized groups. Fresh perspectives on issues of gender are available in the anthology edited by Julia Leslie and Mary McGee (*Invented Identities: The Interplay of Gender, Religion and Politics in India*, 2000). Those interested in the Aryan question will find the anthology edited by Thomas R. Trautmann (*The Aryan Debate*, 2005) particularly useful.

The literature on cultural aspects of early Indian history is prolific. Susan L. Huntington's *The Art of Ancient India: Buddhist, Hindu, Jain* (1985) provides a comprehensive account of traditions of sculpture, architecture, and painting. Vidya Dehejia's *Discourse in Early Buddhist Art: Visual Narratives of India* (1997) is illustrative of fruitful attempts to reinterpret the rich repertoire of visual material from fresh perspectives. The *History of Indian Literature* series, edited by Jan Gonda (1973 onward) and published in 10 volumes, includes several fascicles dealing with early Indian literary traditions, primarily in Sanskrit, but also in Tamil and Pali. Sheldon Pollock's *The Language of the Gods in the World of Men* (2006) addresses issues of the significance of language change and cultural practices in early India, among other things.

There are several lucid introductions to early Indian religious traditions. Depending on his or her interest, the reader may wish to consult *The Sacred Thread—A Short History of Hinduism* by J. L. Brockington (1996), *The Jains* by Paul Dundas (2002), and *Theravada Buddhism* by Richard Gombrich (1988). N. N. Bhattacharyya's *History of the Tantric Religion* (1999) provides an entry point into what is often regarded as one of the most esoteric religious traditions in the subcontinent. Those interested in histories of philosophical ideas can consult the five-volume *History of Indian Philosophy* by Surendranath Dasgupta (1922 onward).

Specific religious traditions have been the subject of detailed analyses. Some examples include *Religious Process: The Puranas and the Making of a Regional Tradition* by Kunal Chakrabarti (2001) and Thomas Coburn's exploration of the goddess tradition (*The Devimahatmya: The Crystallization of the Goddess Tradition*, 1985).

Histories of science and technology in early India are relatively few. Debiprasad Chattopadhyaya's *History of Science and Technology* (1986) is useful as are G. Jan Meulenbeld's *History of Indian Medical Literature* (1999–2002) and David Pingree's *Jyotiḥśāstra* (1981).

Finally, some of the major published primary sources, including archaeological reports, inscriptions, catalogs of coins, and translations of texts, have been listed. The reader who wishes to delve deeper into early Indian history will probably find these helpful.

There is a rich tradition of writing on historical themes related to early India in modern Indian languages as well as in European languages other than English. While the bibliography itself is confined to English-language publications, some of these contain references to scholarship in other languages.

While every effort has been made to list the latest editions and reprints that are easily accessible, it is possible that readers may find other editions, especially as some of the more popular works have been frequently reprinted by publishers, both Indian and foreign, over the years. Reprints of 19th- and early 20th-century publications are indicated by the use of the word *reprint* within parentheses. Readers can also search for online versions of the books as well as consult some of the websites listed at the end of the bibliography, which provide access to a wide range of resources on the history of ancient India.

The names of several cities (which are also important centers of publication) in the subcontinent have been changed in recent times. I have retained the names used in earlier publications. Changes that the reader might find useful to keep in mind are as follows:

Bombay is now Mumbai, Calcutta is Kolkata, Dacca is Dhaka, Madras is Chennai, and Poona is Pune. More recently, Bangalore has become Bengaluru.

GENERAL

History

Basham, A. L. *The Wonder That Was India*. New Delhi: Picador, 2004 (reprint).

Bhattacharyya, Narendra Nath. *Ancient Indian History and Civilization*. New Delhi: Manohar, 1988.

Bongard-Levin, G. M. *Ancient Indian Civilization*. New York: Humanities, 1985.

———. *Complex Study of Ancient India: A Multi-disciplinary Approach*. New Delhi: Ajanta, 1986.

Chattopadhyaya, Brajadulal. *The Making of Early Medieval India*. New Delhi: Oxford University Press, 1994.

———. *Studying Early India: Archaeology, Texts and Historical Issues*. New Delhi: Permanent Black, 2003.

Inden, Ronald. *Imagining India*. Oxford, UK: Basil Blackwell, 1990.

Jha, D. N. *Ancient India in Historical Outline*. New Delhi: Manohar, 2004.

Kenoyer, J. M., and K. Heuston. *The Ancient South Asian World*. New York: Oxford University Press, 2005.

Kosambi, D. D. *The Culture and Civilization of Ancient India in Historical Outline*. New Delhi: Vikas, 1975 (reprint).

———. *An Introduction to the Study of Indian History*. Bombay: Popular Prakashan, 1999 (reprint).

Majumdar, R. C., general ed. *History and Culture of the Indian People*. 11 vols. Bombay: Bharatiya Vidya Bhavan, 1951–1969.

Olivelle, Patrick, ed. *Between the Empires: Society in India 300 BCE to 400 CE*. New York: Oxford University Press, 2006.

Pande, G. C., ed. *The Dawn of Indian Civilization. History of Science, Philosophy and Culture in Indian Civilization*. Vol. 1, Part 1. New Delhi: Munshiram Manoharlal, 1999.

Ray, Niharranjan, Brajadulal Chattopadhyaya, Ranabir Chakravarti, and V. R.

Mani, eds. *A Sourcebook of Indian Civilization*. Calcutta: Orient Longman, 2000.
Satchidananda Murty, K., ed. *Life, Thought and Culture in India (c. AD 300–1000). History of Science, Philosophy and Culture in Indian Civilization*. Vol. 2, Part 1. New Delhi: Motilal Banarsidass, 2002.
Sharma, R. S. *Material Culture and Social Formation in Ancient India*. New Delhi: Macmillan, 1983.
———. *Indian Feudalism c. A. D. 300–1200*. New Delhi: Macmillan, 1985.
———. *India's Ancient Past*. New Delhi: Oxford University Press, 2005.
Shrimali, Krishna Mohan. *The Age of Iron and the Religious Revolution. A People's History of India*. Vol. 3A. New Delhi: Tulika, 2007.
Singh, Upinder. *A History of Ancient and Early Medieval India*. Delhi: Pearson Longman, 2008.
Stein, Burton. *A History of India*. Oxford, UK: Blackwell, 1998.
Thapar, Romila. *Early India: From the Origins to AD 1300*. London: Penguin, 2002.
———. *History and Beyond*. New Delhi: Oxford University Press, 2004.

Archaeology

Agrawal, D. P. *The Archaeology of India*. London: Curzon, 1982.
———. *Man and Environment in India through the Ages*. New Delhi: Books and Books, 1992.
———. *Ancient Metal Technology and Archaeology of South Asia: A Pan-Asian Perspective*. New Delhi: Aryan, 2000.
Agrawal, D. P., and J. S. Kharakwal. *Bronze and Iron Ages in South Asia*. New Delhi: Aryan, 2003.
Agrawal, D. P., and M. G. Yadava. *Dating the Human Past*. Pune, Maharashtra: Indian Society for Prehistoric and Quaternary Studies, 1995.
Allchin, Bridget. *Living Traditions: Studies in the Ethnoarchaeology of South Asia*. New Delhi: Oxford and IBH, 1994.
Allchin, Bridget, and Raymond Allchin. *Origins of a Civilization: The Prehistory and Early Archaeology of South Asia*. New Delhi: Viking, 1997.
Allchin, F. R., ed. *The Archaeology of Early Historic South Asia: The Emergence of Cities and States*. Cambridge, UK: Cambridge University Press, 1995.
Allchin, F. R., and Dilip K. Chakrabarti, eds. *A Source-book of Indian Archaeology*. New Delhi: Munshiram Manoharlal, 1997.
Banerjee, N. R. *The Iron Age in India*. New Delhi: Munshiram Manoharlal, 1965.
Chakrabarti, Dilip K. *The Archaeology of Ancient Indian Cities*. New Delhi: Oxford University Press, 1995.

———. *India: An Archaeological History. Palaeolithic Beginnings to Early Historic Foundations*. New Delhi: Oxford University Press, 1999.

———. *The Oxford Companion to Indian Archaeology*. New Delhi: Oxford University Press, 2006.

Paddayya, K., ed. *Archaeology of India*. New Delhi: Munshiram Manoharlal and Indian Council of Historical Research, 1999.

Possehl, Gregory L. *Radiocarbon Dates for South Asian Archaeology*. Philadelphia: University of Pennsylvania Museum, 1990.

Ray, Himanshu Prabha, and Carla Sinopoli, eds. *Archaeology as History in Early South Asia*. New Delhi: Aryan, 2004.

Tripathi, Vibha. *The Age of Iron in South Asia: Legacy and Tradition*. New Delhi: Aryan, 2001.

Historical Geography

Bhattacharyya, P. K. *Historical Geography of Madhya Pradesh*. New Delhi: Munshiram Manoharlal, 1977.

Chattopadhyaya, Brajadulal. *A Survey of Historical Geography of Ancient India*. Calcutta: Manisha Granthalaya, 1984.

Cunningham, A. *The Ancient Geography of India*. New Delhi: Munshiram Manoharlal, 2002 (reprint).

Gupta, Parmanand. *Geography in Ancient Indian Inscriptions (up to 650 A.D.)* New Delhi: D. K. Publishing, 1973.

———. *Geographical Names in Ancient Indian Inscriptions: A Companion Volume to Geography in Ancient Indian Inscriptions up to 650 A.D.* New Delhi: Concept, 1977.

Law, Bimala Churn. *Historical Geography of Ancient India*. New Delhi: Oriental Books Reprint, 1984 (reprint).

Mangalam, S. J. *Historical Geography and Toponymy of Andhra Pradesh*. New Delhi: Eastern Book Linkers, 1986.

Mulay, Sumati. *Historical Geography and Cultural Ethnography of the Deccan*. Poona, Maharashtra: Deccan College, 1972.

Pandey, M. S. *The Historical Geography and Topography of Bihar*. New Delhi: Motilal Banarsidass, 1963.

Sircar, D. C. *Cosmology and Geography in Early Indian Literature*. Calcutta: Indian Studies, 1967.

———. *Studies in the Geography of Ancient and Medieval India*. New Delhi: Motilal. Banarsidass, 1971.

Subbarayalu, Y. *Political Geography of the Chola Country*. Madras: State Department of Archaeology, 1973.

Historiographical Studies

Allen, Charles. *The Buddha and the Sahibs, the Men Who Discovered India's Lost Religion*. London: Murray, 2002.

Almond, Philip C. *The British Discovery of Buddhism*. Cambridge, UK: Cambridge University Press, 1988.

Bhattacharyya, Narendra Nath. *Indian Religious Historiography*. Vol. 1. New Delhi: Munshiram Manoharlal, 1996.

Chakrabarti, Dilip K. *A History of Indian Archaeology from the Beginning to 1947*. New Delhi: Munshiram Manoharlal, 1988.

———. *Archaeology in the Third World: A History of Indian Archaeology since 1947*. New Delhi: D.K. Printworld, 2003.

Clarke, J. J. *Oriental Enlightenment. The Encounter between Asian and Western Thought*. London: Routledge, 1997.

Cohn, B. S. *Colonialism and Its Forms of Knowledge: The British in India*. Princeton, NJ: Princeton University Press, 1997.

Dikshit, K. N., ed. *Archaeological Perspectives on India since Independence*. New Delhi: Books and Books, 1985.

Ganguly, D. K. *History and Historians in Ancient India*. New Delhi: Abhinav, 1984.

Imam, A. *Sir Alexander Cunningham and the Beginnings of Indian Archaeology*. Dacca: Asiatic Society of Pakistan, 1966.

Keay, John. *India Discovered*. London: HarperCollins, 2001.

Kejariwal, O. P. *The Asiatic Society of Bengal and the Discovery of India's Past*. New Delhi: Oxford University Press, 1988.

Lahiri, Nayanjot. *Finding Forgotten Cities: How the Indus Civilization was Discovered*. New Delhi: Permanent Black, 2005.

Nair, P. T. *James Prinsep: Life and Work*. Calcutta: Firma K. L. Mukhopadhyay, 1999.

Pathak, Vishwambhar Sharan. *Ancient Historians of India: A Study in Historical Biographies*. Jodhpur: Kusumanjali Book World, 1997.

Philips, C. H., ed. *Historians of India, Pakistan and Ceylon*. London: Oxford University Press, 1961.

Ray, Himanshu Prabha. *Colonial Archaeology in South Asia: The Legacy of Mortimer Wheeler*. New Delhi: Oxford University Press, 2007.

Roy, Sourindranath. *The Story of Indian Archaeology 1784–1947*. New Delhi: Archaeological Survey of India, 1961.

Schwab, R. *The Oriental Renaissance: Europe's Rediscovery of India and the East, 1680–1880*. New York: Columbia University Press, 1984.

Settar, S., and Ravi Korisettar, eds. *Indian Archaeology in Retrospect*, Vol. 3, *Archaeology and Interactive Disciplines*. New Delhi: Indian Council of Historical Research and Manohar, 2002.

Sharma, R. K., ed. *Indian Archaeology: New Perspectives*. New Delhi: Agam Kala Prakashan, 1982.

Shrimali, K. M., ed. *Indian Archaeology since Independence*. New Delhi: Association for the Study of History and Archaeology, 1996.

Singh, Upinder. *The Discovery of Ancient India. Early Archaeologists and the Beginnings of Archaeology*. New Delhi: Permanent Black, 2004.

Thakur, V. K. *Historiography of Indian Feudalism: Towards a Model of Early Medieval Indian Economy (c. A.D. 600–1000)*. Patna, Bihar: Janaki Prakashan, 1989.

Thapar, Romila, ed. *Interpreting Early India*. New Delhi: Oxford University Press, 1993.

———, ed. *Recent Perspectives of Early Indian History*. Bombay: Popular Prakashan, 1995.

Journals, Serial Publications

A People's History of India
Ancient Ceylon
Ancient India
Ancient Indian Tradition and Mythology
Ancient Pakistan
Annals of the Bhandarkar Oriental Research Institute
Annual Report of South Indian Epigraphy
Annual Report of the Archaeological Survey of India
Antiquity
Artibus Asiae
Asiatic Researches
Bibliotheca Buddhica
Bulletin of the Deccan College Post-graduate and Research Institute
Bulletin of the School of Oriental and African Studies
Catalogus Catalogorum: An Alphabetical Register of Sanskrit Works and Authors
Comprehensive History of India
Corpus Inscriptionum Indicarum
Descriptive Catalogue of Manuscripts, Bhandarkar Oriental Research Institute
East and West
Electronic Journal of Vedic Studies
Epigraphia Carnatica
Epigraphia Indica
History and Culture of the Indian People
History of Science, Philosophy and Culture in Indian Civilization
History of Religions
Indian Antiquary
Indian Archaeology—A Review

Indian Economic and Social History Review
Indian Historical Quarterly
Indian Historical Review
Indian Journal of the History of Science
Indian Studies Past and Present
Indo-Iranian Journal
Journal of Ancient Indian History
Journal of Central Asia
Journal of Indian History
Journal of Indian Philosophy
Journal of Indo-European Studies
Journal of Oriental Research
Journal of the American Oriental Society
Journal of the Asiatic Society of Bengal
Journal of the Bihar and Orissa Research Society
Journal of the Bihar Research Society
Journal of the Bombay Branch of the Royal Asiatic Society
Journal of the Economic and Social History of the Orient
Journal of the Epigraphic Society of India
Journal of the Indian Society of Oriental Art
Journal of the International Society of Buddhist Studies
Journal of the Numismatic Society of India
Journal of the Oriental Institute of Baroda
Journal of the Pali Text Society
Journal of the Royal Asiatic Society
Journal of the Uttar Pradesh Historical Society
Man and Environment
Marg
Memoirs of the Archaeological Survey of India
New Catalogus Catalogorum: An Alphabetical Register of Sanskrit and Allied Works and Authors
Numismatic Digest
Orissa Historical Research Journal
Pakistan Archaeology
Poona Orientalist
Pragdhara
Purana
Puratattva
Sacred Books of the East
Silk Road Art and Archaeology
Social Science Probings
Social Scientist

South Asia Research
South Asian Archaeology
South Asian Studies
South Indian Inscriptions
Studies in History
Studies in Indian Epigraphy
The Cultural Heritage of India
Vishveshvaranand Indological Journal
World Archaeology

REFERENCE WORKS

Archaeology. *See* Ghosh (1989), Sharma (1998).
Architecture. *See* Meister and Dhaky (1986, 1991, 1996, 1998, 1999).
Epigraphy. *See* Chaudhuri (1966), Sircar (1966).
Geography. *See* Bhattacharyya (1991), Schwartzberg (1991).
Literature. *See* Abhichandani and Dutt (1994), Datta (1987, 1988, 1989), Mohan Lal (1991, 1992), Rengarajan (2006), Sharma (1998).
Philosophy. *See* Jhalakikar (1996), Potter (1981 onward).
Religion. *See* Bhattacharyya (1990, 1999, 2001), Dalal (2006), Dange (1986), Nahar and Ghosh (1988), Vettam Mani (1978), Yamazaki and Ousaka (1999). *See also* VEDAS.
Vedas. *See* Bloomfield (1996), Dandekar (1946, 1961, 1973, 1985, 1993), Kashikar (1990), Macdonnell and Keith (1996), Michaels (1983).

Encyclopedias/Dictionaries

Abhichandani, Param, and K. C. Dutt, eds. *Encyclopaedia of Indian Literature*, Vol. 6. New Delhi: Sahitya Akademi, 1994.
Bhattacharyya, Narendra Nath. *A Glossary of Indian Religious Terms and Concepts*. New Delhi: Motilal Banarsidass, 1990.
———. *Geographical Dictionary: Ancient and Medieval India*. New Delhi: Munshiram Manoharlal, 1991.
———. *Encyclopaedia of Ancient Indian Culture*. New Delhi: Manohar, 1998.
———. *A Dictionary of Indian Mythology*. New Delhi: Munshiram Manoharlal, 2001 (reprint).
———. *Tantrabhidhana: A Tantric Lexicon*. New Delhi: Manohar, 2002.
Buck, Carl Darling. *A Dictionary of Selected Synonyms in the Principal Indo-European Languages*. Chicago: University of Chicago Press, 1949.

Burrow, T., and M. B. Emeneau. *A Dravidian Etymological Dictionary*. Oxford, UK: Clarendon Press, 1984.

Childers, R. C. *A Dictionary of the Pali Language*. Kyoto: Rinsen, 1976 (reprint).

Dalal, Roshen. *The Penguin Dictionary of Religion in India*. New Delhi: Penguin, 2006.

Dange, Sadashiv A. *Encyclopedia of Puranic Beliefs and Practices*. New Delhi: Navrang, 1986.

Datta, Amaresh, chief ed. *Encyclopaedia of Indian Literature*. Vol. 1. New Delhi: Sahitya Akademi, 1987.

———. *Encyclopaedia of Indian Literature*. Vol. 2. New Delhi: Sahitya Akademi, 1988.

———. *Encyclopaedia of Indian Literature*. Vol. 3. New Delhi: Sahitya Akademi, 1989.

Edgerton, Franklin. *Buddhist Hybrid Sanskrit Grammar and Dictionary*. New Haven: Yale University Press, 1953.

Encyclopedic Dictionary of Sanskrit on Historical Principles. Pune, Maharashtra: Deccan College, 1976 onward.

Ghatage, A. M., ed. *A Comprehensive and Critical Dictionary of the Prakrit Languages*. Vol. 1. Pune, Maharashtra: Bhandarkar Oriental Research Institute, 1996.

———. *A Comprehensive and Critical Dictionary of the Prakrit Languages*. Vol. 2. Pune, Maharashtra: Bhandarkar Oriental Research Institute, 2002.

———. *A Comprehensive and Critical Dictionary of the Prakrit Languages*. Vol. 3, Fasc. I and II. Pune, Maharashtra: Bhandarkar Oriental Research Institute, 2002, 2003.

Ghosh, A., ed. *An Encyclopaedia of Indian Archaeology*. 2 vols. New Delhi: Munshiram Manoharlal, 1989.

Jhalakikar, Mahamahopadhyaya Bhimacarya, revised and enhanced by Vasudeva Shastri Abhyankar. *Nyayakosa or Dictionary of Technical Terms in Indian Philosophy*. Poona, Maharashtra: Bhandarkar Oriental Research Institute, 1996.

Joshi, Laxmanshastri, ed. *Dharmakosa*. Vol. 1 (3 parts), *Vyavaharakanda*. Wai, Maharashtra: Prajna Pathasala Mandala, 1937–1941.

———. *Dharmakosa*. Vol. 2 (4 parts), *Upanisat-kanda*. Wai, Maharashtra: Prajna Pathasala Mandala, 1949–1953.

———. *Dharmakosa*. Vol. 3 (5 parts), *Samskarakanda*. Wai, Maharashtra: Prajna Pathasala Mandala, 1959–1984.

———. *Dharmakosa*. Vol. 4 (6 parts), *Rajnitikanda*. Wai, Maharashtra: Prajna Pathasala Mandala, 1973–1979.

———. *Dharmakosa*. Vol. 5, *Varnasramadharmakanda*. Wai, Maharashtra: Prajna Pathasala Mandala, 1988.

Kashikar, R. N. *Srautakosa*. (2 vols. in 3 parts). Pune, Maharashtra: Vaidik Samsodhana Mandala, 1990.

Malalasekara, G. P. *A Dictionary of Pali Proper Names*. London: Luzac, 1960.

Meister, Michael W., and M. A. Dhaky, eds. *Encyclopedia of Indian Temple Architecture*. Vol. 1, Part 2. New Delhi: American Institute of Indian Studies, 1986.

———. *Encyclopedia of Indian Temple Architecture*, Vol. 2, Part 2. New Delhi: American Institute of Indian Studies and Oxford University Press, 1991.

———. *Encyclopedia of Indian Temple Architecture*. Vol. 1, Part 3. New Delhi: Manohar, 1996.

———. *Encyclopedia of Indian Temple Architecture*. Vol. 2, Part 1. New Delhi: Manohar, 1998.

———. *Encyclopedia of Indian Temple Architecture*. Vol. 2, Part 3. New Delhi: Manohar, 1998.

———. *Encyclopedia of Indian Temple Architecture*. Vol. 1, Part 1. New Delhi: Manohar, 1999.

Mohan, Lal, chief ed. *Encyclopaedia of Indian Literature*. Vol. 4. New Delhi: Sahitya Akademi, 1991.

———. *Encyclopaedia of Indian Literature*. Vol. 5. New Delhi: Sahitya Akademi, 1992.

Nahar, P. C., and K. C. Ghosh, eds. *An Encyclopaedia of Jainism*. New Delhi: Satguru, 1988 (reprint).

Potter, Karl H., ed. *Encyclopaedia of Indian Philosophies*. Vol. 3, *Advaita Vedanta upto Samkara and His Pupils*. New Delhi: Motilal Banarsidass, 1981.

———. *Encyclopaedia of Indian Philosophies*. Vol. 1, *Bibliographies*. New Delhi: Motilal Banarsidass, 1995.

———. *Encyclopaedia of Indian Philosophies*. Vol. 2, *Indian Metaphysics and Epistemology*. New Delhi: Motilal Banarsidass, 1995.

———. *Encyclopaedia of Indian Philosophies*. Vol. 8, *Buddhist Philosophy from 100 to 300 A.D*. New Delhi: Motilal Banarsidass, 1999.

———. *Encyclopaedia of Indian Philosophies*. Vol. 9, *Buddhist Philosophy from 350 to 600 A.D*. New Delhi: Motilal Banarsidass, 1999.

———. *Encyclopaedia of Indian Philosophies*. Vol. 11, *Advaita Vedanta from 800 to 1200 A.D*. New Delhi: Motilal Banarsidass, 2007.

Potter, Karl H., Robert E. Buswell, Padmanabh S. Jaini, and Noble Ross Reat, eds. *Encyclopaedia of Indian Philosophies*. Vol. 8, *Buddhist Philosophy upto the Mahavibhanga*. New Delhi: Motilal Banarsidass, 1996.

Potter, Karl H., Harold G. Coward, and K. Kunjunni Raja, eds. *Encyclopaedia of Indian Philosophies*. Vol. 5, *The Philosophy of the Grammarians*. New Delhi: Motilal Banarsidass, 1990.

Potter, Karl H., Gerald James Larson, and Ram Shankar Bhattacharya, eds. *Encyclopaedia of Indian Philosophies*. Vol. 4, *Samkhya, a Dualist Tradition in Indian Philosophy*. New Delhi: Motilal Banarsidass, 1987.

Potter, Karl H., Dalsukh Malvania, and Jayendra Suri. *Encyclopaedia of Indian Philosophies*. Vol. 10, *Jaina Philosophies*. New Delhi: Motilal Banarsidass, 2007.

Ramachandra Rao, S. K. *Encyclopaedia of Indian Iconography: Hinduism-Buddhism-Jainism*. New Delhi: Satguru, 2004 (reprint).

Rengarajan, T. *Dictionary of Indian Epics*. New Delhi: Eastern Book Linkers, 2006.

Sharma, R. K. *Encyclopaedia of Art, Archaeology and Literature in Central India*. 2 vols. New Delhi: Aryan, 1998.

Sircar, D. C. *Indian Epigraphical Glossary*. New Delhi: Motilal Banarsidass, 1966.

Vettam Mani. *Puranic Encyclopaedia*. 2 vols. New Delhi: Motilal Banarsidass, 2002 (reprint).

Indexes

Bloomfield, Maurice. *A Vedic Concordance*. New Delhi: Motilal Banarsidass, 1996 (reprint).

Dikshitar, V. R. R. *Purana Index*. 3 vols. New Delhi: Motilal Banarsidass, 1995 (reprint).

Macdonnell, A. A., and A. B. Keith. *Vedic Index of Names and Subjects*. 2 vols. New Delhi: Motilal Banarsidass, 1996 (reprint).

Michaels, Axel. *A Comprehensive Sulvasutra Word-Index*. Wiesbaden: Steiner, 1983.

Sorensen, S. *An Index to Names in the Mahabharata*. New Delhi: Eastern Book, 2006 (reprint).

Yamazaki, M., and Y. Ousaka. *A Word Index and Reverse Word Index to Early Jain Canonical Texts*. Tokyo: Chuo Academic Research Institute, 1999.

Bibliographies

Biswas, Subhas C., ed. *Bibliographic Survey of Indian Manuscript Catalogues: Being a Union List of Manuscript Catalogues*. New Delhi: Eastern Book Linkers, 1998.

Chaudhuri, Sibadas. *Bibliography of Studies in Indian Epigraphy (1926–50)*. Baroda, Gujarat: Oriental Institute, 1966.

Dandekar, R. N. *Vedic Bibliography*. Vol. 1. Bombay: Karnataka Publishing, 1946.

———. *Vedic Bibliography*. Vol. 2. Pune, Maharashtra: University of Poona, 1961.

———. *Vedic Bibliography*. Vol. 3. Pune, Maharashtra: University of Poona, 1973.

———. *Vedic Bibliography*. Vol. 4. Pune, Maharashtra: University of Poona, 1985.

———. *Harappan Bibliography*. Pune, Maharashtra: Bhandarkar Oriental Research Institute, 1987.

———. *Vedic Bibliography*. Vol. 5. Pune, Maharashtra: University of Poona, 1993.

Gupta, Parameshwari Lal. *Bibliography of Indian Numismatics*. Varanasi, Uttar Pradesh: Numismatic Society of India, 1977.

Patterson, Maureen L. P. *South Asian Civilizations: A Bibliographical Synthesis*. Chicago: University of Chicago Press, 1981.

Puri, B. N. *Kusana Bibliography*. Calcutta: Naya Prokash, 1977.

Yadav, Jagdish S., and Nirmala Yadav. *The Imperial Guptas: A Bibliography*. New Delhi: Manohar, 1997.

Atlases

Chattopadhyaya, Brajadulal, Gautam Sengupta, and Sambhu Chakrabarty, eds. *An Annotated Archaeological Atlas of West Bengal*. New Delhi: Manohar, 2005.

Schwartzberg, J. E., ed. *A Historical Atlas of South Asia*. Chicago: University of Chicago Press, 1991.

ARCHAEOLOGICAL STUDIES

Prehistoric and Protohistoric Archaeology (Except for Harappan)

Agrawal, D. P. *The Copper Bronze Age in India*. New Delhi: Munshiram Manoharlal, 1971.

Agrawal, D. P., and D. K. Chakrabarti, eds. *Essays in Indian Protohistory*. New Delhi: B. R. Publishers, 1979.

Agrawal, D. P., and J. S. Kharakwal. *South Asian Prehistory: A Multidisciplinary Study*. New Delhi: Aryan, 2002.

Agrawal, D. P., and Sheela Kusumgar. *Prehistoric Chronology and Radio-Carbon Dating in India*. New Delhi: Munshiram Manoharlal, 1974.

Allchin, Bridget, Andrew Goudie, and Karunakara Hegde. *The Prehistory and Paleogeography of the Great Indian Desert*. London: Academic Press, 1978.

Allchin, F. R. *Neolithic Cattle Keepers of South India*. Leiden: Brill, 1963.

Chauley, Milan K. *Prehistory and Protohistory of Eastern India*. New Delhi: Agam Kala Prakashan, 2007.

Cooper, Zarine. *Prehistory of the Chitrakot Falls, Central India*. Pune, Maharashtra: Ravish, 1998.

Dani, Ahmad Hasan. *Prehistory and Protohistory of Eastern India: With a Detailed Account of Neolithic Cultures of Mainland Southeast India*. Calcutta: Firma K. L. Mukhopadhyay, 1960.

Dhavalikar, M. K. *The First Farmers of the Deccan*. Pune, Maharashtra: Ravish, 1988.

Habib, Irfan. *Prehistory*. New Delhi: Tulika, 2001.

Murty, M. L. K., ed. *Pre- and Protohistoric Andhra Pradesh up to 500 BC*. Hyderabad: Orient Longman, 2003.

Narasimhaiah, B. *Neolithic and Megalithic Cultures in Tamil Nadu*. New Delhi: Sundeep Prakashan, 1980.

Paddayya, K. *Investigations into the Neolithic Culture of the Shorapur Doab*. Leiden: Brill, 1973.

———. *The Acheulian Culture of the Hunsgi Valley (Peninsular India): A Settlement System Perspective*. Pune, Maharashtra: Deccan College, 1982.

Raju, D. R. *Stone Age Hunter-Gatherers: An Ethno-Archaeology of Cuddapah Region*. Pune, Maharashtra: Ravish, 1988.

Sant, Urmila. *Neolithic Settlement Pattern of North-Eastern and Northern India*. New Delhi: Sarita, 1991.

Settar, S., and Ravi Korisettar, eds. *Indian Archaeology in Retrospect*. Vol. 1, *Prehistory: Archaeology of South Asia*. New Delhi: Manohar, with Indian Council of Historical Research, 2001.

Sharma, A. K. *Prehistoric Delhi and Its Neighbourhood*. New Delhi: Aryan, 1993.

Sharma, Deo Prakash. *Newly Discovered Copper Hoard Weapons of South Asia, c. 2800–1500 B. C.* New Delhi: Bharatiya Kala Prakashan, 2002.

Sharma, R. K., and K. K. Tripathi. *Recent Perspectives on Prehistoric Art in India and Allied Subjects*. New Delhi: Aryan, 1996.

Shinde, Vasant. *Early Settlements in the Central Tapi Basin*. New Delhi: Munshiram Manoharlal, 1998.

Singh, B. P. *Early Farming Communities of the Kaimur*. Jaipur, Rajasthan: Publication Scheme. 2004.

Srivastava, K. M. *Community Movements in Protohistoric India*. New Delhi: Agam Kala Prakashan, 1979.

Tripathi, Vibha. *The Painted Grey Ware: An Iron Age Culture of North India*. New Delhi: Concept, 1976.

The Harappan Civilization

Bisht, R. S. *Banawali: A Look Back into the Pre-Indus and Indus Civilization*. Chandigarh: Haryana Government, 1977.

Chakrabarti, Dilip K. *The External Trade of the Indus Civilization*. New Delhi: Munshiram Manoharlal, 1990.

———. *Indus Civilization Sites in India: New Discoveries*. Mumbai: Marg, 2004.

Dani, A. H., ed. *Indus Civilization: New Perspectives*. Islamabad: Centre for the Study of the Civilization of Central Asia, Quaid-i-Azam University, 1981.

Fairservis, Walter A. *The Harappan Civilization and its Writing: A Model for the Decipherment of the Indus Script*. New Delhi: Oxford and IBH, 1992.

Gupta, S. P. *The Indus-Sarasvati Civilization*. New Delhi: Pratibha Prakashan, 1996.

Habib, Irfan. *The Indus Civilization: Including Other Copper Age Cultures and History of Language Change till c. 1500 BC*. New Delhi: Tulika, 2002.

Jansen, M. *City of Wells and Drains, Mohenjo-Daro: Water Splendor 4500 Years Ago*. Bonn: Verlag und Vertieb, 1993.

Jansen, M., M. Mulloy, and G. Urban, eds. *Forgotten Cities on the Indus: Early Civilization in Pakistan from the 8th to the 2nd millennium BC*. Mainz: Philipp von Zabern, 1991.

Kenoyer, J. M. *Ancient Cities of the Indus Valley Civilisation*. Karachi: Oxford University Press, 1998.

Lahiri, Nayanjot. *The Decline and Fall of the Indus Civilization*. New Delhi: Permanent Black, 2002.

Lal, B. B. *The Earliest Civilization of South Asia: Rise, Maturity and Decline*. New Delhi: Aryan, 1997.

———. *India 1947–1997: New Light on the Indus Civilization*. New Delhi: Aryan, 1998.

Lal, B. B., and S. P. Gupta, eds. *Frontiers of the Indus Civilization*. New Delhi: Books and Books, 1984.

Mahadevan, Iravatham. *The Indus Script: Texts, Concordance and Tables*. New Delhi: Archaeological Survey of India, 1977.

Mughal, M. R. *Ancient Cholistan: Archaeology and Architecture*. Lahore: Ferozsons, 1977.

Osada, Toshiki., ed. *Indus Civilization: Text and Context*. New Delhi: Manohar, 2006.

Parpola, Asko. *Deciphering the Indus Script*. New Delhi: Oxford University Press, 2000.

Possehl, Gregory L., ed. *Harappan Civilization: A Recent Perspective*. New Delhi: Oxford and IBH, and the American Institute of Indian Studies, 1993.

———. *Indus Age: The Writing System*. New Delhi: Oxford and IBH, 1996.

———. *Indus Age: The Beginnings*. New Delhi: Oxford and IBH, 1999.

———. *The Indus Civilization: A Contemporary Perspective*. New Delhi: Vistaar, 2002.

Ratnagar, Shereen. *Enquiries into the Political Organization of Harappan Society*. Pune, Maharashtra: Ravish, 1991.

———. *The End of the Great Harappan Tradition*. New Delhi: Manohar, 2000.

———. *Understanding Harappa: Civilization in the Greater Indus Valley*. New Delhi: Tulika, 2001.

———. *Trading Encounters from the Euphrates to the Indus in the Bronze Age*. New Delhi: Oxford University Press, 2004.

Settar, S., and R. Korisettar, eds. *Indian Archaeology in Retrospect*. Vol. 2, *Protohistory: Archaeology of the Harappan Civilization*. New Delhi: Indian Council of Historical Research and Manohar, 2002.

Sharma, D. P. *Harappan Art*. New Delhi: Sharada, 2007.

Weber, S. A., and W. R. Belcher, eds. *Indus Ethnobiology: New Perspectives from the Field*. Lanham: Lexington Books, 2003.

Wheeler, Mortimer. *The Indus Civilization*. Supplementary volume to the Cambridge History of India. Lahore: Sang e Meel Publications, 1997 (reprint).

Other Works Based on Archaeological Findings: General

Alur, K. R. *Studies in Indian Archaeology and Paleontology*. Dharwad: Shrihari Prakashan, 1990.

Chakrabarti, Dilip K. *Theoretical Issues in Indian Archaeology*. New Delhi: Munshiram Manoharlal, 1998.

Deo, S. B., and K. Paddayya, eds. *Recent Advances in Indian Archaeology*. Pune, Maharashtra: Deccan College, 1985.

Dhavalikar, M. K. *Historical Archaeology of India*. New Delhi: Books and Books, 1999.

Gaur, R. C. *Studies in Indian Archaeology*. Jaipur, Rajasthan: Publication Scheme, 1997.

Jacobsen, J., ed. *Studies in the Archaeology of India and Pakistan*. New Delhi: Oxford and IBH, 1986.

Kennedy, K. A. R., and G. Possehl, eds. *Studies in the Archaeology and Palaeoanthropology of South Asia*. New Delhi: Oxford University Press, 1994.

Kenoyer, J. M., ed. *Old Problems and New Perspectives in the Archaeology of South Asia*. Madison: University of Madison, 1989.

Lad, Gauri. *The Mahabharata and Archaeological Evidence*. Pune, Maharashtra: Deccan College, 1983.

Lahiri, Nayanjot. *The Archaeology of Indian Trade Routes up to c 200 B.C.* New Delhi: Oxford University Press, 1999.

Lal, B. B., and K. N. Dikshit. *Ramayana and Archaeology*. Shimla, Himachal Pradesh: Indian Institute of Advanced Study, 1982.

Rao, S. R. *Progress and Prospects of Marine Archaeology in India*. Goa: National Institute of Oceanography, 1987.

Ray, Amita, and Samir Mukherjee. *Historical Archaeology of India: A Dialogue between Archaeologists and Historians*. New Delhi: Books and Books, 1990.

Ray, Himanshu Prabha. *The Archaeology of Seafaring in Ancient South Asia*. Cambridge, UK: Cambridge University Press, 2003.

Ray, Himanshu Prabha, and J.-F. Salles, eds. *Tradition and Archaeology: Early Maritime Contacts in the Indian Ocean*. New Delhi: Manohar, 1996.

Ray, S. C. *Stratigraphic Evidence of Coins in Indian Excavations and Some Allied Issues*. Varanasi, Uttar Pradesh: Banaras Hindu University, 1959.

Sankalia, H. D. *Ramayana: Myth or Reality?* New Delhi: People's Publishing House, 1973.

Settar, S., and Ravi Korisettar, eds. *Indian Archaeology in Retrospect*. Vol. 3, *Archaeology and Interactive Disciplines*. New Delhi: Indian Council of Historical Research and Manohar, 2002.

Sinha, B. P. *Potteries in Ancient India*. Patna, Bihar: Department of Ancient Indian History and Archaeology, 1969.

Regional Archaeological Studies

Agrawal, D. P., and B. M. Pande, eds. *Ecology and Archaeology of Western India*. New Delhi: Concept, 1977.

Anand, Kumar. *History and Archaeology of Buxar, Bhojpur and Rhotas Regions*. New Delhi: Ramanand Vidya Bhawan, 1995.

Basa, K. K., and P. Mohanty, eds. *Archaeology of Orissa*. Vol. 1. New Delhi: Pratibha Prakashan, 2004.

Chakrabarti, Dilip K. *Ancient Bangladesh: A Study of Archaeological Sources*. New Delhi: Oxford University Press, 1992.

———. *Archaeology of Eastern India: Chhotanagpur Plateau and West Bengal*. New Delhi: Munshiram Manoharlal, 1993.

———. *Archaeological Geography of the Ganga Plain: The Lower and the Middle Ganga*. New Delhi: Permanent Black, 2001.

———. *The Archaeology of the Deccan Routes: The Ancient Routes from the Ganga Plain to the Deccan*. New Delhi: Munshiram Manoharlal, 2005.

Chakrabarti, Dilip K., and S. J. Hasan. *The Antiquities of Kangra*. New Delhi: Munshiram Manoharlal, 1984.

Cooper, Zarine. *Archaeology and History: Early Settlements in the Andaman Islands*. New Delhi: Oxford University Press, 2002.

Dallaporta, Annamaria, and Lucio Marcato. *Archaeological Sites of South Panchala*. Data from Archaeological and Literary Sources. New Delhi: Manohar, 2005.

Dani, Ahmad Hasan. *Recent Archaeological Discoveries in Pakistan*. Paris: UNESCO, 1988.

Datta, Asok. *Black and Red Ware Culture in West Bengal*. New Delhi: Agam Kala Prakashan, 1995.

Gururaja Rao, B. K. *Megalithic Culture in South India*. Mysore: University of Mysore, 1972.

Jettmar, Karl. *Beyond the Gorges of the Indus: Archaeology Before Excavation*. Karachi: Oxford University Press, 2002.

Jettmar, Karl, ed., in collaboration with Ditte Konig and Volker Thewalt. *Antiquities of Northern Pakistan*. Vol. 1. Mainz: Heidelberger Akademie der Wissenschaften, 1989.

Jettmar, Karl, ed., in collaboration with Ditte Konig and Martin Bemmann. *Antiquities of Northern Pakistan*. Vol. 2. Mainz: Heidelberger Akademie der Wissenschaften, 1993.

Jettmar, Karl, ed., in collaboration with Gerard Fussmann. *Antiquities of Northern Pakistan*. Vol. 3. Mainz: Heidelberger Akademie der Wissenschaften, 1994.

Kaul, P. K. *Antiquities of the Chenab Valley in Jammu*. New Delhi: Eastern Book Linkers, 2001.

Kumar, Dilip. *Archaeology of Vaishali*. New Delhi: Ramanand Vidya Bhawan, 1986.

Mani, B. R. *Delhi: Threshold of the Orient: Studies in Archaeological Investigations*. New Delhi: Aryan, 1997.

Mishra, Prabodh Kumar. *Archaeology of Mayurbhanj*. New Delhi: D.K. Printworld, 1997.

Moorti, U. S. *Megalithic Culture of South India: Socio-Economic Perspectives*. Varanasi, Uttar Pradesh: Ganga Kaveri, 1994.

Pal, J. N. *Archaeology of Southern Uttar Pradesh*. Allahabad, Uttar Pradesh: Swabha Prakashan, 1986.

Patil, D. R. *The Antiquarian Remains of Bihar*. Patna, Bihar: K. P. Jayaswal Research Institute, 1963.

Prasad, Ram Chandra. *Archaeology of Champa and Vikramasila*. New Delhi: Ramanand Vidya Bhawan, 1987.

Rajan, K. *Archaeology of Tamil Nadu (Kongu country)*. New Delhi: Book India, 1994.

———. *Archaeological Gazetteer of Tamil Nadu*. Thanjavur, Tamil Nadu: Manoo Pathippakam, 1997.

Roy, T. N. *The Ganges Civilisation: A Critical Archaeological Study of the Painted Grey Ware and Northern Black Polished Ware Periods of the Ganga Plains of India*. New Delhi: Ramanand Vidya Bhawan, 1983.

Sankalia, H. D. *From History to Prehistory at Nevasa*. Poona, Maharashtra: Deccan College, 1960.

———. *Prehistory and Historical Archaeology of Gujarat*. New Delhi: Munshiram Manoharlal, 1987.

Sengupta, Gautam, and Sheena Panja. *Archaeology of Eastern India: New Perspectives*. Kolkata: Centre for Archaeological Studies and Training, Eastern India, 2002.

Sharma, A. K. *Emergence of Early Culture in North-East India: A Study Based on Excavations at Bhaitbari, Meghalaya*. New Delhi: Aryan, 1993.

Sharma, G. R. *History to Prehistory: The Archaeology of the Ganga Valley and the Vindhyas*. Allahabad, Uttar Pradesh: Department of Ancient History, Culture and Archaeology, 1980.

Shukla, K. S. *Archaeology of Unnao District*. New Delhi: B. R. Publishing, 1979.

Singh, B. P. *Life in Ancient Varanasi: An Account Based on Archaeological Evidence*. New Delhi: Sundeep Prakashan, 1985.

Singh, H. N. *The History and Archaeology of Black and Red Ware*. New Delhi: Sundeep Prakashan, 1982.

Singh, Rewant Vikram. *Settlements in the Yamuna-Hindon Doab: An Archaeological Perspective*. New Delhi: B. R. Publishing, 2003.

Singh, S. B. *The Archaeology of the Panchala Region*. New Delhi: Munshiram Manoharlal, 1979.

Singh Deo, Jitamitra Prasad. *Archaeology in Orissa with Special Reference to Nuapada and Kalahandi*. Kolkata: R. N. Bhattacharya, 2006.

Subrahmanyam, R. *Salihundam: A Buddhist Site in Andhra Pradesh*. Hyderabad: Government of Andhra Pradesh, 1964.

Sundara, A. *The Early Chamber Tombs of South India*. New Delhi: University Publishers, 1975.

Suresh, S. *Roman Antiquities in Tamil Nadu*. Chennai: C. P. Ramaswami Aiyar Institute of Indological Research, 1992.

Tripathi, K. K. *Archaeology of Vidisa (Dasarna) Region*. New Delhi: Sharada, 2002.

Wheeler, R. E. M. *Charsada: A Metropolis of the Northwest Frontier*. Oxford, UK: Oxford University Press, 1962.

Yule, Paul. *Early Historic Sites in Orissa*. New Delhi: Pragun Publications, 2006.

STUDIES BASED ON INSCRIPTIONS AND COINS

Agrawal, Jagannath. *Researches in Indian Epigraphy and Numismatics*. New Delhi: Sundeep Prakashan, 1986.

Andersen, Paul Kent. *Studies in the Minor Rock Edicts of Asoka*. Vol. 1, *Critical Edition*. Freiburg: Hedwig Falk, 1990.

Asher, Frederick M., and G. S. Gai, eds. *Indian Epigraphy: Its Bearing on the History of Art*. New Delhi: Oxford University Press and IBH/American Institute of Indian Studies, 1985.

Bajpai, K. D. *Indian Numismatic Studies*. New Delhi: Abhinav, 1976.

Basak, R. G. *Asokan Edicts*. Calcutta: Firma K.L. Mukhopadhyay, 1959.

Carter, Martha L., ed. *A Treasury of Indian Coins*. Bombay: Marg, 1994.

Chakraborti, Haripada. *Early Brahmi Records in India (c. 300 B.C.–c. 300 A.D.): An Analytical Study, Social, Economic, Religious and Administrative*. Calcutta: Sanskrit Pustak Bhandar, 1974.

———. *India as Reflected in the Inscriptions of the Gupta Period*. New Delhi: Munshiram Manoharlal, 1978.

Chattopadhyaya, Brajadulal. *Coins and Currency Systems in South India*. New Delhi: Munshiram Manoharlal, 1977.

Cunningham, A. *Coins of Ancient India: From the Earliest Times Down to the Seventeenth Century A.D.* New Delhi: Asian Educational Services, 2000 (reprint).

Damsteegt, Th. *Epigraphical Hybrid Sanskrit: Its Rise, Spread, Characteristics, and Relationship to Buddhist Hybrid Sanskrit*. Leiden: Brill, 1978.

Dani, Ahmad Hasan. *Indian Palaeography*. New Delhi: Munshiram Manoharlal, 1986.

Dayalan, D. *Computer Application in Indian Epigraphy*. 3 vols. New Delhi: Bharatiya Kala Prakashan, 2005.

Deyell, John. *Living Without Silver: The Monetary History of Early Medieval North India*. New Delhi: Oxford University Press, 1990.

Diskalkar, D. B. *Materials Used for Indian Epigraphic Records*. Poona, Maharashtra: Bhandarkar Oriental Research Institute, 1979.

Dobbins, K. Walton. *Saka-Pahlava Coinage*. Varanasi, Uttar Pradesh: Numismatic Society of India, 1973.

Elliot, Walter. *Coins of South India*. New Delhi: Bharatiya Kala Prakashan, 2005 (reprint).

Guillaume, Olivier. *Analysis of Reasonings in Archaeology: The Case of Graeco-Bactrian and Indo-Greek Numismatics*. New Delhi: Oxford University Press, 1990.

Gupta, Parmaeshwari Lal. *Kusana Coins and History*. New Delhi: D.K. Printworld, 2004.

Handa, Devendra. *Early Coins from Sugh*. New Delhi: Sundeep Prakashan, 2006.

Jain, Rekha. *Ancient Indian Coinage: A Systematic Study of Money Economy from the Janapada Period to the Early Medieval Period (600 BC to AD 1200)*. New Delhi: D.K. Printworld, 1995.

Jenkins, G. K., and A. K. Narain. *Coin Types of the Saka-Pahlava Kings*. Varanasi, Uttar Pradesh: Numismatic Society of India, 1957.

Jha, Amiteshwar, and Dilip Rajgor. *Studies in the Coinage of the Western Ksatrapas*. Nashik: Indian Institute of Research in Numismatic Studies, 1992.

Kant, S. *The Hathigumpha Inscription of Kharavela and the Bhabru Edict of Asoka: A Critical Study*. New Delhi: D.K. Printworld, 2000.

Karashima, Noburu, ed. *Indus Valley to Mekong Delta: Explorations in Epigraphy*. Madras: New Era, 1985.

Karashima, Noburu, Y. Subbarayalu, and Matsui Toro. *A Concordance of the Names in the Cola Inscriptions*. Madurai, Tamil Nadu: Sarvodaya Lakkaiya Pannai, 1978.

Kosambi, D. D. *Indian Numismatics*. New Delhi: Orient Longman, 1981.

Krishnamurthy, R. *Sangam Age Tamil Coins*. Chennai: Garnet, 1997.

Lahiri, N. *Pre-Ahom Assam: Studies in the Inscriptions of Assam between the Fifth and the Thirteenth Centuries A.D*. New Delhi: Munshiram Manoharlal, 1991.

Mahadevan, Iravatham. *Early Tamil Epigraphy. From the Earliest Times to the Sixth Century A.D*. Chennai: Crea-A and the Department of Sanskrit and Indian Studies, Harvard University, Cambridge, MA, 2003.

Mahalingam, T. V. *Early South Indian Palaeography*. Madras: University of Madras, 1974.

———. *A Topographical List of Inscriptions in the Tamil Nadu and Kerala States*. 9 vols. New Delhi: Indian Council of Historical Research, S. Chand, 1985–1995.

Mehendale, M. A. *Asokan Inscriptions in India. (A Linguistic Study, Together with an Exhaustive Bibliography)*. Bombay: University of Bombay, 1948.

———. *Historical Grammar of Inscriptional Prakrits*. Pune, Maharashtra: Deccan College Post-graduate and Research Institute, 1948.

Mirashi, Vasudev Vishnu. *The History and Inscriptions of the Satavahanas and the Western Ksatrapas*. Bombay: Maharashtra State Board for Literature and Culture, 1981.

Mishra, Ratan Lal. *Epigraphical Studies of Rajasthan Inscriptions*. New Delhi: B. R. Publishing, 2003.

Mitchiner, M. B. *The Origins of Indian Coinage*. London: Hawkins, 1973.

———. *Oriental Coins and their Values: Non-Islamic States and Western Colonies, AD 600–1979*. London: Hawkins, 1979.

———. *Coin Circulation in Southernmost India c. 200 BC to AD 1835*. Nashik: Indian Institute of Research in Numismatic Studies, 1995.

———. *The Land of Water—Coinage and History of Bangladesh and Later Arakan, c. 300 BC to the Present Day*. London: Hawkins, 2000.

Mitterwallner, G. von. *Kusana Coins and Kusana Sculptures from Mathura*. Mathura: Mathura Government Museum, 1986.

Mukherjee, B. N. *Kushana Coins in the Land of Five Rivers*. Calcutta: Indian Museum, 1979.

———. *Kusana Silver Coinage*. Calcutta: Indian Museum, 1982.

———. *Studies in the Aramaic Inscriptions of Asoka*. Calcutta: Indian Museum, 1984.

———. *Coins and Currency Systems of post-Gupta Bengal*. New Delhi: Munshiram Manoharlal, 1993.

———. *Numismatic Art of India*. 2 vols. New Delhi: Munshiram Manoharlal, 2007.

Murphy, P. *Kosala State Region c. 600–470 BC: Silver Punchmarked Coinage*. Nashik: Indian Institute for Research in Numismatic Studies, 2001.

Nagaraja Rao, M. S., and K. V. Ramesh. *Copper Plate Inscriptions from Karnataka: Recent Discoveries*. Mysore: Government of Karnataka, 1985.

Narain, A. K., ed. *Local Coins of North India*. Varanasi, Uttar Pradesh: Banaras Hindu University, 1966.

Narain, A. K., and L. Gopal, eds. *Seminar Papers on the Chronology of the Punch-marked Coins*. Varanasi, Uttar Pradesh: Banaras Hindu University, 1966.

Patel, P. G., Pramod Pandey, and Dilip Rajgor. *The Indic Scripts: Palaeographic and Linguistic Perspectives*. New Delhi: D.K. Printworld, 2007.

Radhakrishnan, P. V. *Roman Gold and Silver Coins from India: A Collectors Guide*. Mumbai: Indian Institute of Research and Numismatic Studies, 1999.

Rao, B. S. L. Hanumantha et al. *Buddhist Inscriptions of Andhradesa*. Secunderabad, Andhra Pradesh: Ananda Buddhist Vihara Trust, 1998.

Salomon, Richard. *Indian Epigraphy: A Guide to the Study of Inscriptions in Sanskrit, Prakrit, and Other Indo-Aryan Languages*. New York: Oxford University Press, 1998.

Sarma, I. K. *Coinage of the Satavahana Empire*. New Delhi: Agam Kala Prakashan, 1980.

Singh, Vijaya Laxmi. *Ujjayini: A Numismatic and Epigraphic Study*. New Delhi: Atlantic, 1998.

Sircar, D. C. *Indian Epigraphy*. New Delhi: Motilal Banarsidass, 1965.

———. *Select Inscriptions Bearing on Indian History and Civilization*. Vol. 1, *From the 6th century B.C. to the 6th century A.D*. Calcutta: Calcutta University, 1965.

——— *Inscriptions of Asoka*. New Delhi: Government of India, 1967.

———. *Epigraphic Discoveries in East Pakistan*. Calcutta: Sanskrit College, 1973.

———. *Early Indian Numismatic and Epigraphic Studies*. Calcutta: Indian Museum, 1977.

———. *Select Inscriptions: Bearing on Indian History and Civilization*. Vol. 2. New Delhi: Motilal Banarsidass, 1983.

Sivaramamurti, C. *Indian Epigraphy and South Indian Scripts*. Madras: Government of Madras, 1966.

Somani, Ram Vallabh. *Jain Inscriptions of Rajasthan*. Jaipur, Rajasthan: Rajasthan Prakrit Bharati Sansthan, 1952.

Thakur, Upendra. *Mints and Minting in India*. Varanasi, Uttar Pradesh: Chowkhamba Sanskrit Series, 1972.

Turner, P. J. *Roman Coins from India*. London: Royal Numismatic Society, 1989.

Upasak, C. S. *The History and Palaeography of the Mauryan Brahmi Script*. Nalanda: Nava Nalanda Mahavihara, 1960.

Willis, Michael D. *Inscriptions of Gopaksetra: Materials for the History of Central India*. London: British Museum Press, 1996.

HISTORIES OF DYNASTIES, POLITICAL IDEAS, AND INSTITUTIONS

Political Histories

Altekar, A. S. *Rashtrakutas and Their Times*. Poona, Maharashtra: Oriental Book Agency, 1967.

Bongard-Levin, G. *Mauryan India*. New Delhi: Sterling, 1985.

Bosworth, A. B. *Alexander and the East: The Tragedy of Triumph*. Oxford, UK: Clarendon Press, 1996.

Chattopadhyay, S. *The Achaemenids and India*. New Delhi: Munshiram Manoharlal, 1974.

Devahuti, D. *Harsha: A Political Study*. New Delhi: Oxford University Press, 2001.

Dikshit, Durga Prasad. *Political History of the Calukyas of Badami*. New Delhi: Abhinav, 1980.

Gopal, B. R., ed. *The Rastrakutas of Malkhed*. Mysore: Geetha Book House, 1994.

Gopalan, R. *History of the Pallavas of Kanchi*. Madras: University of Madras, 1928.

Goyal, S. R. *A History of the Imperial Guptas*. Allahabad, Uttar Pradesh: Central Book Depot, 1967.

———. *Kautilya and Megasthenes*. Meerut: Kusumanjali Prakashan, 1985.

Habib, Irfan, and Vivekanand Jha. *Mauryan India*. New Delhi: Tulika, 2005.

Hazra, Kanai Lal. *Asoka as Depicted in His Edicts*. New Delhi: Munshiram Manoharlal, 2007.

Jha, H. N. *The Licchavis*. Varanasi, Uttar Pradesh: Chowkhamba Sanskrit Series Office, 1970.

Lahiri, Bela. *Indigenous States of Northern India (circa 200 BC to 320 AD)*. Calcutta: University of Calcutta, 1974.

Maity, S. K. *The Imperial Guptas and Their Times, c. AD 300–550*. New Delhi: Munshiram Manoharlal, 1975.

Mukherjee, B. N. *Rise and Fall of the Kushana Empire*. Calcutta: Firma K. L. Mukhopadhyay, 1989.

Narain, A. K. *The Indo-Greeks*. Oxford, UK: Oxford University Press, 1957.

———. *The Indo-Greeks: Revisited and Supplemented*. New Delhi: B. R. Publishing, 2003.

Nilakanta Sastri, K. A. ed. *A Comprehensive History of India*. Vol. 2, *The Mauryas and Satavahanas 325 BC–AD 300*. Bombay: Orient Longman, 1957.

———. *The Colas*. Madras: University of Madras, 1975.

———. *The Age of the Nandas and Mauryas*. New Delhi: Motilal Banarsidass, 1996 (reprint).

Pathak, V. S. *History of Kosala up to the Rise of the Mauryas*. New Delhi: Motilal Banarsidass, 1963.

Puri, B. N. *The History of the Gurjara-Pratiharas*. New Delhi: Munshiram Manoharlal, 1986.

———. *Kusanas in India and Central Asia*. New Delhi: Munshiram Manoharlal, 2007.

Ramesh, K. V. *Chalukyas of Vatapi*. New Delhi: Agam Kala Prakashan, 1984.

Rao, M. S. Nagaraja, ed. *The Chalukyas of Badami*. Bangalore: The Mythic Society, 1978.

Raychaudhuri, Hemchandra. *Political History of Ancient India from the Accession of Parikshit to the Extinction of the Gupta Dynasty* (with a commentary by B. N. Mukherjee). New Delhi: Oxford University Press, 1996.

Shastri, Ajay Mitra. *Vakatakas: Sources and History*. New Delhi: Aryan, 1997 (reprint).

———. *The Satavahanas and the Western Kshatrapas*. Nagpur, Maharashtra: Dattsons, 1998.

———. *The Age of the Satavahanas*. 2 vols. New Delhi: Aryan, 1999 (reprint).

Sinha, B. P. *The Decline of the Kingdom of Magadha (c. 455–1000 AD)*. Patna, Bihar: Motilal Banarsidass, 1954.

Tarn, W. W. *The Greeks in Bactria and India*. Cambridge, UK: Cambridge University Press, 1951.

Thakur, Upendra. *The Hunas in India*. Varanasi, Uttar Pradesh: Chowkhamba Sanskrit Series Office, 1967.

Thapar, Romila. *The Mauryas Revisited*. Calcutta: Bagchi, 1987.

———. *Asoka and the Decline of the Mauryas*. New Delhi: Oxford University Press, 2000.

Histories of Political Ideas and Institutions

Aruna, A. *State Formation in the Eastern Deccan*. New Delhi: Bharatiya Kala Prakashan, 2000.

Balambal, V. *Feudatories of South India: 800–1070 A.D*. Allahabad, Uttar Pradesh: Chugh, 1978.

Champakalakshmi, R. *State and Society in Pre-modern South India*. Thrissur, Kerala: Cosmo, 2002.

Ghoshal, U. N. *A History of Indian Political Ideas*. Oxford, UK: Oxford University Press, 1959.

———. *A History of Indian Public Life*. Vol. 2, *The Pre-Maurya and the Maurya Periods*. New Delhi: Oxford University Press, 1966.

Gonda, J. *Ancient Indian Kingship from the Religious Point of View*. Leiden: Brill, 1968.

Govindasamy, M. S. *The Role of Feudatories in Pallava History*. Annamalainagar, Tamil Nadu: Annamalai University, 1965.

———. *The Role of Feudatories in Later Chola History*. Annamalainagar, Tamil Nadu: Annamalai University, 1979.

Heitzman, James. *Gifts of Power: Lordship in an Early Indian State*. New Delhi: Oxford University Press, 2002.

Jha, D. N. *Revenue System in Post-Maurya and Gupta Times*. Calcutta: Punthi Pustak, 1967.

———. *The Feudal Order: State, Society and Ideology in Early Medieval India*. New Delhi: Manohar, 2002.

Kulke, H. *Kings and Cults: State Formation and Legitimation in India and Southeast Asia*. New Delhi: Manohar, 1993.

Mahalingam, T. V. *South Indian Polity*. Madras: Madras University Press, 1967.

Minakshi, C. *Administration and Social Life under the Pallavas*. Madras: Madras University Press, 1977.

Nandi, Ramendra Nath. *State Formation, Agrarian Growth and Social Change in Feudal South India*. New Delhi: Manohar, 2002.

Roy, Kumkum. *The Emergence of Monarchy in North India, 8th to 4th Centuries BC, as Reflected in the Brahmanical Tradition*. New Delhi: Oxford University Press, 1994.

Scharfe, Hartmut. *The State in Indian Tradition*. Leiden: Brill, 1989.

Shanmugam, P. *The Revenue System of the Cholas, 850–1279*. Madras: New Era, 1987.

Sharma, J. P. *Republics in Ancient India 1500 B.C. to 500 B.C*. Leiden: Brill, 1968.

Sharma, R. S. *Origin of the State in India*. Bombay: Bombay University, 1989.

———. *Aspects of Political Ideas and Institutions in Ancient India*. New Delhi: Motilal Banarsidass, 2005 (reprint).

Singh, R. C. P. *Kingship in Northern India (c. 600 A.D.–1200 A.D.)*. New Delhi: Motilal Banarsidass, 1996.

Singh, Sarva Daman. *Ancient Indian Warfare*. New Delhi: Motilal Banarsidass, 1989.

Sinha-Kapur, Nandini. *State Formation in Mewar during the Seventh–Fifteenth Centuries*. New Delhi: Manohar, 2002.

Sircar, D. C. *Studies in the Political and Administrative Systems in Ancient and Medieval India*. New Delhi: Motilal Banarsidass, 1974.

———. *Asokan Studies*. Calcutta: Indian Museum, 1979.

———. *The Emperor and the Subordinate Rulers*. Santiniketan, West Bengal: Visvabharati, 1982.

Smith, R. Morton. *Kings and Coins in India: Greek and Saka Self-Advertisement*. New Delhi: Harman, 1997.

Sparreboom, M. *Chariots in the Veda*. Leiden: Brill, 1985.

Subrahmanian, N. *Sangam Polity*. New Delhi: Asian Publishing, 1966.

Thapar, Romila. *From Lineage to State: Social Formation in the Mid-First Millennium BC in the Ganga Valley*. New Delhi: Oxford University Press, 1990.

Veluthat, Kesavan. *The Political Structure of Early Medieval South India*. New Delhi: Orient Longman, 1993.

Venkatasubramanian, T. K. *Societas to Civitas: Evolution of Political Society in South India*. New Delhi: Kalinga, 1993.

REGIONAL HISTORIES

Adiga, Malini. *The Making of Southern Karnataka: Society, Polity and Culture in the Early Medieval Period AD 400–1030*. Hyderabad, Andhra Pradesh: Orient Longman, 2005.

Bamzai, P. N. K. *Culture and Political History of Kashmir*. Part 1, *Ancient Kashmir*. New Delhi: M. D. Publications, 1994.

Basak, Radhagovinda. *The History of North-Eastern India: Extending from the Foundation of the Gupta Empire to the Rise of the Pala Dynasty of Bengal (c. A.D. 320–760)*. Calcutta: Firma K. L. Mukhopadhyay, 1995 (reprint).

Bhandarkar, R. G. *Early History of the Dekhan*. New Delhi: Asian Educational Services, 1979 (reprint).

Choudhury, P. C. *History of the Civilization of the People of Assam to the 12th century AD*. Gauhati, Assam: Department of History and Antiquarian Studies, Assam, 1966.

Gopalachari, K. *Early History of the Andhra Country*. Madras: University of Madras, 1972.

Grewal, J. S. *Social and Cultural History of the Punjab: Prehistoric, Ancient and Early Medieval*. New Delhi: Manohar, 2004.

Iyengar, P. T. Srinivasa. *History of the Tamils: From the Earliest Times to 600 A.D.* New Delhi: Asian Educational Services, 2001.

Karashima, Noburu. *South Indian History and Society: Studies from Inscriptions A.D. 850–1800*. New Delhi: Oxford University Press, 1985.

Lal, Makkhan. *Settlement History and the Rise of Civilization in the Ganga-Yamuna Doab (1500 B.C.–300 A.D.)*. New Delhi: B. R. Publishing, 1984.

Leela, Shanthakumari S. *History of the Agraharas in Karnataka, 400–1300*. Madras: New Era, 1986.

Majumdar, R. C., ed. *The History of Bengal*. Vol. 1. Dacca: University of Dacca, 1963.

Menon, K. P. Padmanabha. *History of Kerala*. 4 Vols. New Delhi: Asian Educational Services, 2001.

Morrison, B. M. *Political Centers and Cultural Regions in Early Bengal*. Tucson: University of Arizona Press, 1970.

Narayanan, M. G. S. *Re-interpretations in South Indian History*. Trivandrum: College Book House, 1977.

Nilakanta Sastri, K. A. *A History of South India: From Prehistoric Times to the Fall of Vijayanagar*. New Delhi: Oxford University Press, 1997 (reprint).

Pillai, K. K. *The Social History of the Tamils*. Madras: Madras University Publication, 1979.

Pradhan, S. *Orissa: History, Culture and Archaeology*. New Delhi: D.K. Printworld, 1999.

Rajendra Babu, B. S. *Material Culture of the Deccan, with Special Reference to the Satavahana-Ikshvaku Period*. New Delhi: Agam Kala Prakashan, 1999.

Ray, Niharranjan. *History of the Bengali People*. Calcutta: Orient Longman, 1994.

Shastri, H. G. *Gujarat under the Maitrakas of Valabhi*. Vadodara, Gujarat: Oriental Institute, 2000.

Shrimali, Krishna Mohan. *History of Pancala to c. A.D. 550*. Vol. 1, *A Study*. New Delhi: Munshiram Manoharlal, 1983.

———. *History of Pancala to c. A.D. 550*. Vol. 2, *Corpus of the Coins*. New Delhi: Munshiram Manoharlal, 1984.

Singh, M. M. *Life in Northeastern India in Pre-Mauryan Times*. New Delhi: Motilal Banarsidass, 1967.

Singh, Upinder. *Kings, Brahmanas and Temples in Orissa: An Epigraphic Study, AD 300–1147*. New Delhi: Munshiram Manoharlal, 1994.

———. *Delhi: Ancient History*. New Delhi: Social Science Press, 2006.

Srivastava, G. N. *Ancient Settlement Pattern in Orissa, with Special Reference to Bhubaneswar*. New Delhi: Agam Kala Prakashan, 2006.
Subramanian, K. R. *Buddhist Remains in Andhra and the History of Andhra Between 225 and 610 A.D.* New Delhi: Asian Educational Services, 1989.
Yazdani, G., ed. *Early History of the Deccan*. London: Oxford University Press, 1960.

ECONOMIC HISTORY

General

Adhya, G. L. *Early Indian Economics*. Bombay: Asia Publishing, 1966.
Chattopadhyaya, Brajadulal, ed. *Essays in Ancient Indian Economic History*. New Delhi: Munshiram Manoharlal, 1987.
Chaudhary, Radhakrishna. *Economic History of Ancient India*. Patna, Bihar: Janaki Prakashan, 1982.
Das, D. R. *Economic History of the Deccan*. New Delhi: Munshiram Manoharlal, 1969.
Gopal, Lallanji. *The Economic Life of Northern India, c. A.D. 700–1200*. New Delhi: Motilal Banarsidass, 1989.
Jain, D. C. *Economic Life in Ancient India as Depicted in Jaina Canonical Literature*. Vaisali: Research Institute of Prakrit, Jainology and Ahimsa, 1980.
Jha, D. N. *Studies in Early Indian Economic History*. New Delhi: Anupama, 1980.
———. *Economy and Society in Early India: Issues and Paradigms*. New Delhi: Munshiram Manoharlal, 1993.
Maity, S. K. *Economic Life of Northern India in the Gupta Period (c. A.D. 300–550)*. Calcutta: The World Press, 1957.
Mukherjee, B. N. *The Economic Factors in Kushana History*. Kolkata: Progressive Publishers, 2002.
Rai, Jaimal. *The Rural–Urban Economy and Social Changes in Ancient India*. Varanasi, Uttar Pradesh: Bharatiya Vidya Prakashan, 1974.

Rural Economy

Biswas, Atreyi. *Famines in Ancient India*. New Delhi: Gyan, 2000.
Chattopadhyaya, Brajadulal. *Aspects of Rural Settlements and Rural Society in Early Medieval India*. Calcutta: Bagchi, 1990.
Chowdhury, K. A., K. S. Saraswat, and G. M. Buth. *Ancient Agriculture and Forestry in North India*. New Delhi: Asia Publishing, 1977.

Dutta, Saroj. *Land System in Northern India, c. AD 400–c. AD 700*. New Delhi: Munshiram Manoharlal, 1995.

Gopal, L. *Aspects of the History of Agriculture in Ancient India*. Varanasi, Uttar Pradesh: Banaras Hindu University, 1980.

Sahu, Bhairabi Prasad, ed. *Land System and Rural Society in Early India*. New Delhi: Manohar, 1997.

Shrimali, K. M. *Agrarian Structure in Central India and the Northern Deccan (c. A.D. 300–500): A Study in Vakataka Inscriptions*. New Delhi: Munshiram Manoharlal, 1987.

Sircar, D. C., ed. *Land System and Feudalism in Ancient India*. Calcutta: University of Calcutta, 1966.

———. *Landlordism and Tenancy in Ancient and Medieval India as Revealed by Epigraphical Records*. Lucknow, Uttar Pradesh: University of Lucknow, 1969.

Tirumalai, R. *Land Grants and Agrarian Relations in Cola and Pandya Times*. Madras: University of Madras, 1987.

Crafts, Trade, and Cities

Begley, V., and R. de Puma. *Rome and India: Ancient Sea Trade*. New Delhi: Oxford University Press, 1992.

Chakraborti, H. *Trade and Commerce of Ancient India*. Calcutta: Academic Publishers, 1966.

Chakravarti, Ranabir, ed. *Trade in Early India*. New Delhi: Oxford University Press, 2001.

———. *Trade and Traders in Early Indian Society*. New Delhi: Manohar, 2007.

Champakalakshmi, R. *Trade, Ideology, and Urbanization: South India 300 BC to AD 1300*. New Delhi: Oxford University Press, 1996.

Chandra, Moti. *Trade and Trade Routes in Ancient India*. New Delhi: Abhinav, 1977.

Chaudhuri, K. N. *Trade and Civilization in the Indian Ocean from the Rise of Islam to 1700*. New Delhi: Munshiram Manoharlal, 1985.

Cimino, Rosa Maria, ed. *Ancient Rome and India: Commercial and Cultural Contacts between the Roman World and India*. New Delhi: Munshiram Manoharlal, 1994.

Glover, I. C. *Early Trade Between India and Southeast Asia*. Hull: University of Hull, 1989.

Hall, Kenneth R. *Trade and Statecraft in the Age of the Colas*. New Delhi: Abhinav, 1980.

Jain, V. K. *Trade and Traders in Western India (A.D. 1000–1300)*. New Delhi: Munshiram Manoharlal, 1990.

Karashima, Noburu, ed. *Ancient and Medieval Commercial Activities in the Indian Ocean*. Tokyo: Taisho University, 2002.

Mukherjee, B. N. *The External Trade of North-Eastern India*. New Delhi: Harman, 1992.

Prasad, Kameshwar. *Cities, Crafts and Commerce under the Kusanas*. New Delhi: Agam Kala Prakashan, 1984.

Prasad, P. C. *Foreign Trade and Commerce in Ancient India*. New Delhi: Abhinav, 1977.

Ray, Haraprasad. *Trade and Trade Routes Between India and China: c. 140 B.C– A.D. 1500*. Kolkata: Progressive, 2003.

Ray, Himanshu Prabha. *Monastery and Guild: Commerce under the Satavahanas*. New Delhi: Oxford University Press, 1986.

———. *The Winds of Change: Buddhism and the Early Maritime Links of South Asia*. New Delhi: Oxford University Press, 1994.

Ray, Himanshu Prabha, and J. F. Salles, eds. *Tradition and Archaeology—Early Maritime Contacts in the Indian Ocean*. New Delhi: Manohar, 1996.

Sharma, R. S. *Urban Decay in India: c. 300–c. 1000*. New Delhi: Munshiram Manoharlal, 1987.

Sircar, D. C., ed. *Early Indian Trade and Industry*. Calcutta: University of Calcutta, 1972.

Suresh, S. *Symbols of Trade: Roman and Pseudo-Roman Objects Found in India*. New Delhi: Manohar, 2003.

Thakur, Vijay. *Urbanisation in Ancient India*. New Delhi: Abhinav, 1981.

Miscellaneous

Chakravarti, Ranabir. *Warfare for Wealth*. Calcutta: Firma K. L. Mukhopadhyay, 1986.

Deloche, J. *Transport and Communications in India Prior to Steam Locomotion*. 2 vols. New Delhi: Oxford University Press, 1994.

Mukherjee, B. N. *Media of Exchange in Early Medieval North India*. New Delhi: Harman, 1992.

Narang, Bhim Sain. *Concepts of Stridhana in Ancient India*. New Delhi: Parimal, 1990.

Nath, Vijay. *Dana: Gift System in Ancient India (c. 600 B.C.–c. A.D. 300)*. New Delhi: Munshiram Manoharlal, 1987.

Rai, G. K. *Involuntary Labour in Ancient India*. Allahabad, Uttar Pradesh: Chaitanya, 1974.

Sahu, Bhairabi Prasad. *From Hunters to Breeders*. New Delhi: Anamika, 1988.

Tyagi, A. K. *Women Workers in Ancient India*. New Delhi: Radha, 1994.

Vishnoi, Savita. *The Economic Status of Women in Ancient India*. Meerut: Kusumanjali Prakashan, 1987.

SOCIAL HISTORY

General

Auboyer, Jeannnine. *Daily Life in Ancient India: From Approximately 200 BC to AD 700*. New Delhi: Munshiram Manoharlal, 1994.

Banerji, S. C. *Society in Ancient India: Evolution since the Vedic Times Based on Sanskrit, Pali, Prakrit and Other Classical Sources*. New Delhi: D. K. Printworld, 2007.

Bose, A. N. *Social and Rural Economy in Northern India*. 2 vols. Calcutta: Firma K. L. Mukhopadhyay, 1967.

Chakravarti, Uma. *The Social Dimensions of Buddhism*. New Delhi: Oxford University Press, 1987.

———. *Everyday Lives, Everyday Histories: Beyond the Kings and Brahmanas of 'Ancient' India*. New Delhi: Tulika, 2006.

Chanana, Dev Raj. *Slavery in Ancient India*. New Delhi: People's Publishing House, 1990.

Chaudhari, Abhay Kant. *Early Medieval Village Life in North Eastern India (A.D. 600–1200)*. Calcutta: Punthi Pustak, 1971.

Jain, J. *Life in Ancient India as Depicted in the Jain Canon and Commentaries, 6th Century BCE to 17th Century AD*. New Delhi: Munshiram Manoharlal, 1984.

Jha, D. N., ed. *Feudal Social Formation in Early India*. New Delhi: Chanakya Publications, 1987.

Karve, Iravati. *Hindu Society: An Interpretation*. Poona, Maharashtra: Deshmukh Prakashan, 1968.

Narayanan, M. G. S. *Foundations of South Indian Society and Culture*. New Delhi: Bharatiya Book, 1994.

Parasher-Sen, Aloka, ed. *Subordinate and Marginal Groups in Early India*. New Delhi: Oxford University Press, 2004.

———, ed. *Social and Economic History of the Deccan: Some Interpretations*. New Delhi: Manohar, 2007.

Sahu, Bhairabi Prasad, ed. *Iron and Social Change in Early India*. New Delhi: Oxford University Press, 2006.

Sharma, R. S. *Social Changes in Early Medieval India*. New Delhi: People's Publishing House, 1981.

———. *Perspectives in the Social and Economic History of Early India*. New Delhi: Munshiram Manoharlal, 2003 (reprint).

———. *Early Medieval Indian Society: A Study in Feudalism*. Hyderabad, Andhra Pradesh: Orient Longman, 2003.

Thapar, Romila. *Ancient Indian Social History: Some Interpretations*. New Delhi: Orient Longman, 1990.

Wagle, N. *Society at the Time of the Buddha*. Bombay: Popular Prakashan, 1966.

The Aryan Question

Bronkhorst, Johannes, and Madhav M. Deshpande, eds. *Aryan and Non-Aryan in South Asia: Evidence, Interpretation and Ideology*. Cambridge, MA: Harvard University Press, 1999.
Bryant, Edwin. *The Quest for the Origins of Vedic Culture: The Indo-Aryan Migration Debate*. New Delhi: Oxford University Press, 2001.
Bryant, Edwin, and Laurie L. Patton, eds. *The Indo-Aryan Controversy: Evidence and Inference in Indian History*. Richmond: Curzon, 2005.
Dhavalikar, M. D. *The Aryan Myth and Archaeology*. New Delhi: Manohar, 2007.
Erdosy, G., ed. *The Indo-Aryans of Ancient South Asia: Language, Material Culture and Ethnicity*. Berlin: W. De Gruyter, 1995.
Kochhar, Rajesh. *The Vedic People: Their History and Geography*. New Delhi: Orient Longman, 2000.
Kuiper, F. B. J. *Aryans in the Rigveda*. Amsterdam: Rodopi, 1991.
Lal, B. B. *The Homeland of the Aryans: Evidence of Rigvedic Flora and Archaeology*. New Delhi: Aryan, 2005.
Mallory, J. P. *In Search of the Indo-Europeans. Language, Archaeology and Myth*. London: Thames and Hudson, 1989.
Sharma, R. S. *Looking for the Aryans*. Hyderabad, Andhra Pradesh: Orient Longman, 1995.
———. *Advent of the Aryans in India*. New Delhi: Manohar, 2001.
Thapar, Romila, et al. *India: Historical Beginnings and the Concept of the Aryan*. New Delhi: National Book Trust, 2006.
Trautmann, T. R. *Aryans and British India*. New Delhi: Vistaar, 1997.
———. *The Aryan Debate*. New Delhi: Oxford University Press, 2005.

Caste

Chatterjee, Madhumita. *The Kshatriyas in Ancient India*. New Delhi: Munshiram Manoharlal, 2007.
Datta, Swati. *Migrant Brahmanas in Northern India: Their Settlement and General Impact (c. A.D. 475–1030)*. New Delhi: Motilal Banarsidass, 1989.
Das, Veena. *Structure and Cognition: Aspects of Hindu Caste and Ritual*. New Delhi: Oxford University Press, 1987.
Dumont, L. *Homo Hierarchicus: The Caste System and its Implications*. Chicago: University of Chicago Press, 1980.

Hanumanthan, K. R. *Untouchability: A Historical Study up to 1500 AD (with Special Reference to Tamil Nadu)*. Madurai, Tamil Nadu: Koodla, 1979.

Jaiswal, Suvira. *Caste: Origin, Function and Dimensions of Change*. New Delhi: Manohar, 1998.

Klass, Morton. *Caste: The Emergence of the South Asian Social System*. Philadelphia: The Institute for the Study of Human Issues, 1980.

Mukherjee, Prabhati. *Beyond the Four Varnas: The Untouchable in India*. Shimla: Indian Institute of Advanced Study, 1988.

Sharma, R. S. *The State and Varna Formation in the Mid-Ganga Plains: An Ethnoarchaeological View*. New Delhi: Manohar, 1995.

———. *Sudras in Ancient India: A Social History of the Lower Order Down to c. A.D. 600*. New Delhi: Motilal Banarsidass, 2002 (reprint).

Smaje, Chris. *Natural Hierarchies: The Historical Sociology of Race and Caste*. Massachusetts: Blackwell, 2000.

Smith, Brian K. *Classifying the Universe: The Ancient Indian Varna System and the Origins of Caste*. Oxford, UK: Oxford University Press, 1994.

Upadhyaya, G. P. *Brahmanas in Ancient India*. New Delhi: Munshiram Manoharlal, 1979.

Veluthat, Kesavan. *Brahman Settlements in Kerala*. Calicut, Kerala: Sandhya, 1978.

Yamazaki, Gen'ichi. *The Structure of Ancient Indian Society: Theory and Reality of the Varna System*. Tokyo: The Toyo Bunko, 2005.

Gender

Altekar, A. S. *The Position of Women in Hindu Civilization: From Prehistoric Times to the Present Day*. New Delhi: Motilal Banarsidass, 2005 (reprint).

Bhattacharji, Sukumari. *Women and Society in Ancient India*. Calcutta: Basumati, 1994.

Hawley, John S. *Sati: The Blessing and the Curse*. New York: Columbia University Press, 1994.

Jamison, Stephanie. *Sacrificed Wife, Sacrificer's Wife: Women, Ritual and Hospitality in Ancient India*. New York: Oxford University Press, 1996.

Leslie, Julia L., ed. *Roles and Rituals for Hindu Women*. New Delhi: Motilal Banarsidass, 1996.

Leslie, Julia L., and Mary McGee, eds. *Invented Identities: The Interplay of Gender, Religion and Politics in India*. New Delhi: Oxford University Press, 2000.

Major, Andrea, ed. *Sati: A Historical Anthology*. New Delhi: Oxford University Press, 2006.

Moti, Chandra. *The World of Courtesans*. New Delhi: Vikas, 1973.

Orr, Leslie. C. *Donors, Devotees, and Daughters of God: Temple Women in Medieval Tamil Nadu*. New York: Oxford University Press, 2000.
Patton, Laurie, ed. *Jewels of Authority: Women and Textual Tradition in Hindu India*. New Delhi: Oxford University Press, 2002.
Roy, Kumkum, ed. *Women in Early Indian Societies*. New Delhi: Manohar, 1999.
Shah, Kirit K. *The Problem of Identity: Women in Early Indian Inscriptions*. New Delhi: Oxford University Press, 2001.
———, ed. *History and Gender: Some Explorations*. Jaipur, Rajasthan: Rawat, 2005.
Shah, Shalini. *The Making of Womanhood: Gender Relations in the Mahabharata*. New Delhi: Manohar, 1995.
Sharma, Tripat. *Women in Ancient India (from c. A.D. 320 to c. A.D. 1200)*. New Delhi: Ess Ess, 1987.
Singh, A. K. *Devadasi System in Ancient India (A Study of Temple Dancing Girls of South India)*. New Delhi: H. K. Publishers, 1990.
Singh, Sarva Daman. *Polyandry in Ancient India*. New Delhi: Vikas, 1978.
Tripathi, L. K., ed. *Position and Status of Women in Ancient India*. Varanasi, Uttar Pradesh: Banaras Hindu University, Department of Ancient Indian History and Culture, 1988.
Tyagi, Jaya. *Engendering the Early Household: Brahmanical Precepts in the Early Grhyasutras*. Hyderabad, Andhra Pradesh: Orient Longman, 2008.

Miscellaneous

Chatterjee, Mitali. *Education in Ancient India: From Literary Sources of the Gupta Age*. New Delhi: D.K. Printworld, 1999.
Chattopadhyaya, Brajadulal. *Representing the Other? Sanskrit Sources and the Muslims (Eighth to Fourteenth Centuries)*. New Delhi: Manohar, 1998.
Deshpande, Madhav. M. *Sociolinguistic Attitudes in India: A Historical Reconstruction*. Ann Arbor: Karoma, 1979.
———. *Sanskrit and Prakrit: Socio-linguistic Issues*. New Delhi: Motilal Banarsidass, 1993.
Lingat, Robert. *The Classical Law of India*. New Delhi: Oxford University Press, 1998 (translated from the French with additions by J. Duncan M. Derrett).
Mishra, K. C. *Tribes in the Mahabharata: A Socio-cultural Study*. New Delhi: National Publishing House, 1987.
Mookerji, Radha Kumud. *Ancient Indian Education: Brahmanical and Buddhist*. New Delhi: Motilal Banarsidass, 1987 (reprint).
Mukherjee, B. N. *Mathura and Its Society*. Calcutta: Firma K.L. Mukhopadhyay, 1981.
Olivelle, Patrick. *The Asrama System: The History and Hermeneutics of a Religious Institution*. Oxford, UK: Oxford University Press, 1993.

Pandey, Rajbali. *Hindu Samskaras: Socio-religious Study of the Hindu Sacraments*. New Delhi: Motilal Banarsidass, 1987.

Parasher, Aloka. *Mlecchas in Early India: A Study in Attitudes Towards Outsiders up to AD 600*. New Delhi: Munshiram Manoharlal, 1990.

Patil, Sharad. *Dasa-Sudra Slavery: Studies in the Origin of Indian Slavery and Feudalism and Their Philosophy*. New Delhi: Allied Publishers, 1982.

Patkar, Madhukar M. *Narada Brhaspati and Katyayana: A Comparative Study in Judicial Procedure*. New Delhi: Munshiram Manoharlal, 1978.

Ratnagar, Shereen. *The Other Indians: Essays on Pastoralists and Prehistoric Tribal People*. New Delhi: Three Essays Collective, 2004.

Shastri, A. M. *India as Seen in the Kuttanimatam of Damodaragupta*. New Delhi: Motilal Banarsidass, 1975.

Siegel, Lee. *Fires of Love, Waters of Peace: Passion and Renunciation in Indian Culture*. Honolulu: University of Hawaii Press, 1983.

Sircar, D. C. *Studies in the Society and Administration of Ancient and Medieval India*. Vol. 1. Calcutta: Firma K. L. Mukhopadhyay, 1967.

Soundara Rajan, K. V. *Mechanics of City and Village in Ancient India*. New Delhi: Sundeep Prakashan, 1986.

Sternbach, L. *Juridical Studies in Ancient Indian Law*. 2 vols. New Delhi: Motilal Banarsidass, 1996 (reprint).

Syed, A. J., ed. *D.D. Kosambi on History and Society: Problems of Interpretation*. Bombay: University of Bombay, 1985.

Thakur, Upendra. *History of Suicide in India*. New Delhi: Munshiram Manoharlal, 1963.

———. *Introduction to Homicide in India*. New Delhi: Abhinav, 1978.

———. *Buddhist Cities in Early India: Bodh Gaya, Rajagrha, Nalanda*. New Delhi: Sundeep Prakashan, 1995.

Thaplyal, Kiran Kumar. *Village and Village Life in Ancient India*. New Delhi: Aryan, 2004.

Trautmann, T. R., ed. *Kinship and History in South Asia*. Ann Arbor: Centers for South and Southeast Asian Studies, University of Michigan, 1974.

———. *Dravidian Kinship*. New Delhi: Vistaar, 1995.

Vanita, Ruth, and Saleem Kidwai, eds. *Same Sex Love in India: Readings from Literature and History*. New York: St. Martin's, 2000.

CULTURAL DEVELOPMENTS

General

Anand, Mulk Raj, ed. *In Praise of Aihole, Badami, Mahakuta, Pattadakal*. Bombay: Marg, 1980.

Asher, Frederick. M. *The Art of Eastern India, 300–800*. Minneapolis: University of Minnesota Press, 1980.

Banerjee, P. *Rama in Indian Literature, Art and Thought*. 2 vols. New Delhi: Sundeep Prakashan, 1986.

Beck, Elisabeth. *Pallava Rock Architecture and Sculpture*. Pondicherry: Sri Aurobindo Society, 2006.

Chandra, Pramod. *On the Study of Indian Art*. Cambridge, MA: Harvard University Press, 1983.

Coomaraswamy, A. K. *The Arts and Crafts of India and Ceylon*. New York: Farrar, Straus, 1964 (reprint).

———. *History of Indian and Indonesian Art*. New York: Dover, 1985 (reprint).

———. *Jaina Art*. New Delhi: Munshiram Manoharlal, 1994 (reprint).

Dahiya, Neelima. *Arts and Crafts of Northern India: From Earliest Times to c. 200 BC*. New Delhi: B. R. Publishing, 1986.

Dallapiccola, Anna L., ed. *The Shastric Tradition in the Indian Arts*. Wiesbaden: Franz Steiner Verlag, 1989.

Dange, S. A. *Cultural Sources from the Vedas*. Bombay: Bharatiya Vidya Bhavan, 1977.

Davis, Richard. *Lives of Indian Images*. Princeton, NJ: Princeton University Press, 1997.

Dehejia, Vidya. *The Art of the Imperial Cholas*. New York: Columbia University Press, 1990.

Deva, Krishna. *Buddhist Art of India and Nepal*. Varanasi, Uttar Pradesh: Central Institute of Higher Tibetan Studies, 1987.

———. *History and Art: Essays on History, Art, Culture and Archaeology*. New Delhi: Ramanand Vidya Bhawan, 1989.

Dhavalikar, M. K. *Sanchi: Monumental Legacy*. New Delhi: Oxford University Press, 2003.

———. *Satavahana Art*. New Delhi: Sharada, 2004.

Gupta, S. P. *Roots of Indian Art*. New Delhi: B. R. Publication, 1980.

Gupta, S. P., and Shashi Prabha Asthana. *Elements of Indian Art Including Temple Architecture, Iconography and Iconometry*. New Delhi: D. K. Printworld, 2007.

Huntington, Susan L. *The Art of Ancient India: Buddhist, Hindu, Jain*. New York: Weatherhill, 1985.

Misra, R. N. *Ancient Artists and Art Activity*. Shimla: Indian Institute of Advanced Study, 1975.

Nagaswamy, R. *Facets of South Indian Art and Architecture*. New Delhi: Aryan, 2003.

Ray, Amita. *Life and Art of Early Andhradesa*. New Delhi: Agam Kala Prakashan, 1983.

Ray, Niharranjan. *An Approach to Indian Art*. Chandigarh: Punjab University, 1974.

———. *Mauryan and Post-Mauryan Art: A Study in Social and Formal Contrasts*. New Delhi: Indian Council of Historical Research, 1975.

Reddy, R. Chandrasekhara. *Heroes, Cults and Memorials, Andhra Pradesh 300 A.D.–1600 A.D.* Madras: New Era, 1994.

Shrimali, K. M., ed. *Essays in Indian Art, Religion and Society*. New Delhi: Munshiram Manoharlal, 1987.

Smith, Bardwell L., ed. *Essays on Gupta Culture*. New Delhi: Motilal Banarsidass, 1983.

Srinivasan, Doris Meth. *Many Heads, Arms and Eyes: Origin, Meaning and Form of Multiplicity in Indian Art*. Leiden: Brill, 1997.

Tripathi, Aruna. *The Buddhist Art of Kausambi: From 300 BC to AD 550*. New Delhi: D.K. Printworld, 2003.

Vatsyayan, Kapila, ed. *Concept of Space: Ancient and Modern*. New Delhi: Indira Gandhi National Centre for the Arts, 1991.

Williams, Joanna Gottfried. *The Art of Gupta India: Empire and Province*. Princeton, NJ: Princeton University Press, 1982.

Sculpture and Painting

Agrawala, V. S. *Mathura Terracottas*. Varanasi, Uttar Pradesh: Prithivi Prakashan, 1984.

———. *Terracotta Figurines of Ahichchhatra, District Bareilly, Uttar Pradesh*. Varanasi, Uttar Pradesh: Prithivi Prakashan, 1985.

Allchin, F. R., ed. *Gandharan Art in Context: East–West Exchanges at the Crossroads of Asia*. New Delhi: Regency, 1997.

Bakker, Hans. *The Vakatakas: An Essay in Hindu Iconology*. Groningen: Egbert Forsten, 1997.

Banerjea, Jitendra Nath. *Development of Hindu Iconography*. New Delhi: Munshiram Manoharlal, 1974 (reprint).

Banerji, Arundhati. *Early Indian Terracotta Art: Circa 2000–300 B. C, Northern and Western India*. New Delhi: Harman, 1994.

Chakravarty, K. K. *Early Buddhist Art of Bodh Gaya*. New Delhi: Munshiram Manoharlal, 1997.

Champakalakshmi, R. *Vaisnava Iconography in the Tamil Country*. Hyderabad, Andhra Pradesh: Orient Longman, 1981.

Chandra, Pramod. *Stone Sculpture in the Allahabad Museum: A Descriptive Catalogue*. Poona, Maharashtra: American Institute of Indian Studies, 1970.

Coomaraswamy, A. K. *The Dance of Shiva*. New Delhi: Sagar, 1968 (reprint).

———. *Elements of Buddhist Iconography*. New Delhi: Munshiram Manoharlal, 1979 (reprint).

Czuma, Stanislaw J. *Kushana Sculpture: Images from Early India*. Cleveland: Cleveland Museum of Art, 1985.

Dasgupta, C. C. *Prehistoric Terracotta Figurines of South India*. Calcutta: University of Calcutta, 1944.

———. *Origin and Evolution of Indian Clay Sculpture*. Calcutta: University of Calcutta, 1961.

Dehejia, Vidya. *Discourse in Early Buddhist Art: Visual Narratives of India*. New Delhi: Munshiram Manoharlal, 1997.

———. *Representing the Body: Gender issues in Indian art*. New Delhi: Kali for Women, 1997.

———. *Devi the Great Goddess: Female Divinities in South Asian Art*. Ahmedabad, Gujarat: Arthur M. Sackler Art Gallery, 1999.

Dehejia, Vidya, Richard N. Davis, R. Nagaswamy, and Karen Pechilis Prentiss, eds. *The Sensuous and the Sacred: Chola Bronzes from South India*. University of Washington Press, 2002.

Desai, Devangana. *Erotic Sculpture of India: A Socio-cultural Study*. New Delhi: Tata McGraw Hill, 1985.

Deva, Krishna. *Stone Sculpture in the Allahabad Museum*. New Delhi: Manohar, 1996.

———. *Terracottas in the Allahabad Museum*. New Delhi: Abhinav, 1980.

Deva, Krishna, and S. D. Trivedi. *Stone Sculpture in the Allahabad Museum*. New Delhi: Manohar, 1996.

Dhavalikar, M. K. *Masterpieces of Indian Terracotta*. Bombay: D. B. Taraporevala, 1977.

Gupta, P. L. *Gangetic Valley Terracotta Art*. Varanasi, Uttar Pradesh: Prithivi Prakashan, 1972.

Haque, E. *Chandraketugarh: A Treasure-House of Bengal Terracottas*. Dhaka: International Centre for the Study of Bengal Art, 2001.

Jain, Jyotindra, and Eberhard Fischer. *Jaina Iconography*. Leiden: Brill, 1978.

Jayaswal, Vidula. *Kushana Clay Art of the Ganga Plains: A Case Study of Human Forms from Khairadih*. New Delhi: Agam Kala Prakashan, 1991.

———. *Stone Quarry to Sculpturing Workshop: Chunar, Varanasi and Sarnath*. New Delhi: Agam Kala Prakashan, 1998.

Jayaswal, Vidula, and K. Krishna. *An Ethno-Archaeological View of Indian Terracottas*. New Delhi: Agam Kala Prakashan, 1986.

Kala, S. C. *Terracotta Figurines from Kausambi: Mainly in the Collection of the Municipal Museum*. Allahabad, Uttar Pradesh: Municipal Museum, 1950.

Knox, Robert. *Amaravati: Buddhist Sculpture from the Great Stupa*. London: British Museum Press, 1992.

Mathpal, Yashodar. *Rock Art in Kerala*. New Delhi: Aryan, 1998.
Nagaswamy, R. *Masterpieces of Early South Indian Bronzes*. New Delhi: National Museum, 1983.
Pal, Pratapaditya. *The Ideal Image: The Gupta Sculptural Tradition and Its Influence*. New York: Asia Society, 1978.
Rao, T. A. Gopinatha. *Elements of Hindu Iconography*. 2 vols. Varanasi, Uttar Pradesh: Indological Book House, 1971 (reprint).
Ray, Amita. *Aurangabad Sculptures*. Calcutta: Firma K. L. Mukhopadhyay, 1966.
Schlingloff, D. *Studies in the Ajanta Paintings*. New Delhi: Books and Books, 1988.
Sharma, R. C. *The Splendour of Mathura Art and Museum*. New Delhi: D.K. Printworld, 1994.
Sivaramamurti, C. *Indian Sculpture*. New Delhi: Indian Council for Cultural Relations/Allied, 1961.
Tiwari, Usha Rani. *Sculptures of Mathura and Sarnath: A Comparative Study*. New Delhi: Sundeep Prakashan, 1998.

Architecture

Asher, Frederick M. *Bodh Gaya*. New Delhi: Oxford University Press, 2007.
Balasubramaniam, S. R. *Early Cola Temples (A.D. 907–985)*. New Delhi: Orient Longman, 1971.
———. *Middle Cola Temples (A.D. 985–1070)*. New Delhi: Thomson, 1975.
———. *Later Cola Temples (A.D. 1070–1280)*. Madras: Mudgala Trust, 1979.
Bandyopadhyay, Bimal. *Buddhist Centres of Orissa: Lalitagiri, Ratnagiri and Udayagiri*. New Delhi: Sundeep Prakashan, 2004.
Barrett, Douglas. *Early Cola Architecture and Sculpture (866–1014 A.D.)*. London: Faber and Faber, 1975.
Champakalakshmi, R., and Usha Kris. *The Hindu Temple*. New Delhi: Roli, 2001.
Chandra, Satish. *History of Architecture and Ancient Building Materials in India*. 2 parts. New Delhi: Tech Books, 2003.
Coomaraswamy, A. K. *Early Indian Architecture: Cities and City Gates, etc.* New Delhi: Munshiram Manoharlal, 2002 (reprint).
Dallapiccola, A., ed. *The Stupa: Its Religious, Historical and Architectural Significance*. Wiesbaden: Franz Steiner, 1980.
Dehejia, Vidya. *Early Buddhist Rock Temples*. New York: Cornell University Press, 1972.
———. *Early Stone Temples of Orissa*. New Delhi: Vikas, 1979.
———. *Royal Patrons and Great Temple Art*. Bombay: Marg, 1988.

Deo, S. B. *Canons of Architecture and Jaina Monuments*. Dharwad: Prasaranga Karnataka University, 1995.

Deva, Krishna. *Temples of North India*. New Delhi: National Book Trust, 2002.

Fergusson, J. *History of Indian and Eastern Architecture*. London: Murray, 1967 (reprint).

Jayaswal, Vidula. *Royal Temples of the Gupta Period (Excavations at Bhitari)*. New Delhi: Aryan, 2001.

Kak, Ram Chandra. *Ancient Monuments of Kashmir*. New Delhi: Aryan, 2000.

Mahajan, Malati. *A Gate to Ancient Indian Architecture*. New Delhi: Sharada, 2004.

Michell, George. *The Penguin Guide to the Monuments of India*. London: Viking, 1989.

———. *Pattadakal: Monumental Legacy*. New York: Oxford University Press, 2002.

Mitra, Debala. *Buddhist Monuments*. New Delhi: Munshiram Manoharlal, 1980.

———. *Udayagiri and Khandagiri*. New Delhi, Archaeological Survey of India, 1992.

———. *Pandrethan, Avantipur and Martand*. New Delhi: Archaeological Survey of India, 1993.

Nagaraju, S. *Buddhist Architecture of Western India*. New Delhi: Agam Kala Prakashan. 1981.

Nagaswamy, R. *Mahabalipuram* New Delhi: Oxford University Press, 2008.

Roy, Anamika. *Amaravati Stupa*. 2 vols. New Delhi: Agam Kala Prakashan, 1994.

Sarkar, H. *Studies in the Early Buddhist Architecture of India*. New Delhi: Munshiram Manoharlal, 1993.

Sarma, I. K. *Studies in Early Buddhist Monuments and Brahmi Inscriptions of Andhradesa*. Nagpur, Maharashtra: Dattsons, 1988.

Sivaramamurti, C. *The Chola Temples*. New Delhi: Archaeological Survey of India, 1978.

———. *Mahabalipuram*. New Delhi: Archaeological Survey of India, 1992.

Soundara Rajan, K. V. *Architecture of Early Hindu Temples of Andhra Pradesh*. Hyderabad: Government of Andhra Pradesh, 1965.

Srinivasan, K. R. *Cave Temples of the Pallavas*. New Delhi: Archaeological Survey of India, 1965.

Tartakov, Gary Michael. *The Durga Temple at Aihole: A Historiographical Study*. New Delhi: Oxford University Press, 1997.

Textual Traditions

Agrawala, V. S. *India as Known to Panini: A Study of the Cultural Material in the Astadhyayi*. Lucknow, Uttar Pradesh: University of Lucknow, 1953.

Allon, M. *Structure and Function: A Study of the Dominant Stylistic Features of the Prose Portions of the Pali Canonical Sutta Texts and Their Mnemonic Function*. Tokyo: International Institute for Buddhist Studies of the International College for Advanced Buddhist Studies, 1997.

Bhattacharji, Sukumari, *Literature in the Vedic Age*. Vol. 1, *Samhitas*. Calcutta: Bagchi, 1984.

———. *A History of Classical Sanskrit Literature*. Hyderabad, Andhra Pradesh: Orient Longman Ltd., 1993.

Bhattacharyya, N. N. *History of Indian Erotic Literature*. New Delhi: Munshiram Manoharlal, 1975.

Brockington, J. L. *Righteous Rama: The Evolution of an Epic*. New Delhi: Oxford University Press, 1984.

———. *Concepts of the Self in the Ramayana Tradition (Edinburgh Papers in South Asian Studies)*. Edinburgh, UK: University of Edinburgh, 1995.

———. *The Sanskrit Epics (Handbook of Oriental Studies*, Part 2, *South Asia)*. Leiden: Brill, 1998.

———. *Epic Threads*. New Delhi: Oxford University Press, 2000.

Cardona, George. *Panini: A Survey of Research*. New Delhi: Motilal Banarsidass, 1976.

Chandra, K. R. *A Critical Study of the Paumacariya*. Vaishali: Research Institute for Prakrit, Jainism and Ahimsa, 1970.

———. *In Search of the Original Ardhamagadhi*. Ahmedabad, Gujarat: D. M. Prakrit Text Society, 2001.

De, Sushil Kumar. *History of Sanskrit Literature: Prose, Poetry and Drama*. Calcutta: University of Calcutta, 1947.

Derrett, J. Duncan M. *Dharmaśāstra and Juridical Literature*. Vol. 4, Part 2 of *A History of Indian Literature*, edited by J. Gonda. Wiesbaden: Harrassowitz, 1973.

———. *History of Indian Law (Dharmasastra)*. Vol. 2. Fasc. 3 of *A History of Indian Literature*, edited by J. Gonda. Leiden: Brill, 1973.

Devadhar, C. R. *Plays Ascribed to Bhasa: Their Authenticity and Merits*. Poona, Maharashtra: The Oriental Book Agency.

Doniger, Wendy, ed. *Purana Perennis: Reciprocity and Transformation in Hindu and Jaina Texts*. Albany: State University of New York, 1993.

Feller, Danielle. *The Sanskrit Epics: Representation of Vedic Myths*. New Delhi: Motilal Banarsidass, 2004.

Gerow, Edwin. *Indian Poetics*. Vol. 5, Fasc. 3 of *A History of Indian Literature*, edited by J. Gonda. Wiesbaden: Harrassowitz, 1977.

Gonda, Jan, ed. *History of Indian Literature*. 10 vols. in 28 fascicles. Wiesbaden: Harrassowitz, 1973.

Gonda, Jan. *Vedic Literature*. Wiesbaden: Harrassowitz, 1975.

Hart, George L. *Poems of Ancient Tamil: Their Milieu and Their Sanskrit Counterparts*. Berkeley: University of California Press, 1975.

Hinuber, Oskar von. *A Handbook of Pali Literature*. New Delhi: Munshiram Manoharlal, 1996.

Houben, Jan E. B. *Ideology and Status of Sanskrit: Contributions to the History of the Sanskrit Language*. Leiden: Brill, 1996.

Hueckstedt, Robert A. *The Style of Bana: An Introduction to Sanskrit Prose Poetry*. Lanham, MD: University Press of America, 1985.

Inden, Ronald, ed. *Querying the Medieval: Texts and the History of Practices in South Asia*. New York: Oxford University Press, 2000.

Ingalls, Daniel H. H. *Sanskrit Poetry*. Cambridge, MA: Harvard University Press, 1979.

Jain, J. C. *History and Development of Prakrit Literature*. New Delhi: Manohar, 2004 (reprint).

Kane, P. V. *History of Sanskrit Poetics*. New Delhi: Motilal Banarsidass, 1961.

———. *History of Dharmasastras (Ancient and Medieval Religious and Civil Law in India)*. 5 vols. in 7 parts. Poona, Maharashtra: Bhandarkar Oriental Research Institute, 1968–1974.

Lienhard, Siegfried. *A History of Classical Sanskrit Poetry: Sanskrit Pali-Prakrit*. Vol. 3, Fasc. I of *A History of Indian Literature*, edited by J. Gonda. Wiesbaden: Harrassowitz, 1984.

Marr, J. A. *The Eight Anthologies: A Study in Early Tamil*. Madras: Institute of Asian Studies, 1987.

Mehta, Tarla. *Sanskrit Play Production in Ancient India*. New Delhi: Motilal Banarsidass, 1996.

Murti, M. Srimannarayana. *An Introduction to Sanskrit Linguistics: Comparative and Historical*. New Delhi: D.K. Publications, 1990.

Norman, K. R. *Pali Literature*. Wiesbaden: Harrassowitz, 1980.

Oberlies, Th. *Epic Sanskrit*. Berlin: deGruyter, 2004.

Ohira, S. *A Study of the Bhagavati Sutra: A Chronological Analysis*. Ahmedabad, Gujarat: Prakrit Text Society, 1994.

Patkar, Madhukar M. *History of Sanskrit Lexicography*. New Delhi: Munshiram Manoharlal, 1981.

Peterson, Indira Viswanathan. *Design and Rhetoric in a Sanskrit Court Epic: The Kiratarjuniya of Bharavi*. New York: State University of New York Press, 2003.

Pollock, Sheldon, ed. *Literary Cultures in History: Reconstructions from South Asia*. Berkeley: University of California Press, 2003.

———. *The Language of the Gods in the World of Men. Sanskrit, Culture and Power in Premodern India*. New Delhi: Permanent Black, 2006.

Scharfe, Hartmut. *Grammatical Literature*. Vol. 5, Fasc. 2 of *A History of Indian Literature*, edited by J. Gonda. Wiesbaden: Harrassowitz, 1977.

Sharma, Arvind, ed. *Essays on the Mahabharata*. Leiden: Brill, 1991.

Sivaramamurti, C. *Sanskrit Literature and Art: Mirrors of Indian Culture*. New Delhi: Archaeological Survey of India, 1970.

Sternbach, L. *Juridical Studies in Ancient Indian Law*. New Delhi: Motilal Banarsidass, 1965.

Thapar, R. *Sakuntala—Texts, Reading, Histories*. New Delhi: Kali for Women, 1997.

Tieken, Herman. *Kavya in South India: Old Tamil Cankam Poetry*. Groningen: Egbert Forsten, 2001.

Trautmann, T. R. *Kautilya and the Arthasastra—A Statistical Investigation of the Authorship and Evolution of the Text*. Leiden: Brill, 1971.

Warder, A. K. *Indian Kavya Literature*. 3 vols. New Delhi: Motilal Banarsidass, 1972–1977.

Witzel, M., ed. *Inside the Texts, Beyond the Texts*. Cambridge, MA: Harvard University Press, 1997.

Yardi, M. R. *The Ramayana, Its Origin and Growth: A Statistical Study*. Poona, Maharashtra: Bhandarkar Oriental Research Institute, 1994.

Zvelebil, Kamil. *Tamil Literature*. Vol. 10, Fasc. 1 of *A History of Indian Literature*, edited by J. Gonda. Wiesbaden: Harrassowitz, 1974.

———. *Companion Studies to the History of Tamil Literature*. Leiden: Brill, 1992.

Miscellaneous

Alkazi, Roshen. *Ancient Indian Costume*. New Delhi: Art Heritage, 1983.

Chattopadhyay, Siddheswar. *Theatre in Ancient India*. New Delhi: Manohar, 2007.

Nijenhuis, Emmie te. *Indian Music: History and Structure*. Leiden: Brill, 1974.

Rowell, Lewis. *Music and Musical Thought in Early India*. New Delhi: Munshiram Manoharlal, 1998.

RELIGION AND PHILOSOPHY

General

Agrawal, V. S. *Ancient Indian Folk Cults*. Varanasi, Uttar Pradesh: Prithivi Prakashan, 1970.

Arora, U. P. *Motifs in Indian Mythology: Their Greek and Other Parallels*. New Delhi: India Publishing, 1981.

Bhattacharji, Sukumari. *Myths: Vedic, Buddhist and Brahmanical*. Kolkata: Progressive, 2002.

Bhattacharyya, N. N. *Ancient Indian Rituals, and Their Social Contents*. New Delhi: Manohar, 1996.

Derrett, J. Duncan M. *Religion, Law and the State in India*. New York: Free Press, 1968.

Dumont, L. *Religion, Politics and History in India*. Paris: Mouton, 1970.

King, Anna, and John Brockington, eds. *The Intimate Other: Love Divine in Indic Religions*. New Delhi: Orient Longman, 2005.

Kosambi, D. D. *Myth and Reality: Studies in the Formation of Indian Culture*. Bombay: Popular Prakashan, 1962.

Leslie, Julia, ed. *Myth and Mythmaking*. Richmond, VA: Curzon, 1996.

Nandi, R. N. *Religious Institutions and Cults in the Deccan, c. A.D. 600–A.D. 1000*. New Delhi: Motilal Banarsidass, 1973.

———. *Social Roots of Religion in Ancient India*. Calcutta: Bagchi, 1986.

O'Flaherty, Wendy Doniger. *Sexual Metaphors and Animal Symbols in Indian Mythology*. New Delhi: Motilal Banarsidass, 1981.

Ramaswamy, Vijaya. *Walking Naked: Women, Society and Spirituality in South India*. Shimla, Himachal Pradesh: Indian Institute of Advanced Study, 1997.

Roy, U. N., et al., eds. *Ritual Life and Folk Culture in Ancient India: Proceedings of a Seminar Held at Allahabad in 1985*. Allahabad, Uttar Pradesh: Department of Ancient History, Culture and Archaeology, University of Allahabad, 1988.

Sircar, D. C. *Studies in the Religious Life of Ancient and Medieval India*. New Delhi: Motilal Banarsidass, 1971.

Weber, Max. *The Religion of India: The Sociology of Hinduism and Buddhism*. New Delhi: Munshiram Manoharlal, 2000 (reprint).

Vedic and Puranic Traditions

Bailey, Greg. *The Mythology of Brahma*. New Delhi: Oxford University Press, 1983.

Banerji, S. C. *Dharma-sutras: A Study in Their Origin and Development*. Calcutta: Punthi Pustak, 1962.

Basham, A. L. *The Origins and Development of Classical Hinduism*, edited and annotated by Kenneth G. Zysk. New York: Oxford University Press, 1997.

Bhandarkar, R. G. *Vaisnavism, Saivism and Minor Religious Systems*. New Delhi: Munshiram Manoharlal, 2001 (reprint).

Bhattacharji, Sukumari. *Indian Theogony: A Comparative Study of Indian Mythology from the Vedas to the Puranas*. New Delhi: Motilal Banarsidass, 1989.

Biardeau, M. *Hinduism: The Anthropology of a Civilization*. New Delhi: Oxford University Press, 1989.

Brockington, J. L. *The Sacred Thread—A Short History of Hinduism*. New Delhi: Oxford University Press, 1996.

Chakrabarti, Kunal. *Religious Process: The Puranas and the Making of a Regional Tradition*. New Delhi: Oxford University Press, 2001.

Courtright, Paul B. *Ganesa: Lord of Obstacles, Lord of Beginnings*. New York: Oxford University Press, 1985.

Dange, Sadashiv A. *Sexual Symbolism from the Vedic Ritual*. New Delhi: Ajanta, 1979.

Dange, Sindhu S., ed. *Gleanings from Vedic to Puranic Age: Collected Papers of Dr Sadashiv A. Dange*. New Delhi: Aryan, 2002.

Dehejia, Vidya. *Slaves of the Lord: The Path of the Tamil Saints*. New Delhi: Munshiram Manoharlal, 1988.

———. *Antal and Her Path of Love: Poems of a Woman Saint from South India*. Albany: State University of New York Press, 1990.

Eschmann, A., H. Kulke, and G. L. Tripathi, eds. *The Cult of Jagannath and the Regional Tradition of Orissa*. New Delhi: Manohar, 1978.

Goldman, R. P. *Gods, Priests and Warriors: The Bhrigus of the Mahabharata*. New York: Columbia University Press, 1977.

Gonda, J. *Aspects of Early Visnuism*. New Delhi: Motilal Banarsidass, 1993 (reprint).

———. *Visnuism and Sivaism*. New Delhi: Munshiram Manoharlal, 1996 (reprint).

Hardy, Friedhelm. *Viraha Bhakti: The Early History of Krsna Devotion in South India*. New Delhi: Oxford University Press, 1983.

Hazra, Rajendra Chandra. *Studies in Puranic Records on Hindu Rites and Customs*. New Delhi: Motilal Banarsidass, 1975.

Heesterman, J. C. *The Inner Conflict of Tradition: Essays in Indian Ritual, Kingship and Society*. New Delhi: Oxford University Press, 1985.

———. *The Broken World of Sacrifice: An Essay in Ancient Ritual*. Chicago: University of Chicago Press. 1993.

Hiltebeitel, Alf. *The Ritual of Battle: Krsna in the Mahabharata*. Ithaca: Cornell University Press, 1976.

———. *The Cult of Draupadi*. Vol. 1, *Mythologies from Gingee to Kurukshetra*. Chicago: University of Chicago Press, 1988.

———. *The Cult of Draupadi*. Vol. 2, *On Hindu Rituals and the Goddess*. Chicago: University of Chicago Press, 1991.

Jaiswal, Suvira. *The Origin and Development of Vaisnavism: Vaisnavism from 200 BC to AD 500*. New Delhi: Munshiram Manoharlal, 1981.

Jamison, S. W. *The Ravenous Hyenas and the Wounded Sun: Myth and Ritual in Ancient India*. Ithaca: Cornell University Press, 1991.
Kaelber, Walter O. *Tapta Marga: Asceticism and Initiation in Vedic India*. Albany: State University of New York Press, 1989.
Keith, A. B. *The Religion and Philosophy of the Veda and Upanishads*. New Delhi: Motilal Banarsidass, 1998 (reprint).
Nath, Vijay. *Puranas and Acculturation: A Historico-anthropological Perspective*. New Delhi: Munshiram Manoharlal, 2001.
O'Flaherty, Wendy Doniger, ed. *Textual Sources for the Study of Hinduism*. Manchester, UK: Manchester University Press, 1988.
Pathak, V. S. *History of Saiva Cults in North India from Inscriptions (700 A.D. to 1200 A.D)*. Allahabad, Uttar Pradesh: University of Allahabad, 1980.
Rocher, Ludo. *Purana*. Vol. 2, Fasc. 3 of *A History of Indian Literature*, edited by J. Gonda. Wiesbaden: Harrassowitz, 1986.
Smith, Brian K. *Reflections on Resemblance, Ritual and Religion*. New York: Oxford University Press, 1989.
Smith, David. *The Dance of Siva: Religion, Art and Poetry in South India*. Cambridge, UK: Cambridge University Press, 1996.
Sontheimer, Gunther-Dietz, and Hermann Kulke, eds. *Hinduism Reconsidered*. New Delhi: Manohar Publishers, 1989.

Jainism

Bhattacharyya, N. N., ed. *Jainism and Prakrit in Ancient and Medieval India*. New Delhi: Manohar, 1994.
———. *Jain Philosophy: Historical Outline*. New Delhi: Munshiram Manoharlal, 1999.
Chatterjee, Asim Kumar. *A Comprehensive History of Jainism*. 2 vols. Calcutta: Firma K. L. Mukhopadhyay, 1978–1984.
Cort, John, ed. *Open Boundaries: Jaina Communities and Cultures in Indian History*. New York: State University of New York Press, 1998.
———. *Jainas in the World: Religious Values and Ideology in India*. New York: Oxford University Press, 2001.
Deo, Shantaram Bhalchandra. *History of Jaina Monachism from Inscriptions and Literature*. Poona, Maharashtra: Deccan College, 1956.
Dundas, Paul. *The Jains*. London: Routledge, 2002.
Jain, Muni Uttam Kamal. *Jaina Sects and Schools*. New Delhi: Concept, 1975.
Jaini, Padmanabh S. *Gender and Salvation: Jaina Debates on the Spiritual Liberation of Women*. New Delhi: Munshiram Manoharlal, 1992.
Johnson, W. J. *Harmless Souls: Karmic Bondage and Religious Change in Early Jainism with Special Reference to Umasvati and Kundakunda*. New Delhi: Motilal Banarsidass, 1995.

Nagar, Shantilal. *Iconography of Jaina Deities*. 2 vols. New Delhi: B. R. Publishing, 1999.

Ohira, S. *A Study of the Bhagavati Sutra: A Chronological Analysis*. Ahmedabad, Gujarat: Prakrit Text Society, 1994.

Schubring, W. *The Doctrine of the Jainas Described after the Old Sources*. New Delhi: Motilal Banarsidass, 2000.

Settar, S. *Inviting Death: Historical Experiments on Sepulchral Hill*. Dharwar: Institute of Indian Art History, Karnatak University, 1986.

Singh, J. P. *Aspects of Early Jainism (as Known from the Epigraphs)*. Varanasi, Uttar Pradesh: Banaras Hindu University, 1972.

Wagle, N. K., and O Qvarnstrom, eds. *Approaches to Jaina Studies: Philosophy, Logic, Rituals and Symbols*. Toronto: University of Toronto Centre for South Asian Studies, 1999.

Buddhism

Barua, D. K. *An Analytical Study of the Four Nikayas*. New Delhi: Munshiram Manoharlal, 2003.

Bhattacharyya, N. N. *Buddhism in the History of Indian Ideas*. New Delhi: Manohar, 1993.

Blackstone, Kathryn R. *Women in the Footsteps of the Buddha: The Struggle for Liberation in the Therigatha*. New Delhi: Motilal Banarsidass, 2000.

Cabezon, Jose Ignacio, ed. *Buddhism, Sexuality and Gender*. New Delhi: Satguru, 1992.

Dasgupta, Shashibhushan. *An Introduction to Tantric Buddhism*. Calcutta: University of Calcutta, 1974.

Dutt, Sukumar. *Buddhist Monks and Monasteries of India: Their History and Their Contribution to Indian Culture*. New Delhi: Motilal Banarsidass, 1988 (reprint).

Dutta, Nalinaksha. *Early History of the Spread of Buddhism and the Buddhist Schools*. New Delhi: Rajesh Publications, 1980 (reprint).

Gombrich, Richard. *Theravada Buddhism: A Social History from Ancient Benares to Modern Colombo*. London: Routledge & Kegan Paul, 1988.

———. *How Buddhism Began: The Conditional Genesis of the Early Teachings*. London: Athlone, 1996.

Hazra, K. L. *Buddhism in India as Described by the Chinese Pilgrims, A.D. 399–689*. New Delhi: Munshiram Manoharlal, 2002.

———. *Buddhism and Buddhist Literature in Early Indian Epigraphy*. New Delhi: Munshiram Manoharlal, 2004.

Horner, I. B. *Women under Primitive Buddhism*. New Delhi: Motilal Banarsidass, 1975 (reprint).

Lamotte, E. *A History of Indian Buddhism*. Louvain, Belgium: Universal Publishers, 1988.

Nakamura, H. *Indian Buddhism*. New Delhi: Motilal Banarsidass, 1989.
Narain, A. K., ed. *Studies in the History of Buddhism*. New Delhi: B. R. Publishing, 1980.
Niyogi, Pushpa. *Buddhist Divinities*. New Delhi: Munshiram Manoharlal, 2001.
Pande, G. C. *Studies in the Origins of Buddhism*. Allahabad, Uttar Pradesh: University of Allahabad, 1957.
Paul, Diana Y. *Women in Buddhism: Images of the Feminine in the Mahayana Tradition*. Berkeley: University of California Press, 1985.
Sarma, I. K. *Studies in Early Buddhist Monuments and Brahmi Inscriptions of Andhradesa*. Nagpur, Maharashtra: Dattsons, 1988.
Schopen, Gregory. *Bones, Stones and Buddhist Monks: Collected Papers on the Archaeology, Epigraphy and Texts of Monastic Buddhism in India*. Honolulu: University of Hawaii Press, 1997.
Shaw, Miranda. *Passionate Enlightenment: Women in Tantric Buddhism*. Princeton, NJ: Princeton University Press, 1994.
———. *Buddhist Goddesses of India*. New Delhi: Munshiram Manoharlal, 2007.
Strong, J. S. *The Buddha: A Short Biography*. Oxford, UK: Oneworld, 2001.
Talim, Meena. *Women in Early Buddhism*. Bombay: University of Bombay, 1972.
Wayman, Alex, and Hideko Wayman. *The Lion's Roar of Queen Srimala*. New York: Columbia University Press, 1974.
Willis, M., ed. *Buddhist Reliquaries from Ancient India*. London: British Museum, 2000.

Goddess Traditions

Aryan, K. C. *The Little Goddesses (Matrikas)*. New Delhi: Rekha Prakashan, 1980.
Atre, Shubhangana. *The Archetypal Mother: A Systemic Approach to Harappan Religion*. Pune, Maharashtra: Ravish, 1987.
Beane, Wendell Charles. *Myth, Cult and Symbols in Sakta Hinduism: A Study of the Indian Mother Goddess*. New Delhi: Munshiram Manoharlal, 2001.
Bhattacharyya, N. N. *History of the Sakta Religion*. New Delhi: Munshiram Manoharlal, 1996.
———. *Indian Mother Goddess*. New Delhi: Manohar, 1999.
Coburn, Thomas. *The Devimahatmya: The Crystallization of the Goddess Tradition*. New Delhi: Motilal Banarsidass, 1985.
Gatwood, Lynn E. *Devi and the Spouse Goddess: Women, Sexuality and Marriage in India*. New Delhi: Manohar, 1985.
Hawley, John Stratton, and Donna Marie Wulff, eds. *The Divine Consort: Radha and the Goddesses of India*. New Delhi: Motilal Banarsidass, 1984.

Kinsley, David. *Hindu Goddesses: Visions of the Divine Feminine in Hindu Religious Tradition*. Berkeley: University of California Press, 1986.

Kumar, Pushpendra. *Sakti Cult in Ancient India with Special Reference to the Puranic Literature*. Varanasi, Uttar Pradesh: Bharatiya Publishing House, 1974.

Lal, Shyam Kishore. *Female Divinities in Hindu Mythology and Ritual*. Pune, Maharashtra: University of Poona Press, 1980.

Pintchman, Tracy. *The Rise of the Goddess in the Hindu Tradition*. Albany: State University of New York Press, 1994.

Sircar, D. C., ed. *The Sakta Cult and Tara*. Calcutta: University of Calcutta, 1967.

———. *Sakta Pithas*. New Delhi: Motilal Banarsidass, 1973.

Srivastava. M. C. P. *Mother Goddess in Indian Art, Archaeology and Literature*. New Delhi: Agam Kala Prakashan, 1979.

Tiwari, J. N. *Goddess Cults in Ancient India (with Special Reference to the First Seven Centuries AD)*. New Delhi: Sundeep Prakashan, 1985.

Tantricism

Banerji, S. C. *A Brief History of Tantric Literature*. Calcutta: Naya Prokash, 1988.

Bharati, Agehananda. *The Tantric Tradition*. New Delhi: B. I. Publications, 1983.

Bhattacharyya, N. N. *History of the Tantric Religion: A Historical, Ritualistic and Philosophical Study*. New Delhi: Manohar, 1999.

Das, H. V. *Tantricism: A Study of the Yogini Cult*. New Delhi: Sterling, 1981.

Dehejia, Vidya. *The Yogini Cult and Temples: A Tantric Tradition*. New Delhi: National Museum, 1986.

Goudriaan, Teun, and Sanjukta Gupta. *Hindu Tantric and Sakta Literature*. Vol. 2, Fasc. 2 of *A History of Indian Literature*, edited by J. Gonda. Wiesbaden: Harrassowitz, 1981.

Shaw, Miranda. *Passionate Enlightenment: Women in Tantric Buddhism*. Princeton, NJ: Princeton University Press, 1994.

Philosophical Ideas

Balasubramanian, R. *Theistic Vedanta*. Vol. 2, Part 3, *History of Science, Philosophy and Culture in Indian Civilization*. New Delhi: Centre for Studies in Civilizations, 2003.

Bhattacharji, Sukumari. *Fatalism in Ancient India*. Calcutta: Baulmon Prakashan, 1995.

Chattopadhyaya, Debiprasad. *Lokayata: A Study in Ancient Indian Materialism*. New Delhi: People's Publishing House, 1959.

———, ed. *Studies in the History of Indian Philosophy: An Anthology of Articles by Scholars Eastern and Western*. 3 vols. Calcutta: Bagchi, 1991.

Dasgupta, Surendranath. *A History of Indian Philosophy*. 5 vols. New Delhi: Motilal Banarsidass, 1988 (reprint).

Halbfass, Wilhelm. *India and Europe (An Essay in Philosophical Understanding)*. New Delhi: Motilal Banarsidass, 1990.

———. *Tradition and Reflection: Exploration in Indian Thought*. Albany: State University of New York Press, 1991.

Singh, Satya Prakash. *Vedic Vision of Consciousness and Reality*. Vol. 12, Part 3, *History of Science, Philosophy and Culture in Indian Civilization*. New Delhi: Munshiram Manoharlal, 2004.

Thakur, Anantalal. *Origin and Development of the Vaisesika System*. Vol. 2, Part 4, *History of Science, Philosophy and Culture in Indian Civilization*. New Delhi: Motilal Banarsidass, 2003.

Miscellaneous

Basham, A. L. *History and Doctrines of the Ajivikas: A Vanished Indian Religion*. New Delhi: Motilal Banarsidass, 1981.

Mishra, Y. K. *Asceticism in Ancient India: A Study of Asceticism of Different Indian Schools in Philosophical, Religious and Social Perspectives*. Vaishali: Prakrit Jain Institute Research Publication, 1987.

Settar, S., and Gunther D. Sontheimer, eds. *Memorial Stones: A Study of their Origin, Significance and Variety*. Dharwar, Karnataka: Institute of Indian Art History, and Heidelberg: South Asia Institute, University of Heidelberg, 1982.

Zvelebil, K. *The Smile of Murugan*. Leiden: Brill, 1973.

MEDICINE, SCIENCE, AND TECHNOLOGY

Balasubramaniam, R. *The Story of the Delhi Iron Pillar*. New Delhi: Foundation Books, 2005.

Bharadwaj, H. C. *Aspects of Ancient Indian Technology*. New Delhi: Motilal Banarsidass, 1979.

Biswas, Arun Kumar. *Minerals and Metals in Ancient India*. 2 vols. New Delhi: D.K. Printworld, 1996.

Chakrabarti, Dilip K. *Early Use of Iron in India*. New Delhi: Oxford University Press, 1992.

Chakrabarti, Dilip K., and N. Lahiri. *Copper and Its Alloys in Ancient India*. New Delhi: Munshiram Manoharlal, 1996.

Chatterjee, S. K. *Indian Calendric System*. New Delhi: Publications Division, 1998.

Chattopadhyaya, Debiprasad. *The History of Science and Technology in Ancient India. The Beginnings*. Calcutta: Firma K. L. Mukhopadhyay, 1986.

———. *History of Science and Technology in Ancient India: Astronomy, Science and Society*. Calcutta: Firma K. L. Mukhopadhyay, 1996.

Craddock, Paul T., I. C. Freestone, L. K. Gurjar, A. Middleton, and L. Willies. *The Production of Lead, Silver and Zinc in Early India*. Bochum: Deutsches Bergbau Museum, 1989.

Dash, Vaidya Bhagwan. *Studies in the Medicine of Ancient India: Osteology or the Bones of the Human Body*. New Delhi: Concept, 1994.

Dikshit, Moreshwar G. *History of Indian Glass*. Bombay: University of Bombay, 1969.

Gokhale, Shobhana Laxman. *Indian Numerals*. Poona, Maharashtra: Deccan College Post-graduate and Research Institute, 1966.

Kanungo, A. R. *Glass Beads in Ancient India*. Oxford, UK: BAR Series, 2003.

Kuppuram, G. *Ancient Indian Mining, Metallurgy and Metal Industries*. New Delhi: Sundeep Prakashan, 1989.

Meulenbeld, G. Jan. *A History of Indian Medical Literature*. 3 vols. Groningen: Egbert Forsten, 1999–2002.

Mudhol, M. S. *A Technical Study of Megalithic Metal Objects*. Mysore: Directorate of Archaeology and Museums, 1997.

Mukhopadhyaya, Girindranath. *History of Indian Medicine: Containing Notices, Biographical and Bibliographical, of the Ayurvedic Physicians and Their Works on Medicine from the Earliest Ages to the Present Time*. 3 vols. New Delhi: Munshiram Manoharlal, 1994 (reprint).

Pal, Mrinal Kanti. *A Study of the Technology of Some of the Important Traditional Crafts in Ancient and Medieval India*. Calcutta: Indian Publications, 1970.

Pande, G., and Jan Geijerstam, eds. *Tradition and Innovation in the History of Iron Making*. Nainital, Uttarakhand: Pahar, 2002.

Pandey, Lalta Prasad. *History of Ancient Indian Science*. Vol. 1, *Botanical Science and Economic Growth: A Study of Forestry, Horticulture, Gardening and Plant Science*. New Delhi: Munshiram Manoharlal, 1996.

Pingree, David. *Jyotiḥśāstra. Astral and Mathematical Literature*. Vol. 6, Fasc. 4 of *A History of Indian Literature*, edited by Jan Gonda. Wiesbaden: Harrassowitz, 1981.

Ratnagar, Shereen. *Makers and Shapers: Early Indian Technology in the Home, Village and Urban Workshop*. New Delhi: Tulika, 2007.

Sen, Pranab Kumar, ed. *Philosophical Concepts Relevant to Sciences in Indian Tradition*. Vol. 3, Part 4, *History of Science, Philosophy and Culture in Indian Civilization*. New Delhi: Motilal Banarsidass, 2006.

Shastri, Ajay Mitra. *Varahamihira's India*. 2 vols. New Delhi: Aryan, 1996 (reprint).

Shrivastava, Rina. *Mining and Metallurgy in Ancient India*. New Delhi: Munshiram Manoharlal, 2006.

Singh, R. N. *Ancient Indian Glass: Archaeology and Technology*. New Delhi: Parimal, 1989.

Valiathan, M. S. *The Legacy of Caraka*. Hyderabad, Andhra Pradesh: Orient Longman, 2003.

Wujastyk, Dominik. *The Roots of Ayurveda*. New Delhi: Penguin, 2001.

Zysk, Kenneth G. *Asceticism and Healing in Ancient India: Medicine in the Buddhist Monastery*. New Delhi: Oxford University Press, 1990.

———. *Religious Medicine: The History and Evolution of Indian Medicine*. Edison, NJ: Transaction, 1993.

ARCHAEOLOGICAL REPORTS

Prehistoric and Protohistoric Archaeology (Except Harappan Civilization)

Allchin, F. R. *Piklihal Excavations*. Hyderabad: Goverrnment of Andhra Pradesh, 1960.

———. *Utnur Excavations*. Hyderabad: Government of Andhra Pradesh, 1961.

Allchin, F. R., and Jagat Pati Joshi. *Excavations at Malvan: Report of the Archaeological Survey of India and Cambridge University in 1970 on the Gujarat Plain*. New Delhi: Archaeological Survey of India, 1995.

Ansari, Zainuddin Dawood, and M. S. Nagaraja Rao. *Excavations at Sangankallu, 1964–65*. Poona, Maharashtra: Deccan College, 1969.

Dasgupta, P. C. *The Excavations at Pandu Rajar Dhibi*. Calcutta: West Bengal Directorate of Archaeology, 1964.

Dhavalikar, M. K., H. D. Sankalia, and Z. D. Ansari. *Excavations at Inamgaon*. Vol. 1. Pune, Maharashtra: Deccan College, 1988.

Dhavalikar, M. K., Vasant Shinde, and Shubhangana Atre. *Excavations at Kaothe*. Pune, Maharashtra: Deccan College Post-graduate and Research Institute, 1990.

Jarrige, Catherine, J.-F. Jarrige, R. Meadow, and G. Quivron, eds. *Mehrgarh: Field Reports 1974–1985 from Neolithic Times to the Indus Civilization*. Karachi: The Department of Culture and Tourism of Sindh and Department of Archaeology and Museums, French Ministry of Foreign Affairs, 1995.

Nagaraja Rao, M. S. *Protohistoric Cultures of the Tungabhadra Valley: A Report of the Hallur Excavations*. Dharwar: Author, 1971.

Sankalia, H. D. *Excavations at Langhnaj: 1944–63*. Part 1, *Archaeology*. Poona, Maharashtra: Deccan College, 1965.

Sankalia, H. D., S. B. Rao, and Z. D. Ansari. *Chalcolithic Navdatoli*. Pune, Maharashtra: Deccan College, 1971.

Seshadri, M. *Report on the Excavations at T. Narsipur*. Mysore: Department of Archaeology, 1971.

Sharma, G. R., et al. *Beginnings of Agriculture (Epi-Paleolithic to Neolithic): Excavations at Chopani Mando, Mahadaha and Mahagara*. Allahabad, Uttar Pradesh: University of Allahabad, 1980.

Singh, P. *Excavations at Narhan*. New Delhi: Agam Kala Prakashan, 1994.

The Harappan Civilization

Banerji, R. D. *Mohenjodaro: A Forgotten Report*. Varanasi, Uttar Pradesh: Prithivi Prakashan, 1984.

Bhan, Suraj. *Excavations at Mitathal (1968) and Other Explorations in the Sutlej-Yamuna Divide*. Kurukshetra: Kurukshetra University, 1975.

Dales, G. F., and J. M. Kenoyer. *Excavations at Mohenjo Daro, Pakistan, the Pottery*. Philadelphia: University Museum Monograph 53, 1986.

Dhavalikar, M. K., M. R. Raval, and Y. M. Chitalwala. *Kuntasi: A Harappan Emporium on the West Coast*. Pune, Maharashtra: Deccan College Post-graduate and Research Institute, 1996.

Fairservis, Walter A. *Excavations at the Harappan Site of Allahdino: The Seals and Other Inscribed Material*. New York: American Museum of Natural History, 1976.

———. *Excavations at the Harappan Site of Allahdino: The Graffiti, a Model in the Decipherment of the Harappan Script*. New York: American Museum of Natural History, 1977.

Jansen, M. *Mohenjo Daro: Report of the Aachen University Mission 1979–1985*. Leiden: Brill, 1985.

———. *Interim Reports Vol. 2: Reports on Field Work Carried out at Mohenjo-Daro, Pakistan 1983–84 by IsMEO-Aachen University Mission*. Aachen: IsMEO/RWTH, 1987.

Jansen, M., and M. Tosi, eds. *Interim Reports Vol. 3: Reports on Field Work Carried out at Mohenjo-Daro, Pakistan 1983–86 by IsMEO-Aachen University Mission*. Aachen: IsMEO/RWTH, 1988.

Jansen, M., and G. Urban, eds. *Interim Reports Vol. 1: Reports on Field Work Carried Out at Mohenjo-Daro, Pakistan 1982–83 by IsMEO-Aachen University Mission*. Aachen: IsMEO/RWTH, 1984.

Joshi, Jagat Pati. *Excavations at Surkotada 1971–72 and Explorations in Kutch*. New Delhi: Archaeological Survey of India, 1990.

———. *Excavations at Bhagwanpura 1975–75 and other Explorations and Excavations 1975–81 in Haryana, Jammu and Kashmir, and Punjab*. New Delhi: Archaeological Survey of India (Memoirs 89), 1993.

Koskenniemi, Kimmo, and Asko Parpola. *Corpus of Texts in the Indus Script*. Helsinki: Department of Asian and African Studies, University of Helsinki, 1979.

———. *Documentation and Duplicates in the Indus Script*. Helsinki: Department of Asian and African Studies, University of Helsinki, 1980.

———. *A Concordance to the Texts in the Indus Script*. Helsinki: Department of Asian and African Studies, University of Helsinki, 1982.

Koskenniemi, Seppo, Asko Parpola, and Simo Parpola. *Materials for the Study of the Indus Script. A Concordance to the Indus Inscriptions*. Helsinki: Acta Academiae Scientarium Fennicae, 1973.

Lal, B. B., B. K. Thapar, J. P. Joshi, and M. Bala. *Excavations at Kalibangan: The Early Harappan (1960–69)*. New Delhi: Archaeological Survey of India, 2003.

Mackay, E. J. H. *Further Excavations at Mohenjo-daro*. 2 vols. New Delhi: Munshiram Manoharlal, 1998 (reprint).

Marshall, J. *Mohenjo-daro and the Indus Civilization*. 3 vols. New Delhi: Asian Educational Service, 2004 (reprint).

Meadow, R. H., ed. *Harappan Excavations 1986–1990: A Multidisciplinary Approach to Third Millennium Urbanism*. Madison: Prehistory Press, 1991.

Rao, S. R. *Lothal: A Harappan Port Town*. New Delhi: Archaeological Survey of India, 1979.

Vats, M. S. *Excavations at Harappa*. New Delhi: Munshiram Manoharlal, 1997 (reprint).

Other Archaeological Reports

Alam, M. S., and J.-F. Salles, eds. *Franco-Bangladesh Joint Venture Excavations at Mahasthangarh: First Interim Report 1993–1999*. Dhaka: Department of Archaeology, 2001.

Altekar, A. S., and V. K. Mishra. *Report on the Kumrahar Excavations 1951–55*. Patna, Bihar: K. P. Jayaswal Research Institute, 1959.

Begley, V., et al. *The Ancient Port of Arikamedu: New Excavations and Researches, 1989–1992*. Pondicherry: l' Ecole Francais de Extreme Orient, 1996.

Burgess, Jas. *The Buddhist Stupas of Amaravati and Jaggayyapeta in the Krishna District, Madras Presidency, surveyed in 1882*. Archaeological Survey of Southern India, Vol. 1 (1887), Reports, New Imperial Series 6. Varanasi, Uttar Pradesh: Indological Book House, 1970.

Chapekar, B. N. *Report on the Excavations at Ter, 1958*. Poona, Maharashtra: Deccan College, 1969.

Cunningham, Alexander. *Mahabodhi or the Great Buddhist Temple Under the Bodhi Tree at Buddha-Gaya*. Varanasi, Uttar Pradesh: Indological Book House, n.d (reprint).

———. *The Stupa of Bharhut. A Buddhist Monument Ornamented with Numerous Sculptures Illustrative of Buddhist Legend and History in the Third Century B.C.* Varanasi, Uttar Pradesh: Indological Book House, 1962 (reprint).

———. *Archaeological Survey of India Reports*. Calcutta: Office of the Superintendent of Government Printing, 1966–1972 (reprint).

———. *The Bhilsa Topes*. New Delhi: Munshiram Manoharlal Publishers, 1997 (reprint).

Das, S. R. *Rajbadidanga 1962: Excavation Report*. Calcutta: Asiatic Society, 1968.

———. *Archaeological Discoveries from Murshidabad*. Calcutta: Asiatic Society, 1971.

Deglurkar, G. R., and Gouri Lad. *Megalithic Raipur*. Pune, Maharashtra: Deccan College, 1992.

Deo, S. B. *Mahurjhari Excavations*. Nagpur, Maharashtra: University of Nagpur, 1973.

Deo, S. B., and R. S. Gupta. *Excavations at Bhokardan 1973*. Nagpur, Maharashtra: University of Nagpur, 1974.

Deo, S. B., and Jagat Pati Joshi. *Pauni Excavation* (1969–70). Nagpur, Maharashtra: Archaeological Survey of India and Nagpur University, 1972.

Deva, Krishna, and Vijayakanta Mishra. *Vaisali Excavations 1950*. Vaisali: Vaisali Sangh, 1961.

Dikshit, K. N. *Excavations at Paharpur*. New Delhi: Archaeological Survey of India, 1938.

Gaur, R. C. *Excavations at Atranjikhera*. Delhi: Motilal Banarsidass, 1983.

Ghosh, N. C. *Excavations at Satanikota 1977–78*. New Delhi: Archaeological Survey of India, 1986.

Goswami, K. G. *Excavations at Bangarh*. Calcutta: Calcutta University Press, 1948.

Haque, E., S. S. M. Rahman, and S. M. K. Ahsan. *Excavations at Wari-Bateshwar: A Preliminary Study*. Dhaka: International Centre for the Study of Bengal Art, 2001.

Hartel, H. *Excavations at Sonkh*. Berlin: Reimer, 1993.

Howell, J. R. *Excavations at Sannathi 1986–1989*. New Delhi: Archaeological Survey of India, 1995.

Khan, Abdul Waheed. *A Monograph on an Early Buddhist Stupa at Kesanapalli*. Hyderabad: Government of Andhra Pradesh, 1969.

Lal, B. B. *Sringaverapura Excavations*. New Delhi: Archaeological Survey of India, 1963.

Leshnik, L. S. *South Indian 'Megalithic' Burials: The Pandukal Complex*. Wiesbaden: Steiner, 1974.

Marshall, John. *Taxila: An Illustrated Account of Archaeological Excavations Carried Out at Taxila under the Orders of the Government of India between the Years 1913 and 1934*. New Delhi: Motilal Banarsidass, 1975 (reprint).

Marshall, John, and Alfred Foucher. 1982. *The Monuments of Sanchi*. Inscriptions edited, translated, and annotated by N. G. Majumdar. 3 vols. Delhi: Swati, 1982 (reprint).

Mitra, Debala. *Ratnagiri (1958–61)*. 2 vols. New Delhi: Archaeological Survey of India, 1981–1983.

Narain, A. K., and T. N. Roy. *The Excavations at Prahladpur*. Varanasi, Uttar Pradesh: Banaras Hindu University, 1968.

Narain, A. K., and P. Singh. *Excavations at Rajghat*. Varanasi, Uttar Pradesh: Banaras Hindu University, 1977.

Sarkar, H., and B. N. Mishra. *Nagarjunakonda*. New Delhi: Archaeological Survey of India, 1972.

Sarkar, H., and S. P. Nainar. *Amaravati*. New Delhi: Archaeological Survey of India, 1973.

Sastri, T. V. G., et al. *Vaddamanu Excavations*. Hyderabad, Andhra Pradesh: Birla Archaeological and Cultural Research Institute, 1992.

Satyamurthy, T. *The Iron Age in Kerala—A Report on the Mungadu Excavation*. Thiruvananthapuram: Department of Archaeology, 1992.

Sharma, G. R. *Excavations at Kausambi, 1957–58*. Allahabad, Uttar Pradesh: University of Allahabad, 1960.

Sinha, B. P. *Pataliputra Excavations, 1955–56*. Patna, Bihar: Directorate of Archaeology and Museums, 1970.

Sinha, B. P., and S. R. Roy. *Vaisali Excavations: 1958–62*. Patna, Bihar: Directorate of Archaeology and Museums, 1969.

Sinha, B. P., and B. S. Verma. *Sonpur Excavations 1956 and 1959–1962*. Patna, Bihar: Directorate of Archaeology and Museums, 1977.

Sinha, K. K. *Excavations at Sravasti 1959*. Varanasi, Uttar Pradesh: Banaras Hindu University, 1967.

Soundararajan, K. V. *Kaveripattinam Excavations 1963–1973 (A Port City on the Tamil Nadu Coast)*. New Delhi: Archaeological Survey of India, 1994.

Sridhar, T. S., ed. *Alagankulam: Ancient Roman Port of Tamil Nadu*. Chennai: Government of Tamil Nadu.

Srivastava, K. M. *Excavations at Piprahwa and Ganwaria*. New Delhi: Archaeological Survey of India, 1996.

Wadell, Austine L. *Report on the Excavations at Pataliputra, the Palibothra of the Greeks*. New Delhi: Asian Educational Service, 1996 (reprint).

PUBLISHED INSCRIPTIONS AND CATALOGS OF COINS

Agrawal, J. N. *Inscriptions of Haryana, Himachal Pradesh, Punjab, Kashmir and Adjoining Hilly Tracts*. New Delhi: Pratibha Prakashan, 1999.

Allan, J. *A Catalogue of the Indian Coins in the British Museum: Coins of Ancient India*. London: British Museum, 1967 (reprint).

———. *Catalogue of the Coins of the Gupta Dynasty and of Sasanka, King of Gauda*. New Delhi: Munshiram Manoharlal, 1975.

Altekar, A. S. *Catalogue of the Gupta Gold Coins in the Bayana Hoard*. Bombay: Numismatic Society of India, 1954.

Bahadur, Mutua, and Paonam Gunindra Singh. *Epigraphic Records of Manipur*. Vol. 1. Imphal: Mutua Museum, 1986.

Bhandarkar, Devadatta Ramakrishna, Bahadurchand Chhabra, and Govind Swamirao Gai. *Inscriptions of the Early Gupta Kings*. Vol. 3 of *Corpus Inscriptionum Indicarum* (revised edition). New Delhi: Archaeological Survey of India, 1981.

Burgess, Jas, and Bhagwanlal Indraji. *Inscriptions from the Cave-Temples of Western India with Descriptive Notes*. Archaeological Survey of Western India, Reports, Old Series No. 10, 1881. New Delhi: Indological Book House, 1976 (reprint).

Butterworth, Alan, and V. Venugopaul Chetty. *Copper-Plate and Stone Inscriptions of South India*. 3 vols. New Delhi: Caxton, 2006.

Cunningham, Alexander. *Inscriptions of Asoka*. Vol. 1 of *Corpus Inscriptionum Indicarum*. New Delhi: Archaeological Survey of India, 2000 (reprint).

Deambi, B. K. Kaul. *Corpus of Sarada Inscriptions of Kashmir*. New Delhi: Agam Kala Prakashan, 1982.

Fleet, John Faithfull. *Inscriptions of the Early Gupta Kings and Their Successors*. Vol. 3 of *Corpus Inscriptionum Indicarum*. Varanasi, Uttar Pradesh: Indological Book House, 1970 (reprint).

Gai, G. S. *Inscriptions of the Early Kadambas*. New Delhi: Indian Council of Historical Research and Pratibha Prakashan, 1996.

Gokhale, Shobhana Laxman. *Kanheri Inscriptions*. Pune, Maharashtra: Deccan College Post-graduate and Research Institute, 1991.

Gopal, B. R. *Corpus of Kadamba Inscriptions*. Vol. 1. Sirsi: Kadamba Institute of Cultural Studies, 1985.

Guillaume, Olivier, ed. *Graeco-Bactrian and Indian Coins from Afghanistan*. New Delhi: Oxford University Press, 1991.

Hultzsch, E. *Inscriptions of Asoka*. Vol. 1 of *Corpus Inscriptionum Indicarum*. Delhi: Indological Book House, 1969 (reprint).

Jettmar, Karl, ed. *Rock Inscriptions in the Indus Valley*. Mainz: von Zabern, 1989.

Joshi, Jagat Pati, and Asko Parpola. *Corpus of Indus Seals and Inscriptions*. Vol. 1. Helsinki: Suomalainen Tiedeakatemia, Annales Academiae Scientiarum Fennicae, 1987.

Konow, Sten. *Kharosthi Inscriptions With the Exception of Those of Asoka*. Vol. 2, Part 1 of *Corpus Inscriptionum Indicarum*. Varanasi, Uttar Pradesh: Indological Book House, 1969 (reprint).

Krishnan, K. G. *Karandai Tamil Sangam Plates of Rajendrachola I*. New Delhi: Archaeological Survey of India, 1984.

———. *Inscriptions of the Early Pandyas*. New Delhi: Northern Book Centre, 2002.

Lal, Hira. *Inscriptions in the Central Provinces and Berar*. Patna, Bihar: Eastern Books House, 1985 (reprint).

Luders, H. *Mathura Inscriptions* (unpublished papers edited by Klaus L. Janert). Gottingen: Vandenhoeck and Ruprecht, 1961.

———. *Bharhut Inscriptions*. Vol. 2, Part 2 of *Corpus Inscriptionum Indicarum*. Revised by E. Waldschmidt and M. A. Mehendale. Ootacamund: Government Epigraphist for India, 1963.

Mahadevan, Iravatham. *Tamil-Brahmi Inscriptions*. Madras: State Department of Archaeology, Government of Tamil Nadu, 1970.

Mahalingam, T. V. *Inscriptions of the Pallavas*. New Delhi: Indian Council of Historical Research, 1988.

Majumdar, N. G., ed. *Inscriptions of Bengal*. Vol. 3. Rajshahi: The Varendra Research Society, 1929.

Mirashi, Vasudev Vishnu. *Inscriptions of the Kalachuri-Chedi Era*. Vol. 4, Parts 1 and 2 of *Corpus Inscriptionum Indicarum*. Ootacamund: Government Epigraphist for India, 1955.

———. *Inscriptions of the Vakatakas*. Vol. 5 of *Corpus Inscriptionum Indicarum*. Ootacamund, Tamil Nadu: Government Epigraphist for India, 1963.

———. *Inscriptions of the Silaharas*. Vol. 6 of *Corpus Inscriptionum Indicarum*. New Delhi: Director General of the Archaeological Survey of India, 1977.

Mishra, Ram Swaroop. *Supplement to Fleet's Corpus Inscriptionum Indicarum Vol. III (1888): Inscriptions of the Early Gupta Kings and Their Successors*. Part 1, *Bibliography*. Varanasi, Uttar Pradesh: Banaras Hindu University, 1971.

Mittal, A. C. *The Inscriptions of the Imperial Paramaras (800 A.D. to 1320 A.D.)*. Ahmedabad, Gujarat: L. D. Institute of Indology, 1979.

Mukherjee, Ramaranjan, and Sachindra Kumar Maity, eds. *Corpus of Bengal Inscriptions Bearing on the History and Civilization of Bengal*. Calcutta: Firma K. L. Mukhopadhyay, 1967.

Parabrahma Sastry, P. V. *Inscriptions of Andhra Pradesh*. Hyderabad: Government of Andhra Pradesh, 1977–1981.

Paranavitana, S. *Inscriptions of Ceylon: Early Brahmi Inscriptions*. Colombo: Department of Archaeology, Ceylon, 1970.

Peterson, Peter (introduction). *A Collection of Prakrit and Sanskrit Inscriptions [of Kattywar, etc]*. Bhavnagar, Gujarat: State Printing Press, 1896.

Phogat, S. R. *Inscriptions of Haryana*. Kurukshetra, Haryana: Vishal, 1978.

Rajaguru, Satyanarayan. *Inscriptions of Orissa*. 6 vols in 10 parts. Bhubaneswar: Government of Orissa, 1952–1974.

Rama Rao, M. *Inscriptions of Andhradesa*. Tirupati, Andhra Pradesh: Sri Venkatesvara University, 1967–1968.

Ramesan, N. *Copper Plate Inscriptions of Andhra Pradesh Government Museum Hyderabad*. 2 vols. Hyderabad: Government of Andhra Pradesh, 1962–1970.

Ramesh, K. V. *Inscriptions of the Western Gangas*. New Delhi: Indian Council of Historical Research/Agam Kala Prakashan, 1984.

Ramesh, K. V., and S. P. Tewari, eds. *A Copper Plate Hoard of the Gupta Period from Bagh, Madhya Pradesh*. New Delhi: Archaeological Survey of India, 1990.

Rapson, Edward James. *Catalogue of the Coins of the Andhra Dynasty, the Western Ksatrapas, the Traikutaka Dynasty and the "Bodhi" Dynasty*. New Delhi: Munshiram Manoharlal, 1975 (reprint).

Regmi, D. R. *Inscriptions of Ancient Nepal*. New Delhi: Abhinav, 1983.

Rice, B. Lewis. *Mysore Inscriptions*. New Delhi: Navrang, 1983 (reprint).

Roy Chowdhury, Chittaranjan. *A Catalogue of Early Indian Coins in the Asutosh Museum, Calcutta*. Calcutta: University of Calcutta, 1962.

Sahai, Bhagwant. *The Inscriptions of Bihar (from Earliest Times to the Middle of the 13th Century A.D.)*. New Delhi: Ramanand Vidya Bhavan, 1983.

Sarma, I. K., and J. Varaprasada Rao. *Early Brahmi Inscriptions from Sannati*. New Delhi: Harman, 1993.

Sathyanarayana, R. *The Kudimiyamalai Inscription on Music*. Vol. 1, *Sources*. Mysore: Sri Varalakshmi Academy of Fine Arts, 1957.

Satyamurthy, T. *Catalogue of Roman gold coins*. Thiruvananthapuram: Department of Archaeology, Government of Kerala, 1992.

Shah, S. G. M., and Asko Parpola. *Corpus of Indus Seals and Inscriptions*. Vol. 2. Helsinki: Suomalainen Tiedeakatemia, Annales Academiae Scientiayum Fennicae, 1991.

Sharma, Mukunda Madhava. *Inscriptions of Assam*. Gauhati, Assam: Gauhati University, 1978.

Sreenivasachar, P. *A Corpus of Inscriptions in the Telingana Districts of H.E.H. the Nizam's Dominions*. Hyderabad: Government of Andhra Pradesh, 1940, 1942, 1956–1970.

Srinivasan, P. R., and S. Sankaranarayanan. *Inscriptions of the Ikshvaku Period*. Hyderabad: Government of Andhra Pradesh, 1979.

Subramaniam, T. N. *South Indian Temple Inscriptions*. 3 vols in 4 parts. Madras: Government Oriental Manuscript Library, 1953–1957.

Thaplyal, Kiran Kumar. *Inscriptions of the Maukharis, Later Guptas, Puspabhutis and Yasovarman of Kanauj*. New Delhi: Indian Council of Historical Research/Agam Kala Prakashan, 1985.

Tripathi, Snigdha. *Inscriptions of Orissa*. Vol. 1. New Delhi: Motilal Banarsidass, 1997.

———. *Inscriptions of Orissa,* Vol. 2. New Delhi: Pratibha Prakashan, 1999.
Turner, R. L. *The Gavimath and Palkigundu Inscriptions of Asoka*. Hyderabad: Dept. of Archaeology, Government of Hyderabad, 1952.

TEXTS AND TRANSLATIONS

Brahmanical Texts, Sanskrit

Adriaensen, R., H. T. Bakker, and H. Isaacson, eds. *The Skandapurana*. Vol. 1, *adhyayas 1–25*. Groningen: Egbert Forsten, 1998 (critically edited with prolegomena and English synopsis).
Ancient Indian Tradition and Mythology Series, Vols. 1–68. New Delhi: Motilal Banarsidass. (For translations of the *Siva, Linga, Bhagavati, Garuda, Narada, Kurma, Brahmanda, Agni, Varaha, Brahma, Vayu, Padma*, and *Skanda Purana*. General editors J. L. Shastri and G. P. Bhatt).
Bhattacharya, B. *Yaska's Nirukta and the Science of Etymology*. Calcutta: Oxford University Press, 1958.
Bhattacharya, Vibhuti Bhushan, ed. *Baudhayana Sulbasutram*. Varanasi, Uttar Pradesh: Sarasvatibhavan, 1979.
Brough, J. *The Early Brahmanical System of Gotra and Pravara: A Translation of the Gotra-Pravara-Manjari of Purusottama Pandita*. Cambridge, UK: Cambridge University Press, 1953.
Buhler, Georg, trans. *The Sacred Laws of the Aryas as Taught in the Schools of Apastamba, Gautama, Vasistha and Baudhayana*. Sacred Books of the East, Vols. 2 and 14. New Delhi: Motilal Banarsidass, 1984 (reprint).
———, ed. *Apastambiyadharmasutra, with Extracts from Haradatta's Commentary, the Ujjvala,* Parts 1 and 2. Pune, Maharashtra: Bhandarkar Oriental Research Institute, 1997 (reprint).
Caland, W., and Lokesh Chandra. *Sankhayana Srautasutra*. New Delhi: Motilal Banarsidass, 1980.
Coburn, Thomas B. *Encountering the Goddess: A Translation of the Devimahatmya and a Study of Its Interpretation*. New York: State University of New York Press, 1991.
Devi Chand, trans. *The Yajurveda*. New Delhi: Munshiram Manoharlal, 1989.
Doniger, Wendy, and Brian K. Smith. *The Laws of Manu* (translated, with an introduction and notes). New Delhi: Penguin, 1991.
Eggeling, Julius. *The Satapatha Brahmana According to the Text of the Madhyandina School*. New Delhi: Motilal Banarsidass, 1963.
Ganapati, S. V., ed. and trans. *Samaveda: Sanskrit Text in Devanagari with English Translation*. New Delhi: Motilal Banarsidass, 1982.

Garbe, Richard, ed. *Apastamba Srautasutra with Rudradatta's Vrtti*. 3 vols. New Delhi: Munshiram Manoharlal, 1983 (reprint).

Griffith, R. T. H., trans. *Hymns of the Rgveda*. New Delhi: Motilal Banarsidass, 1986 (reprint).

———. *Hymns of the Samaveda*. New Delhi: Munshiram Manoharlal, 1986 (reprint).

———. *Texts of the White Yajurveda on the Vajasaneya Samhita*. New Delhi: Munshiram Manoharlal, 1987 (reprint).

———. *Hymns of the Atharvaveda*. 2 vols. New Delhi: Munshiram Manoharlal, 2002 (reprint).

Haug, M. *The Aitareya Brahmana of the Rig Veda*. Allahabad, Uttar Pradesh: S. N. Vasu, 1922.

Keith, A. B. *The Veda of the Black Yajus School Entitled Taittiriya Samhita*. 2 vols. New Delhi: Motilal Banarsidass, 1967 (reprint).

———. *Rigveda Brahmanas*. New Delhi: Motilal Banarsidass, 1998 (reprint).

Lariviere, Richard W., ed. *The Narada Smrti*. Philadelphia: Department of South Asia Regional Studies, University of Pennsylvania, 1989.

Lokesh Chandra, ed. *Katyayana Srautasutra and Other Vedic Texts*. New Delhi: International Academy of Indian Culture, 1982.

Macdonell, A. A. *The Brhaddevata of Saunaka*. Cambridge, MA: Harvard University Press: Harvard Oriental Series.

Max Muller, Friedrich, general ed. *Sacred Books of the East*. 50 vols. New Delhi: D. K. Publishers, 1995 (reprint).

Miller, Barbara Stoler, trans. *The Bhagavad Gita: Krishna's Counsel in Time of War*. New York: Bantam Classics, 1986.

Mitchiner, John, ed. *The Yuga Purana*. Calcutta: Asiatic Society of Bengal, 2002.

Olivelle, Patrick. *The Codes of Apastamba, Gautama, Baudhayana and Vasistha: Annotated Text and Translation*. New Delhi: Motilal Banarsidass, 2000.

———. *Manu's Code of Law: A Critical Edition and Translation of the Manava-Dharmasastra*. New Delhi: Oxford University Press, 2005.

Peterson, Peter, trans. *Hymns from the Rgveda Samhita*. New Delhi: Bharatiya Kala Prakashan, 2004.

Raghu, Vira, and Lokesh Chandra, eds. *Jaiminiya Brahmana of the Samaveda*. New Delhi: Motilal Banarsidass, 1986.

Sarup, L. *The Nighantu and the Nirukta*. Oxford, UK: Oxford University Press.

Buddhist Texts, Pali

Anguttara Nikaya. See Woodward and Hare (1906–1915).

Cowell, E. B., ed. *Jatakas*. 6 vols. New Delhi: Motilal Banarsidass, 1990 (reprint).

Geiger, W., and M. H. Bode. *The Mahavamsa or the Great Chronicle of Ceylon*. New Delhi: Asian Educational Services, 2000 (reprint).
Horner, I. B., trans. *The Book of the Discipline*. 6 vols. Oxford, UK: Pali Text Society, 1992–1993.
———, trans. *The Collection of the Middle-Length Sayings (Majjhima Nikaya)*. 3 vols. New Delhi: Motilal Banarsidass, 2000 (reprint).
Jayawickrama, N. A., trans. *Vinaya Pitaka Commentary*. Oxford, UK: Pali Text Society, 1986.
Norman, K. R., trans. *Word of the Doctrine (Dhammapada)*. Oxford, UK: Pali Text Society, 1997.
———, ed. and trans. *The Group of Discourses*. Oxford, UK: Pali Text Society, 2001.
———, trans. *Patimokkha*. Oxford, UK: Pali Text Society, 2001.
———, ed. *Elders' Verses*. Oxford, UK: Pali Text Society, 2006.
Oldenberg, H., trans. *Dipavamsa: An Ancient Buddhist Historical Record*. New Delhi: Asian Educational Service, 2001.
Rhys Davids, C. A. F. *Psalms of the Early Buddhists*. Oxford, UK: Pali Text Society, 1980 (reprint).
Rhys Davids, C. A. F., and F. L. Woodward, trans. *The Book of the Kindred Sayings*. 5 vols. Oxford, UK: Pali Text Society, 1993–1995 (reprint).
Rhys Davids, T. W., and C. A. F. Rhys Davids. *Dialogues of the Buddha*. 3 vols. Oxford, UK: Pali Text Society, 1995 (reprint).
Woodward, F. L., and E. M. Hare. *The Book of the Gradual Sayings*. 5 vols. Oxford, UK: Pali Text Society, 1995 (reprint).

Buddhist Texts, Sanskrit

Mitra, R., ed. *The Lalitavistara*. New Delhi: Cosmo, 2004.
Mukhopadhyaya, S. K., ed. *Asokavadana*. New Delhi: Sahitya Akademi, 1963.
Strong, J. S. *The Legend of King Asoka*. Princeton, NJ: Princeton University Press, 1983.

Jaina Texts, Prakrit

Carpentier, J., ed. *Uttaradhyanasutra, Being the First Mula Sutra of the Svetambara Jainas*. Uppsala: Appelsbergs Boktrycheri Aktibolog, 1922.
Chandra, K. R. *Acaranga. Prathama Sruta Skandha: Prathama Adhyayana*. Ahmedabad, Gujarat: Prakrit Jain Vidya Vikas Phamd, 1997.
Deleu, J. *Viyahapannatti (Bhagavai). The Fifth Anga of the Jaina Canon. Introduction, Critical Analysis, Commentary and Indexes*. Brugge: De Tempel, 1970.

Jacobi, Hermann, trans. *Jaina Sutras* (translated from Prakrit). Part 1, *The Acaranga Sutra, the Kalpa Sutra*. New Delhi: Motilal Banarsidass, 1964 (reprint).

Muni, Jambuvijaya, ed. *Thanamgasuttam and Samavayamgasutta*. Bombay: Shri Mahavira Jaina Vidyalaya, 1985.

Muni, Nathmal, ed. *Bhagavati Sutra*. Ladnum: Jain Visva Bharati, 1974.

Muni, Punyavijaya, ed. *Angavijja*. Ahmedabad, Gujarat: Prakrit Text Society, 2000 (reprint).

Schubring, W. *Isibhasiyaim. A Jaina Text of the Early Period*. Ahmedabad, Gujarat: L. D. Institute of Indology, 1974.

Suri, Sagarananda, ed. *Acarangasutram and Sutrakrtangasutram with the Niryukti of Acarya Bhadrabahu Svami*. New Delhi: Motilal Banarsidass, 2007 (reprint).

Literary Texts, Sanskrit

Antoine, Robert. *The Dynasty of Raghu*. Calcutta: Writers Workshop, 1972.

Bhatt, G. H., and U. P. Shah, general eds. *The Valmiki Ramayana: Critical Edition*. 7 vols. Baroda, Gujarat: Oriental Institute, 1958–1975.

Bowles, Adam. *Mahabharata VIII: Karna*. Vol. 1, *Karnaparvan*. New York: Clay Sanskrit Library, 2007.

Buitenen, J. A. B. van, trans. *The Book of the Beginning*. Vol. 1, *Mahabharata*. Chicago: University of Chicago Press, 1973.

———. *The Book of the Assembly Hall*. Vol. 2, *Mahabharata*. Chicago: University of Chicago Press, 1975.

———. *The Book of the Forest*. Vol. 3, *Mahabharata*. Chicago: University of Chicago Press, 1983.

———. *The Book of Virata*. Vol. 4, *Mahabharata*. Chicago: University of Chicago Press, 1983.

———. *The Book of the Effort*. Vol. 5, *Mahabharata*. Chicago: University of Chicago Press, 1983.

Coulson, Michael. *Rakshasa's Ring (Mudraraksasa) by Visakhadatta*. New York: Clay Sanskrit Library, 2005.

Cowell, E. B., and F. W. Thomas, trans. *The Harsacarita of Bana*. New Delhi: Motilal Banarsidass, 1993 (reprint).

Devadhar, C. R., and N. G. Suru, eds. *Raghuvamsa of Kalidasa, Cantos I–IV with Mallinatha's Commentary, Introduction, Translation and Critical and Exhaustive Notes*. Poona, Maharashtra: Aryabhushan, 1934.

Dwivedi, Rewa Prasad, ed. *Raghuvamsa of Kalidasa*. New Delhi: Sahitya Akademi, 1993.

Fitzgerald, J., trans. *The Mahabharata, Book 11: The Book of the Women*. Chicago: University of Chicago Press, 2004.

———, trans. *Book 12. The Book of Peace, Part 1.* Chicago: University of Chicago Press, 2004.

Goldman, Robert, trans. *The Ramayana of Valmiki: An Epic of Ancient India.* Vol. 1. Princeton, NJ: Princeton University Press, 1984.

Goldman, Robert, and Rosalind Lefeber, trans. *The Ramayana of Valmiki: An Epic of Ancient India.* Vol. 4. Princeton, NJ: Princeton University Press, 1994.

Goldman, Robert, and Sheldon Pollock, trans. *The Ramayana of Valmiki: An Epic of Ancient India.* Vol. 2. Princeton, NJ: Princeton University Press, 1987.

———. *The Ramayana of Valmiki: An Epic of Ancient India.* Vol. 3. Princeton, NJ: Princeton University Press, 1991.

Goldman, Robert, and Sally Sutherland, trans. *The Ramayana of Valmiki: An Epic of Ancient India.* Vol. 5. Princeton, NJ: Princeton University Press, 1996.

Heifetz, Hank. *The Origin of the Young God: Kalidasa's Kumarasambhava* (translated with annotations and an introduction). Berkeley: University of California Press, 1985.

Ingalls, Daniel H. H., trans. *Subhasitaratnakosa: An Anthology of Sanskrit Court Poetry.* Harvard. Oriental Series, Vol. 44. Cambridge, MA: Harvard University Press, 1965.

Janaki, S. S., trans. *The Statue: Bhasa's Pratima in English Translation.* Madras: Kuppuswami Sastri Research Institute, 1978.

Johnson, William J. *Mahabharata III. The Forest.* Vol. 4, *Vanaparvan.* New York: Clay Sanskrit Library, 2005.

Johnston, E. H., ed. and trans. *The Buddhacarita or the Acts of the Buddha.* Lahore: University of Punjab, 1936.

———. *The Saundarananda of Asvaghosa.* New Delhi: Motilal Banarsidass, 1975 (reprint).

Kale, M. R., trans. *The Dasakumaracarita of Dandin with a Commentary: With Various Readings, a Literal Translation, Explanatory and Critical Notes, and an Exhaustive Introduction.* New Delhi: Motilal Banarsidass, 1966 (reprint).

———. *The Uttararamacharita of Bhavabhuti with the Commentary of Viraraghava, Various Reading, Introduction, a Literal English Translation, Exhaustive Notes and Appendices.* New Delhi: Motilal Banarsidass, 1993.

———. *Meghaduta of Kalidasa.* New Delhi: Motilal Banarsidass, 2003 (reprint).

Karmakar, R. D., trans. *Raghuvamsa of Kalidasa*, Cantos XI–XIV. Poona, Maharashtra: Aryabhushan Mudranalaya, 1954.

Meiland, Justin. *Mahabharata Vol IX. Shalya.* 2 vols., *Salyaparvan.* New York: Clay Sanskrit Library, 2005, 2007.

Miller, Barbara Stoler, ed. *The Theater of Memory: The Plays of Kalidasa*. New York: Columbia University Press, 1984.

Nathan, Leonard. *Transports of Love: Kalidasa's Meghaduta*. Berkeley: University of California Press, 1977.

Olivelle, Patrick. *Five Discourses on Worldly Wisdom (Pancatantra) by Visnusarman*. New York: Clay Sanskrit Library, 2006.

Onians, Isabelle. *What Ten Young Men Did (Dasakumaracarita) by Dandin*. New York: Clay Sanskrit Library, 2005.

Parab, Kasinath Pandurang, ed. *Harsacarita of Bana*. Bombay: Nirnaya Sagar Press, 1938.

Pilikian, Vaughan. *Mahabharata VII. Drona*. Vol. 1, *Drona Parvan*. New York: Clay Sanskrit Library, 2006.

Smith, David. *The Birth of Kumara (Kumarasambhava) by Kalidasa*. New York: Clay Sanskrit Library, 2005.

Sukthankar, V. S., et al., eds. *Mahabharata*. 19 vols. Pune, Maharashtra: Bhandarkar Oriental Research Institute, 1933–1971.

Vaidya, P. L., ed. *The Ramayana*. Baroda, Gujarat: The Oriental Institute, 1962 onward.

Vasudeva, Somadeva. *The Recognition of Shakuntala (Abhijnanasakuntala) by Kalidasa*. New York: Clay Sanskrit Library, 2006.

Wilmot, Paul. *Mahabharata II. The Great Hall (Sabhaparvan)*. New York: Clay Sanskrit Library, 2006.

Other Sanskrit Texts

Bhadamkar, H. M., and R. G. Bhadamkar, eds. *Yaska's Nirukta with Nighantu, with Durga's commentary*. Poona, Maharashtra: Bhandarkar Oriental Research Institute, 1985 (reprint).

Bhat, R. *Varahamihira's Brhat Samhita*. 2 vols. New Delhi: Motilal Banarsidass, 1993–1995 (reprint).

Doniger, Wendy, and Sudhir Kakar, trans. *Kamasutra*. Oxford, UK: Oxford University Press, 2002.

Feuerstein, Georg. *The Yoga-Sutra of Patanjali: A New Translation and Commentary*. London: Dawson, 1979.

Ghosh, Manomohan. *The Natyasastra: A Treatise on Ancient Indian Dramaturgy and Histrionics*. 2 vols. Calcutta: Manisha Granthalaya Private Ltd, 1995 (reprint).

Hume, Robert Ernest, trans. *The Thirteen Principal Upanisads*. New Delhi: Oxford University Press, 1983 (reprint).

Ingalls, Daniel H. H., Jeffrey Moussaieff Masson, and M. V. Patwardhan, trans. *The Dhvanyaloka of Anandavardhana with the Locana of Abhinavagupta*. Cambridge, MA: Harvard University Press, 1990.

Kangle, R. P. *The Kautiliya Arthasastra*. (3 parts—a critical edition, translation, and study). Bombay: University of Bombay, 1960–1972.

Kielhorn, Franz, ed. *Mahabhasya of Patanjali*. Poona, Maharashtra: Bhandarkar Oriental Research Institute, 1962–1972.

Olivelle, Patrick. *The Early Upaniṣads: Annotated Text and Translation*. New York: Oxford University Press, 1998.

Pingree, D. ed., trans., and commentary. *Yavanajataka of Sphujidhvaya*. Cambridge, MA: Harvard Oriental Series, 1978.

Prasad, Pushpa. *Lekhapaddhati: Documents of State and Everyday Life from Ancient and Medieval Gujarat*. New Delhi: Oxford University Press, 2007.

Radhakrishnan, S. *The Principal Upanisads: Text and English Translation*. New Delhi: Oxford University Press, 1989.

Sadhale, Nalini, trans. *Krishi Parashara*. Secunderabad, Andhra Pradesh: Asian Agri-History Foundation, 1999.

Sharma, Priya Vrat, ed. and trans. *Caraka Samhita: Agnivesa's treatise refined and annotated by Caraka and redacted by Drdhabala*. 4 vols. Varanasi, Uttar Pradesh: Chaukhamba Orientalia, 1981–1994.

Shastri, H., ed. *Amarakosa*. New Delhi: Upal, 1970.

Stein, M. A. *Kalhana's Rajatarangini: A Chronicle of the Kings of Kashmir*. New Delhi: Munshiram Manoharlal, 1960 (reprint).

Vasu, Srisa Chandra, ed. and trans. *The Astadhyayi of Panini*. 2 vols. New Delhi: Motilal Banarsidass, 1996 (reprint).

Wujastyk, Dominik. *The Roots of Ayurveda: Selections from Sanskrit Medical Writings*. New Delhi: Penguin, 1998.

Other Prakrit Texts

Bollee, W. *The Story of Paesi (Paesikahanayam): The Soul and Body in Ancient India. A Dialogue on Materialism, Text, Translation, Notes and Glossary*. Wiesbaden: Harrassowitz, 2002.

Tamil Texts

Dikshitar, V. R. R. *Tirukkural in Tamil and Roman Scripts*. Chennai, Adyar Library, 2000 (reprint).

Hart, George, and Hank Heifetz, trans. and eds. *The Four Hundred Songs of War and Wisdom: An Anthology of Poems from Classical Tamil, the Puranānūru*. New York: Columbia University Press, 2002.

Kailasapathy, R. *Tamil Heroic Poetry*. Chennai: Kumara Book, 2002.

Parthasarathy, R. *The Cilappatikaram: The Tale of an Anklet*. New Delhi: Penguin, 2004.

Peterson, Indira V. *Poems to Śiva: The Hymns of the Tamil Saints*. New Delhi: Motilal Banarsidass, 1991.
Ramanujan A. K., trans. *The Interior Landscape: Love Poems from a Classical Anthology*. London: Peter Owen, 1970.
———. *Poems of Love and War: From the Eight Anthologies and Ten Long Poems of Classical Tamil*. New York: Columbia University Press, 1985.

Foreign Accounts

Beal, Samuel, trans. *Si yu-ki: The Buddhist Records of the Western World*. New Delhi: Munshiram Manoharlal, 2004 (reprint).
———. *Travels of Fah-Hian and Sung-Yun from China to India (400 A.D. and 518 A.D.)*. New Delhi: Low Price, 2005 (reprint).
Casson, L. *The Periplus Maris Erythraei*. Princeton, NJ: Princeton University Press, 1989.
Hui-Li, Yen ts'ung. *The Life of Hsuan Tsang*. New Delhi: Akshaya Prakashan, 2005 (reprint).
Huntingford, G. W. B., trans. *The Periplus of the Erythraean Sea*. London: Hakluyt Society Series, 1980.
Majumdar, R. C. *The Classical Accounts of India*. Calcutta: Firma K. L. Mukhopadhyay, 1960.
———. *Ancient India as Described by Ptolemy*. New Delhi: Munshiram Manoharlal, 2000 (reprint).
McCrindle, J. W., trans. *Ancient India as Described by Megasthenes and Arrian*. Calcutta: Chakrabarty and Chatterjee, 1921.
Schoff, Wilfred H., trans. *The Periplus of the Erythraean Sea*. New Delhi: Oriental Books Reprint, 1974 (reprint).
Takakusu, J., trans. *A Record of the Buddhist Religion as Practised in India and the Malayan Archipelago (AD 671–695) by I-Tsing*. New Delhi: Munshiram Manoharlal, 1998 (reprint).

WEBSITES

asi.nic.in/asi_publ_indian_archaeology.asp (the website of the Archaeological Survey of India, with details on its publications)
www.crl.edu/areastudies/SAMP/collections/archsurv.htm (the website of the Center for Research Libraries, which has records of archaeological reports)
www.harappa.com/indus/kenbiblio.html (one of the most popular websites on the Harappan civilization)

dsal.uchicago.edu/reference/schwartzberg/ (for access to the online version of the *Historical Atlas of South Asia*)
dsal.uchicago.edu/ (for a wealth of resources—texts, visual material, bibliographies, indexes, and dictionaries)
www.palitext.com/ (for Pali texts and translations)
www.whatisindia.com/inscriptions.html (for texts of inscriptions)
namami.nic.in/ (website of the National Mission for Manuscripts, India, for details on Indian manuscript holdings)

About the Author

Kumkum Roy graduated with honors in history from Presidency College, Calcutta, and did her MA and PhD, specializing in ancient Indian history, from the Centre for Historical Studies, School of Social Sciences, Jawaharlal Nehru University, New Delhi, India. Her doctoral dissertation, titled *The Emergence of Monarchy in North India*, was published by the Oxford University Press, New Delhi, in 1994.

Roy taught for several years in colleges in Delhi University before joining as associate professor the Centre for Historical Studies, Jawaharlal Nehru University, in 1999. Her areas of interest include histories of political ideas and institutions, social history with a special focus on issues of gender and kinship, and early textual traditions. She was the recipient of the Commonwealth Academic Staff Fellowship, tenable at the School of Oriental and African Studies, London, in 1994–1995, and a fellowship at the Indian Institute of Advanced Study, Shimla, in 1998. Her publications include an edited anthology, *Women in Early Indian Societies*, and several articles on gender and early Indian textual traditions and kingship. Roy is also associated with programs dealing with pedagogical issues of teaching history.